Ecology and Management of t   ฀ ฀ffalo

One of iconic Africa's Big Five, the African buffalo is the largest African bovine or antelope that occurs throughout most of sub-Sahara and in a wide range of ecosystems from savanna to rainforest. The African buffalo is also one of the most successful large African mammals in terms of abundance and biomass. This species thus represents a powerful model to enhance our understanding of African biogeography and wildlife conservation, ecology and management. Edited by four researchers experienced in different aspects of the African buffalo's biology, this volume provides an exhaustive compilation of knowledge on an emblematic species that stands out as an important component of African natural and human ecosystems. It delivers a global view of the African buffalo and all known aspects of its ecology and management. This book will appeal to students, scholars, scientists and wildlife managers as well as those enthusiastic about the charismatic species. This title is also available as Open Access on Cambridge Core.

ALEXANDRE CARON is a Doctor in Veterinary Medicine and wildlife ecologist specializing in the ecology of infectious disease transmission at the wildlife/livestock interface in the African landscape. For the past 20 years, he has coordinated projects linked to Health Ecology, One Health and Sustainability Science in Southern Africa. He is a permanent researcher at CIRAD (French Agricultural Research Centre for International Development).

DANIEL CORNELIS is a Senior Ecologist specializing in tropical and subtropical wildlife and ecosystems. Over the past 25 years, he has conducted and coordinated projects and studies on wildlife and natural resource management, including the African buffalo. He is a permanent researcher at CIRAD (Montpellier) and scientific advisor for the Foundation François Sommer (Paris).

PHILIPPE CHARDONNET is a Doctor in Veterinary Medicine specializing in tropical animal health and production. He is a co-chair of the IUCN SSC Antelope Specialist Group (ASG) and has over 40 years of experience in wildlife conservation and sustainable use in Africa, Asia, South America and South Pacific. He has co-authored more than 200 publications.

HERBERT H. T. PRINS is Emeritus Professor of Resource Ecology at Wageningen University and Research (WUR), The Netherlands. He was also a Fulbright Scholar at Princeton University, USA; Foundation Fellow at the Royal Melbourne Institute of Technology, Australia; and Honorary Professor in Computational Ecology at the University of KwaZulu-Natal, South Africa. He has co-authored over 500 publications, co-edited 14 books, and wrote *Ecology and Behaviour of African Buffalo* (Chapman & Hall, 1996).

ECOLOGY, BIODIVERSITY AND CONSERVATION

The world's biological diversity faces unprecedented threats. The urgent challenge facing the concerned biologist is to understand ecological processes well enough to maintain their functioning in the face of the pressures resulting from human population growth. Those concerned with the conservation of biodiversity and with restoration also need to be acquainted with the political, social, historical, economic and legal frameworks within which ecological and conservation practice must be developed. The new Ecology, Biodiversity and Conservation series will present balanced, comprehensive, up-to-date and critical reviews of selected topics within the sciences of ecology and conservation biology, both botanical and zoological, and both 'pure' and 'applied'. It is aimed at advanced final-year undergraduates, graduate students, researchers and university teachers, as well as ecologists and conservationists in industry, government and the voluntary sectors. The series encompasses a wide range of approaches and scales (spatial, temporal and taxonomic), including quantitative, theoretical, population, community, ecosystem, landscape, historical, experimental, behavioural and evolutionary studies. The emphasis is on science related to the real world of plants and animals rather than on purely theoretical abstractions and mathematical models. Books in this series will, wherever possible, consider issues from a broad perspective. Some books will challenge existing paradigms and present new ecological concepts, empirical or theoretical models, and testable hypotheses. Other books will explore new approaches and present syntheses on topics of ecological importance.

Ecology and Control of Introduced Plants
Judith H. Myers and Dawn Bazely

Invertebrate Conservation and Agricultural Ecosystems
T. R. New

Ecology and Management of the African Buffalo

Edited by

ALEXANDRE CARON
CIRAD (French Agricultural Research Centre for International Development)

DANIEL CORNELIS
CIRAD (French Agricultural Research Centre for International Development)

PHILIPPE CHARDONNET
Co-chair of the IUCN SSC Antelope Specialist Group

HERBERT H. T. PRINS
Wageningen University

Shaftesbury Road, Cambridge CB2 8EA, United Kingdom

One Liberty Plaza, 20th Floor, New York, NY 10006, USA

477 Williamstown Road, Port Melbourne, VIC 3207, Australia

314–321, 3rd Floor, Plot 3, Splendor Forum, Jasola District Centre,
New Delhi – 110025, India

103 Penang Road, #05-06/07, Visioncrest Commercial, Singapore 238467

Cambridge University Press is part of Cambridge University Press & Assessment,
a department of the University of Cambridge.

We share the University's mission to contribute to society through the pursuit of
education, learning and research at the highest international levels of excellence.

www.cambridge.org
Information on this title: www.cambridge.org/9781316518748

DOI: 10.1017/9781009006828

First published 2023

A catalogue record for this publication is available from the British Library

Library of Congress Cataloging-in-Publication Data
Names: Caron, Alexandre, 1975- editor.
Title: Ecology and management of the African buffalo / edited by Alexandre
Caron, International Centre for Agricultural Research for Development
(CIRAD), Daniel Cornelis, International Centre for Agricultural Research
for Development (CIRAD), Philippe Chardonnet, IUCN SSC Antelope Specialist Group,
Herbert H.T. Prins, Wageningen University, The Netherlands.
Description: Cambridge, United Kingdom ; New York, NY : Cambridge University Press, 2023. |
Series: Ecology, biodiversity and conservation | Includes bibliographical references and index.
Identifiers: LCCN 2023016891 | ISBN 9781316518748 (hardback) |
ISBN 9781009009959 (paperback) | ISBN 9781009006828 (ebook)
Subjects: LCSH: African buffalo – Ecology. | African buffalo – Conservation.
Classification: LCC QL737.U53 E254 2023 | DDC 599.64/3–dc23/eng/20230908
LC record available at https://lccn.loc.gov/2023016891

ISBN 978-1-316-51874-8 Hardback
ISBN 978-1-009-00995-9 Paperback

Contents

Contributors

A. ASEFA
Conservation Ecology, Department of Biology, Philipps-Universität Marburg, Marburg, Germany

M. T. BAH
ASTRE, Univ Montpellier, CIRAD, INRAE, Montpellier, France

R. BALDUS
IUCN SSC Antelope Specialist Group

B. BEECHLER
Carlson College of Veterinary Medicine, Oregon State University, Corvallis, OR, USA

R. G. BENGIS
Retired Chief State Veterinarian, Kruger National Park, South Africa

E. BENNITT
Okavango Research Institute, University of Botswana, Maun, Botswana

H. BONHOTAL
Forêts et Sociétés, University of Montpellier, CIRAD, Montpellier, France; IUCN SSC Antelope Specialist Group

R. BOURGEOIS
Art-Dev, University of Montpellier, Université Paul Valéry Montpellier 3, CIRAD, CNRS, Montpellier, France; CIRAD, UMR ART-Dev, Saint Louis, Senegal; University of Perpignan Via Domitia, CIRAD, Montpellier, France

T. BREUER
World Wide Fund for Nature Germany, Berlin, Germany

A. CARON
ASTRE, University of Montpellier, CIRAD, INRAE, Montpellier, France; Forêts et Sociétés, University of Montpellier, CIRAD, Montpellier, France; Faculdade de Veterinaria, Universidade Eduardo Mondlane, Maputo, Mozambique; IUCN SSC Antelope Specialist Group

P. CHARDONNET
IUCN SSC Antelope Specialist Group Co-Chair

D. CORNELIS
Forêts et Sociétés, University of Montpellier, CIRAD, Montpellier, France; IUCN SSC Antelope Specialist Group; Fondation François Sommer, Paris, France

W. CROSMARY
WWF Germany, Berlin, Germany; IUCN SSC Antelope Specialist Group

M. DE GARINE-WICHATITSKY
ASTRE, University of Montpellier, CIRAD, INRAE, Montpellier, France; Faculty of Veterinary Medicine, Kasetsart University, Bangkok, Thailand

J. F. DE JONG
Wildlife Ecology and Conservation Group, Wageningen University, Wageningen, The Netherlands

P. ELKAN
Wildlife Conservation Society, New York, USA

V. O. EZENWA
Department of Ecology and Evolutionary Biology, Yale University, New Haven, CT, USA

D. FEKADU SHIFERAW
Retired Veterinary Clinical Officer (KKWRC), Zoological Society of London, London, UK

D. FONTEYN
Forêts et Sociétés, University of Montpellier, CIRAD, Montpellier, France; IUCN SSC Antelope Specialist Group, Gland, Switzerland; Forest is Life, Terra Teaching and Research Centre, Gembloux Agro-Bio Tech, Université de Liege, Liege, Belgium

D. FURSTENBURG
Afri Wild Services, Ecology & Zoology Applied Science, Krugersdorp, South Africa

R. FYNN
Okavango Research Institute, Shorobe Road, Sexaxa, Maun, Botswana

F. GAKUYA
Department of Veterinary Science and Laboratories, Wildlife Research and Training Institute, Naivasha, Kenya

E. GANDIWA
Scientific Services, Zimbabwe Parks and Wildlife Management Authority, Harare, Zimbabwe

E. GARINE WICHATITSKY
Paris Nanterre University, Laboratoire d'ethnologie et de sociologie comparative, Nanterre, France

D. GERAADS
CR2P, Muséum National d'Histoire Naturelle, Paris, France

C. GLIDDEN
Department of Integrative Biology, Oregon State University, Corvallis, OR, USA

E. GORSICH
The Zeeman Institute for Systems Biology and Infectious Disease Epidemiology Research, School of Life Sciences, University of Warwick, Warwick, UK

V. GROSBOIS
ASTRE, University of Montpellier, CIRAD, INRAE, Montpellier, France

M. HAUPTFLEISCH
Biodiversity Research Centre, Namibia University of Science and Technology, Windhoek, Namibia

J. W. HEARNE
School of Science, RMIT University, Melbourne, Victoria, Australia

R. HOARE
Independent Consultant, Harare, Zimbabwe

L. C. HOFFMAN
Center for Nutrition and Food Sciences, Queensland Alliance for Agriculture and Food Innovation (QAAFI), The University of Queensland, Gatton, Australia

A. JOLLES
Carlson College of Veterinary Medicine, Oregon State University, Corvallis, OR, USA

M. D. KOCK
International Wildlife Veterinary Services, Greyton, Western Cape, South Africa

R. A. KOCK
Department of Pathobiology and Population Sciences, Royal Veterinary College, London, UK (Retired)

E. KOHI
Tanzania Wildlife Research Institute, Arusha, Tanzania

L. KORTE
International Affairs, Africa Branch, US Fish & Wildlife Service, Washington, DC, USA

O. L. KUPIKA
Okavango Research Institute, University of Botswana, Maun, Botswana

M. LA GRANGE
Independent Consultant; African Wildlife Management and Conservation, Harare, Zimbabwe

N. J. LA GRANGE
African Wildlife Management and Conservation, Harare, Zimbabwe

I. L. LEKOLOOL
Veterinary and Capture Services, Kenya Wildlife Services, Nairobi, Kenya

F. A. LIGATE
Ministry of Natural Resources and Tourism, Tanzania

D. MDETELE
Tanzania Ministry of Fisheries and Livestock, Dodoma, Tanzania

M. MELLETTI
IUCN SSC Wild Pig Specialist Group

J. MICHAUX
Laboratoire de Génétique de la Conservation, Institut de Botanique, Université de Liège (Sart Tilman), Liège, Belgium; UMR CIRAD-INRA 117 ASTRE, Université de Montpellier, Montpellier, France

E. MIGUEL
MIVEGEC, IRD, CNRS, Université de Montpellier, Montpellier, France; CREES Centre for Research on the Ecology and Evolution of Disease – Montpellier, Montpellier, France

L. MONIN
Department of Anthropology, Laboratoire d'Ethnologie et de Sociologie Comparative, Paris Nanterre University, Nanterre, France

J. MOSTERT
African Wildlife Management and Conservation, Harare, Zimbabwe

J. MOSTERT-LA GRANGE
African Wildlife Management and Conservation, Harare, Zimbabwe

B. MUKAMURI
Department of Community and Social Development, University of Zimbabwe, Mount Pleasant, Harare, Zimbabwe

M. MUNYEME
School of Veterinary Medicine, The University of Zambia, Zambia

S. MWIU
Department of Wildlife Populations and Habitat Dynamics, Wildlife Research and Training Institute, Naivasha, Kenya

R. NAIDOO
WWF-US, Washington, DC, USA

T. NEEDHAM
Department of Animal Science and Food Processing, Faculty of Tropical AgriSciences, Czech University of Life Sciences Prague, Prague-Suchdol, Czech Republic

S. NGENE
Department of Wildlife Populations and Habitat Dynamics, Wildlife Research and Training Institute, Naivasha, Kenya

Pa. OBEREM
Dabchick Wildlife Reserve (Pty) Ltd, Pretoria, South Africa

Pe. OBEREM
Dabchick Wildlife Reserve (Pty) Ltd, Pretoria, South Africa

P. OMONDI
Wildlife Research and Training Institute, Naivasha, Kenya

J. OTTENBURGHS
Wildlife Ecology and Conservation Group, Wageningen University, Wageningen, The Netherlands

M. J. S. PEEL
Agricultural Research Council, Animal Production Institute, Rangeland Ecology, Pretoria, South Africa; School of Animal, Plant and Environmental Sciences, University of the Witwatersrand, Johannesburg, South Africa; Applied Behavioural Ecology and Ecosystem Research Unit, University of South Africa, Florida, South Africa

A. PERROTTON
Forêts et Sociétés, University of Montpellier, CIRAD, Montpellier, France

T. PRIN
Fondation François Sommer, Paris, France

H. H. T. PRINS
Department of Animal Sciences, Wageningen University, The Netherlands; IUCN SSC Asian Wild Cattle Specialist Group

P. C. RENAUD
University of Angers, BiodivAG-IRL Rehabs, Angers, France; Sustainability Research Unit, Faculty of Science, George Campus, Nelson Mandela University, George, South Africa

K. ROBERTSON
Kevcat African Wildlife Consultant, Boerne, Texas, USA

A. ROUG
Centre for Veterinary Wildlife Studies and Department of Production Animal Studies, Faculty of Veterinary Science, University of Pretoria, South Africa

F. RUMIANO
ASTRE, University of Montpellier, CIRAD, INRAE, Montpellier, France; TETIS, University of Montpellier, AgroParisTech, CIRAD, CNRS, INRAE, Montpellier, France

P. SCHOLTE
Deutsche Gesellschaft für Internationale Zusammenarbeit (GIZ), Ethiopia; École Régionale Post-Universitaire d'Aménagement et de Gestion Intégrés des Forêts et Territoires Tropicaux, ERAIFT-UNESCO, DR Congo

C. A. SHEPSTONE
Wildlife Nutrition Services, Wonderboom Agricultural Holdings, Pretoria, South Africa

L. SIEGE
German Agency for International Cooperation (Retired); IUCN SSC Crocodile Specialist Group

N. SMITZ
Royal Museum for Central Africa (Biology Department), Tervuren, Belgium

S. P. TADJO
Ministry of Forestry and Wildlife, Garoua, Cameroon

R. TAYLOR
WWF Namibia, Windhoek, Namibia

A. TRAN
ASTRE, University of Montpellier, CIRAD, INRAE, Montpellier, France; TETIS, University of Montpellier, AgroParisTech, CIRAD, CNRS, INRAE, Montpellier, France

P. VAN HOOFT
Wildlife Ecology and Conservation Group, Wageningen University, Wageningen, The Netherlands

E. WIELGUS
ASTRE, University of Montpellier, CIRAD, INRAE, Montpellier, France; Department of Natural Sciences, Manchester Metropolitan University, All Saints, Manchester, UK; CEFE, CNRS, University of Montpellier, University Paul Valéry Montpellier 3, EPHE, IRD, Montpellier, France

Foreword

This book, edited by four researchers experienced in different aspects of African buffalo biology, provides us with the most up-to-date story of what is known and not known of the wild species and how it may be managed for the benefit of humans. It is an extensive compilation of knowledge about a species that is emerging as an important component of African natural and human ecosystems. There are five parts of this story. We are provided with a synthesis of what is known of the conservation and ecology of the African buffalo in nature. Then, we see how this knowledge combined with new information on disease ecology can lead to management in both wild and semi-captive conditions.

After an introduction dealing with the interaction of buffalo and humans, the second part presents new information on the genetics, phylogeny and evolution of the species, confirming now that there are three subspecies – the eastern and southern savanna type, the dwarf forest type of central African forests and the northern savanna type from which the forest form evolved. This leads to a discussion of the conservation status of the species. The third part, the ecology, covers distribution within Africa – increasingly confined to Protected Areas – social organization and population trends, which are largely decreasing due to direct threats from human exploitation and disease, and indirect threats from habitat loss. Populations are also disturbed from their equilibrium by environmental perturbations such as droughts because buffalo are very much water-dependent. There is new information from modern remote-sensing technology on space use, movements and social behaviour. Movements and social behaviour are interlinked – female herds can show small cohesive and sedentary groups with constant membership, as in Uganda and some small montane forest habitats, but they can also form highly flexible herds, of up to 2000 in number. These can split up, reform seasonally, and the groups can intermix. These subgroups have overlapping home ranges. Such herds are found in extensive savanna habitats, and have been shown in southern Africa to perform long-distance migrations.

In the fourth part, new information is presented on the diseases of African buffalo. There are a large number of micro- and macro-parasite species that are endemic in buffalo. Most of these play an important role in expediting the regulation of populations by synergistically interacting with lack of food. There are, however, a few species that cause episodic outbreaks and high mortality, but only a few. Of course, there was once the well-known exotic virus, rinderpest, introduced to Africa in 1889 from Asia, causing catastrophic mortality, but that disease has now been eradicated from the world. We see that buffalo can suffer from diseases contracted from cattle, and equally there are endemic buffalo diseases that can be transmitted to domestic animals. This information is vital for both the conservation of wild populations and the management of domestic herds in the presence of wild buffalo.

The husbandry of African buffalo is covered in the fifth part. Much of this concerns private land, and the legal basis for this is explained – so far mostly in southern African countries. This covers the genetics of populations on private land and the control of parasites and diseases. We are then provided with biological statistics on such production aspects as densities allowable on land, distribution in different habitats, growth and breeding capability. We see the different advantages and disadvantages of these aspects in a comparison with cattle. One of the difficulties with buffalo is how to handle them, being less docile than cattle and more highly stressed; a discussion is offered on how to deal with this problem. The husbandry of buffalo on private land for trophy hunting is outlined.

This book is designed for wildlife students, researchers and managers. The information is valuable for management in wild populations and for situations where buffalo and domestic stock could coexist. Most of the information comes from the savanna subspecies of buffalo. Little is known about the other two types, and especially the miniature forest form. The book ends with a discussion of what we know and what we still have to learn. Nevertheless, we see that there is now a profound knowledge of an African species that could be a valuable asset both for the functioning of natural ecosystems and the livelihoods of African peoples.

Anthony R. E. Sinclair, FRS
Ex-Director of the Biodiversity Research Centre,
University of British Columbia, Vancouver, Canada

Preface

The African buffalo is an emblematic species of African savannas and forests. It has figured in African cultures probably for millennia, and when people from the Middle East and Europe encountered African buffalo, it became the quintessential villain that could transform pampered men into heroes. Indeed, that Francis Macomber (as described by Ernest Hemmingway) had a *short* life after he stood his grounds when facing a charging buffalo is irrelevant; it was a *happy* life. Stories like these and other about 'death in the long grass' ensured the African buffalo's place of honour on that champion rostrum of the Big Five. Indeed, these Big Five are considered the 'worthy adversaries' of our species – the African buffalo alongside the African elephant, lion, leopard and black rhinoceros. Animals of these five species were, according to hunters, valiant, dangerous, perilous, treacherous and mighty antagonists and thus embodied the ideal foes for the manly man, a category of humans into which, at that time, only grudgingly were dauntless women also admitted.

Besides its representations in African and Western cultures, the African buffalo is also a natural resource. It has provided a meat supply for human populations for thousands of years, and continues to do so today. The buffalo resource is also currently being exploited by safari tourism and trophy hunting. This blossoming tourism market in parts of Africa, mainly in southern Africa, has come up with new buffalo 'products' such as the lucrative commerce of disease-free buffalo or animals of high trophy quality. For reasons that are probably unfathomable, Westerners define 'trophy quality' in antelopes, deer and also buffalo by length and size of head appendages. In East Asia, neither form nor size of rhino horn is important for its aphrodisiac powers, and in African cultures, neither the size of the claws nor the whiteness of the fat of the large carnivores is of importance to explain its magical powers. Yet, in some African cultures the killing of an African buffalo as 'enemy of the people', especially when done alone and with a spear, is considered a feat of great significance, allowing for the willingness of women to share their love.

On a more mundane level, the African buffalo is of interest from a One Health perspective, because it is a maintenance host for many important pathogens that can trigger diseases mainly in domestic cattle: bovine tuberculosis, brucellosis and many others including tick-borne diseases such as theileriosis. This raises, and has been raising, concerns at buffalo/cattle/human interfaces all over Africa to the south of the Sahara. As a matter of fact, during the Colonial Era many 'disease-free' buffer zones were created by indiscriminately shooting and eradicating hundreds of thousands of large animals, including African buffalo. This red-line zoning continues even today in South Africa, Namibia, Botswana, Zimbabwe, Angola and Zambia.

Despite its importance in the African landscape and beyond, the species has not 'benefited' from many monographs looking at its ecology and management. Tony Sinclair published a book on this splendid beast with Chicago University Press some 45 years ago, and one of us did the same with Chapman & Hall (now Springer Nature) some 25 years ago. We are very grateful that Tony graced our present book with a Foreword because we consider him a true trailblazer for Nyatology, that is the Science of African Buffalo ('*Nyati*', like '*Mbogo*', being the term for 'African buffalo' in kiSwahili). Since these monographs were published, much water has flowed through the Nile, the Congo and the Niger, and our knowledge has increased considerably. For example, the development of telemetry and remote-sensing techniques has greatly expanded our capacity to track wildlife individuals and social dynamics. For the past 15 years, we have been involved in telemetry studies on African buffalo (and other antelopes) in western and southern Africa. We have gathered one of the most extensive data sets available on the species (more than 200 GPS/satellite collars deployed). The field of genetics has also revolutionized species taxonomy and our understanding of population dynamics at the species and subpopulation levels. We have been involved in studies on the genetics of the African buffalo at the continent and regional levels. From a health ecology perspective, knowledge of the African buffalo's role in the epidemiology of many African diseases, including zoonoses (pathogens that can spread form animal to humans), has also expanded considerably over the last few decades. Finally, the management and ranching of the species, especially in southern Africa, has evolved into a distinct zootechnical field.

We thus felt that there is a huge body of new knowledge with regards to the African buffalo and its interactions with other species, including domestic species and humans, which needed to be synthesized. We

Figure 0.1 Cape African buffalo bull in front of a herd in Hwange National Park, Zimbabwe. © Rudi van Aarde.

also had the opportunity to communicate extensively with other scholars and managers involved with this buffalo species through the AfBIG (African Buffalo Interest Group) under the umbrella of the IUCN SSC Antelope Specialist Group and two symposia that we organized, one in Paris (France: 2014) and one in Windhoek (Namibia: 2016). The cooperation and data sharing by the members of AfBIG that arose out of these gatherings and subsequent interactions through the Internet hugely contributed to the current volume.

The African buffalo represents a very special animal species that needs different management schemes across its range to maintain its populations 'in a favourable conservation status'. Over much of its range, notably in East and southern Africa, its populations are still large and to some extent connected. There, the Cape buffalo can safely be hunted if done judiciously and with good knowledge of the population effects of hunting (Figure 0.1). Then and there, one may assume that the populations of East and southern Africa can be maintained in a favourable conservation status.

The situation with the northern savanna buffalo is much grimmer (Figures 0.2, 0.3 and 0.4). Most populations have been extirpated from their range between Senegal and Ethiopia even though there are still a handful of populations that maintain themselves due to conservation efforts by African governments sometimes supported by overseas'

Figure 0.2 West African savanna buffalo bull in Bandia reserve, Senegal.
© Raymond Snaps.

Figure 0.3 West African savanna buffalo female and calf, W National Park, Niger.
© Daniel Cornélis.

Figure 0.4 Central African savanna buffalo bull, Zakouma National Park, Chad.
© Daniel Cornélis.

organizations. However, while the historical range has shrunk in West
and Central Africa, the populations in some of the few remaining
strongholds have recently shown promising population increase, thus
demonstrating that recovery of the northern savanna buffalo is possible
if the political will and financial resources are available. Regulated hunting may perhaps again play a positive role in the conservation of those
healthy populations. However, the recovery of former ranges and population rebound should have priority over much of the (former) distribution of the northern savanna buffalo.

The third form of the African buffalo, the forest buffalo, occurs in two
disjunct areas, one in the rainforest block to the west of the Dahomey
Gap and the other in the Congo Basin rainforests to the east. Those western populations are nearly extinct now, while those living in the Congo
Basin are still to some extent data-deficient. Yet a picture emerges that
regulated and enforced conservation actions in timber, hunting and oil
concessions may provide these buffalo with the only way to survive if the
National Parks and other protected areas are no longer truly and effectively safeguarded. For this form of African buffalo, population recovery

ought to be of main concern in the forests to the west of the Dahomey Gap. Nevertheless, regulated hunting could play a positive role for forest buffalo of the Congo Basin. However, this necessitates a better understanding of their fundamental ecology and population dynamics.

Because of these very different conservation statuses in the vast range of the species, the African buffalo provides that rare case in which strict conservation, hunting, interaction with livestock, genetic exchange and even breeding for trophies all deserve attention and up-to-date information. This is what we have been aiming for in the current book, for which we have brought together a multidisciplinary team of authors. We thus not only invited ecologists or purely academic geneticists to contribute to the knowledge of this unique species, but also veterinarians, wildlife managers, applied mathematicians, hunters and animal breeders. All these specialists we name 'nyatiologists' to emphasize what they have in common, namely, knowledge of buffalo, be it academic or/ and experiential.

Of very few wild large mammal species their status in the tropics is still so favourable that sustainable use may contribute to their preservation. Yet, in other areas, primarily in the whole of West Africa, their status is now so much in peril that the knowledge about their sustainable use and management garnered in East and southern Africa largely should be used to recreate their former vast numbers. Indeed, sustainable use is only possible when the conservation status of a local population is favourable. We hope that the knowledge and experience reported in this book forms a useful foundation for restoring or maintaining the populations of this marvellous species throughout the whole of the African continent, and we dream of the African buffalo as a symbol of an African renaissance soon emerging from current global changes and social, ecological and political struggles.

H. H. T. Prins, D. Cornélis,
P. Chardonnet and A. Caron

Acknowledgements

We are proud that our edited volume was commissioned by Cambridge University Press through Dr Dominic Lewis and Professor Michael Usher. Ours is one of the last of the long list of contributions to ecological scholarship reaching the scientific community and the public at large due to their vision and stamina. Both Dominic and Michael stood at the helm as the principal commissioning editors of the 'Ecology, Biodiversity and Conservation' series for several years, and we are truly grateful to them for the opportunity to share our collective work in this volume. Yet this collective work could not have been brought to fruition without the consolidating competence of the Antelope Specialist Group and its leadership; this specialist group operates within the remit of the Species Survival Commission of the International Union for Conservation of Nature (IUCN).

Because most of our readership is concentrated in tropical Africa, we wanted to make this book accessible to all even where there are no libraries. We gratefully acknowledge the financial support for Open Access publishing from CIRAD (Centre de coopération internationale en recherche agronomique pour le développement, Montpellier, France) and from the Foundation François Sommer (FFS) (Paris, France). The Foundation François Sommer also financed the costs of the symposium on African buffalo in 2014 in Paris, where the idea for this book was born. The FFS further co-financed the research reported in the doctoral theses of Thomas Prin, Elodie Wielgus and Daniel Cornélis also reported in this book.

We are very thankful for the editing skills and hard work carried out by our language editor Grace Delobel (DipTrans, Montpellier, France), who not only corrected many errors but often suggested clearer and better text. Finally, our Editor at Cambridge University Press, Aleksandra Serocka, often acted as our anchor cable to keep us, the editors, safely tethered to the Press when we were again in different remote places in Africa, often without Internet connections.

1 · *African Buffalo and the Human Societies in Africa: Social Values and Interaction Outcomes*

B. MUKAMURI, E. GARINE
WICHATITSKY, E. GANDIWA,
A. PERROTTON, O. L. KUPIKA AND
L. MONIN

Introduction

The sustainable management of wildlife and other natural resources, including the African buffalo (*Syncerus caffer*), depends largely on the social–ecological context being considered (e.g. McGinnis and Ostrom, 2014), Decision VII/2 of the Convention of Biological Diversity[1]). This context is largely defined by a combination of complex interactions between ecological (e.g. biomass, reproduction rate, climatic factors) and social (e.g. cultural values, norms, needs, practices) parameters and dynamics. These two intertwined dimensions can influence the way natural resources are perceived and subsequently managed, used and studied by actors interacting with natural resources, and vice versa. These interactions may lead to the sustainable use of resources by environmental stewards, or the overexploitation, cruelty and eradication of the natural bounty. Understanding these complex social–ecological dynamics consequently helps facilitate the fair and just conservation and sustainable use of wildlife species.

In this chapter, we bring together experiences on the sustainable use and management of the African buffalo from major regions of the African continent where the African buffalo is found in substantial numbers, especially in the wild and in areas adjacent to protected areas. In the first section, we will explore the socioeconomic values of the African buffalo

---

[1] Principles of Sustainble Use, Convention of Biological Diversity, COP Decision VII/12: www .cbd.int/decision/cop/?id=7749

in its various contexts in Africa. We also examine the African heritage associated with the African buffalo in the form of folklore and poems depicting the interconnectedness of the species' symbolic importance to people. These cultural forms and traditions have been handed down from one generation to another for centuries. However, these African worldviews have been progressively lost in recent natural resource discourses and paradigms framed by the dominant Western worldview (Mtenje and Soko, 1998). Finally, we describe the reality of the relationship between humans and the African buffalo, including the goods and services and the disservices provided by the African buffalo to humans.

Global Names for the African Buffalo

Among African mammals, the African buffalo has one of the largest ranges. Although this range has contracted recently (Chapter 4), it has provided an opportunity for buffalo species and humans to interact for millennia. This scenario developed because people (*Homo sapiens*) likewise inhabited the entire continent (e.g. Taylor, 2011). Beyond their obvious contribution to human diets when hunted, buffalo are part of the cosmology of many African societies, traces of which date back to as early as the Middle Stone Age (Faith, 2008; Dusseldorp, 2010; Chapter 2). Rock paintings by the ancient San communities that roamed sub-Saharan Africa provide evidence of this familiarity with the African buffalo. This relationship transcends African borders, and the African buffalo plays a role in human cultures worldwide. As evidence of its long interface with humanity, the African buffalo is known in different languages across the globe. Figure 1.1 presents a random and small sample of names given to the African buffalo across Africa.

This linguistic diversity based on millennia of interactions between human societies and buffalo reflects the richness of figurative labelling of the buffalo in people's representations. The long experience of African people with wildlife is also reflected in their use of animal-related, figurative terms to describe people. Figurative language is usually used to convey a message in a sarcastic manner and they demonstrate how wild animals are socially integrated into African societies. These labels are also derived from the folklore, songs and stories told by elderly Africans to their children as a way of encouraging desired behaviour and character (Ben-Amos, 1975; Knappert, 1977, 1985; Mtenje and Soko, 1998). Animal-centred figurative language and labels are applied in African societies to denote human attributes such as strength, beauty, height and

Figure 1.1 African names of the buffalo. A few randomly selected names of African buffalo among the 1,000 to 2,000 languages spoken in Africa. The location of the names is approximate due to sometimes wide or multiple location uses and overlap. The Roman alphabet has been intentionally used instead of the international phonetic alphabet. Many more African buffalo names are found in the lexicographic LEXICON database of the African languages by CNRS LLACAN laboratory, which lists 586 names for buffalo with 'buffle' as the entry point in the database and 631 names with 'buffalo' as the entry point (https://reflex.cnrs.fr/Africa/index.php?state=src). For language families, see Z. Frajzyngier, Afroasiatic languages. Oxford Research Encyclopedia – Linguistics (https://doi.org/10.1093/acrefore/9780199384655.013.15). See also Segerer and Flavier (2011–2018), Good (2017) and Dimmendaal (2020).

wit, as well as poverty, ugliness, stupidity, etc. The point here is not that Africans perceive human beings as being equivalent to wild animals, but rather that as Africans live with animals, they draw from animal messages about behaviour, collaboration, networks, social capital, appearance and fecundity (use value).

Animals, both domestic and wild, are therefore a 'living encyclopedia' and source of knowledge. In short, animals serve as 'hermeneutic texts' subject to multiple interpretations, including creating relationships within clans, predicting, impressing, condemning, judging and making important conclusions or recommendations. We remind readers that such euphemisms are also applied to groups, clans, tribes and even nations. The diversity of wildlife in Africa makes it possible to easily match many animal attributes with those of humans. Western readers may refer to the Fables of de la Fontaine, a work published in 1668, translated into every European language, and still widely read today (e.g. Lebrun, 2000).

The characteristics of the African buffalo given by elderly people in Harare (Mukamuri, personal communication, 2021) were undomesticated, unpredictable, assertive, dangerous and powerful. The buffalo is widely acclaimed in southern Africa for being so cruel because of its habit of urinating on the wounds of victims to check whether they are actually dead. If alive, it continues attacking until the adversary dies. Figurative language is also used by hunters in their descriptions of the African buffalo. The words include 'resistant', 'dangerous', 'vengeful' and having a 'piercing look'. In Ghana, however, the buffalo stands for 'uprightness', which is a positive connotation (Benson, 2021).

The African buffalo has also filled and still fills the imaginaries of European hunters. The species belongs to one of the Big Five, a classification of the most dangerous African mammals to hunt. In the book, *Horn of the Hunter*, Robert Ruark (1997) described the African Buffalo as follows: 'He looks at you as if you owe him money. I never saw such malevolence in the eyes of any animal or human being before or since'.[2] From another perspective, Kock (2005, 2014) and Michel and Bengis (2012) described the buffalo as a 'villain', when referring to the menace it causes when spreading diseases at the buffalo–livestock interface (Cortey et al., 2019; Chapter 9). This perception has not favoured the buffalo during some moments in history. For example, in the early twentieth century, entire buffalo populations outside protected areas were culled to control foot-and-mouth disease and rinderpest as part of efforts to boost commercial livestock production (see Chapter 12).

---

[2] www.johnxsafaris.com/hunting/cape-buffalo-hunts/

African Buffalo in Society: Mythology and Symbolism in Africa

Marks (1979) discusses the historical development of a culture among the Bisa of Zambia, which he termed the 'Buffalo Mystique'. Of significance in this culture was the high value placed on both tangible and intangible uses of buffalo, both central to the overall organization of the society. Similarly, in other parts of southern Africa, the close association between people and buffalo can be seen in the wide uses of the animal as a totemic symbol. It is in this region that many ethnic groups use the Nyati totem to organize clans and marriages.

The Bisa of Zambia recognize in the buffalo characteristics of strength, bravery and danger, but they also attribute a powerful 'spiritual' force to the animal. This notion is found in civilizations far removed from West Africa. For the members of the Malinke hunters' brotherhood, the buffalo is endowed with a particularly strong metaphorical spirit or major real element ('*nyama*'; Cissé, 1964), and it is for this same reason that the Hausa of Niger consider it a 'black' animal in the classification of animals based on the power of their spiritual essence (Levy-Luxereau, 1972).

The buffalo also appears in a series of 'horizontal' masks that have been observed over a wide area of West Africa (Frealle, 2002; Figure 1.2). The form of these masks varies, sometimes a buffalo is explicitly represented, notably in the grasslands of Cameroon, but sometimes other species are represented in a stylized manner (McNaughton, 1991). The reference to 'bush cow' appears in several of these masks, which are sometimes representations of hybrids between animals, humans and spirits. The dances and rituals involving the use of these masks are diverse, and although they are often associated with male initiation rituals, this is not their exclusive use. Generally speaking, these masks, especially those based on the form of stylized cattle, are seen as powerful and dangerous entities, associated with the transition from the wild (bush) world to humanized space (Berns and Fardon, 2011). Members of peasant societies have developed a rich cosmology in which the buffalo has a place. A review of myths on the origin of livestock in pastoral societies indicates that for several societies, buffalo are linked to the wild world while cows are associated with humans (Bonte, 2004; Box 1.1). At the other end of the African continent, a Berber myth (Frobenius and Fox, 1937) describes the first two creatures of the world as a buffalo and a heifer, with the former becoming the founding ancestor of wild animals and the latter

Figure 1.2 Anunuma Bush Buffalo Mask performs at a funeral. Tissé, Burkina Faso, 1984 (McNaughton, 1991). Photo by Christopher Roy (used with permission).

that of cattle. Furthermore, cows appear in the increasingly sophisticated costumes worn by the Swazi overlord during the *Ncwala*, the annual rite of royalty that lasts several days (Kuper, 1973). The power and ferocity of the buffalo also are represented in the rich Swazi cosmology.

According to Evans-Pritchard (1940), the Nuer People of South Sudan believe that the buffalo is 'cattle' that destroys people, for 'more people have died for the sake of a cow than for any other cause'. They have a story that tells how, when the beasts broke up their community and each went their own way to live their own lives, Man slew the mother of the Cow and the Buffalo. The Buffalo said she would avenge her mother by attacking men in the bush, but the Cow said that she would remain in the habitations of men and avenge her mother by causing endless disputes about debts, bride–wealth and adultery, which would lead to fighting and deaths among the people. This feud between Cow and Man has gone on from time immemorial, and day by day the Cow avenges the death of her mother by causing the death of men.

Hence, Nuer say of their cattle, 'They will be finished together with mankind', for men will all die on account of cattle and they and cattle will cease together (Evans-Pritchard, 1940).

Box 1.1 *Buffalo Folklore from the Atuot People, Southern Sudan*

Burton (1981) adds to a large basket of buffalo folklores from Africa by narrating one from the Atuot people. According to this folklore, once upon a time, men lived among themselves in their own camp in the forest. But among the animals they kept tethered were buffalo rather than cows. Men had no contact with women, but instead kept vaginas tied to their arms. At the same time, women lived in a camp by themselves by the river, tending herds of cattle, fishing and growing millet. The text continues: 'One day a buffalo calf strayed away from the other animals and did not return that evening. The next morning a man followed its trail, which led to the camp of women. Until this time when women desired sex, they went to the riverside and splashed the foam of the waves between their legs, giving birth to females only. When the man asked if his calf had come into the camp a woman answered no, and while he was satisfied with this reply, he soon took interest in another matter, asking the woman what the separation was between her legs. She answered: "This is vagina" and in turn asked what might be the thing dangling between his legs. When he answered, the man then said to the woman: "You bring that here and let me see if it is sweet." When he later said it was very, very good, all the other women of the camp rushed upon him and they had intercourse with him so much he died. A short while later the women said among themselves: "Now it is time to look after the cows", but each avoided the responsibility, saying: "It is now time to dry the millet so it can be pounded into flour." Then men from the other camp arrived in search of their friend. The women insulted them for thinking that their buffalo were like cows and went on pounding their grain. Seeing that the women appeared to take no interest in the cows, the men stole them. Later in the day each woman sought out a man of her liking and remained with him that evening. The next day, when each man wanted to marry a woman, the senior woman of the camp said: "You have given up your buffalo and that is good. But if you want to marry my daughters then you must give cows to replace them."'

Taboos that forbid the use of buffalo or even coming into close contact with them are also present in some large sections of African communities spread across the continent. For example, some Pygmy groups in Cameroon avoid buffalo because of a commonly held belief that it is inhabited by powerful evil spirits (Duda et al., 2018; see Chapter 16). Southern Africa harbours large ethnic groups, which include the Shona, Shangaan, Sotho and Venda, people who view the buffalo as sacred and who are not allowed to eat or touch the animal because of totemism. However, such taboos are slowly losing their power among people due to modernity and the infusion of other religions, especially Christianity (see also FAO/CIG, 2002). Marks (1979) squarely lays the blame for the destruction of African culture associated with the African buffalo and other wildlife on the emergence of modern institutions of control and in particular the implementation of so-called 'participatory' conservation programmes (Benson, 2021).

The iconic or symbolic nature of the African buffalo is also present in many social spheres such as military units, soccer teams, merchandise such as bicycles and T-shirts, haulage trucks and even buses. Buffalo symbols on such materials are a global feature. An Internet search for such symbols reveals wide and global use of the emblems and symbols. A good example is the 'Buffalo bicycle' (www.buffalobicycle .com), 'built for big loads on tough roads in Africa', with production in Kenya, Malawi, Zambia and Zimbabwe (Figure 1.3). This product borrows characteristics attached to the African buffalo such as robustness and power. Documented examples of the use of buffalo symbols/emblems in the military include the globally popular 'Buffalo soldiers', who were mainly former black slaves in the United States of America at the turn of the nineteenth century.[3] This military unit was eventually immortalized and internationalized by the world-famous reggae musician Robert 'Bob' Nester Marley, who released a song named 'Buffalo Soldier'. The American Buffalo soldiers were widely respected for their bravery and power. More recent military buffalo emblems may be found in present-day Zimbabwe with the buffalo insignia used by the national army's 3rd Infantry Brigade, and in South Africa with that used by the 32nd Battalion of the South African National Defence Force.[4] The same seems also to be the attraction for teams and individuals who wear T-shirts bearing buffalo signs.

---

[3] https://en.wikipedia.org/wiki/Buffalo_Soldier
[4] https://za.pinterest.com/pin/304204149811482618/

Figure 1.3 The 'Buffalo bicycle' is a well-appreciated product in the communal lands of Zimbabwe for its robustness, easiness to fix and adaptation to local conditions. Sengwe Communal Land. © A. Caron.

Buffalo Services: Subsistence and Trophy Hunting in Africa

African Subsistence Hunting

Palaeontological and archaeological evidence suggests that human ancestry in southern Africa dates back four million years, and throughout this time, humanity has hunted for survival (Crader, 1984; Walker, 1995; Plug, 2000; Badenhorst, 2003; Phillipson, 2005). Hunting can be done in pursuit of many benefits, for example maturity rituals, symbolism, recreation or trade, and for food, ecological balance and raising funds for conservation (Di Minin et al., 2016; Wanger et al., 2017; Hsiao, 2020). Despite different levels of compliance by all groups of people, hunting all over the world is regulated by laws and policies and its control is at the core of most wildlife conservation programmes.

Due to its size and abundance in large herds, the African buffalo played a significant role as a protein source for pre-colonial African societies (Marks, 1976, 2016). In Zambia, for example, although agriculture was an important part of the livelihood system, buffalo meat was a stock component in the identity and destiny of Valley Bisa lineage hunters (Marks, 2016). The meat was (and still is) also consumed for its good taste and flavour. Buffalo meat was a major source of protein in Zimbabwe before Africans were banned from buffalo hunting in 1930 (Mutwira, 1989).

Buffalo hunting, as with the hunting of other large animal species, can be dangerous, yet it has remained an important cultural and historical human activity. Hunting connects people with nature and is widely practiced as a maturity ritual for men in many African societies (Atta et al., 2021). The great difficulty, risk and effort involved in hunting buffalo also mean it provides rigorous exercise and adventure and accords a high status to the hunter.

As more and more natural habitats are transformed for human use, and relatively more buffalo populations are consequently found in protected areas (Chapter 4), traditional and subsistence hunting by Africans has increasingly become illegal and is referred to as 'subsistence poaching' or 'illegal hunting'. This phenomenon has put African cultures in a difficult dilemma by impeding them from engaging in important social and traditional activities linked to buffalo hunting, as well as preventing access to valuable protein. Despite the dismal failure of these measures at the local level, scientific studies continue to call for local community involvement in wildlife management, community education, local institutions and benefit-sharing to minimize poaching and compensate for the loss in protein (Hulme and Murphree, 2001; Lunstrum, 2017; Muboko, 2017; Ntuli et al., 2019). However, even if these measures were effective, they cannot compensate for the social and cultural values that have been lost.

Western Trophy Hunting

Interestingly, the experience of Western hunters indicates that the values, risks and perceptions attached to buffalo hunting are cross-cultural. Considered as a pest preventing the establishment of European livestock systems (due to competition and disease transmission) or as a noble thing to hunt, wildlife was targeted by colonial hunting and entire wildlife communities were decimated (Chapter 12). Trophy hunting in Africa developed in the twentieth century as an extreme sport for the perceived 'brave gentlemen', and today is a key management tool for the conservation of large tracts of Africa (Chapter 16). The African buffalo is a key species for trophy hunting in Africa. One reason is that its hunt bears a special aura for practitioners. A person who can take down a buffalo is viewed by some as very brave and a real man among all the other men in the community, in fact, a superhero (Erena et al., 2019).

The danger associated with buffalo hunting is not only associated with buffalo but also with other wild animals and the surrounding environment. Attacks on humans by wild animals, especially buffalo, can lead to permanent injuries or even death. Hunting a buffalo is a hair-raising experience. The sense of danger surrounding buffalo hunting, and hunting in general, is summed up by one writer (Box 1.2). Unfortunately, we could not find any similar accounts written by local African hunters.

Chapter 16 shows the relevance of trophy hunting and the special position of buffalo hunting in the wildlife economy and conservation in Africa. Unfortunately, the price of buffalo hunting is beyond the range of many ordinary traditional African hunters, who therefore cannot reconnect with this thread of their culture through legal and sustainable buffalo hunting. Interestingly, some African countries like Tanzania used to offer low-priced hunting permits to locals. However, the system became fraught with back-door deals whereby some westerners ended up using these permits to hunt buffalo. Innovative economic and social models of trophy hunting in which benefits are fairly shared with local communities and which draw from the knowledge, skills and experience of local individual hunters to provide a special experience to foreign hunters could be a path towards more integration between African cultures and wildlife economies on the one hand, and foreigner and African hunters' values on the other. Such models were partially explored by the CAMPFIRE programme (Communal Area Management Programme for Indigenous Resources) in Zimbabwe in the 1990s.

The CAMPFIRE initiative was an attempt to provide economic value to local human populations through the sustainable use of natural resources such as wildlife. It was first introduced in Zimbabwe in the mid-1980s, later expanded into Botswana and Namibia, and presented comparatively high economic benefits generated notably through buffalo hunting. CAMPFIRE sought to make the hunting of buffalo and other wild animals for sport an economic activity generating revenue for development projects seeking to improve local communities' living conditions and incomes. Despite some internal and external shortcomings, this form of genuine and inclusive public–private community partnerships (PPCPs) offers some opportunities for all stakeholders and

Box 1.2 *Extracts from a Buffalo Hunt Experience, One Among Many that can be Found on the Internet (https://journalofmountainhunting.com/augusts-in-africa/)*

'Looking into a wounded Cape buffalo's discomfortingly intelligent eyes takes you to depths few other animals seem to possess, depths made more profound by the knowledge that this animal is one very much capable of ending your life.'

'With his ferocious temper, treacherous intellect, and stern indifference to the shocking power of all but the most outlandishly large-calibre rifles, the Cape buffalo is routinely touted as the most dangerous member of the African Big Five (…).'

'In open flat country, he may present no serious threat to a hunter sufficiently armed, but you so seldom encounter him on baseball-diamond-like surroundings rather more often he'll be in some swampy thicket or dense forest where he is a clever enough lad to go to cover, and fierce enough to come out of it when it is to his advantage.'

'But when something like that gets into your blood, the rest of life comes to lack an ingredient you never knew, before, that it was supposed to have. I believe it got into mine one evening when we chased a breeding herd in and out of the forest for hours, jumping it and driving it ahead of us, trying to get a good look at one of the bulls in it.'

wildlife conservation (Hulme and Murphree, 2001; Frost and Bond, 2006; Chapter 16). The major limiting factor is a lack of meaningful profit for local households despite the huge challenges they face from living with wildlife (Gandiwa et al., 2013; Poshiwa et al., 2013). Weak local institutions, as well as usurped decision-making and benefit-sharing by politicians and local authorities, were also significant issues that corrupted the CAMPFIRE programme in Zimbabwe (Dzingirai, 1995).

Medicinal Use of the African Buffalo

African buffalo body parts are widely used by traditional healers and shamans as medicines to treat a wide range of diseases and ailments, and frequently as an aphrodisiac (Montcho et al., 2020). Almost all of the buffalo's body parts are used for medicinal purposes, but notably the horns and tails (Atta et al., 2021). The wide use of bones and skulls has been reported in South Africa, particularly among the Xhosa tribe (Nieman et al., 2019). Apart from their use as a putative cure for sickness, buffalo parts are used against witchcraft, bad luck, bad spells and to induce bravery. What is clear is that the use of buffalo parts as putative charms emanates from the characteristics of the animal that humans have observed over many years and their culturally constructed belief systems. These characteristics include its fighting ability, strength and instinctive ability to sense and avert impending danger. A more detailed presentation of claimed medicinal values and other uses of buffalo is presented in Chapter 16.

Buffalo Disservices: Human–Buffalo Conflicts

As with many large vertebrate species, negative interactions between buffalo and humans are often referred to as human–wildlife conflicts (HWCs). The term is omnipresent in the conservation literature (Bhatia et al., 2020), with studies focusing largely – if not only – on imagined conflicts between wild animals and rural populations living at the edge of African protected areas (e.g. Hoare and Du Toit, 2001; Brandon et al., 2010; de Garine-Wichatitsky et al., 2013; Ocholla et al., 2013; Megaze et al., 2017; Matseketsa et al., 2019). Readers will find a profusion of papers and reports explaining the ecological mechanisms of buffalo-related HWCs, the consequences of such conflicts, as well as methods and practices which could reduce their occurrence (e.g. Brandon et al., 2010; Geleta et al., 2019).

Buffalo engage in three types of conflicts with humans: crop raiding, disease transmission to cattle and humans (i.e. zoonoses) and direct accidents when encountering humans. Buffalo are not usually the main wildlife raiding crops (but can be locally), and often are overtaken by elephants, baboons (Mukeka et al., 2018) and especially rodents and insects (Lahm, 1991; Deodatus, 2000). In addition, many years of studies on HWC in Gabon placed the large rodents in the first position of HWC ahead of the elephant (Lahm, 1991), although this could have changed due to demographic changes in elephant populations estimated to be 95,000 in last census (Laguardia et al., 2021). However, any crop raiding can have a significant impact on the food security and livelihoods of farmers living near protected areas (Magama et al., 2018). Secondly, livestock owners living close to buffalo populations often consider the buffalo to be a reservoir for several important diseases that can harm cattle and people (e.g. bovine tuberculosis, foot-and-mouth disease and anthrax; for example de Garine-Wichatitsky et al., 2013; Zumla et al., 2020; Simpson et al., 2021; Chapters 9, 10 and 12). Finally, encounters with buffalo, especially bachelor males, when local residents move around their natural habitat (e.g. to fetch water) can end in death (Dunham et al., 2010; Chomba et al., 2012; Geleta et al., 2019). Although they are sometimes referred to as 'widow maker' or 'black death', buffalo 'only' kill an estimated 200 people each year in Africa, much fewer than crocodiles, hippopotamus and elephants.

Although negative interactions are real, we feel that framing them as conflicts is inadequate. This is largely because it logically calls for conflict resolution methods, often considered 'silver bullet' technical solutions expected to work in all circumstances, but ultimately failing to address context-specific underlying issues (Redpath et al., 2015; Davidar, 2018;). From a sociological perspective, HWCs do not exist independently of the social context where they take place, and in this regard, protected areas and their peripheries are often cultural battlegrounds, with long-lasting historical acts of injustice (Duffy, 2000; Blanc, 2015). Indeed, a central feature of these conflicts is that they involve a plurality of stakeholders whose worldviews, perspectives and agendas are often incompatible (Hill et al., 2017). The notion of HWC is mostly associated with negative interactions involving charismatic animals that reveal the conflicting values and interests held by different groups of people. Few would resort to the HWC narrative to define non-charismatic nuisance animals (e.g. rodents), or animals that all actors consider to be pests and which are managed through traditional animal damage control approaches (e.g. lethal control: Marchini et al., 2014; Redpath et al., 2015). This is partly why these interactions are so complicated to address, because like other social–ecological issues, they can be considered to be 'wicked problems' (Rittel and Webber, 1973).

Perrotton et al. (2017) bring to the fore the wicked nature of buffalo–human conflicts in the western part of Zimbabwe. The authors demonstrate how, although all of the human actors involved acknowledge the reality of a conflictive relationship with and about buffalo, it is impossible to define both the nature and the cause of the conflict. While some actors are concerned about zoonosis, others complain about livestock–buffalo competition for grazing, and for some the 'real' issue is that the presence of livestock in protected areas (instead of buffalo) decreases the attractiveness of the place for tourists who would rather see buffalo. How can the conflict be addressed if we cannot clearly define it? As for the causes to address, for some the root of the problem is the number of cattle on the territory, while for others it is the modalities of access to grazing land, while yet others blame human demography, or the failure of wildlife damage compensation mechanisms, or an obsolete narrative about the wilderness being a pristine place with no trace of human presence that is told to tourists.

Several alternative narratives were proposed and could fit negative interactions with the buffalo: buffalo–livestock competition, human–wildlife competition or human–wildlife coexistence (Madden, 2004). Unfortunately, despite the critiques, the HWC framework remains popular (Bhatia et al., 2020), probably thanks to its simplicity and ease of use to describe a diversity of situations, allowing it to become a buzzword used to amplify conservation initiatives, or to create and maintain a sense of urgency justifying funding (Peterson et al., 2010). Continued use of the term HWC denotes a superfluous or rather fake equality between human beings and wildlife and an attempt to mask the less publicized and real 'human-to-human conflicts', a recurrent 'Cold War' type of relationship located within global, regional and national conservation paradigms, aimed at the exclusion of one group of people by another, especially local communities, but framed as 'wars between people' and 'innocent' wildlife (Gandiwa et al., 2013).

Conclusion

The African buffalo across its vast African range has coexisted with humans for millennia. This coexistence is part of the bestiary of the few imaginaries and mythologies that have managed to reach us. Sometimes, as the obscure brother of the cattle or cow that never agreed to be domesticated, it forms part of the original stories that today define some African cultures. Although other buffalo species have been domesticated in Asia, the African buffalo is broadly perceived or generally considered to be undomesticated, unpredictable, assertive, dangerous and powerful, and these characteristics spill over to the humans (mostly men!) who carry its name or symbolically co-opt its soul. These representations of the species in African cultures seem to have percolated more recently into the imaginaries of European cultures, especially from the angle of hunting and photographic safaris. Despite some of the representations of the species in global culture, African cultural values associated with the buffalo are declining in Africa as these cultures are not perpetuated and are being lost.

The buffalo is also at the centre of services and disservices to different actors, providing uses but also generating conflicts in African landscapes.

An invaluable source of protein for subsistence livelihoods, its access is now mostly forbidden by law to most African users, particularly in southern African countries. However, within the wildlife economy, the buffalo is a key asset that can generate important profits for the beneficiaries of hunting and photographic safaris who are too rarely its former African users (Chapter 16). For animal health services, mostly the products of livestock production systems imported in colonial times, the buffalo represents in some instances a public enemy like the tsetse fly, influencing meat trade policies, land uses and boundaries in many parts of the continent, and once again not for the benefit of local residents (Chapters 9, 10 and 12). The buffalo is also a central species in HWC, creating fear and negative feelings.

The African buffalo is therefore an emblem of the coexistence between humans and nature in Africa. It is feared and respected, hated and loved, hunted, eaten and protected. The 'bush cow' that never accepted to be domesticated, the wild cattle 'made in Africa' still resists human domination and fascinates many.

References

Atta, A.C.-J., O. Soulemane, B. Kadjo, and Y.R. Kouadio (2021). Some uses of the African buffalo *Syncerus caffer* (Sparrman, 1779) by the populations living around the Comoé National Park (North-East Ivory Coast). *Journal of Animal & Plant Sciences* **47**(2): 8484–8496.

Badenhorst, S. (2003). The Archaeofauna from iNkolimahashi Shelter, a Later Stone Age shelter in the Thukela Basin, KwaZulu-Natal, South Africa. *Southern African Humanities* **15**: 45–57.

Ben-Amos, D. (1975). Folklore in African society. *Research in African Literatures* **6**(2): 165–198.

Benson, G. (2021). African traditional religion and natural resource management: the role of totems and deity worship in Ghana. *American Journal of Environment Studies* **4**(1): 13–37.

Berns, M.C. and R. Fardon (2011). Central Nigeria unmasked. Arts of the Benue River Valley. *African Arts* **44**(3): 16–37.

Bhatia, S., M. Stephen, S.M. Redpath, et al. (2020). Beyond conflict: exploring the spectrum of human–wildlife interactions and their underlying mechanisms. *Oryx* **54**(5): 621–628.

Blanc, G. (2015). *Une Histoire environnementale de la nation. Regards croisés sur les parcs nationaux du Canada, d'Éthiopie et de France*. Paris: Publications de la Sorbonne,.

Bonte, P. (2004). Des peuples du bétail. Origines mythiques et pratiques rituelles de l'Élevage en Afrique de l'Est. *Techniques & Culture* [En ligne]: 43–44.

Brandon P.A., P. Scott and A. Antypas (2010). Sitting on the fence? Policies and practices in managing human–wildlife conflict in Limpopo Province, South Africa. *Conservation and Society* **8**(3): 225–240.

Burton, J.W. (1981). The wave is my mother's husband: a piscatorial theme in pastoral nilotic ethnology. *Cahiers d'Études Africaines* **84**: 459–477.

Chomba, C., R. Senzota, H. Chabwela, et al. (2012). Patterns of human wildlife conflicts in Zambia, causes, consequences and management responses. *Journal of Ecology and the Natural Environment* **4**(12): 303–313.

Cissé, Y. (1964). Notes sur les sociétés de chasseurs malinké. *Journal de la Société des Africanistes* **34**(2): 175–226.

Cortey, M., L. Ferretti, E. Pérez-Martín, et al. (2019). Persistent infection of African buffalo (*Syncerus caffer*) with foot-and-mouth disease virus: limited viral evolution and no evidence of antibody neutralization escape. *Journal of Virology* **93**(15): e00563–19.

Crader, D.C. (1984). The zooarchaeology of the storehouse and the dry well at Monticello. *American Antiquity* **49**(3): 542–558.

Davidar, P. (2018). The term human–wildlife conflict creates more problems than it resolves: better labels should be considered. *Journal of Threatened Taxa* **10**(8): 12082–12085.

de Garine-Wichatitsky, M., E. Miguel, B. Mukamuri, et al. (2013). Co-existing with wildlife in transfrontier conservation areas in Zimbabwe: cattle owners' awareness of diseases risks and perceptions of the role played by wildlife. *Comparative Immunology and Microbiology and Infectious Diseases* **36**: 321–332.

Deodatus, F. (2000). Wildlife damage in rural areas with emphasis on Malawi. In H.H.T. Prins, J.G. Grootenhuis, and T.T. Dolan (Eds.), *Wildlife Conservation by Sustainable Use*. Boston: Kluwer, pp. 115–140.

Di Minin, E., N. Leader-Williams and C.J.A. Bradshaw (2016). Banning trophy hunting will exacerbate biodiversity loss. *Trends in Ecology & Evolution* **31**:99–102.

Dimmendaal, G.J. (2020). Nilo-Saharan. In R. Vossen and G.J. Dimmendaal (Eds.), *The Oxford Handbook of African Languages*. Oxford: Oxford University Press, p. 364.

Duda, R., S. Gallois and V. Rayes-Garica (2018). Ethnozoology of bushmeat: importance of wildlife in diet, food avoidances and perception of health among the Baka (Cameroon). *Revue d'ethnoécologie* **14**. https://doi.org/10.4000/ethnoecologie.3976.

Duffy, R. (2000). *Killing for Conservation: Wildlife Policy in Zimbabwe*. James Currey Ltd.

Dunham, K., A. Ghiurghi, R. Cumbi and F. Urbano (2010). Human–wildlife conflict in Mozambique: A national perspective, with emphasis on wildlife attacks on humans. *Oryx* **44**(2): 185-193.

Dusseldorp, G.L. (2010). Prey choice during the South African Middle Stone Age: avoiding dangerous prey or maximising returns? *African Archaeological Review* **27**: 107–133.

Dzingirai, V. (1995). 'Take Back Your Campfire': A Study of Local Level Perceptions to Electric Fencing in the Framework of Binga's CAMPFIRE Programme. CASS Occasional Paper NRM Series, July 1995.

Erena, M.E., H. Jebessa and A. Bekele (2019). Consequences of land-use/land-cover dynamics on range shift of Cape buffalo in Western Ethiopia. *International Journal of Ecology and Environmental Sciences* **45**(2): 123–136.

Evans-Pritchard, E.E. (1940). *The Nuer: A Description of the Modes of Livelihood and Political Institutions of a Nilotic People*. Oxford: Clarendon Press, p. 271.

Faith, J.T. (2008). Eland, buffalo, and wild pigs: were Middle Stone Age humans ineffective hunters? *Journal of Human Evolution* **55**: 24–36.

FAO/CIG. (2002). Assessment of bushmeat trade during the annual closed season on hunting in Ghana (1st August–1st December 2001). Accra, Ghana: Conservation International (www.fao.org/docrep/010/ai793e/ai793e00.htm).

Frealle, P. (2002). *Les animaux dans les masques d'Afrique de l'ouest*. Maison Alfort, Thèse, Ecole Vétérinaire.

Frobenius, L. and D.C. Fox (1937). *African Genesis*. New York: Stackpole Sons.

Frost, G.H. and I. Bond (2006). *CAMPFIRE and the Payment for Environmental Services*. London: International Institute for Environment and Development.

Gandiwa, E., I.M.A. Heitkönig, A.M. Lokhorst, et al. (2013). CAMPFIRE and human–wildlife conflicts in local communities bordering northern Gonarezhou National Park, Zimbabwe. *Ecology and Society* **18**(4): 7.

Geleta, M., H. Jebessa and A. Bekele (2019). Human–buffalo conflict around Jorgo-Wato Protected Forest, western Ethiopia. *Global Veterinaria* **21**: 17–23.

Good, J. (2017). Niger-Congo languages. In R. Hickey (Ed.), *The Cambridge Handbook of Areal Linguistics*. Cambridge: Cambridge University Press, pp. 471–499.

Hill, C.M., A.D. Webber and N.E. Priston (Eds.) (2017). *Understanding Conflicts about Wildlife: A Biosocial Approach* (Vol. 9). New York: Berghahn Books.

Hoare, R.E. and J.T. Du Toit (2001). Coexistence between people and elephants in African savannas. *Conservation Biology* **13**: 633–639.

Hsiao, T. (2020). A moral defense of trophy hunting. *Sport, Ethics and Philosophy* **14**(1): 26–34.

Hulme, D. and M.W. Murphree (2001). *African Wildlife and Livelihoods: The Promise and Performance of Community Conservation*. Oxford: James Currey, p. 336.

Knappert, J. (Ed.) (1977). *Bantu Myths and Other Tales*. Religious texts translations series NISABA 7. Leiden: Brill.

Knappert, J. (1985). *Myths and Legends of Botswana, Lesotho and Swaziland*. Leiden: Brill.

Kock, R.A. (2005). What is the famous wildlife/livestock disease interface? A review of current knowledge. Presented at Southern and East African Experts Panel on Designing Successful Conservation and Development Interventions at the Wildlife/Livestock Interface: Implications for Wildlife, Livestock and Human Health. AHEAD Animal Specialist Group for the Environment and Development Forum. IUCN/SSC Veterinary. Gland, Switzerland and Cambridge, UK, 14–15 September 2003.

Kock, R.A. (2014). African buffalo – a reflexion on pathways to healthy animal harvest and production systems. African Buffalo Symposium Presentations, 5–6 August 2014, Paris.

Kuper, H. (1973). Costume and cosmology: the animal symbolism of the Ncwala. *Man*, **8**(4): 613–630.

Laguardia, A., S. Bourgeois, S. Strindberg, et al. (2021). Nationwide abundance and distribution of African forest elephants across Gabon using non-invasive SNP genotyping. *Global Ecology and Conservation* **32**: e01894.

Lahm, S.A. (1991). Human use of forest resources and local variations of wildlife populations in North-Eastern Gabon. Unpublished report, 6335 Lamda Drive, San Diego, California 92120 USA.

Lebrun, M. (2000). *Regards actuels sur les Fables de La Fontaine* (Vol. 8). Villeneuve d'Ascq: Presses Universitaires Septentrion.

Levy-Luxereau, A. (1972). *Etude ethno-zoologique du pays Hausa en République du Niger*. Paris: Société d'Etudes Ethno-zoologiques et Ethno-botaniques.

Lunstrum, E. (2017). Feed them to the lions: conservation violence goes online. *Geoforum* **79**: 134–143.

Madden, F. (2004). Creating coexistence between humans and wildlife: global perspectives on local efforts to address human–wildlife conflict. *Human Dimensions of Wildlife* **9**: 247–257.

Magama, Y.A., M. Babagana, A.U. Usman, et al. (2018). Assessment of wildlife species mostly involved in human-wildlife conflict around Yankari Game Reserve, Bauchi State, Nigeria. *International Journal of Contemporary Research and Review* **9**(9): 20262–20277.

Marchini, S., B. Ferraz and A. Zimmermann (2014). Planning for coexistence in a complex human-dominated world. In B. Frank, J.A. Glickman and S. Marchini (Eds.), *Human–Wildlife Interactions: Turning Conflict into Coexistence*. Cambridge: Cambridge University Press, p. 414.

Marks, S. (1976). *Large Mammals and a Brave People: Subsistence Hunters in Zambia*. Seattle: University of Washington Press.

Marks, S.A. (1979). Profile and process: subsistence Hunters in a Zambian community. *Africa: Journal of the International African Institute* **49**(1): 53–67.

Marks, S.A. (2016). *Life as Hunt: Thresholds of Identities and Illusions on an African Landscape*. New York: Berghahn Books.

Matseketsa, G., N. Muboko, E. Gandiwa, et al. (2019). An assessment of human–wildlife conflicts in local communities bordering the western part of Save Valley Conservancy, Zimbabwe. *Global Ecology and Conservation* **20**: e00737.

McGinnis, M.D. and E. Ostrom (2014). Social–ecological system framework: initial changes and continuing challenges. *Ecology and Society* **19**(2).

McNaughton, P. (1991). Is there history in horizontal masks? A preliminary response to the dilemma of form. *African Arts* **24**(2): 40–53.

Megaze, A., M. Balakrishnan and G. Belay (2017). Human–wildlife conflict and attitude of local people towards conservation of wildlife in Chebera Churchura National Park, Ethiopia. *African Zoology* **52**(1), 1–8.

Michel, A. and R.G. Bengis (2012). The African buffalo: a villain for inter-species spread of infectious diseases in southern Africa. *The Onderstepoort Journal of Veterinary Research* **79**(2): E1–E5.

Montcho, M., J.P. Ilboudo, E.D. Dayou, et al. (2020). Human use-pressure and sustainable wildlife management in Burkina Faso: a case study of bushmeat hunting in Bobo-Dioulasso. *Journal of Sustainable Development* **13**: 3.

Mtenje, A.I and B. Soko (1998). Oral traditions among the northern region Malawi Ngoni. *Journal of Humanities* **12**: 1–18.

Muboko, N. (2017). The role of transfrontier conservation areas and their institutional framework in natural resource-based conflict management: a review. *Journal of Sustainable Forestry* **36**(6): 583–603.

Mukeka, J.M., J.O. Ogutu, E. Kanga and E. Roskaft (2018). Characteristics of human–wildlife conflicts in Kenya: examples of Tsavo and Maasai Mara regions. *Environment and Natural Resources Research* **8**(3): 148.

Mutwira, R. (1989). Southern Rhodesian wildlife policy (1890–1953): a question of condoning game slaughter? *Journal of Southern African Studies* **15**(2): 250–262.

Nieman, W.A., A.J. Leslie and A. Wilkinson (2019). Traditional medicinal animal use by Xhosa and Sotho communities in the Western Cape Province, South Africa. *Journal of Ethnobiology and Ethnomedicine* **15**: 34.

Ntuli, H., S.C. Jagers, A. Linell, M. Sjöstedt and E. Muchapondwa (2019). Factors influencing local communities' perceptions towards conservation of transboundary wildlife resources: the case of the Great Limpopo Trans-frontier Conservation Area. *Biodiversity and Conservation* **28**: 2977–3003.

Ocholla, G.O., J. Koske, G.W. Asoka, et al. (2013). Assessment of traditional methods used by the Samburu pastoral community in human wildlife conflict management. *International Journal of Humanities and Social Science* **3**(11): 292:302.

Organization for Economic Cooperation & Development, Development. Development Assistance Committee, OECD Staff, & Development (OECD) Staff (2001). *The DAC Guidelines: Poverty Reduction*. Paris: OECD.

Perrotton, A., M. de Garine-Wichatitsky, H. Valls-Fox and C. Le Page (2017). My cattle and your park: codesigning a role-playing game with rural communities to promote multi-stakeholder dialogue at the edge of protected areas. *Ecology and Society* **22**(1).

Peterson, J.N., J.L. Birckhead, K. Leong, et al. (2010). Rearticulating the myth of human–wildlife conflict. *Conservation Letters* **3**(2): 74–82.

Phillipson, D.W. (2005). *African Archaeology* (3rd ed.). Cambridge: Cambridge University Press.

Plug, I. (2000). Overview of Iron Age fauna from the Limpopo valley. *South African Archaeological Society, Goodwin Series* **8**: 117–126.

Poshiwa, X., R.A. Groeneveld, I.M.A. Heitkönig, et al. (2013). Reducing rural households' annual income fluctuations due to rainfall variation through diversification of wildlife use: portfolio theory in a case study of south eastern Zimbabwe. *Tropical Conservation Science* **6**: 201–220.

Redpath, S., S. Bhatia and J. Young (2015). Tilting at wildlife: reconsidering human–wildlife conflict. *Oryx* **49**(2): 222–225.

Rittel, H.W. and M. Webber (1973). Dilemmas in a general theory of planning. *Policy Sciences* **4**: 155–169.

Ruark, R.S. (1997). *Horn of the Hunter: The Story of an African Safari*. Huntington Beach: Safari Press.

Segerer, G. and S. Flavier (2011–2018). *RefLex: Reference Lexicon of Africa, Version 1.1*. Paris: Lyon. http://reflex.cnrs.fr/.

Simpson, G., P.N. Thompson and C. Saegerman (2021). Brucellosis in wildlife in Africa: a systematic review and meta-analysis. *Scientific Reports* **11**: 5960.

Taylor, N. (2011). The origins of hunting and gathering in the Congo basin: a perspective on the Middle Stone Age Lupemban industry. *Before Farming* **2011**(1): 1–21.

Walker, N.J. (1995). *The Late Pleistocene and Holocene Hunter-Gatherers of the Matopos (Studies in African Archaeology 10)*. Uppsala: Societas Archaeologica Upsaliensis.

Wanger, T.C., L.W. Traill, R. Cooney, et al. (2017). Trophy hunting certification. *Nature Ecology & Evolution* **1**: 1791–1793.

Zumla, A., D.S. Hui, I. Esam, et al. (2020). Reducing mortality from 2019-nCoV: host-directed therapies should be an option. *The Lancet* **395**(10224): e35–e36.

Part I
Conservation

D. CORNELIS

The Odyssey of the African Buffalo

The African continent hosts a unique diversified megafaunal assemblage, one which exceeds that of any other biogeographical region of the world. The African buffalo is the largest African bovid and occurs throughout most of sub-Sahara in a wide range of ecosystems, from savanna to rainforest. It exhibits a marked morphological polymorphism across its range, greater than most other African mammals, both in body size and weight, but also in pelage colour and horn shape. The African buffalo is also one of the most successful large African mammals in terms of abundance and biomass. In this context, this species represents a powerful model to enhance our understanding of African biogeography and wildlife conservation.

Buffalo, together with around 80 per cent of ungulates (hoofed mammals), belong to the bovid family, characterized by the presence of two or rarely four unforked horns (at least in the adult male). In Africa, this family, which includes the true antelopes and the African buffalo, emerged some 2.8 million years ago following the increase of open habitats and the expansion of grasslands.

Since the differentiation of African buffalo, which took place some 500,000 years ago, major climate fluctuations during the Quaternary shaped distribution range and caused population oscillations. The expansion of the equatorial rainforest towards eastern Africa during pluvial periods periodically formed a major biogeographical barrier to gene flow between savanna populations. This is why African wildlife species with a continental distribution pattern show a biogeographical pattern structured north and south of the equatorial forest belt. In the African buffalo, this resulted in the emergence of two main genetic lineages: *Syncerus caffer caffer* in eastern and southern Africa, and *S. c. nanus* in western and central Africa.

In addition to climate change, humans and their newly domesticated animals have posed a worldwide ecological threat to wildlife since the beginning of the Holocene epoch (about 12,000 years ago). The Holocene resulted in the extinction of many mammals weighing more than 40 kg. Nevertheless, such a drastic reduction did not occur in Africa, where humans and wildlife had long coevolved (with the exception of some species like the giant long-horned buffalo (*Pelorovis antiquus*); Chapter 2).

In Africa, anthropogenic pressure on African wildlife took on an unprecedented scale from the Neolithic revolution onwards, marked in eastern and southern Africa by the Bantu expansion. From about 3000 BC until AD 1800, human populations originating from present-day Cameroon, Central African Republic and Congo undertook a long series of migrations and settled eastern and southern Africa, which until then had been occupied by small populations of nomadic hunter-gatherers for the past 100,000 years. These migrants brought with them several important commodities and skills, such as domesticated animals (including cattle), cultivation of crops (millet, sorghum, etc.) and the manufacture of metal weapons. This revolution, together with climatic factors, resulted in a strong decline of Cape buffalo populations as shown by recent genetic investigations (Chapter 3).

About 130 years ago, another major crisis hit the African buffalo populations on a continental scale. The introduction of the exotic rinderpest morbillivirus in 1889 by a colonial military expedition to the Horn of Africa caused up to 95 per cent mortality among buffalo populations, wildebeest and cattle across Africa. This was followed by other episodes throughout the twentieth century, until its official eradication in 2011 (last case reported in 2001; Chapter 4). Despite an extremely high mortality rate reported at the continental scale, the Great Rinderpest pandemic apparently had very low impact on the genetic diversity of the African buffalo, as shown by recent studies (Chapter 3). Throughout the twentieth century, buffalo populations gradually recovered, but obviously not to the levels that prevailed before the Great Rinderpest pandemic of the 1880s.

The sub-Saharan human population grew exponentially throughout the twentieth century, increasing from 95 million in 1900 to 1.1 billion by 2020. According to current projections, this figure could reach 1.8 billion in 2050 (i.e. a nearly 20-fold increase in 150 years). To meet the needs of the human populations in Africa and the raw material needs of the rest of the world, many natural habitats have been transformed or severely degraded, and what remains is under increasing pressure. The original distribution range of the African buffalo and wildlife in general therefore was (and still is being) progressively reduced and relegated to protected areas, which today cover around 16 per cent of the total land area. However, in the face of human pressure, the integrity of numerous protected areas has been jeopardised. Hence, the overall number of large mammals in Africa within protected areas decreased by 60 per cent between 1970 and 2005 and by about 85 per cent in Western Africa during that same period.

In response to this major crisis, African governments together with the international community have mobilized in recent decades, and conservation efforts are beginning to bear fruit. As we will see in Chapter 4, African buffalo populations have stabilized overall over the last 20 years. However, these figures conceal major disparities between regions, as well as the concentration of wildlife populations in the besieged fortresses that protected areas have become.

2 · *The Evolutionary History of the African Buffalo: Is It Truly a Bovine?*

H. H. T. PRINS, J. F. DE JONG AND
D. GERAADS

Introduction

If one sees an African buffalo (*Syncerus caffer*) for the first time after see-ing many water buffalo (*Bubalus bubalis*), one could easily believe they are closely related. In 1758, Carolus Linnaeus named the water buffalo scientifically, but he did not classify the African buffalo. The first formal mention is by Anders Sparrmann (1779), a pupil of Linnaeus, who clas-sified the species as *Bos caffer*, just as his mentor had classified the Asian species as *Bos bubalis*. A military artist named Charles Hamilton Smith coined the Latin genus name *Bubalus* for the Asian buffalo in 1827. A nineteenth-century taxonomist, Brian Hodgson, elevated the African buffalo to its own genus, namely, *Syncerus* Hodgson, 1847. What justi-fies the separation of these two 'buffalo' into distinct genera? Strangely enough, two fundamental characters: namely, in *Syncerus* the vomer and the palate are not fused, and the nuchal hair-stream is not reversed (Groves, 1969). Groves states: 'Consequently the generic separation of *Bubalus* from *Syncerus* seems thoroughly justified, and some at least of the similarity between them (such as that in the shape of the horn cores) must be put down to parallelism.' Whether these two fundamental traits have any ecological meaning is unknown, but the case for parallelism is intriguing.

A systematic classification is in principle based on diagnosable (often morphological, thus not necessarily functionally important) characters, mainly of extant species (see Zachos, 2018 for a review). Systematicists decided that the African buffalo should not be classified into one genus with the Asian buffalo, but does the fossil material combined with DNA-based phylogenies provide enough clues to establish the evolutionary history of the African buffalo? Our analysis will show that there is quite some doubt as to whether the African buffalo is related to the Asian buffalo species swarm, or to the larger one comprising wild cattle, yak and bison. The question that arises, of course, is whether taxonomy and systematics have any bearing on ecology and management. We believe it does if, by having knowledge on related species, one can more safely generalize; if not, then systematics at the level of the genus or higher is irrelevant. Indeed, conservation is about species – not genera, families or tribes.

The African buffalo is a large bovid. Mammals are classified as 'bovid' if they have, at least in the adult male, two or rarely four unforked horns. These are composed of bone cores protruding from their skull after 'horn buds' which are covered by a permanent layer of keratin start growing in the skin and fuse with the skull (Davis et al., 2014). Bovids emerged some 18.5 Myr ago (Vrba and Schaller, 2000) or even slightly more recently (Bibi, 2013). Some studies refer to an older emergence of the Bovidae based on material from Mongolia in the Middle Oligocene, thus 26 Myr ago (Trofimov, 1958; see Thomas, 1984), but this is now questioned (Métais et al., 2003). The mammals classified as Bovidae are thought to be related to each other, and the common trait of unforked horns is taken to be a shared, derived character, common between ancestor and descendants. Modern molecular techniques allowed this assumption to be put to the test, resulting in updated insights about the classification of the ~140 bovid species within the approximately 40 genera (Grubb, 1993). Within this group of Bovidae, African buffalo are classified with the subfamily Bovinae, within the tribe Bovini. The other two tribes in that subfamily are the Tragelaphini and the Boselaphini. All other bovids are classified within the subfamily Antilopinae.

Modern molecular techniques show that the subfamily Antilopinae as classified by morphologists has a very different evolutionary, and thus classificatory, structure than previously thought (Ropiquet and Hassanin, 2005; Hassanin, 2014). Enough reasonably well-dated fossils are available to pinpoint some major bifurcations between tribes in time. These phylogenies all suggest that the tribe Bovini is nested together with the Tragelaphini and the Boselaphini in one 'proper' subfamily, the Bovinae (Bibi, 2013; Druica et al., 2016). At first sight, the message about the evolution of the Bovini does not appear to have changed much since publications by Sinclair (1977) and Gentry and Gentry (1978). Yet there is now perhaps more reason to consider the

Bovini as a heterogeneous (non-monophyletic) group, the African buffalo not being closely related to either the water buffalo of Asia (*Bubalus*) or oxen, bisons and yaks. Perhaps it deserves a special tribe, Syncerini, but the evolution of the Bovini is still shrouded in much uncertainty. Five insights play havoc. First, phylogenies based on molecular markers rely heavily on available genetic material. For bovids, to date this material has been taken from living and thus contemporary specimens; fossil material does not yet play a role, except for some very recently extinct species. This means that for extinct tribes or even subfamilies there is no genetic information that has the potential to upset phylogenies that are based on parsimonious calculus (cf. Frantz et al., 2013; Table 2.1). Second, the phylogeny based on mitochondrial DNA shows a short period around 18–15 Myr in which the Boselaphini, Tragelaphini and Bovini separated (Hassanin, 2014; Zurano et al., 2019). It should be realized, however, that the phylogenetic trees based on DNA suggest such divergence to have taken place some 10 million years before the oldest finds of Tragelaphini (second half Late Miocene, *c.*7 Myr) or Bovini (*c.*8 Myr). Furthermore, the calibration of the molecular-based phylogeny is based on fossils from other families mainly (see Zurano et al., 2019 for details) while fossil Boselaphini may be hard to identify, because early forms had few distinctive features. Third, the fossil material itself may indicate that Bovini evolved from Boselaphini several times and not just once (Gentry, 2010). In fact, evidence for this is very slender, but this may nevertheless still be true because there is no evidence that early African Bovini (which are rare and poorly known) are derived from Asian forms. It is quite possible that they derived directly from African Boselaphini (close to *Tragoportax*; see Figure 2.1). Fourth, the number of Bovid species recognized in the fossil material is strongly determined by sampling effort, and there are many more sites for some periods than for others (Patterson et al., 2014). Lastly, within the Bovini tribe there is a worrying lack of clarity about not only the proper naming of species and genera in the fossil material, but also whether particular fossil species and their living descendants should be taken to belong to a particular genus or to another. Much dust has been stirred up on the systematic position of *Pelorovis*. Was it a distinct genus? Did it belong to the genus *Bos*? Did it belong to the genus *Syncerus*? Yet if animal populations cannot be classified into valid species and allocated precise generic status, then concepts like 'competitive exclusion' or 'niche differentiation' become very difficult to apply.

Table 2.1 *Interplay between palaeontology and genetics to deduce a reliable phylogeny. The trade-off one makes between knowledge from genetics and palaeontological knowledge is not straightforward. It may upset established phylogeny, yet it may also strengthen it. If knowledge from palaeontology and genetics (if these have been reached independently) overlap, inference about the past is very strong. If there are mismatches between the two fields of enquiry, a research strategy can be formulated once one realizes the mismatch.*

		Genetics		
		Species that have been allotted an unquestionable place in a phylogeny, thus 'knowns'	Species of which the place in a phylogeny depends on a priori choices	Species of which the genetics has not yet been carried out, thus 'unknowns'
Palaeontology	*Knowns* (i.e. species that have been found and have been classified with confidence)	If there is a match, we have reached a true justified belief (the hallmark of good science). If the two do not match, both fields of knowledge have to actively work together to solve the issues. Exciting new insights can arise: e.g. on the origin of *Bison bonasus* as a possible hybrid species of *Bison priscus* and *Bos primigenius*	Genetics should follow palaeontology and recalculate phylogenies. Bayesian approaches should incorporate prior knowledge from palaeontology	Here future progress in palaeo-DNA will perhaps make very unexpected changes
	Uncertain (i.e. species that have been found but about which the classification is unsure)	Palaeontology should incorporate knowledge from genetics to decide on the best place of such a species in an existing phylogeny	Danger exists that there is false certainty in published phylogenies by geneticists	A general state of ignorance predominates
	Unknowns (i.e. species that have not yet been found or identified)	Phylogenies based on absent species may give a false sense of certainty	Phylogenies based on absent species may give a false sense of certainty	'Unknown unknowns', which may upset any established phylogeny

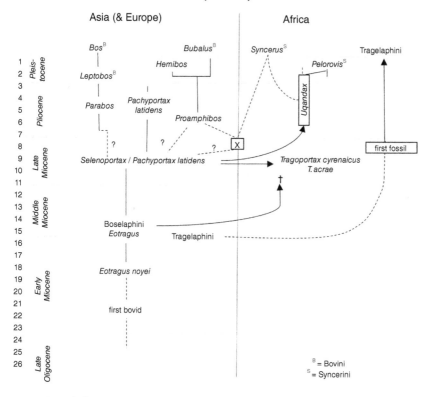

Figure 2.1 Phylogeny of the Bovini and Syncerini. During the Pleistocene members of the genus *Bos* ventured into Africa too (see text). The separation between Boselaphini and Bovini or Syncerini is very unclear.

The Genus *Pelorovis* and the *Syncerus antiquus* Conundrum

We start with *Pelorovis* and the issues surrounding its phylogenetic position to better understand the evolution of *Syncerus*. The most important insight that emerges is that there was a second species of *Syncerus*, namely *S. antiquus*, in much of Africa that went extinct only very recently, in the last two millennia. It overlapped in space and in time with the extant African buffalo.

Hans Reck started the excavations in Olduvai (Tanzania) and found the remains of a large mammal, which he named *Pelorovis* ('frightful sheep'). Later, Gentry (1967) classified *Pelorovis* with the Bovini, but thought it to be very distantly related to the Asian Bovini. *Pelorovis* may have been derived from *Simatherium* (Geraads, 1992) like the African buffalo *Syncerus*. The difficulty of Bovini classification is well underscored by the struggle palaeontologists have in allocating the different species of

Pelorovis to their classificatory nook: does a fossil belong to *Pelorovis* or to *Bos* or *Syncerus*, and, alternatively, should the genus *Pelorovis* be seen as an independent genus, or do the species of this genus better fit in *Bos* or *Syncerus*? Indeed, an identical specimen may be classified as *Pelorovis* or as *Simatherium* (Gentry, 2010), showing the opaqueness of the systematics and phylogeny of the Bovini (see Table 2.1).

Seven species of *Pelorovis* have been named. *Pelorovis oldowayensis* is the best-known form; it has long, regularly curved horncores, first emerging almost posteriorly but recurving forwards, with a total span that can reach 2 m. It is best represented in Olduvai, but also in other Eastern African sites and in Israel (Geraads, 1986). *Pelorovis turkanensis* has shorter horns; it overlaps in time with the former species, but appears earlier. The North African '*Bos*' *bubaloides*, '*Bos*' *praeafricanus* and *Pelorovis howelli* (Hadjouis and Sahnouni, 2006) are almost certainly identical with one or the other East African forms. *Pelorovis kaisensis* from Uganda and perhaps Ethiopia differs in its virtually straight horns (Geraads and Thomas, 1994; Alemseged et al., 2020). The origin of the genus is unclear, especially because the distinction between the earlier African *Ugandax* and *Simatherium* dwindled recently with the discovery of more fossils. The last species to go extinct was *Pelorovis antiquus* (a.k.a. *Homoiceras antiquus*, *H. baineii* or *H. nilsonii*: Rossouw, 2001). However, this species may be better understood as *Syncerus antiquus*. Neither Gentry (2010) nor Klein (1994) were convinced that this was correct, but at present the leading verdict is that one could accept this view. *S. antiquus* had a wide distribution, and survived in northern Africa till recent times (Figure 2.2). A very late drawing of it may have been from Egypt just prior to the first Pharaoh from the so-named Amratian Civilization (~3600 BCE; see Childe, 1958, figure 1.9). Lovely rock art from the desert of Algeria shows scenes, including bulls fighting (e.g. Brodrick, 1948, p. 37).

In the Early Pleistocene beds in Arabia, a very large bovid has been found that is classified as *Pelorovis* cf. *oldowayensis* (Thomas et al., 1998). This may be an early proof of an outward migration of members of the genus *Pelorovis*, together with the 'Ubeidiya occurrence. Intriguingly, it had very large feet apparently adapted to move on soft substrates' (Thomas et al., 1998). The case shows how nomenclature intertwines with dating: the finds described by Thomas et al. (1998), and interpreted on the basis of morphological data as being close to *P. oldowayensis*, were later re-interpreted because the beds from which the fossils were extracted were dated later in time and were thus allocated to *Syncerus antiquus* (Stewart et al., 2019). This latter approach to classification is, in our opinion, incorrect. Similarly, molars of a smaller species that looked like those

Figure 2.2 In rocky massifs in the Sahara, petroglyphs (engravings in the rock) of animal species are quite widespread. This rock art was made when the Sahara was covered by savannas or steppes, and thus shows many species that are now only known from the Sahel or East Africa. Among these are depictions of *Syncerus* (or *Pelorovis*) *antiquus*, which is now extinct but was once widespread. (a) *S. antiquus* from I-n-Habeter, Mesāk, Libya. Photo Jean-Loïc Le Quellec. (b) Rock engraving of *S. antiquus* from Tilizzāyen, Mesāk, Libya. Photo Jean-Loïc Le Quellec (used with permission).

of *S. caffer* were classified as *S. antiquus* because *S. antiquus* is known from south-west Asia but *S. caffer* is not (Stewart et al., 2019). However, Geraads (1986) also identified *Pelorovis oldowayensis* from the Early Pleistocene in a nearby area, namely Israel, and later Martínez-Navarro et al. (2012) confirmed the identification, but assigned the species to *Bos*.

This raises the issue of the relationships of *Pelorovis* with *Bos*, a mostly Eurasian genus that includes, besides the modern cattle and aurochs, several wild, endangered southern Asian species and fossil species in the same area. In Africa, unquestionable early representatives of the genus are *Bos buiaensis* from Eritrea, dated to 1 Myr (Martínez-Navarro et al., 2010), a Middle Pleistocene *B. primigenius* from Tunisia dated to 0.7 Myr (Martínez-Navarro et al., 2014) and a species from the lower Awash Valley of Ethiopia, which is close to the southern Asian extinct species *B. acutifrons* (Geraads et al., 2004).

The Tunisian find is almost certainly a Eurasian immigrant (*pace* Martínez-Navarro et al., 2014), while the fact that the Eastern African forms were found close to the Aden straits strongly suggests that they are Asian immigrants. Detailed studies of the geology of the Bab-al-Mandab (the entry to the Red Sea from the Gulf of Aden) show that the straits between the Horn of Africa and the Hadhramaut, where a shallow sill is positioned (the Hanish Sill), remained submerged during the Pleistocene (Al-Mikhlafi et al., 2018). Yet during glacial periods, the straits were 'sufficiently narrow for both sides of the channel to have been visible at all times' and only about 1–3 km wide (Lambeck et al., 2011), thus making it feasible that Asian species of *Bos* crossed here into Africa. Note that the occurrence of *S. c. nanus* until a century ago on Bioko Island, some 35 km off the mainland in the Gulf of Guinea, cannot be taken as an example of buffalo being able to cross such a distance at sea, because Bioko Island was linked to the mainland until the beginning of the Holocene (Ceríaco et al., 2020). Nevertheless, buffalo are good swimmers, and are able to cross wide rivers like the Nile and the Zambesi.

By contrast, Martínez-Navarro et al. (2007, 2010) envisage an evolutionary line of the genus *Bos* starting as *Bos (P.) turkanensis* (Late Pliocene), *B. (P.) oldovayensis* (Early Pleistocene), *B. (P.) buiaensis* (Early Pleistocene) and thence *Bos primigenius* (the Aurochs) and also *Bos planifrons* (which more often is taken as the direct ancestral form of *Bos primigenius namadicus* – the Indian form of the aurochs which developed into *Bos indicus*, the zebu). The important consequence of accepting this interpretation is that the direct ancestors of cattle and zebu evolved in Africa and not in Asia. This would agree with the parsimony analysis on morphological characters performed by Geraads (1992), which showed them to be close on the cladograms. However, the detailed study by Gentry (1967) showed that the cranial morphology of *P. oldowayensis* is very different from that of *Bos*, and it is likely that their closeness on cladograms results from parallelisms. Furthermore, the contemporaneity of the last representatives of the former species with *Bos buiaensis* make an ancestral–descendant relationship extremely unlikely (Geraads, 2018). Moreover, this reasoning sits very uncomfortably with studies that base their reasoning on genetics: *B. primigenius*, cattle and zebu all fit snugly within the phylogenies of the other Asian *Bos* species (cf. Van der Made, 2013). After carefully considering the arguments and fossil material, Tong et al. (2018) conclude that *B. primigenius* was not derived from species that have been classified as *Pelorovis*, and support the view that *B. primigenius* evolved in South Asia, as does Van der Made (2013). Likewise, Bar-Yosef and Belmaker (2016) maintain the position that *B. primigenius* appeared in southwestern Asia as early as 1.2 Myr BP, and it continually occurred in this region until the Late Pleistocene. They recognize *B. buiaensis* in the Jordan Valley much later, namely 0.5–0.8 Myr, but as stated, this could well have been a *Pelorovis*. Indeed, many authors have stated that *Pelorovis (Syncerus) antiquus* was part of the mammal assemblage of the Pleistocene Levant.

Is there good reason to accept the view that *Pelorovis antiquus* should be considered as *Syncerus antiquus* as deduced by Peters et al. (1994) but rejected by Klein (1994)? The predecessor (but not necessarily ancestor) of *P. antiquus* was *P. oldovayensis*. This species was already present in the Levant (Bar-Yosef and Belmaker, 2016) and perhaps in Arabia (Thomas et al., 1998) in the Early Pleistocene. Yet, Martínez-Navarro and Rabinovich (2011) argue to classify this species as *S. antiquus*; however, their publication does not present arguments other than opinion. The original argument put forward by Peters et al. (1994) to view *P. antiquus* merely as a form of *S. caffer*, or as a separate species *S. antiquus*, was mainly based on the observation that the postcranial skeleton hardly differed from *S. caffer* (Peters et al., 1994). However, this is a weak argument, because 'The similarity in the postcranial skeleton known from *Bos*, *Bison* and *Bubalus arnee* is surprising considering that, according to an analysis of mitochondrial DNA, the separation of the *Bubalus–Syncerus* clade from the *Bos–Bison* clade goes back to the Middle Miocene' (Van der Made et al., 2016; see also Von Koenigswald et al., 2019). The main argument of Klein (1994) was that the two species coexisted for a long time, and if both were to be viewed as *Syncerus*, then that would not have been possible. This is, however, based on an old 'rule' of competitive exclusion formulated by Charles Darwin but for which there is no firm evidential support (Prins and Gordon, 2014a, 2014b). Note that species of the same genus can very well coexist, as exemplified by Lechwe and Puku or Plains Zebra and Grevy's zebra in Africa, or for that matter by the many different *Anas* spp., *Anser* spp., *Corvus* spp., etc. in the Boreal zone.

Yet we also have not read convincing arguments to accept the view that *Pelorovis antiquus* was merely another African buffalo or even a more drought-adapted subspecies of the present-day African buffalo (cf. Peters et al., 1994). Indeed, the stance one takes with respect to the systematic position of *P. antiquus* affects the way the evolutionary history of *S. caffer* is interpreted. Note that this has little to do with accepting or rejecting the narrow species concept proposed by Groves and Grubb (2011, p. 1 ff.). However, Gentry (2010) takes *P. antiquus* (grudgingly) as *S. antiquus*, even though he does not present arguments for (or against) this view. However, this evidence is murky, because it depends so much on interpretation in the case of the fossil Bovini material. This implies that one has to consider two alternative scenarios in the evolution of *Syncerus*: namely, one with *S. antiquus* as a species coexisting with *S. caffer* and living in the same area as *B. primigenius* in northern Africa, and the other in which *Syncerus* never reached the areas to the north of the Sahara but that the relevant 'buffalo' species in that area was *P. antiquus*.

Miocene Origins of the African Buffalo

How far back in time can one trace the ancestry of the African buffalo? It may have appeared reasonably clear 50 years ago (Sinclair, 1977, p. 22), but the crucial issue is whether the African buffalo really fits into the Bovini (together with the Asian buffalo and the wild cattle swarm). On the basis of DNA, it can be deduced that the last common ancestors of the Bovini and the Tragelaphini (species like the present-day kudu, bushbuck and eland antelope) lived some 18 Myr (Bibi et al., 2009) or 15 Myr ago (Zurano et al., 2019), but the first fossil material comes from *Eotragus*, which is classified as a Boselaphine (like the present-day nilgai). Between the oldest species, *E. noyei* from Pakistan (18 Myr), and the next species, *E. sansaniensis* from France (15.2 Myr), there is a gap of 3 million years, which is as long as the duration of the entire Pleistocene (Solounias and Moelleken, 1992). Then there is another enormous time gap of some 6 million years to a genus named *Selenoportax/Pachyportax*, again from Pakistan (9 Myr; Bibi et al., 2009). An ancestral relation between *Pachyportax* and *Parabos* (thought to be ancestral to *Leptobos*, *Bos* and *Bison* and perhaps to *Proamphibos* leading to *Bubalus*) has been surmised, but the evidence is weak. From *Pachyportax* onwards, the fog of the fossil record lifts a bit. But just when one seemed to be back on firm footing, Gentry (2010) dropped a bombshell by pointing out that there is a fair chance that the Bovini are not even monophyletic. Indeed, Geraads (1992) had already shown that the relationship between Asian and African buffalo is not well supported. In other words, after decades of hard field work and thinking, the early history of the Bovini is not yet clear regardless of what phylogenies based on present-day DNA seem to suggest. Later we will show that cross-fertilization data between African and Asian buffalo also point to a very weak relationship within the group of organisms that are classified as Bovini.

The genus *Eotragus* was a long-lived one with a very wide distribution, ranging from Europe to China, Pakistan and Israel to Kenya (Solounias et al., 1995). The genus *Tethytragus* was similar to *Eotragus*, but evolutionary perhaps not a Boselaphine, and even though *T. langai* still falls within the class of brachydont herbivores, it was more hypsodont than *Eotragus* and may already have been a grazer (DeMiguel et al., 2011, 2012). Yet it appears that the early 'invasion' of Africa by Boselaphini at the beginning of the Middle Miocene did not lead to today's Bovini in Africa. They may have arisen from a second 'invasion' of Boselaphini at the end of the Middle Miocene (Thomas, 1984; Gentry, 2010).

The next genus to consider is *Pachyportax*, which lived during the end of the Miocene. The genus has also been classified within the Boselaphini, but it appears that the Boselaphini are not a homogeneous tribe (Bibi et al., 2009). *Pachyportax latidens* was a large Boselaphine during the Late Pliocene (7–3.5 Myr) of the Siwalik Hills of Pakistan with strongly developed molars for chewing roughage (Ikram et al., 2017). At the same time, there was another Boselaphine in the Siwaliks with less hypsodont molars, which was of the genus *Tragoportax*. European *Tragoportax* at least are large forms, and have rather long legs (perhaps similar to the nilgai). There were quite a number of other putative Boselaphini species at that time in the Siwalik mammal assemblage (Batool et al., 2016), but whether they were truly Boselaphine is uncertain (Bibi et al., 2009). Miocene Bovini show mesowear patterns that are similar to present-day browsers and mixed-feeders, and the molars were not yet very hypsodont (Bibi, 2007). Indeed, Solounias and Dawson-Saunders (1988)

elegantly showed how masticatory morphology features relating to intermediate feeding and grazing adaptations evolved in parallel several times
and independently from primitive browsing conditions. According to
these authors, this did not happen in a savanna-type landscape but in
the broad-leaved forests and woodlands there (in Greece). Bibi's (2007)
palaeoecological reconstruction is that these early Bovini started utilizing
open C_3 vegetation with C_3 grasses. Indeed, C_4 grasses became important only later (Barry et al. 2002), and Bibi (2007) speculates that because
the hypsodont index only reached values indicating pure grazing around
8 Myr ago, this behaviour started with the emergence of C_4 grassland at
that time. However, the abrasion patterns of the molars do not support
this (Bibi, 2007). The driving evolutionary force may have been the
strengthening of the monsoonal system due to the uplift of the Tibetan
Plateau (Searle, 2017) leading to resource scarcity during the dry season
(Bibi, 2007). The fire-dominated and grazer-induced grasslands came
into existence only about 2 Myr ago in Africa (Spencer, 1997).

In Libya, *Tragoportax cyrenaicus* lived about 7 Myr ago; the species
was perhaps derived from the West Eurasian form (Gentry, 2010). From
South Africa, *T. acrae* has been reported (also known as *Mesembriportax
acrae*, but cladistically sitting more comfortably with *Tragoportax*: Spassov
and Geraads, 2004). *Tragoportax* had a very large range, from Spain to
China, and from southern Asia to southern Africa (Batool et al., 2016). In
the Siwaliks, the lineage of *Tragoportax* changed from a C_3 browser at 8
Myr to a C_4 grazer at 7.5 Myr. By 6.5 Ma, most frugivores and/or browsers had disappeared even though areas of C_3 vegetation remained until at
least 4.5 Myr on the flood plain (Patnaik, 2013; cf. Saarinen, 2019).

Sinclair (1977, p. 22), based on Pilgrim (1939) and Thenius (1969,
cited in Sinclair, 1977), suggested that *Parabos* was the ancestor of the
African Bovini (*Pelorovis*, *Syncerus*) but also of the Eurasian *Bos* and
Bubalus. The fact that much older Bovini have been found in Pakistan,
namely some 8 Myr ago (Bibi, 2007), and that no *Parabos* has been found
outside Europe and the Middle East, pleads against accepting the genus
Parabos as ancestral to modern Bovini. This is reinforced by the fact that
it seems to be seen better as belonging to the Boselaphini than to the
Bovini (Gromolard, 1980; Gromolard and Guerin, 1980; Geraads, 1992).
Moreover, *Parabos* still occurred much later in time than the separation
of *Syncerus* and *Bubalus*. It appears that Boselaphines disappeared from
the African continent at the end of the Miocene (Gentry, 1990; Bibi,
2007 – the Miocene ends 5.3 Myr), unless there was a lineage leading to
the present-day African buffalo.

The Pliocene Ancestors of *Syncerus*

Genetic data suggest a separation of *Bubalus* and *Syncerus* some 8.8 Myr ago (Hassanin, 2014) or even a million years earlier (Zurano et al., 2019), or (on the basis of cytochrome-c analyses) some 6 Myr ago (Druica et al., 2016), thus in the Miocene. Among the oldest African Bovines, *Ugandax* cf. *gautieri* (see Thomas, 1984) has been reported from Lukeino, as early as about 6 Myr (Pickford and Senut, 2001); this species had much morphological similarity with *Simatherium demissum* from South Africa (Thomas, 1984; cf. Geraads, 1992). *Ugandax* may have been derived from the *Selenoportax–Pachyportax* lineage from the Siwaliks (Thomas, 1984; Gentry, 2010), but Bibi (2009, p. 332) states that it was also very similar to *Proamphibos lachrymans* (the putative ancestor of the Asian buffalo). Bibi (2009, p. 339) poses that *Proamphibos lachrymans* was the last common ancestor of the African and Asian buffalo. *Proamphibos* was substantially larger than *Pachyportax* (Bibi, 2009, p. 339).

There was a suite of species within the genus *Ugandax* or closely related (*U. [S.] demissum* from Early Pliocene South Africa; *U. coryndonae* from the Middle Pliocene, Ethiopia; *U. gautieri* from Uganda, of about 5 Myr; *Simatherium kohllarseni* from the Middle Pliocene of Tanzania and Kenya; and *S. shungurense* from the Late Pliocene of Ethiopia; Geraads et al., 2009a). Yet the evolutionary link between *Ugandax–Simatherium* and *Syncerus* also is not well supported by cladistic analyses (Geraads, 1992).

Ugandax coryndonae is perhaps the best known of the Pliocene African Bovini, represented by a large number of specimens from Ethiopia (Gentry, 2006; Geraads et al., 2009b, 2012). This species may have lived until the Pleistocene, 2.5 Myr ago (Bibi, 2009, p. 335). In other words, the notion that *Ugandax* could have given rise to *Syncerus* (Gentry, 2006) is not well supported by cladistic analysis, and is further undermined by the earliest records of *Syncerus* perhaps overlapping in time with those of *Ugandax* (Gentry, 2010; Bibi et al., 2017).

The deduction that a Middle Pliocene emigration took place by a *Syncerus*-type buffalo from Africa into the Caucasus (Vislobokova, 2008), and from there to Eastern Europe (Evlogiev et al., 1997), by a species classified as *Eosyncerus ivericus* is most likely not justified because the material appears to be Caprine (Bukhsianidze and Koiava, 2018).

So, back to *Proamphibos*. During the Pliocene, this large bovine lived in the foothills of the Himalayas and the floodplains of the Indus and Ganges (Khan et al., 2009). Two species have been distinguished, namely, the less advanced form (with regards to skull and horn morphology) *P. lachrymans* and the more advanced *P. kashmiricus* (Pilgrim, 1939; Khan and

Akhtar, 2011). The body mass of *Proamphibos* was about 200 kg (Dennell et al., 2005). Later (i.e. younger) finds of *P. lachrymans* have been reclassified as *Damalops palaeindicus*, not belonging within the Bovini but to the Alcelaphini (the hartebeest group); the presence of *Proamphibos* as late as 0.8 Myr ago is thus factually refuted. Apparently, it did not co-occur with *Hemibos* (neither with *H. acuticornis* nor with *H. triquetricornis*) and also not with *Bubalus* in Siwalik deposits (Badam, 1977: his table 2; also, in figure 17.11 of Patnaik, 2013). The genus *Proamphibos* is thus considered to be more ancient than the genus *Hemibos* (cf. Bibi, 2009, p. 338). The genus *Hemibos* was considered to include the direct ancestor of *Bubalus*, and perhaps especially of the Anoa of Sulawesi (Groves, 1976). Evidence of co-occurrence of *Hemibos* with *Bubalus*, however, pleads against this. There is no evidence that members of the genus *Hemibos*, which appears to have derived from *Proamphibos*, migrated to Africa or were involved in any way in the evolution of African Bovini and *Syncerus* in particular.

An independent lineage, not leading to *Syncerus* but perhaps related, was present in northern Africa in the form of *Leptobos syrticus*. Gentry (1990), Duvernois (1992) and Geraads (1992) concluded that it should not be maintained within the genus *Leptobos*; they prefer to not assign it to a genus, but conclude a similarity with *Syncerus*. '*Leptobos*' *syrticus* may be related to *Jamous kolleensis* from Pliocene Chad, but this latter species does not show clear affinity with *Syncerus* (Geraads et al., 2009a). *Jamous kolleensis* was a medium-sized bovine, still with rather primitive molars (Geraads et al., 2009a). Because the Eurasian genus *Leptobos*, so important for understanding the evolution of *Bos* including *Bison*, apparently did not otherwise play a role in the evolution of *Pelorovis* or *Syncerus*, we do not deal with it in this chapter.

Thus, *Proamphibos*, or less likely *Ugandax*, is perhaps the link between Asian and African buffalo that geneticists identified to have lived some 8 Myr ago. Cladistic analysis of many fossil forms, modern *Bubalus* and modern *Syncerus* do not well support a strong relationship between Asian and African buffalo (Geraads, 1992). A putative separation some 8 Myr ago is an ancient one for mammals in contrast to birds because the former have prezygotic and postzygotic barriers and the latter prezygotic ones only. These postzygotic barriers are confirmed through embryo transfer experiments (see below), so the genetic distance is really to be reckoned in millions of years. On the basis of a careful analysis of karyotype evolution, it also appears that African and Asiatic buffalo evolved along two different and independent routes, as their centric fusions involved different homoeologous chromosomes (Iannuzzi et al., 2009).

African Buffalo *Syncerus caffer* – Pleistocene and Holocene Fossil Material

So, neither a cladistic analysis of many fossil and modern forms nor studies on nuclear DNA and embryology support a strong relationship between African and Asian buffalo. The ancestry of Asian buffalo, through its descending from *Hemibos*, which was derived from *Proamphibos*, appears reasonably well-founded. The ancestry of the African buffalo is shrouded in opacity. As sketched out, the Pliocene forms *Ugandax* led to *Simatherium* and may have led from there to *Syncerus*, but this link is not well supported by cladistic analyses (Geraads, 1992). Fossil *Syncerus*, such as at Shungura and Olduvai, had no large basal bosses (as the modern Cape buffalo *Syncerus c. caffer*) (Gentry, 1990). Gentry even states that these *Simatherium* were small and short-horned similar to the forest buffalo *S. c. nanus* of today. Whether they form an unbroken lineage to the present forest buffalo is not known, but this is very unlikely given the way that *S. c. nanus* is genetically nested within the other living African buffalo (Van Hooft et al., 2002). Recent genetic studies (reviewed in Prins and Sinclair, 2013) suggest that *S. c. nanus* is the older form and *S. c. caffer* only arose some 150,000 years ago. Whether the two forms (a *nanus*-like one and a *caffer*-like one), as suggested by Gentry (1990), really have been present for a long time seems to be contradicted by genetic analyses (see e.g. Van Hooft et al., 2002). In Chapter 8, Prins, Ottenburghs and Van Hooft revise their opinion, and conclude that *S. c. nanus* is a derived form, while *S. c. aequinoctialis* may be closest to the ancestral form.

The first species that can be classified as *Syncerus* may have been *Syncerus acoelotus*. Geraads et al. (2009a) state that it was as large as the modern *S. caffer* but with less-advanced horns. However, because fossils are not plentiful and the remains are fragmentary, classification remains fraught with issues. Indeed, Gentry (1985) compared Shungura Member C (~2.7 Ma) *Syncerus* horn cores to those of *Syncerus acoelotus*, named from the much younger Olduvai Bed II (~1.5 Ma), but later, Gentry (2010) referred to them as *Simatherium shungurense*. Bibi et al. (2017) re-examined some of the Shungura material and state that they prefer Gentry's (1985) opinion, so they choose to see these fossils again as *Syncerus acoelotus*. A possible very early find of *S. caffer* is from northern Sudan near Dongola; the authors were convinced it was not a *Pelorovis (S.) antiquus* but a true African buffalo (Chaix et al., 2000), but the age of the site is poorly supported. We are not aware of any palaeontological material that can be ascribed to some of the other existing forms of *S. caffer*, to wit *S. c. mathewsi* or *S. c. brachyceros*. Unless material is unearthed, one has to rely on genetic analyses to reconstruct the history of the morphological differentiation within the species. The scant sample sizes on morphology that Groves and Grubb (2011, p. 122 ff.) rely on to distinguish *S. brachyceros* or *S. mathewsi* as separate species are certainly not convincing.

We mentioned earlier that phylogenies based on DNA do not take into consideration the DNA sequences of extinct species if genetic material is no longer available (see Table 2.1). So even where, for example, Bibi (2013) took into account three *Bubalus* species (when there are five or six) into his phylogeny, he did not (and could not) include a whole suite of recently extinct species (some 10 from China: Dong et al., 2014) or the three species that went extinct 2–1 Myr ago (from southern Asia: Van den Bergh et al., 2001; Patnaik, 2013). This relative 'blindness' may cause an optimally parsimonious phylogeny to be an imperfect reconstruction of evolution in reality. This is no criticism of such work, to the contrary, but a call for even better integrating palaeontology with genetics (Table 2.1).

The whole group of (wild) cattle and bison combines well, but ancestors of the wild South-East Asian cattle, bison and West Asian cattle apparently speciated at one short period of time, which cannot be resolved hierarchically (MacEachern et al., 2009). A major issue is extensive hybridization between the whole group of cattle, zebu, yak, gaur, banteng, wisent and bison. Indeed, closely related species (as established by genetic analyses) show hardly any or no barriers to cross-breeding. Species that diverged longer ago show infertility in the male offspring but none in the female offspring. Back-crosses are then very well possible, and this may explain the frequently observed introgression of genetic material in one species from another. Species that are only distantly related cannot cross-breed; in a number of cases, it has been found that in-vitro fertilization is then possible, but the embryo only survives briefly in vitro. These results are further supported by embryo transplantations of 'normal' embryos of one species implanted into a cow of another species.

As expected, this technique shows that embryos of *Bos taurus indicus* transferred to *B. t. taurus* cows result in fully normal parturitions (Summers et al., 1983). Likewise, *B. gaurus* embryos have been transferred to *B. taurus* cows without any problems (Stover et al., 1981). However, pregnancy of embryos of *Bison bison* that were transferred to *B. taurus* cows were terminated sometime between 60 and 100 days (Dorn, 1995). This does not mean that they are not frequently born, because they are, and are named 'beefalo'. Sanders (1925) already reported that male offspring of bison–cattle hybrids (at that time named catalo) frequently were either aborted, stillborn or died very young. Crosses between yak and cattle also often result in increased abortion (Zhang, 2000), yet the offspring that survives is valuable, because they are strong (personal observation).

Water buffalo and cattle are genetically much more distant. Indeed, the pregnancy of *Bubalus bubalis* embryos transferred to *B. taurus* cows terminated after 37 days (Drost et al., 1986). After in-vitro fertilization, embryos of crosses between cattle and water buffalo only survive to the blastocyst state (Kochhar et al., 2002), and to the morula state only in in-vitro fertilization of cattle with African buffalo sperm (Owiny et al., 2009). Indeed, African buffalo are more distantly related to the other Bovini than to Asian buffalo.

In other words, prezygotic barriers are nearly absent between the different species of *Bos* and *Bison*, but postzygotic barriers become increasingly severe with increasing genetic (and evolutionary) distance. We deduce from this that postzygotic barriers become an overwhelming barrier between Bovini that are separated by more than 5 Myr or more, and that prezygotic barriers become an issue after a divergence of some 2 Myr. This appears to be about the same as in wild pigs (*Sus*; Frantz et al., 2013), and very different from birds like ducks (Kraus et al., 2012) or geese (Ottenburghs et al., 2017), where postzygotic barriers do not play a (major) role against horizontal gene transfer (see also Syvanen, 2012; Stewart et al., 2019). Because the Bovini hold much interest in terms of livestock production, perhaps more is known about 'evolution in progress' with this species group than with nearly any other. The picture that emerges is not a simple evolutionary tree, but a system more akin to 'reticulated evolution' (Buntjer et al., 2002).

Using microsatellite data, Ritz et al. (2000) put forward that some 2.5 million years ago, water buffalo and African buffalo had a common ancestor. Their data show that the genetic distance between African buffalo and species of the genus *Bos* appears to be equal. More recent research not using microsatellites but nuclear genome sequences suggests that the groups (*Bubalus* plus Syncerus) and (*Bos* plus *Bison*) split very much earlier, namely around five to nine million years ago (Bibi, 2013). The findings of Ritz et al. (2000) are even more difficult to understand if one realizes that a short genetic distance can point to hybridization. Hybridization between *Syncerus* and *Bos*, however, is very unlikely given the outcome of the fertilization and transplantation experiments alluded to above. An alternative explanation is that because these two genera split relatively recently, the genetic makeup is so similar because of incomplete lineage sorting (MacEachern et al., 2009; Bibi, 2013).

Perhaps the true phylogenetic relationship must be derived through other techniques, as was done by Buntjer et al. (2002). They used amplified fragment length polymorphism (AFLP) to generate nuclear DNA fingerprints that display variation of loci dispersed over the nuclear genome of the different species. They did not use algorithms that necessitate solving a tree, and also think that a 'consequence of reticulation is that a tree topology is not adequate for representing the phylogeny'. The Bovini thus form a prime case of 'evolution in action' in which there is a hugely successful group of morphologically very distinct species through which exchange of adaptive or non-adaptive genes can move within the 'supra species' *Bos* (*sensu* Kraus et al., 2012). However, the African buffalo is not part of the species swarm of cattle, gaur, zebu, banteng, yak, wisent and bison that form the Bovini. It is evolutionarily so far removed from that group of Palaearctic and Oriental Bovini that it may be thought as a single surviving species in a tribe 'Syncerini'. Does that have any repercussions for understanding their ecology or management better? We seriously doubt this, because the amount of ecological knowledge garnered from wild Asian buffalo in their native environment is negligible. The wild Asian species is nearly extinct, and little progress has been made to reintroduce them into the wild. In other words, the African buffalo may be irreplaceable and for understanding it, one cannot plagiarize knowledge from other Bovini.

References

Al-Mikhlafi, A.S., L.R. Edwards and H. Cheng (2018). Sea-level history and tectonic uplift during the last-interglacial period (LIG): inferred from the Bab al-Mandab coral reef terraces, southern Red Sea. *Journal of African Earth Sciences* **138**: 133–148.

Alemseged, Z., J.G. Wynn, D. Geraads, et al. (2020). Fossils from Mille-Logya, Afar, Ethiopia, elucidate the link between Pliocene environmental changes and *Homo* origins. *Nature Communications* **11**: 1–12.

Badam, G.L. (1977). Fossils of the Upper Sivalik and the problem of the boundary between the Neogene and the Quaternary System in India [original in Russian]. *Bulletin of the Commission for the Study of the Quaternary* **47**: 37–42.

Bar-Yosef, O. and M. Belmaker (2016). Early and Middle Pleistocene faunal and hominins dispersals through southwestern Asia. *Quaternary Science Reviews* **30**: 1318–1337.

Barry, J.C., M.E. Morgan, L.J. Flynn, et al. (2002). Faunal and environmental change in the Late Miocene Siwaliks of northern Pakistan. *Paleobiology* **28**: 1–71.

Batool, A., M.A. Khan, M.A. Babar, et al. (2016). New Bovid fossils from the Late Miocene Hasnot (Siwaliks, Pakistan). *Palaeoworld* **25**: 453–464.

Bibi, F. (2007). Origin, paleoecology, and paleobiogeography of early Bovini. *Palaeogeography, Palaeoclimatology, Palaeoecology* **248**: 60–72.

Bibi, F. (2009). Evolution, systematics, and paleoecology of bovinae (Mammalia: Artiodactyla) from the Late Miocene to the recent. PhD thesis, Yale University.

Bibi, F. (2013). A multi-calibrated mitochondrial phylogeny of extant Bovidae (Artiodactyla, Ruminantia) and the importance of the fossil record to systematics. *BMC Evolutionary Biology* **13**: 166.

Bibi, F., M. Bukhsianidze, A.W. Gentry, et al. (2009). The fossil record and evolution of Bovidae: state of the field. *Palaeontologia Electronica* **12**: 1–11.

Bibi, F., J. Rowan and K. Reed (2017). Late Pliocene Bovidae from Ledi-Geraru (Lower Awash Valley, Ethiopia) and their implications for Afar paleoecology. *Journal of Vertebrate Paleontology* **37**: e1337639, 1–23.

Brodrick, A.H. (1948). *Prehistoric Painting*. London: Avalon Press.

Bukhsianidze, M. and K. Koiava (2018). Synopsis of the terrestrial vertebrate faunas from the Middle Kura Basin (Eastern Georgia and Western Azerbaijan, South Caucasus). *Acta Palaeontologica Polonica* **63**: 441–461.

Buntjer, J.B., M. Otsen, I.J. Nijman, et al. (2002). Phylogeny of bovine species based on AFLP fingerprinting. *Heredity* **88**: 46–51.

Ceríaco, L.M., J. Bernstein, A.C. Sousa, et al. (2020). The reptiles of Tinhosa Grande islet (Gulf of Guinea): a taxonomic update and the role of Quaternary sea level fluctuations in their diversification. *African Journal of Herpetology* **69**: 200–216.

Chaix, L., M. Faure, C. Guerin and M. Honegger (2000). Kaddanarti, a Lower Pleistocene assemblage from Northern Sudan. Recent research into the Stone Age of North-Eastern Africa. *Studies in African Archaeology* **7**: 33–46.

Childe, V.G. (1958). *New Light on the Most Ancient East* (4th rev. ed.). London: Routledge and Kegan Paul.

Davis, E.B., K.A. Brakora and K.T. Stilson (2014). Evolution, development and functional role of horns in cattle. In M. Melletti and J. Burton (Eds.), *Ecology, Evolution and Behaviour of Wild Cattle: Implications for Conservation*. Cambridge: Cambridge University Press, pp. 72–81.

DeMiguel, D., B. Azanza and J. Morales (2011). Paleoenvironments and paleoclimate of the Middle Miocene of central Spain: a reconstruction from dental wear of ruminants *Palaeogeography, Palaeoclimatology, Palaeoecology* **302**: 452–463.

DeMiguel, D., I.M. Sánchez, D.M. Alba, et al. (2012). First evidence of *Tethytragus* Azanza and Morales, 1994 (Ruminantia, Bovidae), in the Miocene of the Vallès-Penedès Basin (Spain). *Journal of Vertebrate Paleontology* **32**: 1457–1462.

Dennell, R.W., R. Coard, M. Beech, et al. (2005). Locality 642, an Upper Siwalik (Pinjor Stage) fossil accumulation in the Pabbi Hills, Pakistan. *Journal of the Palaeontological Society of India* **50**: 83–92.

Dong, W., J. Liu, L. Zhang and Q. Xu (2014). The Early Pleistocene water buffalo associated with *Gigantopithecus* from Chongzuo in southern China. *Quaternary International* **354**: 86–93.

Dorn, C.G. (1995). Application of reproductive technologies in North American Bison (*Bison bison*). *Theriogenology* **43**: 13–20.

Drost, M., J.M. Wright and R.P. Elsden (1986). Intergeneric embryo transfer between water buffalo and domestic cattle. *Theriogenology* **25**: 13–23.

Druica, R., M. Ciorpac, D. Cojocaru, et al. (2016). The investigation of cytochrome b gene in order to elucidate the taxonomic uncertainties between European bison (*Bison bonasus*) and its relatives. *Romanian Biotechnological Letters* **22**: 12116–12125.

Duvernois, M.P. (1992). Mise au point sur le genre *Leptobos* (Mammalia, Artiodactyla, Bovidae); implications biostratigraphiques et phylogénétiques. *Geobios* **25**: 155–166.

Evlogiev, J., A. Glazek, A. Sulimski and T. Czyzewska (1997). New localities of vertebrate fauna in the Quaternary sediments in the vicinity of Rouse (North-East Bulgaria). *Geologica Balcanica* **27**: 61–68.

Frantz, L.A.F., J.G. Schraiber, O. Madsen, et al. (2013). Genome sequencing reveals fine scale diversification and reticulation history during speciation in *Sus. Genome Biology* **14**: 1–12.

Gentry, A.W. (1967). *Pelorovis oldowayensis* Reck, an extinct bovid from East Africa. *Bulletin of the British Museum (Natural History), Geology* **14**: 245–299.

Gentry, A.W. (1985). The Bovidae of the Omo Group deposits, Ethiopia (French and American collections). In Y. Coppens and F.C. Howell (Eds.), *Les Faunes Plio-Pleistocenes de la basse Vallee de l'Omo (Ethiopie); I: Perissodactyles-Artiodactyles (Bovidae).* Paris: CNRS, pp. 119–191.

Gentry, A.W. (1990). Evolution and dispersal of African Bovidae. In G.A. Bubeník and A.B. Bubeník (Eds.), *Horns, Pronghorns, and Antlers: Evolution, Morphology, Physiology, and Social Significance.* New York: Springer, pp. 195–227.

Gentry, A. W. (2006). A new bovine (Bovidae, Artiodactyla) from the Hadar Formation, Ethiopia. *Transactions of the Royal Society of South Africa* **61**: 41–50.

Gentry, A.W. (2010). Bovidae. In L. Werdelin and W.J. Sanders (Eds.), *Cenozoic Mammals of Africa.* Berkeley: University of California Press, pp. 741–796.

Gentry, A.W. and A. Gentry (1978). Fossil Bovidae (Mammalia) of Olduvai Gorge, Tanzania, parts I and II. *Bulletin of the British Museum (Natural History), Geology* **29**: 289–446; **30**: 1–83.

Geraads, D. (1986). Ruminants pléistocènes d'Oubeidiyeh. In E. Tchernov (Ed.), *Les Mammifères du Pléistocène inférieur de la Vallée du Jourdain à Oubeidiyeh. Mémoires et Travaux du Centre de Recherche Français de Jérusalem* **5**: 143–181.

Geraads, D. (1992). Phylogenetic analysis of the tribe Bovini (Mammalia: Artiodactyla). *Zoological Journal of the Linnean Society* **104**: 193–207.

Geraads, D. (2018). Faunal change in Eastern Africa at the Oldowan–Acheulean transition. The emergence of the Acheulean in East Africa and beyond. In R. Gallotti and M. Mussi (Eds.), *The Emergence of the Acheulean in East Africa and Beyond: Contributions in Honor of Jean Chavaillon, Vertebrate Paleobiology and Paleoanthropology.* Cham: Springer, pp. 183–194.

Geraads, D., A. Alemseged, D. Reed, et al. (2004). The Pleistocene fauna (other than Primates) from Asbole, lower Awash Valley, Ethiopia, and its environmental and biochronological implications. *Geobios* **37**: 697–718.

Geraads, D., C. Blondel, H.T. Mackaye, et al. (2009). Bovidae (Mammalia) from the Lower Pliocene of Chad. *Journal of Vertebrate Paleontology* **29**: 923–933.

Geraads, D., R. Bobe and K. Reed (2012). Pliocene Bovidae (Mammalia) from the Hadar Formation of Hadar and Ledi-Geraru, Lower Awash, Ethiopia. *Journal of Vertebrate Paleontology* **32**: 180–197.

Geraads, D., D. Melillo and Y. Haile-Selassie (2009). Middle Pliocene Bovidae from Hominid-bearing sites in the Woranso-Mille area, Afar region, Ethiopia. *Palaeontologia Africana* **44**: 59–70.

Geraads, D. and H. Thomas (1994). Bovidés du plio-pléistocène d'Ouganda. In *Geology and Palaeobiology of the Albertine Rift Valley, Uganda-Zaire, Vol. II: Palaeobiology.* Orléans: CIFEG Occas. Publ., pp. 383–407.

Gromolard, C. (1980). Une nouvelle interprétation des grands Bovidae (Artiodactyla, Mammalia) du Pliocène d'Europe occidentale classés jusqu'à présent dans le genre *Parabos: Parabos cordieri* (de Christol) emend.,? *Parabos boodon* (Gervais) et *Alephis lyrix* n. gen., n. sp. *Geobios* **13**: 767–775.

Gromolard, C. and C. Guérin (1980). Mise au point sur *Parabos cordieri* (de Christol), un bovidé (Mammalia, Artiodactyla) du Pliocène d'Europe occidentale. *Geobios* **13**: 741–755.

Groves, C.P. (1969). Systematics of the *Anoa* (Mammalia, Bovidae). *Beaufortia* **17**: 1–12.

Groves, C.P. (1976). The origin of the mammalian fauna of Sulawesi (Celebes). *Z. Säugetierkunde* **41**: 201–216.

Groves, C.P. and P. Grubb (2011). *Ungulate Taxonomy*. Baltimore: John Hopkins University Press.

Grubb, P. (1993). Family Bovidae. In D.E. Wilson and D.A.M. Reeder (Eds.), *Mammal Species of the World. A Taxonomic and Geographic Reference* (2nd ed.). Washington: Smithsonian Institution Press, pp. 393–414.

Hadjouis, D. and M. Sahnouni (2006). *Pelorovis howelli* nov. sp. (Mammalia, Artiodactyla): a new bovine from the Lower Pleistocene site of Aïn Hanech (El-Kherba locus), north-eastern Algeria. *Geobios* **39**: 673–678.

Hassanin, A. (2014). Systematics and evolution of Bovini. In M. Melletti and J. Burton (Eds.), *Ecology, Evolution and Behaviour of Wild Cattle: Implications for Conservation*. Cambridge: Cambridge University Press, p. 20.

Hodgson, B.H. (1847). On various genera of the ruminants. *Journal of the Asiatic Society of Bengal* **16**: 685–711.

Ikram, T., F. Safdar, M.A. Babar, et al. (2017). Fossil molars of *Pachyportax* (Boselaphini, Bovidae) from Middle Siwalik Subgroup of Pakistan. *Biologia (Pakistan)* **63**: 147–150.

Iannuzzi, L., W.A. King and D. Di Berardino (2009). Chromosome evolution in domestic bovids as revealed by chromosome banding and FISH-mapping techniques. *Cytogenetic and Genome Research* **126**: 49–62.

Khan, M.A. and M. Akhtar (2011). *Proamphibos kashmiricus* (Bovini: Bovidae: Mammalia) lower case from the Pinjor formation of Pakistan. *Pakistan Journal of Zoology* **43**: 615–621.

Khan, M. A., M. Iqbal, A. Ghaffar and M. Akhtar (2009). *Proamphibos* (Bovini, Bovidae, Mammalia) from the Tatrot Formation in the Upper Siwaliks of Pakistan. *Journal of Animal and Plant Sciences* **19**: 104–107.

Klein, R.G. (1994). The long-horned African buffalo (*Pelorovis antiquus*) is an extinct species. *Journal of Archaeological Science* **21**: 725–733.

Koenigswald, W. von, A.H. Schwermann, M. Keiter and F. Menger (2019). First evidence of Pleistocene *Bubalus murrensis* in France and the stratigraphic occurrences of *Bubalus* in Europe. *Quaternary International* **522**: 85–93.

Kochhar, H. P. S., K.A. Rao, A.M. Luciano, et al. (2002). In vitro production of cattle–water buffalo (*Bos taurus–Bubalus bubalis*) hybrid embryos. *Zygote* **10**: 155–162.

Kraus, R.H.S, H.H.D. Kerstens, P. van Hooft, et al. (2012). Widespread horizontal genomic exchange does not erode species barriers among sympatric ducks. *BMC Evolutionary Biology* **12**: 1–10.

Lambeck, K., A. Purcell, N.C. Flemming, et al. (2011). Sea level and shoreline reconstructions for the Red Sea: isostatic and tectonic considerations and implications for hominin migration out of Africa. *Quaternary Science Reviews* **30**: 3542–3574.

MacEachern, S., J. McEwan and M. Goddard (2009). Phylogenetic reconstruction and the identification of ancient polymorphism in the Bovini tribe (Bovidae, Bovinae). *BMC Genomics* **10**: 177.

Martínez-Navarro, B., J.A. Pérez-Claros, M.R. Palombo, et al. (2007). The Olduvai buffalo *Pelorovis* and the origin of *Bos*. *Quaternary Research* **68**: 220–226.

Martínez-Navarro, B. and R. Rabinovich (2011). The fossil Bovidae (Artiodactyla, Mammalia) from Gesher Benot Ya'aqov, Israel: out of Africa during the Early–Middle Pleistocene transition. *Journal of Human Evolution* **60**: 375–386.

Martínez-Navarro, B., L. Rook, M. Papini and Y. Libsekal (2010). A new species of bull from the Early Pleistocene paleoanthropological site of Buia (Eritrea): parallelism on the dispersal of the genus *Bos* and the Acheulian culture. *Quaternary International* **212**: 169–175.

Martínez-Navarro, B., M. Belmaker and O. Bar-Yosef (2012). The Bovid assemblage (Bovidae, Mammalia) from the Early Pleistocene site of Ubeidiya, Israel: biochronological and paleoecological implications for the fossil and lithic bearing strata. *Quaternary International* **267**: 78–97.

Martínez-Navarro, B., N. Karoui-Yaakoub, O. Oms, et al. (2014). The early Middle Pleistocene archeopaleontological site of Wadi Sarrat (Tunisia) and the earliest record of *Bos primigenius*. *Quaternary Science Reviews* **90**: 37–46.

Métais, G., P.O. Antoine, L. Marivaux, et al. (2003). New artiodactyl ruminant mammal from the Late Oligocene of Pakistan. *Acta Palaeontologica Polonica* **48**: 375–382.

Ottenburghs, J., R.H.S. Kraus, P. van Hooft, et al. (2017). Avian introgression in the genomic era. *Avian Research* **8**: 30.

Owiny, O.D., D.M. Barry, M. Agaba and R.A. Godke (2009). In vitro production of cattle×buffalo hybrid embryos using cattle oocytes and African buffalo (*Syncerus caffer caffer*) epididymal sperm. *Theriogenology* **71**: 884–894.

Patnaik, R. (2013). Indian Neogene Siwalik mammalian biostratigraphy. In X. Wang, L.J. Flynn and M. Fortelius (Eds.), *Fossil Mammals of Asia: Neogene Biostratigraphy and Chronology*. New York: Columbia University Press, pp. 423–444.

Patterson, D.B., J.T. Faith, R. Bobe and B. Wood (2014). Regional diversity patterns in African bovids, hyaenids, and felids during the past 3 million years: the role of taphonomic bias and implications for the evolution of *Paranthropus*. *Quaternary Science Reviews* **96**: 9–22.

Peters, J., A. Gautier, J.S. Brink and W. Haenen (1994). Late Quaternary extinction of ungulates in sub-Saharan Africa: a reductionist's approach. *Journal of Archaeological Science* **21**: 17–28.

Pickford, M. and B. Senut (2001). The geological and faunal context of Late Miocene hominid remains from Lukeino, Kenya. *Comptes Rendus de l'Académie des Sciences-Series IIA-Earth and Planetary Science* **332**: 145–152.

Pilgrim, G.E. (1939). The fossil Bovidae of India. *Palaeontologia Indica NS* **26**: 1–356.

Prins, H.H.T. and I.J. Gordon (2014a). Testing hypotheses about biological invasions and Charles Darwin's two-creators ruminations. In H.H.T. Prins and I.J. Gordon (Eds.), *Invasion Biology and Ecological Theory: Insights from a Ccontinent in Transformation*. Cambridge: Cambridge University Press, pp. 1–19.

Prins, H.H.T. and I.J. Gordon (2014b). A critique of ecological theory and a salute to natural history. In H.H.T. Prins and I.J. Gordon (Eds.), *Invasion Biology and Ecological Theory: Insights from a Continent in Transformation*. Cambridge: Cambridge University Press, pp. 497–516.

Prins, H.H.T. and A.R.E. Sinclair (2013). *Syncerus caffer* African buffalo. In J.S. Kingdon and M. Hoffmann (Eds.), *Mammals of Africa. Vol. 6. Pigs, Hippopotamuses, Chevrotain, Giraffes, Deer and Bovids*. London: Bloomsbury, pp. 125–136.

Ritz, L.R., M.L. Glowatzki-Mullis, D.E. MacHugh and C. Gaillard (2000). Phylogenetic analysis of the tribe Bovini using microsatellites. *Animal Genetics* **31**: 178–185.

Ropiquet, A. and A. Hassanin (2005). Molecular phylogeny of caprines (Bovidae, Antilopinae): the question of their origin and diversification during the Miocene. *Journal of Zoological Systematics and Evolutionary Research* **43**: 49–60.

Rossouw, L. (2001). The extinct giant long-horned buffalo of Africa (*Pelorovis antiquus*). *Culna* **56**: 14–15.

Saarinen, J. (2019). The palaeontology of browsing and grazing. In I.J. Gordon and H.H.T. Prins (Eds.), *The Ecology of Browsing and Grazing II*. Cham: Springer, pp. 5–59.

Sanders, A.H. (1925). The taurine world. *National Geographic Magazine* **48**: 591–710.

Searle, M. (2017). Geological origin and evolution of the Himalayas. In H.H.T. Prins and N. Tsewang (Eds.), *Bird Migration across the Himalayas: Wetland Functioning Amidst Mountains and Glaciers*. Cambridge: Cambridge University Press, pp. 145–154.

Sinclair, A.R.E. (1977). *The African Buffalo: A Study of Resource Limitation of Populations*. Chicago: Chicago University Press.

Solounias, N. and B. Dawson-Saunders (1988). Dietary adaptations and paleoecology of the Late Miocene ruminants from Pikermi and Samos in Greece. *Palaeogeography, Palaeoclimatology, Palaeoecology* **65**: 149–172.

Solounias, N. and S.M. Moelleken (1992). Tooth microwear analysis of *Eotragus sansaniensis* (Mammalia: Ruminantia), one of the oldest known bovids. *Journal of Vertebrate Paleontology* **12**: 113–121.

Solounias, N., J.C. Barry, R.L. Bernor, E.H. Lindsay and S.M. Raza (1995). The oldest bovid from the Siwaliks, Pakistan. *Journal of Vertebrate Paleontology* **15**: 806–814.

Sparrmann, A. (1779). *Bos caffer*, et nytt species af Buffel, ifrån Caput bonei spei. *Kongl. Vetensk. Acad. Handl.* **40**: 79–84.

Spassov, N. and D. Geraads (2004). *Tragoportax* PILGRIM, 1937 and *Miotragocerus* STROMER, 1928 (Mammalia, Bovidae) from the Turolian of Hadjidimovo, Bulgaria, and a revision of the Late Miocene Mediterranean Boselaphini. *Geodiversitas* **26**: 339–370.

Spencer, L.M. (1997). Dietary adaptations of Plio-Pleistocene Bovidae: implications for hominid habitat use. *Journal of Human Evolution* **32**: 201–228.

Syvanen, M. (2012). Evolutionary implications of horizontal gene transfer. *Annual Review of Genetics* **46**: 341–358.

Stewart, M., J. Louys, G.J. Price, N.A. Drake, H.S. Groucutt and M.D. Petraglia (2019). Middle and Late Pleistocene mammal fossils of Arabia and surrounding regions: implications for biogeography and hominin dispersals. *Quaternary International* **515**: 1229.

Stover, J., J. Evans and E.P. Dolensek (1981). Interspecies embryo transfer from the gaur to domestic Holstein. *Proceedings of the American Association of Zoo Veterinarians*: 122–124.

Summers, P.M., J.N. Shelton and J. Edwards (1983). The production of mixed-species *Bos taurus–Bos indicus* twin calves. *Animal Reproduction Science* **6**: 79–89.

Thomas, H. (1984). Les Bovidae (Artiodactyla: Mammalia) du Miocène du sous-continent indien, de la péninsule Arabique et de l'Afrique: biostratigraphie, biogéographie et écologie. *Palaeogeography, Palaeoclimatology, Palaeoecology* **45**: 251–299.

Thomas, H., D. Geraads, D. Janjou, et al. (1998). First Pleistocene faunas from the Arabian Peninsula: An Nafud desert, Saudi Arabia. *Earth and Planetary Sciences* **326**: 145–152.

Tong, H.W, X. Chen, B. Zhang and F.G. Wang (2018). New fossils of *Bos primigenius* (Artiodactyla, Mammalia) from Nihewan and Longhua of Hebei, China. *Vertebrata PalAsiatica* **56**: 69–92.

Trofimov, B.A. (1958). New Bovidae from the Oligocene of central Asia. *Vertebrata PalAsiatica* **2**: 243–247.

Van den Bergh, G.D., J. de Vos and P.Y. Sondaar (2001). The Late Quaternary palaeogeography of mammal evolution in the Indonesian Archipelago. *Palaeogeography, Palaeoclimatology, Palaeoecology* **171**: 385–408.

Van der Made, J. (2013). Faunal exchanges through the Levantine Corridor and human dispersal: the paradox of the late dispersal of the Acheulean industry. In *Proceedings of the International Conference 'Africa: Cradle of humanity, recent discoveries'*, pp. 255–294. Travaux Centre National Recherche Prehistoriques, Anthropologiques et Historiques N.S. 18, Ministère de la Culture, Algiers.

Van der Made, J., T. Torres, J.E. Ortiz, et al. (2016). The new material of large mammals from Azokh and comments on the older collections. In Y. Fernández-Jalvo, T. King, L. Yepiskoposyan and P. Andrews (Eds.), *Azokh Cave and the Transcaucasian Corridor*. Cham: Springer, pp. 117–162.

Van Hooft, W.F., A.F. Groen and H.H.T. Prins (2002). Phylogeography of the African buffalo based on mitochondrial and Y-chromosomal loci: Pleistocene origin and population expansion of the Cape buffalo subspecies. *Molecular Ecology* **11**: 26–270.

Vislobokova, I.A. (2008). The major stages in the evolution of artiodactyl communities from the Pliocene–Early Middle Pleistocene of northern Eurasia: Part 1. *Paleontological Journal* **42**: 297–312.

Vrba, E.S. and G.B. Schaller (2000). Phylogeny of Bovidae based on behavior, glands, skulls, and postcrania. In E.S. Vrba and G.B. Schaller (Eds.), *Antelopes, Deer, and Relatives: Fossil*

Record, Behavioral Ecology, Systematics, and Conservation. New Haven: Yale University Press, pp. 203–222.

Zachos, F.E. (2018). Species concepts and species delimitation in mammals. In F. Zachos, and R. Asher (Eds.), *Mammalian Evolution, Diversity and Systematics.* Berlin: Walter de Gruyter, pp. 1–16.

Zhang, R.C. (2000). Interspecies hybridization between yak, *Bos taurus* and *Bos indicus* and reproduction of the hybrids. In X.X. Zhao and R.C. Zhang (Eds.), *Recent Advances in Yak Reproduction.* International Veterinary Information Service (IVIS): e-book.

Zurano, J.P., F.M. Magalhães, A.E. Asato, et al. (2019). Cetartiodactyla: updating a time-calibrated molecular phylogeny. *Molecular Phylogenetics and Evolution* **133**: 256–262.

3 · *Taxonomic Status of the African Buffalo*

J. MICHAUX, N. SMITZ AND P. VAN HOOFT

Introduction

Because the African buffalo (*Syncerus caffer*) exhibits extreme morphological variability across its range (e.g. body size and weight, coat colouration, horn size and curvature), its taxonomic status has been the subject of many debates over time (reviewed in Chapter 2). The most recent update of the IUCN Red List recognized four African buffalo subspecies: *S. c. nanus*, *S. c. brachyceros*, *S. c. aequinoctialis* and *S. c. caffer*. Two genetic clusters can be identified based on maternally inherited mitochondrial DNA (mtDNA): one cluster encompassing the three subspecies from West and Central Africa (*S. c. nanus*, *S. c. brachyceros*, *S. c. aequinoctialis*); the other cluster consisting of the *S. c. caffer* subspecies from East and Southern Africa. The amount of genetic differentiation between these two clusters is typical of that of subspecies in other African bovids (Smitz et al., 2013). The same picture emerges with the paternally inherited Y-chromosome: three haplotypes (genetic variants) among West and Central African populations and one unique haplotype among East and Southern African populations (Van Hooft et al., 2002). Thus, with both mtDNA and Y-DNA *S. c. caffer* emerges as a distinct genetic cluster. The only exception may be *S. c. caffer* in Angola and Namibia. There, two mtDNA haplotypes and one Y-haplotype typical of West and Central Africa were observed (Van Hooft et al., 2002). However, these latter observations should be taken with caution considering these genotypes were derived from zoo animals.

Nevertheless, the spatial genetic pattern based on microsatellites (polymorphic genetic markers residing on non-sex chromosomes) is different. Among *S. c. caffer* populations, genetic variation is mainly clinal (Van Hooft et al., 2021). This clinal variation is characterized by a linear relationship between genetic distance (pairwise F_{ST}: the proportion

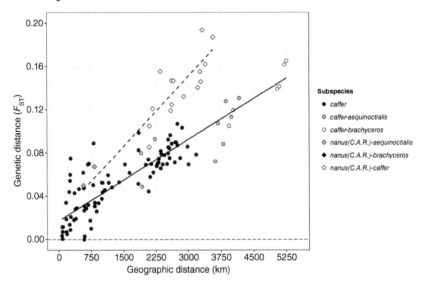

Figure 3.1 Increase of pairwise F_{ST} with geographic distance (isolation-by-distance): among savanna-dwelling populations (i.e. excluding *S. c. nanus*): $R^2 = 0.83$ (solid line), between the *S. c. nanus* population from Central African Republic (C.A.R.) and the savanna-dwelling populations: $R^2 = 0.85$ (dashed line). Regression is weighted by 'square root of number of genotyped individuals per population pair X number of shared genotyped microsatellites per population pair'. Only population pairs are included with weight >102 in case of savanna-dwelling populations and with weight >48 in case pairs including the *S. c. nanus* population from C.A.R. In all cases, sample size per population ≥5 with number of microsatellites per population pair varying between 8 and 18. Data from Van Hooft et al. (2021) and unpublished data from Smitz et al. (2014b). Genotype data came from different laboratories, which when also coming from the same population permitted allele alignment by matching each microsatellite's allele frequencies while preserving size order (Van Hooft et al., 2021).

of the total genetic variation per population pair, that is between the two populations) and geographic distance, a pattern also known as isolation-by-distance, with the latter explaining as much as 78 per cent of the variation. This clinal pattern even extends to the populations of *S. c. brachyceros* and *S. c. aequinoctialis*, which like *S. c. caffer* also occur on savannas ($R^2 = 0.83$, Figure 3.1). Predicted pairwise F_{ST} gradually increases to ~0.15 at 5,300 km. Genetic distances involving the *S. c. nanus* population from the Central African Republic (Ngotto Forest Reserve) are also clinal ($R^2 = 0.85$, Figure 3.1), but twice as large in comparison to those involving only savanna-dwelling populations. This is probably due to a combination of low population density and reduced gene flow in rainforests compared to savannas. The only exceptions to these clinal patterns are populations with elevated F_{ST} values ($F_{ST} > 0.2$ beyond 2000 km distance; not shown in Figure 3.1) due to small size, isolation or a bottleneck, as observed with the populations from HiP (Hluhluwe-iMfolozi Park, South Africa; Van Hooft et al., 2019), Nairobi National Park (Kenya; Heller et al,. 2010) and Lékédi Park (Gabon).

Thus, at the level of neutral genetic markers in savanna-dwelling buffalo, neither the subspecies nor buffalo in the contact zones between them appear as distinct genetic clusters. As has been proposed in human genetics (Handley et al., 2007), one should abandon the traditional island model of population differentiation (treating populations as discrete random mating units) when explaining genetic structure in relation to historical gene flow (in the case of African buffalo before 1870). The observed linear relationship between genetic and geographic distance indicates that, historically, the savanna-dwelling buffalo populations constituted one large metapopulation with continuous gene flow over limited distance, in which 'limited' is defined as less than the lifetime dispersal distance.

The clinal pattern of genetic variation seems to be in conflict with studies that describe population genetic structure as discontinuous or clustered (Heller et al., 2010; Smitz et al., 2014a). It is possible that genetic clusters are an artefact of a discontinuous sampling scheme (Pritchard et al., 2000; Kopec, 2014). On the other hand, clinal and clustered depictions of genetic structure are not necessarily mutually exclusive (Handley et al., 2007). Genetic structure may also be described using a synthetic model, in which most population differentiation can be explained by gradual isolation-by-distance, with some discontinuities due to historical or recent geographic barriers (e.g. human-induced population fragmentation). However, clusters probably explain only a small fraction of the variation when there is a strong underlying pattern of isolation-by-distance; a fraction which in case of African buffalo is no more than 0.17 (1 minus R^2) (Handley et al., 2007).

The question of how many subspecies of buffalo can be recognized depends on the subspecies concept to which one adheres. If one merely relies on the notion of heritable geographic variation in phenotype (Patten, 2015), then almost any number of subspecies can be justified, as long the phenotypic traits used in subspecies designation are heritable and confined to specific areas. On the other hand, if one uses partial restricted gene flow and clearly delineated genetic clusters as additional criteria (Haig et al., 2006), then no more than three subspecies may be recognized: (1) *S. c. caffer* of the East and Southern African savannas (a separate cluster with mitochondrial and Y-chromosomal markers), (2) *S. c. nanus* of the West and Central African rainforests (restricted gene flow indicated by relatively high F_{ST} values) and (3) the northern savanna buffalo of the West and Central African savannas (currently assigned to two different subspecies: *S. c. brachyceros* and *S. c. aequinoctialis*). Prins et al. (Chapter 2) propose to name the latter *Syncerus caffer umarii*. Considering that *S. c. nanus* is not phylogenetically distinct from the northern savanna buffalo, one may even argue that all of the buffalo from West and Central Africa, irrespective of habitat, should be lumped into one subspecies as suggested in Smitz et al. (2014a). Irrespective of subspecies designation, which appears quite subjective according to the selected criteria and to the interpretation of the obtained results, the West and Central African buffalo should be recognized as a separate Conservation Unit (see next section).

Phylogeography and Evolutionary History of the African Buffalo

Phylogeography is the study of the geographic distribution of genetic lineages (Avise, 2000). As mentioned above, the African buffalo is genetically divided in two main lineages, one encompassing the buffalo distributed in West, Central and possibly southwestern Africa (Angola and Namibia; hereafter called the WC cluster) and another one including buffalo roaming East and southern African savannas (hereafter referred to as the ES cluster). This clear genetic discontinuity has led to the recognition of two management units (Moritz, 1994) deserving specific conservation efforts (Van Hooft et al., 2002; Smitz et al., 2013). Each management unit is characterized by a unique evolutionary history, which can be investigated using molecular tools. In fact, genomes retain records of demographic changes and evolutionary processes that have shaped present-day diversity within the species. Reconstructing the species' evolutionary history allows us to determine the effect of recent and past climatic events, as well as of human activities. Over the last decades, some congruent results were obtained when investigating the signature left in the buffalo genomes by past and recent events using various DNA markers (i.e. mtDNA fragments, Y-chromosomal loci, autosomal microsatellites, mitogenomes and whole genomes). In this section we review the present understanding of the effect of these events in a chronological way (from the past to the recent). However, note that inferring history and linking demographic changes to specific historical events can hardly be achieved with more than some thousand years of certainty.

The species is widespread in sub-Saharan Africa, physically able to disperse through a wide range of habitats, from sea level to the limits of forests on the highest mountains (Sinclair, 1977; Prins, 1996) and morphologically able to rapidly adapt in evolutionary terms to different ecological conditions (Smitz et al., 2013). Its distribution is limited by the availability of permanent sources of water. Drought is considered to be a major cause of ungulate mortality, with short-term rainfall fluctuations proven to significantly affect both vegetation indices and buffalo dynamics (Dublin and Ogutu, 2015; Abraham et al., 2019; see Chapter 7). Additionally, while it was long believed to be strongly philopatric, forming large aggregations remaining on separate home ranges and with few interchanges (male-biased dispersal; Estes, 1991; reviewed in Chapter 6), according to collaring studies in Botswana, 5 of 75 (7 per cent) female buffalo showed long-distance movement, with distances from 120 km to over 200 km, and 5 of 32 (16 per cent) herd-switching. The latter is supported by a high mtDNA diversity among females within herds in Kruger Nation Park (KNP, South Africa). Consequently, the African buffalo shows high gene flow over evolutionary timescales, reflected by low genetic differentiations between populations within lineages (Simonsen et al., 1998; Van Hooft et al., 2002; Smitz et al., 2013; de Jager et al., 2021) – in fact, the lowest among African mammals studied, as reviewed in Smitz et al. (2013) and Lorenzen et al. (2012).

During the Pleistocene, oscillations in the precipitations governing the physiography of Africa – the major vegetation zones being savannas and tropical forests (Moreau, 1963; Dupont and Agwu, 1992; DeMenocal, 2004; Dupont, 2011; Lehmann et al., 2011; Staver et al., 2011) – are believed to be the main drivers of population expansion in savanna species during cool and dry phases (interpluvials/glacial) and contraction during wet and warm phases (pluvials/interglacials). This is in agreement with the fact that congruent phylogeographical patterns across taxonomic groups and trophic levels have been observed, suggesting similar forces shaped species' evolutionary histories (reviewed in Lorenzen et al., 2012). Repeated shifts of the two major vegetation zones facilitated the emergence and evolution of many bovid taxa (Vrba, 1995; Bobe et al., 2002; Bobe and Behrensmeyer, 2004). These considerable fluctuations have promoted divergence within and between the two buffalo lineages (WC versus ES clusters); the latter north-south structuration has been identified across multiple species associated with savanna ecosystems (Lorenzen et al., 2012). Periodic separation by an equatorial forest belt during moist pluvials could have acted as a barrier to gene flow (populations isolated in refugia), with secondary contacts during dry interpluvials (Arctander et al. 1999; Van Hooft et al., 2002; Lorenzen et al., 2012). The overlapping or suture zone between WC and ES buffalo clusters is proposed to be located in East Africa (Smitz et al., 2013), a region identified as a melting pot of long-diverged lineages across many taxa – for example, the kob, *Kobus kob* (Lorenzen et al., 2007, 2012). Despite the lack of contemporary barriers to gene flow (supported by the aforementioned clinal genetic structure at autosomal microsatellites), lineages appear conserved, with female gene flow estimated to be in the order of no more than five mitochondrial genomes per generation since divergence (Smitz et al., 2013).

Some inferred demographic changes shaping the pattern of divergence and distribution of the species could be dated and linked to historical climatic, environmental and/or anthropogenetic events. The most ancient identified expansion pre-dated the above-mentioned divergence between the WC and ES clusters, and started approximatively one million years ago to continue until ~500 kyr (de Jager et al., 2021). This period was marked by a shift between arid and moist conditions toward less extreme cycles leading to the development of a more stable savanna environment, allowing for the expansion of the buffalo ancestor (see Chapter 2). The genetic divergence between the WC and ES clusters was dated to around 130–300 kyr, resulting from populations isolated in allopatry in savanna refugia (Van Hooft et al., 2002; Smitz et al., 2013). These particular core areas were characterized by long-standing savanna habitat enabling the continued survival of savanna-adapted taxa (Lorenzen et al., 2012). Because Pleistocene-dated fossils resemble buffalo of the present-day WC cluster, the ES cluster (or Cape buffalo) might have derived from a stock of savanna buffalo from WC (Gentry, 1978; Kingdon, 1982). Likewise, the forest dwarf buffalo (*S. c. nanus* – WC cluster) turned out to be an advanced form derived from savanna buffalo, rather than being the ancestor of all living African buffalo (Smitz et al., 2013; see Chapter 2). African buffalo refugia were purportedly proposed in present-day Uganda and Central African Republic, where present-day populations display the highest genetic diversities within the species (Smitz et al., 2013). Yet, both sampling size and species distribution coverage in West Central Africa have been limiting factors in all conducted studies, presumably linked to the difficulty of collecting material for DNA-based investigations from these regions. Further efforts are recommended to fill knowledge gaps, based on the use of a new generation of molecular markers made available by technological advances in the field of genome sequencing.

The aforementioned refugia played an important role in the dispersal of the lineages. A first westward expansion event of the WC cluster after divergence occurred in the late to middle Pleistocene (~100 kyr) along two routes, into the forest belt and the Western Sahel region, hence adapting morphologically to colonize new habitats (Smitz et al., 2013). The latter can be associated with the shift from persistent rainforest in both dry and wet periods before ~220 kyr to its reduction and replacement by savanna after ~220 kyr (Dupont and Agwu, 1992; Dupont et al., 2000; DeMenocal, 2004). Unlike the WC cluster, the southward expansion of the ES cluster occurred after a core was retained in Eastern Africa, probably unable to colonize this part of the continent due to extremely arid conditions between 135 and 90 kyr. A demographic decline in the ES cluster was even identified around 100 kyr, proposed to be a consequence of a series of mega-droughts registered in East Africa around that time, to which the African buffalo is especially sensitive (de Jager et al., 2021). After aridity decreased, reaching near modern conditions around 60 kyr (Cohen et al., 2007; Scholz et al., 2007), the development of large savanna-type grasslands allowed for an expansion of the ES cluster around 50 kyr (Van Hooft et al., 2002; Smitz et al., 2013) or 80 kyr (Heller et al., 2012; de Jager et al., 2021). Another, non-exclusive hypothesis is that the expansion could have followed the extinction of the giant long-horned buffalo (*Peloveris antiquus*), which dominated savannas until the late Pleistocene, as supported by fossil data (Kingdon, 1982; Klein, 1995; Van Hooft et al., 2002; see Chapter 2). This expansion was concurrent with the expansion of humans between 80 and 10 kyr (Heller et al., 2012). It therefore refutes an adverse ecological effect of Palaeolithic humans (Heller et al., 2012). Finally, it is worth pointing out that the finding of *Syncerus*-like fossil records in Southern Africa pre-dating this expansion (Porat et al., 2010) might indicate multiple colonization–extinction events in the region, following habitat suitability (Smitz et al., 2013). Local loss of populations in Southern Africa and subsequent recolonization from an East core was also suggested for the hartebeest *Alcelaphus buselaphus*, the topi *Damaliscus lunatus* and the giraffe *Giraffa camelopardalis* (Arctander et al., 1999; Pitra et al., 2002; Brown et al., 2007).

Following this expansion phase, a strong signal of population decline was identified within the ES cluster, in the order of 75–98 per cent (Heller et al., 2008, 2012). This major decline was not detected in the studies of Van Hooft et al. (2002) and Smitz et al. (2013), although discrepant demographic signals can be obtained from different types of molecular markers and databases. This major bottleneck occurred around ~5000 years ago (Heller et al., 2008, 2012). The mid-Holocene aridification, marked by a pronounced transition from warm and wet (the Holocene Climatic Optimum – DeMenocal et al., 2000) to drier conditions around 4500 years ago (Marchant and Hooghiemstra, 2004; Burroughs, 2005; Kiage and Liu, 2006), was identified as a possible driver of the effective population size decline. In addition to the climate-mediated decline hypothesis, the explosive growth in human population size and their domestic bovines (the Neolithic revolution – Finlay et al., 2007; Scheinfeldt et al., 2010) and correspondingly rapid decline in buffalo populations from 5 kyr onwards, could represent an alternative explanation (Heller et al., 2012). Together, they could have driven humans, domesticated cattle and large savanna mammals into closer contact around remaining water sources, leading to ecological competition and possible spill-over of exotic diseases from cattle to buffalo. This two-phased dynamic (expansion/decline) was also observed in other drought-intolerant species, such as the savanna elephant *Loxondonta africana* and baboon *Papio cynocephalus* (Storz et al., 2002; Okello et al., 2008), indicating a community-wide collapse.

Various studies indicate that the African buffalo from Southern Africa have relatively high frequencies of deleterious alleles throughout their genome, which negatively affect male body condition and disease resistance (Van Hooft et al., 2014, 2018, 2019, 2021). These high frequencies are attributed to an underlying sex-ratio meiotic gene-drive system. Meiotic drivers are selfish genetic elements that, by distorting meiosis, favour transmission of the chromosome on which they reside. In the case of sex chromosomes, this results in distorted primary sex ratios, as observed in KNP and HiP (Van Hooft et al., 2010, 2019). High frequencies of deleterious alleles indicate that environmental stressors such as drought and diseases have been consistently acting as selective agents for long periods of time. Despite this, most populations of African buffalo seem to have been large in the recent evolutionary past and to be stable after their recovery from the rinderpest pandemic of 1889–1895. This seems to support the view, advocated by some population geneticists, that deleterious alleles and genetic diversity in general play a smaller role in ecology, at least with respect to demographics, than one might expect (Agrawal and Whitlock, 2012; Teixeira and Huber, 2021).

Note that overall, less is known for the WC cluster because available studies are limited by the sampling size and geographical coverage for this region, as well as by the type of DNA marker investigated, limiting the possible inferences (Van Hooft et al., 2002; Smitz et al., 2013). To our knowledge, two ongoing studies involving the investigation of genome-wide single nucleotide polymorphism (SNP) data and whole genomes (WGS) undertaken by the research teams of L. Morrison (University of Edinburgh) and of J. Michaux (University of Liège) might uncover some additional events which shaped the evolutionary history of the WC cluster.

Population Genetic Structure at Local Scale and Linked to Recent Events

The African buffalo has suffered important population losses during the last century, impacting all of the subspecies mentioned above. Of the more than 3 million buffalo that roamed the continent in the nineteenth century (Lessard et al., 1990), only around one million presently survive (Chapter 4).

Habitat loss and poaching are the main challenges currently threaten-ing the species. Habitat loss can be due to anthropogenic factors (Alroy, 2001; Godfrey and Jungers, 2003; Surovel et al., 2005) or to climatic changes (Meijaard, 2003; Barnosky et al., 2004; Lovett et al., 2005; Vanacker et al., 2005), as for example the increasing drought observed in Africa since the 1990s (rain is the ecologically most important climate variable in most of Africa). The African buffalo, a species highly sensitive to drought (Ogutu et al., 2008), exhibits important climate-mediated population decline as demonstrated by a decrease in the Masai Mara population from 10,000 to 2400 individuals during the severe drought of 1993–1994 (East, 1999). This last factor was associated with other drivers like enhanced encroachments of pastoralists/cattle and commercial farms and changes in governance systems, which further aggravated the situa-tion (Chapter 12).

Fragmentation of the natural habitat into small patches also endangers the populations by increasing genetic drift, resulting in loss of genetic diversity and consequently leading to a reduction in the evolutionary potential of the species (Frankham et al., 1999; Hedrick, 2005). For exam-ple, around 75 per cent of all buffalo (estimated to be around 900,000 animals) are currently located in protected areas (i.e. national parks (NPs) and game reserves; East, 1999), with many populations completely iso-lated each from another (Chapter 4). These reduced population sizes due to human-induced population fragmentation have a strong impact on local genetic diversity. In Kenya and Uganda, a significant correlation between park area and microsatellite heterozygosity (fraction of individuals with two different alleles per microsatellite) was observed, with populations in small parks (<400 km^2) having a genetic diversity reduced by ~5 per cent compared to the population of the Masai Mara–Serengeti ecosystem (Heller et al., 2010). This amount of reduction in genetic diversity was also observed among the buffalo from the Ngorongoro Crater, Tanzania (Ernest et al. 2012). In South Africa, genome-wide diversity in the populations from HiP (~4500 buffalo) and Addo NP (~800 buffalo) is 19 per cent and 31 per cent smaller, respectively, in comparison to the KNP population (~40,900 buffalo) due to historical population bottlenecks (de Jager et al., 2021). Other small isolated populations with reduced genetic diversity are those in Arusha NP (Kenya, ~1800 buffalo in the early 1970s; Ernest et al., 2012) and Campo-Ma'an (Cameroon, <100 buffalo; Bekhuis et al., 2008), which show ~15 per cent reduction in mtDNA diversity compared to nearby populations (Smitz et al., 2013). It is therefore safe to assume that genetic drift affects population in smaller conservancies more rapidly than in larger ones. It is also expected that this genetic erosion will become significantly more progressive in the near future (Heller et al., 2010). Suppression or restriction of gene flow by confinement into small areas could also have an ethological impact, disturbing the behaviour of natural dispersion in response to seasonal variations in food availability (Sinclair, 1977; Halley et al., 2002; Ryan et al., 2006; Heller et al., 2010).

The introduction of non-native species, such as domestic cattle, besides generating direct competition for natural resources, also poses severe problems due to the introduction of pathogens. Indeed, domestic cattle and African buffalo are related closely enough to cause considerable challenges in terms of disease transmission. It was notably the case of the rinderpest morbillivirus introduced in 1889 by a colonial military expedition to Ethiopia (Branagan and Hammond, 1965; Sinclair, 1977; Prins, 1996). The African buffalo has probably been one of the African species that has suffered most from this disease (extreme regional reductions in population density, paired to many local extinctions; Wenink et al., 1998), with the most severe collapse occurring in the 1890s when mortality rates estimated between 90 per cent and 95 per cent were registered over the continent (Mack, 1970; Sinclair, 1977; Plowright, 1982; Prins and Van der Jeugd, 1993; Shigesada and Kawasaki, 1997; O'Ryan et al., 1998; Winterbach, 1998).

Some studies investigated the impact of rinderpest epidemics on the genetic diversity of the African buffalo. Results contrasted between no reported genetic signature of a recent bottleneck (Simonsen et al., 1998; Van Hooft et al., 2000; Heller et al., 2008) to the observation of a population decline caused by the rinderpest epidemic (Heller et al., 2012; de Jager et al., 2021). Nevertheless, all studies still reported high genetic diversities (O'Ryan et al., 1998; Simonsen et al., 1998; Wenink et al., 1998; Van Hooft et al., 2000, 2002; Heller et al., 2008, 2012; Smitz et al., 2013; Smitz et al., 2014a; de Jager et al., 2021). Even though the continent-wide pandemic reportedly caused important buffalo mortalities (with death rates in some localities possibly as high as 90 per cent; Lessard et al., 1990; Estes, 1991; Prins, 1996; O'Ryan et al., 1998), the absence of a pronounced effect on the genetic diversity might result from a possible overestimation of the severity of the pandemic in terms of population decline, but also from a rapid population regrowth combined with high interpopulation gene flow, reintroducing rare alleles and distorting the genetic signal of bottleneck (Van Hooft et al., 2000; Heller et al., 2008). This is supported by the observation that survivors recolonized their range, being so productive that by 1920 the species was again numerous (Sinclair, 1977; Estes, 1991). For example, in the KNP, area survival estimates were off by at least a factor of 10, considering the high number of mitochondrial and Y-chromosomal haplotypes observed in the present-day population.

High genome-wide nucleotide diversity in KNP is indicative of a large long-term effective population size of ~48,000 individuals (de Jager et al., 2021). Because within-population nucleotide diversity is largely determined by the total size of a metapopulation, this effective population size is probably indicative for the subspecies as whole (Strobeck, 1987). The aforementioned linear relationship between genetic and geographic distance (Figure 3.1) indicates that this effective population size varies little between the different savanna-dwelling subspecies. However, effective population size is probably considerably smaller for the small *S. c. nanus* subspecies, considering the relative isolation and small sizes of the forest-dwelling populations as indicated by the relatively large genetic distances observed with microsatellites.

Conclusion

The evolutionary history of the African buffalo began a long time ago, between one million and 500,000 years ago. It started with an expansion throughout sub-Saharan Africa, probably during cool and dry phases (interpluvials/glacial) as these periods favoured the development of more constant savanna environments. Later, around 130–300 kyr, population isolations in savanna refugia led to an allopatric differentiation and to the appearance of two main genetic lineages (the WC and EC clusters). These lineages spread again from Central African refugia, in sub-Saharan Africa during the late to middle Pleistocene along different routes: into the forest belt and the Western Sahel regions, for the WC cluster, and in the south of the continent for the EC one. Following this expansion phase, a strong signal of population decline was identified within the ES cluster around ~5000 years ago. This decline could be linked to the mid-Holocene aridification of Africa, but also to the explosive growth in the population sizes of humans and their domestic bovines (the Neolithic revolution), which also happened during this period. In more recent times, during the last century, the African buffalo also suffered important population losses. Habitat loss and poaching are the main challenges currently threatening the species. Habitat loss can mainly be due to anthropogenic factors or, to a lesser degree, climatic changes. Other aspects like the introduction of non-native species, such as domestic cattle, besides generating direct competition for natural resources, also had a deep impact on the Africa buffalo's survival due to the introduction of pathogens.

Concerning the taxonomic aspect, genetic studies tend to propose either two (*S. c. caffer* of the East and Southern African savanna and *S. c. nanus*, in Western and Central Africa), or three (*S. c. caffer* of the East and Southern African savannas; *S. c. nanus* of the West and Central African rain forests; and *S. c. umarii* in the savanna buffalo of the West and Central African savannas) subspecies. However, irrespective of subspecies designation, which appears quite subjective, the Eastern and Southern populations, the West and Central African forest buffalo and the West and Central African savanna buffalo should be recognized as three separate Conservation Units. Indeed, the global conservation status of the West Central African forest buffalo is not as good as that for the West Central African savanna buffalo (Chapter 4). Its conservation context is also quite distinct from that of the West Central African savanna buffalo. A particular conservation status for the forest buffalo group is therefore needed.

From a genetic point of view, the main challenges for the conservation and management of the African buffalo are the development of new genetic markers, such as the study of whole-genome sequences, which will give an even more precise information concerning the evolutionary history of the African buffalo and the relationships among the different conservation units. The comparison of neutral as well as selective genetic traits will also help to better understand the impact of artificial hybridization among different African buffalo morphotypes, which are developed in some areas to obtain particular hunting trophies (in the frame of game farming activities). In a more general context, another important challenge will be to promote the integration of genetic studies in conservation practices (i.e. important to retain high genetic diversity and gene flow for long-term conservation – and better consider the impact of habitat fragmentation and land use and major drought events).

References

Abraham, J.O., G.P. Hempson and A.C. Staver (2019). Drought-response strategies of savanna herbivores. *Ecology and Evolution* **9**(12): 7047–7056.

Agrawal, A.F. and M.C. Whitlock (2012). Mutation load: the fitness of individuals in populations where deleterious alleles are abundant. *Annual Review of Ecology, Evolution and Systematics* **43**(115): 2012.

Alroy, J. (2001). A multispecies overkill simulation of the end-Pleistocene megafaunal mass extinction. *Science* **292**(5523): 1893–1896.

Arctander, P., C. Johansen and M. Coutellec-Vreto (1999). Phylogeography of three closely related African bovids (tribe Alcelaphini). *Molecular Biology and Evolution* **16**(12): 1724–1739.

Avise, J.C. (2000). *Phylogeography: The History and Formation of Species.* Cambridge, MA: Harvard University Press.

Barnosky, A.D., P.L. Koch, R.S. Feranec, et al. (2004). Assessing the causes of late Pleistocene extinctions on the continents. *Science* **306**(5693): 70–75.

Bekhuis, P.D.B.M., C.B. De Jong and H.H.T. Prins (2008). Diet selection and density estimates of forest buffalo in Campo-Ma'an National Park, Cameroon. *African Journal of Ecology* **46**(4): 668–675.

Bobe, R. and A.K. Behrensmeyer (2004). The expansion of grassland ecosystems in Africa in relation to mammalian evolution and the origin of the genus *Homo*. *Palaeogeography, Palaeoclimatology, Palaeoecology* **207**(3–4): 399–420.

Bobe, R., A.K. Behrensmeyer and R.E. Chapman (2002). Faunal change, environmental variability and late Pliocene hominin evolution. *Journal of Human Evolution* **42**(4): 475–497.

Branagan, D. and J. Hammond (1965). Rinderpest in Tanganyika: a review. *Bulletin of Epizootic Diseases of Africa. Bulletin des Epizooties en Afrique* **13**(3): 225–246.

Brown, D.M., R.A. Brenneman, K.-P. Koepfli, et al. (2007). Extensive population genetic structure in the giraffe. *BMC Biology* **5**: 57.

Burroughs, W. (2005). *Climate Change in Prehistory: The End of the Reign of Chaos.* Cambridge: Cambridge University Press.

Cohen, A. S., J.R. Stone, K.R.M. Beuning, et al. (2007). Ecological consequences of early Late Pleistocene megadroughts in tropical Africa. *Proceedings of the National Academy of Sciences of the United States of America* **104**(42): 16422–16427.

DeMenocal, P., J. Ortiz, T. Guilderson, et al. (2000). Coherent high- and low-latitude climate variability during the Holocene warm period. *Science* **288**: 2198–2202.

DeMenocal, P.B. (2004). African climate change and faunal evolution during the Pliocene–Pleistocene. *Earth and Planetary Science Letters* **220**(1–2): 3–24.

Dublin, H.T. and J.O. Ogutu (2015). Population regulation of African buffalo in the Mara–Serengeti ecosystem. *Wildlife Research* **42**(5): 382–393.

Dupont, L. (2011). Orbital scale vegetation change in Africa. *Quaternary Science Reviews* **30**(25–26): 3589–3602.

Dupont, L. and C.O.C. Agwu (1992). Latitudinal shifts of forest and savanna in N. W. Africa during the Brunhes chron: further marine palynological results from site M 16415. *Vegetation History and Archaeobotany* **1**(3): 163–175.

Dupont, L.M., S. Jahns, F. Marret, et al. (2000). Vegetation change in equatorial West Africa: time-slices for the last 150 ka. *Palaeogeography, Palaeoclimatology, Palaeoecology* **155**(1–2): 95–122.

East, R. (1999). *African Antelope Database*. Edited by IUCN/SSC. Vol. 21. Antelope Specialist Group. Gland, Switzerland and Cambridge, UK: IUCN.

Ernest, E.M., H. Haanes, S. Bitanyi, et al. (2012). Influence of habitat fragmentation on the genetic structure of large mammals: evidence for increased structuring of African buffalo (*Syncerus caffer*) within the Serengeti ecosystem. *Conservation Genetics* **13**(2): 381–391.

Estes, R.D. (1991). *The Behavior Guide to African Mammals*. Berkeley: University of California Press.

Finlay, E.K., C. Gaillard, S.M.F. Vahidi, et al. (2007). Bayesian inference of population expansions in domestic bovines. *Biology Letters* **3**(4): 449–452.

Frankham, R., K. Lees, M.E. Montgomery, et al. (1999). Do population size bottlenecks reduce evolutionary potential? *Animal Conservation Forum* **2**(4): 255–260.

Gentry, A.W. (1978). Bovidae. In: V.J. Maglio and H.B.S. Cook (Eds.), *Evolution of African Mammals*. Cambridge, MA: Harvard University Press, pp. 540–572.

Godfrey, L.R. and W.L. Jungers (2003). The extinct sloth lemurs of Madagascar. *Evolutionary Anthropology: Issues, News, and Reviews: Issues, News, and Reviews* **12**(6): 252–263.

Handley, L.J.L., A. Manica, J. Goudet, et al. (2007). Going the distance: human population genetics in a clinal world. *Trends in Genetics* **23**(9): 432–439.

Haig, S.M., E.A. Beever, S.M. Chambers, et al. (2006). Taxonomic considerations in listing subspecies under the U.S. Endangered Species Act. *Conservation Biology* **20**(6): 1584–1594.

Halley, D.-J., M.E.J. Vandewalle, M. Mari and C. Taolo (2002). Herd-switching and long-distance dispersal in female African buffalo *Syncerus caffer*. *African Journal of Ecology* **40**(1): 97–99.

Hedrick, P. (2005). 'Genetic restoration': a more comprehensive perspective than 'genetic rescue'. *Trends in Ecology & Evolution* **20**(3): 109.

Heller, R., E.D. Lorenzen, J.B. Okello, et al. (2008). Mid-Holocene decline in African buffalos inferred from Bayesian coalescent-based analyses of microsatellites and mitochondrial DNA. *Molecular Ecology* **17**(22): 4845–4858.

Heller, R., A. Brüniche-Olsen and H.R. Siegismund (2012). Cape buffalo mitogenomics reveals a Holocene shift in the African human–megafauna dynamics. *Molecular Ecology* **21**(16): 3947–3959.

Heller, R., J.B. Okello and H. Siegismund (2010). Can small wildlife conservancies maintain genetically stable populations of large mammals? Evidence for increased genetic drift in geographically restricted populations of Cape buffalo in East Africa. *Molecular Ecology* **19**: 1324–1334.

de Jager, D., B. Glanzmann, M. Möller, et al. (2021). High diversity, inbreeding and a dynamic Pleistocene demographic history revealed by African buffalo genomes. *Scientific Reports* **11**(1): 4540.

Kiage, L.M. and K.-B. Liu (2006). Late Quaternary paleoenvironmental changes in East Africa: a review of multiproxy evidence from palynology, lake sediments, and associated records. *Progress in Physical Geography* **30**(5): 633–658.

Kingdon, J. (1982). *East African Mammals: an Atlas of Evolution in Africa, Vol III Part C (Bovids)*. London: Academic Press.

Klein, R.G. (1995). Mammalian extinctions and Stone Age people in Africa. In: P.S. Martin and R.G. Klein (Eds.), *Quaternary Extinctions: a Prehistoric Revolution*. Tucson: The University of Arizona Press, pp. 553–573.

Kopec, M. (2014). Clines, clusters, and clades in the race debate. *Philosophy of Science* **81**(5): 1053–1065.

Lehmann, C.E.R., S.A. Archibald, W.A. Hoffmann, et al. (2011). Deciphering the distribution of the savanna biome. *The New Phytologist* **191**(1): 197–209.

Lessard, P., R. L'Eplattenier, R.A. Norval, et al. (1990). Geographical information systems for studying the epidemiology of cattle diseases caused by *Theileria parva*. *The Veterinary Record* **126**(11): 255–262.

Lorenzen, E.D., R. De Neergaard, P. Arctander, et al. (2007). Phylogeography, hybridization and Pleistocene refugia of the kob antelope (*Kobus kob*). *Molecular Ecology* **16**(15): 3241–3252.

Lorenzen, E.D., R. Heller and H.R. Siegismund (2012). Comparative phylogeography of African savannah ungulates. *Molecular Ecology* **21**(15): 3656–3670.

Lovett, J.C., G.F. Midgley and P. Barnard (2005). Climate change and ecology in Africa *African Journal of Ecology* **43**(3): 167–169.

Mack, R. (1970). The great African cattle plague epidemic of the 1890s. *Tropical Animal Health and Production* **2**: 210–219.

Marchant, R. and H. Hooghiemstra (2004). Rapid environmental change in African and South American tropics around 4000 years before present: a review. *Earth-Science Reviews* **66**(3): 217–260.

Meijaard, E. (2003). Mammals of south-east Asian islands and their Late Pleistocene environments. *Journal of Biogeography* **30**(8): 1245–1257.

Moreau, R.E. (1963). The distribution of tropical African birds as an indicator of past climatic changes. In: *African Ecology and Human Evolution*. London: Routledge, p. 15.

Moritz, C. (1994). Defining 'Evolutionarily Significant Units' for conservation. *Trends in Ecology and Evolution* **10**: 373–375.

O'Ryan, C., E.H. Harley, M.W. Bruford, et al. (1998). Microsatellite analysis of genetic diversity in fragmented South African buffalo populations. *Animal Conservation* **1**(2): 85–94.

Ogutu, J.O., H.-P. Piepho, H.T. Dublin, et al. (2008). Rainfall influences on ungulate population abundance in the Mara–Serengeti ecosystem. *The Journal of Animal Ecology* **77**(4): 814–829.

Okello, J.B., G. Wittemyer, H.B. Rasmussen, et al. (2008). Effective population size dynamics reveal impacts of historic climatic events and recent anthropogenic pressure in African elephants. *Molecular Ecology* **17**(17): 3788–3799.

Patten, M.A. (2015). Subspecies and the philosophy of science. *The Auk: Ornithological Advances* 132(2): 481–485.

Pitra, C., A.J. Hansen, D. Lieckfeldt, et al. (2002). An exceptional case of historical outbreeding in African sable antelope populations. *Molecular Ecology* **11**(7): 1197–1208.

Plowright, W. (1982). The effect of rinderpest and rinderpest control on wildlife in Africa. In M.A. Edwards and U. McDonnell (Eds.), *Animal Disease in Relation to Animal Conservation*. Symposia of the Zoological Society of London, Vol. 50. London: Academic Press, pp. 1–28.

Porat, N., M. Chazan, R. Grün, et al. (2010). New radiometric ages for the Fauresmith industry from Kathu Pan, southern Africa: implications for the Earlier to Middle Stone Age transition. *Journal of Archaeological Science* **37**(2): 269–283.

Prins, H.H.T. (1996). *Ecology and Behaviour of the African Buffalo: Social Inequality and Decision Making*. Wildlife Ecology and Behaviour Series Vol. 1. London: Chapman & Hall.

Prins, H.H.T. and H.P. van der Jeugd (1993). Herbivore population crashes and woodland structure in East Africa. *Journal of Ecology* **81**(2): 305–314.

Pritchard, J.K., M. Stephens and P. Donnelly (2000). Inference of population structure using multilocus genotype data. *Genetics* **155**(2): 945–959.

Ryan, S.J., C.U. Knechtel and W.M. Getz (2006). Range and habitat selection of African buffalo in South Africa. *Journal of Wildlife Management* **70**(3): 764–776.

Scheinfeldt, L.B., S. Soi and S. Tishkoff (2010). Working toward a synthesis of archaeological, linguistic, and genetic data for inferring African population history. *Proceedings of the National Academy of Sciences of the United States of America* **107**(Suppl_2): 8931–8938.

Scholz, C.A., T.C. Johnson, A.S. Cohen (2007). East African megadroughts between 135 and 75 thousand years ago and bearing on early-modern human origins. *Proceedings of the National Academy of Sciences of the United States of America* **104**(42): 16416–16421.

Shigesada, N. and K. Kawasaki (1997). *Biological Invasions: Theory and Practice*. Oxford: Oxford University Press.

Simonsen, B.T., H.R. Siegismund and P. Arctander (1998). Population structure of African buffalo inferred from mtDNA sequences and microsatellite loci: high variation but low differentiation. *Molecular Ecology* **7**(2): 225–237.

Sinclair, A.R.E. (1977) *The African Buffalo: A Study of Resource Limitation of Populations*. Chicago: University of Chicago Press.

Smitz, N., C. Berthouly, D. Cornélis, et al. (2013). Pan-African genetic structure in the African buffalo (*Syncerus caffer*): investigating intraspecific divergence. *PLoS One* **8**(2): e56235.

Smitz, N., D. Cornélis, P. Chardonnet, et al. (2014a). Genetic structure of fragmented southern populations of African Cape buffalo (*Syncerus caffer caffer*). *BMC Evolutionary Biology* **14**(1): 1–19.

Smitz, N, D. Cornélis, P. Chardonnet, et al. (2014b). Genetic structure of the African buffalo (*Syncerus caffer*) at continental and population scales: an evolutionary and conservation approach. In: M. Melletti and J. Burton (Eds.), *Ecology, Evolution and Behaviour of Wild Cattle: Implications for Conservation*. Cambridge: Cambridge University Press, pp. 410–430.

Staver, A.C., S. Archibald and S. Levin (2011). Tree cover in sub-Saharan Africa: rainfall and fire constrain forest and savanna as alternative stable states. *Ecology* **92**(5): 1063–1072.

Storz, J.F., M.A. Beaumont and S.C. Alberts (2002). Genetic evidence for long-term population decline in a savannah-dwelling primate: inferences from a hierarchical Bayesian model. *Molecular Biology and Evolution* **19**(11): 1981–1990.

Strobeck, C. (1987). Average number of nucleotide differences in a sample from a single subpopulation: a test for population subdivision. *Genetics* **117**(1): 149–153.

Surovell, T., N. Waguespack and P.J. Brantingham (2005). Global archaeological evidence for proboscidean overkill. *Proceedings of the National Academy of Sciences* **102**(17): 6231–6236.

Teixeira, J.C. and C.D. Huber (2021). The inflated significance of neutral genetic diversity in conservation genetics. *Proceedings of the National Academy of Sciences* **118**(10): e2015096118.

Vanacker, V., M. Linderman, F. Lupo, et al. (2005). Impact of short-term rainfall fluctuation on interannual land cover change in sub-Saharan Africa. *Global Ecology and Biogeography* **14**(2): 123–135.

Van Hooft, W.F., A.F. Groen and H.H.T. Prins (2000). Microsatellite analysis of genetic diversity in African buffalo (*Syncerus caffer*) populations throughout Africa. *Molecular Ecology* **9**: 2017–2025.

Van Hooft, W.F., A.F. Groen and H.H.T. Prins (2002). Phylogeography of the African buffalo based on mitochondrial and Y-chromosomal loci: Pleistocene origin and population expansion of the Cape buffalo subspecies. *Molecular Ecology* **11**(2): 267–279.

Van Hooft, P., H.H.T. Prins, W.M. Getz, et al. (2010). Rainfall-driven sex-ratio genes in African buffalo suggested by correlations between Y-chromosomal haplotype frequencies and foetal sex ratio. *BMC Evolutionary Biology* **10**(1): 1–11.

Van Hooft, P., B.J. Greyling, W.M. Getz, et al. (2014). Positive selection of deleterious alleles through interaction with a sex-ratio suppressor gene in African buffalo: a plausible new mechanism for a high frequency anomaly. *PLoS One* **9**(11): e111778.

Van Hooft, P., E.R. Dougherty, W.M. Getz, et al. (2018). Genetic responsiveness of African buffalo to environmental stressors: a role for epigenetics in balancing autosomal and sex chromosome interactions? *PLoS One* **13**(2): e0191481.

Van Hooft, P., W.M. Getz, B.J. Greyling, et al. (2019). A natural gene drive system influences bovine tuberculosis susceptibility in African buffalo: possible implications for disease management. *PLoS One* **14**(9): e0221168.

Van Hooft, P., W.M. Getz, B.J. Greyling, et al. (2021). A continent-wide high genetic load in African buffalo revealed by clines in the frequency of deleterious alleles, genetic hitch-hiking and linkage disequilibrium. *PLoS One* **16**(12): e0259685.

Vrba, E.S. (1995). The fossil record of African antelopes (Mammalia, Bovidae) in relation to human evolution and paleoclimate. In: E.S. Vrba, G.H. Denton, T.C. Partridge and L.H. Burckle (Eds.), *Paleoclimate and Evolution*. New Haven: Yale University Press, pp. 385–424.

Wenink, P.W., A.F. Groen, M.E. Roelke-Parke, et al. (1998). African buffalo maintain high genetic diversity in the major histocompatibility complex in spite of historically known population bottlenecks. *Molecular Ecology* **7**(10): 1315–1322.

Winterbach, H. (1998). Research review: the status and distribution of Cape buffalo *Syncerus caffer caffer* in southern Africa. *South African Journal of Wildlife Research* 28(3): 82–88.

4 · *Conservation Status of the African Buffalo: A Continent-Wide Assessment*

D. CORNELIS, P.C. RENAUD, M. MELLETTI, D. FONTEYN, H. BONHOTAL, M. HAUPTFLEISCH, A. ASEFA, T. BREUER, L. KORTE*, P. SCHOLTE, P. ELKAN, E. KOHI, S. MWIU, S. NGENE, P. OMONDI, S.P. TADJO, T. PRIN, A. CARON, H.H.T. PRINS AND P. CHARDONNET

Introduction

In this chapter, we provide an update on the distribution and abundance of the African buffalo at the scale of the entire African continent. For this purpose, we conducted a literature search to uncover published information. We also carried out an extensive survey of national and international agencies and field experts in the 37 countries that are within the buffalo's distribution range.

We collected abundance data from 163 protected areas or protected area complexes for the period 2001–2021. These data are mainly based on aerial counts using standardized methods, and occasionally on estimates provided by experts. We also obtained information on the presence of buffalo in 711 localities (inside and outside protected areas) for the period 2001–2021. These data and metadata were compiled in a database that is available upon request (Cornélis et al., 2023).

We present the distribution and abundance of each of the four subspecies of African buffalo. We are naturally aware that the validity of the 'subspecies' concept is under debate, and we refer to Chapters 2 and 14 for a discussion about the number of subspecies and their status. For the

---

* The views expressed are solely those of the authors and do not necessarily represent the views of the institutions represented.

sake of consistency with earlier studies on buffalo distribution (East, 1998; Cornélis et al., 2014), our results are presented in accordance with the latest IUCN subspecies range (IUCN SSC Antelope Specialist Group, 2019). Therefore, maps of this chapter reproduce the geographical boundaries of the four subspecies published by the IUCN Red List of Threatened Species (IUCN SSC Antelope Specialist Group, 2019). Although clearly delineated on paper, the boundaries between subspecies' distribution ranges are in fact blurry on the ground. In case of inconsistency or doubt about the assignment of a population to a 'subspecies' (especially in transitional areas), we explicitly acknowledge this in the text.

Historical Distribution

Endemic to the African continent, the buffalo is one of the most successful mammals in terms of geographical distribution, abundance and biomass. Its range covers almost all natural ecosystems south of the Sahara. It mainly inhabits savannas with high herbaceous biomass, but also occupies dry shrubland as well as grassy clearings in dense tropical rainforests, and can live at altitudes above 2500 m, such as in Aberdare National Park in Kenya. The African buffalo penetrates arid biomes where surface water is permanently available. Overlaying the African buffalo's current continental range with mean annual rainfall (Figure 4.1) shows that 95 per cent of the buffalo's range comprises areas with more than 450 mm of rainfall (min: 150 mm; max: 4000 mm).

African buffalo formerly occupied the entire savanna zone stretching between Senegal, Gambia and Guinea and Ethiopia and Eritrea, and from there south to the Cape of Good Hope, with the exception of drylands. African buffalo did not colonize islands such as Zanzibar or Mafia, although they did colonize Bioko Island (Equatorial Guinea), from where they were extirpated sometime between 1860 and 1910 (Butynski et al., 1997).

There is no palaeontological evidence of the presence of the African buffalo in North Africa or the Nile Valley to the north of Khartoum (Prins and Sinclair, 2013). In North Africa, the aurochs (*Bos primigenius*; wild ancestor of domestic cattle) occupied a similar niche (Gautier, 1988), perhaps preventing the buffalo's spread to the north. Buffalo could have expanded their range in eastern and southern Africa during the last ice age due to the extinction of possible competitors, such as *Pelorovis antiquus* and *Elephas reckii* (for more details on evolution see Chapter 2; Klein, 1988, 1994; Prins, 1996).

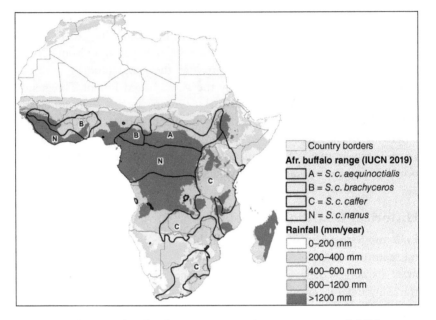

Figure 4.1 African buffalo distribution range in relation to average rainfall for 1970–2000. Sources: Fick and Hijmans (2017) and IUCN SSC Antelope Specialist Group (2019).

Present Distribution

In areas of high human densities, people and their activities caused large discontinuities to arise in the historical distribution of African buffalo (Figure 4.2). Although according to our estimates its population remains above 500,000 individuals, and has been above that level since at least the last human generation (East, 1998; Cornélis et al., 2014), the species' distribution range has been severely reduced since the nineteenth century. As there were no reliable estimates of its total population prior to the assessment undertaken by East (1998), we cannot determine whether the current population is smaller than that which existed prior to the Great Rinderpest epidemic of the 1880s (e.g. Prins, 1996; Prins and Sinclair, 2013). The shrinkage of the species' range was the result of the combined effects of anthropogenic impacts such as rangeland conversion, poaching, disease outbreaks and political unrest, and climatic events such as droughts. At present, most savanna populations (i.e. the three subspecies except *S. c. nanus*) are confined to protected areas (including trophy hunting areas).

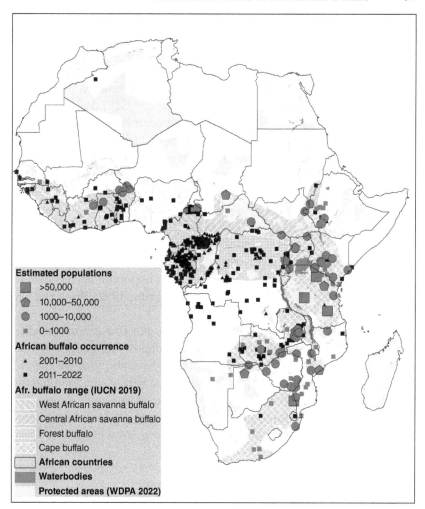

Figure 4.2 Continental distribution and abundance of African buffalo. The two classes of occurrence (2001–2010 and 2011–2022) refer only to the date of the source and do not signify a change in status between classes. Note that in certain other chapters of this book, the West African savanna buffalo and the Central African savanna buffalo are considered together and are referred to as the 'Northern savanna buffalo'. Sources: UNEP-WCMC and IUCN (2022) and IUCN SSC Antelope Specialist Group (2019).

Since the nineteenth century, the expansion of livestock has gradually generated direct competition for space and resources and has led to large and destructive epidemics in African buffalo populations. Exotic rinderpest was historically the most devastating disease for buffalo populations throughout Africa, leading to extreme reductions in population densities and local extinctions. The most severe population collapse occurred in the 1890s, with mortality rates estimated at 90–95 per cent across the continent (Sinclair, 1977; Prins and van der Jeugd, 1993; Winterbach, 1998). This was followed by other episodes throughout the twentieth century. The World Organization for Animal Health (WOAH, formerly OIE) declared rinderpest eradicated in Africa in 2011 (last case reported in 2001). Rinderpest was the first animal disease to have been globally eliminated, and the second disease after human smallpox to have been globally eradicated. Both diseases are caused by viruses. During the twentieth century, efforts to limit the transmission to cattle of several pathogens, such as foot and mouth disease (FMD) and trypanosomiasis (Taylor and Martin, 1987), also actively reduced the geographic distribution of buffalo in several countries due to large-scale culling operations and the erection of veterinary fences.

Outright competition for range use and overexploitation by all sorts of poachers including local pastoralists also were important drivers behind the degradation of the buffalo's status (e.g. Prins, 1992; Prins and De Jong, 2022; Scholte et al., 2022).

Recent climate fluctuations, such as the droughts that affected Sahelian and Sudanese regions at the end of the 1960s and southern Africa in 1992 (Dunham, 1994; Mills et al., 1995; Chapter 8), have also strongly affected buffalo populations over the past few decades. Finally, yet importantly, armed conflicts, the feeding of armies and labourers during peacetime, the traffic of weapons and the bushmeat trade have strongly contributed to the reduction of buffalo populations in some areas (e.g. Prins et al., in review).

West African Savanna Buffalo (*S. c. brachyceros*)

In the 1970s and 1980s, this subspecies still locally occurred in Sahelo-Sudanian savannas and gallery forests, including those found in south-eastern Senegal, northern Côte d'Ivoire, southern Burkina Faso, Ghana, northern Benin, the extreme south of Niger, Nigeria (very locally), the northern part of Cameroon and Central African Republic (west of Chari River) (East, 1998). It is worth noting that the West African savanna buffalo (Figure 4.3) was (and still is) therefore also found in Central Africa, which underlines the inconsistency of this appellation (Figures 4.4 and 4.6).

Presently, most known populations remain in five main strongholds. Two of these are complexes hosting national parks (NP) and neighbouring trophy hunting areas: (1) W–Arly–Pendjari NPs (WAP) in

(a)

(b)

Figure 4.3 West African savanna buffalo in W National Park, Niger. © Daniel Cornélis.

Burkina Faso–Benin–Niger; and (2) Bouba N'djidda–Bénoué–Faro NPs in Cameroon. The remaining three strongholds are single NPs: (3) Niokolo-Koba NP in Senegal; (4) Comoé NP in Côte d'Ivoire; and (5) Mole NP in Ghana. In the other protected areas of the above-mentioned

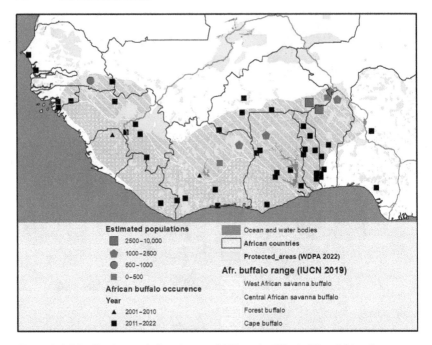

Figure 4.4 Distribution and abundance of African buffalo in West Africa. Sources: UNEP-WCMC and IUCN (2022) and IUCN SSC Antelope Specialist Group (2019).

countries, and in Nigeria, Togo and Sierra Leone, the presence of buffalo is limited to a few scattered residual populations. At present, the populations in the remaining strongholds are isolated from each other and the distribution of the West African savanna buffalo has shrunk overall. A positive finding emerging from our investigation is that the buffalo populations inside four of these five strongholds are, when compared with 2013 figures, either constant (Niokolo-Koba NP) or increasing (Comoé NP, WAP complex, Mole NP). On the downside, the populations in Northern Cameroon appear to be decreasing.

Central African Savanna Buffalo (*S. c. aequinoctialis*)

This subspecies still locally populates Central African countries within the Sahelo-Sudanian savannas and gallery forests: southeast Chad, northern Central African Republic (east of Chari River), northern Democratic Republic of Congo (DRC), south-east Sudan and western Ethiopia (Figures 4.5 and 4.6). The subspecies is now extinct in Eritrea. Most presently known populations remain in two main strongholds: Zakouma

(a)

(b)

Figure 4.5 Central African savanna buffalo in Zakouma National Park, Chad.
© Daniel Cornélis.

NP in Chad and Garamba NP in DRC. In Ethiopia, the decline of several populations has been offset by the recent discovery of several populations outside the known range (see Ethiopia section below).

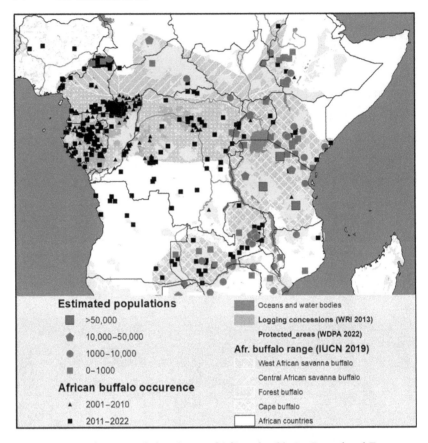

Figure 4.6 Distribution and abundance of African buffalo in Central and Eastern Africa. Sources: UNEP-WCMC and IUCN (2022) and IUCN SSC Antelope Specialist Group (2019).

Forest Buffalo (*S. c. nanus*)

The distribution range of the forest buffalo comprises two separate regions in West and Central Africa (Figures 4.4, 4.6 and 4.7). In West Africa, fragmented and isolated populations persist in the relict rainforest belt, while the population's stronghold is located in the Central African countries of the Congo Basin (Cornélis et al., 2014; IUCN SSC Antelope Specialist Group, 2019). In the Congo Basin, forest buffalo occur in the south of the Central African Republic, western Uganda, Democratic Republic of Congo, Republic of Congo, southern Cameroon, Equatorial Guinea and Gabon.

In West Africa, the subspecies persists in Benin, Ghana, Guinea, Guinea-Bissau, Côte d'Ivoire, Liberia, Nigeria and Sierra Leone (see below). Forest

(a)

(b)

Figure 4.7 Forest buffalo in Odzala National Park, The Republic of Congo. ©
Christophe Morio, with permission.

(a)

(b)

Figure 4.8 (a) Cape buffalo in Ngorongoro Conservation Area, Tanzania.
© Christophe Morio, with permission. (b) Cape buffalo in Okavango Delta
(Botswana). © Emily Bennitt, with permission.

buffalo are highly associated with forest clearings and riverine forests (Prins and Reitsma, 1989; Blake, 2002; Melletti et al., 2007, 2008; Bekhuis et al., 2008; Korte, 2008a). In several poorly explored areas, gaps remain in the scientific knowledge of the distribution and status of forest buffalo.

Contrary to the savanna buffalo, recent estimates of the population size of forest buffalo are available only for a few areas in the Congo Basin and their accuracy is low. Indeed, unlike aerial surveys carried out in savanna areas, surveys methods in forest environment are currently unable to provide reliable population estimates. Such estimates may become available for a larger number of sites once more appropriate techniques are implemented, such as distance sampling via camera

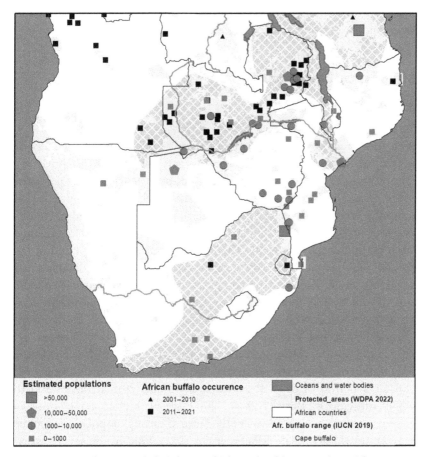

Figure 4.9 Distribution and abundance of African buffalo in southern Africa. Sources: UNEP-WCMC and IUCN (2022) and IUCN SSC Antelope Specialist Group (2019).

traps, capture–mark–recapture methods using genetic fingerprinting, and methods to formally capture information from local experts (e.g. indigenous people and local communities living in the rainforests).

Cape Buffalo (*S. c. caffer*)

The Cape buffalo's range encompasses East and Southern Africa and covers 17 countries (Figures 4.6, 4.8 and 4.9). In East Africa, Cape buffalo populations occur in southwestern Ethiopia, southern Somalia, Uganda, Kenya, Tanzania, Rwanda and Burundi. In southern Africa, this subspecies is distributed in Mozambique, Malawi, Zambia, southwest Angola, north-east Namibia, northern Botswana, Zimbabwe and South Africa. The current population in Eswatini (formerly known as Swaziland) was reintroduced after extirpation.

Abundance Per Country

West Africa

Burkina Faso

West African savanna buffalo formerly occurred widely in the open woodlands of the Niger basin and southern districts (Sidney, 1965; East, 1998). Starting from the 1980s, the population has been restricted to the southernmost areas of the country. At the national level, the buffalo population comprises around 6000 individuals. Their presence is recorded in six different localities, all conservation areas (national park, protected forest, game ranch or trophy hunting area). The largest populations are located in the eastern conservation areas: Arly complex with about 4950 individuals (0.5 ind./km^2) and W Burkina Faso complex with about 300 animals (0.8 ind./km^2) (Ouindeyama, 2021). The presence of buffalo is reported in central and western conservation areas (Nazinga Game Ranch, Bougouriba, Comoé-Lareba and Tuy Mouhoun areas) but in very low densities and isolated populations (Dahourou and Belemsobgo, 2020). In Nazinga Game Ranch, the total population is around 150 individuals (PAPSA, 2018).

After a period of growth between 2003 and 2015 (from ~4800 to ~8900 individuals; Bouché et al., 2003, 2015), buffalo populations of eastern conservation areas recently faced a strong population decline (~5300 individuals; Ouindeyama et al., 2021). Due to the severe worsening of the security situation, the protected areas are facing an increase in threats of banditry, adding new forms of violent interactions with protected area management teams.

Côte d'Ivoire

West African savanna buffalo formally occurred throughout the northern region (Sidney, 1965; East, 1998), but their populations have collapsed and are now isolated in a few protected areas. The main population is located in Comoé NP with an estimated 1450 individuals (0.1 ind./km²; OIPR, 2019), which has increased slightly since 2010 (then about 900 individuals; N'Goran et al., 2010) and 2016 (1200 individuals; Bouché, 2016). The presence of buffalo has been recorded in Lamto and Marahoué NPs, but their numbers were not reported and are thought to be very low. Interestingly, a population of about 300 individuals was reported in N'Zi River Lodge Voluntary Nature Reserve near Bouaké (2.1 ind./km²) and is known to be growing (Louis and Karl Diakité, personal communication, 2021).

The few observations of the forest buffalo subspecies are reported from the residual blocks of forest in the south of the country. This holds especially for Tai NP, where transect counts gave an estimated population size of ~500 individuals (0.09 ind./km²) in 1999–2004, with lower estimates based on transect dung counts of ~200 individuals (Hoppe-Dominik et al., 2011). In striking contrast, recent detailed surveys only reported indirect signs, suggesting a collapse of the buffalo population (Tiedoue et al., 2019, 2020).

Between 2019 and 2021, a wildlife survey on foot was conducted throughout Côte d'Ivoire (ONFI, 2021). The data from this survey for African buffalo came mainly from indirect observations (tracks and dung) for which the risk of confusion with livestock was considered high (Gilles Moynot, ONFI, personal communication), and therefore are not included here.

Benin

West African savanna buffalo ranged in the past throughout the northern region (East, 1998), but populations are now restricted to Pendjari and W-Benin complexes (both complexes include the eponymous NPs and surrounding trophy hunting areas). The Pendjari complex has an estimated population of about 7200 individuals (1.2 ind./km²), while in the W-complex some 1500 buffalo were counted (0.2 ind./km²; Ouindeyama et al., 2021). The three main aerial surveys conducted over the last two decades in northern Benin show that buffalo populations have doubled since the early 2000s (2003: ~4600 individuals; 2015: ~8200 individuals; 2021: ~8650 individuals; Bouché et al., 2003, 2015; Ouindeyama et al., 2021).

Records of forest buffalo mainly refer to old observations located in the centre and southern sectors of Benin (PAPFCA, 2007; Sinsin et al., 2010). The last observations of forest buffalo were reported during a ground survey carried out in the Forest of Agoua (Central Benin) in 2013 in which about 100 individuals scattered over 12 herds were seen (Natta et al., 2014). Further investigation is needed because buffalo are regularly observed in several spots in the southern and central parts of the country (Félicien Amakpe, personal communication).

Gambia

No recent information was received from this country. To our knowledge, the West Africa savanna buffalo subspecies is now extinct in Gambia (Jallow et al., 2004).

Ghana

Buffalo formerly occurred throughout Ghana, with the West African savanna buffalo in the northern and eastern savannas, and the forest buffalo in the southwestern forests (Sidney, 1965; East, 1998). The species is now restricted to a few protected areas.

The major surviving population of the savanna buffalo occurs in Mole NP with an estimated 1400 animals (0.3 ind./km^2; Hauptfleisch and Brown, 2019), and an increasing trend during the last decade (from about 700 individuals: Bouché, 2006). Small populations persist in the following savanna protected areas: Bui National NP (~60; 0.03 ind./km^2), Yerada–Kenikeni Forest Reserve (~30; 0.03 ind./km^2), Kyabobo NP (~50; 0.1 ind./km^2), Digya NP (~120; 0.03 ind./km^2) and Bomfobiri Wildlife Sanctuary (~30; 0.6 ind./km^2) (David Kpelle, Ghana Forestry Commission, personal communication). Some individuals also have been spotted in the Kogyae Strict Nature Reserve (Danquah et al., 2015) and Kalakpa Reserve (Afriyie et al., 2021).

The status of the forest buffalo is unclear. Its presence was reported in Subri River Forest Reserve in 2011 (Buzzard and Parker, 2012), but more recent information does not exist.

Guinea

African buffalo once occurred widely, with the West African savanna buffalo in the north intergrading to the forest buffalo in the south-west and south-east. It has been eliminated in most of its former range by overhunting and habitat destruction (East, 1998) and remains in pockets of relict populations spread throughout the country. The savanna buffalo is known to be present in Haut Niger NP (Nefzi, 2020) and Moyen-Bafing NP (Wild Chimpanzee Foundation, 2021); however, without numerical information. Forest buffalo is present in Ziama Biosphere Reserve, the largest primary rain forest of the country, next to Liberia (Nefzi, 2020). It has also been observed recently in Tokounou, Tiro and Nialia subprefectures (Catherine André, personal communication), but no numerical estimates are available. However, we suspect that both savanna and forest subspecies may be present elsewhere in the country.

Guinea-Bissau
Intermediate forms between the West African savanna buffalo and the forest buffalo formerly occurred widely in the forest–savanna mosaic of Guinea-Bissau (East, 1998). The species still occurs widely in the south and is reasonably common in some areas, for example Cufada Lagoons Natural Park, Cantanhez Forest (da Silva et al., 2021) as well as Boe Region (Coppens, 2015), but no numerical estimates are available. No information was found from the northern part of the country.

Liberia
Only forest buffalo are known to occur in Liberia. In this country, the African buffalo was reported to occur sparsely in the 1960s (Sidney, 1965). A national survey carried out in 1989/1990 recorded the presence of the species in poorly accessible and high-altitude forests of the south-east and north-west (Anstey, 1991 cited by East, 1998). The contraction of its distribution range in recent decades appears to be due to civil war, unrest and widespread poaching. We have no recent information on its status, except observations by camera traps in the Grebo-Krahn NP forest in 2020 (Wild Chimpanzee Foundation; www.youtube.com/watch?v=QtYUSk53p2Q).

Niger
In the early twentieth century, West African savanna buffalo occurred in the south-western tip of Niger (Niger River basin and along parts of the Nigeria border; East, 1998). It has since disappeared from most of its former range and survives only in the W-Niger complex (W-NP and Tamou Total Reserve), where the last population estimate was about 350 individuals (0.1 ind./km^2; Ouindeyama et al., 2021). A

comparison with aerial counts conducted over the past two decades suggests a strong reduction in numbers since 2015 (2003: ~1200 individuals; 2015: ~1100 individuals; 2021: ~350 individuals; Bouché et al., 2003, 2015; Ouindeyama et al., 2021).

Nigeria

In the early twentieth century, the African buffalo was reported to be very common throughout Nigeria, from coastal evergreen forests (forest buffalo subspecies) to shrubby savannas in the north of the country (savanna buffalo subspecies). During the 1960s, the same author reports its occurrence in all suitable habitats, except for the southern coastal districts (Sidney, 1965). In the late twentieth century, East (1998) reported populations reduced to small, generally declining populations in a few protected areas.

For the West African savanna buffalo, the findings reported by East in 1999 still apply in 2022. The subspecies maintains an extremely limited distribution in northern Nigeria with a presence recorded only in three sites that are far from each other: Yankari Game Reserve, Kainji Lake NP and Gashaka Gumti NP (Andy Dunn, Naomi Matthews and Stuart Nixon, personal communication). The prospects for restoring the populations of Kainji Lake NP are poor due to their isolation from other populations and to the insecurity prevailing when this book went to press. Gashaka Gumti NP borders Faro NP in Cameroon, where about 600 individuals were estimated to occur (Elkan et al., 2015). A transfrontier conservation strategy could pave the way for the restoration of a viable buffalo population in Gashaka Gumti NP when the political and security contexts on both sides of the border so allow.

The forest buffalo was once widespread in most southern areas of Nigeria (Sidney, 1965), but has been eliminated from most of its former range and reduced to small, generally declining populations in a few protected areas (East, 1998). To date, this subspecies seems mainly localized in Cross River NP (4000 km^2), where presence was reported from 2001 to 2019 (Eniang et al., unpublished data; Eniang et al., 2017; Bassey, 2019). In this NP bordering Cameroon, only 131 records of forest buffalo were reported for all years combined during line transect surveys (namely, in 2001, 2005, 2009, 2013; Eniang et al., 2017). Only one forest buffalo observation was reported in the Mbe Mountains corridor (linking the Afi Mountain Wildlife Sanctuary and the Okwangwo Division of Cross River NP) during a 2019 year-round anti-poaching patrol (Eban, 2020). Buffalo presence was recently reported in Okomu NP in south-central Nigeria (Akinsorotan et al., 2021). In other words, the forest buffalo is near to extinction in Nigeria.

Senegal
West African savanna buffalo were formerly widespread in the southern savannas of this country (East, 1998). The Senegalese buffalo population seems to have been isolated from other populations for some time (Sidney, 1965). Nowadays, populations have drastically declined and most buffalo are now only located in Niokolo–Koba NP. This protected area, where buffalo populations reached about 1000 individuals in the late 1960s (Dupuy, 1971) now hosts about 500 buffalo (0.06 ind./km²; Rabeil et al., 2018). These figures are quite similar to those observed 12 years earlier (~500 individuals (0.05 ind./km²), Renaud et al., 2006). Some buffalo are present in the private fenced reserves of Bandia (ranging from 80 to 134 individuals; 3 ind./km²; Raymond Snaps, personal communication; Holubová, 2019) and Fathala (40; 1.7 ind./km²; Holubová, 2019). The Bandia buffalo originated from 10 individuals translocated from Niokolo–Koba NP in 2000. It is worth noting that a relict population of savanna buffalo can still be found in the Faleme trophy hunting area (Philippe Chardonnet, personal communication).

Sierra Leone
Forest buffalo may still have occurred until a decade ago, mainly in the north of the country in 2009 and 2010 (Brncic et al., 2015). No recent information is available from this country.

Togo
Until the mid-1950s, the African buffalo was found in most parts of the country (Baudenon, 1952). Although classified as West African savanna buffalo, this author observed an important morphological gradient across the country, with black-coated buffalo in the north and red-coated buffalo in the south. According to East (1998), African buffalo survived in small to moderate numbers in the country's protected areas until the early 1990s, but were expected to be close to extinction in the late 1990s.

From our investigations, it appears that African buffalo are still present in small numbers in several protected areas. In the two northern regions (Savanne and Kara), small populations were reported in Oti–Kéran NP (MERF, 2013) and Djamdè Faunal Reserve (MERF, 2014). In the Central Region, observations were made in Fazao–Malfakassa NP (Atsri et al., 2013) and Abdoulaye Game Faunal Reserve (MERF, 2017). Further south in the Plateaux Region, Amou Mono classified forest (MERF, 2016) and Togodo complex of protected areas (GIZ, 2017) also host small numbers.

Central Africa

Cameroon

Buffalo formerly occurred more or less throughout the country, except for the more arid parts of the far north (Sidney, 1965), with the West African savanna buffalo in northern and central Cameroon and the forest buffalo in the southern forests, which cover about half the country's area (East, 1998). In Cameroon, the savanna buffalo is now restricted to conservation areas in the North Region. In contrast, the forest buffalo is still present in forest areas sparsely populated by humans, especially in the South and East provinces, and to a lesser extent in the south-west province.

At the beginning of the twentieth century, West African savanna buffalo used to be common in the Logone floodplain, Far North Cameroon. However, in 1935, the African buffalo was already rare in the area, and no longer occurred when Waza NP was created in 1968 (Scholte, 2005). Remaining buffalo are located in the Bouba Ndjidda–Bénoué–Faro complex (North Province) with an overall estimated number of 2500 individuals (0.11 ind./km^2; Elkan et al., 2015 for Bénoué and Faro; Grossmann et al., 2018 for Bouba Ndjidda). It is hard to evaluate the proportion of animals within national parks or trophy hunting areas, but the last surveys (2015, 2018) tend to show that Bouba Ndjidda and Faro NPs still host buffalo, while for Bénoué, all individuals were spotted in the trophy hunting areas and none in the national park. The general trend seems to show a decrease in the population, estimated at 4000 individuals in 2008 (0.18 ind./km^2; Omondi et al., 2008).

Over the past 15 years, the presence of the forest buffalo was reported in most of the protected areas and numerous logging concessions.

In south-west and north-west provinces (border with Nigeria), buffalo are present in Korup NP (Astaras, 2009) and were also sighted in a logging concession located north of the park. Further north, buffalo presence was reported in the Black Bush Area of Waindow in 2014

(Chuo and Angwafo, 2017). These buffalo populations appear to be more scattered and isolated as they are surrounded by areas of high human population density. In this respect, it should be noted that no observations of buffalo have been reported recently in the West, Littoral and Central provinces, all of which are heavily populated. However, it is plausible that buffalo populations remain in the northern part of Central Province in the triangle formed by the Mpem-Djim, Mbam-Djerem, and Deng-Deng NPs. The presence of buffalo was observed there in a logging concession in 2004 (Cornélis et al., 2023).

In the South province, buffalo are present in Campo–Ma'an NP (650 km^2), where population sizes were estimated by Bekhuis et al. (2008) with 20 individuals only (densities 0.01–0.04 ind./km^2) and by Van der Hoeven, de Boer and Prins (2004) at 0.07–1.27 ind./km^2. The presence of buffalo was also reported in several logging concessions located on the periphery of the park (Cornélis et al., 2023). Further east, forest buffalo also were reported in a logging concession located north of Mangame Wildlife sanctuary.

In the south-eastern end of the country (East Province), forest buffalo are present in Dja Biosphere Reserve (Bruce et al., 2017, 2018) and have been sighted in several logging concessions located south of the reserve over the past 15 years (Cornélis et al., 2023). Forest buffalo were reported in Nki and Boumba-Bek NPs in 2015 (Imbey et al., 2019; Ngaba and Tchamba, 2019; Hongo et al., 2020) and Lobeke NP (Gessner et al., 2013). The area surrounding these three protected areas is almost entirely allocated to logging. The presence of buffalo also has been reported in many logging concessions over the past 15 years (Cornélis et al., 2023).

Central African Republic

The Central African Republic (CAR) is the only country where three subspecies of buffalo occur.

The West African savanna buffalo subspecies used to be widespread in the west of the country next to the border with Cameroon, although its West African name looks odd in a Central African country. Nowadays, information is lacking about this subspecies in CAR, but it is certainly and by far the least represented of the three subspecies present in CAR. It may be reasonable to think that buffalo are present next to the Cameroon border because there are Trophy Hunting Areas (*Zones d'Intérêt Cynégétique*) on the Cameroon side with buffalo quota and offtake.

Central African savanna buffalo were historically widespread in all Central African savannas (East, 1998). Presently, residual buffalo populations are apparently restricted to the far Northern complex (Bamingui–Bangoran and Manovo–Gounda St Floris NPs and surrounding trophy hunting areas) and in the Southeast complex (Chinko Basin).

In the Northern complex, the population numbers declined from ~19,000 individuals (0.3 ind./km^2) in 1985 (Douglas-Hamilton et al., 1985) to ~13,000 (0.2 ind./km^2) in 2005 (Renaud et al., 2005), after which it collapsed to 13 individuals only in 2017 (Elkan et al., 2017). Given the level of insecurity in the region, it may have now gone extinct.

In the Southeast complex, buffalo populations strongly declined between 2012 and 2017 due to the invasion of the area by transhumant herders from South Darfur, Sudan (Aebischer et al., 2020). Conservation efforts undertaken by African Parks since 2014 have reversed the trend in the Chinko conservation area (6000 km^2), where the buffalo population was estimated at over 4000 buffalo in 2022 (Thierry Aebischer, personal communication).

The huge uninhabited wilderness areas in between those residual complexes are composed of trophy hunting areas where buffalo were present and hunted before the 2012 war started. However, no recent information on buffalo presence or abundance is available.

Although a large part of potential suitable areas has not been surveyed recently, the conservation status of the Central African savanna buffalo should be considered as under major threat in the Central African Republic (see also Scholte et al., 2022).

Forest buffalo are mainly localized in the south-west tip of the country, covered by rainforests. Over the past 15 years, the presence of the forest buffalo was reported in all protected areas and most of the logging concessions of this region (Cornélis et al., 2023). Buffalo are encountered in the Dzanga-Sangha Protected Area complex, including recent records in the Special Reserve of Dzanga-Sangha (Melletti et al. 2007 Beudels-Jamar et al., 2016). Forest buffalo were also reported from the south-east part of the country, where forest and savanna intermingle: Bangassou forest (Roulet, 2006) and the thick riverine forests of the upper Mbomou River (Philippe Chardonnet, personal communication).

Chad

Central African savanna buffalo were formerly widespread in the south of the country from Lake Chad to Salamat (Sidney, 1965). However, buffalo were extirpated from most of their original range by agricultural and livestock expansions as well as drought (East, 1998). The largest population, estimated at ~15,500 individuals (5 ind./km²), is located in Zakouma NP (Fraticelli et al., 2021). In this protected area, the buffalo population tripled in 15 years, showing an average annual growth rate of 7 per cent. In January 2022, 905 buffalo were translocated from Zakouma NP to restock the nearby Siniaka-Minia wildlife reserve (Naftali Honig, personal communication).

The last survey in Sena Oura NP did not encounter any buffalo (Elkan et al., 2015). Some buffalo were reported in the far south province of Logone Oriental near Monts de Lam and Baïbokoum in 2021 (Matuštíková, 2021), suggesting that buffalo populations of Bamingui-Bangoran/Manovo-Gounda St Floris in the Central African Republic and of Bouba N'djidda complex in Cameroon could have some connection through southern Chad.

Democratic Republic of Congo
Forest buffalo seem to be widespread in the Democratic Republic of Congo (DRC; informally known as 'Congo-Kinshasa'), but with a patchy distribution because DRC is one of the most densely populated countries in the Congo Basin. This may be due to a combination of both human pressure (e.g. poaching, meat harvesting for logging camps and for other extractive industries) and a lack of knowledge.

In the south-western section of the DRC forest block (Maï-Ndombe and Equateur Provinces), the presence of buffalo was reported in Tumba-Ledima Reserve (ICCN and WWF, 2016a) and Ngiri Triangle Reserve (T. Breuer, personal observation). The presence of the forest buffalo was recorded during the forest management surveys of many logging concessions over the past 15 years, particularly in the western and south-eastern parts of Mai-Ndombe Province (Cornélis et al., 2023).

In the south-central section of the DRC forest block (north of Kasai and Sankuru provinces, south of Tshuapa Province), forest buffalo were recently reported in Salonga NP (Bessone et al., 2020) and the Tshuapa–Lomami–Lualaba landscape (John Hart, personal communication). Although highly possible, the presence of buffalo was not reported (to our knowledge) from Sankuru Reserve.

In the south-east section of the DRC forest block (Maniema and South Kivu Provinces), forest buffalo were reported in Kahuzi–Biega NP (Spira et al., 2018), Kasongo and Pangi priority areas (ICCN and WWF, 2017a), the Itombwe NR (ICCN and WWF, 2016b) and in the Luama–Kivu region (ICCN and WWF, 2017b).

In the north-central section of the DRC forest block, the presence of buffalo has been confirmed in a dozen places of Tshopo Province over the last 15 years by several studies (van Vliet et al., 2012; Nebesse, 2016) and forest management surveys (Cornélis et al., 2023). Further west, its presence was recorded in Abumonbazi Reserve (province of Nord-Ubangi; ICCN and WWF, 2015a) and in a logging concession ('09/11-Baulu') located south of Lomako–Yokokala Reserve (north of Tshuapa Province; Cornélis et al., 2023).

In the eastern section of the DRC forest block, forest buffalo were reported north of Maiko NP (Naomi Matthews and Stuart Nixon, personal communication) and in the southern section of Virunga NP (Mikeno Sector; Hickey et al., 2019). Further north (Ituri province), buffalo were reported in Okapi Wildlife Reserve (Madidi et al., 2019).

Interestingly, the presence of buffalo also has been reported south of the current 'official' (IUCN SSC Antelope Specialist Group, 2019) range of the forest buffalo, in trophy hunting areas: Bombo Lumene (ICCN and WWF, 2017c), Bushimaie (ICCN and WWF, 2016c), and Swa-Kibula (ICCN and WWF, 2015b) as well as in Mangai Nature Reserve (ICCN and WWF, 2015c) and Kaniama Elephant Refuge (ICCN and WWF, 2016d). The taxonomic status of these populations is unclear.

Central African savanna buffalo formerly occurred on the edge of the dense forest along the northern and eastern borders of the country (East, 1998). Much hunted and regularly infected with rinderpest, buffalo populations became isolated in Garamba NP (Northern border), where Sudanese meat hunters reduced the population from 53,000 in 1976–83 to 26,000 in 1995 (East, 1998). Nowadays, Garamba NP and adjacent trophy hunting areas (~14,800 km^2) host about 9400 buffalo (0.6 ind./ km^2; Ngoma et al., 2021). The population in Garamba NP may have increased slightly from some 6000 individuals in 2012 (Bolaños, 2012) with improved protection of the park. Population estimates in Bili–Uere NP are unknown, but most probably low with a few small groups left (Elkan et al., 2013b; Jef Dupain, personal communication, 2018).

Cape buffalo – in the east of the DRC, along the border with Uganda, the central plains of Virunga NP are host to a population of savanna buffalo located in a zone of introgression between several subspecies and which we have assigned to the 'caffer' subspecies. The population of Virunga NP has decreased from about 2100 individuals in 2010 (Plumptre et al., 2010) to about 600 (Wanyama et al., 2014).

In the southern savannas, the population of Upemba NP is less well monitored, but we think it is very small as only 15 individuals were spotted in 2009 (Vanleeuwe et al., 2009). East (1998) stated that buffalo were eliminated from the Kundelungu NP population and we have not received any contradicting information.

Equatorial Guinea

There is evidence of the former widespread occurrence of forest buffalo on Bioko Island, Equatorial Guinea, but no indication of a surviving population was found during 4.5 months of field surveys there between 1986 and 1992 (Butynski et al., 1997). Due to overhunting, buffalo were probably already extirpated from the island between 1860 and 1910.

In the mainland region of the country, the forest buffalo formerly occurred throughout Mbini (Rio Muni). It has been eradicated from parts of its range but seems to have survived locally within the remaining forested areas, including Monte Alen NP until the end of the 1990s (East, 1998).

Gabon

Gabon is a sparsely populated country, 88 per cent of which is covered by equatorial forests. The country is home to a largely preserved biodiversity. Thirteen national parks were created in 2002 and protected areas cover 15 per cent of the country (41,000 km^2). About half of the country (~142,000 km^2) is dedicated to logging (WRI, 2013). Forest buffalo populations are widely distributed in Gabon both inside and outside protected areas, including logging and oil concessions (Prins and Reitsma, 1989). Except for Akanda NP, located 30 km north of Libreville, the presence of the forest buffalo has been documented in all of the national parks over the past 15 years (Christy et al., 2008; Vanthomme et al., 2013; Nakashima, 2015; Hedwig et al., 2018). For this country, we reviewed 42 reports of biodiversity inventories conducted on foot by international forestry consultancy companies in logging concessions between 2000 and 2017 (unpublished and confidential reports). Almost all of these inventories recorded evidence of buffalo presence. These observations are supported by recent surveys conducted in several logging concessions using camera traps (Houngbégnon, 2015; Nunez et al., 2019; Fonteyn et al., 2021; Naomi Matthews and Stuart Nixon, personal communication).

Estimates of buffalo populations were carried out in a forest–savanna mosaic area of Lopé NP (North sector 70 km^2) where Korte (2008b) estimated about 300 individuals in 18 herds with a density of 5 ind./ km^2. In forest areas at Lopé NP, White (1994) estimated a density of 0.42 ind./km^2. In the Réserve de Faune de Petit Loango, Morgan (2007) found a density of 1.7 ind./km^2. Prins and Reitsma (1989) reported a forest buffalo density of 0.51 ind./km^2, but absolute numbers could not be established reliably.

Republic of Congo

Republic of Congo (informally known as 'Congo-Brazzaville') is a sparsely populated country, 70 per cent of which is covered by equatorial forests. The central part of the country is made up of the so-called Bateke plateaus, which are covered with savanna grassland and riverine forests.

In the northern part of the country, which is very sparsely populated, the forests of the Congolese basin are home to widely distributed buffalo populations. Forest buffalo are present in all of the protected areas: Odzala-Kokoua NP (Chamberlan et al., 1995), Nouabalé-Ndoki NP (Blake, 2002), Ntokou-Pikounda NP (Malonga and Nganga, 2008), and Lac Tele Reserve (Devers and Van de Weghe, 2006). Between these protected areas, upland forests are allocated to logging. For this area, we reviewed 10 biodiversity survey reports conducted between 2005 and 2019 by international forestry consultancy companies in 10 logging concessions (unpublished and confidential reports). All of them recorded evidence of buffalo presence. In northern Congo, Blake (2002) recorded densities between 0.01 and 0.04 ind./km^2 at Nouabalé-Ndoki NP, while Chamberlan et al. (1995) estimated the buffalo population of Odzala-Kokoua NP at around 500 individuals (0.4 ind. km^2).

From the central part of the country, little information is available on the presence of forest buffalo in the savannas and gallery forests of the Bateke Plateau. However, Mathot et al. (2006) report buffalo presence in the Lessio-Luna Wildlife Sanctuary bordering the Lefini Reserve.

In the southern part of the country, forest buffalo are present in Conkouati-Douli NP (Devers and Van de Weghe, 2006) and Kouilou Department (Orban et al., 2018). In Niari and Lekoumou Departments, the biodiversity survey reports conducted in the logging concessions between 2005 and 2019 on foot also reported evidence of buffalo presence.

East Africa

Burundi

A resident population of cape buffalo has been living for a long time and continues to do so today in the narrow strip of Ruvubu NP, Eastern Burundi (Nzigidahera et al., 2020).

Ethiopia

African buffalo populations have long been restricted to the south-western and western parts of the country, along the borders of Kenya, South Sudan and Sudan (Sidney, 1965). East (1998) reported that the main populations can be found in Omo and Mago NPs. Buffalo do also occur in montane forests and swampy wetlands, such as in the Chebera Churchura (Megaze et al., 2018) and Gambella NPs (TFCI, 2010; Rolkier et al., 2015). Currently their distribution is largely confined to protected areas with a total estimated population of about 15,000 (around 5000 *S. c. aequinoctialis* and 10,000 *S. c. caffer* – Table 4.1).

Ethiopia is a contact zone between the Cape buffalo and the Central African savanna buffalo where the two subspecies intergrade. The presence of intermediate phenotypes and the absence of geographical barriers make classification difficult. For the sake of consistency with earlier studies on buffalo distribution (East, 1998; Cornélis et al., 2014), our results are presented in accordance with the current IUCN subspecies range (IUCN SSC Antelope Specialist Group, 2019), but this is one of the areas where the 'subspecies concept' loses meaning for African buffalo.

The largest population of Cape buffalo is found in Chebera Churchura NP (~5200 animals; Megaze et al., 2017). Significant populations are also found in other formally protected areas, such as Omo NP (~800 animals; Tola, 2020), Mago NP (~850 animals; Tsegaye, 2020). In addition, about 2000 buffalo are estimated to be in the Tama wildlife reserve that connects Omo and Mago NPs (Girma Timer, personal communication). Finally, the Weleshet-Sala controlled trophy hunting area holds about 1100 individuals (Kebede et al., 2011).

Significant populations of Central African savanna buffalo are found in Gambella NP (~1400 animals; TFCI, 2010). Reports from two newly established national parks indicate the presence of about 1700 buffalo in Maokomo Nature Reserve (Wendim, 2015). The presence of several hundred buffalo was also confirmed by a count in Dati Wolel NP (Gonfa et al., 2015), but the population estimate is not reliable. Buffalo observations were also recently reported from Alatash NP along the border with Sudan (Bauer et al., 2018).

During the last decade, several Central African savanna buffalo populations have been reported north-east of their earlier established (IUCN SSC Antelope Specialist Group, 2019) distribution range. Two Controlled Hunting Areas (CHAs) hold a reasonable number of buffalo: Haro Aba Diko CHA (~900 individuals; Kebede and Tsegaye, 2012) and Beroye CHA (~600 individuals; Kebede et al., 2013). A population of at least 60 buffalo was reported in Didessa NP (Wendim, 2018) and a herd of seven animals was repeatedly observed in Jorgo-Wato National Forest Priority Area (Jebessa, 2015; Erena et al., 2019). Finally, Lafto Forests area hosts about 340 buffalo (Dandena and Dinkisa, 2014). Yet we repeat that 'subspecies' designation in this country is shaky due to intergradation.

Kenya

The Cape buffalo was formerly widespread throughout southern and central Kenya, and on isolated, forested hills and mountains in the north. In the 1990s, the population became largely confined to protected areas, except in Laikipia and Lamu districts (East, 1998). The status of buffalo in Kenya has recently been updated during a national wildlife census undertaken between April and July 2021. Several aerial total counts covered nearly 60 per cent of Kenya's land mass (Waweru et al., 2021). Results show that the Cape buffalo is distributed in almost all of the wildlife ecosystems surveyed, except in the northern counties of Mandera, Wajir, Turkana as well as the Nasolot-Kerio Valley ecosystem. About 41,700 buffalo were counted.

In Kenya, seven conservation areas host populations of over 1000 buffalo, respectively, Maasai Mara ecosystem (~11,600), Tsavo ecosystem (~8000), Lake Nakuru NP (~6500), Laikipia–Samburu–Marsabit ecosystem (~6300), Lamu–Lower Tana and Garissa ecosystem (~3000), Meru ecosystem (~2600) and Naivasha–Nakuru ranches (~1500). These seven ecosystems account for about 95 per cent of Kenya's total buffalo population. Three conservation areas contain a few hundred buffalo, namely Nairobi NP (~1000), Amboseli–Magadi ecosystem (~500) and Ruma NP (~400). Small populations occur in other protected areas, such as Athi–Kapiti ecosystem, Mwea National Reserve, Shimba Hills National Reserve and Oldonyo Sabuk NP. Other populations have not been estimated over the years because the technique of aerial surveys is not well suited for dense forests and nature of the terrain of Aberdares,

Mount Kenya, and Mount Elgon forested areas or Forest Reserves such as Mukogodo, Ngare Ndare Arabuko Sokoke and Boni Dodori. For this reason, but also because some buffalo strongholds were not surveyed under optimal visibility conditions (e.g. Lamu–Lower Garissa and Tana River Ecosystem with about 13,800 buffalo in 2015), the above-mentioned figure for the Kenyan population of buffalo is likely underestimated.

According to the latest national census (Waweru et al., 2021), buffalo in Kenya are now largely confined to protected areas. In the Mara ecosystem, 70 per cent of all buffalo were found in the Maasai Mara National Reserve, while the remaining 30 per cent were recorded from the Maasai Mara community conservancies. In the Tsavo ecosystem, 80 per cent of the buffalo population was found inside the protected areas. In the Laikipia–Samburu–Marsabit–Meru ecosystem, 69 per cent of the population was counted in ranches, 27 per cent in the protected areas and 3 per cent in community/settlement areas.

In Kenya, buffalo populations suffered a sharp contraction in the 1990s because of severe drought and the very last rinderpest events. For example, the Mara population was reduced from 12,200 to 3100 by the 1993–94 drought (East, 1998) and has since shown good recovery (~11,600 animals in 2021). The buffalo population in Nakuru NP has recovered and has consistently increased from about 2200 buffalo in the year 2000 to the current population of about 6400 individuals at a density of 51.3 buffalo/km^2 (a continental record for the present; Lake Manyara National Park in Tanzania reached nearly twice as much: Prins and Douglas-Hamilton, 1990). In contrast, the Tsavo population decreased from an estimated 34,600 in 1991 to 5500 in 1997 (East, 1998) with no strong evidence of recovery so far (~8000 in 2021). Although the Kenyan population shows a cumulative increase of about 40 per cent between 2008 and 2021, recovering the numbers from the early 1990s (approximately 95,000 buffalo) is challenging in a context of increasing competition with humans and cattle for resources (water, space and forage; Waweru et al., 2021). The effects of the 2022 drought with some heavy buffalo mortality in, for example, Lewa Downs (Susan Brown, personal communication), were not yet known when we finalized this chapter.

Rwanda
The Cape buffalo formerly occurred at high densities in Akagera and Volcanoes NPs. The population of Akagera NP, estimated to number 10,000 in 1990 (East, 1998), subsequently declined due to the 1994

genocide and political unrest. The park also faced a two-thirds reduction in size to about 1120 km^2. Since 2002, buffalo numbers have been increasing again, reaching ~3400 individuals in 2019 (Macpherson, 2019).

In Volcanoes NP, a dung count undertaken in 2004 suggested a population of ~900 (2.0 ind./km^2; Owiunji et al., 2005). We are not aware of more recent surveys, but given the excellent protection of Volcanoes NP, as testified by the increasing number of mountain gorillas, we assume that the number of buffalo remained constant. In contrast, the buffalo was reported extinct at Lake Kivu shore and nearby forests (including Gishwati–Mukura) as well as Nyungwe NP (Cockar, 2022).

Somalia

The Cape buffalo formerly occurred in the south of the country in areas with permanent water along the lower Shebelle and lower Juba Rivers (Fagotto, 1980). At the end of the twentieth century, agricultural settlement and hunting pressure eliminated the buffalo from most of its former range, except in the Bushbush NP area (now Lag Badana NP), where it occurred in good numbers (East, 1998). Buffalo presence was recently reported in Lag Badana National Park and surrounding areas in Jubalan (Gedow et al., 2017), but the total number was not reported.

South Sudan

Sidney (1965) reported that large herds of Central African savanna buffalo were commonly found in grassy plains. Although variations in numbers could be found, the subspecies population was very healthy in South Sudan, with probably several tens of thousands of individuals. Small migrations between the rainy and dry seasons were also observed. East (1998) also reported large populations of several thousand individuals in the main South Sudan protected areas (Boma NP and Shambe Nature Reserve), but warned that meat hunting pressure was very high. This declining trend appears to remain in process. Fay et al. (2007) recorded ~10,200 buffalo in the protected areas of Southern Sudan (mainly in Zeraf and Sambe game reserves), while aerial reconnaissance surveys spotted only 285 individuals in 2013 and none in 2016 (Elkan et al., 2013a, 2016). From this we infer that the conservation status of the Central African savanna buffalo should be considered under major threat in South Sudan.

Sudan
The Central African savanna buffalo is historically present in the south-eastern tip of Sudan along the border with Ethiopia. Bauer et al. (2018) reported observations of African buffalo in the Dinder–Alatash trans-boundary protected area (13,000 km^2; Sudan and Ethiopia) during five field trips undertaken between 2015 and 2018.

Tanzania
Although once common throughout the country, the range of the Cape buffalo covered less than half its area of distribution at the end of the last century, with an estimated population of 342,000 individuals (East, 1998). Tanzania today is still the country with by far the largest number of buffalo, with an estimated population of at least 240,000 individuals. The country has established a dense network of protected areas covering slightly more than 30 per cent of the land surface area (MNRT, 2021) and implementing a range of nature conservation models with both (i) consumptive use of wildlife in Game Reserves, Game Controlled Areas and Wildlife Management Areas (WMAs) and (ii) non-consumptive use of wildlife in National Parks and Ngorongoro Conservation Area.

Tanzania is the only country with single populations of buffalo exceeding 50,000 individuals (Figure 4.6). There are three of these strongholds: (i) the Serengeti Ecosystem (~23,700 km^2) in the north-ern part of the country hosts a population of about 69,000 individ-uals (TAWIRI, 2021a), (ii) the Selous–Mikumi Ecosystem (~74,000 km^2) in the south-east of the country has a population of about 66,800 individuals (TAWIRI, 2019a) and (iii) the adjacent Katavi–Rukwa and Ruaha–Rungwa Ecosystems (~83,000 km^2) located in the west-centre of the country hold a population of about 53,000 individuals (TAWIRI, 2022).

Nearby the Serengeti Ecosystem, the Tarangire–Manyara Ecosystem (~15,500 km^2) also hosts an important buffalo population, estimated at about 19,000 individuals (TAWIRI, 2020). Mkomazi NP (~2800 km^2) in the north-east supports about 600 individuals (TAWIRI, 2019b). Saadani NP and Wami Mbiki WMA on the coast host about 1000 individuals (Edward Kohi, personal communication). By contrast, the last census undertaken in West Kilimanjaro–Lake Natron Ecosystem (~10,000 km^2) reported a population of 46 buffalo only (TAWIRI, 2021b), a very low number largely due to cattle encroachment (Prins and De Jong, 2022).

In the north-western part of the country, the Malagarasi–Muyovozi Ecosystem hosts an important buffalo population, estimated at about 28,300 individuals (Edward Kohi, personal communication). The recently created Burigi–Chato NP (2200 km^2) west of Lake Victoria along the border with Rwanda has a small number of buffalo, as well as Rubondo Island NP in Lake Victoria (Edward Kohi, personal communication). At the northwestern tip of the country, Ibanda Kyerwa NP (200 km^2) supports about 215 buffalo (Edward Kohi, personal communication).

Finally, several mountainous and/or densely forested areas host buffalo populations of which the recent numbers are unknown: Arusha NP and Mount Meru Forest Reserve, Kilimanjaro NP and Udzungwa Mountains NP. Therefore, given these knowledge gaps, the estimates provided for Tanzania should be considered as minimum values.

In 2022, the conservation status of buffalo in Tanzania is uneven. On the positive side, (i) not only is Tanzania the only country holding single populations of over 50,000 buffalo, but there are three of these populations in the country; and (ii) several ecosystems show positive trends with growing buffalo populations, for example Serengeti Ecosystem. On a more worrying side, the overall national trend of buffalo is on the decrease due to (i) severe encroachment by livestock tending to replace buffalo in several ecosystems (Prins, 1992; Musika et al., 2021, 2022; Prins and De Jong, 2022) and (ii) steady agricultural expansion and associated settlements.

Uganda

The Cape buffalo was formerly widespread in large numbers in savannas, with putative intermediates with the forest buffalo in the southwest (Greater Virunga Landscape) (East, 1998). However, genetic samples so far have not yet recognized these putative hybrids in Uganda (see Chapter 3). It is noteworthy that western Uganda is a zone of introgression between several subspecies where the taxonomy is subject to controversy.

Cape buffalo are now confined to three conservation areas. In Queen Elizabeth NP (2110 km^2), the most recent survey reported ~15,800 buffalo (Wanyama et al., 2014) and the population seemed to be increasing from the ~10,300 reported in 2010 (Plumptre et al., 2010). In Murchison Falls NP and surrounding wildlife reserves (5030 km^2), an aerial survey undertaken in 2016 resulted in an estimate of ~15,200 buffalo (Lamprey et al., 2020), and the population also seemed to be increasing (from ~9200 in 2010 (Rwetsiba and Nuwamanya, 2010). Finally, in Kidepo NP and Karenga Community Wildlife area (2400 km^2), the last survey reported ~7500 individuals, mainly located inside the park (~6600; Wanyama et al., 2019). The trend is also up in Kidepo NP (from ~3800 in 2008 to ~6600 in 2019; WCS Flight Programme, 2008). These three conservation areas (together ~9400 km^2) host a population of about 38,500 buffalo (4 buffalo/km^2). Smaller populations were also recently reported in Lake Mburo Conservation Area (1290 km^2 with ~1500 buffalo; Kisame et al., 2018a) and Pian Upe Wildlife Reserve (no estimate; Kisame et al., 2018b). Hence, the total number of Cape buffalo in Uganda is now about 40,000 head, which compares very favourably to the estimate of about 22,000 a few decades ago (East, 1998).

The presence of forest buffalo was recently confirmed in Semuliki NP in 2020 (Naomi Matthews and Stuart Nixon, personal communication). No forest buffalo presence was reported from Mgahinga Gorilla NP since 2003 (Hickey et al., 2019) or from Kibale NP from 2013 to 2021 (Rafael Reyna-Hurtado and Jean-Pierre d'Huart, personal communication). In the latter park, records of buffalo inside the forest are related to savanna buffalo coming from Queen Elizabeth NP through the Dura corridor.

Southern Africa

Angola

Apart from the arid coastal strip in the southwest, African buffalo formerly occurred very widely, with the Cape buffalo in the south and intermediate forms with the forest buffalo in the north (East, 1998). During the civil war (1975–2002), thousands of buffalo were slaughtered by the Angolan army for food. Since the 2000s, buffalo populations have remained low due to widespread poaching, habitat degradation, human encroachment and the presence of land mines. However, very little information is available on the status of buffalo in this country, especially in the central plateau and the northern and eastern regions.

Cape buffalo are still relatively common in the south-eastern parts of Angola, especially in the Mucusso region and in Mavinga and Luengue-Luiana NPs (Funston et al., 2017; Beja et al., 2019; Petracca et al., 2020), but their actual numbers have not been assessed. Naidoo et al. (2014) report frequent movements of Cape buffalo between Angola and Namibia, particularly along the northern banks of the Okavango River, and west of the Cuando River. Large herds (over 1000 animals) were also reported to aggregate in the southeast of Luiengi–Luiana NP along the Kwando River just before the rainy season (Roland Goetz, personal communication).

In the northern Quiçama region, there were an estimated 8000 so-called 'forest buffalo' prior to the civil war of 1975–2002 (Braga-Pereira et al., 2020). During the war, uncontrolled poaching severely reduced the populations, which are now confined to a few small herds in Quiçama NP (Groom et al., 2018), Luando Natural Integral Reserve (Elizalde et al., 2019) and Cangandala NP (David Elizalde, personal communication). Although surprising at this latitude, recent photographs of buffalo taken by camera traps in Quiçama NP and Luando Natural Integral Reserve confirm the presence of buffalo that phenotypically correspond to the forest buffalo (David Elizalde, personal communication). Outside protected areas, recent sightings of buffalo were reported in the north-western section of the country, in the region of Mussera (Zaire Province), Quissafo-Ndalatando and Cassoxi (Cuanza Norte Province), and in the Pingano Mountains (Uige Province) (David Elizalde, personal communication).

Botswana

Cape buffalo are found only north of 20° S in the Okavango–Chobe region and wildlife movements are constrained by veterinary fences erected to control the spread of livestock diseases. In a 2018 aerial total count covering northern Botswana (~103,700 km^2, including Moremi Game Reserve, Chobe NP, Makgadikgadi Nxai Pan NP and surrounding WMAs), the buffalo population was estimated to be some 28,500 individuals (Chase et al., 2018). For the record, a similar survey undertaken in 2010 reported an estimate of 39,600 individuals (Chase, 2011), while East (1998) reported about 27,000 head. It thus appears that the population is fairly constant.

Eswatini (Swaziland)

Cape buffalo were reintroduced in Swaziland, where the indigenous population was extirpated (Tambling et al., 2016). They now occur in the Mkhaya Private Game Reserve (~20 animals, 0.2 ind./km^2; Tal Fineberg, personal communication, 2021).

Lesotho

Buffalo was extirpated from this country (Tambling et al., 2016), but historically it had occurred here even though it was no longer present a few decades ago (East, 1998).

Malawi

In the late 1990s, the Cape buffalo was confined to protected areas such as Lengwe, Kasungu and Nyika NPs as well as Nkhotakota and Vwaza Marsh Game Reserves. Their population was estimated at about 1850 individuals (East, 1998).

To our knowledge, buffalo occur today in Majete and Nkhotakota Wildlife Reserves as well as Liwonde and Kasungu NPs. In Majete Wildlife Reserve, where 306 buffalo were reintroduced between 2006 and 2010, the buffalo population was estimated at ~1800 individuals in 2020 (Sievert and Adenorff, 2020). Between 2016 and 2017, over 100 buffalo were moved from Majete Wildlife Reserve and Liwonde NP to Nkhotakota Wildlife Reserve as part of a rehabilitation programme undertaken by African Parks. Similarly, 80 buffalo were translocated from Liwonde to Kasungu NP in 2022 as part of a restoration programme (African Parks, personal communication).

Mozambique

Cape buffalo populations occurred throughout the country until the 1970s, but suffered greatly from 25 years of war (independence war 1964–1974 then civil war 1977–1992) (East, 1998). Buffalo are well present in the northern part of the country (Niassa and Cabo Delgado Provinces). In Niassa Special Reserve, they were successively estimated at 6800 (2009), 6200 (2011) and 7100 (2014) individuals (Craig, 2011a; Grossmann et al., 2014a), with a density surprisingly more than five times lower than in the neighbouring Selous complex in Tanzania. In Quirimbas NP and adjacent areas, aerial sample counts undertaken in 2011 and 2014, respectively, reported 0 and 88 buffalo observations with no population estimate (Craig, 2011b; Grossmann et al., 2014b). We did not obtain figures for the buffalo occurring in the Chipanje Chetu community-based natural resource management initiative (6500 km²) north-west of Niassa Special Reserve, and for the numerous hunting blocks outside the reserve in the two northern provinces.

Further south, in Zambezia Province, Gilé National Reserve embarked on a restoration programme by reintroducing extinct large mammal species such as buffalo: 67 buffalo were reintroduced in 2012 and 2013–2020 from the Marromeu complex (the National Reserve and numerous trophy hunting areas) and Gorongosa NP, then 47 buffalo from the trophy hunting areas within the Niassa Special Reserve (Chardonnet et al., 2017; Fusari et al., 2017). The population in the now Gilé NP was estimated at about 139 individuals in 2017 (Macandza et al., 2017). Mahimba Game Reserve, north bank of Zambezi River, would also host around 850 individuals (Grant Taylor, personal communication). In Tete Province, an aerial survey conducted in 2014 south and north of Lake Cahora Bassa and Magoe NP including the Tchuma Tchato community programme reported 4300 buffalo (Grossmann et al., 2014c).

The largest African buffalo population of Mozambique is located south (right bank) of Zambezi River (Manica and Sofala Provinces). At the mouth of the Zambezi River into the Indian ocean (the famous Zambezi delta), the open floodplains of the Marromeu Game Reserve and surrounding trophy hunting areas ('*Coutadas*') host about 21,300 individuals according to the latest aerial total count (Macandza et al., 2020). Gorongosa NP was restocked between 2006 and 2011 with 186 buffalo from Kruger and Limpopo NPs (Carlos L. Pereira, personal communication). An aerial total count conducted in 2020 reported 1200 buffalo (Stalmans and Peel, 2020). Finally, the trophy hunting areas located northwest of Gorongosa NP likely hold about 1000 buffalo (Willie Prinsloo, Joao Simoes Almeida and Grant Taylor, personal communication).

The Great Limpopo Transfrontier Conservation Area lies in South-Central and Southern Mozambique. In its northern section (Inhambane Province), a restoration programme has been underway since 2017 in Zinave NP, where the buffalo was extinct, with the reintroduction of 250 buffalo from Marromeu Reserve and surrounding trophy hunting areas (Mike La Grange, personal communication). A 2021 Zinave census reported 479 buffalo in the core sanctuary area (Antony Alexander, personal communication). Further south (Gaza Provinces), Banhine NP is estimated to host about 200 buffalo (Joao Simoes Almeida, personal communication). The Chicualacuala trophy hunting areas, located along Gonarezhou NP (Zimbabwe) also contain around 800 buffalo, but this figure is variable because the population undertakes seasonal migrations through Gonarezhou NP (Anthony Marx and Joao Simoes Almeida, personal communication). Finally, two areas adjacent to Kruger NP (South Africa) also host significant buffalo populations. The first is the Limpopo NP, with a population estimated around 5000 based on the 2018 census (Antony Alexander, personal communication). The second is the Great Lebombo Conservancy (including Sabie Game Park) with around 2000 buffalo (Joao Simoes Almeida, personal communication).

In the south-eastern tip of the country (Maputo Province), around 250 buffalo have been reintroduced in the Maputo Special Reserve since 2016 and their population is estimated at 300 (Antony Alexander, personal communication). Finally, around 50 individuals are present in Namaacha Catuane Community Area (close to the borders with Eswatini and South Africa; Joao Simoes Almeida, personal communication).

Buffalo are also present in numerous *fazendas do bravio* (private game ranches) and *Coutadas* (State-owned protected areas leased and managed by the private sector for hunting tourism). Most of these areas are unfenced, so nearly all buffalo in Mozambique are wild and free-ranging.

Overall, the buffalo has been experiencing a spectacular post-civil-war recovery in Mozambique since 1992, mainly by reintroductions where the species had become extinct, and by reinforcements of rump populations. In recent years, buffalo translocations have been conducted frequently in Mozambique. Some of the buffalo originate from South Africa, but most are indigenous, coming from trophy hunting areas within the Marromeu complex and the Niassa Special Reserve.

Namibia
Because the availability of perennial water is a key requirement for African buffalo, much of Namibia is not suitable for naturally occurring populations of Cape buffalo, except for the Caprivi Strip in the south and the area along the border with Angola in the north. As with probably all African buffalo populations, those in Namibia were drastically reduced during the 1890s rinderpest epidemic. Small herds survived along the perennial rivers of the far north-eastern Kavango East and Zambezi regions (Martin, 2002). By 1934, their distribution had spread somewhat west and southwards to include what is now known as Kavango West, and small seasonal populations in Ohangwena, Omusati and Oshikoto regions (Shortridge, 1934). Any further natural expansion was halted by the erection of a veterinary control fence in the 1960s to protect commercial cattle ranching from the central north southwards. The only exception to the present day has been the reintroduction of two isolated herds in the Waterberg Plateau Park and the Nyae-Nyae communal conservancy. In Waterberg, the founder population of 48 individuals were sourced gradually between 1981 and 1991 from the disease-free Addo Elephant NP population in South Africa at a rate of approximately four a year, while four animals were added to Waterberg from a zoo in then Czechoslovakia in 1986, and 11 from Willem Prinsloo Game Reserve in South Africa, also in 1986 (Martin, 2008). The location of the herd on the plateau

bordered by sandstone cliffs does not allow the buffalo to move from the plateau. In Nyae-Nyae, 30 individuals from a natural population in the area were fenced off in 1996. Only one individual tested positive for FMD, and was destroyed (Martin, 2008). The Waterberg population has grown to at least 800 individuals, and the Nyae-Nyae population to about 250 head, both considered disease-free (Kenneth Uiseb, personal communication). The Zambezi and Kavango populations move freely into and from Angola and Botswana within the Kavango–Zambezi (KAZA) transboundary conservation area (Naidoo et al., 2014). The current estimate in Namibia's portion of KAZA is 7500 individuals based on a 2019 aerial census (Craig and Gibson, 2019). This represents a steady increase from 4500 in 2014 and 5500 in 2015 (Craig and Gibson, 2014, 2015).

South Africa

Cape buffalo were historically present throughout the country except for the arid western section. Free-ranging Cape buffalo were extirpated from their former range and are now totally confined within fenced areas (except Kruger NP along the Zimbabwe and Mozambique borders). At the end of the 1980s and beginning of the 1990s, the total number of buffalo in the country was about 50,000 head (East, 1998). Based on the data collected, the present buffalo population stands at an estimated 121,000 heads, distributed between national parks (~40,000; 28 per cent), game parks (~26,000; 10 per cent) and privately owned game farms (~75,000; 62 per cent) (Chapter 14; Cornélis et al., 2023).

About 96 per cent of the national parks' population is located in Kruger NP (~32,800; Ferreira et al., 2021). The rest are located in the following national parks (Ferreira et al., 2021): Addo (~450), Mokala (~500), Marakele (~250), Mountain Zebra (~90) and Camdeboo (~30). Populations in the parks are fairly constant despite population controlling factors such as bovine tuberculosis and the effects of droughts (see Chapter 8).

Several private game reserves (Sabi Sand, Klaserie, Thornybush, etc.) set alongside the unfenced western boundary of Kruger NP (the so-called 'APNR' – Association of Private Nature Reserves, 1800 km^2 together with the NP named 'Greater Kruger') also host about 6000 buffalo (Mike Peel, personal communication). This complex as a whole (~21,000 km^2) therefore hosts a population of approximately 58,000 buffalo. Further south in KwaZulu–Natal, Hluhluwe–Imfolozi Park (960 km^2) carries about 6400 buffalo (Dave Druce, personal communication).

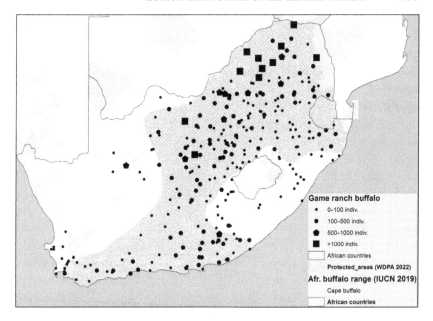

Figure 4.10 Distribution and abundance of African buffalo in private care (game ranches) in South Africa. Sources: UNEP-WCMC and IUCN (2022), IUCN SSC Antelope Specialist Group (2019) and South African Veterinary services (personal communication).

Buffalo in private care (privately owned game ranches) number about 75,000 individuals in 2022 (Peter Oberem, personal communication; Chapter 14). This population is distributed among 3144 game properties (2980 of which contain disease-free buffalo). About half (53 per cent) of the game ranches that hold buffalo are located in Limpopo Province, followed by North West Province (12 per cent) and Free State (11 per cent) (Figure 4.10). Many of these enclosed subpopulations are intensively managed (i.e., with intensive and selective breeding; Chapter 14); they are from an IUCN Red List assessment point of view supernumerary (cf. Tambling et al., 2016), but some of the relatively untrammelled populations can still be of importance for restocking wilderness areas.

Zambia

Nowadays, the Cape buffalo in Zambia is largely confined to national parks and trophy hunting areas that in this country are named Game Management Areas (GMAs), with populations estimated around 40,000 in the late 1990s (East, 1998). According to the latest available estimates, the buffalo population in this country has remained constant since then. The bulk of the population (~30,000) is located in the Luangwa Valley ecosystem (32,800 km^2), mainly North and South Luangwa NPs and surrounding GMAs (DNPW, 2016). Important populations (~6400 over 45,000 km^2) also occur in the Kafue ecosystem, mainly (97 per cent) in Kafue NP (Busanga Plains, Chunga and Ngoma Headquarters, and areas adjacent to Mufunta and Kasonso Busanga GMAs; DNPW, 2019). The Zambian section of the Lower Zambezi ecosystem hosts about 4800 buffalo over 2500 km^2, with the bulk of the population (80 per cent) located in Chiawa GMA (DNPW, 2016). Several other areas in the country host populations of a few hundred animals. East of the Kafue ecosystem, Kafue Flats wetlands (5600 km^2: Blue Lagoon and Lochinvar NPs Kafue Flats GMA) host about 900 head (Shanungu et al., 2015). West of the Luangwa Valley ecosystem, Bangweulu swamps host about 400 head (APN and DNPW, 2019). Finally, about 200 buffalo range in the Liuwa Plain NP and surrounding Upper West Zambezi GMA (APN and DNPW, 2020). To our knowledge, no recent information is available on the populations located between lakes Mweru and Tanganyika in the north of the country, but the total population appears to be constant.

Zimbabwe

Cape buffalo are now exclusively located in large protected area complexes in the northern (Northwest Matabeleland, Sebungwe region and Lower Zambezi Valley) and southern (South East Lowveld) sections of the country. During the period that covers the estimates of East (1998), the total number of buffalo was ~50,000. According to the most recent estimates, Zimbabwe currently hosts about 30,000–35,000 buffalo (Dunham et al., 2015a, 2015b, 2015c; Cumming, 2016; Dunham and van der Westhuizen, 2018). The populations in the northern part of the country (about 15,000) are free-ranging in State-protected areas and communal land under the CAMPFIRE programme, while most southern populations (about 18,000) are fenced-in within State and private land (commercial conservancies). The northern region faced a severe decline over the last 20 years (from about 42,000 in 2001 (Dunham et al., 2015a, 2015b, 2015c) to the present 15,000 head). In contrast, the numbers have been increasing in the southern section of the country. Three protected areas – Gonarezhou NP, Bubye Valley Conservancy

and Save Valley Conservancy – host two-thirds of the southern populations. There, buffalo recovered well from the devastating effects of the
drought of 1992 (see East, 1998).

Trends in Abundance over the Last Decades

In this chapter, we have presented the most recent information available
on the abundance and distribution of the African buffalo. We have also
presented the trends observed where such information was available,
usually at the local level. To do this, we drew on the published scientific
literature, and collected and compiled a substantial amount of information from the grey literature (unpublished reports). We also contacted
numerous organizations and field experts, to whom we express our sin-
cere thanks (see below).

Although we believe that this synthesis is the most comprehensive to
date, it is still not exhaustive. The puzzle remains especially incomplete
in areas of ongoing or recent armed conflict, or in the large, often inaccessible areas of tropical forest where buffalo populations are small and
diffuse. Consequently, the absence of buffalo sightings in a given area
does not mean that buffalo are absent, but rather that no presence information was reported to us despite our investigations and many queries
in our network (AFbIG members and others). Conversely, sightings of
buffalo in previously unrecorded areas (e.g. Congo Basin) are simply
the result of access to previously unavailable information.

Making temporal comparisons is also complex because few protected
areas are monitored on a regular basis using robust and standardized
approaches. Access to information is also a challenge. Although most
often funded by public bodies and/or intended for public bodies, wildlife count reports are rarely published. Reports also rarely present dis-
aggregated data, making temporal comparisons by area difficult (e.g.
abundance inside versus outside protected areas).

Despite these limitations, a brief summary of the situation and regional
trends is presented below.

Savanna Buffalo

The savanna buffalo population is estimated in 2022 at over 595,000
individuals, after deduction of the 75,000 buffalo under intensive private
management in South Africa (q.v.; Table 4.1). Its abundance is roughly
equivalent to that estimated 25 years ago (625,000) by East (1998). With

Table 4.1 *Abundance of the savanna subspecies of the African buffalo (three savanna subspecies:* brachyceros, aequinoctialis *and* caffer*) based on the most recent data available and comparison with earlier global assessments.*

	East (1998)	Cornélis et al. (2014)	Cornélis et al. (2023)
S. c. brachyceros	>20,000	>17,000	>20,500
Benin	>2000	4600	8200
Burkina Faso	1600	5000	5300
Cameroon	3200	4000	2500
Gambia	Ex	Ex	Ex
Ghana	C	700	1400
Guinea	V	X	X
Guinea-Bissau	X	U	U
Côte d'Ivoire	8300	900	1500
Mali	120	Ex	Ex
Niger	500	1200	1100
Nigeria	>200	>170	X
Senegal	>4000	460	500
Togo	U/R	X	X
S. c. aequinoctialis	>59,000	>23,000	>34,000
Central African Republic	19,000	4000	>4000
Chad	1000	8000	16,000
DRC	39,000	6000	9400
Eritrea	Ex	Ex	Ex
Ethiopia	X	4000	5000
South Sudan	>100	U	X
Sudan			X
S. c. caffer	>545,000	>447,000	>540,000
Angola	<500	X	X
Botswana	27,000	40,000	29,000
Burundi	500	Uk	X
DRC	No data	2000	600
Ethiopia	2300	3600	10,000
Kenya	>20,000	>17,000	42,000
Malawi	>3000	Uk	3000
Mozambique	10,000	23,000	45,000
Namibia	1000	6000	9000
Rwanda	1200	R	3500
Somalia	U	Uk	X
South Africa	28,500 (★)	52,000 (★★)	46,000 (★★★)
Eswatini	U	Uk	R
Tanzania	>342,000	>189,000	>240,000
Uganda	>20,000	23,000	38,000
Zambia	>40,000	>29,000	41,000

Table 4.1 (*cont.*)

	East (1998)	Cornélis et al. (2014)	Cornélis et al. (2023)
Zimbabwe	50,000	63,000	33,000
Total	>625, 000	>487,000	595,000

Legend: (C): Common; (Ex): Extinct; (R): rare; (U): uncommon; (Uk): unknown; (V): occurs only as a vagrant; (X): definitely present but abundance unknown; (★; ★★, ★★★): estimates excluding the 2500, 26,000 and 75,000 buffalo in game ranches/farms, respectively.

an estimated population of over 540,000 individuals, the Cape buffalo is by far the most abundant subspecies (91 per cent of the total), far ahead of the West (>20,000; 3 per cent) and Central (>34,000; 6 per cent) African savanna buffalo; for the forest buffalo, we do not dare to make a numerical assessment.

Tanzania is the country where the Cape buffalo is the most abundant, with an estimated population of over 240,000 individuals (44 per cent of the Cape buffalo subspecies), followed by South Africa (46,000), Mozambique (45,000), Kenya (42,000) and Zambia (41,000).

It is worth noting that four ecosystems contain more than 50,000 savanna buffalo. Three of these '5-star' ecosystems are in Tanzania: the Serengeti Ecosystem (~69,000; ~24,000 km^2), the Selous–Mikumi Ecosystem (~67,000; ~74,000 km^2) and the complex composed by the adjacent Katavi–Rukwa and Ruaha–Rungwa Ecosystems (~53,000; ~83,000 km^2). The other '5-star' ecosystem is the Kavango–Zambezi Transfrontier Conservation Area (KAZA, southern Africa; ~52,000; ~520,000 km^2).

Despite the apparent constancy of Cape buffalo abundance on a global scale, contrasts appear on a national scale (Table 4.1). A comparison with estimates made 25 years ago (East, 1998) suggests that some national buffalo stocks have increased significantly, such as those of Namibia (+800 per cent), Mozambique (+350 per cent), Ethiopia (+335 per cent), Rwanda (+190 per cent), South Africa (+60 per cent) and Uganda (+90 per cent). In contrast, some national buffalo stocks have declined substantially, such as in Tanzania (−30 per cent) and Zimbabwe (−34 per cent). However, these trends should be treated with great caution given the biases associated with these estimates. In Ethiopia, for example, part of the increase in numbers is due to the discovery of buffalo outside their previously established distribution range.

The same observation applies to the West African savanna buffalo. Despite a population apparently similar to that estimated 25 years ago, some countries have witnessed an increase in population (Benin: 310 per cent; Burkina Faso: 224 per cent; Niger: 127 per cent) and others a decrease (Senegal: −87 per cent; Côte d'Ivoire: −82 per cent). The largest buffalo population is located in WAP Regional Park (28,350 km^2), Benin, Burkina Faso, Niger. This complex comprises 3 National Parks ('W', Arly and Pendjari) and several neighbouring trophy hunting areas, with a buffalo population estimated at about 15,000 individuals (Bouché et al., 2015; Ouindeyama et al., 2021). Secondary strongholds are located in Cameroon (Bouba Ndjidda–Bénoué–Faro NP and neighbouring trophy hunting areas, ~2500), Ghana (Mole NP, ~1400), Côte d'Ivoire (Comoé NP, ~1200) and Senegal (Niokolo–Koba NP, ~500) (see country sections for details).

Finally, the most worrying situation is probably that of the Central African savanna buffalo, which has nearly halved in abundance over the last 25 years. The collapse of the population in the Central African Republic (−80 per cent) has only been partially offset by the increase (albeit spectacular: +1600 per cent) in Chad (Zakouma NP), and to a lesser but promising extent by the recent recovery of populations in DRC (Garamba NP). Today, half of the residual population of this subspecies is located in a single protected area (Zakouma NP).

Forest Buffalo

As pointed out above, estimating the abundance of forest buffalo is challenging, not to mention ascertaining a trend. Indeed, in dense tropical forest, populations are spatially dispersed, in small herds, in very dense habitats, and are distributed over a very large geographical area.

In the residual forest block of West Africa, we obtained very little information on the presence of the forest buffalo. The forest buffalo is restricted to limited and isolated patches of forest with small populations. In this circumstance, it is likely that forest buffalo in West Africa might be decreasing in much of its distribution range due to a combination of poaching for bushmeat trade, habitat loss and degradation.

In Central Africa, our investigations have shown that the forest buffalo is still well represented in areas with low human density, from the Atlantic coast to south-east Cameroon and up to the border of CAR and Republic of Congo, both in protected areas and adjoining logging and hunting concessions. Of the 235 locations of forest buffalo that we have collected in Central Africa during our review, 45 per cent are located within the Greater TRIDOM-TNS, a vast contiguous block of mainly intact moist forest covering 250,000 km² (11 per cent of Central African forest block) and straddling four countries (Cameroon, Central African Republic, Gabon and Republic of Congo; European Commission, 2015). This vast area is thus probably the most strategic stronghold for the conservation of the forest buffalo in Central Africa.

Conservation Status, Challenges and Opportunities

The latest 10-year update of the conservation status of the African buffalo has led to its downgrading from 'Least concern' to 'Near threatened' (IUCN SSC Antelope Specialist Group, 2008, 2019). The African buffalo is therefore now placed at level 2 on a seven-step threat risk scale. As we have just seen, this global conservation status masks significant regional disparities that result from different combinations of environmental and human factors. In the following sections, we look at the main drivers of these contrasted trajectories. As both the West and Central Africa buffalo are globally confronted with similar factors (and are also very close from a genetic and phenotypic perspective, see Chapter 3), we have grouped them together in a single section called 'northern savanna buffalo'.

Northern African Savanna Buffalo (*S. c. brachyceros* and *S.c. aequinoctialis*)

The current distribution area of the northern African savanna buffalo is very fragmented and most populations are located within a few protected areas. This situation is the consequence of a strong anthropic pressure, in a context where poor soils limit biomass production (Chapter 5). The near extinction of the African buffalo in Nigeria, the most densely populated country in West Africa (Figure 4.11), is the culmination of similar processes taking place progressively throughout the region.

The protected areas in the savannas of West and Central Africa are particularly challenged by the increasing expansion of cash crops (e.g. cotton, groundnut) at their periphery, but also by the expansion of livestock husbandry. The massive movements of livestock in the immediate periphery and within protected areas has been a recurrent and growing problem in recent decades (Bouché et al., 2012; Aebischer et al., 2020). The increasing effective control of sleeping sickness (African trypanosomiasis) has facilitated the rising number of livestock (Gouteux et al., 1994; Cuisance, 1996; Reid et al., 2000; Courtin et al., 2010), the geographical

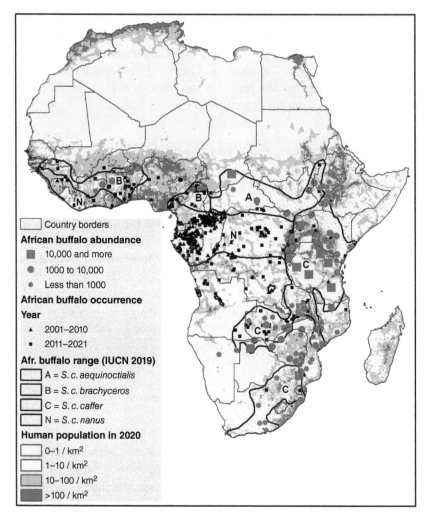

Figure 4.11 African buffalo distribution range in relation to human population density in 2020. Sources: Center for International Earth Science Information Network (2016) and IUCN SSC Antelope Specialist Group (2019).

range of which was previously greatly reduced to the benefit of trypano-tolerant wild species such as the African buffalo (Chapter 9).

Against this backdrop, the conservation of wildlife in general and African buffalo in particular is highly dependent on effective governance and management systems. Unfortunately, in a global context of poverty, poor governance, insecurity, corruption and centralized management, most protected areas in West and Central Africa lack public and private investment (Scholte,

2022). This situation is amplified by the fact that protected area networks are globally oversized in Central Africa, which holds the world record for the highest number of protected areas over 10,000 km². For example, the complex of protected areas in the north of Central African Republic (Manovo-Gounda St Floris, Bamingui Bangoran and adjacent gazetted Trophy Hunting Areas) covers 42,000 km², which represents half of the size of the region (80,000 km²). Such conservation overstretches, when combined with one of the highest poverty levels in the world, poorly developed infrastructure and massive and regular insecurity outbreaks, makes the conservation dilemma acute in Central Africa. In this context, it is estimated that West and Central African protected areas operate with 10 per cent of the resources needed for their sustainable management (Scholte, 2022).

Despite this bleak picture, targeted conservation efforts have managed to stabilize or even substantially increase buffalo populations in a few protected areas, today considered strongholds for biodiversity conservation in West and Central Africa. Over the last few decades, these protected areas have benefited from the support of public donors (such as the European Union or USAID). This support is now amplified by private investments in the form of public–private partnerships in the long term. The most striking example is the non-governmental organization (NGO) African Parks, which is successfully committed in long-term public–private conservation partnerships with governments in several countries such in Benin (Pendjari and W NPs), DRC (Garamba NP), Chad (Zakouma NP, Siniaka Minia Faunal Reserve and Aouk Aoukalé Faunal Reserve) and Central African Republic (Chinko Wildlife Refuge and Vovodo Hunting Area). It is also worth noting that protected areas organized in well-connected complexes with mixed management regimes (such as National Parks buffered and interconnected by functional trophy hunting areas) also tend to have stable buffalo populations (e.g. W–Arly–Pendjari complex or Bouba Ndjidda–Benoue–Faro complex).

So far, the strategy of focusing such conservation efforts over time on a few strongholds while waiting for better days is paying off. In this context, supporting sustainably a few more relevant strongholds (in Senegal, Cameroon, South Sudan, Central African Republic or Ethiopia) would help secure northern savanna buffalo populations, and in turn, a representative sample of ecosystems and species in this subregion. Once political stability is restored, regaining lost space around strongholds by diversifying conservation models (hopefully more participatory and inclusive) and restoring full sovereignty to national administrations seems the most realistic option to target (Scholte et al., 2022).

Forest Buffalo (*S. c. nanus*)

In West Africa, habitat loss and degradation are major threats to forest buffalo. The Guinean forests that run from Sierra Leone to Cameroon cover approximately 93,000 km^2 of natural vegetation, which represents only 15 per cent of its original cover (Mittermeier et al., 2005; Aleman et al., 2018).

The situation is less critical in Central Africa, which has historically been less disturbed, and where less than 9 per cent of the rainforest area has been lost since 2000 (Dalimier et al., 2022). However, since 2009, the annual rate of forest degradation has increased in all Central African countries. If the rate of forest degradation observed over the past 10 years continues, the Democratic Republic of Congo could lose 33 per cent of its undisturbed rainforest by 2050 (Vancutsem et al., 2020) as a result of agricultural expansion (Perrings and Halkos, 2015), infrastructure development and extractive industries (Malhi et al., 2013).

Hunting for wild meat or bushmeat is also a threat to forest buffalo in West and Central Africa, where many rural populations depend on wildlife for meat (van Vliet et al., 2016). Although poorly assessed, subsistence hunting and poaching are likely to have a strong impact on the forest buffalo insofar as the larger (and thus more profitable) species are generally the most sought after, especially when sold in big city markets. For example, buffalo meat was reported to be among the most expensive meat among ungulates in Bangui (Central African Republic; Fargeot et al., 2017) as well as in Kinshasa (DRC) and Brazzaville (Republic of the Congo; Gluszek et al., 2021).

Insecurity and the presence of armed groups are known to greatly amplify the pressure on forest buffalo, especially because military weapons are more suitable for hunting buffalo than traditional 12-gauge guns. For example, poaching by armed groups during the periods of rebellion in Yangambi landscape (DRC) led to the complete extirpation of buffalo (van Vliet et al., 2018).

In West Africa, our investigations show that the forest buffalo are clearly dependent on conservation efforts (protected areas and wildlife laws) to prevent extinction. The lack of effective conservation measures currently leaves forest buffalo critically endangered. In contrast, the conservation status of the forest buffalo is less of a concern in Central Africa as it benefits from better preserved habitats and less anthropogenic pressure, particularly West of the Congo basin. Several protected areas also benefit from long term public–private partnerships such as Nouabalé–Ndoki and Odzala NPs in the Republic of Congo, or Salonga NP in the Democratic Republic of Congo (Scholte, 2022).

Finally, although logging is often detrimental to wildlife because of easier access for poaching (Kleinschroth at al., 2019), it is likely that a moderate opening of the forest canopy allows the forest buffalo to access more profitable food resources, as shown for large primates (Bekhuis et al., 2008; Haurez et al., 2014). In this context, the developing forest certification in Central Africa opens up interesting conservation perspectives for wildlife in general and for forest buffalo populations in particular.

Cape Buffalo (*S. c. caffer*)

Our investigations show that the conservation status of the African buffalo remains satisfactory in most of the countries in its geographical range. However, with a few exceptions, the Cape buffalo is now mainly confined to protected areas. Despite increasing human pressure, the integrity of protected areas is better respected in Eastern and Southern Africa, where conflicts and insecurity are less prevalent than in Western and Central Africa. The Cape buffalo populations also globally benefit from better soils conditions, particularly in East Africa where volcanic soils provide more profitable forage (Chapter 5). However, eastern and southern Africa are subject to severe droughts that have repeatedly affected buffalo populations in recent decades (Prins and Sinclair, 2013; Cornélis et al., 2014). In a context where the frequency and amplitude of these events could increase in the near future due to climate change, buffalo populations – a water-dependent species – could be strongly and durably affected in Eastern and southern Africa and beyond (Sintayehu, 2018).

The good conservation status of the fauna in general and the buffalo in particular has made it possible for several countries to develop a thriving industry based on nature tourism (viewing and hunting; Chapter 16). In addition, the successful development of community-based natural resources management (CBNRM) programmes since about 25 years in several countries of the Cape buffalo range is to some extent responsible for the rather good conservation status of the subspecies in the two regions, for example the CAMPFIRE programme in Zimbabwe; Game Management Areas in Zambia; communal conservancies in Namibia; and Wildlife Management Areas in Tanzania. The role of Trophy Hunting Areas is often overlooked in the success of wildlife management, especially buffalo. The private ownership of buffalo in game ranches and the private management of buffalo in trophy hunting areas are powerful drivers of thriving buffalo populations (Chapter 16). Many National Parks of the Eastern and southern regions are embedded in networks of

Trophy Hunting Areas (another category of Protected Areas) functioning as buffer zones and socioecological corridors between National Parks. Such complexes make much stronger conservation tools than isolated National Parks. Within this context, mass translocation has become a common tool for wildlife management in southern Africa for either reintroduction of the species or reinforcement of small populations. A striking example is Mozambique, where large buffalo herds thriving in trophy hunting areas within the Marromeu complex and Niassa Special Reserve were translocated to Gilé and Zinave National Parks.

Acknowledgements

We are grateful to all the organizations and individuals who kindly contributed information and materials to this study. African Parks network (Jean-Marc Froment, Angela Gaylard, Joanne Dube, Jean Labuschagne and Thierry Aebischer) and Forest Resource Management (Nicolas Bayol and Alexandra Pasquier) kindly provided us with very useful information in their many areas of intervention. We also warmly thank the following individuals for their contributions: Joao Simoes Almeida, Félicien Amakpe, Catherine André, Dagmar Andres-Brümmer, Matt Becker, Emily Bennitt, Alain Billand, Robin Bouckaert, Susan Brown, Dave Bruce, David Brugière, Tim Caro, Nicola Carruthers, Simon Chamaille-Jammes, Mike Chase, Erwan Cherel, Marc Colyn, Alayne Cotterill, Ian Craig, Benoit Demarquez, Jean Pierre d'Huart, Louis and Karl Diakité, Kevin Dunham, Andy Dunn, Jef Dupain, David Elizalde, Samuel Ferreira, Eric Forni, Alessandro Fusari, Jamie Gaymer, Roland Goetz, Danny Govender, John Hart, Philipp Henschel, Naftali Honig, Howard Hunter, Richard Kock, David Kpelle, Nick La Grange, Alain and Kewin Lefol, Peter Lindsey, Dolmia Malachie, Roseline Mandisodza-Chikerema, Anthony Marx, Naomi Matthews, Menard Mbende, Rachel Mc Robb, Christophe Morio, Naomi Moss, Gilles Moyot, Victor Narat, Stuart Nixon, Nyambe Nyambe, Peter Oberem, Valentin Omasombo, Mike Peel, Carlos L. Pereira, Willie Prinsloo, Julie Price, Rafael Reyna-Hurtado, Lee-Anne Robertson, Holly Rosier, Hamish Rudland, Edward Sayer, Scott Schlossberg, Twakundine Simpamba, Raymond Snaps, Ian Stevenson, Grant Taylor, Dorian Tilbury, Girma Timer, Kenneth Uiseb, Jean-Claude Urvoy, Wouter van Hoven, Louis van Schalkwyk, David Wilkie, Fabrice Yapi, Kim Young-Overton and Craig Zytkow. A project like this is perhaps impossible without the help of e-mail and the Internet, and we exchanged more than 1500 messages. The mind boggles when one tries to imagine how Rod East undertook his massive 1998 assessment not only for buffalo but for all African antelopes. It took us two years thanks to modern technology, whereas Rod needed 15. We dedicate this chapter to the memory of Rod, who was honoured with the Sir Peter Scott Award for Conservation Merit shortly before he died. More importantly, his work now allows us to assess in which countries conservation of buffalo works, and where it does not. Indeed, humans may need awards but buffalo need protection: thank you, Rod!

References

Aebischer, T., T. Ibrahim, R. Hickisch, et al. (2020). Apex predators decline after an influx of pastoralists in former Central African Republic hunting zones. *Biological Conservation* **241**: 108326.

Afriyie, J.O., M.O. Asare, E. Danquah, and H. Pavla (2021). Assessing the management effectiveness of three protected areas in Ghana. *Conservation and Society* **19**: 13–24.

Akinsorotan, O.A., V.A. Odelola, O.E. Olaniyi, and B.G. Oguntuase (2021). Human–wildlife conflicts and rural livelihood in Okomu national park, Edo state, Nigeria. *IOP Conference Series: Earth and Environmental Science* **655**(1): 012097.

Aleman, J.C., M.A. Jarzyna, and A.C. Staver (2018). Forest extent and deforestation in tropical Africa since 1900. *Nature Ecology & Evolution* **2**: 26–33.

Alistair, D.G. and N. Bereket (1996). Trends in large herbivore numbers of Omo and Mago national parks. Ministry of Agriculture, technical reports: 20.

Anstey, S. (1991). Large mammal distribution in Liberia: The findings of a preliminary national survey. WWF/FDA wildlife survey report. WWF International (Gland, Switzerland).

APN and DNPW (2019). Aerial survey report for Black Lechwe and other large herbivores in the Bangweulu Wetlands November 2019. African Parks Network and Department of National Parks and Wildlife.

APN and DNPW (2020). Aerial census report. October 2020 Liuwa Plain National Park. African Parks Network and Department of National Parks and Wildlife.

Astaras, C. (2009). *Ecology and Status of the Drill (Mandrillus leucophaeus) in Korup National Park, Southwest Cameroon: Implications for Conservation*. PhD thesis, Faculty of Mathematics and Natural Sciences, Georg-August-University of Göttingen.

Atsri, H., K. Adjossou, K. Tagbi, et al. (2013). *Inventaire faunique et forestier, études écologiques et cartographiques du Parc National de Fazao-Malfakassa*. Bern: Fondation Franz Weber.

Bassey, E. (2019). *Cross River National Park (Okwangwo Division) Annual Report: 2019*. WCS.

Baudenon, P. (1952). Notes sur les bovidés du Togo. *Mammalia* **16**: 49–61.

Bauer, H., A.A. Mohammed, A. El Faki, et al. (2018). Antelopes of the Dinder–Alatash transboundary Protected Area, Sudan and Ethiopia. *Gnusletter* **35**(1): 26–30.

Beja, P., P.V. Pinto, L. Veríssimo, et al. (2019). The mammals of Angola. In B. Huntley, V. Russo, F. Lages, and N. Ferrand (Eds.), *Biodiversity of Angola*. Cham: Springer, pp. 357–443.

Bekhuis, P.D.B.M., C.B. de Jong, and H.H.T. Prins (2008). Diet selection and density estimates of forest buffalo in Campo-Ma'an National Park, Cameroon. *African Journal of Ecology* **46**: 668–675.

Bessone, M., H.S. Kühl, and G. Hohmann (2020). Drawn out of the shadows: surveying secretive forest species with camera trap distance sampling. *Journal of Applied Ecology* **57**: 963–974.

Beudels-Jamar, R.C., R.-M. Lafontaine, H. Robert, et al. (2016). *Identification des zones de grande valeur de biodiversité à l'intérieur et dans la périphérie de l'Assiette de Coupe provisoire du permis 190 de la compagnie Sinfocam, limitrophe au Parc national de Dzanga-Sangha, APDS RCA*. Belgium: WWF, ZSL.

Blake, S. (2002). Forest buffalo prefer clearings to closed canopy forest in the primary forest of northern Congo. *Oryx* **36**: 81–86.

Bolaños, N.C. (2012). Garamba National Park: aerial animal census 2012. African Parks.

Bouché, P. (2006). *Mole Wildlife Survey. Northern Savannah Biodiversity Conservation Project*. Gland: IUCN, p. 42.

Bouché, P. (2016). *Comptage aérien de la faune du Parc national de la Comoé et des deux zones de biodiversité*. Bonn: Deutsche Gesellschaft für Internationale Zusammenarbeit (GIZ) GmbH.

Bouché, P., C. Lungren, B. Hien, and P. Omondi (2003). Aerial total count of the "W"–Arli–Pendjari–Oti–Mandouri–Keran (WAPOK) ecosystem in West Africa. Mike-Paucof project.

Bouché, P., R. Nzapa Mbeti Mange, F. Tankalet, et al. (2012). Game over! Wildlife collapse in northern Central African Republic. *Environmental Monitoring and Assessment* **184**(11): 7001–7011.

Bouché, P., H. Frederick, and E. Kohi (2015). *Inventaire aérien de l'écosystème W-Arly-Pendjari Juin 2015*. Buffalo, NY: Vulcan, WCS: Elephants Without Borders.

Braga-Pereira, F., C.A. Peres, J.V. Campos-Silva, et al. (2020). Warfare-induced mammal population declines in Southwestern Africa are mediated by species life history, habitat type and hunter preferences. *Scientific Reports* **10**: 15428.

Brncic, T., B. Amarasekaran, A. McKenna, et al. (2015). Large mammal diversity and their conservation in the human-dominated land-use mosaic of Sierra Leone. *Biodiversity and Conservation* **24** (10): 2417–2438.

Bruce, T., R. Amin, T. Wacher, et al. (2018). Using camera trap data to characterise terrestrial larger-bodied mammal communities in different management sectors of the Dja Faunal Reserve, Cameroon. *African Journal of Ecology* **56**: 759–776.

Bruce, T., T. Wacher, H. Ndinga, et al. (2017). *Camera-trap Survey for Larger Terrestrial Wildlife in the Dja Biosphere Reserve, Cameroon*. London: Zoological Society of London (ZSL) and Yaoundé, Cameroon: Ministry of Forests and Fauna (MINFOF).

Butynski, T., C. Schaaf, and G. Hearn (1997). African buffalo *Syncerus caffer* extirpated on Bioko Island, Equatorial Guinea. *Journal of African Zoology* **111**: 57–61.

Buzzard, P.J. and A.J.A. Parker (2012). Surveys from the Subri River Forest Reserve, Ghana. *African Primates* **7**: 175–183.

Center for International Earth Science Information Network (2016). *Gridded population of the world, version 4 (GPWv4): Population count*. Palisades, NY: NASA Socioeconomic Data and Applications Center (SEDAC), Center for International Earth Science Information Network (CIESIN), Columbia University.

Chamberlan, C., C. Maurois, and C. Marechal (1995). Étude mammologique dans le Parc national d'Odzala. Programme ECOFAC (Congo).

Chardonnet, P., A. Fusari, J. Dias, et al. (2017). *Lessons Learned from the Reintroduction of Large Mammals in Gilé National Reserve, Mozambique*. Saint-Louis, Senegal: SSIG 17.

Chase, M. (2011). *Dry Season Fixed-Wing Aerial Survey of Elephants and Wildlife in Northern Botswana, September–November 2010*. Kasane, Botswana: Elephant Without Borders.

Chase, M., S. Schlossberg, R. Sutcliffe, and E. Seonyatseng (2018). *Dry Season Aerial Survey of Elephants and Wildlife In Northern Botswana*. Kasane, Botswana: Elephant Without Borders.

Christy, P., S. Lahm, O. Pauwels, and J.V. Weghe (2008). *Checklist of the Amphibians, Reptiles, Birds and Mammals of the National Parks of Gabon*. Tielt: Smithsonian Institution Lannoo SA.

Chuo, D.M. and T.E. Angwafo (2017). Status of large mammals: case study of gorilla (*Gorilla gorilla diehi*), chimpanzee (*Pan troglodytes ellioti*) and buffalo (*Syncerus caffer*), Menchum South, NW Cameroon. *International Journal of Environment, Agriculture and Biotechnology* **2**: 1523–1539.

Cockar, Z.S. (2022). A checklist of the mammals of Rwanda. *Journal of East African Natural History* **111** (1): 1–17.

Coppens, B. (2015). Report on the ornithological importance of the Boé region, Guinea-Bissau. Fieldwork from January to July 2015. Fondation Chimbo.

Cornélis, D., M. Melletti, L. Korte, et al. (2014). African buffalo (*Syncerus caffer* Sparrman, 1779. In M. Melletti and J. Burton (Eds.), *Ecology, Evolution and Behaviour of Wild Cattle: Implications for Conservation*. Cambridge: Cambridge University Press, pp. 326–372.

Cornélis, D.; Melletti, M.; Renaud, P.C.; Fonteyn, D.; Bonhotal, Hannah; Prins, H.; Chardonnet, P.; Caron, A., 2023, The African buffalo database, https://doi.org/10.18167/DVN1/AK1NQY, CIRAD Dataverse

Courtin, F., J.-B. Rayaissé, I. Tamboura, et al. (2010). Updating the northern tsetse limit in Burkina Faso (1949–2009): impact of global change. *International Journal of Environmental Research and Public Health* **7**(4): 1708–1719.

Craig, G.C. (2011a). Aerial Survey of Wildlife in the Niassa Reserve, Mozambique, October 2011. Sociedade para a Gestao e Desenvolvimento da Reserva do Niassa.

Craig, G.C. (2011b). Aerial survey of Quirimbas National Park and adjacent areas; annex 2 of the aerial survey of wildlife in the Niassa game reserve. WWF Mozambique.

Craig, G.C. and D.S. Gibson (2014). Aerial survey of elephants and other wildlife in the Zambezi Region September/October 2014. Ministry of Environment and Tourism (Namibia).

Craig, G.C. and D.S. Gibson (2015). Aerial survey of elephants and other wildlife in the Zambezi Region September/October 2015. Ministry of Environment and Tourism (Namibia).

Craig, G.C. and D.S. Gibson (2019). Aerial survey of elephants and other wildlife in the Zambezi Region September/October 2019. Ministry of Environment and Tourism (Namibia).

Cuisance, D. (1996). Réactualisation de la situation des tsé-tsé et des trypanosomoses africaines au Tchad. Rapport no. 96–024. CIRAD-EMVT, Montpellier.

Cumming, D. (2016). The buffalo–cattle interface in Zimbabwe: a preliminary review. AHEAD (Animal and Human Health for the Environment And Development) Program.

Dahourou, L.D. and U. Belemsobgo (2020). *Etude sur les chaînes de valeurs de la viande de brousse et des produits d'animaux sauvages au Burkina Faso (Version provisoire)*. Rome: FAO.

Dalimier, J., F. Achard, B. Delhez, et al. (2022). Répartition des types de forêts et évolution selon leur affectation. In R. Eba'a Atyi, F. Hiol Hiol, G. Lescuyer, et al. (Eds.), *Les forêts du bassin du Congo: état des forêts 2021*. Bogor, Indonesia: CIFOR.

Dandena, T. and T. Dinkisa (2014). *Report on Ecological and Socio-Economic Assessment in Tulu Lafto forests of Horo Guduru Wellega Zone: A Feasibility Study for Consideration to Designate a Protected Area*. Addis Ababa, Ethiopia: OFWE.

Danquah, E. and J.A. Owusu (2015). Distribution of buffalo in the Kogyae Strict Nature Reserve, Ghana. *Applied Research Journal* **1**: 20–26.

Da Silva, M.J.F., T. Minhos, R. Sa, et al. (2021). A qualitative assessment of Guinea-Bissau's hunting history and culture – and their implications for primate conservation. *African Primates* **15**: 1–18.

Devers, D. and J. Weghe (2006). Les forêts du Bassin du Congo: Etat des forêts 2006. Partenariat des forêts pour le Bassin du Congo. COMIFAC/EC/USAID/Coopération française, Kinshasa, République Démocratique du Congo.

DNPW (2019). Aerial survey of elephant and large terrestrial herbivores in the Kafue and Sioma Ngwezi Ecosystem. Department of National Parks & Wildlife.

DNPW (2016). The 2015 aerial census of elephants and other large mammals in Zambia: volume II. Population estimates for other large mammals and birds. Department of National Parks and Wildlife (Chilanga, Zambia).

Douglas-Hamilton, I., J.-M. Froment, G. Doungoube, and J. Root (1985). Recensement aérien de la faune dans la Zone Nord de la République Centrafricaine. ECOFAC.

Dunham, K.M. (1994). The effect of drought on the large mammal populations of Zambezi riverine woodlands. *Journal of Zoology* **234**: 489–526.

Dunham, K.M., C.S. Mackie, and G. Nyaguse (2015). Aerial survey of elephants and other large herbivores in the Zambezi Valley (Zimbabwe): 2014. Parks and Wildlife Management Authority. Zimbabwe and Great Elephant Survey, Paul G. Allen Project (Harare).

Dunham, K.M., C.S. Mackie, G. Nyaguse, and C. Zhuwau (2015a). Aerial survey of elephants and other large herbivores in north-west Matabeleland (Zimbabwe). Zimbabwe and GreatElephant Survey, Paul G. Allen Project (Harare).

Dunham, K.M., C.S. Mackie, G. Nyaguse, and C. Zhuwau (2015b). Aerial survey of elephants and other large herbivores in the Sebungwe (Zimbabwe). Zimbabwe and Great Elephant Survey, Paul G. Allen Project (Harare).

Dunham, K.M. and H.F. Westhuizen (2018). Aerial survey of elephants and other Large herbivores in Gonarezhou National Park (Zimbabwe) and some adjacent areas: 2018. Gonarezhou Conservation Trust, Gonarezhou National Park (Chiredzi, Zimbabwe).

Dupuy, A.R. (1971). *Le Niokolo-Koba: premier grand parc national de la République du Sénégal.* Dakar: GIA.

East, R. (1998). *African Antelope Database.* Edited by IUCN/SSC. Vol. *Antelope Specialist Group.* Gland, Switzerland and Cambridge, UK: IUCN.

Eban, J. (2020). *Mbe Mountains Annual Report: January–December 2019.* New York: Wildlife Conservation Society.

Elizalde, S., D. Elizalde, E. Lutondo, et al. (2019). Luando Natural Integral Reserve, Angola – a large and medium sized mammal survey. Instituto Nacional de Biodiversidade e Areas de Conservação (INBAC)/The Range Wide Conservation Programme for Cheetah and African Wild Dogs (RWCP).

Elkan, P., R. Fotso, C. Hamley, et al. (2015). Aerial surveys of wildlife and human activity across the Bouba N'djidda–Sena Oura–Benoué–Faro Landscape Northern Cameroon and Southwestern Chad 2015. Government of Cameroon, Great Elephant Census – Paul G. Allen Foundation and Wildlife Conservation Society.

Elkan, P., C. Hamley, S. Mendiguetti, et al. (2013a). Aerial recce surveys of wildlife and human activity in key areas of Sudd 2013. Government of South Sudan, USAID, and Wildlife Conservation Society.

Elkan, P., C. Hamley, S. Mendiguetti, et al. (2016). Aerial surveys of wildlife and human activity in key areas of South Sudan Boma, Badingilo, Nimule, Southern and Shambe National Parks, and Loelle Proposed Protected Area 2015–2016. Government of South Sudan, USAID, Great Elephant Census – Paul G. Allen Foundation and Wildlife Conservation Society.

Elkan, P., R. Mwinyihali, S. Mendiguetti, et al. (2013b). Aerial reconnaissance survey of wildlife, human activity and habitat across the Bili–Uéré Protected Area Complex, Democratic Republic of Congo (April 2013). Institut Congolais pour la Conservation de la Nature and Wildlife Conservation Society.

Elkan, P., H. Vanleeuwe, O. Eldar, et al. (2017). Sondage aérien de la faune, des habitats et des activités humaines dans les zones clefs du Nord Centrafrique. WCS & Agreco/Ecofaune.

Eniang, E., C. Ebin, A. Nchor, et al. (2017). Distribution and status of the African forest buffalo *Syncerus caffer nanus* in south-eastern Nigeria. *Oryx* **51**(3): 538–541.

Erena, M., A.A.D. Bekele and H.J. Debella (2019). Diet composition of forest inhabiting Cape buffalo (*Syncerus caffer caffer*) in western Ethiopia. *International Journal of Ecology and Environmental Sciences* **45**(2): 165–178.

European Commission (2015). *Larger than Elephants. Inputs for the Design of an EU Strategic Approach to Wildlife Conservation in Africa: Synthesis.* Luxembourg: Publications Office of the European Union.

Fagotto, F. (1980). The caffer buffalo and its habitat in Somalia. *Atti della Societa Toscana Scienze Naturali Memorie B* **87**: 161–79.

Fargeot, C., N. Drouet-Hoguet, and S. Le Bel, (2017). The role of bushmeat in urban household consumption: insights from Bangui, the capital city of the Central African Republic. *Bois et Forêts Des Tropiques* **332**, 31–42.

Fay, M., P. Elkan, M. Marjan, and F. Grossmann (2007). Aerial surveys of wildlife, livestock, and human activity in Southern Sudan. USFWS and GoSS.

Ferreira, S., C. Greaver, C. Bissett, J. Hayes, J.M. Herbst, and N. Mzileni (2021). Large vertebrate abundances in SanParks in 2020/20121. Scientific Services. South African National Parks. Summary Report.

Fick, S.E. and R.J. Hijmans (2017). WorldClim 2: new 1-km spatial resolution climate surfaces for global land areas. *International Journal of Climatology* **37**(12): 4302–4315.

Fonteyn, D., C. Vermeulen, N. Deflandre, et al. (2021). Wildlife trail or systematic? Camera trap placement has little effect on estimates of mammal diversity in a tropical forest in Gabon. *Remote Sensing in Ecology and Conservation* **7**: 321–336.

Fraticelli, C., O. Ourde, J. Arnulphy, et al. (2021). Dry Season Aerial Total Count of Zakouma National Park, Chad, 2021. African Parks Network (Johannesburg).

Funston, P., P. Henschel, L. Petracca, et al. (2017). The distribution and status of lions and other large carnivores in Luengue–Luiana and Mavinga National Parks, Angola. KAZA TFCA Secretariat.

Fusari, A., C. Lopes Pereira, J. Dias, et al. (2017). Reintroduction of large game species to Gilé National Reserve, Mozambique. In IUGB 33rd Congress, Montpellier, 22–25 August 2017.

Gautier, A. (1988). "L'exploitation saisonnière des ressources animales pendant le paléolithique supérieur dans la vallée du Nil égyptien." L'animal dans l'alimentation humaine: Les critères des choix. Actes du colloque international de Liège, 26–29 novembre 1986 (*Anthropozoologica* Numéro Spécial).

Gedow, A.O., J. Leeuw, and G. Koech (2017). Assessment of the biodiversity in terrestrial and marine landscapes of the proposed Lag Badana National Park and surrounding areas, Jubaland, Somalia. ICRAF working paper No. 251.

Gessner, G., R. Buchwald, and G. Wittemyer (2013). Assessing species occurrence and species-specific use patterns of bais (forest clearings) in Central Africa with camera traps. *African Journal of Ecology* **52**: 59–68.

GIZ (2017). *Plan d'aménagement et de gestion 2016–2025 du complexe d'aires protégées de Togodo. Réserve de Biosphère Transfrontalière du Delta du Mono.* Deutsche Gesellschaft für Internationale Zusammenarbeit (GIZ) GmbH.

Gluszek, S., J. Viollaz, and M.L. Gore (2021). Using conservation criminology to understand the role of restaurants in the urban wild meat trade. *Conservation Science and Practice*, **3**(5): e368.

Gonfa, G., T. Gadisa, and T. Habitamu (2015). The diversity, abundance and habitat association of medium- and large-sized mammals of Dati Wolel National Park, Western Ethiopia. *International Journal of Biodiversity and Conservation* **7**(2): 112–118.

Gouteux J.P., F. Blanc, E. Pounekrozou, et al. (1994). Tsé-tsé et élevage en République Centrafricaine : le recul de *Glossina morsitans submorsitans* (Diptera, Glossinidae). *Bulletin de la Société de Pathologie Exotique* **87**: 52–56.

Groom, R., D. Elizalde, S. Elizalde, et al. (2018). Quiçama National Park, Angola. A large and medium sized mammals survey. INBAC/RWCP (Luanda, Angola).

Grossmann, F., H. Fopa Kueteyem, A. Vailia Nguertou, et al. (2018). *Aerial Survey of Wildlife and Human Activity in the BSB Yamoussa Landscape, Cameroon, Dry Season 2018.* New York: Wildlife Conservation Society.

Grossmann, F., C. Lopes Pereira, D. Chambal, et al. (2014a). *Aerial Survey of Elephant, Other Wildlife and Human Activity in the Niassa National Reserve and Adjacent Areas.* New York: Wildlife Conservation Society.

Grossmann, F., C. Lopes Pereira, D. Chambal, et al. (2014b). *Aerial Survey of Elephant, Other Wildlife and Human Activity in Quirimbas National Park and the Western Corridor.* New York: Wildlife Conservation Society.

Grossmann, F., C. Lopes Pereira, D. Chambal, et al. (2014c). *Aerial Survey of Elephant, Other Wildlife and Human Activity in the Tete Province Areas South and North of Lake Cahora Bassa and Magoe National Park.* New York: Wildlife Conservation Society.

Haurez, B., C.-A. Petre, C. Vermeulen, et al. (2014). Western lowland gorilla density and nesting behavior in a Gabonese forest logged for 25 years: implications for gorilla conservation. *Biodiversity and Conservation* **23**(11): 2669–2687.

Hauptfleisch, M. and C. Brown (2019). Wildlife Census for Mole National Park 16–18 September 2019. Namibia University of Science and Technology.

Hedwig, D., I. Kienast, M. Bonnet, et al. (2018). A camera trap assessment of the forest mammal community within the transitional savannah-forest mosaic of the Batéké Plateau National Park, Gabon. *African Journal of Ecology* **56**(4): 777–790.

Hickey, J.R., A.C. Granjon, L. Vigilant, et al. (2019). Virunga 2015–2016 surveys: monitoring mountain gorillas, other select mammals, and illegal activities. Kigali, Rwanda.

Hoeven, C.A., W.F. Boer, and H.H.T. Prins (2004). Pooling local expert opinions for estimating mammal densities in tropical rainforests. *Journal for Nature Conservation* **12**: 193–204.

Holubová, Z. (2019). *Assessment of Selected Methods for Monitoring of Large African Ungulates.* Master's thesis, Czech University of Life Sciences, Faculty of Tropical AgriSciences.

Hongo, S., Z.S.C. Dzefack, L.N. Vernyuy, et al. (2020). Use of multi-layer camera trapping to inventory mammals in rainforests in southeast Cameroon. *African Study Monographs* **60**: 21–37.

Hoppe-Dominik, B., H.S. Kühl, G. Radl, and F. Fischer (2011). Long-term monitoring of large rainforest mammals in the biosphere reserve of Taï National Park, Côte d'Ivoire. *African Journal of Ecology* **49**: 450–458.

Houngbégnon, F.G.A. (2015). *Gestion de la faune sauvage et du secteur de la viande de brousse en Afrique-Centrale. Étude diagnostique de durabilité. Village de Ngokoéla (Ovan), Gabon.* Master GAED (Mondialisation, Dynamiques Spatiales et Développement Durable dans les pays du Sud), La Sorbonne.

ICCN and WWF (2015a). Evaluation du massif forestier du Nord Ubangi. Programme d'appui au Réseau des Aires Protégées. Institut Congolais de la Conservation de la Nature and World Wildlife Fund.

ICCN and WWF (2015b). Évaluation du domaine et réserve de chasse de Swa-Kibula. Programme d'appui au Réseau des Aires Protégées. Institut Congolais de la Conservation de la Nature and World Wildlife Fund.

ICCN and WWF (2015c). Évaluation des aires protégées de Mangaï et Gungu. Programme d'appui au Réseau des Aires Protégées. Institut Congolais de la Conservation de la Nature and World Wildlife Fund.

ICCN and WWF (2016a). Revue des stratégies de conservation des valeurs naturelles de l'espace Tumba–Lediima. Programme d'appui au Réseau des Aires Protégées. Institut Congolais de la Conservation de la Nature and World Wildlife Fund.

ICCN and WWF (2016b). Statut de la grande faune de la réserve naturelle d'Itombwe. Programme d'appui au Réseau des Aires Protégées. Institut Congolais de la Conservation de la Nature and World Wildlife Fund.

ICCN and WWF (2016c). Evaluation des aires protégées de Bushimaie. Programme d'appui au Réseau des Aires Protégées. Institut Congolais de la Conservation de la Nature and World Wildlife Fund.

ICCN and WWF (2016d). Evaluation du refuge à éléphants de Kaniama. Programme d'appui au Réseau des Aires Protégées. Institut Congolais de la Conservation de la Nature and World Wildlife Fund.

ICCN and WWF (2017a). Évaluation des zones prioritaires de Pangi et Kasongo. Programme d'appui au Réseau des Aires Protégées. Institut Congolais de la Conservation de la Nature and World Wildlife Fund.

ICCN and WWF (2017b). Evaluation des aires protégées de Luama–Kivu. Programme d'appui au Réseau des Aires Protégées. Institut Congolais de la Conservation de la Nature and World Wildlife Fund.

ICCN and WWF (2017c). Evaluation des aires protégées de Bombo–Lumene. Programme d'appui au Réseau des Aires Protégées. Institut Congolais de la Conservation de la Nature and World Wildlife Fund.

Imbey, M.O., J.Y.N. Mbezele, Y.A. Ahanda, et al. (2019). Suivi écologique de la dynamique des grands et moyens mammifères dans les clairières du parc national de Boumba Bek: cas du complexe de clairières de Pondo. *Journal of Applied Biosciences* **144**: 14755–14763.

IUCN SSC Antelope Specialist Group (2008). *Syncerus caffer*. The IUCN Red List of Threatened Species 2008.

IUCN SSC Antelope Specialist Group (2019). *Syncerus caffer*. The IUCN Red List of Threatened Species 2019.

Jallow, A., O. Touray, and M. Jallow (2004). An update of the status of antelopes in The Gambia. In B. Chardonnet and P. Chardonnet (Eds.), *Antelope Survey Update*. Paris, France, pp. 18–20. IUCN/SSC Antelope Specialist Group Report.

Jebessa, H.D. (2015). New range of the African buffalo (*Syncerus caffer sparrman*, 1772) in the upper Blue Nile valley, Western Ethiopia – a preliminary study. *SINET, Ethiopian Journal of Science* **38**(1): 61–66.

Kebede, A., T. Timer and A. Gebre-Michael (2011). *Report on Wildlife Census in Weleshet–Sala Controlled Hunting Area. South Nations Nationalities and People's Regional State*. Addis Ababa, Ethiopia: Ethiopian Wildlife Conservation Authority.

Kebede, A. and B. Tsegaye (2012). *Wildlife Census Report in the Haro Aba Diko Controlled Hunting Area in Illubabor zone of the Oromia Regional State of Ethiopia*. Addis Ababa, Ethiopia: EWCA and OFWE.

Kebede, A., E. Wendim, Z. Abdulwahid, et al. (2013). *Wildlife Census in Beroye Proposed Controlled Hunting Area (Oromia Regional State)*. Addis Ababa, Ethiopia: Ethiopian Wildlife Conservation Authority.

Kisame, F., F. Wanyama, E. Buhanga and A. Rwetsiba (2018a). *Ground Counts for Medium to Large Mammals in Lake Mburo Conservation Area*. Kampala: Uganda Wildlife Authority.

Kisame, F.E., F. Wanyama, E. Buhanga and A. Rwetsiba (2018b). *Ground Counts for Medium to Large Mammals in Pian Upe Wildlife Reserve, Karamoja, Uganda*. Kampala: Uganda Wildlife Authority.

Klein, R.G. (1988). The archaeological significance of animal bones from Acheulean sites in southern Africa. *African Archaeological Review* **6**: 3–25.

Klein, R.G. (1994). The long-horned African buffalo (*Pelorovisantiquus*) is an extinct species. *Journal of Archaeological Science* **21**: 725–733.

Kleinschroth, F., N. Laporte, W.F. Laurance, et al. (2019). Road expansion and persistence in forests of the Congo Basin. *Nature Sustainability* **2**(7): 628–634.

Korte, L. (2008a). Habitat selection at two spatial scales and diurnal activity patterns of adult female forest buffalo. *Journal of Mammalogy* **89**: 115–125.

Korte, L. (2008b). Variation of group size among African buffalo herds in a forest–savanna mosaic landscape. *Journal of Zoology* **275**: 229–236.

Lamprey, R., D. Ochanda, R. Brett, et al. (2020). Cameras replace human observers in multi-species aerial counts in Murchison Falls, Uganda. *Remote Sensing in Ecology and Conservation* **6**: 529–545.

Macandza, V.A., C.M. Bento, R.M. Roberto, et al. (2017). *Relatório da contagem aérea de fauna bravia na reserva nacional do Gilé*. Maputo, Mozambique: Centro De Estudos De

Agricultura E Gestão De Recursos Naturais (CEAGRE), Faculdade De Agronomia E Engenharia Florestal (FAEF), Universidade Eduardo Mondlane (UEM), Administração Nacional Das Áreas De Conservação (ANAC).

Macandza, V.A., C.P. Ntumi, F.P.S. Mamugy, et al. (2020). *Marromeu Complex Wildlife Census Report.* Mozbio, Republic of Mozambique: Ministry of Land and Environment, ANAC, FNDS.

Macpherson, D. (2019). *Aerial Wildlife Census of Akagera National Park, Rwanda – August 2019.* Namitete, Malawi: Cluny Wildlife Management Services.

Madidi, J., F. Maisels, F. Kahindo, et al. (2019). *Inventaires des Grands Mammifères et de l'Impact Humaine, Réserve de Faune à Okapis, 2018.* Rapport technique No.: 01/BION/RFO/2019. Kinshasa, DRC: WCS DRC.

Malhi, Y., S. Adu-Bredu, R.A. Asare, et al. (2013). African rainforests: past, present and future. *Philosophical Transactions of the Royal Society B: Biological Sciences* **368**(1625): 20120312.

Malonga, R. and I. Nganga (2008). *Potentialités naturelles de la Foret de Ntokou–Pikounda. Synthèse des résultats des études de faisabilité du projet de création d'une aire protégée.* Kinshasa, DRC: WCS-Congo and CNIAF-MEF.

Martin, M. (2002). *Species Management Plan for Southern Savanna Buffalo (Syncerus caffer caffer).* Windhoek, Namibia: Ministry of Environment and Tourism.

Martin, R. (2008). *Transboundary Species Project: Southern Savanna Buffalo. Species Report for Southern Savanna Buffalo in Support of The Transboundary Mammal Project of the Ministry of Environment and Tourism.* Windhoek, Namibia: Namibia Nature Foundation and the World Wildlife Fund's Living in a Finite Environment (LIFE) Programme.

Mathot, L., F. Ikoli and B.R. Missilou (2006). *Rapport annuel de monitoring de la faune du Projet Lésio–Louna.* Port Lympne: The John Aspinall Foundation.

Matuštíková, M. (2021). *Mapping of Water Sources Available for wildlife.* Master's thesis. Faculty of Tropical AgriSciences, Czech University of Life Sciences, Prague.

Megaze, A., M. Balakrishnan, and G. Belay (2018). Current population estimate and distribution of the African buffalo in Chebera Churchura National Park, Ethiopia. *African Journal of Ecology* **56** (1): 12–19.

Melletti, M., V. Penteriani, and L. Boitani (2007). Habitat preferences of the secretive forest buffalo (*Syncerus caffer nanus*) in Central Africa. *Journal of Zoology* **271**: 178–186.

Melletti, M., V. Penteriani, M. Mirabile, and L. Boitani (2008). Effects of habitat and season on the grouping of forest buffalo resting places. *African Journal of Ecology* **47**: 121–124.

MERF (2013). *Evaluation de l'efficacité de la gestion d'Oti–Kéran et Oti–Mandouri (Togo). Projet PNUD/FEM: 'Renforcement du rôle de conservation du système national d'aires protégées du Togo'.* Lomé, Togo: Ministère de l'environnement et des ressources forestières.

MERF (2014). *Cinquième rapport national sur la diversité biologique du Togo (2009–2014).* Lomé, Togo: Ministère de l'environnement et des ressources forestières (MERF).

MERF (2016). *Plan d'aménagement et de gestion de l'aire protégée de Amou–Mono.* Lomé, Togo: Ministère de l'environnement et des ressources forestières (MERF).

MERF (2017). *Plan d'aménagement et de gestion de l'aire protégée d'Abdoulaye (réserve de faune).* Lomé, Togo: Ministère de l'environnement et des ressources forestières (MERF).

Mills, M., H. Biggs, and I. Whyte (1995). The relationship between rainfall, lion predation and population trends in African herbivores. *Wildlife Research* **22**: 75–87.

Mittermeier, R., P. Gil, M. Hoffmann, et al. (2005). *Hotspots Revisited: Earth's Biologically Richest and Most Endangered Terrestrial Ecoregions: Conservation International.* Sierra Madre: Cemex, p. 315.

MNRT (2021). United Republic of Tanzania: Ministry of Natural Resources and Tourism. Accessed August, 29 2022. www.maliasili.go.tz/about/category/ministry-overview.

Morgan, B.J. (2007). Group size, density and biomass of large mammals in the Réserve de Faune du Petit Loango, Gabon. *African Journal of Ecology* **45**: 508–518.

Musika, N.V., J.V. Wakibara, P.A. Ndakidemi, and A.C. Treydte (2021). Spatio-temporal patterns of increasing illegal livestock grazing over three decades at Moyowosi Kigosi Game Reserve, Tanzania. *Land* **10**(12): 1325.

Musika, N.V., J.V. Wakibara, P.A. Ndakidemi, and A.C. Treydte (2022). Using trophy hunting to save wildlife foraging resources: a case study from Moyowosi–Kigosi Game Reserves, Tanzania. *Sustainability* **14**(3): 1288.

N'Goran, K.P., N.R. Maho, Y.C. Kouakou, et al. (2010). *Etat des ressources naturelles du Parc National de la Comoé et de sa zone périphérique. Rapport de l'inventaire faunique par survol aérien; mars 2010*. Abidjan, Côte d'Ivoire: Wild Chimpanzee Foundation, GTZ & OIPR.

Naidoo, R., P. Preez, G. Stuart-Hill, and P. Beytell (2014). Movements of African buffalo (*Syncerus caffer*) in the Kavango–Zambezi Transfrontier Conservation Area. *African Journal of Ecology* **52**(4): 581–584.

Nakashima, Y. (2015). Inventorying medium- and large-sized mammals in the African lowland rainforest using camera trapping. *Tropics* **23**(4): 151–164.

Natta, A., S. Nago and P. Keke (2014). Structure et traits ethnozoologiques du buffle de forêt (*Syncerus caffer nanus*) dans la forêt classée d'Agua (Centre Bénin). *Sciences Naturelles et Agronomie*, **4**(1): 39–52.

Nebesse, C. (2016). Caractérisation de la viande de brousse prélevée du village Basukwambula (PK 92) au village Baego (PK147) sur l'axe Kisangani–Ituri. MSc thesis, Faculté des Sciences, Université de Kisangani.

Nefzi, T. (2020). *Etude des potentialités touristiques des aires protégées de la Guinée*. Guinée: Ministère de l'Environnement des Eaux et Forêts.

Ngaba, M.Y. and M. Tchamba (2019). Etude de faisabilité de la mise en place d'un site écotouristique dans le parc national de Boumba-Bek: cas des clairières forestières de Pondo. *International Journal of Biological and Chemical Sciences* **13**(7): 3177–3192.

Ngoma, A., A. Diodio, K.L. Dieudonné, et al. (2021). *An assessment of intermediate and large mammal population sizes across the Garamba National Park and adjacent protected areas*. Kinshasa, Democratic Republic of Congo: Institut Congolais pour la Conservation de la Nature, African Parks, USAID.

Nunez, C.L., G. Froese, A.C. Meier, et al. (2019). Stronger together: comparing and integrating camera trap, visual, and dung survey data in tropical forest communities. *Ecosphere* **10** (12).

Nzigidahera, B., D. Mbarushimana, B. Habonimana, and F. Habiyaremye (2020). *Habitats du Parc National de la Ruvubu au Burundi. Guide sur la flore pour le suivi de la dynamique des habitats du PNR*. Bruxelles: Institut royal des Sciences naturelles de Belgique.

OIPR (2019). *Inventaire aérien de la grande faune du parc national de la Comoé et des sites de Warigue et mont Tingui*. Abidjan: Office Ivoirien des Parcs et des Réserves (OIPR) and Coopération Allemande.

Omondi, P., E.K. Bitok, M.R.M. Tchamba, and B.B. Lambert (2008). *The Total Aerial Count of Elephants and Other Wildlife Species in Faro, Benoué and Bouba Ndjida National Parks and Adjacent Hunting Blocks in Northern Cameroon*. Yaounde, Cameroon: WWF and Cameroon Ministry of Forestry and Wildlife.

ONFI (2021). *Inventaire forestier et faunique national (Côte d'Ivoire). Rapport final de l'inventaire faunique – Livrable no. 55 Janvier 2019–Juin 2021*. Nogent-sur-Marne: ONF International.

Orban, B., G. Kabafouako, R. Morley, et al. (2018). Common mammal species inventory utilizing camera trapping in the forests of Kouilou Département, Republic of Congo. *African Journal of Ecology* **56**(4): 750–754.

Ouindeyama, A., J. Chevillot, J.D. Akpona, et al. (2021). Inventaire Aérien des grands mammifères et du bétail du complexe W–Arly–Pendjari, Benin–Burkina Faso. African Parks Network, Johannesburg, South Africa.

Owiunji, I., D. Nkuutu, D. Kujirakwinja, et al. (2005). The Biodiversity of the Virunga Volcanoes. Unpublished report. New York: Wildlife Conservation Society.

PAPFCA (2007). *Plan d'Aménagement Participatif de la Forêt Classée d'Agoua. Projet d'aménagement des massifs forestiers d'Agoua, des Monts Kouffé et de Wari-Maro.* Cotonou, Bénin: MEPN/DGFRN.

PAPSA (2018). Rapport d'évaluation des tendances évolutives des espèces fauniques sur la période de 2010 à 2017, dans la forêt classée et ranch de gibier de Nazinga. projet PAPSA. Ministère de l'Environnement, de l'Economie Verte et du Changement Climatique, Ouagadougou, Burkina Faso.

Perrings, C. and G. Halkos (2015). Agriculture and the threat to biodiversity in sub-Saharan Africa. *Environmental Research Letters* **10**(9): 095015.

Petracca, L., P. Funston, P. Henschel, et al. (2020). Modeling community occupancy from line transect data: a case study with large mammals in post-war Angola. *Animal Conservation* **23**: 420–433.

Plumptre, A., D. Kujirakwinja, D. Moyer, et al. (2010). *Virunga Landscape Large Mammal Surveys, 2010.* New York: US Fish and Wildlife Service WCS, UWA, CITES/MIKE.

Prins, H.H.T. (1992). The pastoral road to extinction: competition between wildlife and traditional pastoralism in East Africa. *Environmental Conservation* **19**: 117–123.

Prins, H.H.T. (1996). *Ecology and Behaviour of the African Buffalo.* London: Chapman & Hall.

Prins, H.H.T. and J.F. De Jong (2022). The ecohistory of Tanzania's northern Rift Valley – can one establish an objective baseline as endpoint for ecosystem restoration? In C. Kiffner, M.L. Bond, and D.E. Lee (Eds.), *Tarangire: Human–Wildlife Coexistence in a Fragmented Landscape.* Cham: Springer Nature, pp. 129–161.

Prins, H.H. and I. Douglas-Hamilton (1990). Stability in a multi-species assemblage of large herbivores in East Africa. *Oecologia* **83**(3): 392–400.

Prins, H.H.T. and H.P. Jeugd (1993). Herbivore population crashes and woodland structure in East Africa. *Journal of Ecology* **81**: 305–314.

Prins, H.H.T. and J.M. Reitsma (1989). Mammalian biomass in an African equatorial forest. *Journal of Animal Ecology* **58**: 851–861.

Prins, H.H.T. and A. Sinclair (2013). The African buffalo: species profile. In M.H. Knight, J. Kingdon, and M. Hoffmann (Eds.), *Mammals of Africa. Pigs, Hippopotamuses, Chevrotain, Giraffes, Deer and Bovids.* London: Bloomsbury, pp. 125–136.

Prins, H.H.T., Y. Wato, L. Kenana and R. Chepkwony (in review). Is the collapse of large mammal populations in Sibiloi National Park and the Chalbi Desert (Kenya) caused by local people or climate change? *African Journal of Ecology.*

Rabeil, T., P. Hejcmanová, M. Gueye, et al. (2018). *Inventaire combiné terrestre et aérien Parc National du Niokolo-Koba, Sénégal.* Dakar: Direction des Parcs Nationaux, Randgold resources.

Reid, R.S., R.L. Kruska, U. Deichmann, et al. (2000). Human population growth and the extinction of the tsetse fly. *Agriculture, Ecosystems & Environment* **77**(3): 227–236.

Renaud, P.C. (2007). *Omo National Park Report for the Wet Season Aerial Survey.* Gembloux, Belgium: Ethiopia African Parks Foundation, Nature+ et Université de Gembloux.

Renaud, P.-C., M.B. Gueye, P. Hejcmanová, et al. (2006). *Inventaire aérien et terrestre de la faune et relevé des pressions au Parc National du Niokolo Koba.* Johannesburg: African Parks.

Renaud, P.C., M. Fay, A. Abdoulaye, et al. (2005). *Recensement aérien de la faune dans les préfectures de la région Nord de la République Centrafricaine.* Bruxelles, Belgium: AGRECO/UE.

Rolkier, G.G., K. Yehestial, and R. Prasse (2015). Habitats map of distributions of key wild animal species of Gambella National Park. *International Journal of Innovative Research and Development* **4**(4): 240–259.

Roulet, P.A. (2006). Plan d'aménagement de la Zone Cynégétique Villageoise (ZCV) de Mourou-Fadama, Sud-Est RCA. Projet PILED/RICAGIRN-FB/Fonds Français pour l'Environment Mondial, Paris, France.

Rwetsiba, E. and A. Nuwamanya (2010). Aerial surveys of Murchison Falls Protected Area, Uganda, March 2010. *Pachyderm* **47**: 118–123.

Scholte, P. (2005). *Floodplain Rehabilitation and the Future of Conservation & Development. Adaptive Management of Success in Waza-Logone, Cameroon.* Tropical Resource Management Papers 67. Wageningen, The Netherlands: Wageningen University and Research Centre.

Scholte, P. (2022). Fifteen years of delegated protected area management in West and Central Africa: five recommendations to guide maturity. *Oryx* **56**: 1–9.

Scholte, P., O. Pays, S. Adam, et al. (2022). Conservation overstretch and long-term decline of wildlife and tourism in the Central African savannas. *Conservation Biology* **36**(2): e13860.

Shanungu, G.K., C. Kaumba, and R. Beilfuss (2015). *Current Population Status and Distribution of Large Herbivores and Floodplain Birds of the Kafue Flats Wetlands, Zambia: Results of the 2015 Wet Season Aerial Survey.* Chilanga, Zambia: Zambia Wildlife Authority.

Shortridge, G.C. (1934). *The Mammals of South West Africa: A Biological Account of the Forms Occurring in That Region.* London: W. Heinemann.

Sidney, J. (1965). *The Past and Present Distribution of Some African Ungulates.* London: Zoological Society.

Sievert, O. and J. Adenorff (2020). *Majete Wildlife Reserve, Malawi, Aerial Census 2020.* Johannesburg, South Africa: Lilongwe Wildlife Trust and African Parks Network.

Sinclair, A.R.E. (1977). *The African Buffalo. A Study of Resource Limitation of Populations.* Chicago: University of Chicago Press.

Sinsin, B., D. Kampmann, A. Thiombiano,and S. Konaté (2010). *Atlas de la Biodiversité de l'Afrique de l'Ouest. Tome I: Benin.* Cotonou & Frankfurt/Main: BIOTA.

Sintayehu, D.W. (2018). Impact of climate change on biodiversity and associated key ecosystem services in Africa: a systematic review. *Ecosystem Health and Sustainability* **4**(9): 225–239.

Spira, C., G. Mitamba, A. Kirkby, et al. (2018). *Inventaire de la biodiversité dans le parc national de Kahuzi–Biega République Démocratique du Congo.* New York: Wildlife Conservation Society.

Stalmans, M. and M. Peel (2020). *Aerial Wildlife Count of the Gorongosa National Park.* Mozambique: Afrecology & USAID Mozambique.

Tambling, C., J. Venter, J. Toit, and M. Child (2016). A conservation assessment of *Syncerus caffer caffer.* In M.F. Child, L. Roxburgh, E. Do Linh San, D. Raimondo, and H.T. Davies-Mostert (Eds.), *The Red List of Mammals of South Africa, Swaziland and Lesotho.* South Africa: South African National Biodiversity Institute and Endangered Wildlife Trust, pp. 1–7.

Taylor, R.D. and R.B. Martin (1987). Effects of veterinary fences on wildlife conservation in Zimbabwe. *Environmental Management* **11**: 327–334.

TAWIRI (2019a). *Aerial Survey of Large Animals in the Mkomazi National Park, Wet Season, 2019. TAWIRI Aerial Survey Report.* Arusha, Tanzania: Tanzania Wildlife Research Institute.

TAWIRI (2019b). *Aerial Wildlife Survey of Large Animals and Human Activities in the Selous–Mikumi Ecosystem, Dry Season 2018. TAWIRI Aerial Survey Report.* Arusha, Tanzania: Tanzania Wildlife Research Institute.

TAWIRI (2020). *Aerial Wildlife Census in the Tarangire–Manyara Ecosystem, Wet Season, 2019. TAWIRI Aerial Survey Report.* Arusha, Tanzania: Tanzania Wildlife Research Institute.

TAWIRI (2021a). *Aerial Elephant, Buffalo and Giraffe Total Count Census in the Serengeti Ecosystem, Wet Season, 2020. TAWIRI Aerial Survey Report.* Arusha, Tanzania: Tanzania Wildlife Research Institute.

TAWIRI (2021b). *Aerial Survey in The West-Kilimanjaro–Natron Landscape, Wet Season, 2021. Tawiri Aerial Survey Report.* Arusha, Tanzania: Tanzania Wildlife Research Institute.

TAWIRI (2022). *Aerial Survey of Large Animals and Human Activities in the Ruaha–Rungwa and Katavi–Rukwa Ecosystems, Tanzania. Dry Season, 2021.* Arusha, Tanzania: Tanzania Wildlife Research Institute.

TFCI (2010). *Aerial Survey Report: Gambella Reconnaissance 2009 & Census 2010.* TransFrontier Conservation Initiative. Addis Ababa: Ethiopian Wildlife Conservation Authority.

Tiedoue Manouhin, R., A. Diarrassouba, and A. Tondossama (2020). *Etat de conservation du Parc national de Taï: Résultats du suivi écologique, Phase 14.* Soubré, Côte d'Ivoire: Office Ivoirien des Parcs et Réserves/Direction de Zone Sud-ouest.

Tiedoue Manouhin, R., S. Kone Sanga, A. Diarrassouba, and A. Tondossama (2019). *Etat de conservation du Parc national de Taï: Résultats du suivi écologique, Phase 13.* Soubré, Côte d'Ivoire: Office Ivoirien des Parcs et Réserves/Direction de Zone Sud-ouest.

Tola, A. (2020). *Species Diversity, Population Size and Density of Medium and Large Mammals of Mago National Park, South West Ethiopia.* MSc thesis, Hawassa University Wondo Genet College of Forestry and Natural Resource, Wondo-Genet.

Tsegaye, E. (2020). *Species Diversity, Population Size and Density of Medium and Large Mammals of Omo National Park, South West Ethiopia.* MSc thesis, Hawassa University Wondo Genet College of Forestry and Natural Resource, Wondo-Genet.

UNEP-WCMC and IUCN (2022). *Protected Planet: The World Database on Protected Areas (WDPA)* [On-line]. Cambridge: UNEP-WCMC and IUCN. Available at: www.protectedplanet.net.

Vancutsem, C., F. Achard, J.-F. Pekel, et al. (2020). Long-term (1990–2019) monitoring of tropical moist forests dynamics. *bioRxiv* 2020.09.17.295774.

Vanleeuwe, H., P. Henschel, C. Pélissier, et al. (2009). *Recensement des grands mammifères et des impacts humains. Parcs nationaux de l'Upemba et des Kundelungu République Démocratique du Congo.* Kampala, Uganda: Wildlife Conservation Society.

Vanthomme, H., J. Kolowski, L. Korte, and A. Alonso (2013). Distribution of a community of mammals in relation to roads and other human disturbances in Gabon, Central Africa. *Conservation Biology* 27: 281–291.

Van Vliet, N., D. Cornélis, H. Beck, et al. (2016). Meat from the wild: extractive uses of wildlife and alternatives for sustainability. In R. Mateo, B. Arroyo, and J.T. Garcia (Eds.), *Current Trends in Wildlife Research, Wildlife Research Monographs, Volume 1.* Cham: Springer, pp. 225–265.

Van Vliet, N., J. Muhindo, J. Kambale Nyumu, et al. (2018). Mammal depletion processes as evidenced from spatially explicit and temporal local ecological knowledge. *Tropical Conservation Science* 11: 1940082918799494.

Van Vliet, N., C. Nebesse, S. Gambalemoke, et al. (2012). The bushmeat market in Kisangani, Democratic Republic of Congo: implications for conservation and food security. *Oryx* 46: 196–203.

Wanyama, F., E. Balole, P. Elkan, et al. (2014). *Aerial Surveys of the Greater Virunga Landscape.* New York, NY: WCS, UCCN & UWA.

Wanyama, F., E.F. Kisame and D. Owor (2019). *Aerial Surveys of Medium–Large Mammals in Kidepo Valley National Park and Karenga Community Wildlife Area.* Kampala: Uganda Wildlife Authority.

Waweru, J., P. Omondi, S. Ngene, et al. (2021). *National Wildlife Census 2021 Report.* Nairobi: The Wildlife Research and Training Institute (WRTI) and Kenya Wildlife Service (KWS).

WCS Flight Programme (2008). *Aerial Surveys of Kidepo National Park, Lipan Controlled Hunting Area & Madi Corridor, March–April 2008.* Kampala, Uganda: Wildlife Conservation Society.

Wendim, E. (2015). *Maokomo Nature Conservation Area 2015.* Addis Ababa: Ethiopian Wildlife Conservation Authority.

Wendim, E. (2018). *Assessment of Wildlife and Socioeconomic in Didessa (Bijimiz) National Park.* Addis Ababa: Ethiopian Wildlife Conservation Authority.

White, J.T.L. (1994). Biomass of rain forest mammals in the Lopé Reserve, Gabon. *Journal of Animal Ecology* **63**: 499–512.

Wild Chimpanzee Foundation (2021). La faune du Parc National du Moyen-Bafing, Guinée. La faune du Parc National du Moyen-Bafing, Guinée – Fauna of the Moyen-Bafing National Park, Guinea. www.youtube.com/watch?v=Ui-S6krni_o

Winterbach, H.E.K. (1998). Research review: the status and distribution of Cape buffalo (*Syncerus caffer caffer*) in southern Africa. *South African Journal of Wildlife Research* **28**(3): 82–88.

WRI (2013). Aménagement forestier au Gabon. Situation en juillet 2013. http://data.wri .org/forest_atlas/gab/poster/gab_poster_2013_fr.pdf.

Part II
Ecology

H. H. T. PRINS

Introduction

When satellite technology became widely available, many animals studied revealed surprising behaviour and showed up in unexpected places. Likewise, modern genome studies on kinship relations show that the spreading of genes cannot easily be explained by visual observation. This raises the question whether erstwhile interpretations of animal movements and social organization stand the test of time. Dispersal (the movement of individuals away from their place of birth) is an influential life-history trait that alters the spatial distribution of species, individuals and, if followed by reproduction, alleles. Knowledge of dispersal behaviour, in terms of frequency, distance and direction, is essential for understanding population dynamics, structure and genetics, but can one-time deductions on social structure still be trusted? Likewise, can satellite-derived observations be trusted? Indeed, satellite-based remote sensing (RS) interpretations of vegetation and vegetation change over time are notorious for their dependency on underlying (often poorly known) algorithms. While RS specialists are mostly aware of the pitfalls, ecologists are not and merrily draw conclusions where RS specialists caution care. Since the beginning of modern ecology in the 1960s, African buffalo have been subject to observational studies, but the technologies that have been developed since the 1990s seem to question older interpretations. In this section, we examine the idea that buffalo may be migratory in some places. Older literature also showed this, but the deployment of GPS collars appears to reveal even more migratory behaviour.

The same GPS-collaring data may also lead to a different interpretation of the social organization of buffalo than previously posited. In that case, genetic data (see Part I) also appear to underpin the notion that buffalo may be less of a herding species, in which females live their lives in cohesive societies that undergo fission–fusion processes, than earlier interpretations indicated, but show more fluidity and less natal philopatry. It is of great importance to validate the GPS-based data. From other extensive data analyses on these types of data, we know that data cleaning is essential before one interprets GPS data, and we thus recommend that analyses of these types of data have a clear description of how raw data were transposed into the data used for the analyses. Compared to past literature, much more attention has been given in recent papers to the justification of the statistical methods used. Reliance on modern technology should lead to a similar openness about how data are acquired. Data handling may affect the trustworthiness of conclusions, as was demonstrated so aptly in climatology when the Antarctic ozone hole was erased from the data.

In the same vein, not enough is yet known about the effects on buffalo physiology, brain processes and behavioural (ab-)normality of chasing, darting and immobilizing African buffalo. The chapters presented are unique in the sense that we bring together for the first time ecologists, students of behaviour, animal handlers, veterinarians and physiologists in the hope that they all can learn from one another. We, as editors, thus hope that the disciplinary knowledge from these different specialities percolate into a fuller understanding of the technologies that (field) scientists use, so that they can draw well-informed conclusions on African buffalo.

This is also shown in the chapter on population dynamics. It is not easy to make a good life table of a species if there are no hard and fast rules to establish age estimates of individuals. Nor is it easy to apply mathematical models if one does not fully grasp the underlying assumptions. And if these assumptions do not incorporate the reality of the African savannas, with their recurrent droughts and permanent non-equilibrium states, then completely erroneous estimates of safe harvesting rates, not to mention estimates of 'maximum sustainable offtakes', could easily be made. Indeed, the latter concepts hail from environments where equilibrium dynamics govern systems and populations show a stable population structure; for African buffalo, that would appear to be another universe.

Diving deeper into evolutionary time, this section also provides a podium to discuss how to deal with the considerable morphological variation displayed by African buffalo. Through the simple mechanism of isolation by distance (see Part I), one might expect variation from a species with such an enormous geographical range, but neither the editors nor any of the authors advocate for the resurrection of 'micro-species' as were exuberantly discerned in the 1930s and again even more recently. If for conservation reasons (and not for postage stamp collecting) different forms need to be identified, then the smallest number of 'subspecies' that can be discerned on ecological and genetic grounds appears to be three (the northern savanna buffalo, the forest buffalo and the Cape buffalo). Ecologically speaking, they live under quite different natural selection pressures. These can be translated into different conservation challenges. It is too early, however, to translate these into us being able to precisely formulate differences in management challenges for the three different forms. Apart from the economic, financial and game handling challenges (Part IV), the lack of knowledge on African buffalo physiology (including thermal stress and precise food requirements) and its three 'subspecies' continues to prevent management based on science. As demonstrated by the chapters in this section, knowledge on the ecology of this fascinating species continues to widen. We certainly have made progress since M. Taute published his work in 1913 and F. Vaughan-Kirby in 1917, but when one century of research can be summarized in less than 100 pages, we think there is still much to learn.

5 · *Habitat, Space Use and Feeding Ecology of the African Buffalo*

R. TAYLOR, E. BENNITT, R. FYNN,
L. KORTE*, R. NAIDOO, A. ROUG AND
D. CORNELIS

Introduction

Spatial distribution and movement patterns of wild ungulates are strongly dependent on the spatial and temporal heterogeneity of biotic and abiotic resources (Bailey et al., 1996; Fryxell et al., 2004). In most African ecosystems, feeding, drinking and resting places are subject to high seasonal variability and can be spatially segregated at certain times of the year. In this context, animals adopt space-use, movement and activity strategies that allow them to minimize detrimental effects of the main limiting factors to reach, at different scales, suitable trade-offs between several constraints and needs that must be addressed simultaneously (Godvik et al., 2009; Massé and Côté, 2009).

Ungulates, like the vast majority of higher vertebrates, do not move erratically through the environment, but restrict their movements to sites much smaller in size than their locomotion capabilities allow, and which they mostly exploit over a long period. Based on this, Burt (1943) conceptualized the concept of home range as 'the area traversed by the individual in its normal activities of food gathering, mating, and caring for young'. The home range is thus the spatial result of the movements and behaviours that an individual (or a social group) expresses at different spatiotemporal scales to survive and reproduce, in other words to maximize its (their) selective value. The home range is a central concept

---

* The views expressed are solely those of the authors and do not necessarily represent the views of the institutions represented.

in ecology because it materializes a link between the movement of an animal and the resources necessary for its survival and reproduction.

In this chapter, we present the current state of knowledge on the space-use and feeding ecology of the African buffalo. This chapter also introduces some behavioural traits required for the comprehensiveness of this chapter, and which are further developed in other chapters. Most of what we know today about the behavioural ecology of savanna buffalo comes from studies focused on the Cape buffalo. In contrast, the ecology of the West and Central African savanna buffalo remains thus far poorly investigated. For this reason, and because several behavioural traits are similar within savanna buffalo subspecies, we present all savanna subspecies in one section, while the forest buffalo is the subject of a separate section.

Habitat

African buffalo live in a wide range of habitats, from open grasslands to rainforests, including all intermediate vegetation types: scrublands, woodlands and deciduous forests. African buffalo persist in semi-arid environments, as long as surface water is available within 20–40 km, year round (Cornélis et al., 2014).

Biomass or production of savanna ecosystems, such as buffalo populations, is positively correlated with mean annual rainfall and the soil quality (Coe et al., 1976; Sinclair, 1977; Grange and Duncan, 2006; Winnie et al., 2008). In similar water regime conditions, the nutrient content of vegetation and primary production are much lower on poor than on rich soils (Breman and De Wit, 1983; Le Houérou, 2008). The low biomass of wild ungulates in savanna ecosystems of West Africa (compared to those of volcanic areas in East Africa) mainly results from poorer soil conditions (Bell, 1982; East, 1984; Fritz, 1997).

Savanna Buffalo

Savanna buffalo are mainly found in habitats with a high herbaceous biomass. In eastern and southern Africa, suitable grasses for Cape buffalo are found in several types of woodland, such as mopane (*Colophospermum mopane*), miombo (*Brachystegia* spp.), acacia (*Acacia* spp.) and *Baikiaea* spp. In West and Central Africa, savanna buffalo live in a variety of habitats ranging from typical Sahelian shrub savannas (*Combretum* spp., *Terminalia* spp, *Acacia* spp.) to Sudanian woodlands (e.g. *Isoberlinia doka*, *Daniellia oliveri*, *Burkea africana*).

Forest Buffalo

Forest buffalo are forest-dwellers, inhabiting rainforests with grassy glades, watercourse areas and mosaics of equatorial forests and savannas. This subspecies is absent (or present at very low densities) in continuous forests (Blake, 2002; Melletti, Penteriani and Boitani, 2007; Melletti, 2008).

Suitable habitats for forest buffalo are mosaics of forest with equatorial savannas or clearings, which consist of grassy vegetation and shrubs (Reitsma, 1988; Blake, 2002). Blake (2002) at Noubale–Ndoki National Park (NP) found high buffalo abundance close to open grassy areas with low abundance in the closed canopy forest, suggesting it is unsuitable for forest buffalo. A significant relationship between buffalo and natural forest clearings was also reported at Dzanga–Ndoki NP, where clearings were the centre of buffalo home ranges. In addition, no signs of buffalo presence were recorded over 500 m from clearings (Melletti, Penteriani and Boitani, 2007; Melletti 2008). In Cameroon, buffalo rarely penetrated into the forest more than 300 m from logging roads, which were the main feeding sites for buffalo (Bekhuis et al., 2008).

Behaviour

Savanna Buffalo

African savanna buffalo are gregarious animals living in herds, and core members include adult females, subadults, juveniles and calves. Young females are known to maintain post-weaning bonds with their mother until the birth of their first calf, and probably longer. In contrast, young males gradually become independent, and are likely to form subadult male groups within the mixed herd. At the age of about 4–5 years (occasionally earlier), the males temporarily leave the herd to form bachelor groups of 2–20 individuals (sometimes more). The elder males (from about 10 years) sometimes permanently leave the herd, but this behaviour is not systematic (Sinclair, 1977; Prins, 1996). Adult males competing for females leave the herd once their body condition decreases. Bachelor groups spend more time foraging and recover physical condition by foraging on patches of habitat too small and sometimes too risky for the herd, such as dense riparian woodland (Prins, 1996; Turner et al., 2005; see Chapter 6 for more details).

Savanna buffalo herd size varies across their distribution from as few as 20 to as many as 2000 individuals in the floodplains of eastern and southern Africa (Sinclair, 1977; Prins, 1989, 1996). In West Africa (WAP Regional Park), the mean herd size was about 45 individuals when excluding bachelor males, and the largest herds were estimated to contain about 150 individuals (Cornélis et al., 2011). Similar figures were reported for Central African savanna buffalo, except in floodplain areas such as Zakouma NP (Chad), where herds up to 800 individuals were observed (D. Cornélis, personal observation).

Forest Buffalo

Forest buffalo form small and stable herds of 3–25 individuals (Melletti, Penteriani, Mirabile and Boitani, 2007; Korte, 2008b; Melletti, 2008). Herds generally comprise several adult females with their young and one or two bulls (Dalimier, 1955; Blake, 2002; Melletti, Penteriani and Boitani, 2007). In Lopé National Park, Gabon, the mean group size for the 18 herds was 12 ± 2 (range of means = 3–24; Korte, 2008a). Larger herds were shown to contain a higher proportion of open habitat within their home range.

Although observations of solitary individuals (males and females) were reported, there is no evidence of the occurrence of sexual segregation in herds. Males apparently access profitable resources all year long and do not leave the mixed herds to form bachelor groups.

Home Range and Movements

The African buffalo is generally considered a sedentary species. In buffalo, home range (HR) size and movements (either seasonal or daily) are related to the spatiotemporal distribution of key resources. As pointed out previously, space use tends to be largely constrained by access to water in most study locations.

Savanna Buffalo Subspecies

Savanna buffalo herds exhibit HRs that generally range between 50 and 350 km^2 (see Table 6.1 in Chapter 6). The larger HRs are generally observed in areas where resources are spatially segregated, which forces herds to undertake seasonal movements (see below). In contrast, males living in bachelor groups use smaller patches of habitat and form smaller HRs (0.5 and 4 km^2; Grimsdell, 1969; Sinclair, 1977; Taylor, 1985; Naidoo et al., 2012a).

In some systems, the HR size of mixed herds increases during the rainy season and decreases during the dry season (Naidoo et al., 2012b; Roug et al., 2020). During the rainy season, forage and water are abundant across the landscape and herds can move freely to find productive areas, whereas water availability often limits movement during the dry season, constraining buffalo to areas close to permanent water sources. In other systems that either have abundant natural surface water or extensive man-made water networks, buffalo HR sizes will increase during the dry season as they search for optimal foraging grounds (Ryan et al., 2006).

Some buffalo populations migrate between seasonal HRs (Cornélis et al., 2011; Bennitt et al., 2016; Sianga et al., 2017), although the exact migration pattern is not always consistent across years (Roug et al., 2020). Some buffalo populations were shown to undertake partial migration, meaning that within a group (or subpopulation), some will be migrant and others resident (Cornélis et al., 2011). Some groups exhibiting intermediate or partially migratory behaviour were qualified as 'expanders' (Naidoo et al., 2012b).

Naidoo et al. (2014) report several seasonal movements of buffalo from the Kavango–Zambezi Transfrontier Conservation Area (KAZA TFCA) that are the longest documented distances for this species. A female collared on the Kwando River floodplains in Namibia during the dry season moved 87 km west along the Caprivi Strip before returning to her dry season range, a round trip journey of >170 km. The following wet season, she again moved ~87 km south into Botswana, before returning to the same dry season range for a different >170 km journey.

The most frequent pattern of buffalo seasonal movements is the use of extensive upland woodland and savanna systems during the wet season, which support more abundant high-quality grasses. Once grasses and waterholes in wooded savannas have dried out, buffalo move to lowland habitats, such as extensive wetlands, riparian areas and lake shore grasslands where sufficient soil moisture for plant growth and green forage persists into the dry season (Vesey-FitzGerald, 1960; Taylor, 1985; Prins, 1996; Cornélis et al., 2011; Sianga et al., 2017). During drought years, buffalo resort to eating more productive and less digestible forage in the form of tall robust grasses and sedges and even reeds. They will resort to browsing in the absence of sufficient grass (Jarman and Jarman, 1973; Stark, 1986).

For example, in Ruaha National Park (Tanzania), Cape buffalo showed strong association with habitats near dry season water sources, whereas they were distributed widely across the park during the wet season (Roug et al., 2020). As cool drier seasons advance, herds may move progressively towards localized concentrations of remaining suitable grazing resources and water supplies, with increasing herd size.

In W Regional Park (Burkina Faso, Benin, Niger), the movements of seven West African savanna buffalo breeding herds were monitored using GPS collars (Cornélis et al., 2011). In the dry season, herds were shown to range close (within 5.3 ± 2.0 km, mean ± SD) to segments of permanent rivers. At the onset of the monsoon rains, all herds but one (which had year-round access to suitable resources along the Niger River) performed a larger (35 ± 10 km) south-west movement in response to a large-scale directional gradient of primary production. Furthermore, the establishment of wet season HRs appears conditioned by a threshold (~10 per cent) in the availability of perennial grasses, underlining the key role played by this resource for buffalo.

This was also observed for wet season ranges of buffalo in northern Botswana, where buffalo favoured areas >15 km from permanent water that have the highest cover of high-quality perennial grasses (Sianga et al., 2017). This is likely because leafy perennial grasses facilitate maximum intake for a large-bodied herbivore that relies on a tongue-sweep strategy to increase bite size.

Several recent studies based on GPS tracking have highlighted the occurrence of one-way movements over long distances, akin to dispersion. In the KAZA TFCA, two GPS-tracked females (among 30 females and five males tracked) undertook a long-range (~200 km) dispersal from the Kwando and Kavango Rivers in Namibia towards the Okavango Delta (Naidoo et al., 2014). In the Great Limpopo TFCA, a total of 66 GPS collars were deployed during 2008–2013 on females (47 adults, 19 subadults; Caron et al., 2016). Among this sample, three subadults were reported to leave the HR of their herd and disperse over 90 km.

Perhaps the most remarkable long-range movements came from female adult animals tagged in Mahango National Park, Namibia that exited via a break in the park fence in 2011. Numerous sightings of these animals suggest they moved as a group from north-eastern Botswana into Khaudum National Park. From there, the animals split into two groups, with one group observed in Angola near the Kavango River, around 250 km from where they had been ear-tagged. Another ear-tagged animal was eventually shot in an agricultural area in the Otjozondjupa Region in central Namibia. This location was a staggering 500 km from where she was tagged, far outside what is considered current buffalo range in Namibia (Martin, 2002).

Although the occurrence of large-amplitude dispersions is probably inherent to the spatial behaviour of some buffalo, it cannot be excluded at this stage of knowledge that some of these movements result from disorientation due to the anaesthesia required to fit the GPS collars.

Forest Buffalo Subspecies

HR data are limited for forest buffalo because there are few sites where direct observation is possible due to the forest habitat and the animal's elusive nature (Blake, 2002; Melletti, Penteriani, Mirabile and Boitani, 2007; Korte, 2008b). Melletti, Penteriani, Mirabile and Boitani (2007) report an HR of 8 km^2 for a herd of 24 buffalo at Danzga-Ndoki NP (Central African Republic). Based on seven radio-collared adult female forest buffalo at Lopé National Park, Gabon, over a two-year period (2002–2004), HRs of female forest buffalo averaged 4.6 km^2 with little HR range overlap (Korte, 2008b). Space use within HRs varies with season, with a preference for marshes during the wet season (September through February) and for forest in the dry season (March through August).

Forest buffalo HRs are thus much smaller than those of the savanna subspecies. It is likely that this pattern, common to all studies, results from the spatial arrangement of suitable resources in dense tropical forest, but also to less pronounced seasonality of the environment.

Activity Patterns

African buffalo display a large array of activity modes, including feeding, resting/ruminating, relocating between foraging areas, vigilance, wallowing and drinking. The relative proportions of these activity modes are mainly driven by spatiotemporal changes in the quality and availability of resources, interspecific competition, weather conditions and predation pressure (Sinclair, 1977; Prins, 1996; Ryan and Jordaan, 2005; Owen-Smith et al., 2010).

Savanna Buffalo Subspecies

Daily Movements

Previous investigations on the daily movement rates of buffalo herds (based on short-term sampling, radiotelemetry or path retracement) reported contrasted results. Taylor (1989) reported mean distances moved over a 24-hour period of <4 km compared to >6 km elsewhere (Sinclair, 1977; Conybeare, 1980). These authors reported that proximity of both food and water influence movements, and that bachelor males tend to move much less than herds. In South Africa (Kruger NP), buffalo herds were estimated to move 3.5 km per day during the dry season and 3.1 km during the wet season (Ryan and Jordaan, 2005). In contrast, in Cameroon (Benoué NP), Stark (1986) estimated a buffalo herd to travel on average 7.2 km per day during the rainy season and 5.6 km during the dry season.

More recently, Cornélis et al. (2011) showed that GPS-tracked adult female savanna buffalo ($n = 7$) in West Africa (W Regional Park) travelled on average 6.5 ± 0.5 km (mean ± SD) per day at an annual scale. Analyses showed no significant differences between herds. In contrast, analyses at a subannual scale globally emphasized interesting trends in movement speed. Daily speed peaked around the dry–wet season transition (8.4 ± 0.5 km), either during the late dry season phases or during the early wet season phases. Minimum daily values (4.8 ± 0.4 km) were observed in most herds during the phases corresponding to the late wet season or just after. The daily movement speed thus followed in all herds a decreasing pattern between dry–wet and wet–dry season transitions.

Similar patterns were reported in Ruaha NP, where daily movements of GPS-tracked herds averaged 4.6 km with the longest distances (mean 6.9 km) travelled during November at the end of the dry season and beginning of the wet season. The shortest daily distances (mean 3.6 km) travelled occurred in the wet season in April–June (Roug et al., 2020).

Grazing and Ruminating

Ruminant ungulates such as buffalo spend a large proportion of their time feeding, and must additionally allocate time to ruminating, which results in an overall total time (feeding + ruminating) of 70–80 per cent (Beekman and Prins, 1989; Prins, 1996). In savanna buffalo, most studies report feeding time accounting for 35–45 per cent of the 24-hour activity budget (Grimsdell and Field, 1976; Sinclair, 1977; Mloszewski, 1983; Stark, 1986; Prins, 1996; Winterbach and Bothma, 1998; Ryan and Jordaan, 2005; Bennitt, 2012).

Grazing most often takes place in the early morning and late afternoon, and during the first half of the night, suggesting that buffalo cease feeding during the hottest part of the day and during the coolest part of the night for thermoregulation purposes. Note that an exception to this feeding pattern was observed at Lake Manyara NP (Tanzania), with the main grazing bout occurring between 10:00 and 14:00 hours (Prins, 1996). In most studies, buffalo herds appear to spend an equal or greater proportion of time feeding at night than during the day (Sinclair, 1977; Taylor, 1985; Prins and Lason, 1989; Ryan and Jordaan, 2005). At a seasonal scale, most authors reported a trend towards more time spent feeding in the dry than the wet season in response to lower vegetation quality and quantity and decreased intake rates. Other modes of activity such as resting, rumination and vigilance are not mutually exclusive, thus making it hard to individualize ratios and to compare across studies.

Most studies reported average rumination times of around 30–35 per cent of the 24-hour activity budget (Sinclair, 1977; Prins, 1996; Winterbach and Bothma, 1998; Ryan and Jordaan, 2005). Seasonal trends in rumination time are the subject of debate; Sinclair (1977) reported that buffalo spend more time ruminating during the dry season, whereas Beekman and Prins (1989) found the opposite.

Thermoregulation

Buffalo generally cease feeding during the hottest part of the day and during the coolest part of the night for thermoregulation purposes. During the hottest hours of the day, mixed herds generally seek shade (Sinclair, 1977). Contrary to females and young, males generally wallow during the hottest time of the day for periods lasting up to three hours. This practice is more effective in temperature regulation than the use of shade (Sinclair, 1977).

In West Africa (WAP Regional Park), the daily activity patterns of buffalo herds were explored using biorhythm indices derived from GPS location data and activity sensors (Cornélis et al., 2011). At a daily scale, herds were equally active during night and day, and were mostly crepuscular, with two main active periods per day (dawn and dusk). Buffalo rested during the hottest hours of the day, and the duration of the resting bout was particularly marked during the hot dry season (Figure 5.1; Cornélis et al., 2014).

Water Resources and Drinking Activity

In many savanna regions of Africa, pronounced seasonal variability in rainfall results in wildlife being restricted to floodplains and other habitats adjacent to permanent surface water in the dry season. Nearly 100

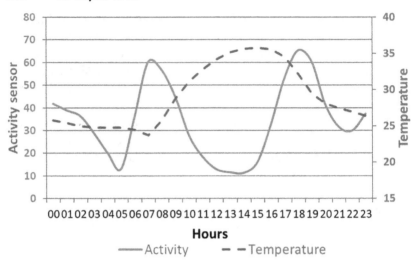

Figure 5.1 Average daily activity of a buffalo cow tracked in the WAP transfrontier conservation area (Burkina Faso, Benin, Niger) from March 2007 to February 2008 (using temperature and activity sensors embedded in the GPS collar). The first peak of activity started at dawn and the second finished after dusk, both lasting on average about 3–4 hours. Source: Cornélis, D. (2011). Ecologie du déplacement du buffle de savane ouest-africain (*Syncerus caffer brachyceros*). PhD, Université de Montpellier 2, Montpellier.

per cent of the biomass density of large water-dependent grazing herbivores has been found within a 15 km radius from surface water (Western, 1975). Nevertheless, while rarely quantified, ephemeral water sources far from permanent surface water also allow wildlife to exploit forage and other resources further afield, influencing their distribution, abundance and movement (Naidoo et al., 2020; Rumiano et al., 2021).

African buffalo are water-dependent: they can sweat profusely (Taylor, 1970), the water content of their faeces is high (about 80 per cent: Prins, 1996) and their body water turnover rate is high (King, 1979). They have to drink at least every two days, taking about 45 litres daily, and they are not able to survive on the moisture content of their food (Prins, 1996).

Previous studies on drinking reported contrasted hourly patterns. In Hwange NP (Zimbabwe), equipped with pumped artificial surface water supplies, Weir and Davidson (1965) found during the dry season that buffalo drank in the late afternoon (16:30–20:00) with a shorter peak early in the morning (08:30–10:30). In Kruger NP (South Africa), Ryan and Jordaan (2005) found two main periods of diurnal drinking (the early morning and mid-morning) and their observations suggest more time devoted to drinking during the day than at night. In contrast, Winterbach and Bothma (1998) found in Willem Pretorius game reserve (South Africa) that buffalo drank in the early afternoon. Grimsdell and Field (1976) also found that herds in Rwenzori NP (Uganda) drank in the mid-morning. In one study, buffalo were shown to modulate hourly drinking patterns according to the risk of predation by preferentially avoiding waterholes during high-risk hours of the day (dawn and dusk), when lions were likely to be in their vicinity (Valeix et al., 2009).

A detailed analysis of drinking behaviour was reported by Taylor (1989) in Matusadona NP (Zimbabwe), where Lake Kariba provides permanent water supplies for buffalo, in addition to seasonal rivers and pans that hold water in pools. During the hot dry season, herds drank once during the daytime, either around midday or between 16:00 and 19:00. The average drinking time took 20 minutes. In the wet season buffalo herds were a greater distance away from permanent water (mean 2.8 km) than during the dry season, when the mean distance from permanent water was 1.3 km. The converse held for seasonal water supplies. Buffalo herds were closer to these (1.5 km) in the wet season but further away in the dry season (2.4 km). This is to be expected because buffalo disperse during the wet season when abundant food and water resources are widespread, but concentrate on the lakeshore during the dry season where the only readily available food and water resources are present (Taylor, 1989).

For bachelor males, over 50 per cent of drinking bouts occurred between 10:00 and 14:00 with a peak from 11:00 to 12:00. Males drank throughout the day from before 06:00 until 20:00 and in the early morning hours at 02:00–03:00 (Taylor, 1989). During the wet season an individual may drink 2–3 times from the lake's edge, but usually once in the morning and once in the afternoon. During the cooler months, drinking during the day usually occurred only once, either late morning or at midday. As the hot season progressed, the number of drinking bouts increased to two or three in the morning and afternoon. Drinking bouts for individual males were, on average, of 1–3 minutes' duration.

Overall, however, in the literature reviewed, there appears to be no clear seasonal trends in drinking frequency among savanna buffalo.

Forest Buffalo Subspecies

Much less is known about the movement and activity of forest buffalo compared to savanna populations. In Dzanga–Ndoki NP (Central African

Republic), a study of a single buffalo herd showed that daily distances travelled by buffalo were generally very short (i.e. 500–1500 m) and were mainly restrained to clearings and surrounding areas (Melletti, 2008). The maximum distance travelled during a 24-hour tracking period was about 4000 m. Like savanna buffalo, forest buffalo wallow in the late afternoon; however, they spend more time in wallows during the dry season (Melletti, Penteriani, Mirabile and Boitani, 2007; Korte, 2008a).

Feeding Ecology

Buffalo are ruminants, essentially feeding on grass and roughage. This species is capable of subsisting on pastures too coarse and too tall for most other herbivores (Bothma, 2002), and as a 'bulk grazer' they ingest around 2.2 per cent of their body mass daily. This represents on average 6.5 kg for a forest buffalo of 300 kg, 11 kg for a West or Central African buffalo of 500 kg and 15 kg for a Cape buffalo of 700 kg.

Buffalo are very efficient grazers (their adapted dentition and a mobile tongue allowing the ingestion of high quantities of grass in a short amount of time). Optimal feeding conditions for buffalo prevail when the grass forms swards and leaf heights reach and exceed 10 cm, as in flood plains or in forest glades (Prins, 1996). However, buffalo cannot cut pastures as short as other species. The African buffalo thus occupies an important niche, opening up habitats that are preferred by short-grass grazers (Prins, 1996; Estes, 1991). Their primary competitors are cattle *Bos taurus*, African elephant *Loxodonta africana*, plains zebra *Equus quagga* and wildebeest *Connochaetes taurinus* (Sinclair, 1977; de Boer and Prins, 1990; Plumptre and Harris, 1995; Prins, 1996).

Savanna (Cape, West and Central African) Buffalo

In savanna buffalo, optimal dietary conditions occur during the rainy season, while the end of the long dry season is a period of food scarcity (both in quantity and quality; Prins and Sinclair, 2013). Detailed diet studies conducted in eastern and southern Africa indicated that buffalo are resource limited and constrained by a minimum dietary protein concentration of 7–8 per cent to make fermentation in the rumen possible (Sinclair, 1977; Prins, 1996). In such a situation, buffalo thus face a trade-off of quality and quantity in obtaining an appropriate protein-to-fibre ratio in their diet (Redfern et al., 2006; Ryan et al., 2012). During the dry season, savanna buffalo are generally forced to become more selective, and to partially switch their diet to browse (see below). Despite this, buffalo were reported to live at or below nitrogen requirements for prolonged periods, accounting for visibly losing body condition (Prins, 1989; Ryan, 2006; Ryan et al., 2012). In natural ungulate communities, the regulation of populations is driven by two processes: a control by available food resources ('bottom-up regulation') on the one hand, and a control by predation ('top down' regulation) on the other (Hunter and Price, 1992). In the case of savanna buffalo, most authors agree that resources play a dominant role in the regulation of populations (Sinclair et al,. 2003; Hopcraft et al., 2010).

There is moderate consensus in feeding studies on Cape buffalo about the preferred grass species. Usually species that are avoided contain low nutritious quality or the presence of aromatic oils (Prins, 1996). During the dry season, usual food resources are of poor quality, due to lignifications and high standing biomass. During this period, floodplain species (e.g. *Leersia hexandra*) and riverine forest species (e.g. *Setaria sphacelata*) become important. In areas with upwelling groundwater, species such as *Cyperus laevigatus* may also form a mainstay in the dry season (Prins and Sinclair, 2013). Buffalo prefer grasses such as *Cynodon dactylon*, but may also eat broad-leaved grasses, such as *Panicum maximum*. Sinclair, in the Serengeti, reported that buffalo preferred soft, nutritious grass such as *Digitaria macroblephora*. Although there is little information on seasonal changes on diet, Sinclair (1977) analysed stomach contents and showed that Cape buffalo select more grass leaf at the end of the rainy season. Finally, Taylor (1985) found that grasslands dominated by *Panicum repens* were the best habitat on the shores of Lake Kariba (Matusadona NP, Zimbabwe). In Cape buffalo, the diet of the different age/sex classes does not appear to differ and dry matter food intake ranges between 1.2 per cent and 3.5 per cent of body mass, similarly to other ruminants, but subject to food quality (Sinclair, 1977; Prins and Beekman, 1989).

Few studies investigated the feeding ecology of West and Central African buffalo. In West Africa (WAP Regional Park), habitat selection analysis emphasized the importance of perennial grasses (e.g. *Andropogon gayanus*; Cornélis et al., 2011). In this study, a gradient in primary production appeared to determine large-scale movements of herds at the onset of the wet season, but its action clearly was modulated by the proportion of perennials available. Buffalo herds were shown to establish early wet season HRs at locations where this proportion reached a 9 per cent threshold. At Benoué NP (Cameroon), Stark (1986) similarly reported a very high proportion of grasses in the diet, particularly *Andropogon gayanus*, which represented 51 per cent of the volume ingested in the dry season, versus 40 per cent in the wet season. At Zakouma NP (Chad), Gillet (1969) noted a preference for *Setaria anceps* (particularly new shoots after fire) and *Andropogon gayanus*, but also *Vetiveria nigritana*. In the dry season, the unburned straws of *Echinochloa obtusiflora* appeared to be preferred.

Savanna buffalo are primarily grazers, but partially switch to browse when grasses become tall and lignified (Field, 1972; Leuthold, 1972; Sinclair, 1977; Mloszewski, 1983; Hashim, 1987; Prins, 1996). Shrub and tree leaves have been shown to contain higher protein (nitrogen) content than dry grasses during the dry season (Kone et al., 1990; Prins, 1996). As mentioned above, the contribution of nitrogen from browse facilitates the fermentation of fibrous grass in the rumen, which they eat in high quantities during the dry season. According to Estes (1991), the browse can represent up to 5 per cent of the total diet, but higher figures were reported in several sites (e.g. 26 per cent in dry season in Cameroon; Taylor, 1985). A wide range of species of shrubs and trees are consumed throughout African savanna, including *Grewia* spp., *Heeria* spp., *Colophospermum mopane*, *Combretum* spp., *Capparis* spp. and *Piliostigma* spp. (Pienaar, 1969; Jarman, 1971; De Graaf et al., 1973; Taylor and Walker, 1978; Ryan, 2006). In drier habitats in the Eastern Cape, buffalo appear to be adapted to eat woody species because grassy vegetation is scarce. In this particular habitat, during the dry season, up to 33 per cent of their diet comprises species such as *Acacia* sp., *Plumbago* sp. and *Grewia* sp.

In some areas buffalo can maintain or create 'grazing lawns' if the feeding interval is short enough (Prins, 1996). Evidence of this 'returning' behaviour has also been described for buffalo in Kruger NP and Klaserie Private Nature Reserve in South Africa (Bar-David et al., 2009). They may also create favourable lawns in conjunction with other large herbivores such as elephants at Lake Rukwa, Tanzania (Vesey-FitzGerald, 1960) and Benoué NP in central Cameroon (H. H. T. Prins, personal observation).

Geophagy has been reported at several sites, where clay or substrates rich in iron may explain this preference. On Mount Kenya, geophagy is reported in the bamboo belt (2100–3000 m), where clay soils are rich in iron and aluminium (Grimshaw et al., 1995). This rare activity is carried out mainly by solitary individuals on Mount Kenya (Mahaney, 1987). In Lent Valley in Kilimanjaro, buffalo enter into caves rich in sodium bicarbonate and chew off the soda deposits.

Forest Buffalo

Few data exist on the feeding ecology of forest buffalo because direct observations are rarely feasible in rainforest habitats. Blake (2002) in Noubale–Ndoki NP and Melletti (2008) in Dzanga–Ndoki NP observed buffalo feeding mainly on Poaceae and Cyperaceae within clearings, in particular on *Rhyncospora corymbosa*, *Kyllinga* sp. and *Cyperus* sp. Blake (2002) also recorded several species of Marantaceae, including *Marantochloa purpurea*, *M. cordifolia*, *M. filipes* and *Halopegia azurea*. In addition, species of the Commelinaceae family such as *Commelina diffusa* and *Palisota brachythyrsa* and a species of algae (*Spirogyra* sp.) were recorded. Melletti (2008) also found indirect signs of feeding activity on *Commelina* sp and *Palisota* sp. in the understory of *Gilbertodendrum dewevrei* mono-dominant forest.

Bekhuis et al. (2008) used micro-histological faecal analysis in a two-month study to determine the diet of forest buffalo at Campo-Ma'an NP in southern Cameroon. They found that the most important part of the diet was composed of graminoids (43 per cent, with *Leptochloa caerulescens* representing 15 per cent of the total diet), non-graminoid monocots (21 per cent, mainly Commelinaceae such as *Palisota* spp.), dicotyledoneous plants (33 per cent, mainly leaves) and cryptogamous plants (3 per cent). The composition of the diet suggests that the buffalo fed mainly along logging roads and river banks (Bekhuis et al., 2008). Using a similar method at Lopé NP (Gabon), Lustenhouwer (2008) and van der Hoek et al. (2013) found that the majority of plants consumed by forest buffalo were monocotyledons, primarily grasses (Poaceae) and sedges (Cyperaceae), with a low portion of dicotyledonous plants in the diet. In the same study area, van der Hoek et al. (2013) emphasized the importance of savanna habitat, noting that controlled burning is a key tool for maintaining open areas.

Thus far, no evidence of the existence of grazing lawns was found in the different studies focused on the feeding ecology of forest buffalo, even in areas of high density such as Lopé NP (L. Korte and M. Melletti, personal observations).

Conclusion

The African buffalo is endowed with an amazing adaptability, which probably explains why this species is one of the most successful large African mammals in terms of geographical distribution, abundance and biomass. On an evolutionary scale, African buffalo have adapted their phenotype across their distribution range, which covers almost all natural ecosystems south of the Sahara. For example, the mass ratio between the large Cape buffalo and the small forest buffalo is about 2.7 to 1. With the exception of the elephant, few species have an equivalent mass range across their distribution area. The African buffalo has also managed to adapt its behaviour to the different ecosystems in which it lives. For example, in dense tropical forests where food resources are scarce and aggregated, the African buffalo forms small herds of 5–20 animals. In contrast, in the rich pastures of the savanna floodplains, the African buffalo can gather in herds of up to 2000 animals.

The space-use behaviour of buffalo herds also differs strongly according to the spatial arrangement of resources. In areas where buffalo access profitable resources all year long, the herds settle in home ranges of a few square kilometres. In contrast, in areas where resources are spatially segregated, buffalo occupy home ranges of several hundreds of square kilometres. In some regions, buffalo undertake seasonal movements of several dozen kilometres. Such migrations may be only partial within a population, meaning that it is not undertaken by all herds.

At a seasonal and daily scale, buffalo are also able to modulate their social behaviour within the herd according to the availability of resources. The herd splits into subgroups and reforms within the contours of a long-lasting (multiannual) home range, according to mechanisms that remain largely unexplored (Chapter 6). Finally, within their seasonal home range, we also saw that buffalo can regulate their diet and activity patterns according to the quality and quantity of food resources, as well as according to abiotic factors such as temperature.

Thus, despite reported regional declines in buffalo population numbers due, inter alia, to climate change, habitat fragmentation, livestock development and diseases, the species may be flexible enough to adapt to the wide range of challenges it faces and will face in the coming decades.

References

Bailey, D.W., J.E. Gross, E.A. Laca, et al. (1996). Mechanisms that result in large herbivore grazing distribution patterns. *Journal of Range Management* **49**: 386–400.

Bar-David, S., I. Bar-David, P.C. Cross, et al. (2009). Methods for assessing movement path recursion with application of African buffalo in South Africa. *Ecology Letters* **90**: 2467–2479.

Beekman, J.H. and H.H.T. Prins (1989). Feeding strategies of sedentary large herbivores in East Africa, with emphasis on the African buffalo (*Syncerus caffer*). *African Journal of Ecology* **27**(2): 129–147.

Bekhuis, P.D.B.M., C.B. Jong, and H.H.T. Prins (2008). Diet selection and density estimates of forest buffalo in Campo-Ma'an National Park, Cameroon. *African Journal of Ecology* **46**: 668–675.

Bell, R.H.V. (1982). The effect of soil nutrient availability on community structure in African ecosystems. In B.J. Huntley and B.H. Walker (Eds.), *Ecology of Tropical Savannas*. Berlin: Springer-Verlag, pp. 193–216.

Bennitt, E. (2012). *The Ecology of African Buffalo (Syncerus caffer) in the Okavango Delta, Botswana*. PhD dissertation, School of Biological Sciences, University of Bristol, UK.

Bennitt, E., M.C. Bonyongo, and S. Harris (2016). Effects of divergent migratory strategies on access to resources for Cape buffalo (*Syncerus caffer caffer*). *Journal of Mammalogy* **97**(6): 1682–1698.

Blake, S. (2002). Forest buffalo prefer clearings to closed-canopy forest in the primary forest of northern Congo. *Oryx* **36**(1): 81–86.

Bothma, J.d.P. (2002). *Game Ranch Management*. Edited by J.P. du Bothma. 4th. ed. Pretoria: Van Schaik.

Breman, H. and C. De Wit (1983). Rangeland productivity and exploitation in the Sahel. *Science* **221**(4618): 1341.

Burt, W. (1943). Territoriality and home range concepts as applied to mammals. *Journal of Mammalogy* **24**(3): 346–352.

Caron, A., D. Cornélis, C. Foggin, et al. (2016). African buffalo movement and zoonotic disease risk across Transfrontier Conservation Areas, Southern Africa. *Emerging Infectious Diseases* **22**(2): 277.

Coe, M.J., D.H. Cumming, and J. Phillipson (1976). Biomass and production of large African herbivores in relation to rainfall and primary production. *Oecologia* **22**(4): 341–354.

Conybaere, A. (1980). Buffalo numbers, home range and daily movement in the Sengwa Research area, Zimbabwe. *South African Journal of Wildlife Research* **10**: 89–93.

Cornélis, D., S. Benhamou, G. Janeau, et al. (2011). Spatiotemporal dynamics of forage and water resources shape space use of West African savanna buffaloes. *Journal of Mammalogy* **92**(6): 1287–1297.

Cornélis, D., M. Melletti, L. Korte, et al. (2014). African buffalo (*Syncerus caffer*). In M Melletti and J. Burton (Eds.), *Ecology, Evolution and Behaviour of Wild Cattle: Implications for Conservation*. Cambridge: Cambridge University Press, pp. 326–372.

Dalimier, P. (1955). *Les buffles du Congo Belge*. Bruxelles: Institut des Parcs Nationaux du Congo Belge.

de Boer, W.F. and H.H.T. Prins (1990). Large herbivores that strive mightily but eat and drink. *Oecologia* **82**: 264–274.

De Graaf, G., K. Schultz,and P. van der Waet (1973). Notes on rumen contents of Cape buffalo *Syncerus caffer* in the Addo Elephant National Park. *Koedoe* **16**(1): 45–58.

East, R. (1984). Rainfall, soil nutrient status and biomass of large African savanna mammals. *African Journal of Ecology* **22**(4): 245–270.

Estes, R.D. (1991). *The Behavior Guide to African Mammals*. Berkeley: University of California Press.

Field, C. (1972). The food habits of wild ungulates in Uganda by analyses of stomach contents. *African Journal of Ecology* **10**(1): 17–42.

Fritz, H. (1997). Low ungulate biomass in west African savannas: primary production or missing megaherbivores or large predator species? *Ecography* **20**(4): 417–421.

Fryxell, J.M., J.F. Wilmshurst, and A.R.E. Sinclair (2004). Predictive models of movement by serengeti grazers. *Ecology* **85**(9): 2429–2435.

Gillet, H. (1969). La végétation du parc national de Zakouma (Tchad) et ses rapports avec les grands mammifères. *La Terre et la Vie* **4**: 373–485.

Godvik, I.M., L.E. Loe, J.O. Vik, et al. (2009). Temporal scales, trade-offs, and functional responses in red deer habitat selection. *Ecology Letters* **90**: 699–710.

Grange, S. and P. Duncan (2006). Bottom up and top down processes in African ungulate communities: resources and predation acting on the relative abundance of zebra and grazing bovids. *Ecography* **29**(6): 899–907.

Grimsdell, J. (1969). *Ecology of the Buffalo, Syncerus caffer, in Western Uganda.* PhD dissertation, Cambridge University.

Grimsdell, J. and C. Field (1976). Grazing patterns of buffaloes in the Rwenzori National Park, Uganda. *African Journal of Ecology* **14**(4): 339–344.

Grimshaw, J., N. Cordeiro, and C. Foley (1995). The mammals of Kilimanjaro. *Journal of East African Natural History* **84**(2): 105–139.

Hashim, I. (1987). Relationship between biomass of forage used and masses of faecal pellets of wild animals in meadows of the Dinder National Park. *African Journal of Ecology* **25**(4): 217–223.

Hopcraft, J.G.C., H. Olff, and A. Sinclair (2010). Herbivores, resources and risks: alternating regulation along primary environmental gradients in savannas. *Trends in Ecology & Evolution* **25**(2): 119–128.

Hunter, M.D. and P.W. Price (1992). Playing chutes and ladders: heterogeneity and the relative roles of bottom-up and top-down forces in natural communities. *Ecology* **73**(3): 723–732.

Jarman, M. and P. Jarman (1973). Daily activity of impala. *African Journal of Ecology* **11**(1): 75–92.

Jarman, P. (1971). Diets of large mammals in the woodlands around Lake Kariba, Rhodesia. *Oecologia* **8**(2): 157–178.

King, J. (1979). Game domestication for animal production in Kenya: field studies of the body-water turnover of game and livestock. *The Journal of Agricultural Science* **93**(1): 71–79.

Kone, A., D. Richard, and H. Guerin (1990). Teneurs en constituants pariétaux et en matières azotées des ligneux fourragers d'Afrique occidentale. Seizième congrès international des herbages, Versailles.

Korte, L. (2008a). Habitat selection at two spatial scales and diurnal activity patterns of adult female forest buffalo. *Journal of Mammalogy* **89**: 115–125.

Korte, L. (2008b). Variation of group size among African buffalo herds in a forest–savanna mosaic landscape. *Journal of Zoology* **275**: 229–236.

Le Houérou, H.N. (2008). *Bioclimatology and Biogeography of Africa.* Berlin: Springer Verlag.

Leuthold, W. (1972). Home range, movements, and food of a buffalo herd in Tsavo National Park. *East African Wildlife Journal* **10**: 237–243.

Lustenhouwer, I. (2008). *Diet Composition and Parasite Occurrence in the Forest Buffalo (Syncerus caffer nanus) in Lopé National Park, Gabon.* Thesis, Resource Ecology Group, Wageningen University.

Mahaney, W.C. (1987). Behaviour of the African buffalo on Mount Kenya. *African Journal of Ecology* **25**: 199–202.

Martin, M. (2002). *Species Management Plan for Southern Savanna Buffalo (Syncerus caffer caffer).* Windhoek: Ministry of Environment and Tourism (Namibia).

Massé, A. and S.D. Côté (2009). Habitat selection of a large herbivore at high density and without predation: trade-off between forage and cover? *Journal of Mammalogy* **90**: 961–970.

Melletti, M. (2008). *Habitat Use and Behaviour of Forest Buffalo (Syncerus caffer nanus) in Dzanga–Ndoki National Park, Central African Republic.* PhD dissertation, University of Rome, 'La Sapienza', Italy, and Department of Conservation Biology, E.B.D., C.S.I.C. Seville, Spain.

Melletti, M., V. Penteriani, and L. Boitani (2007). Habitat preferences of the secretive forest buffalo (*Syncerus caffer nanus*) in Central Africa. *Journal of Zoology* **271**: 178–186.

Melletti, M., V. Penteriani, M. Mirabile, and L. Boitani (2007). Some behavioral aspects of forest buffalo (*Syncerus caffer nanus*): from herd to individual. *Journal of Mammalogy* **88**(5): 1312–1318.

Mloszewski, M.J. (1983). *The Behavior and Ecology of the African Buffalo.* Cambridge: Cambridge University Press.

Naidoo, R., A. Brennan, A.C. Shapiro, et al. (2020). Mapping and assessing the impact of small-scale ephemeral water sources on wildlife in an African seasonal savannah. *Ecological Applications* **30**(8): e02203.

Naidoo, R., P. Du Preez, G. Stuart-Hill, et al. (2014). Long-range migrations and dispersals of African buffalo (*Syncerus caffer*) in the Kavango–Zambezi Transfrontier Conservation area. *African Journal of Ecology* **52**: 12163.

Naidoo, R., P. Du Preez, G. Stuart-Hill, et al. (2012a). Home on the range: factors explaining partial migration of African buffalo in a tropical environment. *PLoS One* **7**(5): e36527.

Naidoo, R., P.D. Preez, G. Stuart-Hill, et al. (2012b). Factors affecting intraspecific variation in home range size of a large African herbivore. *Landscape Ecology* **27**: 1523–1534.

Owen-Smith, N., J.M. Fryxell, and E.H. Merrill (2010). Foraging theory upscaled: the behavioural ecology of herbivore movement. *Philosophical Transactions of the Royal Society B: Biological Sciences* **365**: 2267–2278.

Pienaar, U.V. (1969). Observations on developmental biology, growth and some aspects of the population ecology of African buffalo (*Syncerus caffer caffer* Sparrman) in the Kruger National Park. *Koedoe* **12**: 29–52.

Plumptre, A. and S. Harris (1995). Estimating the biomass of large mammalian herbivores in a tropical montane forest: a method of faecal counting that avoids assuming a 'steady state' system. *Journal of Applied Ecology* **32**(1): 111–120.

Prins, H.H.T. (1989). Buffalo herd structure and its repercussions for condition of individual African buffalo cows. *Ethology* **81**: 47–71.

Prins, H.H.T. (1996). *Ecology and Behaviour of the African Buffalo.* London: Chapman & Hall.

Prins, H.H.T. and J.H. Beekman (1989). A balanced diet as a goal of grazing: the food of the Manyara buffalo. *African Journal of Ecology* **27**: 241–259.

Prins, H.H.T. and G.R. Lason. (1989). Dangerous lions and nonchalant buffalo. *Behaviour* **108**: 262–296.

Prins, H. and A. Sinclair (2013). The African buffalo: species profile. In M.H. Knight, J. Kingdon, and M. Hoffmann (Eds.), *Mammals of Africa. Pigs, Hippopotamuses, Chevrotain, Giraffes, Deer and Bovids.* London: Bloomsbury, pp. 125–136.

Redfern, J., S. Ryan, and W. Getz (2006). Defining herbivore assemblages in the Kruger National Park: a correlative coherence approach. *Oecologia* **146**(4): 632–640.

Reitsma, J. (1988). Forest vegetation of Gabon. Tropenbos Technical Series (Netherlands).

Roug, A., E.A. Muse, D.L. Clifford, et al. (2020). Seasonal movements and habitat use of African buffalo in Ruaha National Park, Tanzania. *BMC Ecology* **20**(1): 1–13.

Rumiano, F., C. Gaucherel, P. Degenne, et al. (2021). Combined use of remote sensing and spatial modelling: when surface water impacts buffalo (*Syncerus caffer caffer*) movements in savanna environments. *International Archives of the Photogrammetry, Remote Sensing and Spatial Information Sciences* **43**(B3–2021): 631–638.

Ryan, S.J. (2006). *Spatial Ecology of African Buffalo* (Syncerus caffer) *and Their Resources in a Savanna Landscape.* PhD dissertation, University of California.

Ryan, S.J., P.C. Cross, J. Winnie, et al. (2012). The utility of normalized difference vegetation index for predicting African buffalo forage quality. *The Journal of Wildlife Management* **76**: 1499–1508.

Ryan, S.J. and W. Jordaan (2005). Activity patterns of African buffalo (*Syncerus caffer*) in the Lower Sabie region, Kruger National Park, South Africa. *Koedoe* **48**(2): 117–124.

Ryan, S., C. Knechtel, and W. Getz (2006). Seasonal and interannual variation in the home range and habitat selection of African buffalo (*Syncerus caffer*) in the Klaserie Private Nature Reserve, South Africa. *Journal of Wildlife Management* **70**: 764–776.

Sianga, K., R.W. Fynn, and M.C. Bonyongo (2017). Seasonal habitat selection by African buffalo Syncerus caffer in the Savuti–Mababe–Linyanti ecosystem of northern Botswana. *Koedoe: African Protected Area Conservation and Science* **59**(2): 1–10.

Sinclair, A. (1977). *The African Buffalo. A Study of Resource Limitation of Populations.* Chicago: University of Chicago Press.

Sinclair, A., S. Mduma, and J.S. Brashares (2003). Patterns of predation in a diverse predator–prey system. *Nature* **425**(6955): 288–290.

Stark, M.A. (1986). Daily movement, grazing activity and diet of savanna buffalo, *Syncerus caffer brachyceros* in Benoue National Park, Cameroon. *African Journal of Ecology* **24**: 255–262.

Taylor, C.R. (1970). Dehydration and heat: effects on temperature regulation of East African ungulates. *American Journal of Physiology – Legacy Content* **219**(4): 1136–1139.

Taylor, R.D. (1985). *The Response of Buffalo,* Syncerus caffer *(Sparrman) to the Kariba Lakeshore Grassland (*Panicum repens *L.) in Matusadona National Park.* PhD dissertation, University of Zimbabwe.

Taylor, R.D. (1989). Buffalo and their food resources: the exploitation of Kariba lakeshore pastures. *Symposia of the Zoological Society of London* **61**: 51–71.

Taylor, R.D. and B. Walker (1978). Comparisons of vegetation use and herbivore biomass on a Rhodesian game and cattle ranch. *Journal of Applied Ecology* **15**: 565–581.

Turner, W.C., A.E. Jolles, and N. Owen-Smith (2005). Alternating sexual segregation during the mating season by male African buffalo (*Syncerus caffer*). *Journal of Zoology* **267**(03): 291.

Valeix, M., H. Fritz, A.J. Loveridge, et al. (2009). Does the risk of encountering lions influence African herbivore behaviour at waterholes? *Behavioral Ecology and Sociobiology* **63**(10): 1483–1494.

van der Hoek, Y., I. Lustenhouwer, K.J. Jeffery and P. van Hooft (2013). Potential effects of prescribed savannah burning on the diet selection of forest buffalo (*Syncerus caffer nanus*) in Lopé National Park, Gabon. *African Journal of Ecology* **51**(1): 94–101.

Vesey-FitzGerald, D.F. (1960). Grazing succession among East African game animals. *Journal of Mammalogy* **41**(2): 161–172.

Weir, J. and E. Davidson (1965). Daily occurrence of African game animals at water holes during dry weather. *African Zoology* **1**(2): 353–368.

Western, D. (1975). Water availability and its influence on the structure and dynamics of a savannah large mammal community. *African Journal of Ecology* **13**(3–4): 265–286.

Winnie, J.A., P. Cross, and W. Getz (2008). Habitat quality and heterogeneity influence distribution and behavior in African buffalo (*Syncerus caffer*). *Ecology* **89**(5): 1457–1468.

Winterbach, H.E.K. and J.D. Bothma (1998). Activity patterns of the Cape buffalo *Syncerus caffer caffer* in the Willem Pretorius Game Reserve, Free State. *South African Journal of Wildlife Research* **28**(3): 73–81.

6 · *African Buffalo Social Dynamics: What Is a Buffalo Herd?*

A. CARON, E. BENNITT, E. WIELGUS,
D. CORNELIS, E. MIGUEL AND
M. DE GARINE-WICHATITSKY

Introduction

The ecology of the African buffalo (*Syncerus caffer*) has been the focus of extensive research studies over the past 50 years (Grimsdell, 1969; Sinclair, 1977; Taylor, 1985; Prins, 1996), including some more observational ones (e.g. Mloszewski, 1983). The species' grouping patterns have historically been described as follows: *mixed or breeding herds* constitute the main social units, consisting of adult females, weaned and subadult individuals of both sexes (subadults are between 3 and 5 years of age) and a small proportion of adult males; *bachelor groups* gather males (two or more) 4 years of age and above; they gravitate around mixed herds, joining them mainly for mating and leaving them to escape intra-species and gender competition and to improve their resource offtake efficiency until the next mating opportunity (Prins, 1996; Turner et al., 2005). Bachelor groups tend to have a transient composition, with individuals associating for periods ranging between a few hours and several months. Bachelor groups can interact with several mixed herds ensuring gene flow at the inter-herd level (Van Hoof et al., 2003; Halley and Mari, 2004; Turner et al., 2005). The mixed/breeding herd is classically defined by its home range, which has little interannual variation, and on which it interacts with bachelor groups, and a static and stable group size often affected by temporary and seasonal fusion–fission patterns (Prins, 1989a; Cross et al., 2004; Tambling et al., 2012). However, some aspects of this planet- and satellite-like framework have recently been challenged by observational studies.

In addition, the lack of a clear set of definitions regarding the entities composing buffalo assemblages prevent a clear and comparative approach. For example, two mixed herds can be described as either fusing or as one 'herd' being joined by another 'group' or 'subgroup', and the new entity is sometimes called a 'large or mega herd'. The complexity associated with reliably and accurately identifying individual buffalo within large groups and regularly estimating the number of individuals associated with a focal animal (e.g. followed by telemetry) explains the difficulty with understanding group/individual dynamics within mixed herds. In this chapter, we will present a revised conceptual framework for buffalo social systems based on recent knowledge and interpretation. This conceptual framework will present the facts and hypotheses and highlight the gaps in knowledge to map the way forward in our understanding of African buffalo social dynamics.

Mixed Herds of African Buffalo

Mixed or *breeding herd* of African buffalo are the common terms used for a group of buffalo with a core social unit consisting of adult females. We will start by reviewing recent data from telemetry studies to shed light on what is known and unknown about these mixed herds.

A Mixed Herd is Composed of Adult Females Sharing a Home Range

In Gonarezhou National Park (GNP), Zimbabwe in 2008–2009, nine adult female *Syncerus caffer caffer* were equipped with GPS collars in four presumably different groups spotted from a helicopter (1, 2, 3 and 3 individuals in each group, respectively). Animals of these age and sex categories are expected to be most strongly bound to mixed herds (Sinclair, 1977; Prins, 1996; Fortin et al., 2009; but see Cross et al., 2004, 2005). The GPS acquired hourly locations over 405 days. The annual home range (HR) was computed (up to the 0.95 isopleth) for each collared individual using a movement-based kernel density estimation method (Benhamou and Cornélis, 2010). HR overlap between individuals was estimated using Bhattacharyya's affinity index (Benhamou et al., 2014). When displayed together (Figure 6.1), the HR of the nine females captured in four groups cluster easily in two HRs, which define the HRs of two mixed herds. Individual HRs strongly overlap within each mixed herd (74.4–80 per cent; and 59.3–68.6 per cent).

Observations from GNP were included in a larger study based on 47 adult female buffalo from three national parks (NPs) in Zimbabwe and

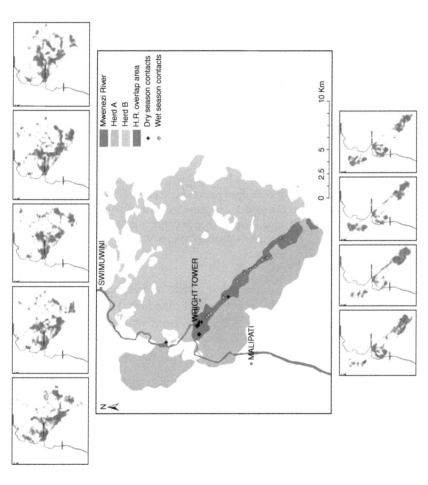

Figure 6.1 In yellow–reddish gradient, nine individual adult females African buffalo annual home range (HR) captured in Gonarezhou NP, Zimbabwe in 2008; central larger map, HR of the two mixed herds after superposition of individual HR. Source: Author.

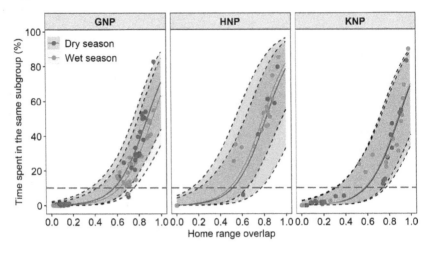

Figure 6.2 Relationship between the time spent in the same subgroup and HR overlap among pairs of *Syncerus caffer caffer*, *n* = 47 adult female buffalo from Gonarezhou, Kruger and Hwange NPs (Zimbabwe, South Africa); points represent the observed values for each dyad per year and per season. Solid lines represent the predictions from the model, and grey dashed lines represent 95 per cent confidence intervals. Horizontal blue dashed line indicates the cut-off value of 10 per cent of time spent in the same subgroup. (From Wielgus et al., 2020.)

South Africa, which confirmed that adult female buffalo belonging to the same mixed herds shared at least 60 per cent of their HR. However, when observing adult female dyad dynamics (i.e. collared adult females two by two) within each mixed herd, the proportion of time spent together (simultaneous locations within 1000 m) in relation to HR overlap remained highly variable between dyads (Figure 6.2; Wielgus et al., 2020). In GNP and Kruger NP (KNP), females sharing between 60 per cent and 80 per cent of their HR spent, respectively, between 10–40 per cent and 10–70 per cent of their time together in each park. Cross et al. (2004, 2005) found similar patterns of fusion–fission dynamics within mixed herds.

In the Okavango Delta (OD), Botswana, hourly GPS data were collected from 15 buffalo cows between 2007 and 2010. Based on HR overlap, two mixed herds were identified, one resident and the other migratory (Bennitt et al., 2018). Analysis using the methods of Wielgus et al. (2020) showed that buffalo dyads with approximately 30–90 per cent HR overlap spent between 3 per cent and 80 per cent of their time within 1000 m of each other. These data fit well with the definition of a mixed herd being composed of individuals sharing the same HR (Sinclair, 1977).

Mixed Herds' Home Range Overlap is Generally Small

The African buffalo is usually considered a non-territorial species, but studies investigating space sharing between neighbouring mixed herds have reported contrasting results. At Lake Manyara NP, Tanzania (Prins, 1996), in Chobe NP, Botswana (Halley et al., 2002), at Klaserie Private Nature Reserve, South Africa (Ryan et al., 2006) and in Niassa National Reserve, Mozambique (Prins, personal communication), herds tended to occupy distinct and exclusive HRs with little overlap. In contrast, in Rwenzori NP, Uganda (Grimsdell, 1969) and Sengwa Wildlife Research Area, Zimbabwe (Conybeare, 1980), a large spatial overlap has been reported between HRs of neighbouring mixed herds (but these may have been offshoots of mixed herds). Seasonal changes in the use of space between neighbouring mixed herds and their temporal dynamics, however, are less understood.

Recently, the use of GPS technology on adult females has provided more accurate measures of the temporal dynamics between neighbouring herds. In a West African buffalo population living in W Regional Park, Niger, two neighbouring herds had very little direct contact within a 500-m spatial window, and for less than an hour despite the quite large overlap (21 per cent) of their HRs (Cornélis et al., 2011). In KNP and GNP, HR overlaps between individuals belonging to different mixed herds were very small, ranging from 3 per cent to 8 per cent (Figure 6.1). These results are in agreement with observations in Manyara NP, Tanzania (Prins, 1996). A recent study based on long-term GPS-tracking of adult females in KNP and the OD has confirmed strong spatial segregation of HRs of neighbouring Cape buffalo herds, and short-term behavioural avoidance (Wielgus et al., 2021). Cape buffalo formed relatively distinct herds occupying unique and separated HRs, with minimal overlap and very few direct contacts. Interestingly, and for the first time, this study highlighted that herds tended to avoid areas used by another herd in the previous two days during both the dry and wet seasons. Indirect contacts (i.e. use by two collared individuals of the same area at different times) between the neighbouring herds occurring within one month were more frequent than direct contacts.

Exchanges of Individuals between Mixed Herds Do Exist

Despite the temporal avoidance and the low spatial overlap between the HR of neighbouring mixed herds, dispersal events connecting mixed herds have been observed. From direct observations, Cross et al. (2004) reported contacts and exchanges between neighbouring mixed herds within a two-year period. Caron et al. (2016) reported three occurrences of dispersal by juvenile female buffalo out of 19 juvenile cows tagged or fitted with a GPS collar in KNP and GNP (Figure 6.3). These observations are corroborated by reports by game farmers and managers of juvenile females being spotted in small groups around wildlife farms or along veterinary fences in Zimbabwe (Caron, personal observation). Naidoo et al. (2014) also reported long-range movement of female buffalo (age unknown) in Namibia and Botswana, some without apparent return to their former HR. In Ruaha NP in Tanzania and in Chobe NP and the OD in Botswana, herd switching was also observed (Halley et al., 2002; Bennitt et al., 2018; Roug et al., 2020). In southern KNP, the annual dispersal rates in two herds by adult females were 14 per cent and 19 per cent, respectively, and younger adult cows were more likely to disperse (Spaan et al., 2019). These results indicate that adult and juvenile females do change herds, with juvenile cows engaging in this behaviour more frequently. An outbreeding behaviour prior to first reproduction could explain this difference. However, the composition (other individuals of the same or different age or sex, if any) of the group accompanying the tracked females in these studies is unknown. In addition, it is not known in this study if these female dispersal events are also mirrored by male dispersal events.

Social Dynamics within Mixed Herds Are More Fluid Than Expected

Based on the studies in GNP, KNP and Hwange NP (HNP), adult female dyads within a mixed herd were shown to be sometimes loosely associated, and that dyad association patterns varied between sites (Figure 6.3). For example, a majority of loose dyad associations were found in GNP and KNP (with 15–50 per cent of time spent together within a mixed herd) and the OD (most dyads with >30 per cent HR overlap spent <30 per cent of the time together) versus more lasting dyad association in HNP (with the majority of dyads spending 40–65 per cent of time together).

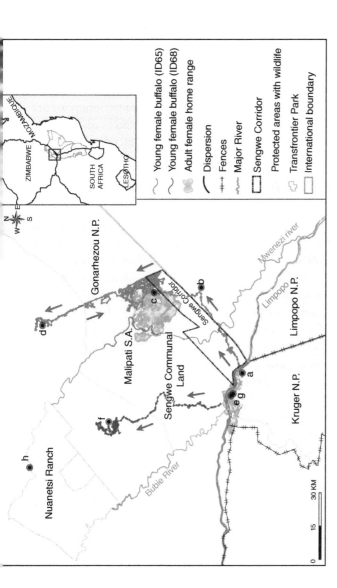

Figure 6.3 Study area encompassing part of Mozambique, South Africa and Zimbabwe. The inset map shows the location of the Great Limpopo Transfrontier Conservation Area within southern Africa. Brown areas represent the home ranges of five satellite collar-equipped adult female African buffalo, representative of the five herds followed for the study in Kruger National Park (NP; n = 3) and Gonarezhou NP (n = 2). Because of overlap among the herds, boundaries for the five herds cannot be seen. Data for the other adult female buffalo in the study are not represented. The home range of Kruger NP herds spans the Limpopo River between South Africa and Zimbabwe. Long-distance movements of three subadult female buffalo are shown. Arrows indicate the direction of movements for two buffalo; sites of capture and resighting are shown for the third buffalo. A complete description of the movements of these three buffalo is provided in the expanded figure legend online (wwwnc.cdc.gov/EID/article/22/2/14-0864-F1.htm).

These results challenge previous works that proposed a more cohesive definition of mixed herds (Grimsdell, 1969; Sinclair, 1977; Prins, 1996). The fact that intraherd associations for adult cows seem to be looser than expected in Figure 6.2 indicates either that the social dynamics within the mixed herds studied in southern Africa differed from those of the mixed herds studied in eastern Africa, or that these previous studies, which did not use precise individual tracking, could not detect such dyad dynamics. Another interpretation could be that in more recent times, the disturbances created by humans at the periphery or in protected areas (most buffalo mixed herds followed in Figure 6.3 live on the periphery of protected areas) have impacted the social dynamics of mixed herds compared to earlier studies implemented in the heart of more intact protected areas.

Gaps in Knowledge and Hypotheses about Mixed Herds

If a mixed herd is not the cohesive social unit within which individuals spend most of their time together, it could hypothetically be the case within a smaller social unit, which we will define as a *core group* and within which individuals would spend most of their time together (Korte, 2009; Table 6.1).

Adult females, calves and juveniles of both sexes and possibly adult males can potentially belong to this core group (Grueter et al., 2017). The existence of these core groups (or 'basic herds' or 'subgroups') has already been suggested (Sinclair, 1977; Mloszewski, 1983). Several storylines could explain why individual buffalo would spend most of their time together. First, core herds could be based on kinship, containing mothers and several generations of their offspring, with young females staying with their mothers until the birth of their first calf and perhaps longer, and juvenile males leaving this association earlier (Sinclair, 1977; Mloszewski, 1983; Prins, 1996). Second, individuals having the same metabolic requirements could spend time together. However, this second storyline would imply that core groups are not stable over time as individual metabolic requirements can vary (e.g. with reproductive status). Third, some behaviours could benefit clusters of individuals that would spend more time together; such behaviours could concern anti-predation or anti-parasite, competition avoidance and information sharing on food resources, among others. These storylines are not mutually exclusive and various authors have described mixed herds as a composition of family groups, juvenile groups (male or female) and single males.

Table 6.1 *Information about studied African buffalo populations across their range; classes are (1) habitat where water is not a limiting factor; (2) woodland/forest habitat; (3) habitat with water as a limiting factor during the dry season. Site gives area name and country. Water provides the average annual rainfall and the availability of water during the dry season. Habitat heterogeneity provides the proportion of grassland in the home range. HR = home range (minimum and maximum recorded) including acronym of the methodology used to measure the HR.*

Site	Country	Subspecies	Study years	Dominant habitat	Water during dry season (average rainfall in mm)	Home range min, max/ method	Mixed herd size	Largest observed association	Long-distance movement	Herd switching	Type of social units	Class	Source
Matusadona NP	Zimbabwe	*S. c. caffer*	1973–1983	Open grassland	Lake Karimba (400–800 mm)	60–110 km^2 (MCP*)	>500		NA	NA	NA	Mixed herd	1	Taylor, 1985
Hwange NP	Zimbabwe	*S. c. caffer*	2010–2015	Woodland and bushland savannas	Pumped waterholes (600 mm)	27–161 km^2 (seasonal; BBMM** 90%)	50–250 (at capture)	800+	115 km (adult female)	NA	Mixed herd	3	Miguel et al., 2013, 2017; Valls-Fox et al., 2018; Wielgus et al., 2020, 2021
Gonarezhou– North Kruger NP	Zimbabwe South Africa	*S. c. caffer*	2008–2015	Open grassland, woodlands	River pools (600 mm)	8–82 km^2 (seasonal; BBMM 90%)	20–250	250	96 km (juvenile females)	Yes	Mixed herd	3	Miguel et al., 2013; Caron et al., 2016; Wielgus et al., 2020, 2021

(*cont.*)

Table 6.1 (*cont.*)

Site	Country	Subspecies	Study years	Dominant habitat	Water during dry season (average rainfall in mm)	Home range min, max/ method	Mixed herd size	Largest observed association	Long-distance movement	Herd switching	Type of social units	Class	Source
Kruger NP	South Africa	S. c. *caffer*	2002–2013	Open grassland, woodlands	River pools (600–1000 mm)	40–70 km² (95% LoCoH★★★) 100–460 km² (100% UD)	Mean between 250 and 550 Median dry season = 45 (range: 1–1200) Median wet season = 4.5 (range = 1–250)	1200	110 km (dispersal, young adult females)	NA	Mixed herd	3	Hughes et al., 2017; Winnie et al., 2008; Spaan et al., 2019
Klaserie Private Nature Reserve	South Africa	S. c. *caffer*	1995–2000	Open grassland, woodlands	Pumped waterholes/ river pools (486 mm)	103–266 km² (MCP) 197–342 km² (FKE 95%#) 83–251 km² (LoCoH)	180–225	400	NA	NA	Mixed herd	3	Ryan et al., 2006
Caprivi strip	Namibia Botswana	S. c. *caffer*	2007–2010	Open grassland, woodlands	Perennial rivers (650 mm)	5.5–564 km² (r-LoCoH)	NA	NA	100–200 km (females)	Yes	Mixed herd	1?	Naidoo et al., 2012a, 2012b, 2014
Okavango Delta	Botswana	S. c. *caffer*	2007–2010	Open grassland	Okavango Delta (450 mm)	100–280 km² (seasonal; r-LoCoH)	100–200	2000+	50 km (migration)	Yes	Mixed herd	1	Bennitt et al., 2016, 2018
Serengeti Greater Ecosystem	Tanzania Kenya	S. c. *caffer*	1966–1973	Open grassland	Few perennial rivers (500–1000 mm)	222 km² (MCP)	50–400	1750	NA	NA	Mixed herd	3?	Sinclair, 1977

Site	Country	Subspecies	Years	Habitat	Water source	Home range	Group size	N	Movement	Migratory	Herd type	N	Reference
Ruaha NP	Tanzania	*S. c. caffer*	2014–2016	Miombo/*Commiphora*–*Combretum* woodland/acacia savanna	Perennial rivers (500–800 mm)	73–601 km² (seasonal, 95% BBMM)	100–1000	NA	Migratory, expander	Yes	Mixed herd	3	Roug et al., 2020
Manyara NP	Tanzania	*S. c. caffer*	1981–1985	Open grassland	Manyara Lake (620 mm)	NA	12–980	980	40–50 km (adult bulls)	No	Mixed herd Bachelor group	1	Prins, 1996
W NP	Niger	*S. c. equinocalis*	2007–2008	*Combretum* shrub savanna/Sudanian vegetation	River pools (685–850 mm)	168–503 km² (MCP)	16–76	150	30–50 km (migration)	NA	Mixed herd	3	Cornélis et al., 2011
Lope NP	Gabon	*S. c. nanus*	2002–2004	Tropical forest	Perennial water sources	2.41–10.56 km² (MCP) 2.30–7.64 km² (LoCoH)	12 ± 2	44	NA	Yes	Mixed herd	2	Korte, 2008
Ndanza-Ndoki	Central African Republic	*S. c. nanus*	2002–2004	Tropical forest	Perennial water sources (1365 mm)	8 km² (MCP-type)	16–24	NA	NA	NA	Mixed herd	2	Melleti et al., 2007

*Minimum Convex Polygon; ** Brownian Bridge Models; *** Local nearest-neighbour convex-hull construction; #Fixed Kernel Estimator 95%; ##Kernel-based utilization distribution.

Field observations provide indications about the size of core groups based on the smallest units observed. In the savannas of GNP, Zimbabwe, groups of 20–40 buffalo were regularly seen during a study between 2007 and 2012 (Caron, personal observation). In tropical forests of Lope NP in Gabon, Korte (2008) observed a mean group size of 12 (range 3–24) *Syncerus caffer nanus* individuals per group. In the Guinean–Congolian Forest of Central African Republic, Melletti et al. (2007) studied over two years a herd of the same *S. c. nanus* subspecies comprising 16 individuals (one adult male, nine adult females, five juveniles and one calf) that only increased to 24 individuals through reproduction within the herd. Most buffalo groups observed in the OD contained 50–200 individuals (54 per cent of groups; Bennitt et al., 2016). The core group's size (and composition) may vary between buffalo subspecies and geographical areas. Kinship could form the basis of mixed herds, with several core groups sharing the same HR but intermingling at times.

Against this kinship hypothesis is the observation that individuals collared in the same group (i.e. individuals that were together at the time of darting and fitting GPS collars) at the beginning of a study engage in highly heterogeneous fusion–fission dynamics (Prins, 1989a). Wielgus et al. (2020) analysed the associations of 4–6 individual buffalo collared in the same groups in GNP, HNP and KNP and found almost no stability in dyad observations. In addition, genetic characterization of individuals (both males and females) captured in the same herds in GNP and KNP revealed low levels of genetic relatedness, which were similar to relatedness values between individuals from different herds. This suggests that herds may contain many unrelated buffalo (Wielgus et al., personal communication). The combination of genetic and GPS data has also shown that the strength of female–female associations studied within three herds was not strongly influenced by their genetic relatedness. However, these observations should be considered cautiously, as few individuals from the same herd were both simultaneously monitored and genotyped ($n =$ 3, 4 and 6 individuals in each herd). Sinclair (1977) observed mixed herd size variation around focal marked individuals through direct observation and aerial photographs. Herd size varied throughout the year and between HR areas, ranging from 90 to 428 individuals (Sinclair, 1977). In the same study, two cases were reported of buffalo being darted and then joining a herd different from their original one. They were chased by the hosting herd and remained at the periphery of the herd (and one was quickly killed by a lion). In contrast, Grimsdell (1969) found a relative stability of mixed herd size and composition in Queen Elizabeth NP, Uganda during a one-year study.

A better understanding of what constitutes a mixed herd therefore requires understanding of its inner dynamics and the existence or not of core groups. Currently available data indicate that buffalo herds experience very frequent fusion–fission dynamics, which seem to contradict the core group existence, with the exception of the very close association between mothers and calves. This fluidity also seems to exist at a higher order: numerous observations of groups of 1000–2000 individual buffalo suggest that distinct mixed herds could undergo fusion (Sinclair, 1977; Chardonnet, personal communication; Table 6.1). While there are few continuous observation data available on these mega herds, it seems that their existence is temporary and responds to environmental drivers (Table 6.1). Given the little overlap observed between adjacent herds (less than 8 per cent of the HR), the gathering of several mixed herds raises the question of the HR of these temporary mega herds. It could span over more than one mixed herd's HR or concentrate at very specific times on highly concentrated resources (see subsequent sections).

Knowledge of *bachelor groups*, the specific male-based social unit, has not significantly improved in recent years, mainly due to the reduced longevity of telemetry devices fitted on male buffalo (i.e. collars usually fail within a few weeks after deployment, probably due to the specific aggressive behaviour and strength of adult males; Taolo, 2003). Bachelor group size ranges from a couple of individuals up to 51, with 20 already being an unusual observation (Sinclair, 1977; Prins, 1989a; Hughes et al., 2017). Larger bachelor groups might form as a response to high levels of predation pressure from lions that prefer buffalo prey. They represent social associations based partially on similar metabolic requirements, that is to build on strength to face better odds of reproduction when joining mixed herds (i.e. re-entrant consecutive polygyny; Prins, 1989b). Sinclair indicated that in the Serengeti they could represent 5.7 per cent and 15 per cent of the adult male and total populations, respectively (Sinclair, 1977), proportions that increased during the dry season.

On the Difficulty of Understanding Social Dynamics in Buffalo

The ability of the African buffalo to cope with contrasting environmental conditions throughout most sub-Saharan ecosystems by modulating a large array of biological traits (weight, herd and HR sizes, etc.)

highlights a high degree of behavioural plasticity. This plasticity, which allows the buffalo to enjoy a very wide distribution range in Africa (>200 mm rainfall), is a factor that challenges the understanding of the social dynamics of this species (Prins, 1996). In this context, one main challenge is the ability to sample social movements and interactions at different scales and over time, between and within ecosystems, between and within adjacent social units, and finally within cohesive social units.

More recent research presented here has benefited from the use of GPS collaring technology, which provides almost continuous, accurate information on the location of each collared animal. However, it does not provide information about the group size or individual composition around the focal individual equipped with a GPS collar. Therefore, a dyad identified by telemetry does not indicate whether focal individuals associate in dyads within a defined social group (e.g. a core group). A limit to this technology is that the impact on the behaviour of individuals chased and darted from a helicopter to deploy collars has not been extensively measured and could trigger short-and longer-term behavioural responses that could blur the social dynamics studied (e.g. effect on mortality; Oosthuizen et al., 2009).

In addition, there is a large number of indices to quantify the overlap between HRs (e.g. Fieberg and Kochanny, 2005), which can also be delimited in many ways, for example using minimum convex polygon (MCP) and utilization distribution (UD) methods. Recently, alternative methods that more explicitly consider the temporal component of movement data have been proposed, including the Brownian bridges methods (Benhamou and Cornélis, 2010). The variability of methods can restrain understanding of social dynamics at the species level because comparisons between studies using distinct methods or applications are limited. For example, we used data from the telemetry studies described above (Bennitt et al., 2018; Wielgus et al., 2020) to compare four empirical HR estimation methods: MCP, a fixed kernel utilization density method (KUD with least squares cross-validation, LSCV), a local convex-hull construction method (r-LoCoH) and Brownian random bridge model method (BRBMM) for 99, 90 and 50 per cent isopleths. These methods demonstrated the potentially different size estimates of the HR that we can obtain using the same data sets. In general, annual HRs obtained using BRBMM and KUD were substantially smaller than those estimated from MCP (e.g. 3.2 and 2.5 times greater than BRBMM and KUD, respectively, for the

90 per cent isopleth) and LoCoH (e.g. 2.2 and 1.7 times greater than BRBMM and KUD, respectively, for the 90 per cent isopleth), irrespective of the isopleth used to define the bounds. For these same data, the degree of overlap between seasonal HRs calculated with Bhattacharyya's affinity index was greater than when calculated with the Utilization Distribution Overlap Index (UDOI). A similar comparison was conducted by Ryan et al. (2006), with the MCP method giving a larger range size than the LoCoH method. In the future, standardizing variables should be used to facilitate comparisons between populations and improve our understanding of buffalo herd definition.

Additionally, GPS collars can provide key information about proximity between buffalo dyads, which can be interpreted in the context of social associations, enabling the identification of fusion–fission events (Bennitt et al., 2018; Wielgus et al., 2020). However, these studies rely on an external definition of a proximity and temporal threshold determining whether buffalo dyads are 'together' or 'apart', and variation in this threshold can alter interpretation. Definitions of fusion–fission events should therefore be informed by buffalo detection capabilities rather than those of observers, which could lead to new interpretations of buffalo social systems. Knowledge is still missing to determine at what distance buffalo still perceive themselves as being together or not (e.g. what is the threshold beyond which an individual will react to a flight behaviour by the mixed herd?).

Determining the evolution of group size around a focal individual is also a crucial parameter to explore fusion–fission dynamics. Regular direct observation can in principle estimate this parameter if the focal individual is easily identifiable (e.g. with a color tag or collar; Grimsdell, 1969; Prins, 1996). However, recent studies tend to focus on telemetry technology to remotely follow buffalo movements. This technology falls short of identifying group size and individuals moving or not in association with the collared individuals. Therefore, group size estimations around focal individuals will require direct observation studies or approaches combining telemetry and unmanned aerial vehicles, for example capturing regularly the group size around the collared individuals after locating it. The advent of proximity sensors should be a powerful tool for understanding social dynamics in African buffalo. These sensors record when two collared animals are close to each other according to the specified spatial threshold, and their lower cost compared to GPS technology makes it possible to monitor simultaneously a larger number of individuals, which is especially relevant for this species (Prange et al., 2006; Hamede et al., 2009; Walrath et al., 2011). Additionally, when synchronized with GPS data (collected on some animals), the use of proximity sensors can help better identify the location of fusion and fission events, and therefore, the external drivers of fusion–fission dynamics.

Fluidity in Group Dynamics and Its Drivers – Conceptual Framework

Given the female-based social units described in the previous sections, and using the highly dynamic fusion–fission patterns of adult females observed with telemetry, Figure 6.4 presents a revised framework including the level of fluidity in social dynamics. In recent studies, the number of fusion–fission events between dyads of cows (dyads were considered together if at 1 km or less at the same time log) belonging to the same herd ranged on average between 4.04 and 5.73 per month during the dry season and 8.22 and 10.30 per month during the wet season in GNP, HNP and KNP (Wielgus et al., 2020); and in the OD, the mean number of fusion events per dyad ranged between 2.7 and 5.5 during the different seasons of 2008 and 2009 (dyads were considered together if at 300 m or less at the same time log; Bennitt et al., 2018). These data would indicate fusion–fission dynamics corresponding to the right-end panel of Figure 6.4.

These dynamics both respond to a set of external factors, reviewed in the next section, and result from individual decision making (Cross et al., 2005). A dominance of fusion events will cause the formation of larger groups, whereas frequent fission events will lead to smaller groups. Prins (1996) observed in Manyara NP, Tanzania, that larger herds tended to split more often than smaller herds. Individual decisions may be triggered by resource competition within mixed herds, predation risk (e.g. the larger the group in open habitat, the lesser the predation risk per individual), kinship bonding (e.g. related to the core group concept), activity synchronizing and access to collective knowledge to deal with habitat heterogeneity and access to vital resources. Investigating the position of individuals within the herd, Prins (1996) hypothesized about the use of fission by rear individuals to 'overcome social inequality' of not accessing good resources compared to animals at the front. Apart from this, knowledge of how buffalo decide whether to stay in an association or not remains scarce.

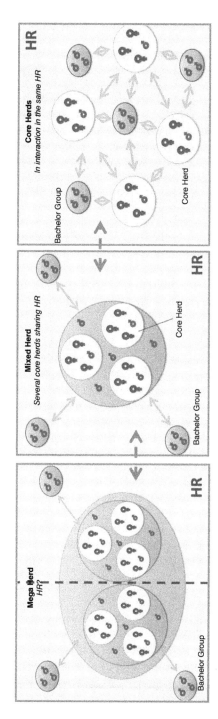

Figure 6.4 Framework of social units and dynamics of African buffalo. The three female–based social units (i.e. core, mixed and mega herds) are presented in a fluid diagram. We hypothesize that there is a fluidity between these social units in the same buffalo grouping, depending on drivers discussed in this chapter. Source: Authors.

External Drivers of Fusion–Fission Dynamics

Resource Distribution and Habitat Heterogeneity

Resource availability is closely related to variation in social organization in social ungulates (Jedrzejewski et al., 2006; Isvaran, 2007; Fortin et al., 2009). When forage and water are relatively scarce and/or distributed in small, distant patches, animals are expected to form smaller groups and aggregate in areas or during times where or when resources are abundant. Interestingly, studies investigating temporal variation in group size in African buffalo described seasonal changes in group size that hint at the role of resource condition as a driver of fusion–fission dynamics (e.g. Sinclair, 1977; Melletti et al., 2007; Hughes et al., 2017). However, they reported contrasting results depending on the geographical areas and the subspecies. For instance, while *S. c. caffer* groups from Klaserie Private Nature Reserve (South Africa; Ryan et al., 2006) and Serengeti NP (Serengeti; Sinclair, 1977) occurred in larger herds during the wet season, the opposite was reported in *S. c. caffer* groups from Chobe NP (Botswana; Halley et al., 2002) as well as in *S. c. nanus* herds living in Dzanga–Ndoki NP (Central African Republic; Melletti et al., 2007). Conversely, Korte (2008) reported that *S. c. nanus* herds were relatively stable between seasons at Lopé NP (Gabon). Irrespective of the group size, the monitoring of adult females in KNP, GNP and HNP revealed seasonal differences in the underlying patterns of fusion–fission events within herds, with higher fusion–fission dynamics during the wet season, while fusion–fission dynamics in the OD did not vary seasonally (Bennitt et al., 2018; Wielgus et al., 2020). This suggests that environmental heterogeneity affects buffalo group dynamics, but in different ways depending on the geographical areas.

In social ungulates, larger and tighter groups are more common in open habitats where visibility is higher than in closed habitats. Large group sizes facilitate social cohesion, improve protection against predators and parasites (e.g. ticks, flies) and possibly provide access to more abundant forage for grazing (Jarman, 1974; Isvaran, 2007; Pays et al., 2007; Sueur et al., 2011). A tendency for buffalo to occur in larger groups in open habitats, such as grassland, as well as in more homogeneous areas has been noticed in Hluhluwe–iMfolozi Game Reserve during both dry and wet seasons (Dora, 2004). Therefore, one hypothesis is that as the habitat opens and turns into more (larger patches of) grasslands, fusion-fission dynamics will tend to create larger herds, up to mega herds, compared to woodland habitats hosting smaller mixed herds (Figure 6.4).

This hypothesis is also supported by field observations in Matusadona NP, Zimbabwe (Taylor, 1985), Serengeti NP, Tanzania (Sinclair, 1977) and forest buffalo in Gabon (Korte, 2008). Mloszewski (1983) proposed three types of herds depending on the habitat: open grassland habitat that allows the largest herds with water available throughout (e.g. OD or Matusadona NP); well-watered woodland habitat hosting smaller herds (e.g. forest buffalo in tropical forests); and drier habitats where the need to regularly commute between water and pasture encourages smaller herds and the greatest degree of herd discipline (e.g. GNP, HNP or KNP; Table 6.1). GPS monitoring of adult females revealed that habitat openness had a minor effect on the patterns of associations among individuals and the location of fusion–fission events. Similarly, in the same study, although the scarcity of water during the dry season in such habitats might be expected to affect the social dynamics of buffalo, a significant, but weak, effect of distance to water on the patterns of associations and the location of fusion–fission events between adult females was observed (Wielgus et al., 2020).

Bachelor groups often concentrate around small patches of good-quality grazing, too small for larger herds to exploit (Taylor, 1985; Prins, 1996).

Predation and Parasitism

The 'ecology of fear' has detailed the behavioural and ecological trait changes of numerous prey species and their consequences in response to predators in temperate and tropical ecosystems (Buck et al., 2018). For instance, Tambling et al. (2012) documented the changes in the behaviour of S. c. caffer following the reintroduction of lions (*Panthera leo*) into the Addo Elephant National Park, South Africa. Buffalo responded by increasing group sizes and switching habitat preferences towards more open grasslands during lions' hunting hours, which countered the initial high levels of predation on juvenile buffalo experienced just after the reintroduction of the predator.

Although parasites (broadly including micro- and macroparasites) can also cause hosts to adopt defensive strategies that reduce infection risks, the 'ecology of disgust' has not yet provided strong empirical and theoretical evidence of the causes and consequences of such anti-parasite behaviours (Buck et al., 2018). The 'encounter-dilution' effect provides protection when the probability of detection of a group does not increase in proportion to an increase in group size provided that the parasites (or predator) do not offset the encounter effect by attacking more members of the group (Mooring and Hart, 1992). This mechanism could provide larger groups of buffalo with some added protection against parasites that actively seek their hosts, such as biting flies (e.g. tabanids, *Glossina* spp). The 'selfish herd' effect provides protection from predators to animals that are in the centre of a group (Hamilton, 1971), which also protects against biting parasites (Mooring and Hart, 1992). Ungulate hosts have evolved adaptive strategies to minimize their exposure to parasites (Gunn and Irvine, 2003; Fritzsche and Allan, 2012), and the adoption of such grouping and foraging strategies could provide some protection to buffalo herds against free-living stages of significant ectoparasites, such as ticks in southern African savanna ecosystems (de Garine-Wichatitsky et al., 1999; de Garine-Wichatitsky, 2000).

In conclusion, analysing the causes and consequences of predation and parasitism on African buffalo grouping strategies is not trivial. Despite relatively abundant literature documenting the effects of parasites on buffalo populations, including detailed surveys of the complex interactions between parasites (Jolles et al., 2008; Ezenwa et al., 2019; Chapter 11), there is a need for further empirical data specifically documenting group size variations of buffalo herds and their epidemiological consequences. Furthermore, it is likely that some consequences of buffalo herding strategies may differ fundamentally between predation and parasitism, with contrasted consequences depending on the mode of transmission of parasites (density- versus frequency-dependent transmission; Heesterbeek and Roberts, 1995).

Anthropological Drivers

Although few buffalo populations remain unaffected by human activities, little is known about the impact of human activities and infrastructures on fusion–fission dynamics in African buffalo. Naidoo et al. (2012a, 2012b) explored the influence of infrastructure such as (wildlife management or veterinary) fences, roads, fires, cultivated areas and homesteads on the dispersal and home range of African buffalo in the Caprivi strip in Bostwana/Namibia, and noted that they all influenced buffalo movements and HRs as no through zones (e.g. fence, roads) or no-go zones (e.g. villages or recently burnt areas). In Zimbabwe, in HNP, KNP and GNP studies, African buffalo were seldom seen outside of protected areas (Miguel et al., 2017; Valls-Fox et al., 2018). In Figure 6.1, the right-hand side boundary for both herds is a railway line doubled with a dirt road crossing through the GNP; no adult female buffalo ever crossed that line even after coming very close to it (Caron, personal observation). Buffalo regularly cross over the poorly maintained veterinary fence around the OD, most likely seeking productive forage, and several individual male buffalo were seen in Maun in 2021. In Kasane town, Botswana, buffalo just ignore the tarmac main road (Chardonnet, personal communication).

Besides the impact of humans on buffalo movements and HRs, little is known about the impact of cattle encounters on fusion–fission dynamics in buffalo mixed herds. Over most of their current distribution in sub-Saharan Africa, the ranges of buffalo and cattle populations extensively overlap, and they often share forage and grazing resources (Chapter 10). However, at a fine scale, there are few field observations of free-ranging buffalo mingling with cattle on the same grazing grounds, drinking together from the same waterholes, or any other activity implying close direct contact between individuals from the two species. On the contrary, most field evidence indicates that buffalo tend to avoid areas occupied by cattle herds. For instance, a spoor survey conducted to monitor the movements of wildlife and livestock across the damaged FMD fence of southern GNP found that cattle and buffalo used different sections of the damaged fence (Chigwenhese et al., 2016), while Hibert et al. (2010) demonstrated a similar trend, with a clear separation of buffalo from cattle tended even at large scales in the WNP in West Africa. At a finer scale, Valls-Fox et al. (2018) were able to further quantify the movement patterns of sympatric free-roaming buffalo and herded cattle using GPS empirical data combined with spatial modelling, according to seasonal changes of surface water availability in an interface area of HNP. As expected, both cattle and buffalo preferred open grassland habitats found close to water, but buffalo avoidance of cattle varied seasonally. During the rainy season, buffalo avoided cattle completely at the HR scale, whereas during the dry season, when cattle ranged further into the protected area in search of forage, buffalo and cattle spatial overlap increased as water dependence took precedence over avoidance (Valls-Fox et al., 2018). The same study observed a more nocturnal use by buffalo of shared pastures between both species, at a time when cattle are penned in 'kraals' close to their owner's homestead. Although it is still unclear whether buffalo avoid cattle, or possibly their herders, dogs or other associates, and what cues they use to detect and minimize contacts, this could open perspectives for the management of wildlife–livestock interfaces (Sitters et al., 2009; Caron et al., 2021). Valls-Fox et al. (2018) suggested that long-term planning of both artificial water provisioning and traditional cattle-herding practices could help maintain spatial segregation and thus mitigate conservation conflicts such as pathogen transmission, crop-raiding and livestock depredation. Finally, if, when encounters occur, they result in fusion–fission events as observed when one encounters buffalo groups, one would expect that the size of buffalo groups closer to park boundaries would be smaller than those further from boundaries.

Conclusion

Since Prins (1996), the understanding of the dynamics of mixed herds of buffalo has evolved, mainly due to breakthroughs in telemetry technology. Associations of buffalo are now considered more fluid than the initial idea of a stable mixed herd fixed in a home range. Individual buffalo belonging to a mixed herd participate in extensive fusion–fission events and can spend less than 30 per cent of their time together. In addition, dyads are not stable over time and patterns of individuals' association within mixed herds are not clear. A mixed herd is therefore better defined by a fixed home range shared by individuals, and mixed herd switching by young or adult females has been observed on several occasions (Table 6.1). Individuals within mixed herds may associate based on kinship or shared metabolic requirements, and attempts to test these hypotheses have been inconclusive so far. These two non-exclusive hypotheses should attract more attention in future studies. These interpretations are mainly based on studies in southern Africa and their replication in other regions where the species occur would be welcome.

The dynamics of fusion–fission events within mixed herds are largely driven by habitat heterogeneity and the quality and quantity of grazing and surface water (Winnie et al., 2008). The size of grazing patches and water points determine the size of mixed herds that can crop them, and their distribution across space trigger fusion–fission dynamics. Additional drivers such as predation, parasitism or fires also influence mixed herd dynamics. However, most African buffalo populations today are exposed to some degree of human activity (traditional and trophy hunting, cattle grazing, roads, fences and fire to name a few). Human activities have been shown to impact buffalo movements, home ranges and daily activities (Naidoo et al., 2012a; Valls-Fox et al., 2018). The fluidity of the buffalo social system as updated in this chapter may help the species to adapt to changing environments and expanding buffalo/cattle/human interfaces (Figure 6.5). However, given the potential impact of climate

Figure 6.5 Herd of Cape African buffalo observed from a helicopter, central Botswana. © Rudi van Aarde.

change on water availability in Africa (James and Washington, 2013), the drier conditions that will be experienced in semi-arid ecosystems in the coming decades may alter external drivers (e.g. intensity of buffalo/cattle/human interfaces) and herd dynamics (less), home range (larger) and group size (smaller) (Naidoo et al., 2012a; Roug et al., 2020; Wielgus et al., 2020).

Some large buffalo populations also remain unstudied. For example, 21,000 buffalo are estimated in Maromeu National Reserve in Mozambique and 12,000 in Zakouma National Park (Chapter 4). Forest buffalo are largely understudied despite their importance to confirm or not the existence of a core group for the species. Studies on these populations could shed light on the 'natural' ecology of buffalo populations in different contexts, as some remain relatively free of human impact.

In 1977, Sinclair concluded: 'we need more data on the degree to which animals move between herds and whether there are characteristic gene frequencies for each herd'. These needs are still valid today, and one could add 'how animals move within herds'. Future studies will benefit from more advances in telemetry, using cheaper devices (e.g. ear tags, proximity tags), new technologies (e.g. drones to regularly estimate group size around focal/collared individuals), new information sources (e.g. sound recorders) and non-invasive genetic studies to enhance our knowledge of buffalo social dynamics. These future studies should not forget that longitudinal observational studies based on fieldwork by researchers will always bring additional information that new technologies promoting remote access to data tend to occult.

References

Benhamou, S. and D. Cornélis (2010). Incorporating movement behavior and barriers to improve kernel home range space use estimates. *Journal of Wildlife Management* **74**(6): 1353–1360.

Benhamou, S., M. Valeix, S. Chamaillé-Jammes, et al. (2014). Movement-based analysis of interactions in African lions. *Animal Behaviour* **90**: 171–180.

Bennitt, E., M.C. Bonyongo and S. Harris (2016). Effects of divergent migratory strategies on access to resources for Cape buffalo (*Syncerus caffer caffer*). *Journal of Mammalogy* **97**(6): 1682–1698.

Bennitt, E., M.C. Bonyongo, S. Harris and L. Barrett (2018). Cape buffalo (*Syncerus caffer caffer*) social dynamics in a flood-pulsed environment. *Behavioral Ecology* **29**(1): 93–105.

Buck, J., S. Weinstein and H. Young (2018). Ecological and evolutionary consequences of parasite avoidance. *Trends in Ecology & Evolution* **33**(8): 619–632.

Caron, A., J. Angel Barasona, E. Miguel, et al. (2021). Characterisation of wildlife–livestock interfaces: the need for interdisciplinary approaches and a dedicated thematic field. In J. Vicente, K.C. Vercauteren and C. Gortázar (Eds.), *Diseases at the Wildlife–Livestock Interface: Research and Perspectives in a Changing World*. Cham: Springer International Publishing, pp. 339–367.

Caron, A., D. Cornélis, C. Foggin, et al. (2016). African buffalo movement and zoonotic disease risk across Transfrontier Conservation Areas, southern Africa. *Emerging Infectious Diseases* **22**(2): 277–280.

Chigwenhese, L., A. Murwira, F.M. Zengeya, et al. (2016). Monitoring African buffalo (*Syncerus caffer*) and cattle (*Bos taurus*) movement across a damaged veterinary control fence at a Southern African wildlife/livestock interface. *African Journal of Ecology* **54**(4): 415–423.

Conybeare, A.B. (1980). Buffalo numbers, home range and daily movement in the Sengwa Wildlife Research Area, Zimbabwe. *South African Journal of Wildlife Research* **10**(3–4): 89–93.

Cornélis, D., S. Benhamou, G. Janeau, et al. (2011). Spatiotemporal dynamics of forage and water resources shape space use of West African savanna buffalo. *Mammalogy* **92**(6): 1287–1297.

Cross, P., J.O. Lloyd-Smith, J.A. Bowers, et al. (2004). Integrating association data and disease dynamics in a social ungulate: bovine tuberculosis in African buffalo in the Kruger National Park. *Annales Zoologici Fennici* **41**: 879–892.

Cross, P., J.O. Lloyd-Smith, P.L.F. Johnson and W.M. Getz (2005). Duelling time scale of host movement and disease recovery determine invasion of disease in structured populations. *Ecology Letters* **8**: 587–595.

de Garine-Wichatitsky, M. (2000). Assessing infestation risk by vectors. Spatial and temporal distribution of African ticks at the scale of a landscape. *Annals of the New York Academy of Sciences* **916**: 222–32.

de Garine-Wichatitsky, M., T. De Meeus, J.F. Guegan and F. Renaud (1999). Spatial and temporal distributions of parasites: can wild and domestic ungulates avoid African tick larvae? *Parasitology* **119**: 455–466.

Dora, C.A. (2004). *The Influences of Habitat Structure and Landscape Heterogeneity on African Buffalo (Syncerus cgffer) Group Size in Hiuhiuwe-iMfolozi Game Reserve, South Africa.* MSc, Environmental Sciences, Oregon State University.

Ezenwa, V.O., A.E. Jolles, B.R. Beechler, et al. (2019). The causes and consequences of parasite interactions: African buffalo as a case study. In K. Wilson, A. Fenton and D. Tompkins (Eds.), *Wildlife Disease Ecology: Linking Theory to Data and Application.* Cambridge: Cambridge University Press, pp. 129–160.

Fieberg, J. and C.O. Kochanny (2005). Quantifying home-range overlap: the importance of the utilization distribution. *The Journal of Wildlife Management* **69**(4): 1346–1359.

Fortin, D., M.-E. Fortin, H.L. Beyer, et al. (2009). Group-Size-mediated habitat selection and group fusion–fission dynamics of bison under predation risk. *Ecology* **90**(9): 2480–2490.

Fritzsche, A. and B.F. Allan (2012). The ecology of fear: host foraging behavior varies with the spatio-temporal abundance of a dominant ectoparasite. *EcoHealth* **9**(1): 70–74.

Grimsdell, J. (1969). *Ecology of the Buffalo, Syncerus caffer, in Western Uganda.* Unpublished PhD thesis, Cambridge University.

Grueter, C.C., X. Qi, B. Li and M. Li (2017). Multilevel societies. *Current Biology* **27**(18): R984–R986.

Gunn, A. and R.J. Irvine (2003). Subclinical parasitism and ruminant foraging strategies – a review. *Wildlife Society Bulletin* **31**: 117–126.

Halley, D.-J. and M. Mari (2004). Dry season social affiliation of African buffalo bulls at the Chobe riverfront, Botswana. *South African Journal of Wildlife Research* **34**(2): 105–111.

Halley, D.-J., M.E.J. Vandewalle, M. Mari and C. Taolo (2002). Herd-switching and long-distance dispersal in female African buffalo *Syncerus caffer. African Journal of Ecology* **40**(1): 97–99.

Hamede, R.K., J. Bashford, H. McCallum and M. Jones (2009). Contact networks in a wild Tasmanian devil (*Sarcophilus harrisii*) population: using social network analysis to reveal seasonal variability in social behaviour and its implications for transmission of devil facial tumour disease. *Ecology Letters* **12**(11): 1147–1157.

Hamilton, W.D. (1971). Geometry for the selfish herd. *Journal of Theoretical Biology* **31**(2): 295–311.

Heesterbeek, J. and M. Roberts (1995). Mathematical models for microparasites of wildlife. *Ecology of Infectious Diseases in Natural Populations* **90**: 122.

Hibert, F., C. Calenge, H. Fritz, et al. (2010). Spatial avoidance of invading pastoral cattle by wild ungulates: insights from using point process statistics. *Biodiversity and Conservation* **19**(7): 2003–2024.

Hughes, K., G.T. Fosgate, C.M. Budke, et al. (2017). Modeling the spatial distribution of African buffalo (*Syncerus caffer*) in the Kruger National Park, South Africa. *PLoS One* **12**(9): e0182903.

Isvaran, K. (2007). Intraspecific variation in group size in the blackbuck antelope: the roles of habitat structure and forage at different spatial scales. *Oecologia* **154**(2): 435–444.

James, R. and R. Washington (2013). Changes in African temperature and precipitation associated with degrees of global warming. *Climatic Change* **117**(4): 859–872.

Jarman, P.J. (1974). The social organisation of antelope in relation to their ecology. *Behaviour* **48**(3–4): 215–267.

Jedrzejewski, W., H. Spaedtke, J.F. Kamler, et al. (2006). Group size dynamics of red deer in Białowieża primeval forest, Poland. *The Journal of Wildlife Management* **70**(4): 1054–1059.

Jolles, A.E., V.O. Ezenwa, R.S. Etienne, et al. (2008). Interactions between macroparasites and microparasites drive infection patterns in free-ranging African buffalo. *Ecology* **89**(8): 2239–2250.

Korte, L. (2008). Variation of group size among African buffalo herds in a forest–savanna mosaic landscape. *Journal of Zoology* **275**(3): 229–236.

Korte, L. (2009). Herd-switching in adult female African forest buffalo *Syncerus caffer nanus. African Journal of Ecology* **47**: 125–127.

Melletti, M., V. Penteriani, M. Mirabile and L. Boitani (2007). Some behavioral aspects of forest buffalo (*Syncerus caffer nanus*): from herd to individual. *Journal of Mammalogy* **88**(5): 1312–1318.

Miguel, E., V. Grosbois, A. Caron, et al. (2013). Contacts and foot and mouth disease transmission from wild to domestic bovines in Africa. *Ecosphere* **4**(4): art51. https://doi.org/10.1890/es12-00239.1.

Miguel, E., V. Grosbois, H. Fritz, et al. (2017). Drivers of foot-and-mouth disease in cattle at wild/domestic interface: Insights from farmers, buffalo and lions. *Diversity & Distributions* **23**(9): 1018–1030.

Mloszewski, M.J. (1983). *The Behavior and Ecology of the African Buffalo*. Cambridge: Cambridge University Press.

Mooring, M.S. and B.L. Hart (1992). Animal grouping for protection from parasites: selfish herd and encounter-dilution effects. *Behaviour* **123**(3–4): 173–193.

Naidoo, R., P. Du Preez, G. Stuart-Hill, et al. (2012a). Home on the range: factors explaining partial migration of African buffalo in a tropical environment. *PLoS One* **7**(5): e36527.

Naidoo, R., P. Du Preez, G. Stuart-Hill, et al. (2012b). Factors affecting intraspecific variation in home range size of a large African herbivore. *Landscape Ecology* **27**(10): 1523–1534.

Naidoo, R., P. Du Preez, G. Stuart-Hill, et al. (2014). Long-range migrations and dispersals of African buffalo (*Syncerus caffer*) in the Kavango–Zambezi Transfrontier Conservation Area. *African Journal of Ecology* **52**(4): 581–584.

Oosthuizen, W.C., P.C. Cross, J.A. Bowers, et al. (2009). Effects of chemical immobilization on survival of African buffalo in the Kruger National Park. *Journal of Wildlife Management* **73**(1): 149–153.

Pays, O., S. Benhamou, R. Helder and J.-F. Gerard (2007). The dynamics of group formation in large mammalian herbivores: an analysis in the European roe deer. *Animal Behaviour* **74**: 1429–1441.

Prange, P., T. Jordan, C. Hunter and S.D. Gehrt (2006). New radiocollars for the detection of proximity among individuals. *Wildlife Society Bulletin* **34**(5): 1333–1344.

Prins, H.H.T. (1989a). Buffalo herd structure and its repercussions for condition of individual African buffalo cows. *Ethology* **81**: 47–71.

Prins, H.H.T. (1989b). Condition changes and choice of social environment in African buffalo bulls. *Behaviour* **108**(3–4): 297–324.

Prins, H.H.T. (1996). *Ecology and Behaviour of the African Buffalo.*: London: Chapman & Hall.

Roug, A., E.A. Muse, D.L. Clifford, et al. (2020). Seasonal movements and habitat use of African buffalo in Ruaha National Park, Tanzania. *BMC Ecology* **20**(1): 6.

Ryan, S.J., C.U. Knechtel and W.M. Getz (2006). Range and habitat selection of African buffalo in South Africa. *Journal of Wildlife Management* **70**(3): 764–776.

Sinclair, A.R.E. (1977). *The African Buffalo. A Study of Resource Limitation of Populations*. Chicago: University of Chicago Press.

Sitters, J., I.M.A. Heitkönig, M. Holmgren and G.S.O. Ojwang' (2009). Herded cattle and wild grazers partition water but share forage resources during dry years in East African savannas. *Biological Conservation* **142**(4): 738–750.

Spaan, R.S., C.W. Epps, V.O. Ezenwa and A.E. Jolles (2019). Why did the buffalo cross the park? Resource shortages, but not infections, drive dispersal in female African buffalo (*Syncerus caffer*). *Ecology and Evolution* **9**(10): 5651–5663.

Sueur, C., A.J. King, L. Conradt, et al. (2011). Collective decision-making and fission–fusion dynamics: a conceptual framework. *Oikos* **120**(11): 1608–1617.

Tambling, C.J., D.J. Druce, M.W. Hayward, et al. (2012). Spatial and temporal changes in group dynamics and range use enable anti-predator responses in African buffalo. *Ecology* **93**(6): 1297–1304.

Taolo, C.L. (2003). *Population Ecology, Seasonal Movements and Habitat Use of the African Buffalo (Syncerus caffer) in Chobe National Park, Botswana.* PhD dissertation, Department of Biology, Faculty of Natural Sciences and Technology, Norwegian University of Science and Technology.

Taylor, R.D. (1985). *The Response of Buffalo, Syncerus caffer (Sparrman) to the Kariba Lakeshore Grassland (Panicum repens L.) in Matusadona National Park.* PhD dissertation, University of Zimbabwe.

Turner, W.C., A.E. Jolles and N. Owen-Smith (2005). Alternating sexual segregation during the mating season by male African buffalo (*Syncerus caffer*). *Journal of Zoology* **267**(03): 291.

Valls-Fox, H., S. Chamaillé-Jammes, M. de Garine-Wichatitsky, et al. (2018). Water and cattle shape habitat selection by wild herbivores at the edge of a protected area. *Animal Conservation* **21**(5): 365–375.

Van Hoof, W.F., A.F. Groen and H.H.T. Prins (2003). Genetic structure of African buffalo herds based on variation at the mitochondrial D-loop and autosomal microsatellite loci: evidence for male-biased gene flow. *Conservation Genetics* **4**(4): 467–477.

Walrath, R., T.R. Van Deelen and K.C. VerCauteren (2011). Efficacy of proximity loggers for detection of contacts between maternal pairs of white-tailed deer. *Wildlife Society Bulletin* **35**(4): 452–460.

Wielgus, E., A. Caron, E. Bennitt, et al. (2021). Inter-group social behavior, contact patterns and risk for pathogen transmission in Cape buffalo populations. *Journal of Wildlife Management* **85**(8): 1574–1590.

Wielgus, E., D. Cornélis, M. de Garine-Wichatitsky, et al. (2020). Are fission–fusion dynamics consistent among populations? A large-scale study with Cape buffalo. *Ecology and Evolution* **10**(17): 9240–9256.

Winnie, J.A.J., P. Cross and W. Getz (2008). Habitat quality and heterogeneity influence distribution and behavior in African buffalo (*Syncerus caffer*). *Ecology* **89**(5): 1457–1468.

7 · Population Dynamics of Buffalo: The Effects of Droughts and Non-Equilibrium Dynamics

J. W. HEARNE, M. J. S. PEEL
AND H. H. T. PRINS

Introduction

Population dynamics is concerned with changes in a population over time. Understanding these dynamics facilitates the early detection of growing or declining trends in a population. If necessary, appropriate control or protection strategies can then be introduced timeously to deal with undesirable trends (Mertens, 1985; Jolles, 2007). This is needed both for the conservation of African buffalo (*Syncerus caffer*) and for designing optimal strategies for their harvesting (e.g. hunting) or even ranching (Chapters 13 and 16).

Several studies (e.g. Sinclair, 1977; Mertens, 1985) collected data in the field and subsequently processed these data to produce life tables of buffalo populations. For humans, actuaries use life tables to determine the expected life expectancy of an individual, and hence perhaps the appropriate life insurance premium for that individual to pay. Due to practical difficulties in collecting data, life tables for buffalo are generally less accurate than those for humans. More importantly, in wildlife management the *purpose* of life tables is different. Forecasting is essential for good management and life table data can be used in a model to project a population into the future. Even for this purpose, however, the utility of such a model is limited. Population dynamics of buffalo populations are frequently event-driven. For example, droughts, disease and poaching may invalidate any forecast based on life tables. Moreover, wildlife managers require scenario-based rough estimates rather than precise population projections into the future. *Roughly* what proportion of a herd will die if a severe drought occurs next year? Hence, should any intervention be considered? Indeed, for a herd of 500 buffalo, the answer to this last question is not likely to differ whether there is an expected loss of 105 or 125 animals.

Investigating the dynamics of a population usually involves the use of mathematical models. There is a diverse array of such models. Therefore, before commencing any formulation or use of a model it is important to be very clear about its purpose. What are the questions for which one seeks answers? What understanding of system behaviour is sought? Only once the aims and the purpose of the model are clear can the appropriate type of model be chosen.

In this chapter, we first discuss various exogenous factors that disrupt population trajectories. We focus particularly on drought and disease. This is followed by a discussion on the constraints that these factors play in the types and goals of models that can provide any useful insight. Finally, we show the importance of age structure in determining population dynamics. We will illustrate how aggregated population data might in fact mislead observers.

Factors Affecting Population Dynamics

Droughts

The rinderpest outbreak in Africa in the 1890s reached southern Africa around 1896, peaked in 1897–1898 and severely impacted artiodactyl populations in Africa. Stevenson-Hamilton (1929) reported that the disease '...reduced the already much depleted buffalo herds to about a dozen individuals' in what is now Kruger National Park (KNP). Impressive conservation efforts during the early twentieth century and the recovery of rangelands following the large-scale, disease-related grazer die-off contributed to the recovery of game populations. However, African buffalo remain susceptible to drought (Sinclair, 1977; Smuts, 1982; Walker et al., 1987; Prins, 1996; Peel and Smit, 2020; Smit et al., 2020). As the doyen of South African nature conservation, James Stevenson-Hamilton observed, 'During the severe drought at the end of 1935, when the rains failed completely, and the Lower Sabie area was quite bare of grass, the buffaloes suffered terribly' (Stevenson-Hamilton, 1947, p. 85). This pattern of sensitivity to drought is further illustrated by, among others, Walker et al. (1987) describing the impact of the severe 1981–1984 drought, exacerbated by water provision, that affected most of southern Africa, causing extensive grass mortality and grazer mortality in particular. Peel and Smit (2020) describe declines in the buffalo population of between 77 per cent in an area that was minimally managed and declines of 29 per cent and 35 per cent, respectively, in areas where management removals were carried out before the 2014/15–2016/17 drought developed fully. Furthermore, regional buffalo population declines were highest in areas with a high density of artificially provided water points and associated low herbaceous biomass (Smit et al., 2020).

Stevenson-Hamilton (1947, p. 85) further states, 'Such few calves as were born did not survive...'. This is a very pertinent observation, yet more detailed observations appear to indicate that recently weaned juveniles are the first to die, followed by suckling calves, both groups being very susceptible to drought conditions (Prins and Peel, personal observations at numerous places during some droughts). During the 1969–1970 drought in KNP, Smuts (1982) once observed five buffalo calves dying while the herd was moving between two water points some 9 km apart. Further, observations of calves wandering through the veld alone were common, as they could not keep up with the herds moving over large areas in search of food and water. The proportions of calf and juvenile groups in the buffalo population were extremely low after the 2014/15–2015/16 drought, and these statistics feature in our detailed discussion of individual protected areas.

We examined three protected area (PA) scenarios under varying environmental and management regimes in the same semi-arid savanna (Lehmann et al., 2011; Luvhuno et al., 2018) in the Lowveld of South Africa as described by Stevenson-Hamilton (1947). The three PAs represent an environmental gradient with decreasing long-term mean annual rainfall from south to north (PA 1: 631 mm, PA 2: 552 mm and PA 3: 430 mm). While focusing on what we consider the 'long' 2014/15 and 2015/16 droughts, it is important to describe the conditions prior to the onset of the drought. For all three PAs, the two-year pre-drought mean varied from wet (PA 1 and PA 2) to very wet (PA 3). The rainfall received as a percentage of the long-term mean annual rainfall in year one of the drought varied between 54 per cent for the wetter south to around 77 per cent for the 'drier' central and northern areas. The second year of the drought showed the same pattern for the PAs, with the 'wetter' southern PA 1 receiving 38 per cent, the central fenced PA 2 57 per cent and the drier northern PA 3 65 per cent of the mean annual rainfall, respectively. The post-drought rainfall was at the mean annual rainfall for PA 1 and marginally below the mean for PA 2 and PA 3. Rainfall correlates well with the grass standing crop (GSC) – the two-year pre-drought mean for the GSC ranged from 123 per cent for PA 1, 159 per cent for PA 2 and 152 per cent for PA 3. The entry point to the drought in terms of grass availability was thus very favourable (Figure 7.1a–f). Year 1 of the drought was characterized by marked declines in the GSC,

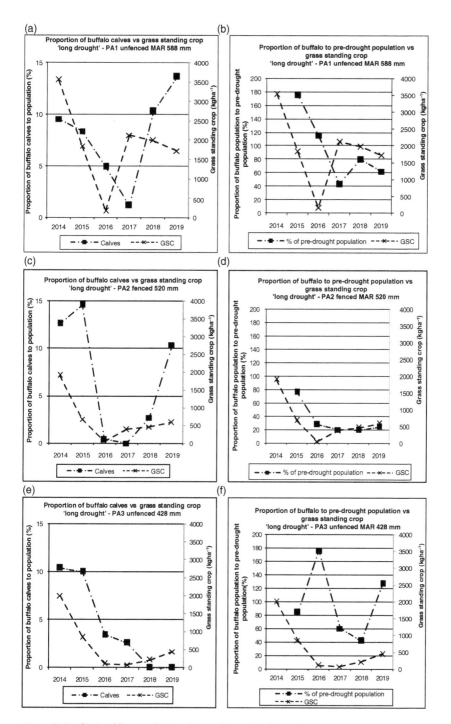

Figure 7.1(a–f) Buffalo population data and rangeland conditions pre-, during and post-drought on three protected areas in the Lowveld of South Africa. Source: Authors.

ranging from 70, 67 to 72 per cent of the long-term mean for PAs 1–3, respectively. The second drought year precipitated an almost complete failure of the grassland crop with the mean GSC ranging from 7, 6 to 9 per cent for PAs 1–3, respectively. Recovery of the GSC post-drought again tracked a return to improved rainfall conditions (Figure 7.1a–f). Similar precipitous declines in standing crop (and subsequent yearling mortality) were observed in Tarangire National Park (Tanzania) in 1992 when minimal perennial grass cover was left, and in KNP in 1993 and again in 2004 with similar effects (Prins, personal observation). The periodicity of the droughts in the southern African climatic system is well illustrated in Malherbe et al. (2020), where it appears to be associated with the Southern Atlantic Oscillation (see also Gandiwa et al., 2016 and Poshiwa et al., 2013). Droughts in East Africa do not show clear periodicity (Prins and Loth, 1988) because rainfall there is driven much more by monsoonal effects over the Indian Ocean.

We evaluated how buffalo numbers changed after a drought event in the three PAs located in the Lowveld of South Africa and located along a south–north gradient. In our study, we considered buffalo numbers and the susceptible calf groups (up to 2 years old). Buffalo numbers were calculated as a percentage of the pre-drought number (Figure 7.1a, c and e) and for calves as a percentage of the population as a whole (Figure 7.1b, d and f).

In PA 1 (Figure 7.1a – wetter, and open to KNP), the population maintained itself in the first year of the drought, followed by a marked decline in the second year, but the population remained healthy. It was only during the winter of the second year of drought with the collapse of the grass layer that the numbers declined spectacularly. The latter was a result of a combination of movement out of the heavily stocked PA 1 into the adjacent KNP (less artificial water point provision and lower animal densities), and drought-related mortality through starvation and predation due to the animals' weakened condition. The proportion of calves present in the population was maintained during the first year of the drought (favourable drought entry conditions), declined markedly in the second year and plummeted in the first post-drought year, a function of the die-off in the winter of year two and reflected in recovery year two post-drought as the rangelands recovered (Figure 7.1b). The recovery of the 'rested' rangeland in these wetter southern areas was illustrated by the return to pre-drought calf proportions in the second post-drought year. The overall reduced population size after the drought indicates that the older age classes also lost individuals, likely caused by increased predation and starvation.

In PA 2 (Figure 7.1c – intermediate rainfall and fenced), 98 buffalo (11 per cent of the population) were removed on recommendation between 2014 and 2015 with an additional 28 animals removed in 2016 (11 per cent of a much-reduced population). While these removals were commendable, they did not prevent marked declines in year one of the drought and steep declines in the following two years resulting in levels of around 20 per cent of pre-drought numbers up to three years post-drought. We consider that this situation was due to the heavy prevailing stocking rates at the start of the drought and rapid declines in the grass layer at the onset of the drought due to the fenced situation, resulting in drought-related mortality through predation on weakened animals and starvation. The proportion of calves present in the population was maintained in the first year of the drought (favourable drought entry conditions), declined steeply in the second year of drought and year one post-drought (to 0 per cent) with minimal recovery in year two post-drought and improvement in only year three post-drought but to levels still below pre-drought (Figure 7.1d). The population contin- ued to recover slowly due to numbers below the exponential phase of the growth curve in this fenced PA. Without supplementation from outside sources, the rangeland would have rested in this wetter, albeit fenced central area. We would expect the population to recover, the rate dependent on the prevailing rainfall conditions and associated range condition that in turn affects how quickly the growth curve reaches exponential.

In PA 3 (Figure 7.1e, drier open to KNP) there was a decline in the number of buffalo in the first year of the drought followed by an increase in the second year of drought. This is anomalous as the grass layer was already severely limiting and probably the result of buffalo moving through the area at the time of the count from the surround- ing drier waterless areas where conditions were more severe. The steep decline in the buffalo population was therefore only recorded in the first-year post-drought and continued in the second-year post-drought due to a continued decline in the grass layer combined with movement out of the PA (see e.g. Hilbers et al., 2015), predation due to the animals being in a weakened condition and starvation. This pattern was only reversed in the third-year post-drought. Although the buffalo popula- tion 'increased' in year two of the drought, the proportion of calves was very low, supporting the argument that the animals present in this PA were in all likelihood moving through the area in search of water and grazing. The proportion of calves present in the population was maintained in the first year of the drought (favourable drought entry conditions), declined steeply in the second year of drought and continued to decline markedly for the three years post-drought (3, 2.6 and 0 per cent; Figure 7.1f). We contend that the slower recovery of the population is a function of the slower recovery in the calf component and even greater susceptibility to drought in these drier, less-resilient areas.

Disease

Buffalo are remarkably resistant to indigenous diseases, but can be negatively affected by anthrax (*Bacillus anthracis*; e.g. Hugh-Jones and De Vos, 2002; Clegg et al., 2007). They are not known to succumb easily to different forms of trypanosomes transmitted by tsetse flies (see Garcia et al., 2018). These parasitic forms, some of which may cause sleeping sickness in humans, are destroyed by phagocytes (Young et al., 1975), but other forms of trypanotolerance may occur (e.g. Murray et al., 1984). They are also resistant to other diseases like corridor disease caused by *Theileria p. parva* and East Coast fever caused by *T. p. lawrenci*. East Coast fever was introduced into South Africa in 1902 by infected cattle imported from East Africa to restock depleted cattle numbers after the rinderpest epidemic of 1896 (Lawrence, 1979). The subsequent epidemic lead to an estimated 5.5 million cattle deaths (Potgieter et al., 1988) but no buffalo epidemic was reported. Buffalo are also resistant to *Anaplasma* forms (Sisson, 2017). For an overview of other diseases, see Chapters 9 and 12. Some exotic diseases, however, were disastrous and buffalo had no immunity or resistance. Rinderpest was the most notorious, with a death toll exceeding 90 per cent (Prins, 1996, p. 122 and references therein). The disease has been eradicated. Other exotic diseases, however, did not affect buffalo too badly. A case in point is bovine tuberculosis (bTB). We thus think that diseases exert a rather constant pressure in contrast to droughts that are punctuated events with frequently severe consequences for young buffalo in particular.

Implications for Modelling

Clearly, there are many factors that may cause major losses in population numbers. Furthermore, it is rare to find two consecutive decades within which such a loss does not occur. Consequently, a population in the wild will mostly, if not always, be in some transitional stage. Thus, transient dynamics will dominate rather than any form of density-dependent growth or equilibrium, and concepts of carrying capacity become irrelevant. In such situations, any analysis involving aggregation of age groups may lead to incorrect conclusions. Population trajectories are affected by how age structures are distributed. Two populations that have the same total number of head at some point in time might exhibit very different dynamic behaviour for several years thereafter due to the populations having different age structures. Distinguishing a population by age groups is therefore important both from a data and a modelling perspective, and the more precise, the better. In the following sections, we will explore these issues further.

Modelling

We constructed a model to gain insight into the relationship between aggregated population data, such as that available from a field survey, and the age structure of a population. We looked at the implications for forecasting population trends as well as for drawing conclusions about possible density effects. To have a clear, uncluttered focus on this, we considered a population for which the following assumptions hold for the solution period:

- No migration
- No losses due to disease, predation, culling, poaching or other exogenous factors
- No constraining limits related to space and grazing resources within the time
- A population large enough so that we can ignore stochastic changes in vital rates.

We also assumed that there would be enough males in a population to service the females. In this case, the population dynamics are determined by the females.

Leslie Model

Let $\underline{x}(t)$ denote the vector whose ith element, $x_i(t)$, is the female population in age group i at time t. We can project the population in each age group forward one year by the following equation:

$$\underline{x}(t+1) = A\underline{x}(t) \qquad (7.1)$$

The matrix A is known as a Leslie matrix (Caswell, 2001). With subscripts denoting the age groups, a Leslie matrix comprises the following:

- The first row of A contains the specific fecundity rates
- The ith row of A contains the survival rate s_{i-1} in column $i-1$
- All other elements of the matrix A are zero.

Thus:

$$A = \begin{bmatrix} f_1 & f_2 & f_3 & \cdots & f_{18} & f_{19} \\ s_1 & 0 & 0 & \cdots & 0 & 0 \\ 0 & s_2 & 0 & \cdots & 0 & 0 \\ & & \ddots & & & \\ 0 & 0 & 0 & \cdots & s_{18} & 0 \end{bmatrix} \qquad (7.2)$$

Stationary Age-Structure

From mathematical theory (Caswell, 2001), we know that applying equation (7.1) repeatedly for $t = 1, 2, 3, \ldots$ will eventually lead to a *stationary age structure*. By this, we mean that the population in each age group as a proportion of the total population remains constant even as the total population might grow or decline. These proportions (i.e., the age structure) can be obtained by calculating the eigenvector of matrix A corresponding to its largest eigenvalue, λ. Furthermore, the value of λ yields information about the annual growth rate of the population. If $\lambda = 1$, the population will remain constant, whereas a value of λ greater than or less than one indicates that the population is growing or declining, respectively.

Ricker Model

A population subject to density-dependent growth is frequently modelled using the Ricker model:

$$p(t+1) = p(t)\exp^{r(1-p(t)/K)} \qquad (7.3)$$

where p is the population, r is the intrinsic annual growth rate and K is the maximum stocking rate, often referred to as the carrying capacity. For unbounded populations, K is infinitely large. In this case, the relationship between λ and r is given by:

$$r = \log(\lambda) \tag{7.4}$$

This quantity will be referred to simply as the growth rate for the remainder of this chapter.

Data

Data from three different studies were used in the analyses that follow: namely, Serengeti National Park (Sinclair, 1977), Hluhluwe–iMfolozi Park (Jolles, 2007) and Virunga National Park (Mertens, 1985). These data are shown in Figure 7.2 (precise values are given in the Appendix, Table A7.1).

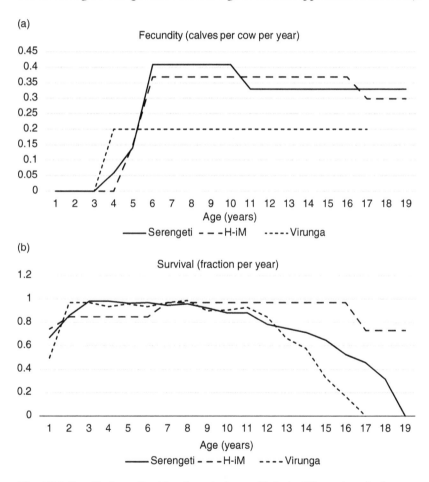

Figure 7.2 Specific fecundity (a) and survival rates (b) for buffalo as given in three different studies: Serengeti (Sinclair, 1977), Hluhluwe–iMfolozi (Jolles, 2007) and Virunga (Mertens, 1985). The age group refers to the age of the animals in a cohort.

Small adjustments have been made to the age groups in Jolles (2007) to facilitate comparison.

Analysis

There are three parts to this section. First, we explore the population dynamics using the Serengeti data and make some observations. In the second and third parts, we examine some of the conclusions drawn in the studies of Jolles (2007) and Mertens (1985), respectively.

Serengeti

The data in Sinclair (1977) were a result of several years of work in the Serengeti during the 1960s. It is the most cited work on the fecundity and survival rates of the African buffalo.

Substituting the Serengeti fecundity and survival rates into the matrix (7.2), we find the largest eigenvalue λ and the corresponding eigenvector. The eigenvector corresponds to the *stationary age distribution*, which we will use as starting values for simulating the population dynamics. The eigenvalue $\lambda = 1.054$ implies a growth rate of 5.4 per cent for this stationary age distribution. However, as discussed, populations are subject to frequent disruptions. After such a disruption, how long will it take before the population returns to this stationary age distribution? We consider two plausible scenarios to explore this question.

Serengeti Scenario 1 – A Short Drought
Starting with a stationary age distribution, a population is subject to a short, acute drought of 6 months. This results in the deaths of a major proportion of the recently weaned calves. Specifically, in our model, 75 per cent of the second and third age classes die immediately after the start of year 2.

To simplify the visual representation of the results we aggregate the 19 age groups as follows: calves (group 1), juveniles (groups 2–4), subadults (group 5) and adults (groups 6–19). A division of adults into 'young' cows (groups 6–10) and 'old' cows is used for some results. This division corresponds to specific fecundity rates as given by Sinclair and shown in Figure 7.2.

It can be observed in Figure 7.3a that more than a decade after the drought event, the population has not yet returned to its previous growth rate. In Figure 7.3b, we note that the age structure of the population is

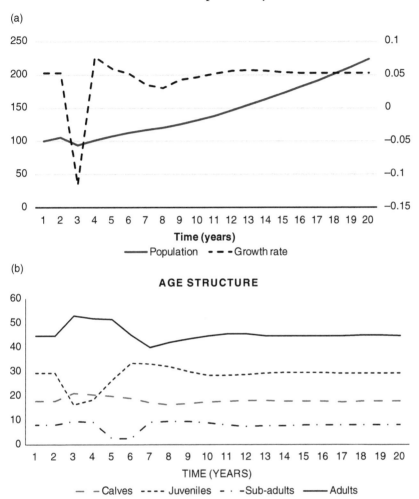

Figure 7.3 The effect of a short, acute drought on the dynamics of a population initially in a stable age distribution. (a) Growth rate, (b) age structure. Source: Authors.

also unsettled. A consequence of this is that the number of calves produced per cow fluctuates as shown in Figure 7.4a. Why should this be, given that the specific fecundity rate for each year-age group is constant?

Dividing the 'adult' group into 'young' (groups 6–10) and 'old' (groups 11–19), we observe in Figure 7.4b that the proportion of cows in each group fluctuates over the solution period. As the 'young' and 'old' cows have different specific fecundity rates of 0.41 and 0.33, respectively, changes in the proportions of each group cause a change in the *average* number of calves produced per adult cow.

(a)

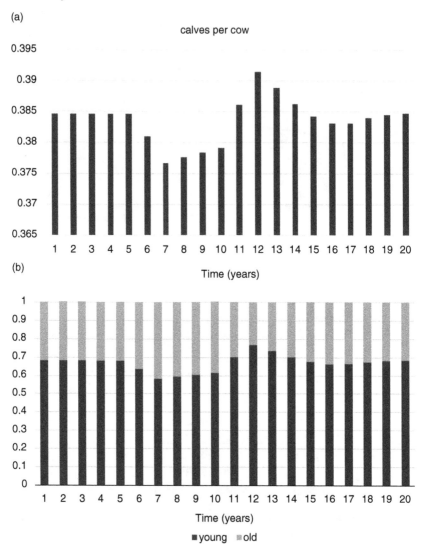

Figure 7.4 (a) Fluctuations in the rate of calf production by a herd of buffalo cows. (b) Changes in the proportion of high fecundity 'young' cows to 'old' cows. Source: Authors.

Serengeti Scenario 2 – A Long Drought

Starting with a stationary age distribution, a population is subjected to a severe drought lasting 2 years. This results in high mortality for recently weaned calves. Specifically, we impose in the model a die-off of 75 per cent of females in groups 2 and 3 in year 2. This is followed in year 3 by

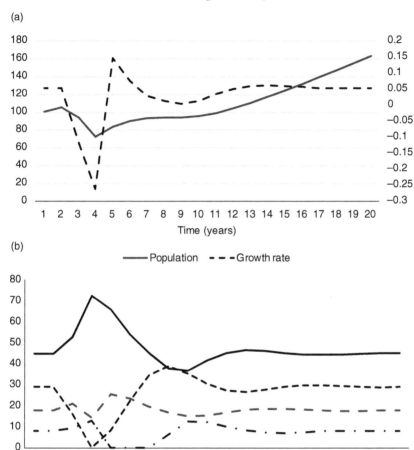

Figure 7.5 Fluctuations in (a) population and growth rate and (b) age structure.
Source: Authors.

a complete die-off of all calves and juveniles, that is all animals in groups 1–4, and 50 per cent of cows staying barren.

In some respects, Figures 7.5 and 7.6 show exaggerated versions of the effects already noted in scenario 1, but there is more to learn from these results.

Suppose a field study commences in year 4 and is concluded in year 10. Further, suppose that no other data were available other than that obtained over the six-year study period. Observing the population

(a)

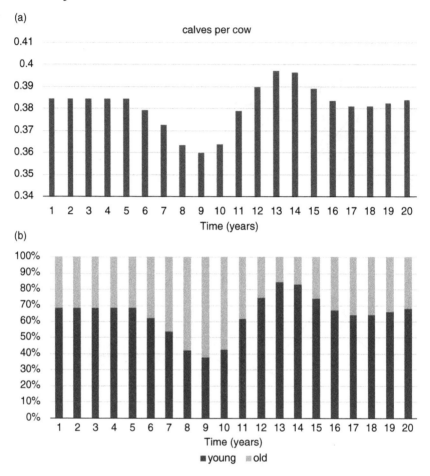

(b)

Figure 7.6 (a) Number of calves produced per adult cow each year. (b) Composition of the adult female population. Source: Authors.

trajectory (Figure 7.5a) over this period, it is easy to conclude (wrongly) that population growth is density-dependent. In fact, a Ricker model with $K = 95$ and $r = 0.61$ gives an almost perfect fit to these data. The declining number of calves produced per cow over this period (Figure 7.6a) would tend to confirm a conclusion that the population is subject to density-dependent growth. And yet there is no density effect built into the model that generated these results as can be seen from the population trajectory beyond year 11. The transient dynamics of a disturbed population can easily mislead.

Discussion of the Serengeti Cases

- Even a short disturbance (6-month drought) affects the population dynamics for more than a decade.
- A study of 6 years may produce trajectories that lead to misconceptions about the longer-term prospects of a population.
- With no density constraints on a population, transient changes in the age structure may lead to a population trajectory mimicking density-dependent growth over a period lasting a few years.
- Specific fecundity rates cannot be accurately determined using aggregated adult age groups for populations in transition.

Hluhluwe–iMfolozi

Demographic data from 826 buffalo in 12 herds in the Hluhluwe–iMfolozi Park, captured in 2001–2002, were used by Jolles (2007) to parameterize an age-structured population model. The stationary age distribution predicted by the model is, according to Jolles, 'very similar to the age distribution observed in the captured population sample'. Jolles goes on to use some of her results to provide evidence of density-dependent population growth. We analyse whether these conclusions stand up to further scrutiny.

The first problem we come across is in the age-structured population data given in Jolles (2007) and shown in Table 7.1. Let us assume that the given number of subadults (= 42) is correct. The survival rate for the juvenile group is given as 0.85. Thus, to get 42 subadults we would need to have 42/0.85 = 49.4 juveniles in the age range from 3.5 to 4.5 years. Similarly, the population in the age range from 5.5 to 6.5 years would be 42 × 0.85 = 35.7 and the next year class would be 35.7 × 0.97 = 34.6. We can continue in this way and determine the numbers in all age groups. Then aggregating these into broader groups, we get the 'Revised' values given in Table 7.1. As can be seen, these numbers differ significantly from the values reported by Jolles.

Is it possible to understand the discrepancy in the two sets of values in Table 7.1 using the simple model presented earlier by equations 7.1 and 7.2? The first step to take is to substitute the fecundity and survival rates determined by Jolles, given in Figure 7.2, into the Leslie matrix (equation 7.2).

The largest eigenvalue of the Leslie matrix in this case indicates a growth rate of 3.4 per cent per annum. This is less than the average 6.8 per cent recorded over the period from 1957 to 2004. The associated

Table 7.1 *Age structure for African buffalo in Hluhluwe-iMfolozi Park, South Africa as reported by Jolles (2007). The revised estimates for the number of buffalo in the different age classes (N) were obtained by assuming the subadult number of 42 (the number published) is correct and then using the survival data provided in the same article for each year-age group to generate the numbers in the 'Revised' column as described in the previous paragraph.*

Age (years)	Jolles (N)	Revised (N)
Calves (<1)	136	109
Juveniles (1 ≥ 4.5)	366	256
Subadults (>4.5–5.5)	42	42
Mature (>5.5)	247	408

Table 7.2 *The stationary age structure for Hluhluwe–iMfolozi Park, South Africa as calculated on the basis of the Leslie model compared with field data reported by Jolles (2007). Values shown (rounded to the nearest integer) are percentages of the total population.*

Age (years)	Leslie model (%)	Data (Jolles) (%)
Calves (<1)	17	17
Juveniles (1 ≥ 4.5)	30	46
Subadults (>4.5–5.5)	7	5
Mature (>5.5)	47	31

stationary age structure is given in Table 7.2 where it is compared with the field data. This difference suggests that a stationary age distribution had not been attained at the time the field data were recorded. This is not surprising given droughts and removals over this period.

Let us now impose on this system the same drought described in Serengeti – scenario 2 to investigate the population dynamics. For this, we used equation 7.1 with the same Leslie matrix comprising the fecundity and survival rates. We assume an initial population of 100 head and determine the age distribution from the eigenvector of the Leslie matrix. Some results are shown in Figure 7.7.

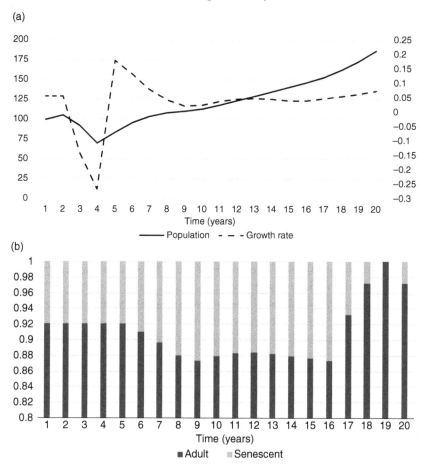

Figure 7.7 (a) Fluctuations in the population and its growth rate. (b) The relative proportion of 'adult' cows (6–16 years old) to 'senescent' cows (17+ years). Source: Authors.

We observe in Figure 7.7a that during years 4–11 the population displays a trajectory that might easily be interpreted as density-dependent growth. Applying a Ricker model with $K = 117$ and $r = 0.45$ gives an almost perfect fit to the population trajectory over this 7-year period, and yet the population trajectory has been generated by a model that has no density-dependence as is apparent in later years. How can we explain this?

The changes in growth rate observed in Figure 7.7a are purely a result of changes in the age structure. It can be seen in Figure 7.7b that the proportion of 'adult' cows (6–16 years old) is depressed between the years 5 and 17. Recall from Figure 7.2 that 'adult' cows in Hluhluwe have a specific fecundity rate of 0.37 compared with only 0.3 for 'senescent' cows. Therefore, the number of calves produced by a population, and thus the growth rate of the whole population, will be affected by the ratio of 'adult' cows to 'senescent' cows.

Finally, it should be noted in Figure 7.7b that the population has not settled into a stationary age structure nearly two decades after the drought.

Discussion of the Hluhluwe–iMfolozi Case

- If we have accurate fecundity and survival rates, we can easily test whether a population has attained a stationary age structure. The number in any age group multiplied by the survival rate should give the number in the next age group. This will be true for all age groups if we have a stationary age structure.
- It takes nearly two decades after a severe year drought before the population settles into a stationary age structure.
- Due to the frequency of droughts a population is likely to always be in a transient state.
- For populations in a transient state, determining vital rates from aggregated data can be misleading. Furthermore, even a field study with a 7-year duration might yield data that lead to an incorrect conclusion of density-dependent growth.

Virunga

In an analysis of buffalo in Virunga National Park in the Democratic Republic of the Congo (then Zaire), Mertens concluded in 1985 that the structure of the population had remained approximately stable over the past 25 years. Let us investigate this further. We apply to the matrix A, given in equation 7.1, the lifetable data constructed by Mertens (Figure 7.2), which differs to some extent from that of Sinclair (1977).

As described previously, the stationary age structure can be obtained by calculating the eigenvector of matrix A corresponding to its largest eigenvalue, λ. Furthermore, the value of λ can be used in equation 7.4 to calculate the growth rate of the population.

Table 7.3 *Comparison of the stationary age structure of African buffalo in Virunga National Park, Democratic Republic of Congo obtained by our model with the field data of Mertens (1985).*

Age groups (year)	Model (%)	Mertens (%)
<1 (Young)	14.5	8.7
≥1–4 (Immatures)	22.2	15.9
>4–17 (Adults)	63.3	75.4

For the data given in Figure 7.2, we obtain the value of the largest eigenvalue $\lambda = 0.974$. This implies that the population will experience a continuing decline once it has settled into a stationary age structure. Although Mertens provides vital rates for 17 age groups, his population counts and age structure are given in only three groups: 'young' (0–1 years), 'immatures' (1–4 years) and 'adults' (4+ years). Clustering age groups from the eigenvector to enable a direct comparison with Mertens' data, we get Table 7.3.

The two age structures in Table 7.3 differ. To explore this, we first note that the age structure reported by Mertens shows that the proportion of each group differs by less than 3 per cent from two previous findings at Virunga National Park in 1960 and 1978–1979. Therefore, we set initial population values close to those of Mertens and used the Virunga vital rates given in Figure 7.2. We then applied equation 7.1 repeatedly to project the population forward in time. The simulations were performed for 30 years, but it is clear from the results that the age groups stabilized after about 25 years as shown in Figure 7.8.

In reporting his data, Mertens allowed for the possibility that his fecundity data were a bit too low and that Sinclair's values might be more accurate. We thus replaced Virunga fecundity data in Figure 7.2 with those for Serengeti to determine whether this reduces the difference between the model output and the field data. In fact, this replacement increased the discrepancy further, as shown in Table 7.4 (Model 1 as compared to the output based on Merten's data). Using Serengeti data for both fecundity and survival also did not improve matters (Model 2 in Table 7.4).

Table 7.4 *Comparison of the stationary age structure determined from population counts in Virunga National Park, the Democratic Republic of Congo by Mertens (1985) and that obtained using a Leslie matrix model. Model 1 used Mertens' survival data but with Sinclair's (1977) fecundity data. Model 2 used Sinclair's data on fecundity as well as on survival.*

Age group (year)	Mertens (%)	Model 1 (%)	Model 2 (%)
<1 (Young)	8.7	19	18
≥1–4 (Immatures)	15.9	26.3	29
>4–17 (Adults)	75.4	54.7	53

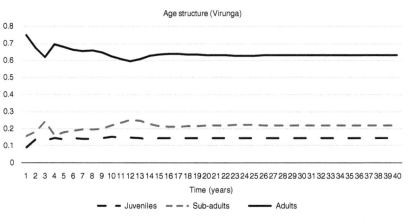

Figure 7.8 Changing age structure over 30 years. Compared with the initial structure at $t = 1$, both juveniles and subadults ended up representing higher percentages of the population, while adults are lower. Source: Authors.

Discussion of the Virunga Case

- Starting with the age structure recorded, it takes nearly two decades before the population settles. It then settles into an age structure that differs from that recorded by Mertens.
- Given this inconsistency and the frequent disturbances to buffalo populations, it seems unlikely that the age structure of the Virunga population was stable over 25 years as claimed. We conclude this, even though the broad population structure recorded by Mertens was similar to that recorded 25 years earlier.

Conclusion

We have noted that factors such as disease, predation, poaching and droughts all have severe effects on buffalo populations, but that droughts (because they occur punctuated in time) have the most intriguing consequences. These events happen frequently. Three major droughts, for example, have occurred in less than four decades in the Greater Kruger National Park (Malherbe et al., 2020; Smit et al., 2020) and severe droughts were also reported by Stevenson-Hamilton (1947) decades previously. Such droughts may increase in frequency with climate change in some parts of the range of the African buffalo, but perhaps not in others. With such disruptions, populations are always in a state of transition (and in a form of non-equilibrium dynamics: see for example Ellis and Swift, 1988; Desta and Coppock, 2002; Vetter, 2005). Their age structures are thus always changing. Even without further disruptions, it might take more than a couple of decades before a population settles into a stationary age structure.

In this chapter, we have shown the importance of detailed age structure modelling in determining population trajectories. Time series analysis of aggregated populations may lead to significantly incorrect conclusions. This includes, for example, misleading 'evidence' for density-dependence for a case where, in fact, there was no such effect at all.

A concern highlighted by this analysis is that in the field it is often difficult to distinguish the exact ages of individuals. This might also have implications for calculating vital rates. Suppose fecundity starts declining from age 15 and we cannot distinguish between 14- and 16-year-olds. Then simply counting calves and adults will not give a specific fecundity rate that will hold for a different mix of 14- and 16-year-olds.

We also have shown that vital rates determine an age structure. If the survival rate, say 0.9, in a particular age group with 100 individuals is known, then the next older age group should comprise 90 individuals *a year later*. If the population is in equilibrium and hence the age structure is stationary, the older group will contain 90 individuals *now*. Thus, if numbers in the older group differ from 90 then we know that the population is still in a state of transition.

In conclusion, we contend that understanding the population dynamics of buffalo requires detailed knowledge of the age structure. Furthermore, any data on vital rates should record the extent to which age groups have been aggregated. Any studies on population dynamics using these data should explore the full range of disaggregation possible that is consistent with the aggregated data. Only then can firm statements be made about the population dynamics. Indeed, while it is easy to do some arm-waving about 'climate change' and stating that 'there will be more droughts in Africa', it is much more difficult to replace comfortable thinking about 'carrying capacity' by the realization that animal populations in many parts of Africa are in a state of non-equilibrium dynamics, and that a drought some years ago is still playing havoc with the population dynamics. Nonetheless, choosing the wrong (mathematical) model for predicting future numbers, setting offtake numbers (e.g. for hunting quota) or even temporary destocking strategies may have severe repercussions for the sustainability of a harvesting operation, for example, or for calculating gene flow in a population.

Appendix

Table A7.1 *Specific fecundity and survival rates for buffalo as given in three different studies: Serengeti (Sinclair, 1977), Hluhluwe–iMfolozi (Jolles, 2007) and Virunga (Mertens, 1985). The age group refers to the age of the animals in a cohort.*

Study	Serengeti		Hluhluwe–iMfolozi		Virunga	
Age group	Fecundity	Survival	Fecundity	Survival	Fecundity	Survival
1	0	0.670	0	0.74	0	0.50
2	0	0.860	0	0.85	0	0.97
3	0	0.981	0	0.85	0	0.97
4	0.06	0.979	0	0.85	0.2	0.94
5	0.14	0.962	0.15	0.85	0.2	0.96
6	0.41	0.970	0.37	0.85	0.2	0.94
7	0.41	0.944	0.37	0.97	0.2	0.97
8	0.41	0.959	0.37	0.97	0.2	0.99
9	0.41	0.925	0.37	0.97	0.2	0.90
10	0.41	0.880	0.37	0.97	0.2	0.91
11	0.33	0.884	0.37	0.97	0.2	0.93
12	0.33	0.783	0.37	0.97	0.2	0.85
13	0.33	0.745	0.37	0.97	0.2	0.67
14	0.33	0.714	0.37	0.97	0.2	0.58
15	0.33	0.650	0.37	0.97	0.2	0.33
16	0.33	0.527	0.37	0.97	0.2	0.17
17	0.33	0.458	0.3	0.73	0.2	0.00

Table A7.1 (cont.)

Study	Serengeti		Hluhluwe–iMfolozi		Virunga	
Age group	Fecundity	Survival	Fecundity	Survival	Fecundity	Survival
18	0.33	0.318	0.3	0.73	–	–
19	0.33	0.000	0.3	0.73	–	–

References

Caswell, H. (2001). *Matrix Population Models: Construction, Analysis, and Interpretation.* Sunderland, MA: Sinauer.

Clegg, S.B., P.C.B. Turnbull, C.M. Foggin and P.M. Lindeque (2007). Massive outbreak of anthrax in wildlife in the Malilangwe Wildlife Reserve, Zimbabwe. *Veterinary Record* **160**: 113–118.

Desta, S. and D.L. Coppock (2002). Cattle population dynamics in the southern Ethiopian rangelands, 1980–97. *Rangeland Ecology and Management/Journal of Range Management Archives* **55**: 439–451.

Ellis, J.E. and D.M. Swift (1988). Stability of African pastoral ecosystems: alternate paradigms and implications for development. *Rangeland Ecology and Management/Journal of Range Management Archives* **41**: 450–459.

Garcia, H.A., C.M. Rodrigues, A.C. Rodrigues, et al. (2018). Remarkable richness of trypanosomes in tsetse flies (*Glossina morsitans morsitans* and *Glossina pallidipes*) from the Gorongosa National Park and Niassa National Reserve of Mozambique revealed by fluorescent fragment length barcoding (FFLB). *Infection, Genetics and Evolution* **63**: 370–379.

Gandiwa, E., I.M.A. Heitkönig, P.H. Eilers and H.H.T Prins (2016). Rainfall variability and its impact on large mammal populations in a complex of semi-arid African savanna protected areas. *Tropical Ecology* **57**: 163–180.

Hilbers, J.P., F. van Langevelde, H.H.T. Prins, et al. (2015). Modeling elephant-mediated cascading effects of water point closure. *Ecological Applications* **25**: 402–415

Hugh-Jones, M.E. and V. De Vos (2002). Anthrax and wildlife. *Revue Scientifique et Technique-Office International des Epizooties* **21**: 359–384.

Jolles, A.E. (2007). Population biology of African buffalo (*Syncerus caffer*) at Hluhluwe-iMfolozi Park, South Africa. *African Journal of Ecology* **45**: 398–406.

Lawrence, J.A. (1979). The differential diagnosis of the bovine theilerias of southern Africa. *Journal of the South African Veterinary Association* **50**: 311–313.

Lehmann, C.E.R., S.A. Archibald, W.A. Hoffmann and W.J. Bond (2011). Deciphering the distribution of the savanna biome. *New Phytologist* **191**: 197–209.

Luvhuno, L., R. Biggs, N. Stevens and K. Esler. (2018). Woody encroachment as a social–ecological regime shift. *Sustainability* **10**: 2221.

Malherbe, J., I.P. Smit, K.J. Wessels and P.J. Beukes (2020). Recent droughts in the Kruger National Park as reflected in the extreme climate index. *African Journal of Range and Forage Science* **37**: 1–17.

Mertens, H. (1985). Structures de population et tables de survie des buffles, topis et cobs de buffon au parc national des Virunga, Zaire. *Revue d'écologie* **40**: 3–50.

Murray, M., J.C.M. Trail, C.E. Davis and S.J. Black (1984). Genetic resistance to African trypanosomiasis. *Journal of Infectious Diseases* **149**: 311–319.

Peel, M.J.S. and I.P. Smit (2020). Drought amnesia: lessons from protected areas in the eastern Lowveld of South Africa. *African Journal of Range and Forage Science* **37**: 81–92.

Poshiwa, X., R.A. Groeneveld, I.M.A. Heitkönig, et al. (2013). Wildlife as insurance against rainfall fluctuations in a semi-arid savanna setting of southeastern Zimbabwe. *Tropical Conservation Science* **6**: 108–125.

Potgieter F.T., W.H. Stoltsz, E.F. Blouin and J.A. Roos (1988). Corridor disease in South Africa: a review of the current status. *Journal of the South African Veterinary Association* **59**: 155–160.

Prins, H.H.T. (1996). *Behaviour and Ecology of the African Buffalo: Social Inequality and Decision Making*. London: Chapman & Hall.

Prins, H.H.T. and P.E. Loth (1988). Rainfall patterns as background to plant phenology patterns in the Masai ecosystem of northern Tanzania. *Journal of Biogeography* **15**: 451–463.

Sinclair, A. (1977). *The African Buffalo: A Study of Resource Limitation of Populations*. Chicago: Chicago University Press.

Sisson, D. (2017). *Health and Fitness Effects of Anaplasma Species Infection in African Buffalo (Syncerus caffer)*. MSc thesis, Melbourne Veterinary School.

Smit, I.P.J, M.J.S. Peel, S.M. Ferreira, et al. (2020). Megaherbivore response to droughts under different management regimes: lessons from a large African savanna. *African Journal of Range and Forage Science* **37**: 65–80.

Smuts, G.L. (1982). *Lion*. Johannesburg: Macmillan.

Stevenson-Hamilton, J. (1929). *The Low-Veld: Its Wildlife and Its People*. London: Cassell and Co.

Stevenson-Hamilton, J. (1947). *Wildlife in South Africa*. London: Hamilton and Co.

Vetter, S. (2005). Rangelands at equilibrium and non-equilibrium: recent developments in the debate. *Journal of Arid Environments* **62**: 321–341.

Walker, B.H., R.H. Emslie, R.N. Owen-Smith and R.J. Scholes (1987). To cull or not to cull: lessons from a southern African drought. *Journal of Applied Ecology* **24**: 381–401.

Young, A.S., G.K. Kanhai and D.A. Stagg (1975). Phagocytosis of trypanosoma (*Nannomonas congolense*) by circulating macrophages in the African buffalo (*Syncerus caffer*). *Research in Veterinary Science* **19**: 108–110.

8 · The Environments of the African Buffalo, with Different Selection Forces in Different Habitats

H. H. T. PRINS, J. OTTENBURGHS
AND P. VAN HOOFT

Introduction

Every first-year text book in ecology informs students that every species has its own niche. This is sometimes taken further with the assertion that every species also has its own function (whatever that means). In this chapter, we ask what the 'niche' is of the African buffalo *Syncerus caffer*. However, 'the African buffalo' is not a homogeneous species because there is much morphological variation within the species. This variation is to some extent geographically restrained, and hence scientists have distinguished 'subspecies'. Due to the recent proliferation of 'recognized' subspecies and species, the reader should be aware that the recognizing and naming of taxa, which used to be safely in the hands of systematicists and taxonomists, has become politicized (see O'Brien and Mayr, 1991; Gippoliti and Amori, 2007). Under U.S. legislation, there may be a need to recognize and name taxa because any *named* taxon that may deserve protection can get it, but unnamed taxa cannot. Indeed, the U.S. Endangered Species Act considers any subspecies of fish or wildlife or any distinct population segment as an entity available for protection (Schwartz and Boness, 2017). To our knowledge, this does not apply to legislation in African buffalo range states, and so there is no conservation need for distinguishing many or few subspecies of African buffalo.

In the scientific literature, there are currently five recognized forms or subspecies of African buffalo, namely, *matthewsii*, *aequinoctialis*, *brachyceros*, *caffer* and *nanus* (Prins and Sinclair, 2013). Confusingly, the Safari Club International trophies system (SCI) also recognizes five subspecies, but they are not the same (see below). Ecologically speaking, we know next to nothing about *matthewsii*; this subspecies occurs in mountainous areas to the north of Lake Kivu as far as the Virunga Mountains. Whether it is justified to separate it from *caffer* is unclear (Prins and Sinclair, 2013); there is no scientific literature available to state whether this form has special ecological requirements, except if we consider the buffalo of Virunga National Park (a.k.a. Albert NP) in the Democratic Republic of the Congo (DRC) and of Parc National des Volcans in Rwanda as *matthewsii* too. In that case, the ecological literature does not provide clues to see it as functionally different from *caffer* (see e.g. Mertens, 1985; Mugangu et al., 1995; Plumptre, 1995; Treves et al., 2009).

Another blank spot in our knowledge on buffalo ecology concerns *aequinoctialis*. This subspecies occurs north of the Congo rainforest between the Chari River in the west and the Nile in the east. Phenotypically it looks very much like *caffer*, but on the basis of mitochondrial DNA clustering it resembles *nanus/brachyceros* (Smitz et al., 2013). One study on the diet of this subspecies has been published (Hashim, 1987) and does not give reason to think it is different from the diet of *caffer*.

Further to the west, from Senegal to the Chari River in southwest Chad, to the north of the Guinea rainforest, roams the third form, namely *brachyceros* (the West African bush cow). Again, we do not know much about this subspecies ecologically speaking save for the information provided in the PhD thesis of Cornélis (2011). This subspecies may grade into the *aequinoctialis* form east of Lake Chad, noting that the buffalo is nearly extinct within the Lake Chad Basin with the exception of some incursions from elsewhere (Chardonnet and Lamarque, 1996); genetically speaking, it intergrades with *nanus* (the forest buffalo) of both the Guinea rainforest and the Congo rainforest. Of this latter subspecies we have reasonable knowledge. The SCI system does not recognize *matthewsii* and splits the West African bush cow into two subspecies, namely, *S. c. brachyceros* and *S. c. planiceros*.

And finally there is *caffer* (the Cape buffalo), of which much is known. Its karyotype suggests that it is the most recently derived form. It is the only subspecies with a fusion between chromosomes 5 and 20 (2n = 52), and it lacks the polymorphism for a 1;13 fusion, as observed in *Syncerus caffer nanus* (2n = 54–56; Wurster and Benirschke, 1968; Anon., 2004; Pagacova et al., 2011). Hybrids between *nanus* and *aequinoctialis* have been produced in zoos (Gray, 1972; Anon., 2004), as well as between *nanus* and *caffer* (Cribiu and Popescu, 1980).

There are gradual changeovers but also sharp boundaries between the different forms. By and large, three types can be recognized based on body mass, namely, the small *S. c. nanus* (adults 265–320 kg), the inter-mediate *S. c. brachyceros* plus *S. c. aequinoctialis* (adults 300–600 kg) and the massive *S. c. caffer* (adult cows up to 500 kg, adult bulls from 650 kg to 900 kg; Cornélis et al., 2014).

The unclear allocation of individuals to these five forms (*matthewsii, aequinoctialis, brachyceros, caffer* and *nanus*) is well illustrated by comparing Smithers (1983 – who only recognizes '*caffer*' and '*nanus*'), the Rowland Ward trophies system (Smith, 1986 – with a northern savanna buffalo, a southern one and the forest buffalo; basically the same as Grubb, 1972), Ansell's (1972) system (which does not recognize '*matthewsii*') and finally the exuberance celebrated by Groves and Grubb (2011), who elevated every form to its own species, thus revelling in the same super species-splitting that was witnessed 100 years ago (Prins, 1996). Would these different forms then have different niches?

Now, what is a 'niche'? Confusingly, there are three niche con-cepts in ecology, to wit, the Grinellian niche concept, the Eltonian one and the Hutchinsonian one (see Prins and Gordon, 2014, p. 7ff.). The Grinellian niche concept reflects the habitat in which an organism lives, the Eltonian one stresses the functional attributes of the species and its position in a food web, while the Hutchinsonian niche is defined by the resources and environmental requirements of an individual of a species to live and reproduce. In this chapter, we lean towards the Hutchinsonian niche concept, but we use the 'niche' concept loosely.

It thus would be reasonable to believe that if there are different sub-species of the African buffalo because they are morphologically distinct, then they have different 'niches'. An alternative explanation could be that environmental history 'accidentally' led to vicariance, thus result-ing in phenotypically different forms that were isolated long enough to be genetically sufficiently distinct to justify 'subspecies status', but they (still) have the same 'niche'. Yet the null hypothesis should not be forgotten, namely, that the (normally) morphological characters that systematicists use to distinguish species or subspecies have no functional meaning (Gould and Lewontin, 1979).

An Ultrashort Recapitulation of the Evolutionary History of These Forms

The most direct ancestor of *S. caffer* was *S. acoelotus*; Geraads et al. (2009) state that it was as large as the modern *S. caffer*. *S. acoelotus* was a Plio-Pleistocene species in Africa that disappears from the fossil record about

600,000 years ago (see Kullmer et al., 1999: Late Pliocene; Bunn et al., 2010; cf. Bibi et al., 2017: Early Pleistocene; O'Regan et al., 2005: Middle Pleistocene; Chaix et al., 2000: Middle Pleistocene). This may coincide with the expansion of the present-day species between 1,000,000 and 500,000 years ago as deducted by genetics (Chen et al., 2019; de Jager et al., 2021). *S. acoelotus* may have led to a second *Syncerus* species too, namely *S. antiquus*. This latter species went extinct only about 2000 years ago, and may have been a more drylands-adapted species (see Chapter 2). The other species, namely, *S. caffer*, is extant. In the Lake Turkana basin, the last record of *S. acoelotus* was about 1.6 Myr ago, and the first *S. caffer* about 1.2 Myr ago (Bobe and Behrensmeyer, 2004). The genetics and palaeontology of *S. caffer* shows that it apparently could expand its range to southern Africa when *S. antiquus* went extinct. *S. antiquus* also was able to cross the Sahara Desert, most likely in periods when the desert was much greener, and may even have entered the Middle East (for details see Chapter 2). The first occurrence of *S. c. caffer* is from Melkbos, South Africa, from the Upper Pleistocene (Hendey, 1969; see Groves, 1992). However, there is the possibility that *Syncerus caffer* and *S. acoelotus* were both derived from an earlier genus, namely *Ugandax* (see Chapter 2).

Genetics shows that 'subspeciation' may have arisen as long as about one million years ago (de Jager et al., 2021) or as recently as 200 kyr (Smitz et al., 2013; de Jager et al., 2021), but does not provide evidence (yet) whether *S. c. nanus* is more ancestral than the other *Syncerus* forms (*pace* Van Hooft et al., 2002; Smitz et al., 2013, even though they suggest that *nanus* is the derived form). The observations that the older *S. acoelotus* had the same size as the present *S. caffer*, and that the older forms that looked like *S. caffer* are known from the Lake Turkana Basin (Bobe and Behrensmeyer, 2004) nearly overlapping with the present-day range of *S. c. aequinoctialis*, thus allow for the scenario that the present-day buffalo with the simplest horns (*S. c. aequinoctialis*) is genetically closest to the ancestral form. On the basis of genetic analyses, this was already suggested by Smitz et al. (2013), and prior to that by Groves (1992 – slightly confusingly, he put forward that this was spp. *brachyceros*, but he did not distinguish spp. *aequinoctialis* from spp. *brachyceros*). Groves (1992) puts this transition from *S. acoelotus* to *S. c. aequinoctialis* at 130 kyr. The observation that (pure?) *nanus* buffalo have one pair of chromosomes less than at least *aequinoctialis* and *caffer* (we could find no evidence for *brachyceros*) due to a recent fusion (Anon., 2004) also points towards the derived status of the forest buffalo.

In such a scenario, *S. c. nanus* could be the result of dwarfing (as has been observed on islands with the Asian buffalo and humans in the rainforest, e.g. pygmies). Additionally, it cannot be ruled out, we think, that *S. c. brachyceros* represents a hybrid of *S. c. nanus* and *S. c. aequinoctialis* (a pattern that is very well known from Asian bovines). Indeed, the genetic distances between these three subspecies are very small (Van Hooft et al., 2002; Smitz et al., 2013). However, there is no evidence for two separated lineages of dwarf buffalo and large buffalo that were separated for a very long time as has been put forward (for a discussion see Chapter 2).

On the basis of the above, different storylines can be constructed, namely: (1) there was a large buffalo species ('*acoelotus*') that evolved into '*caffer*' and '*antiquus*'. *Antiquus* was a species adapted to dry conditions and could outcompete *caffer* under these conditions. When *antiquus* went extinct, *caffer* took over parts of its range but is nowadays limited by the isohyet of 350 mm. It could not cross the Sahara, and along the Nile it encountered the aurochs (*Bos primigenius*), which prevented *caffer*'s establishment to the north of Khartoum. Storyline (2) is different, with the original large buffalo *acoelotus* able to infiltrate the rainforest (perhaps at times when the forest was reduced to gallery forest only). There, secondary dwarfing took place. At times when the rainforest nearly disappeared (e.g. during the Last Glacial Maximum), the range of the buffalo was probably restricted to one or two refuges in present-day CAR, northern Congo and Uganda (Smitz et al., 2013). In such a small area, possibly no more than 1500 km across, hybridization could easily have taken place with *aequinoctialis*, thus leading to the form *brachyceros*. The further west one travels, the lesser is the expected imprint of *aequinoctialis*, thus leading to a possible cline. Alternatively, storyline (3) narrates that after *S. caffer* evolved into a form that looked like *S. c. aequinoctialis*, it developed into the large Cape buffalo (*S. c. caffer*), but also expanded into the Congo Basin where dwarfing took place, producing *S. c. nanus*. Storyline (4) is different. It narrates that there was a large buffalo species ('*acoelotus*') that evolved into '*antiquus*'. However, there was an even older species (so, not *acoelotus*), say, *Ugandax* (see Chapter 2) that evolved into *Syncerus acoelotus* and also into *S. caffer*, which was much smaller and looked like *S. c. nanus*. Note that this putative predecessor has not been unearthed. This *S. c. nanus* than lived in the ancestral rainforest, from which it radiated into the north to form *S. c. brachyceros* and *S. c. aequinoctialis*, and into the east to form *S. c. caffer* (which then expanded towards the Cape).

Storylines (1), (2) and (3) make the point that the forest buffalo are the product of dwarfing; storyline (4) emphasizes that the northern and eastern savanna buffalo became adapted to C_4 grasses in their diet and had to adapt to a large new predator, namely the lion (*Panthera leo*), because its descendants moved into the savanna after they had evolved in the rainforest (see below on the different 'niches'). On purpose we do not use the word 'hypothesis' but 'storyline' because too much is unknown. However, the ramifications are startling, because these storylines result in very different insights into the buffalo's 'adaptations'. Thornhill's is nonetheless a stark reminder of the difficulties one faces in deriving notions about adaptation from present-day niche occupation:

A Darwinian adaptation is an organism's feature that was functionally designed by the process of evolution by selection acting in nature in the past. Functional design rules out explanations of drift, incidental effect, phylogenetic legacy and mutation. Elucidation of the functional design of an adaptation entails an implicit reconstruction of the selection that made the adaptation. Darwinian adaptations and other individual traits may be currently adaptive, maladaptive or neutral. (Thornhill, 2007)

The Environmental Envelopes of African Buffalo

For the present discussion, we discern three environmental envelopes (an important part of the Hutchinsonian niche) for the three major forms of the buffalo, namely, the forest buffalo (*nanus*), the northern savanna buffalo (*brachyceros* and *aequinoctialis*) and the Cape buffalo (*caffer*) (Table 8.1). Judging from distribution maps of the different forms of buffalo, we generally know at which altitudes they occur or once occurred. Altitude is the main determinant of ambient temperature. For the forest buffalo, we assume that they generally occur below 500 m altitude. However, there may be forest buffalo on the slopes of Mt Cameroon (an isolated volcano of 4000 m altitude) and they do or did occur on Mt Nimba (a 1750-m high mountain on the border between Ivory Coast and the Republic of Guinea; the area is now overrun by refugees) and perhaps in the Masisi Region (eastern DRC; dominated by civil war and resource extraction; P. Chardonnet, personal communication). The northern savanna buffalo also is a lowland form, but it occurs up to 1000 m above sea level in, for instance, the Bouba Njida area (northern Cameroon; P. Chardonnet, personal communication). Yet, this is below the C_3-grass zone (see Van der Zon, 1992).

On the basis of the environmental envelope parameters of Table 8.1, we posit that forest buffalo run the real risk of getting overheated when

Table 8.1 *Approximate climate envelopes of the three main forms of African buffalo; we have taken S. c. aequinoctialis and S. c. brachyceros together as 'northern savanna buffalo'. The lethal zones (based on what we know of cattle) may be reached due to a combination of temperature and air humidity for the forest buffalo; for the northern savanna buffalo the lethal temperatures can be reached during heatwaves with dry air. Cape buffalo have been known to freeze to death, but we do not know of the heat index being excessed.*

	Elevation range (m a.s.l.)	Minimum temperature and cold waves bracketed (°C)	Maximum temperature and heatwaves bracketed (°C)	Radiation heat flux	Rainfall regime (mm yr^{-1})	Air humidity	Wind/ moving air
Forest buffalo	0–700	18	32 (35)	Very low	1000–9000	70–95	Absent
Northern savanna buffalo	100–1000	(6) 30	42 (52)	Very high	400–1000	15–70	Present
Cape buffalo	0–5000	(–5) 10	38 (47)	Very high	400–1000	50–80	Present

Relative Humidity %	Air temperature°C										
	21	24	27	29	32	35	38	41	43	46	49
0	18	21	23	26	28	31	33	35	37	39	42
10	18	21	24	27	29	32	35	38	41	44	47
20	19	22	25	28	31	34	37	41	44	49	54
30	19	23	26	29	32	36	40	45	51	57	64
40	20	23	26	30	34	38	43	51	58	66	
50	21	24	27	31	36	42	49	57	66		
60	21	24	28	32	38	46	56	65			
70	21	25	29	34	41	51	62				
80	22	26	30	36	45	58					
90	22	26	31	39	50						
100	22	22	33	42							

Serious risk to health – heatstroke imminent

Prolonged exposure and activity could lead to heatstroke

Prolonged exposure and activity may lead to fatigue

Figure 8.1 Heat risk assessment for people. The figures inside the cells are the temperatures (°C) as experienced. Thousands of cattle have died from heat stroke in India and Australia. The combined effect of relative air humidity and temperature is slightly different for cattle and people, but as we do not know the exact relationship in buffalo, we use this for illustrative purposes. From Diffey (2018) © 2018 John Wiley & Sons A/S. Published by John Wiley & Sons Ltd. For more on this issue, see for example Du Preez et al. (1990), Hubbard et al. (1999) or Allen et al. (2013).

the temperature is high and air humidity is very high (thus preventing evaporative heat loss; see Figure 8.1). Buffalo do not have much sweating or panting abilities. In the much more unvarying warm circumstances of a tropical lowland rainforest, wallowing offers much fewer cooling opportunities (because of the higher temperature of standing water but also because of the windless circumstances) than in a savanna where water bodies can cool at night, and more breeze occurs. The northern savanna buffalo can take shelter against high heat loading through direct sunshine by finding places with a breeze and/or shade. Yet these buffalo, we posit, also run a high risk of dying from heat stress during heat waves (Figure 8.1).

Finally, the Cape buffalo runs the risk of being exposed to cold and frost. This is especially important in its southern range, but also high in the mountains of the volcanoes of East Africa.

From this, it follows that it is likely that there is selection pressure for buffalo (and humans, elephants and hippos) to be as small as possible in the tropical lowland rainforest, but in the savanna it would be advantageous to be large (see Table 8.6). The reasons are that in a tropical lowland rainforest where evaporative heat loss is often impossible, heat loss must be achieved through radiation. A large body surface to mass ratio (typical for small animals) is then advantageous; heat can barely dissipate at night because there can be no radiation towards the sky (and thus outer space) due to dense foliage and clouds. In a savanna, however, evaporative loss is possible and body heat can dissipate at night, while a large body mass prevents rapid overheating. Indeed, in areas where there is no hunting, buffalo can be seen resting and grazing during the middle of the day in the full sun even when it is 32°C. Central African rainforest pygmies also separated only recently (i.e. about 70 kyr: Perry and Verdu, 2017; to 190 kyr: Hsieh et al., 2016) from Bantu. Yet, the adaptive significance of small stature in humans in rainforests is far from clear (see e.g. Hsieh et al., 2016; Bergey et al., 2018; Patin and Quintana-Murci, 2018). It is also unclear as to whether the African forest elephant (*Loxodonta africana cyclotis* a.k.a. *L. cyclotis*), genetically perhaps distinct from the African savanna elephant (*L. a. africana*, a.k.a. *L. africana*; but see Debruyne, 2005), is a similar case of dwarfing. Grubb et al. (2000) consider the forest form to be more primitive than the savanna form, which, if correct, would mean that the dwarfing was not recent. There is, by the way, insufficient evidence for the existence of the pygmy elephant ('*L. pumilio*'; Debruyne et al., 2003), so it is unclear whether parallels may be drawn between the case of the African elephant and the emergence of the forest buffalo. The pygmy hippo (*Choeropsis liberiensis*) also is not a dwarfed form of the large *Hippopotamus amphibius*, but is a descendant of a much older, original form that is hardly related to the modern mega-sized hippo (Boisserie, 2005). True dwarfed hippos did occur on Mediterranean islands (Petronio, 2014). The idea could be entertained that dwarfing of buffalo in the rainforest took place because of poorer quality food. Yet food quality in the rainforest of Cameroon, judging by its species composition (Bekhuis et al., 2008) was about equal to or better than that of savanna buffalo (Prins, 1996), and generally it is assumed that larger ruminants (because they have a slower throughput rate) can cope with poorer-quality food. In other words, it is not plausible that a dwarfing of African buffalo after broadening their niche into the tropical rainforest was a reaction to food quality.

It is unlikely that very high amounts of rainfall pose a problem to forest buffalo. They can swim well, and their large splayed hooves offer sufficient movement possibilities in very wet and muddy terrains. Yet we have observed them taking shelters in grottoes in Cameroonian rain forests (H. Prins, personal observation).

The Food of the African Buffalo Subspecies

For the diet of the different forms of the African buffalo, one must pay attention to differential occurrence across its range of C_3 grasses versus C_4 grasses because of their impact on digestibility and intake. Moreover, there appear to be differences in the inclusion of browse (including forbs) for the different buffalo forms. The main difference between the subspecies is that the northern savanna forms have a diet comprised of C_4 grasses; they take also 10–15 per cent browse in the dry season (de Iongh et al., 2011; this is nearly completely in the form of the buds and fruits of Caesalpineacea in Benoué NP, Cameroon: Erik Klop, personal communication). Indeed, the range of *S. c. brachyceros* is typically below 500 m altitude, and that of *S. c. aequinoctialis* between 200 and 800 m a.s.l. The Cape buffalo also takes about 10 per cent browse (mainly in the dry season: Prins, 1996) while in the non-montane areas below 2000 m altitude, the grasses they forage on are also of the C_4 type. However, above 3000 m and in wetlands, the grasses are of the C_3 type in East Africa (Tieszen et al., 1979); further south this shift occurs at about 2800 m (Morris et al., 1993). An estimated 10 per cent of the original range of *S. c. caffer* is higher than 3000 m a.s.l., and about 30 per cent above 2500 m, so a substantial proportion of the diet of buffalo before the expansion of human agriculture may have been comprised of C_3 grass (see altitude maps in SEDAC n.d.). Note that the map of the ratio of C_3 over C_4 plants in Africa proposed by Shanahan et al. (2016) cannot be used for this comparison because it includes trees and shrubs (most of which use the C_3 photosynthetic pathway). The rainforest grass species that comprise the diet of the forest buffalo are mainly the C_3 type (Bocksberger et al., 2016). The digestibility of C_3 grasses is much higher than that of C_4 grasses. In other words, diets of the different subspecies are subtly different (Table 8.2).

In East and South Africa, probably all terrain higher than 1500 m but lower than 3500 m has been taken over by agriculture since the

Table 8.2 *The different subspecies of buffalo basically have different diets. The different photosynthesis pathways of C_3 and C_4 grasses have major repercussions for digestibility of the food and intake rates (see text). A sizeable proportion of the original distribution area of the Cape buffalo was above 3000 m altitude before agriculture displaced them.*

	Percentage browse	Type of grass
Forest buffalo	~30% (Bekhuis et al., 2008)	C_3 photosynthetic pathway
Northern savanna buffalo	~10% (de Iongh et al., 2011)	C_4 photosynthetic pathway
Cape buffalo	~10% (Prins, 1996)	Below 2000 m altitude: C_4 photosynthetic pathway Above 3000 m altitude: C_3 photosynthetic pathway

start of the Iron Age up until the present. These are so-called Tropical Highlands (see for a map: IFPRI, 2015). On the basis of this, we posit that before the current fragmentation of the range of the African buffalo due to human expansion, some populations of the subspecies *caffer* could easily have moved up to areas with C_3 grasses during the dry season, while other populations could have used that type of grass year-round. These buffalo must thus have been buffered against the negative effects of a pronounced dry season. The northern savanna buffalo (*aequinoctialis* but especially *brachyceros*), on the other hand, would have suffered much more from droughts and the dry season in general. Indeed, a migration centred on rivers would have been a good 'evolutionary answer' to that challenge (as was found by Cornélis, 2011, for *S. c. brachyceros*). Proper migratory behaviour of *S. c. caffer* has not been reported, although there is a hint of it from the early 1960s in northern Tanzania's Lake Manyara region, where a migration may have been centred on the Tarangire River (Prins, 1996). Short-distance migrations of *S. c. caffer* have also been reported from woodlands at a relative short distance from the Okavango Delta and from the Linyanti Swamps, both in Botswana (see Chapter 5 for details). It is not known to the present authors whether buffalo forage on C_3 grasses in these riverine systems or swamps. Altitudinal seasonal migration (still) occurred between the Rift Valley bottom lands and adjacent high-altitude areas (volcanoes and Ngorongoro Crater highlands) of northern Tanzania in the 1970s and 1980s (P. Chardonnet, personal observations and personal communication). These higher areas abound(ed) in C_3 grasses (see Clayton, 1970; Clayton et al., 1974).

The intake of C_3 grasses has two very important advantages over C_4 grasses: first, the digestibility of C_3 grasses is considerably higher, and second, intake is determined to a large extent by rumen fill, which appears to be mainly determined by NDF (neutral detergent fibre). C_4 grasses are more fibrous than C_3 grasses (see e.g. García et al., 2014 for a review). The throughput rate also is much lower if the fibre content (as in C_4 grasses) is higher (Blaxter, 1962, p. 196). In other words, everything being equal, it is easier for *S. c. caffer* and *S. c. nanus* to acquire energy for lactation and growth than for *S. c. brachyceros* or *S. c. aequinoctialis*. However, for *nanus* there may be a disadvantage to forage of highly digestible grass because the heat of digestion could be higher than if foraging on food that is slower to digest (see Blaxter, 1962).

The Competitors of the African Buffalo Subspecies

Because the different forms of African buffalo live in such different environments (habitats), the animal species they (potentially) share resources with are very different. A little is known already about the habitat requirements of the enormous array of African herbivores, but a striking pattern is that the habitat requirements of these many species coupled with historical processes (and chance) has led to a spatially very variable distribution of these species (see Prins and Olff, 1998). The African buffalo has (together with the leopard *Panthera pardus* and the African elephant) the widest of all distributions of African large mammals, thus overlapping with a very variable suite of other herbivores. This insight leads to the conclusion that possible competition with most species can hardly have shaped the evolutionary pathway of African buffalo because the population of African buffalo is characterized by relatively small genetic distances, particularly within subspecies (Smitz et al., 2013), and has been vast for hundreds of thousands of years (Chen et al., 2019; de Jager et al., 2021). In Table 8.3 we present a non-exhaustive overview of the 'constant' (i.e. occurring everywhere) potential competitors for the three African buffalo forms, and the 'variable' ones (i.e. large herbivorous species that do not occur everywhere in the range of a particular subspecies).

While we posit that the 'variable competitors' on a species level do not exert particular selective pressure, as an ensemble they could do so because in no habitat is a particular 'subspecies' of buffalo free from these variable competitors. Their omnipresent competitor is the African elephant in its two forms (*Loxodonta* [a.] *africana* and *L.* [a.] *cyclotis*). Adults

Table 8.3 *African buffalo are large grazers with a variable admixture of browse (from woody species and from herbs) in their diet. Some herbivore mammalian species share resources with them, which we tabulated only for those species heavier than 50 kg and with some grass in their diet. Of these, the 'constant competitors' co-occur with African buffalo (or did so in the recent 5000 years or so) nearly everywhere (species names in bold). Other potentially competing species, which we termed the 'variable competitors', co-occur with buffalo only here and there. In this table we split the 'northern savanna buffalo' in to S. c. aequinoctialis and S. c. brachyceros.* N = *number of species that may show overlap in resource use with a particular form of buffalo. Species are arranged alphabetically.*

	Adult mass 50–100 kg	Adult mass 100–200 kg	Adult mass 200–400 kg	Adult mass >400 kg	N
Forest buffalo (250–300 kg)	**Bushbuck** Sitatunga		Bongo Okapi	**African elephant** **Hippopotamus**	6
Northern savanna buffalo: *brachyceros* (300–600 kg)	**Bushbuck** Kob Sitatunga	Hartebeest Topi (korrigum) Roan antelope Waterbuck	Bongo Giant eland	**African elephant** **Hippopotamus**	11
Northern savanna buffalo: *aequinoctialis* (400–700 kg)	**Bushbuck** Kob Nile lechwe Sitatunga	Greater kudu Hartebeest Roan antelope Topi (Tiang) Waterbuck	Bongo Giant eland	**African elephant** **Hippopotamus** Northern white rhino	14
Cape buffalo (500–800 kg)	Blesbok Bohor reedbuck **Bushbuck** Grant's gazelle Gerenuk Hirola Impala Mountain nyala Nile lechwe Nyala Puku Sitatunga Southern lechwe Lesser kudu Southern reedbuck	Black wildebeest Bontebok greater kudu Hartebeest Roan antelope Sable antelope Topi Waterbuck	Blue wildebeest Common eland Grant's zebra Mountain zebra Plains zebra	**African elephant** **Hippopotamus** Southern white rhino	32

are always much heavier (respectively, 3000–6000 kg and 2700 kg) and have much more browse in their diet. So this may suggest that buffalo would encounter a negative selection pressure against increasing in size. Their main 'constant' competitor may be or has been the hippo (*Hippopotamus amphibius*). They are true grazers and twice as heavy as buffalo, thus preventing buffalo from getting heavier (see Olff et al., 2002). All of their other competitors are smaller or do not compete over most of the range of the populations of the three forms (Table 8.3). Outside of the rainforest, their most important potential competitor would be the two species of eland. The giant eland is a browser over nearly the entire year, while the common eland is a browser during the dry season when food is scarce. From this we conclude that the other herbivores would exert stabilizing selection on the body mass of the different forms of African buffalo (see also Prins and Olff, 1998). They potentially have a very important facilitatory role for the species mentioned to the left of the column in which the different buffalo subspecies are located (cf. Prins and Olff, 1998; Olff et al., 2002). This is especially the case for the Cape buffalo.

The Predators of the African Buffalo Subspecies

The three main types of African buffalo, namely the forest buffalo, the northern savanna buffalo and the Cape buffalo, live in very different worlds, or, better expressed, cohabited until very recently before the collapse of nature conservation in West Africa in very different worlds. The main difference is that adult forest buffalo are basically predator-free (except for man). Lions (*Panthera leo*) are absent from the tropical rainforest proper. The African golden cat (*Caracalla aurata*) with its maximum body mass of only 16 kg is no match, but a 90-kg leopard is. Leopard density may be approximately equal in rainforest and savanna environments (e.g. Jenny, 1996 for rainforest versus Balme et al., 2007, for savanna), but spotted hyaena (*Crocuta crocuta*), a formidable predator in savannas, are absent from rainforests proper (see map in Varela et al., 2009), as are wild dogs (a.k.a. painted dog, *Lycaon pictus*; Woodroffe et al., 1997). The forest buffalo may encounter African dwarf crocodiles (*Osteolaemus tetraspis*), which are likely to be insignificant predators, like the West African slender-snouted crocodile (*Mecistops cataphractus*), the Central African one (*M. leptorhynchus*) or even the sacred crocodile (*Crocodylus suchus*).

The northern savanna buffalo had to deal with lions until this large predator basically went extinct, as the Cape buffalo still must do. Lions

Table 8.4 *The different subspecies of African buffalo share their habitat with different predators. We have taken S. c. aequinoctialis and S. c. brachyceros together as 'northern savanna buffalo'. The subspecies with the biggest horns, namely, the Cape buffalo seems to live in the most dangerous environment.*

	Predator of adults	Predator of calves
Forest buffalo	None	Leopard, African python
Northern savanna buffalo	Lion	Leopard, spotted hyena, African wild dog, African python
Cape buffalo	Lion, Nile crocodile	Leopard, spotted hyena, African wild dog, African python

are large predators (adult females about 115 kg and adult males about 220 kg). Wild dogs are now next to extinct nearly anywhere in West and Central Africa (Woodroffe et al., 1997). We do not think the sacred crocodile was much of a threat to the northern savanna buffalo, nor were African wild dogs before they went functionally extinct in West and Central Africa. The much larger Nile crocodile (*C. niloticus*) appears to be a predator for the Cape buffalo. Finally, the African python (*Python sebae*) may perhaps be an occasional threat to calves of all buffalo subspecies. Spotted hyena and African wild dogs prey on buffalo calves and juveniles in the northern, eastern and southern savannas, but are rarely a threat to adult buffalo (Table 8.4). The different jackal species are insignificant.

From this it follows that there has been a selection pressure for becoming big in the savannas to escape predation from lions and perhaps Nile crocodiles. In the rainforest we believe that the predation pressure has not been high, and buffalo would only have run a risk of major predation if they had attained the size of duiker antelopes.

Are the Subspecies of the African Buffalo Functionally Different?

Currently, maximally five subspecies are considered to be relevant for a discussion on what the African buffalo 'is'. These are *Syncerus caffer caffer* (the Cape buffalo), *S. c. nanus* (the forest buffalo), *S. c. brachyceros* (the West African bush cow), *S. c. aequinoctialis* (the Nile buffalo) and *S. c. matthewsii* (the mountain buffalo). The last one is morphologically not well distinguishable from the nominate subspecies, and functionally ecological research does not provide any clue as to why it would be different if we take the

Table 8.5 *The relationship with other mammals of the African buffalo depends on the subspecies (we have taken S. c.* brachyceros *and S. c.* aequinoctialis *together in this table). Data on predatory species are from Table 8.4, data on species that can be facilitated or species that can be competitive are from Table 8.3. We use the term 'embeddedness' instead of 'connectedness' because the latter is local food-web–dependent while ours is based on major regions (i.e. West African Guinea and Sudan savanna, West and Central rainforest and the whole region from Ethiopia to the Cape).*

	Predatory species of adults	Predatory species of calves	Large mammal species that can be competitive	Large mammal species that can be facilitated by buffalo foraging	Embeddedness
Forest buffalo	0	2	4	2	8
Northern savanna buffalo	1	4	4	4	13
Cape buffalo	2	4	8	7	21

Virunga buffalo as *matthewsii*. If not, and the subspecies must be found closer to Lake Tanganyika, then it comprises a blank spot in our knowledge.

The forest buffalo *S. c. nanus* of the rainforests of Central Africa and West Africa are functionally very different from the nominate subspecies. Actually, they are morphologically and functionally so different that most ecologists would not reject species status. Genetics, however, shows how intrinsically they are related to the nominate subspecies (Van Hooft et al., 2002; Smitz et al., 2013). Their difference does not show up as much in their habitat use (see Korte, 2008; Bekhuis et al., 2008: they mainly use the small savannas in the forest, logging roads and open marshes) than in their relationship with other species of the assemblage, while their morphology adheres to a common pattern of 'forest species'. They have a more reddish coat colour, conspicuous white ear fringes (like the riverine bush pig *Potamochoerus porcus*), small body size, smaller incisor width, more 'streamlined' and smaller horns, and live in much smaller group sizes.

The two forms of the northern savannas pose more problems because so little is known of the ecology of this species in these areas (but see Cornélis, 2011). Yet the role of the different forms is well illustrated in Table 8.5. Cape buffalo appear to be located in the richest web (they show the highest degree of 'embeddedness'), while the forest buffalo is perhaps only loosely connected to the other species in the rainforest, possibly indicative that it only recently entered the forest.

The Different Subspecies of the African Buffalo in a Human Context

Humans evolved in Africa; the genus to which we belong is about three million years old (nicely summarized in Dunsworth, 2010). The genus *Syncerus* is likely younger (Chapter 2). If the ancestral species of *Syncerus caffer* was *S. acoelotus*, then there is no convincing evidence that it was hunted by humans (Bobe and Behrensmeyer, 2004). *Homo* may have started controlling fire some 1.2 Myr ago (James et al., 1989), as long as the oldest record of *S. caffer* (see above).

The *Homo–Syncerus* relationship has thus been a long-standing one. In the pre-Modern, this interaction was comprised of one that benefited buffalo when fire modified the vegetation to their benefit, producing more palatable grass, perhaps less tsetse flies and less shrubbery or even forest. Buffalo suffered from humans when they became better at killing large game. Different ways of killing became available over time, for example throwing stones to stampede a herd over a cliff (which can only be done if cliffs are available, for example in the Drakensberg region or some places along the coast in Transkei for instance). We do not think that spears ever made much of an impact on the level of populations even though we are aware that some men single-handedly killed a buffalo bull with a spear (Mr ole-Konchella as young warrior of the Masai did long before he became the Director of Tanzania National Parks; H. Prins, personal communication). Running prey to ground with weapons is an unlikely strategy for killing buffalo (Bunn and Pickering, 2010). Bow-and-arrow technology is perhaps 300 kyr old (Lombard and Haidle, 2012). We are not aware of successful bow-and-arrow hunting with traditional bows, in contrast to European-style long-bows or modern crossbows. Using poisons on arrows, however, is a successful strategy, as was demonstrated by traditional Hadza-hunters near Lake Eyasi (H. Prins, personal observation; cf. O'Connell et al., 1988). Bambote hunters of Zambia successfully kill buffalo with this technique (Terashima, 1980). Indeed, when a good market developed for ivory, Kamba started elephant hunting with poisoned arrows (Steinhart, 2000). The oldest written description of buffalo refers to a similar hunting technique:

[In the Kingdom of Mali] there are undomesticated buffalo which are hunted like wild beasts, in the following fashion. They carry away little calves such as may be reared in their houses, and when they want to hunt the buffaloes they send out one of these calves to the place where the buffaloes are so that they may see it, make towards it, and become used to it because of the unity of the species which is a cause of association. When they have become used to it the hunters shoot them with poisoned arrows. Having cut out the poisoned place, that is, where the arrow has struck and round about it, they eat the flesh. (al-Umari ~1347 CE, translated by Levitzion and Hopkins, 2000, p. 264)

Netting is a viable strategy to capture game, for instance in a rainforest, but needs large groups of cooperating people (H. Prins, personal observation; Abruzzi, 1979) and the largest prey thus taken may be bushbuck *Tragelaphus sylvaticus* (Terashima, 1980; Sato, 1983). Traditional spring traps can catch prey as heavy as bushbuck and yellow-backed duiker *Cephalophus silvicultur* (H. Prins, personal observation; Sato, 1983). Pre-Modern hunting techniques were likely to be sustainable (Hitchcock, 2000).

We posit that it is really with the invention of steel wire (by Wilhelm Albert in 1834), the gin trap and the shotgun that buffalo started directly suffering from people. Leg traps made of steel wire attached to long lines of hundreds to thousands of metres of steel cable can play havoc with buffalo (for a description see Sinclair, 1977, p. 25). In some hunting concessions, concessionaires removed tens of thousands of steel wire snares in northern Tanzania (Hurt and Ravn, 2000). The impact of using snares on a population can be severe (cf. Mduma ert al., 1998). The old-fashioned shotgun basically eradicated buffalo from South Africa, and even just before the independence of Mozambique, the Portuguese shot some 50,000 buffalo for potential gain. Storehouse rooms filled with hooves and dried scrota skins were still a macabre reminder in 1993 (H. Prins, personal observation).

Through agriculture, humans started domineering the landscape. Instead of simply a supply of proteins and fat, buffalo started becoming a nuisance when they damaged crops. Because browse is unimportant in their diet (see above), they would hardly have been an issue to beans, peas or yams. However, even native species such as sorghum would not be very attractive to buffalo because many varieties are high in prussic acid and lignin. Millet, on the other hand, is a good fodder source. Agriculture and associated iron smelting only became important in West Africa around 500 BCE, around 500 CE in the Great Lakes area, around 1000 CE in small mountainous pockets in East Africa, and even later in South Africa. In the rainforest zone, the savanna environment slowly but surely disappeared during the Holocene, and agriculture even disappeared (e.g. Tutin and White, 1998). Slash-and-burn cultivation, so important in western Africa, enabled the expansion of the Guinea savanna and the Sudan savanna, allowing the expansion of buffalo habitat. In other words, African buffalo may have benefited from humans perhaps until the advent of Modern days. In contrast to East and southern Africa, the West African kingdoms all used cavalry since about 1000 CE, indicative of well-developed grasslands (Fisher, 1972; Ukpabi, 1974; Sayer, 1977), but how much buffalo hunting on horseback took place is not known even though they used stirrups. Plains Indians in North America were only able to have a devastating impact on American bison when they adopted horseback hunting.

The Cape buffalo, however, may have started suffering from humans more than the northern savanna buffalo (which benefited from forest conversion). The advent of pastoralism from the Sudan towards the Cape was a slow process (at a rate of about 5 km per generation; Prins, 2000), but as cattle and buffalo largely use the same resources, and as people are able to monopolize water sources, pastoralists can outcompete grazers like buffalo (Prins, 1992; Prins and de Jong, 2022).

Speculation on Further Subspeciation of the African Buffalo

Table 8.6 summarizes of the selection forces on the different forms of buffalo that we envisage.

What would the consequences be of *S. c. nanus* becoming smaller? We would not be amazed that it might be able to cope better with climate warming, and become much smaller before encountering serious negative effects from bushbuck and sitatunga (*T. spekii*; both as potentially competing species) or leopards (as major predator).

Yet in a world where people allowed the northern savanna buffalo to continue to live in protected areas, the reality of the West African context would perhaps be that the absence of sufficient shade or wallowing holes would make their lives unbearable, but the extreme scarcity or even absence of predators and competing species would not hinder further evolution towards bigger sizes. Indeed, in West Africa today the lion is nearly extinct, and potentially competing species (Table 8.3) are very rare. The east and southern savanna buffalo, if well-protected, could also well become bigger under natural selection (Table 8.6).

Table 8.6 *Putative selection forces on body mass of the different forms of the African buffalo in the different habitats where they live.*

	Heat management	Food management	Competitor management	Predator management	Overall selection
Forest buffalo	Selection to become bigger	Selection to become smaller	Stabilizing selection	**No** selection	Become smaller
Northern savanna buffalo	Selection to **become bigger**	Selection to **become bigger**	Stabilizing selection	Selection to **become bigger**	Become bigger
Cape buffalo	Selection to **become bigger**	Selection to **become bigger**	Stabilizing selection	Selection to **become bigger**	Become bigger

We started this attempt to understand the differences between the forms or subspecies of the African buffalo with three storylines. We did not want to use the term 'hypothesis' because in science a hypothesis is a strong presumption preferably based on theory or a set of coherent observations. Too much is missing from the palaeontological records to formulate a proper hypothesis concerning the evolutionary (in contrast to genetical) relationship between the subspecies or forms of the African buffalo. The Popperian instrument of falsifying also is not in our toolkit, so we have to fall back on the concept of plausibility instead of falsifiability. We do this to stimulate research into the question of whether subspecies are ecologically (not classificatory) speaking meaningful entities without claiming 'proof' (see Walton, 1988, 2001), yet the concept of 'plausibility' may become more important in science than it was before (see Sinatra and Lombardi, 2020).

Storyline 2 is of importance here. It states that the original large buffalo *Syncerus acoelotus* was able to infiltrate the rainforest (perhaps at times when the forest was reduced to only gallery forest during one of the Glacial Periods; about 150 kyr; de Jager et al., 2021). Indeed, present-day forest buffalo mainly use small savannas in the rainforest, which savannas have been shrinking in size during the Holocene (Tutin and White, 1998). Secondary dwarfing took place there and the subspecies *S. c. nanus* arose. At times when the rainforest nearly disappeared (e.g. during the Last Glacial Maximum), hybridization took place with *S. c. aequinoctialis* leading to the form *S. c. brachyceros*. The further west one travels, the lesser the imprint of *S. c. aequinoctialis* is expected to be visible in *S. c. brachyceros*, leading to a cline. So, how plausible does it sound that dwarfing of the descendants of *S. acoelotus* took place in the rainforest but not in the savanna? Table 8.6 summarizes our feeling that dwarfing (or better stated: miniaturization) would be under positive selection. The genetics of both dwarfing (Boegheim et al., 2017) and miniaturization (Bouwman et al., 2018; see also Boden, 2008) are well understood in cattle and other species. 'Dwarfing' is often associated with negative effects, but miniaturization much less so. Miniaturization has been observed in Asian buffalo (weighing only 200 kg: Anilkumar et al., 2003) and in cattle (mini zebu's weighing only 150–250 kg: Boden, 2008; Porter et al., 2016). Selection can result quickly in small forms (Miniature Texas Longhorns, n.d.).

Why would we posit the notion that *Syncerus caffer brachyceros* could be viewed as a 'hybrid (sub-)species'? There are a number of reasons to think so. The first is that when the present-day Sahara was a savanna, other species of buffalo existed there, namely *S. antiquus*, where it lived with the now extinct *Equus mauritianum* and the white rhino (*Ceratotherium simum*). Because no fossil material of *S. c. brachyceros* (or *S. c. aequinoctialis*) is available, we do not know whether there was a zone to the south with *S. c. nanus*, a zone to the north with *S. antiquus*, and in between a zone with the two present-day subspecies (*brachyceros* and *aequinoctialis*). We do not find this very plausible because it assumes quite a lot. Intriguingly, the West African Guinea Savanna (between isohyets 1200 and 900 mm) and Sudan Savanna (between isohyets 900 and 600 mm), presently the habitat of *S. c. brachyceros* and *S. c. aequinoctialis*, appears to be largely man-made and rather recent due to people bringing slash-and-burn cultivation and fire management to this zone (Klop and Prins, 2008). If we are correct, then *S. c. brachyceros* especially, and to a lesser extent *S. c. aequinoctialis*, can be viewed as hybrid 'species' similar to the European wisent (or European bison, *Bison bonasus*). Indeed, based on mitochondrial DNA, the European wisent nests more strongly with *Bos taurus* than with *Bison bison* (Bibi, 2013; Zuranoa et al., 2019); similar results were found using nuclear DNA (Druica et al., 2016). The scenario in this case is that wisent arose as a hybrid between the aurochs (*Bos primigenius*) and the Steppe bison (*Bison [Bos] priscus*; see Verkaar et al., 2004), even though not all geneticists agree. The modern *B. bison* may also be the result of hybridization between two subspecies of *B. antiquus*, namely, *B. a. antiquus* and a subspecies that evolved from *B. antiquus* into *B. a. occidentalis* (McDonald, 1981, p. 82). Presently, hybridization takes place between the lowland anoa (*Bubalus depressicornis*) and the mountain anoa (*B. quarlesi*) even though they are characterized by a very large divergence time of some 2 Myr (Kakoi et al., 1994; Tanaka et al., 1996) after they putatively immigrated into Sulawesi independently of each other (Takenaka et al., 1987). Similarly, a hybrid zone exists between the two different species of Asian water buffalo, namely, the 'river form' *B. bubalis* and the 'swamp form' *B. carabenensis* (Mishra et al., 2015; Kumar et al., 2020). Microsatellite data seem to show that these two buffalo 'species' were already separated some 1.6 million years ago (Ritz et al., 2000), while cytochrome-b data indicate a separation between 1.7 and 1 Myr (Schreiber et al., 1999). Nuclear data, underpinning their separation, also shows much introgression between these two forms (MacEachern et al., 2009). In other words, much precedent exists for thinking that hybridization can result in new forms or species in large buffalo-like animals, strengthening the plausibility of its occurrence at the root of the existence of the bush cow (*S. c. brachyceros*).

An important consideration here is that the Guinea Savanna and Sudan Savanna are to a very large extent man-made environments due to shifting agriculture, slash-and-burn cultivation and intense use of fire (see Sankaran et al., 2005; Klop and Prins, 2008; Laris, 2008). Grasses become quickly unpalatable when growing during the wet season, reaching heights of 2 m or more (see Penning de Vries and Djitèye, 1982; Olff et al., 2002). Further north lies the Sahel, but that is too dry for buffalo, and does not offer enough food for buffalo in the dry season (or for many of the East African grazers such as zebra; cf. Klop and Prins, 2008). To describe the influence of human-induced habitat changes on the incidence of hybridization, the botanist Edgar Anderson (1948) coined the phrase 'hybridization of the habitat'. Indeed, numerous hybridization events are the outcome of anthropogenic actions (Ottenburghs, 2021). In general, novel environments – whether induced by human actions or not – can offer opportunities for the evolution of hybrid plant species, as has already long been put forward regarding the recolonization of deglaciated areas after a glacial period (see e.g. Daubenmire, 1968; Young, 1970; Kallunki, 1976; Fredskild, 1991; Gussarova et al., 2008). A notable example involves the Arunachal macaque (*Macaca munzala*), a presumed hybrid between *M. radiata* and a member of the *M. assamensis/thibetana* group, which occupies a specialized ecological niche in mountain forests (Chakraborty et al., 2007). Similarly, the transgressive phenotype of the hybrid rodent species *Lophuromys melanonyx* allowed it to invade a new habitat zone (Lavrenchenko, 2008). These examples and additional cases of rapid hybrid speciation in other taxonomic groups (Comeault and Matute, 2018; Ottenburghs, 2018; Nevado et al., 2020) indicate that the hybrid origin of the *brachyceros* is a plausible storyline.

Conclusion

O'Brien and Mayr (1991) provide guidelines to help think about subspecies: 'Members of a subspecies share a unique geographic range or habitat, a group of phylogenetically concordant phenotypic characters, and a unique natural history relative to the subdivisions of the species.' We believe that we have made the case that this applies to *S. c. nanus* and *S. c. caffer*. We are less convinced about a distinction between *S. c. brachyceros* and *S. c. aequinoctialis*; although they fall into two mtDNA clades, their nuclear DNA does not reveal distinction (Chapter 3). We do not believe that *S. c. matthewsii* should be maintained as a possible subspecies because phenotypically it is not very different from *S. c. caffer* and it also does not have a unique natural history. O'Brien and Mayr (1991) continue with 'Because they [the subspecies] are below the species level, different subspecies are reproductively compatible … are normally allopatric.' Indeed, evidence of genetic barriers between *nanus* and *caffer* is insufficient, which thus precludes independent species status for these two forms. There is in effect gene flow between *nanus* and *caffer* because there are mtDNA haplotypes that are characteristic in *nanus* found in *caffer* and vice versa (Smitz et al., 2013), and there is thus successful hybridization. O'Brien and Mayr (1991) end by stating that 'most subspecies will be monophyletic, however they may also derive from ancestral subspecies hybridization'. We believe that this is happening and has happened with *nanus* and *brachyceros*, but also with *aequinoctialis*. This then would be our motivation to lump the northern savanna buffalo into one subspecies like Smith (1986) has done previously. In our weighing, we included not only genetic but also ecological and historical reasoning as advocated by O'Brien and Mayr (1991). Because the Syrian Mameluke geographer Ibn Fadl Allah al-Umari was the first to write about these buffalo around 1337 CE (737 AH) (Levitzion and Hopkins, 2000, p. 264), we propose to name it in his honour *Syncerus caffer umarii*, but will leave a formal decision of course to a taxonomist.

The selection forces for the forest buffalo appear to be very different than for the savanna buffalo; the former are expected to further dwarf if that is genetically possible, while the latter would benefit under natural conditions to increase in size. The critical environmental factor is that they should continue having access to sufficient water for cooling. The human impact had been negligible on all forms of buffalo until the relentless expansion of arable agriculture, monopolization of water resources and the widespread availability of steel for snares and gin traps. Indeed, if humans were to go extinct, there would be a bright future for buffalo.

References

Abruzzi, W.S. (1979). Population pressure and subsistence strategies among the Mbuti Pygmies. *Human Ecology* **7**: 183–189.

Allen, J.D., S.D. Anderson, R.J. Collier and J.F Smith (2013). Managing heat stress and its impact on cow behavior. In *28th Annual Southwest Nutrition and Management Conferenc* **68**: 150–159.

Anderson, E. (1948). Hybridization of the habitat. *Evolution* **2**: 1–9.

Anilkumar, K., K.M. Syman Mohan, K. Ally and C.T. Sathian (2003). Composition and mineral levels of the milk of Kuttanad dwarf buffaloes of Kerala. *Buffalo Bulletin* **22**: 67–70.

Anonymous. (2004). Congo buffalo *Syncerus caffer nanus* (*nana*). http://placentation.ucsd.edu/congo.html (accessed 2 April 2021).

Ansell, W.F.H. (1972). Order Artiodactyla. In J. Meester and H.W. Setzer (Eds.), *The Mammals of Africa: An Identification Manual*. Washington, DC: Smithsonian Institute.

Balme, G., L. Hunter and R. Slotow (2007). Feeding habitat selection by hunting leopards *Panthera pardus* in a woodland savanna: prey catchability versus abundance. *Animal Behaviour* **74**: 589–598.

Bekhuis, P.D.B.M., C. de Jong and H.H.T. Prins (2008). Diet selection and density estimates of forest buffalo in Campo-Ma'an National Park, Cameroon. *African Journal of Ecology* **46**: 668–675.

Bergey, C.M., M. Lopez, G.F. Harrison, et al. (2018). Polygenic adaptation and convergent evolution on growth and cardiac genetic pathways in African and Asian rainforest hunter-gatherers. *Proceedings of the National Academy of Sciences* **115**: E11256–E11263.

Bibi, F. (2013). A multi-calibrated mitochondrial phylogeny of extant Bovidae (Artiodactyla, Ruminantia) and the importance of the fossil record to systematics. *BMC Evolutionary Biology* **13**:166.

Bibi, F., J. Rowan and K. Reed (2017). Late Pliocene Bovidae from Ledi-Geraru (Lower Awash Valley, Ethiopia) and their implications for Afar paleoecology. *Journal of Vertebrate Paleontology* **37**: e1337639.

Blaxter, K.L. (1962). *The Energy Metabolism of Ruminants*. London: Hutchinson and Co.

Bobe, R. and A.K. Behrensmeyer (2004). The expansion of grassland ecosystems in Africa in relation to mammalian evolution and the origin of the genus *Homo*. *Palaeogeography, Palaeoclimatology, Palaeoecology* **207**: 399–420.

Bocksberger, G., J. Schnitzler, C. Chatelain, et al. (2016). Climate and the distribution of grasses in West Africa. *Journal of Vegetation Science* **27**: 306–317.

Boden, D.W.R. (2008). Miniature cattle: for real, for pets, for production. *Journal of Agricultural and Food Information* **9**: 167–183.

Boegheim, I.J., P.A. Leegwater, H.A. van Lith and W. Back (2017). Current insights into the molecular genetic basis of dwarfism in livestock. *The Veterinary Journal* **224**: 64–75.

Boisserie, J.R. (2005). The phylogeny and taxonomy of Hippopotamidae (Mammalia: Artiodactyla): a review based on morphology and cladistic analysis. *Zoological Journal of the Linnean Society* **143**: 1–26.

Bouwman, A. C., H.D. Daetwyler, A.J. Chamberlain, et al. (2018). Meta-analysis of genome-wide association studies for cattle stature identifies common genes that regulate body size in mammals. *Nature Genetics* **50**(3): 362.

Bunn, H.T., A.Z.P. Mabulla, M. Domínguez-Rodrigo, et al. (2010). Was FLK North levels 1–2 a classic "living floor" of Oldowan hominins or a taphonomically complex palimpsest dominated by large carnivore feeding behavior? *Quaternary Research* **74**: 355–362.

Bunn, H. T. and T.R. Pickering (2010). Bovid mortality profiles in paleoecological context falsify hypotheses of endurance running–hunting and passive scavenging by early Pleistocene hominins. *Quaternary Research* **74**: 395–404.

Chaix, L., M. Faure, C. Guerin and M. Honegger (2000). Kaddanarti, a lower Pleistocene assemblage from northern Sudan. In L. Krzyzaniak, K. Kroeper and M. Kobusiewicz (Eds.), *Recent Research into the Stone Age of Northeastern Africa*. Studies in African Archaeology, vol. 7. Poznań: Poznań Archaeological Museum, pp. 33–46.

Chakraborty, D., U. Ramakrishnan, J. Panor, et al. (2007). Phylogenetic relationships and morphometric affinities of the Arunachal macaque *Macaca munzala*, a newly described primate from Arunachal Pradesh, northeastern India. *Molecular Phylogenetics and Evolution* **44**: 838–849.

Chardonnet, P. and F. Lamarque (1996). Wildlife in the Lake Chad Basin. In I. De Zborowski (Ed.), *Livestock Atlas of the Lake Chad Basin*. Montpellier: CIRAD-EMVT-CTA, pp. 109–124.

Chen L, Q. Qiu, Y. Jiang, et al. (2019). Large-scale ruminant genome sequencing provides insights into their evolution and distinct traits. *Science* **364**: eaav6202.

Clayton, W.D. (1970). *Flora of Tropical East Africa. Gramineae (Part 1)*. London: Crown Agents for Oversea Governments and Administrations.

Clayton, W.D., S.M. Phillips and S.A. Renvoize (1974). *Flora of Tropical East Africa. Gramineae (Part 2)*. London: Crown Agents for Oversea Governments and Administrations.

Comeault, A.A. and D.R. Matute (2018). Genetic divergence and the number of hybridizing species affect the path to homoploid hybrid speciation. *Proceedings of the National Academy of Sciences* **115**: 9761–9766.

Cornélis, D. (2011). *Ecologie du Déplacement du Buffle de Savane ouest-africain Syncerus caffer brachyceros*. Doctoral dissertation, UM2.

Cornélis, D., M. Melletti, L. Korte, et al. (2014). African buffalo (*Syncerus caffer* Sparrman, 1779). In M. Melletti and J. Burton (Eds.), *Ecology, Evolution and Behaviour of Wild Cattle*. Cambridge: Cambridge University Press, pp. 326–372.

Cribiu, E.P. and C.P. Popescu (1980). Chromosome constitution of a hybrid between East African buffalo (*Syncerus caffer caffer*) and dwarf forest buffalo (*Syncerus caffer nanus*). *Annales de Genetique et de Selection Animale* **12**: 291–293.

Daubenmire, R. (1968). Some geographic variations in *Picea sitchensis* and their ecologic interpretation. *Canadian Journal of Botany* **46**: 787–798.

Debruyne, R. (2005). A case study of apparent conflict between molecular phylogenies: the interrelationships of African elephants. *Cladistics* **21**: 31–50.

Debruyne, R., A. Van Holt, V. Barriel and P. Tassy (2003). Status of the so-called African pygmy elephant (*Loxodonta pumilio* (Noack 1906)): phylogeny of cytochrome b and mitochondrial control region sequences. *Comptes Rendus Biologies* **326**: 687–697.

Diffey, B.L. (2018). Time and place as modifiers of personal UV exposure. *International Journal of Environmental Research and Public Health* **15**(6):1112.

Druica, R., M. Ciorpac, D. Cojocaru, et al. (2016). The investigation of cytochrome b gene in order to elucidate the taxonomic uncertainties between European bison (*Bison bonasus*) and its relatives. *Romanian Biotechnological Letters* **22**: 12116–12125.

Dunsworth, H.M. (2010). Origin of the genus *Homo*. *Evolution: Education and Outreach* **3**: 353–366.

Du Preez, J.H., P.J. Hattingh, W.H. Giesecke and B.E. Eisenberg (1990). Heat stress in dairy cattle and other livestock under southern African conditions. III. Monthly temperature–humidity index mean values and their significance in the performance of dairy cattle. *Onderstepoort Journal of Veterinary Research* **57**: 243–248.

Fisher, H.J. (1972). 'He swalloweth the ground with fierceness and rage': the horse in the Central Sudan. I. Its introduction. *Journal of African History* **13**: 367–388.

Fredskild, B. (1991). The genus *Betula* in Greenland – Holocene history, present distribution and synecology. *Nordic Journal of Botany* **11**: 393–412.

García, S.C., M.R. Islam, C.E.F. Clark and P.M. Martin (2014). Kikuyu-based pasture for dairy production: a review. *Crop and Pasture Science* **65**: 787–797.

Geraads, D., C. Blondel, H.T. Mackaye, et al. (2009). Bovidae (Mammalia) from the lower Pliocene of Chad. *Journal of Vertebrate Paleontology* **29**: 923–933.

Gippoliti, S. and G. Amori (2007). The problem of subspecies and biased taxonomy in conservation lists: the case of mammals. *Folia Zoologica* **56**: 113–117

Gould, S.J. and R.C. Lewontin (1979). The spandrels of San Marco and the Panglossian paradigm: a critique of the adaptationist programme. *Proceedings of the Royal Society of London. Series B. Biological Sciences* **205**: 581–598.

Gray, A.P. (1972). *Mammalian Hybrids: A Check-List with Bibliography* (2nd ed.). Slough: Commonwealth Agricultural Bureaux.

Groves, C.P. (1992). How old are subspecies? A tiger's eye-view of human evolution. Perspectives in Human Biology 2. *Archaeology in Oceania* **27**: 153–160.

Groves, C.P. and P. Grubb (2011). *Ungulate Taxonomy*. Baltimore: John Hopkins University Press.

Grubb, P. (1972). Variation and incipient speciation in the African buffalo. *Zeitschrift für Säugetierkunde* **37**: 121–144.

Grubb, P., C.P. Groves, J.P. Dudley and J. Shoshani (2000). Living African elephants belong to two species: *Loxodonta africana* (Blumenbach, 1797) and *Loxodonta cyclotis* (Matschie, 1900). *Elephant* **2**: 1–4.

Gussarova, G., M. Popp, E. Vitek and C. Brochmann (2008). Molecular phylogeny and biogeography of the bipolar *Euphrasia* (Orobanchaceae): recent radiations in an old genus. *Molecular Phylogenetics and Evolution* **48**: 444–460.

Hashim, I.M. (1987). Relationship between biomass of forage used and masses of faecal pellets of wild animals in meadows of the Dinder National Park. *African Journal of Ecology* **25**: 217–223.

Hendey, Q.B. (1969). Quaternary vertebrate fossil sites in the south-western Cape Province. *The South African Archaeological Bulletin* **24**: 96–105.

Hitchcock, R.K. (2000). Traditional African wildlife utilization: subsistence hunting, poaching, and sustainable use. In H.H.T. Prins, J.G. Grootenhuis and T.T. Dolan (Eds.), *Conservation of Wildlife by Sustainable Use*. Boston: Kluwer Academic, pp. 389–415.

Hooft, W.F. van, A.F. Groen and H.H.T. Prins (2002). Phylogeography of the African buffalo based on mitochondrial and Y-chromosomal loci: Pleistocene origin and population expansion of the Cape buffalo subspecies. *Molecular Ecology* **11**: 267–270.

Hsieh, P., K.R. Veeramah, J. Lachance, et al. (2016). Whole-genome sequence analyses of Western Central African Pygmy hunter-gatherers reveal a complex demographic history and identify candidate genes under positive natural selection. *Genome Research* **26**: 279–290.

Hubbard, K.G., D.E. Stooksbury, G.L. Hahn and T.L. Mader (1999). A climatological perspective on feedlot cattle performance and mortality related to the temperature–humidity index. *Journal of Production Agriculture* **12**: 650–653.

Hurt, R. and P. Ravn (2000). Hunting and its benefits: an overview of hunting in Africa with special reference to Tanzania. In H.H.T. Prins, J.G. Grootenhuis and T.T. Dolan (Eds.), *Conservation of Wildlife by Sustainable Use*. Boston: Kluwer Academic, pp. 295–313.

IFPRI (2015). Agro-ecological zones for Africa South of the Sahara. HarvestChoice and International Food Policy Research Institute (IFPRI). https://dataverse.harvard.edu/file .xhtml?persistentId=doi:10.7910/DVN/M7XIUB/GCVTBIandversion=3.1).

Iongh, H.H. de, C.B. de Jong, J. van Goethem, et al. (2011). Resource partitioning among African savanna herbivores in North Cameroon: the importance of diet composition, food quality and body mass. *Journal of Tropical Ecology* **27**: 503–513.

Jager, D. de, B. Glanzmann, M. Möller, et al. (2021). High diversity, inbreeding and a dynamic Pleistocene demographic history revealed by African buffalo genomes. *Scientific Reports* **11**: 1–15.

James, S.R., R.W. Dennell, A.S. Gilbert, et al. (1989). Hominid use of fire in the Lower and Middle Pleistocene: a review of the evidence. *Current Anthropology* **30**: 1–26.

Jenny, D. (1996). Spatial organization of leopards *Panthera pardus* in Taï National Park, Ivory Coast: is rainforest habitat a 'tropical haven'? *Journal of Zoology* **240**: 427–440.

Kakoi, H., T. Namikawa, A. Takenaka, et al. (1994). Divergence between the anoa of Sulawesi and the Asiatic water buffaloes, inferred from their complete amino acid sequences of hemoglobin 13 chains. *Journal of Zoological Systematics and Evolutionary Research* **32**: 1–10.

Kallunki, J.A. (1976). Population studies in *Goodyera* (Orchidaceae) with emphasis on the hybrid origin of *G. tesselata*. *Brittonia* **28**: 53–75.

Klop, E. and H.H.T. Prins (2008). Diversity and species composition of West African ungulate assemblages: effects of fire, climate and soil. *Global Ecology and Biogeography* **17**: 778–787.

Korte, L.M. (2008). Habitat selection at two spatial scales and diurnal activity patterns of adult female forest buffalo. *Journal of Mammalogy* **89**: 115–125.

Kullmer, O., K.O. Sandrock, F. Schrenk and T.G. Bromage (1999). The Malawi Rift: biogeography, ecology and co-existence of *Homo* and *Paranthropus*. *Anthroplogie* **37**: 221–231.

Kumar, D.R., M.J. Devadasan, T. Surya, et al. (2020). Genomic diversity and selection sweeps identified in Indian swamp buffaloes reveals its uniqueness with riverine buffaloes. *Genomics* **112**: 2385–2392.

Laris, P. (2008). An anthropogenic escape route from the "Gulliver Syndrome" in the West African savanna. *Human Ecology* **36**: 789–805.

Lavrenchenko, L.A. (2008). Mammals of Ethiopian plateau as a model for evolutionary studies. In: *Sovremennye problemy biologicheskoi evolyutsii (Current Problems of Biological Evolution)*. Moscow: GDM, pp. 149–184.

Levitzion, N. and J.F.P. Hopkins (Eds.) (2000) *Corpus of Early Arabic Sources for West African History*. Princeton: Markus Wiener.

Lombard, M. and M.N. Haidle (2012). Thinking a bow-and-arrow set: cognitive implications of Middle Stone Age bow and stone-tipped arrow technology. *Cambridge Archaeological Journal* **22**: 237–264.

MacEachern, S., J. McEwan and M. Goddard (2009). Phylogenetic reconstruction and the identification of ancient polymorphism in the Bovini tribe (Bovidae, Bovinae). *BMC Genomics* **10**: 177.

McDonald, J.N. (1981). *North American Bison: Their Classification and Evolution*. Berkeley: University of California Press.

Mduma, S., R. Hilborn and A.R.E. Sinclair (1998). Limits to exploitation of Serengeti wildebeest and implications for its management. In D.M. Newbery, H.H.T. Prins and N.D. Brown (Eds.), *Dynamics of Tropical Communities*. Oxford: Blackwell Science, pp. 243–265.

Mertens, H. (1985). Structures de population et tables de survie des buffles, topis et cobs de Buffon au Parc National des Virunga, Zaïre. *Revue d'écologie (Terre Vie)* **40**: 33–51.

Miniature Texas longhorns (n.d.) https://en.wikipedia.org/wiki/Miniature_Texas_Longhorn (accessed 9 March 2021).

Mishra, B.P., P.K. Dubey, B. Prakash, et al. (2015). Genetic analysis of river, swamp and hybrid buffaloes of north-east India throw new light on phylogeography of water buffalo (*Bubalus bubalis*). *Journal of Animal Breeding and Genetics* **132**: 454–466.

Morris, C.D., N.M. Taintoi and S. Boleme (1993). Classification of the eastern alpine vegetation of Lesotho. *African Journal of Range and Forage Science* **10**: 47–53.

Mugangu, T., M. Hunter and J. Gilbert (1995). Food, water, and predation: a study of habitat selection by Buffalo in Virunga National Park, Zaïre. *Mammalia (Paris)* **59**: 346–362.

Nevado, B., S.A. Harris, M.A. Beaumont and S.J. Hiscock (2020). Rapid homoploid hybrid speciation in British gardens: the origin of Oxford ragwort (*Senecio squalidus*). *Molecular Ecology* **29**: 4221–4233.

O'Brien, S.J. and E. Mayr (1991). Bureaucratic mischief: recognizing endangered species and subspecies. *Science* **251**: 1187–1188.

O'Connell, J.F., K. Hawkes and Jones (1988). Hadza scavenging: implications for Plio/Pleistocene hominid subsistence. *Current Anthropology* **29**: 356–363.

Olff, H., M.H. Ritchie and H.H.T. Prins (2002). Global environmental determinants of diversity in large herbivores. *Nature* **415**: 901–904.

O'Regan, H.J., L.C. Bishop, A. Lamb, et al. (2005). Large mammal turnover in Africa and the Levant between 1.0 and 0.5 Ma. *Geological Society, London, Special Publications* **247**: 231–249.

Ottenburghs, J. (2018). Exploring the hybrid speciation continuum in birds. *Ecology and Evolution* **8**: 13027–13034.

Ottenburghs, J. (2021). The genic view of hybridization in the Anthropocene. *Evolutionary Applications* **14**(10): 2342–2360.

Pagacova, E., H. Cernohorska, S. Kubickova, et al. (2011). Centric fusion polymorphism in captive animals of family Bovidae. *Conservation Genetics* **12**: 71–77.

Patin, E. and L. Quintana-Murci (2018). The demographic and adaptive history of central African hunter-gatherers and farmers. *Current Opinion in Genetics and Development* **53**: 90–97.

Penning de Vries, F.W.T. and M.A. Djitèye (1982). *La Productivité des Pâturages Sahéliens: une étude des sols, des végétations et de l'exploitation de cette ressource naturelle*. Wageningen: PUDOC.

Perry, G.H. and P. Verdu (2017). Genomic perspectives on the history and evolutionary ecology of tropical rainforest occupation by humans. *Quaternary International* **448**: 150–157.

Petronio, C. (2014). Note on the taxonomy of Pleistocene hippopotamuses. *Journal of Mountain Ecology* **3**: 53–55.

Plumptre, A.J. (1995). The chemical composition of montane plants and its influence on the diet of the large mammalian herbivores in the Pare National des Volcans, Rwanda. *Journal of Zoology* **235**: 323–337.

Porter, V., L. Alderson, S.J.G. Hall and D.P. Sponenberg (2016). *Mason's World Encyclopedia of Livestock Breeds and Breeding* (6th ed.). Wallingford: CABI.

Prins, H.H.T. (1992). The pastoral road to extinction: competition between wildlife and traditional pastoralism in East Africa. *Environmental Conservation* **19**: 117–123.

Prins, H.H.T. (1996). *Behaviour and Ecology of the African Buffalo: Social Inequality and decision Making*. London: Chapman & Hall.

Prins, H.H.T. (2000). Competition between wildlife and livestock. In H.H.T. Prins, J.G. Grootenhuis and T.T. Dolan (Eds.), *Conservation of Wildlife by Sustainable Use*. Boston: Kluwer Academic, pp. 51–80.

Prins, H.H.T. and I.J. Gordon (2014). Testing hypotheses about biological invasions and Charles Darwin's two-creators ruminations. In H.H.T. Prins and I.J. Gordon (Eds.), *Invasion Biology and Ecological Theory: Insights From a Continent in Transformation*. Cambridge: Cambridge University Press, pp. 1–19.

Prins, H.H.T. and J.F. de Jong (2022). The ecohistory of Tanzania's northern Rift Valley – can one establish an objective baseline as endpoint for ecosystem restoration? In C. Kiffner, M.L. Bond and D.E. Lee (Eds.), *Tarangire: Human–Wildlife Coexistence in a Fragmented Landscape*. Cham: Springer Nature, pp. 129–161.

Prins, H.H.T. and H. Olff (1998). Species richness of African grazer assemblages: towards a functional explanation. In D.M. Newbery, H.H.T. Prins and N.D. Brown (Eds.), *Dynamics of Tropical Communities*. British Ecological Society Symposium Vol. 37. Oxford: Blackwell Science, pp. 449–490.

Prins, H.H.T. and A.R.E. Sinclair (2013). *Syncerus caffer* African buffalo. In J.S. Kingdon and M. Hoffmann (Eds.), *Mammals of Africa. Vol. 6. Pigs, Hippopotamuses, Cevrotain, Giraffes, Deer and Bovids*. London: Bloomsbury, pp. 125–136.

Ritz, L.R., M.L. Glowatzki-Mullis, D.E. MacHugh and C. Gaillard (2000). Phylogenetic analysis of the tribe Bovini using microsatellites. *Animal Genetics* **31**: 178–185.

Sankaran, M., N.P. Hanan, R.J. Scholes, et al. (2005). Determinants of woody cover in African savannas. *Nature* **436**: 846–849.

Sato, H. (1983). Hunting of the Boyela, slash-and-burn agriculturalists, in the central Zaire forest. *African Study Monographs* **4**: 1–54.

Sayer, J.A. (1977). Conservation of large mammals in the Republic of Mali. *Biological Conservation* **12**: 245–263.

Schreiber, A., I. Seibold, G. Nötzold and M. Wink (1999). Cytochrome b gene haplotypes characterize chromosomal lineages of anoa, the Sulawesi dwarf buffalo. *Journal of Heredity* **90**: 165–176.

Schwartz, M.K. and D.J. Boness (2017). Marine mammal subspecies in the age of genetics: introductory remarks from the associate editor and editor-in-chief of *Marine Mammal Science*. *Marine Mammal Science* **33**: 7–11.

SEDAC (n.d.). Socioeconomic Data and Applications Center (SEDAC). https://sedac .ciesin.columbia.edu/data/set/nagdc-population-landscape-climate-estimates-v3/ maps?facets=region:africa (accessed 3 April 2014).

Shanahan, T.M., K.A. Hughen, N.P. McKay, et al. (2016). CO_2 and fire influence tropical ecosystem stability in response to climate change. *Scientific Reports* 6: 1–8.

Sinatra, G.M. and D. Lombardi (2020). Evaluating sources of scientific evidence and claims in the post-truth era may require reappraising plausibility judgments. *Educational Psychologist* 55: 120–131.

Sinclair, A.R.E. (1977). *The African Buffalo: A Study of Resource Limitation.* Chicago: Chicago University Press.

Smith, S.J. (1986). *Rowland Ward's Records of Big Game: Africa and Asia.* Johannesburg: Rowland Ward Publications.

Smithers, R.H.N. (1983). *Die Soogdiere van die Suider-Afrikaanse Substreek.* Pretoria: University of Pretoria.

Smitz, N., C. Berthouly, D. Cornélis, et al. (2013). Pan-African genetic structure in the African buffalo (*Syncerus caffer*): investigating intraspecific divergence. *PLoS One* 8(2): e56235.

Steinhart, E.I. (2000). Elephant hunting in 19th-century Kenya: Kamba society and ecology in transformation. *The International Journal of African historical Studies* 33: 335–349.

Takenaka, O., M. Hotta, Y. Kawamoto, et al. (1987). Origin and evolution of the Sulawesi macaques 2. Complete amino acid sequences of seven β chains of three molecular types. *Primates* 28: 99–109.

Tanaka, K., C.D. Solis, J.S. Masangkay, et al. (1996). Phylogenetic relationship among all living species of the genus *Bubalus* based on DNA sequences of the cytochrome b gene. *Biochemical Genetics* 34: 443–452.

Terashima, H. (1980). Hunting life of the Bambote: an anthropological study of hunter-gatherers in a wooded savanna. *Senri Ethnological Studies* 6: 223–268.

Thornhill, R. (2007). The concept of an evolved adaptation. In G.R. Bock and G. Cardew (Eds.), *Characterizing Human Psychological Adaptations.* London: John Wiley, pp. 4–22.

Tieszen L.L., M.M. Senyimba, S.K. Imbamba and J.H. Troughton (1979). The distribution of C_3 and C_4 grasses and carbon isotope discrimination along an altitudinal and moisture gradient in Kenya. *Oecologia* 37: 337–350.

Treves, A., A.J. Plumptre, L.T. Hunter and J. Ziwa (2009). Identifying a potential lion *Panthera leo* stronghold in Queen Elizabeth National Park, Uganda, and Parc National des Virunga, Democratic Republic of Congo. *Oryx* 43: 60–66.

Tutin, C.E.G. and L.J.T. White (1998). Primates, phenology and frugivory: past and future patterns in the Lopé Reserve, Gabon. In D.M. Newbery, H.H.T. Prins and N.D. Brown (Eds.), *Dynamics of Tropical Communities.* Oxford: Blackwell Science, pp. 309–337.

Ukpabi, S.C. (1974). The military in traditional African Societies. *Africa Spectrum* 9: 200–217.

Van der Zon, A.P. (1992). *Graminées du Cameroun.* PhD thesis, Wageningen University.

Varela, S., J. Rodríguez and J.M. Lobo (2009). Is current climatic equilibrium a guarantee for the transferability of distribution model predictions? A case study of the spotted hyena. *Journal of Biogeography*, 36: 1645–1655.

Verkaar, E.L.C., I.J. Nijman, M. Beeke, et al. (2004). Maternal and paternal lineages in crossbreeding bovine species. Has wisent a hybrid origin? *Molecular Biology and Evolution* 21: 1165–1170.

Walton, D.N. (1988). Burden of proof. *Argumentation* 2: 233–254.

Walton, D.N. (2001). Abductive, presumptive and plausible arguments. *Informal Logic* 21: 141–169.

Woodroffe, R., J.R. Ginsberg and D.W. Macdonald (Eds.) (1997). *The African Wild Dog: Status Survey and Conservation Action Plan.* Gland: IUCN.

Wurster, D.H. and K. Benirschke (1968). Chromosome studies in the superfamily Bovoidea. *Chromosoma* 25:152–171.

Young, S.B. (1970). On the taxonomy and distribution of *Vaccinium uliginosum.* *Rhodora* 72: 439–459.

Zuranoa, J.P., F.M. Magalhãesa, A.E. Asato, et al. (2019). Cetartiodactyla: updating a time-calibrated molecular phylogeny. *Molecular Phylogenetics and Evolution* 133: 256–262.

Part III
Diseases

A. CARON

African Buffalo and Diseases, and the Villain is...

All iconic wildlife species trigger an array of positive and negative feelings, beliefs and values in humans. The lion is the king of the savanna, powerful and dangerous but benevolent towards his subjects. The African buffalo, on the other hand, is aggressive, naughty and treacherous. These perceptions do not only draw their strength from the ferocious opponent that the buffalo represents when hunted. They also are deeply rooted in the perceived relationship between the buffalo and infectious diseases, and the negative representations associated with the buffalo as a villainous animal spreading pathogens to livestock. In Africa, and perhaps even beyond, no other species crystallizes so many of perceptions about the health risks that need to be controlled to produce livestock. Managing buffalo populations, by culling them, physically disconnecting them from livestock and protecting livestock from their diseases, has been one of the priorities of colonial and post-colonial veterinary services since their creation at the end of the nineteenth century. This section of the book aims to review the current state of knowledge on the relationship between the buffalo and infectious diseases, and then to reflect on old paradigms and opportunities provided by new knowledge and global contexts.

To do so, we first needed to present recent data and synthetize knowledge about the role of buffalo in infectious diseases in Africa. The buffalo is a species that co-evolved with African pathogens and their vectors, developing resistance and tolerance mechanisms that has allowed it to survive across the continent in different habitat types. However, it is far from clear that the buffalo is a maintenance host for all or many endemic pathogens. Gaps in knowledge still exist despite the massive amount of work that has been done on the species. With regard to European and

Asian pathogens that have been imported into Africa since the beginning of the colonial era, buffalo have once again proved to be a quite resistant species. The one exception was the deadly and now extinct rinderpest, which hammered buffalo populations in Africa. The picture that emerges from this section is that compared to exotic cattle breeds, the buffalo is a quite robust species well adapted to the African terrain. As a result, in the current intensive livestock production systems promoted in Africa, the buffalo needs to be separated from livestock because of its maintenance of some diseases detrimental for livestock production. Does the same hold for extensive subsistence farming systems?

The last decades have seen the emergence of a relatively larger number of behavioural studies looking at the buffalo/cattle interface in relation to pathogen ecology. These studies have been concentrated in southern and eastern Africa and are largely absent in other regions. They require interdisciplinary collaboration bridging ecology, spatial epidemiology and social sciences, among others. The replication of these studies in different ecosystems has indicated that buffalo tend to avoid cattle, leading to very few observations of direct contacts (only the odd story of a buffalo bull hanging around a cattle herd, but probably not a common event). Buffalo tend to use similar grazing and water sources because cattle are penned ('corralled', 'kraaled') at night, adapting their behaviour to the contexts of wildlife/livestock interfaces. This means that potential interspecies transmission is more likely to involve pathogens that are indirectly transmitted (e.g. through the environment or vectors). This new science of the wildlife/livestock interface still needs some development. More data-heavy modelling will help the testing of management options for these interfaces, such as manipulating key resources (e.g. water, grazing) or strategically controlling the disease in cattle (e.g. seasonal vaccination protecting cattle when contacts with buffalo are the highest). The integration of non-invasive tools and genomics should considerably impact the understanding of these buffalo/cattle interfaces.

The entanglement of the buffalo in grievances because it was thought (unjustifiedly) to cause sanitary issues had the advantages of concentrating a huge amount of disease ecology work on the species. Today, the buffalo belongs to the top five species in the world studied for *in vivo* coinfection. Its gregarious social organization and phylogenetic proximity with cattle, with whom they share a large part of their pathogen burden, makes the buffalo a formidable subject to investigate the little-known interactions of important viruses, mycoplasmas, other bacteria and parasites in coinfected individuals and populations. Interesting coinfection properties emerge from these studies that emphasize potential cooperation or competition between pathogens through the intermediary of the host immune systems and the relevance of the infection history of the host to determine the community of pathogens that it harbours. The knowledge and hypotheses produced by these studies can inform not only the management of buffalo and buffalo/cattle interfaces (e.g. shall we manage pathogens in buffalo populations or not), but also the nascent field of pathogen community ecology.

After weighing and sifting through the evidence, it would appear that the African buffalo is probably not the health villain invented by colonial administrations. Its coexistence with Western livestock production systems is probably impossible and has been fought against during the twentieth century. But what have been the costs and benefits for African societies? Is the species that is well-adapted to the African environment the problem, or is it the imported breed that needs to be kept under unsustainable conditions to stay productive? The twenty-first century has started with the prospect of massive global changes for the century to come that will threaten societies and their productive systems. There is a chance that Africans and African societies could emerge stronger from this challenging era, and the buffalo could be a flagship of this transformation.

9 · Infections and Parasites of Free-Ranging African Buffalo

R. G. BENGIS, F. GAKUYA, M. MUNYEME,
D. FEKADU SHIFERAW, R. A. KOCK AND
P. CHARDONNET

Introduction

Infections in free-ranging African wildlife with pathogens normally associated with wild animals or domestic livestock can arbitrarily be assigned to four or possibly even five categories, as follows.

- *Wildlife-maintained infections*: African indigenous infections without disease expression in sylvatic hosts, such as South African Territory (SAT) types of foot and mouth disease (FMD), African theileriosis, African swine fever, African horse sickness, bovine malignant catarrh fever and African trypanosomiasis.
- *Alien, exotic or foreign animal infections*: some of the best examples of this category are certain pathogens historically alien to sub-Saharan Africa that were probably introduced onto the African continent with the importation of domestic livestock from Eurasia during the colonial era. Indigenous African free-ranging mammals, within similar taxonomic groupings to these domesticated hosts, are generally immunologically naïve to these foreign pathogens, and may suffer significant morbidity and mortality when exposed to these disease agents. Examples include rinderpest (may it rest in peace), bovine tuberculosis, bovine brucellosis, peste des petits ruminants (PPR), bovine papillomatosis and canine distemper, which may impact both wildlife and domestic species.
- *Multi-species infections*: these infections usually occur on most continents and may affect both wildlife and domestic livestock. Transmission can thus occur in both directions, although certain regional dominant role players have been identified. These infections are generally cyclical in nature, and the epidemic cycles appear to be related to population densities of one or more host species, as well as climatic factors.

Uniquely, these infections generally have a fatal outcome in both wildlife and domestic livestock and are frequently zoonotic. Some of the these diseases, such as anthrax and rabies, have been documented in African buffalo (*Syncerus caffer*).

- *Newly emerging or recently detected infections*: these infections have been detected only recently, such as encephalomyocarditis in elephants (*Loxodonta africana*), arthropod-borne flavi- and bunyaviruses in several wildlife species, parafilariasis in African buffalo and feline immuno-deficiency virus infection in wild felids. They also include infections that have relatively recently crossed the species barrier, such as canine distemper in lions (*Panthera leo*) and bovine papillomatosis in giraffe (*Giraffa camelopardalis*), zebra (*Equus zebra*), sable antelope (*Hippotragus niger*) and buffalo.

- Finally, *truly novel diseases* such as spongiform encephalopathies seen in cervids in North America and more recently in Norway and Sweden, but not yet seen in African wildlife.

Infectious Diseases Impacting African Buffalo

Rinderpest

Rinderpest, the great cattle plague pandemic of 1889–1905, was introduced with infected cattle from southern Asia to feed troops on military expeditions around the Horn of Africa (Hutcheon, 1902). Much has been written about the massive die-offs of both indigenous cattle, wild ruminants and suids across most regions of Africa, and the massive social, political and economic repercussions resulting from the huge livestock losses (Mack, 1970). The livelihoods of nomadic pastoralists were devastated. Countless wild artiodactyls also perished, with buffalo, tragelaphs (spiral horned antelope), wildebeest, hippotragines and wild suids being the most severely affected (Kock, 2006). Being social ruminants that occur in large herds, buffalo were massively affected by this close-contact transmitted morbillivirus, and in many cases, only small relict populations survived in remote pockets or were entirely extirpated from their former ranges (Stevenson-Hamilton, 1957). Impacts were also seen on some keystone species, including migrating East African wildebeest (*Connochaetes taurinus*). This disease had major impacts on the scale of migration and the habitat, with resultant transformation in vegetation types and distribution (Holdo et al., 2009). This disease may have contributed to certain wildlife distribution anomalies, such as the formation of isolated metapopulations of species such as sable antelope, roan antelope (*Hippotragus equinus*), greater kudu (*Tragelaphus strepsiceros*) and nyala (*Tragelaphus angasii*). Rinderpest was declared officially eradicated in 2011, the first animal disease to be so (FAO report, 2011).

Bovine Tuberculosis

Bovine tuberculosis (bTB) in wildlife in sub-Saharan Africa is probably a foreign animal disease introduced into southern Africa with colonial cattle breeds imported from Europe during the eighteenth and nineteenth centuries. The first report of bTB in wildlife in southern Africa was in greater kudu and common duiker (*Silvicapra grimmia*) in the eastern Cape Province of South Africa (Paine and Martinaglia, 1929), and then again in greater kudu in the same region in 1940 (Thorburn and Thomas, 1940). This region apparently had a high prevalence of bTB in cattle at that time. The first report of bTB in African buffalo came from the Queen Elizabeth National Park (NP) in Uganda (Guilbride et al., 1963), and confirmed in 1965 (Thurlbeck et al., 1965). The disease spilled over into common warthogs (*Phacochoerus africanus*) and has persisted to this day (Woodford, 1982a, 1982b). BTB was also discovered in free-ranging Kafue lechwe (*Kobus leche kafuensis*) in Zambia in 1972 and 1977 (Gallagher et al., 1972; Clancey, 1977), and confirmed later (Munyeme et al., 2010). Subsequent screening of buffalo from the Greater Kafue NP yielded nothing (Munang'andu et al., 2011). In South Africa, the disease was first detected in buffalo in the Hluhluwe/Imfolosi Park in Kwazulu-Natal Province in the 1980s, and in Kruger (KNP) in 1990 (Bengis et al., 1996). It appears as though these wildlife populations became infected by contact with infected cattle. The outbreak in Kruger followed recorded outbreaks of bTB in cattle on farms south of the Crocodile River (southern boundary of KNP) during the early 1960s, and again in the 1980s (State veterinary reports). During these periods, outbreaks of buffalo-associated theileriosis were also reported in cattle on these farms, indicating that buffalo and cattle had shared range and vector ticks. Subsequently in Kruger, the disease spread through all of the buffalo herds from the extreme south to the far north of the park, and eventually into Zimbabwe (Gonarezhou National Park), over a period of 19 years (de Garine-Wichatitsky et al., 2010; Figure 9.1). Systematic sampling of buffalo herds in the different regions of the KNP between

Figure 9.1 Advanced pulmonary tuberculosis in African buffalo. © R. Bengis.

2003 and 2011 demonstrated a gradient of the prevalence of infection, with a 35 per cent prevalence in the south where the disease first entered, 20 per cent in the central district and 3 per cent in the far north. Spillover infection also has been detected in 15 other species. Only buffalo and lechwe appear to have become true sylvatic maintenance hosts of bTB, while greater kudu and warthog appear to have maintenance host potential, if their population densities are high enough. The long-term effects of this chronic progressive disease on African wildlife host populations at sustained high prevalence rates are unknown. Initially there was concern that bTB may negatively affect the population dynamics and structure of buffalo herds and lion prides in KNP. To date, however, no negative impact has been detected at the population level in Kruger, illustrating the resilience of these species. However, due to the veterinary control measures imposed, this disease has definitely had an impact on translocation of wildlife out of what are now endemic bTB areas in South Africa. The disease has also been reported in buffalo, warthogs, Uganda kob (*Kobus kob thomasi*) and olive baboon (*Papio anubis*) in Uganda, and in buffalo, Masai giraffe (*Giraffa camelopardalis tippelskirchi*) and topi (*Damaliscus lunatus jimela*) in the greater Serengeti Ecosystem and in Kenya (Meunier et al., 2017). These are unfenced systems and the prevalence of disease appears to be relatively stable (Meunier, 2017), although no intensive sampling has been reported. In Ethiopia, although bTB is endemic in cattle, no infection was detected in a small sample of buffalo from Omo/Mago NP, also an open system.

Brucellosis

In the African wildlife context, only *Brucella abortus bovis* and *B. melitensis* have been recorded in wildlife (Simpson et al., 2021). Both these organisms have zoonotic potential, although no cases of human infection from buffalo have been reported.

Bovine brucellosis caused by *B. abortus bovis* is a foreign chronic animal disease thought to have been introduced into sub-Saharan Africa by the importation of European cattle breeds by colonial settlers during the eighteenth and nineteenth centuries. This chronic disease has also crossed the interface with wildlife, and is now endemic in wildlife in several countries. In sub-Saharan Africa, *Brucella* sero-positivity has been demonstrated in bovids, 12 antelope species, four carnivore species, baboons, black and white rhinoceros, hippopotamus (*Hippopotamus amphibius*) and zebras. Of all of these, only African buffalo and possibly Kafue lechwe appear to be reservoir species that are able to maintain infection in the absence of infected cattle (Simpson et al., 2021).

In KNP, *Brucella* sero-positivity has been detected in most buffalo herds (De Vos and van Niekerk, 1969), and at sero-prevalence rates of up to 23 per cent (Herr and Marshall, 1981). Similar to the disease in cattle, experimental infection with brucellosis causes late-term abortions in buffalo heifers, as well as in buffalo cows during the first pregnancy after infection (Gradwell et al., 1977). In addition, it was observed that calves born through the following pregnancy tend to be weak and poor survivors. Brucellosis in buffalo may also affect synovial structures causing arthritic conditions such as carpal hygromata, and may cause severe lameness (Figure 9.2). This has been observed in both eastern and southern African buffalo populations (Kock, personal communication). In Zimbabwe, clinical disease also has been reported in eland and waterbuck (Condy and Vickers, 1972). Brucellosis caused by *B. melitensis* has only been detected in farmed sable antelope on several Eastern Cape wildlife ranches (Glover et al., 2020).

Figure 9.2 Brucella Carpel Hygroma in African buffalo. © R. Bengis.

Anthrax

Anthrax is historically one of the oldest documented diseases, and the life cycle of the causative bacterium, *Bacillus anthracis*, has both biotic and abiotic components. The abiotic component is the resistant dormant spore phase, which occurs in regions with predominantly alkaline soils and high calcium and moisture content. These spores can survive almost indefinitely in this dormant state in the soil. The biotic component is the exponential amplification phase, which takes place within the mammalian body, and appears to be the essential reproductive phase (De Vos and Turnbull, 2004), although germination and amplification of anthrax bacteria in certain soil-dwelling *Amoebas* has been reported (Dey et al., 2012). Anthrax outbreaks have been documented in most domestic species in the absence of a wildlife link. Similarly, localized to extensive outbreaks have occurred in various wildlife populations with no livestock link. Large-scale outbreaks may cross the interface, especially where livestock and wildlife share ranges and resources (Mukarati et al., 2020). With regard to buffalo, anthrax has been reported in buffalo populations in KNP, in Gonarezhou NP in Zimbabwe, in the Okavango ecosystem in Botswana, in the Caprivi system in Namibia and in Luangwa valley NP in Zambia. In East Africa, anthrax has been recorded in Uganda, Tanzania, Kenya and Ethiopia. In Kenya,

Figure 9.3 Anthrax in African buffalo. Note blood coming from nose and generalized putrefactive swelling. © R. Bengis.

an anthrax outbreak in 2015 at Lake Nakuru NP resulted in the death of 745 out of the 4500 buffalo in the park, with a species-specific mortality rate of 17 per cent (Muturi et al., 2018). An analysis of temporal and spatial distribution of anthrax outbreaks among Kenya wildlife revealed that out of the 51 outbreaks, 23.5 per cent involved buffalo (Gachohi et al., 2019).

In Mago NP in Ethiopia, anthrax outbreaks originating from cattle and sheep from nearby pastoralists killed more than 1617 (in 1999) and 563 (in 2000) wild animals from 21 species, including buffalo. About 20 people, including one scout, from the area who handled or ate the carcasses, including one scout, were infected and developed severe skin lesions, but recovered after treatment (Shiferaw et al., 2002).

In a review of seven documented anthrax outbreaks in KNP between 1960 and 2010, buffalo featured as the second most common species affected in an analysis of the carcass counts. Greater kudu were the most frequently affected species in these Kruger outbreaks (Bengis, personal communication; Figure 9.3).

In Africa, human anthrax is generally contracted when people handle or consume carcasses of infected livestock or of any wildlife that have succumbed during an outbreak, and this would include buffalo in light of the susceptibility of this species as mentioned.

Buffalo appear to become infected mainly by ingestion of contaminated water, contaminated grazing or by mechanical transmission by biting flies. Buffalo are exquisitely sensitive to the exotoxins produced during the exponential replication phase of the anthrax organisms, and unlike other ruminants, will often die before developing substantial bacteremia. This makes it important for laboratories to microscopically scan buffalo diagnostic blood smears thoroughly if this disease is suspected. The post-mortem signs commonly seen with buffalo that have died of anthrax include sudden death, tarry black blood that does not clot exuding from the natural orifices and swollen carcasses from rapid putrefaction. Suspected anthrax carcasses should not be opened.

Other Bacterial Diseases

There are several other bacterial diseases that have been sporadically reported in African buffalo. Localized bacterial abscesses caused by a variety of organisms do occur, usually as a result of bacterial infection of penetrating wounds. With the exception of anthrax, bacterial infections that cause systemic disease have rarely been reported in free-ranging buffalo. Those that have been detected include haemorrhagic septicaemia caused by *Pasteurella multocida* and bacterial entero-colitis caused by entero-pathogenic *Escherichia coli* or *Salmonella* spp. (Mitchell et al., 2021). In addition, malignant oedema/gas gangrene, caused by toxigenic *Clostridia*, have been sporadically reported following blunt traumatic injury and bruising.

Buffalo and Other Wildlife-Maintained Infections

In this discussion, it is important to realize that only a few wildlife species have been identified and positively implicated in the maintenance and transmission of these diseases. These include the African savanna buffalo, wild suids including warthogs and bush pigs, brindled wildebeest, black wildebeest (*Connochaetes gnou*), bushbuck, the various species of zebra and possibly greater kudu.

Foot-and-Mouth Disease

In the case of FMD in sub-Saharan Africa, cattle-derived imported Eurasian serotypes A and O coexist with African serotypes SAT1, 2 and 3 (SAT for South African Territory). The pivotal role played by the African buffalo as a sylvatic maintenance host of the SAT group of FMD viruses was identified in the late 1960s, and initial findings in various buffalo populations were published by Condy (1971), Hedger (1972) and Falconer and Child (1975). This was followed by further publications on the characterization of the viruses in several buffalo subpopulations in eastern and southern Africa (Anderson et al., 1979; Vosloo et al., 1996; Thomson and Bastos, 2004). Most buffalo populations in southern Africa, with the exception of those relict populations that survived the rinderpest in the Eastern Cape and Kwazulu/Natal Provinces of South Africa, have been shown to be infected. Random serological sampling of buffalo herds in KNP in South Africa, the Okavango delta in Botswana and the Zambezi valley in Zimbabwe demonstrate that over 95 per cent of those free-ranging buffalo have antibodies to at least one, but frequently two or even all three SAT virus serotypes, by the age of 12 months. Surveys in West, Central and East Africa showed a similar picture (Bronsvoort et al., 2008). In addition, FMD viruses of all three serotypes can regularly be isolated from oro-pharyngeal probang samples collected from these buffalo, and this carrier state may last for years (Jolle et al., 2021). The virus apparently survives almost indefinitely in certain dendritic cells of the tonsils, even in the presence of humoral antibodies. Most free-ranging buffalo show no clinical signs of infection.

Thus, until recently, there could be no doubt that infected buffalo herds were the ultimate source of all FMD infections in naive livestock, and most SAT-type FMD outbreaks in livestock could also be traced back to interface buffalo contact (Guerrini et al., 2019). However, more recently, it would appear that certain SAT virus topotypes have adapted to cattle, and several outbreaks have recently occurred in South Africa without any identifiable buffalo contact (Thomson, personal communication). This has been confirmed in Kenya (Wekesa et al., 2015). They found that FMDV serotypes O, A, SAT1 and SA2 were circulating among cattle in Kenya and cause disease, but only SAT1 and SAT2 viruses were successfully isolated from clinically normal buffalo. The buffalo isolates were also genetically distinct from isolates obtained from cattle. In another study in Kenya, Omondi et al. (2020) investigated the epidemiology of FMDV in buffalo, including the role of buffalo in the circulation of FMDV in livestock populations. By sequencing the virus' VP1 coding region from blood and oropharyngeal fluids collected from wild buffalo and sympatric cattle in central Kenya, they were able to show that FMDV has a high seroprevalence in buffalo and targeted cattle populations. In addition, serotype SAT1 and SAT2 sequences from buffalo and serotype O and A sequences from sympatric cattle were recovered. These results further confirmed the findings of Wekesa et al. (2015), because amongt sympatric buffalo and cattle, no SAT1 or 2 sequences found in buffalo were found in cattle, which suggests that transmission of FMDV from buffalo to sympatric cattle in this region is rare. Similarly, there was no evidence that serotype O and A sequences found in cattle were transmitted to buffalo. Serotypes A and O have also been introduced with infected cattle into Ethiopia and other countries in the region. In Ethiopia, serology confirmed the presence of antibodies to serotypes A, SAT1 and SAT2 in clinically normal buffalo in Mago/Omo NP, whereas in neighbouring cattle, which have a seropositivity prevalence of between 5.6 per cent and 42.7 per cent with endemic distributions, serotypes O, A, SAT1 and SAT2 were documented (Sahle, 2004; Abdela, 2017). More recently (2021), Eurasian serotype O has been reported in cattle in Zimbabwe, Namibia and Mozambique.

FMD is rarely a fatal disease in cattle except for occasional calf mortalities, but it certainly does impact animal production, as dairy cows dry up and beef cattle lose condition. It is therefore not generally considered to be an important disease among pastoralists and subsistence farmers. However, due to FMD international control regulations (through the WOAH (World Organization for Animal Health, founded as the OIE (Office International of Epizootics)) directed by northern hemisphere countries, subsistence farmers living close to buffalo populations in Africa have been negatively impacted. Fortunately, in recent years there has been an increasing realization among world leaders that globalization is perpetuating the dominance of the developed world, and there is a genuine desire to address poverty issues in Africa (Ferguson et al., 2013; Thomson et al., 2013a, 2013b; Chapter 12).

Buffalo-Associated Theileriosis

Theileria parva is a tick vector-borne protozoan infection of buffalo. It is transmitted by *Rhipicephalus appendiculatus* and *R. zambesiensis*, which are three-host ticks. It is naturally a silent infection in buffalo, but is highly pathogenic and causes an acute fatal disease in cattle, especially the European cattle breeds (Neitz et al., 1955). It is generally a dead-end disease in these cattle, because they die before the lymphoid tissue-associated schizonts can produce erythrocyte-associated merozoites (small piroplasms), and are therefore unable to infect the vector ticks to maintain circulation of the infection. Small clustered outbreaks of buffalo-associated theileriosis still occur today in southern and East Africa where there is a buffalo/cattle interface. However, cattle-adapted strains have now also evolved, which cause the diseases known as East Coast fever (ECF) and Zimbabwe theileriosis (January disease). These diseases can circulate independently in cattle without any buffalo presence because these *Theileria parva* variants can complete their life cycle in cattle, produce small piroplasms, and are therefore able to infect the tick vectors (Irvin and Cunningham, 1981). ECF occurs widely through the range of the same main vectors (*R. appendiculatus* and *R. zambesiensis*) in East and southern Africa north of the Zambezi River. In these regions, ECF, together with heartwater and trypanosomiasis, remain the greatest disease obstacle to agricultural development and prosperity. However, *T. parva* is absent in West Africa and most of Central Africa, including the whole Congo basin, because *R. appendiculatus* is absent. In Central Africa, the disease is only present in the far eastern side, above 500 m in the region of the Great Lakes: Burundi, Rwanda, Kivu in eastern DRC. This is a disease of great concern to most pastoralists in the affected countries because it has the potential to threaten food security. ECF was also introduced with cattle movement to regions south of the Zambezi River in 1901/02, but after resulting in the death of 1.25 million of the 4 million cattle present in the affected territories, was subsequently eradicated at great expense to governments and both farmers and pastoralists. From an agriculturalist/pastoralist perspective, this was a disaster, but for conservation and environmental objectives, these diseases have ensured that large tracts of land in Africa remain ecologically intact and viable, a vital element in the desired long-term recovery from anthropogenic impacts that are of such contemporary global concern. These diseases were eventually eradicated from southern Mozambique in 1917, from Rhodesia in 1954 and from South Africa in 1955 (Lawrence, 1992), but continue to circulate in cattle north of the Zambezi River.

There are other theilerias frequently found in buffalo blood samples, such as *T. mutans* (transmitted by *Amblyomma* spp.) and *T. taurotragi* (transmitted by *R. appendiculatus*). Both of these parasites generally cause benign infection in cattle. Buffalo-associated *T. taurotragi* also generally results in a mild infection in cattle, but occasionally causes a disease called turning sickness in young cattle, characterized by nervous signs, such as circling, head pressing, ataxia, paralysis and uni- or bilateral blindness (Lawrence and Williamson, 2004).

Trypanosomiasis

Trypanosomiasis is a very important disease of cattle (known as nagana), camels (known as surra), horses, pigs and dogs in parts of sub-Saharan

Africa, and certain *Trypanosoma* species may also affect humans (causing sleeping sickness disease). The various *Trypanosoma* spp. have different transmission modes, including biological transmission by tsetse flies, an insect genus endemic to Africa that had time to co-evolve with buffalo (*T. brucei* and *T. congolense, T. vivax*), and mechanical transmission by other biting flies of three main families, Tabanidae (genera *Chryspos, Haematopota* and *Tabanus*), Stomoxynae (genera *Stomoxys* and *Haematobia*) and Hippoboscidae (genera *Melophagus* and *Hippobosca*) (all previous plus *T. evansi*) (Itard, 1981). With non-tsetse biting flies, trypanosomiasis expands well beyond the tsetse fly-infested areas.

Historically, the distribution of tsetse flies (known as tsetse belts) profoundly shaped and limited the distribution of livestock, and consequently severely hampered the development of the livestock industry. However, the situation has changed dramatically in the last decades under pressure from two main driving forces: (i) the drastic reduction of the tsetse distribution range, due notably to the destruction of their habitat such as forest galleries for agriculture (Gouteux et al., 1994; Cuisance, 1996; Reid et al., 2000), tsetse eradication campaigns, the global climate change (Courtin et al., 2010) and for savanna tsetse species such as *Glossina morsitans*, the disappearance of large game (Itard, 1981); and (ii) the development and now widespread use of trypanocide drugs, both preventive and curative, which allow large transhumant cattle herds to graze in tsetse-infested areas during the dry season, including in Protected Areas, and leads to the degradation of the pastoral rangeland though excessive bushfire, overgrazing, tree felling, etc.

Preferred wildlife hosts of tsetse flies include African buffalo, wild porcines, spiral horned antelopes (*Tragelaphs* spp.), elephants, black rhinoceros and hippopotami, and these species are all capable of surviving well within the tsetse belts. They frequently develop significant infection rates with detectable parasitaemias, but without developing disease, and may therefore serve as natural maintenance hosts for the various *Trypanosome* spp. Interestingly, the respective historical distribution ranges of African buffalo and tsetse flies largely match (Olubayo, 1991). Buffalo and tsetse flies have co-evolved in the same ecological system for millenaries to the mutual advantage of the three stakeholders, the parasite, its vector and its host, with the consequence of having made the buffalo both a maintenance host and one resistant to the parasite. The mechanisms of trypano-resistance of the African buffalo have been partially investigated (e.g. Olubayo, 1991; Redruth et al., 1994; Wang et al., 2000; Guirnalda et al., 2007).

Trypano-tolerant cattle breeds, all of them humpless *Bos taurus* (e.g. N'dama and Baoulé cattle), as well as trypano-tolerant goat and sheep breeds, have evolved in pastoral societies, mainly in West Africa, but also in Central and East Africa (Murray et al., 1979). They are, however, not trypano-resistant and may potentially serve as maintenance hosts.

An important conservation corollary is that many of the remaining and relatively pristine wildlife conservation areas in Africa owe their very existence to the presence of this disease, which made these areas unsuitable for agricultural expansion or human habitation (Chapter 12). However, as seen above, the situation is changing drastically with the wide use of trypanocide drugs. Pastoralists no longer hesitate to enter deep inside tsetse-infested Protected Areas with large cattle herds. To quote only one striking example from Cameroon, before trypanocid drugs no livestock entered Bouba Ndjidda NP and the seven surrounding Hunting Areas due to heavy tsetse infestation, while in 2015 the wildlife aerial census of these Protected Areas counted 526,233 (over half a million) head of cattle (Wildlife Conservation Society, Ministry of Forests and Wildlife and Ecole de Faune de Garoua, 2015), which was 21 times more than in 2008 (Omondi et al., 2008), despite the continued presence of tsetse flies there today.

With the contemporary shrinkage of the distribution range of tsetse flies, their main remaining strongholds are now largely Protected Area complexes, which also are the residual strongholds of the African buffalo. In these restricted situations, the coevolution of the tryptic 'buffalo/tsetse/trypanosome' is maintained, including the resistance of buffalo to the disease, and buffalo remain there as a maintenance host and maybe even a bridge host. The question is raised whether these Protected Areas can now be regarded as maintenance sites, including for Human African Trypanosomiasis (HAT). HAT originating from wildlife has been explored to some extent, but only in a very limited number of wild species like bushbuck (Heisch et al., 1958). Much remains to be investigated with regards to the possible role of wildlife, including buffalo, in the maintenance of *Trypanosoma brucei gambiense*, which is responsible for HAT in West and Central Africa.

Peste des petits ruminants

The peste des petits ruminants (PPR) virus is closely related to the rinderpest virus (serologically indistinguishable with screening enzyme-linked immunosorbent assays, or ELISAs), from which it likely evolved (rinderpest of small ruminants) over recent centuries in West Africa. It spread to much of the rest of Africa and Asia, and this pandemic has gathered pace over the last two decades, entering East Africa and spreading south and across Asia, reaching the China seaboard in 2013. Serological surveys of wildlife, including mostly buffalo, during the rinderpest eradication campaign showed cross neutralization between rinderpest and PPR antibodies, and ELISA tests during epidemio-surveillance produced confusing results. Once differentiated, this confirmed widespread infection of wild artiodactyls, buffalo included, in Africa with the PPR virus where livestock were infected, and evidence suggests the small ruminants spilled the virus into adjacent wildlife populations (Kock, 2006; Mahapatra et al., 2015; Fernandez Aguilar et al., 2020). Buffalo were no exception and have shown the highest true prevalence for PPR virus infection among sampled species (Jones et al., 2021). No evidence of disease in African buffalo is reported, while only rare and, epidemiologically unconfirmed, reports of PPR disease have been made in sub-Saharan Africa in free-ranging antelope, notably gazelle in Sudan (Asil et al., 2019).

Malignant Catarrhal Fever

In Africa, the most important cause of malignant catarrhal fever (MCF) in cattle in the context of this chapter is wildebeest-associated MCF caused by *Alcelaphine Herpesvirus 1*. There is also a sheep-associated MCF affecting cattle caused by *Ovine Herpesvirus 2*. The important role played by wildebeest (*Connachaetes* spp.) in the maintenance and seasonal shedding of *Alcelaphine Herpesvirus 1* has been elucidated (Plowright et al., 1960; Plowright, 1967; Mushi et al. 1980). Free-ranging African buffalo in multi-species systems may be infected with this virus and sero-convert, but do not develop overt clinical signs of disease, or detected viral persistence, and thus appear totally unimportant in the maintenance or transmission of this important viral disease of cattle. West and Central Africa are outside the wildebeest distribution range and MCF infection has not been reported in buffalo there.

Rabies

Rabies is an ancient disease, and recognizable descriptions of it can be traced back to early Chinese, Egyptian, Greek and Roman records (Wilkinson, 1988). In sub-Saharan Africa, sylvatic rabies has been diagnosed in 33 carnivorous species and 23 herbivorous species, including

African buffalo (Mitchell et al., 2021), with regional variation in dominant epidemiological role players (Swanepoel, 2004). In spite of this, by far the largest number of rabies cases reported in the developing world occur in domestic dogs. In Africa, endemic rabies (caused by both viverid and canid biotypes) has been identified in certain communal burrow-dwelling wildlife species such as the yellow mongoose, and in bat-eared fox as well as various jackal species. African buffalo appear to be incidentally infected and do not appear to play any role in the maintenance of this infection.

Buffalo Involvement in Other Important Livestock Diseases

Tick-borne Diseases

Heartwater (Cowdriasis, Ehrlichia/Rickettsia ruminantium *Infection)*
Heartwater is a tick-transmitted rickettsial infection, and is one of the most important diseases of domesticated ruminants in sub-Saharan Africa. This disease causes high morbidity and significant mortality in cattle (especially *Bos taurus* types), as well as in sheep and goats, throughout the range of its biological vectors, which are present in most of sub-Saharan Africa with the exception of the extremely arid zones. The important biological vectors are Ixodid ticks of the genus *Amblyomma*, which are three-host ticks. Interestingly, in West and Central Africa, the historical distribution area of buffalo largely matches with the range of *A. variegatum* (annual rainfall over 500 mm). Some *Amblyomma* are specific to buffalo and suspected to be vectors, namely *A. splendidum* in forest buffalo (*Syncerus caffer nanus*), *A. astrion* in Central African savanna buffalo (*S. c. aequinoctialis*), *A. cohaerens* in East African buffalo and *A. hebraeum* in Southern African buffalo (Morel, 1981).

Free-ranging African buffalo, together with giraffe, black wildebeest, blesbok and eland that occur within the distribution range of the *Amblyomma* ticks, frequently harbour this rickettsial organism without developing the disease. The infection in these species is generally subclinical due to the evolution of disease resistance over millennia and the development of an endemically stable host/pathogen relationship. Helmeted guineafowl, leopard tortoises and scrub hares, which are the preferred hosts of the larval and nymph stages of this vector, may also harbour this pathogen (Oberem and Bezuidenhout, 1987). All of these silent carriers may potentially serve as sources of infection for the vector ticks, which theoretically could infect livestock in an open interface situation where livestock and wildlife share range and resources. However, it appears from recorded spatial and temporal patterns of disease outbreaks that the major source of infection for the vectors causing most livestock outbreaks are in fact the domestic livestock themselves, and this perpetuates the cycle of infection and disease.

Anaplasmosis

Both *Anaplasma marginale* subsp. *centrale* and *A. marginale* are regularly found in buffalo blood samples. Eygelaar et al. (2015) report prevalence rates of 30 per cent for *A. marginale* subsp. *centrale* and 20 per cent for *A. marginale* in free-ranging buffalo in northern Botswana. These pathogens can be transmitted by several one-host and multi-host ticks of the genus *Rhipicephalus*; they can also be mechanically transmitted by biting insects, mainly by biting flies of the families Tabanidae and Stomoxynae, less so by mosquitoes (Morel, 1981). *A. marginale* is pathogenic in cattle, causing severe anaemia and icterus, mainly in older dairy and beef cattle of the *Bos taurus* type. This disease is commonly known as 'dry gall sickness'. In endemic areas, most calves are generally immune. *A. marginale* subsp. *centrale* infection is usually apathogenic in cattle, and is in fact used in a blood-based vaccine for cattle. It appears that buffalo have become incidentally infected by ticks that have fed on infected cattle and play a minor role, if any, in the maintenance of this disease. Buffalo do not develop any clinical signs of infection.

Babesiosis

The babesioses are tick-borne infections caused by intra-erythrocytic protozoal parasites of the genus *Babesia*. Four species are known to infect cattle in southern Africa, namely *B. bovis*, *B. bigemina*, *B. occultans* and an as yet unnamed species. *B. bovis* and *B. bigemina* are highly pathogenic and both cause redwater disease in cattle, but they have never been documented in African buffalo. Other pathogenic *Babesia* occur in sheep, goat, pigs and equids. Therefore, buffalo do not appear to play any role in the epidemiology of these two important cattle diseases. However, *B. occultans*, which causes benign infections in cattle, is also frequently found in buffalo, and a prevalence of 23 per cent has been reported in 120 buffalo blood samples collected in Northern Botswana (Eygelaar et al., 2015). The vector of *B. occultans* is *Hyalomma marginatum rufipes*, a two-host tick with a wide distribution range in southern Africa.

African Insect-Borne (Arbo-) Virus Diseases

Serological studies have shown that a whole host of wild artiodactyls, including African buffalo, are able to be infected with several of these insect-borne viruses, but the infections are naturally subclinical, indicating innate resistance or low pathogenicity in these wildlife species. These diseases include lumpy skin disease (LSD), caused by a capripox virus, bluetongue and epizootic haemorrhagic disease caused by orbiviruses, bovine ephemeral fever caused by a rhabdovirus, Rift Valley fever (RVF) caused by a phlebovirus and congenital arthrogryphosis/hydrancephaly caused by Akabane virus. In addition, some recent investigations have looked into the involvement of buffalo in certain Flavivirus and Bunyavirus infections.

Lumpy Skin Disease

Davies (1991) reported the detection of antibodies to LSD in buffalo in an endemic LSD area, but no clinical disease. In South Africa, serosurveys of 440 free-ranging buffalo from KNP were all negative for serum-virus neutralizing antibody. In addition, experimental infection of sero-negative buffalo gave negative results (Howell and Coetzer, unpublished results). These animals did not even sero-convert. From these observations, it can be concluded that African buffalo are not susceptible to this virus and play no role in the epidemiology of this important disease of cattle.

Bluetongue

Serum-virus neutralizing antibodies have been detected in African buffalo, as well as many other wild sympatric ruminants (Davies and Walker, 1974). However, clinical disease has not been reported, and the role of these wild ruminants in the epidemiology of this livestock disease remains speculative.

Ephemeral Fever

Also known as three-day stiff sickness, ephemeral fever occurs in most sub-Saharan countries in the form of epizootics in cattle. In between these epizootics, limited foci of disease may be encountered and there is evidence of sero-conversion in sentinel herds. The examination of a range of wild ruminant sera showed evidence of neutralizing antibody in 54 per cent of buffalo, 62 per cent of waterbuck (*Kobus ellipsiprymnus*), 9 per cent of wildebeest and 2.8 per cent of hartebeest (*Alcelaphus buselaphus*) (Davies et al., 1975). An interesting observation is that there were sero-conversions in waterbuck and buffalo in samples collected before the previous cattle epizootic of the disease. This would appear to indicate that the virus was circulating in wild ruminant populations during a period when no clinical disease was observed in cattle. Thus wild ruminants, including buffalo, may play a maintenance role during inter-epizootic periods.

Rift Valley Fever

Rift Valley fever is a zoonotic mosquito-borne virus disease of livestock and wild ruminants that has been identified as a risk for international spread. Typically, the disease occurs in geographically limited outbreaks associated with high rainfall events, and can cause massive losses of livestock. It is unclear how the RVF virus persists during interepidemic periods, but cryptic low-level cycling of the virus in livestock and/or wildlife populations may play a role. What is known is that the RVF virus can be efficiently maintained by certain floodwater breeding Aedine mosquitoes. In these mosquitoes, male/female sexual transmission as well as transovarial transmission of virus occurs. The eggs are laid on grasses, sedges and mud on the edge of rainwater pans, and these eggs are dormant and require a drying-out period followed by re-wetting to hatch. The time course for this drying out and re-wetting follows climatic cycles and may be weeks, months, years or even decades, and this is probably the main maintenance mechanism during the interepidemic periods (Linthicum et al., 1984, 1985).

In 1999, an abortion storm caused by the RVF virus occurred at a disease-free buffalo breeding project in KNP, followed by a second outbreak at another buffalo breeding project just south of the park. Serological surveys in free-ranging buffalo in KNP revealed generally low levels of sero-positivity that spiked during these outbreaks (Beechler et al., 2015). In addition, several other aborted buffalo foetuses were also positive for RVF (Mitchell et al., 2021). Sero-positivity also has been detected in a range of other wild ungulates in South Africa (Swanepoel, 1976) and Zimbabwe (Caron et al., 2013). In Kenya, a sero-prevalence of around 15 per cent of RVF virus neutralizing antibodies has been detected in buffalo (Evans et al., 2008; Britch et al., 2013). Many buffalo live in endemic RVF areas, and this could explain the seroconversion to this mosquito-borne disease. It is notable that other wildlife such as gazelles living outside these endemic regions can suffer clinical disease during periods of epizootic expansion, although this has not been observed in sympatric buffalo. It also has been observed that significant mortality from RVF occurred when naive scimitar-horned oryx (*Oryx damma*) were translocated into the RVF endemic area of Chad from the UAE, whereas the long-term resident oryx appeared resistant (Chardonnet, personal communication).

In 2010, during a major outbreak of RVF in the Orange Free State and Northern Cape Provinces in South Africa, apart from heavy livestock losses, RVF-associated abortions and mortality were recorded in ranched buffalo, eland (*Taurotragus oryx*), sable antelope, waterbuck, springbok (*Antidorcas marsupialis*), blesbok (*Damaliscus dorcas phillipsi*) and bontebok (*D. d. dorcas*), as well as exotic fallow deer, llamas and alpacas. Whether buffalo or any of these other species play a role in low-level maintenance cycling of the RVF virus during the interepizootic period remains speculative.

Mycoplasma

Contagious bovine pleuropneumonia (CBPP), caused by *Mycoplasma mycoides* subsp. *mycoides*, is one the three great historic cattle plagues of the world (OIE, 2022a), and Contagious caprine pleuropneumonia (CCPP), caused by *M. capricolum* subsp. *capripneumoniae*, is one of the most severe diseases of goats (OIE, 2022b). Moreover, these two diseases have gained renewed attention since the eradication of rinderpest and the PPR eradication programme. The African buffalo is not susceptible to CBPP and does not play any role in its transmission. In contrast with CBPP, which affects cattle only, CCPP also affects a number of wild ungulates, including some African antelopes; however, it is not known to affect the African buffalo. It is difficult to evaluate the prevalence of these mycoplasma diseases in wildlife due to sampling and transportation constraints. However, the use of specific serological tests and PCR may improve information in wildlife.

Emerging Infectious Diseases

So-called emerging animal infectious diseases include recently detected diseases (often in new geographies), variants of known diseases, diseases that have recently crossed the 'species barrier' and finally, truly novel diseases. With regard to African buffalo, the following emerging infectious diseases have been reported.

Figure 9.4 Papillomatosis on an African buffalo. © R. Bengis.

Bovine Papillomatosis

Infection with bovine papilloma virus types 1 or 2, causing cutaneous lesions in giraffe, Cape mountain zebra (*Equus zebra zebra*), sable antelope and African buffalo, have been described and confirmed by histopathology and immunohistochemistry. These cutaneous lesions varied from single or multiple wart-like growths to massive sarcoids (Williams et al., 2011; Figure 9.4). This is a good example of a cattle disease that has crossed the species barrier.

Diseases Caused by Akabane and Related Simbu-Group Viruses

In KNP, several buffalo calves with arthrogryposis and hydranencephaly were born at a buffalo breeding facility. These congenital defects are frequently a result of *in utero* infection of the foetus with Akabane virus during certain critical stages of development. There is no reason to suspect that these congenital deformities do not also occur in freeranging buffalo, but are rarely seen because most new-born animals with congenital defects are taken out by predators. In a sero-survey for Akabane virus infection in African wildlife, neutralizing antibody was detected in 222/979 buffalo (22.7 per cent; Al-Busaidy et al., 1987).

In the past decade, mortalities associated with neurological clinical signs have been reported in several free-ranging wildlife species, including a variety of antelope, warthogs, white rhinoceros and African buffalo. Histopathology demonstrated a viral encephalitis characterized by glial apoptosis, neuronal degeneration and/or cerebral oedema (Mitchell et al., 2021). A Shuni virus of the Simbu group has been implicated.

Diseases Caused by Flaviviruses

Bovine viral diarrhoea virus (BVDV) and antibody have been detected in a whole range of free-ranging ruminants (Hamblin and Hedger, 1979), and in Africa, some buffalo and wildebeest populations suffer high infection rates (Hyera et al., 1992). In a recent report (Mitchell et al., 2021), two aborted buffalo foetuses and one neonatal mortality were confirmed to be caused by BVDV, using immunohistochemistry.

Macroparasitic Infections in African Buffalo

When reading this paragraph, what needs to be appreciated is that all free-ranging wildlife are 'biological packages' that are infected subclinically by a variety of endo- and ectoparasites. African buffalo are no exception, and host numerous different nematodes, cestode and trematode worms and several external parasites (Boomker et al., 1996). What is important is that most of these parasites do not appear to deleteriously affect the health of free-ranging wildlife in any way. In free-ranging multi-species wildlife systems, certain mammalian species may be susceptible to certain parasitic infections, and the uptake of larvae or ova by non-patent species functions as a natural balancing mechanism that reduces infection burden and helps to reduce parasite loads resulting in sustainable host/parasite relationships. In addition, in the co-infection context in which most wild species live, multiple minor parasitic infections may result in parasitic competition or in immune stimulation, both of which attenuate parasitic pathogenesis and minimize the effect on the host health (Chapter 11).

It is beyond the scope of this chapter to attempt to tabulate and describe all of the macro-parasites that have been detected in African buffalo, and we will limit our discussion to include mainly those parasitic infections of buffalo that are overtly visible in the live animal or in the dead animal carcass.

Ixodid Ticks

Most free-ranging wildlife are parasitized to a greater or lesser extent by one or more of the life-cycle stages of ixodid ticks. Certain species, such as African buffalo, giraffe and black and white rhinos, are preferred hosts for the adult stage of several of these ixodid ticks, which is the reproductive stage of these ticks. Adult ticks of the important genera *Amblyomma*, *Rhipicephalus* and *Hyalomma* are frequently found on these host species. In a study conducted in Ethiopia's Mago/Omo National Park (Shiferaw and Kock, 2002), seven species of ticks, namely *Amblyomma cohaerence*, *A. lepidum*, *A. variegatum*, *A. nuttali*, *A. gemma*, *Rhipicephalus pravus*, *R. pulchaellus* and *R. evertsi*, were collected from buffalo. In southern Africa, *A. hebraeum*, *R. appendiculatus* and *R. zambeziensis* are the most common buffalo ticks. In Central African Republic, *A. variegatum*, *A. astrion*, *R. longus*, *R. muhsamae*, *R. cliffordi*, *R. lunatus*, *Hyalomma nitidus* and *H. rufipes* have been described on 100 per cent of 85 examined buffalo (Thal, 1971).

Parafilaria bassoni Infection

Parafilaria bassoni is a spirurid nematode that infects the skin and subcutaneous tissues of buffalo, causing bleeding skin nodules (Figure 9.5). These bleeding nodules are associated with gravid female worms ovipositing embryonated eggs. These lesions occur mainly on the dorsum and lateral sides of the buffalo. Complications of these lesions develop in a low percentage of buffalo due to secondary bacterial infections forming subcutaneous abscesses, or as a consequence of a Type 1 hypersensitivity reaction that may result in vascular occlusion, and skin infarction with the development of cutaneous ulcers, which often become enlarged by oxpecker worry. A sero-survey using a *Parafilaria* ELISA in the Greater KNP Complex demonstrated that this parasite occurs in buffalo populations throughout this complex at a seroprevalence rate of approximately 34 per cent (Keet et al., 1997).

Psoroptic Mange

Psoroptic mange is caused by a large sarcoptiform mite, *Psoroptes pienaari*, commonly found on buffalo. This is a large mite that can be seen with

Figure 9.5 Parafilaria skin ulceration on an African buffalo. © R. Bengis.

the naked eye. This mite is most commonly found on the head, neck, shoulders and rump of buffalo, and causes a pruritic scaley alopecia (hair loss), frequently giving the skin a thickened, hairless, greyish appearance.

Demodectic Mange

Demodectic mange is caused by the parasitic mite *Demodex caffer*, which inhabits the hair follicles in the skin of buffalo, and when present in large numbers may cause nodular parasitic and sebaceous cysts (Figure 9.6). These cutaneous skin nodules are most commonly seen in the younger age classes, and are generally limited to the head, neck and shoulder regions, but in severe cases, may be present over the entire animal (Dräger and Paine, 1980). If one of these nodules is incised and lateral pressure applied, a thick, creamy white material exudes, which consists of sebaceous cells and masses of *Demodex* mites. In a study in KNP,

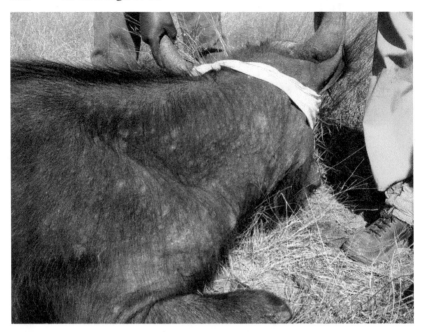

Figure 9.6 Nodular demodex on a captured African buffalo. © R. Bengis.

approximately 50 per cent of 203 buffalo examined had clinical signs varying from few to multiple skin nodules (Wolhuter et al., 2009).

Parasites Commonly Seen in Buffalo Carcasses

Buffalo serve as intermediate hosts for a number of tapeworms and enteric protozoa of sympatric predators, which are the definitive hosts. Cysticercosis usually seen in the muscles of the forelimbs, diaphragm and heart muscle of buffalo are the intermediate stages of the tapeworms of lions, leopards and hyaenas, such as *Taenia regis*, *T. gonyamai* and *T. crocutae*. In some regions where there is a close interface between buffalo and humans, cysticerci of the human tapeworm, *T. saginata*, have also been found in buffalo.

Two trematodes of common pathological importance for livestock are frequent in buffalo with no clinical signs, namely the giant fluke (*Fasciola gigantea*) and the small fluke (*Dicrocoelium hospes*), which are found in buffalo livers, often together and sometimes in a massive infestation. In Central African Republic, 12 of 33 inspected buffalo (36.3 per cent) were affected by both flukes with no apparent clinical signs (Thal, 1971).

Other trematodes of the genus *Schistosoma* also are frequently found in the mesenteric blood vessels of buffalo, again causing no clinical signs.

Hydatidosis and Coenurus Cerebralis

Hydatid and coenural cysts are parasitic cysts occasionally observed in buffalo carcasses. These cysts are the intermediate stage of the wild predator and domestic dog tapeworms, *Echinococcus granulosis* and *T. multiceps*. Hydatid cysts are most commonly found in the liver, lung and occasionally brain of buffalo, and may be large and multiple. Coenural cysts are much less common, and may be found in the brain or subcutaneous tissues.

Sarcosporidiosis

Sarcosporidia are protozoal parasites that have a two-host life cycle. The sexual reproductive cycle takes place in the small intestine of predators, and sporocysts are passed in their faeces and contaminate the environment. These sporocysts are then ingested by grazing herbivores and undergo asexual replication to form merozoites, which in turn form the sarcocysts in the muscle. Sarcocysts are cysts filled with thousands of bradyzoites, and it is these that will infect a predator when the muscle tissue is eaten, and thus the life cycle is completed. In the African buffalo, large macrocysts caused by *Sarcocystis fusiformis* (preliminary identification) are most commonly seen in the tongues and pharyngeal muscles of older buffalo, but can occur elsewhere (Quandt et al., 1997). Most buffalo appear to be infected, and these macrocysts are a common finding at meat inspection and may result in partial condemnation of the carcass.

Pentastome Larvae

The larval stages of a pentastome parasite of the paranasal sinuses of large carnivores, *Linguatula serrata*, are frequently found in the mesenteric lymph nodes, liver and cardiac chambers of African buffalo at meat inspection.

Conclusions and Summary

We hoped to provide a comprehensive view of infections and macroparasites of African buffalo, although significant gaps remain in our knowledge. All in all, the African buffalo is a resilient and hardy species that is well adapted to harsh African conditions and pathogen challenges. Much of its reputation as a disease villain is not warranted, and its qualities as a resource for nature, ecosystems and humanity speak for themselves.

References

Abdela, N. (2017). Sero-prevalence, risk factors and distribution of foot–mouth disease in Ethiopia. *Acta Tropica* **169**: 125–132.

Al-Busaidy, S., C. Hamblin and W.P. Taylor (1987). Neutralising antibodies to Akabane virus in free-living wild animals in Africa. *Tropical Animal Health and Production* **19**(4): 197–202.

Anderson, E.C., W.J. Doughty, J. Anderson and R. Paling (1979). The pathogenesis of FMD in African Buffalo and the role of this species in the epidemiology of the disease in Kenya. *Journal of Comparative Pathology* **89**: 541–550.

Asil, R.M., M. Ludlow, A. Ballal, et al. (2019). First detection and genetic characterization of peste des petits ruminants virus from dorcas gazelles "Gazella dorcas" in the Sudan, 2016–2017. *Archives of Virology* **164**(10): 2537–2543.

Beechler, B.R., R. Bengis, R. Swanepoel, et al. (2015). Rift Valley Fever in the Kruger National Park. Do buffalo play a role in the inter-epidemic circulation of the virus? *Transboundary and Emerging Diseases* **62**(1): 24–32.

Bengis, R.G., N.P.J. Kriek, D.F. Keet, et al. (1996). An outbreak of bovine tuberculosis in a free-living African buffalo (*Syncerus caffer*) population in the Kruger National Park: a preliminary report. *Onderstepoort Journal of Veterinary Research* **63**: 15–18.

Boomker, J., I.G. Horak, B.L. Penzhorn and D.F. Keet (1996). Parasites of African buffalo: a documentation. In B.L. Penzhorn (Ed.), *Proceedings of a Symposium on the African Buffalo as a Game Ranch Animal*, 26 October 1996. Pretoria: Onderstepoort.

Britch, S.L., Y.S. Binepal, M.G. Ruder, et al. (2013). Rift Valley fever risk map model and seroprevalence in selected wild ungulates and camels from Kenya. *PLoS One* **8**(6): e66626.

Bronsvoort, B.M.D., S. Parida, S. McFarland, et al. (2008). Serological survey for foot-and-mouth disease in wildlife in East Africa and parameter estimation of the Cedi test NSP ELISA for buffalo. *Clinical and Vaccine Immunology* **15**(6): 1003–1011.

Caron, A., E. Miguel, C. Gomo, et al. (2013). Relationship between burden of infection in ungulate populations and wildlife/livestock interfaces. *Epidemiology and Infection* **141**(7): 1522–1535.

Clancey, J.K. (1977). The incidence of tuberculosis in lechwe (marsh antelope). *Tubercle* **58**(3): 151–156.

Condy, J.B. (1971). A study of FMD in Rhodesian wildlife. F.R.C.V.S. thesis.

Condy, J.B. and D.B. Vickers (1972). Brucellosis in Rhodesian wildlife. *Journal of the South African Veterinary Medicine Association* **3**: 175–179.

Courtin, F., J.B. Rayaissé, I. Tamboura, et al. (2010). Updating the northern tsetse limit in Burkina Faso (1949–2009): impact of global change. *International Journal of Environmental Research and Public Health* **7**(4): 1708–19.

Cuisance D. (1996). Réactualisation de la situation des tsé-tsé et des trypanosomoses africaines au Tchad. Rapport no. 96–024. CIRAD-EMVT, Montpellier.

Davies, F. (1991). Lumpy skin disease, an African capripox virus disease of cattle. *British Veterinary Journal* **147**(6): 489–503.

Davies, F.G., T. Shaw and P. Ochieng (1975). Observations on the epidemiology of ephemeral fever in Kenya. *Journal of Hygiene* **75**: 231–235.

Davies, F.G. and A.R. Walker (1974). The distribution in Kenya of bluetongue disease and antibody and the Culicoides vector. *Journal of Hygiene* **72**: 265–272.

de Garine-Wichatitsky, M., A. Caron, C. Gomo, et al. (2010). Bovine tuberculosis in buffaloes, Southern Africa. *Emerging Infectious Diseases* **16**(5): 884–5.

De Vos, V. and P.C.B. Turnbull (2004). Anthrax. In J.A.W. Coetzer and R.C. Tustin (Eds.), *Infectious Diseases of Livestock*. Cape Town: Oxford University Press, pp. 1788–1818.

De Vos, V. and C.A.W.J. van Niekerk (1969). Brucellosis in the Kruger National Park. *Journal of the South African Veterinary Medicine Association* **40**: 331–334.

Dey, R., P.S. Hoffman and J.J. Glomski (2012). Germination and amplification of anthrax spores by soil-dwelling amoebas. *Applied and Environmental Microbiology* **78**(22): 8075–8081.

Dräger, N. and G.D. Paine (1980). Demodicosis in African buffalo (*Syncerus caffer*) in Botswana. *Journal of Wildlife Diseases* **16**: 521–524.

Evans, A., F. Gakuya, J.T. Paweska, et al. (2008). Prevalence of antibodies of Rift Valley fever in Kenyan wildlife. *Epidemiology and Infection Journal* **136**(9): 1261–1269.

Eygelaar, D., F. Jori, M. Mokopaseto, et al. (2015). Tick-borne haemoparasites in African buffalo (*Syncerus caffer*) from two wildlife area in Northern Botswana. *Parasites and Vectors* **8**:26.

Falconer, J. and G. Child (1975). A survey of FMD in wildlife in Botswana. *Mammalia* **39**: 51–58.

FAO (2011). Rinderpest eradicated – what next. www.fao.org/news/story/en/item/80894/icode/

Ferguson, K.J., S. Cleaveland, D.T. Haydon, et al. (2013). Evaluating the potential for the environmentally sustainable control of foot and mouth disease in Sub-Saharan Africa. *Ecohealth* **10**(3): 314–322.

Fernandes Aguilar, X., M. Mahapatra, M. Begovoeva, et al. (2020). Peste des Petits Ruminants at the wildlife–livestock interface in the northern Albertine Rift and Nile basin, East Africa. *Viruses* **12**(3): 293.

Gachohi, J.M., F. Gakuya, I. Lekolool, et al. (2019). Temporal and spatial distribution of anthrax outbreaks among Kenyan wildlife, 1999–2017. *Epidemiology and Infection* **147**: e249.

Gallagher, J., I. Macadam, J. Sayer and L.P. van Lavieren (1972). Pulmonary tuberculosis in free-living Lechwe antelope in Zambia. *Tropical Animal Health and Production* **4**(4): 204–213.

Glover, B., M.D. Macfarlane, R.G. Bengis, et al. (2020). Investigation of of *Brucella melitensis* in sable antelope (*Hippotragus niger*) in South Africa. *Microorganisms* **8**: 1494.

Gouteux J.P., F. Blanc, E. Pounekrozou, et al. (1994). Tsé-tsé et élevage en République Centrafricaine : le recul de *Glossina morsitans submorsitans* (Diptera, Glossinidae). *Bulletin de la Société de Pathologie Exotique* **87**: 52–56.

Gradwell, D.V., A.P. Schutte, C.A.W.J. Van Niekerk and D.J. Roux (1977). The isolation of *Brucella abortus*, biotype1 from African buffalo in the Kruger National Park. *Journal of the South African Veterinary Medicine Association* **48**:41–43.

Guerrini, L., D.M. Pfukenyi, E. Etter, et al. (2019). Spatial and seasonal patterns of FMD primary outbreaks in cattle in Zimbabwe between 1931 and 2016. *Veterinary Research* **50**(1): 73.

Guilbride, P.D.L., D.H.L. Rollinson, E.G. McAnulty, J.G. Alley and E.A. Wells (1963). Tuberculosis in the free living African (Cape) buffalo (Syncerus caffer caffer Sparrman). *Journal of Comparative Pathology and Therapeutics* **73**: 337–348. https://doi.org/10.1016/S0368-1742(63)80036-3.

Guirnalda, P., N.B. Murphy, D. Nolan and S.J. Black (2007). Anti-*Trypanosoma brucei* activity in Cape buffalo serum during the cryptic phase of parasitemia is mediated by antibodies. *International Journal of Parasitology* **37**(12):1391–1399.

Hamblin, C. and S. Hedger (1979). The prevalence of antibodies to bovine viral diarrhoea/mucosal disease virus in African wildlife. *Comparative Immunology, Microbiology and Infectious Diseases* **2**: 295–303.

Hedger, R.S. (1972). FMD and the African buffalo. *Journal of Comparative Pathology* **82**: 19–28.

Heisch, R.B., J.P. McMahon and P.E.C. Manson-Bahr (1958). The isolation of *Trypanosoma rhodesiense* from a bushbuck. *British Medical Journal* **2**(5106): 1203–1204.

Herr S. and C. Marshall (1981). Brucellosis in free-living African buffalo (*Syncerus caffer*): a serological survey. *Onderstepoort Journal of Veterinary Research* **48**: 133–134.

Holdo, R.M., A.R.E. Sinclair, A.P. Dobson, et al. (2009). A disease-mediated trophic cascade in the Serengeti and its implications for Ecocystem C. *PLoS Biology* **7**(9): e1000210.

Hutcheon, D. (1902). Rinderpest in South Africa. *Journal of Comparative Pathology* **15**: 300–324.

Hyera, J.M.K., B. Liess, E. Anderson and K.N. Hirji (1992). Prevalence of antibodies to bovine viral diarrhoea virus in some wild ruminants in northern Tanzania. *Bulletin of Animal Health and Production in Africa* **40**: 143–151.

Irvin, A.D. and M.P. Cunningham (1981). East Coast Fever. In M. Ristic and I. McIntyre (Eds.), *Diseases of Cattle in the Tropics*. The Hague: Martinus Nijhoff, p. 662.

Itard, J. (1981). Les trypanosomoses animales africaines. In *Précis de parasitologie vétérinaire tropicale*. Paris: Institut d'Élevage et de Médicine vétérinaire des Pays tropicaux, Ministère de la Coopération en du Développment, pp. 305–465.

Jolle, A., E. Gorsich, S. Gubbins, et al. (2021). Endemic persistence of a highly contagious pathogen, foot-and-mouth disease in its wildlife host. *Science* **374**(6563): 104–109.

Jones, B.A., M. Mahapatra, J. Keyyu, et al. (2021). Peste des petits ruminants virus infection at the wildlife–livestock interface in the Greater Serengeti Ecosystem, 2015–2019. *Viruses* **13**: 838.

Keet, D.F., J. Boomker, N.P.J. Kriek, et al. (1997). Parafilariosis in African buffaloes (*Syncerus caffer*). *Onderstepoort Journal of Veterinary Research* **64**: 217–225.

Kock, R.A. (2006). Rinderpest and wildlife. In T. Barret, P.P. Pastoret and W. Taylor (Eds.), *Rinderpest and Peste des Petits Ruminants, Plagues of Large and Small Ruminants. Biology of Animal Infections*. London: Elsevier, pp. 144–162.

Lawrence, J.A. (1992). History of bovine theileriosis in southern Africa. In R.A.I. Norval, B.D. Perry and A.S. Young (Eds.), *The Epidemiology of Theileriosis in Africa*. London: Academic Press.

Lawrence, J.A. and S.M. Williamson (2004). Turning sickness, *Theileria taurotragi* infection and *Theileria mutans* infection. In J.A.W. Coetzer and R.C. Tustin (Eds.), *Infectious Diseases of Livestock* (2nd ed.). Cape Town: Oxford University Press, pp. 475–482.

Linthicum, K.J., F.G. Davies, C.L. Bailey and A. Kairo (1984). Mosquito species encountered in a flood grassland dambo in Kenya. *Mosquito News* **44**: 589–595.

Linthicum, K.J., F.G. Davies, A. Kairo and C.L. Bailey (1985). Rift valley fever virus (family Bunyaviridae genus *Phlebovirus*) isolations from Diptera collected during an inter-epizootic period in Kenya. *Journal of Hygiene* **95**: 197–209.

Mack, R. (1970). The great African cattle plague epidemic of the 1890's. *Tropical Animal Health and Production* **2**: 210–219.

Mahapatra, M., K. Sayalel, M. Muniraju, et al. (2015). Spillover of peste des petits ruminants virus from domestic to wild ruminants in the Serengeti Ecosystem, Tanzania. *Emerging Infectious Diseases* **21**(12): 2230–4.

Meunier, N. (2017). Characterising the epidemiology of bovine tuberculosis at a wildlife–livestock interface in and around the Queen Elizabeth National Park, Uganda. PhD dissertation, Royal Veterinary College, University of London.

Meunier, N.V., P. Sebulime, R.G. Whiteand and R. Kock (2017). Wildlife–livestock interactions and risk areas for cross-species spread of bovine tuberculosis. *Onderstepoort Journal of Veterinary Research* **84**(1): e1–e10.

Mitchell, E.P., J. Steyl, D.B. Woodburn, et al. (2021). Pathological findings in African Buffalo (*Syncerus caffer*) in South Africa. *Journal of the South African Veterinary Association* **92**(1): 1–11.

Morel, P.C. (1981). Maladies à tiques du bétail en Afrique. In *Précis de parasitologie vétérinaire tropicale*. Paris: Institut d'Elevage et de Médecine vétérinaire des Pays tropicaux, Ministère de la Coopération et du Développement, pp. 473–717.

Mukarati, N.L., G. Matope, M. de Garine-Wichatitsky, et al. (2020). The pattern of anthrax at the wildlife–livestock–human interface in Zimbabwe. *PLoS Neglected Tropical Diseases* **14**(10): e0008800.

Munang'andu, H.M., V. Siamudaala, W. Matandiko,et al. (2011). Comparative intradermal tuberculin testing of free-ranging African buffaloes (*Syncerus caffer*) captured for ex situ conservation in the Kafue Basin Ecosystem in Zambia. *Veterinary Medicine International* **2011**: 385091.

Munyeme, M., J.B. Muma, V.M. Siamudaala, et al. (2010). Tuberculosis in Kafue lechwe antelopes (*Kobus leche kafuensis*) of the Kafue Basin in Zambia. *Preventative Veterinary Medicine* **95**(3–4): 305–308.

Murray, M., W.I. Morrison, P.K. Murray, et al. (1979). Trypanotolerance – a review. *World Animal Review* **31**: 2–12.

Mushi, E.Z., L. Karstad and D.M. Jesset (1980). Isolation of bovine malignant catarrhal virus from ocular and nasal secretions of wildebeest calves. *Research in Veterinary Science* **29**: 161–171.

Muturi, M., J. Gachohi, A. Mwatondo, et al. (2018). Recurrent anthrax outbreaks in humans, livestock and wildlife in the same locality, Kenya, 2014–2017. *The American Journal of Tropical Medicine and Hygiene* **99**(4): 833.

Neitz W.O., A.S. Canham and E.B. Kluge (1955). Corridor disease: a fatal form of bovine theileriosis encountered in Zululand. *Journal of the South African Veterinary Medicine Association* **26**: 79–87.

Oberem, P.T. and J.D. Bezuidenhout (1987). Heartwater in hosts other than domestic ruminants. *Onderstepoort Journal of Veterinary Research* **54**: 271–275.

OIE. (2022a). Contagious bovine pleuropneumonia. www.oie.int/en/disease/contagious-bovine-pleuropneumonia/

OIE. (2022b). Contagious caprine pleuropneumonia. www.oie.int/fileadmin/Home/eng/Animal_Health_in_the_World/docs/pdf/Disease_cards/CONTAGIOUS_CAPRINE_PLEURO.pdf

Olubayo R.O. (1991). Expression of trypanotolerance by African wild bovidae with special reference to the buffalo (*Syncerus caffer*). PhD thesis, Utrecht University. 194 pp.

Omondi P., E.K. Bitok, M. Tchamba, et al. (2008). Total aerial count of elephants and other wildlife species in Faro, Benoue and Bouba Ndjida national parks and adjacent hunting blocks in northern Cameroon. Technical report, MINFOF and WWF.

Omondi, G., F. Gakuya, J. Arzt, et al. (2020). The role of African buffalo in the epidemiology of foot-and-mouth disease in sympatric cattle and buffalo populations in Kenya. *Transboundary and Emerging Diseases* **67**(5): 2206–2221.

Paine, R. and G. Martinaglia (1929). Tuberculosis in wild buck living under natural conditions. *Journal of the South African Veterinary Medicine Association* 1: 87.

Plowright, W. (1967). Malignant catarrhal fever in East Africa III. Neutralising antibody in free-living wildebeest. *Research in Veterinary Science* **8**: 129–136.

Plowright, W., R.D. Ferris and G.R. Scott (1960). Blue wildebeest and the aetiological agent of bovine malignant catarrhal fever. *Nature* **188**: 1167–1169.

Quandt, S., R.G. Bengis, M. Stolte, et al. (1997). Sarcocystis infection of the African buffalo (*Syncerus caffer*), in the Kruger National Park, South Africa. *Acta Parasitologica* **42**(2): 68–73.

Redruth, D., J.G. Grootenhuis, R.O. Olubayo, et al. (1994). African buffalo serum contains novel trypanocidal protein. *Journal of Eukaryotic Microbiology* **41**(2): 95–103.

Reid, R.S., R.L. Russell, U. Kruska, et al. (2000). Human population growth and the extinction of the tsetse fly. *Agriculture, Ecosystems and Environment* **77**: 227–236.

Sahle, M. (2004). *An Epidemiological Study on the Genetic Relationships of Foot-and Mouth Disease Viruses in East Africa.* University of Pretoria.

Shiferaw, F., S. Abditcho, A. Gopilo and M.K. Laurenson (2002). Anthrax outbreak in Mago National Park, southern Ethiopia. *Veterinary Record* **150**: 319–320.

Shiferaw, F. and R.A. Kock (2002). Survey of ticks in wild animals in Ethiopia. Proceedings of Pace Wildlife Training Workshop. *Joint Meeting of Pace and The Wildlife Disease Association of Africa and The Middle East*, 29 November–3 December 2002. Mount Meru Hotel, Arusha, Tanzania.

Simpson, G., P.N. Thompson, C. Saegerman, et al. (2021). Brucellosis in wildlife in Africa: a systematic revue and meta-analysis. *Scientific Reports* **11**(1): 1–16.

Stevenson-Hamilton, J. (1957). *Wildlife in South Africa*. London: Hamilton and Co., p. 17.

Swanepoel, R. (1976). Studies on the epidemiology of Rift Valley fever. *Journal of the South African Veterinary Medicine Association* **47**: 93–94.

Swanepoel, R. (2004). Rabies. In: J.A.W. Coetzer and R.C. Tustin (Eds.), *Infectious Diseases of Livestock* (2nd ed.). Cape Town: Oxford University Press, pp. 1123–1182.

Thal, J. (1971). Les maladies similaires à la Peste bovine, étude et lutte, Ndélé, RCA. Rapport final. Projet FAO-PNUD CAF 12. IEMVT, Maisons Alfort, France.

Thomson, G.R. and D.S. Bastos (2004). Foot and mouth disease. In: J.A.W. Coetzer and R.C. Tustin (Eds.), *Infectious Diseases of Livestock* (2nd ed.). Cape Town: Oxford University Press, pp. 1324–1365.

Thomson, G.R., M.L. Penrith, M.W. Atkinson, et al. (2013a). Balancing livestock production and wildlife conservation in and around southern Africa's transfrontier conservation areas. *Transboundary and Emerging Diseases* **60**(6): 492–506.

Thomson, G.R., M.L. Penrith, M.W. Atkinson et al. (2013b). International trade standards for commodities and products derived from animals: the need for a system that integrates food safety and animal disease risk management. *Transboundary and Emerging Diseases* **60**(6): 507–515.

Thornburn J.A. and A.D. Thomas (1940). Tuberculosis in the Cape kudu. *Journal of the South African Veterinary Medicine Association* XI(1): 3–10.

Thurlbeck, W.M., C. Butas, E.M. Mankiewicz and R.M. Laws (1965). Chronic pulmonary disease in the wild buffalo (Syncerus caffer) in Uganda. *American Review of Respiratory Disease* **92**(5): 801–805.

Vosloo, W., A.D. Bastos, E. Kirkbride, et al. (1996). Persistent infection of African buffalo (*Syncerus caffer*) with SAT-type foot-and-mouth disease viruses: rate of fixation of mutations, antigenic change and interspecies transmission. *Journal of General Virology* **77**(7): 1457–1467.

Wang, Q., E. Hamilton, S.J. Black (2000). Purine requirements for the expression of Cape buffalo serum trypanocidal activity. *Comparative Biochemistry and Physiology C Toxicology and Pharmacology* **125**(1): 25–32.

Wekesa, S.N., A.K. Sangula, G.J. Belsham, et al. (2015). Characterisation of recent foot-and-mouth disease (FMD) viruses from African buffalo (*Syncerus caffer*) and cattle in Kenya: evidence for independent virus populations. *BMC Veterinary Research* **11**(1): 1–15.

Wildlife Conservation Society, Ministry of Forests and Wildlife and Ecole de Faune de Garoua (2015). Aerial Surveys of Wildlife and Human Activity Across the Bouba N'djida–Sena Oura–Benoue–Faro Landscape Northern Cameroon and Southwestern Chad, April–May 2015.

Wilkinson, L. (1988). Understanding the nature of rabies. In J.B. Campbell and K.M. Charlton (Eds.), *Rabies*. Boston: Kluwer, pp. 1–23.

Williams, J.H., E. van Dyk, P.J. Nel,et al. (2011). Pathology and immunohistochemistry of papillomavirus-associated cutaneous lesions in Cape mountain zebra, giraffe, sable antelope and African buffalo in South Africa. *Journal of the South African Veterinary Association* **82**(2): 97–106.

Wolhuter, J., R.G. Bengis, B.K. Reilly and P.C. Cross (2009). Clinical demodicosis in African buffalo (*Syncerus caffer*) in the Kruger National Park. *Journal of Wildife Diseases* **45**(2): 502–504.

Woodford, M.H. (1982a). Tuberculosis in wildlife in the Ruwenzori National Park, Uganda (Part 1). *Tropical Animal Health and Production* **14**: 81–88.

Woodford, M.H. (1982b). Tuberculosis in Wildlife in the Ruwenzori National Park (Part II). *Tropical Animal Health and Production* **14**: 155–160.

10 · *Characterization of Buffalo/Cattle Interactions for Assessing Pathogen Transmission*

A. CARON, F. RUMIANO, E. WIELGUS,
E. MIGUEL, A. TRAN, M. T. BAH,
V. GROSBOIS AND M. DE
GARINE-WICHATITSKY

Introduction

African buffalo (*Syncerus caffer*) and domestic cattle (*Bos taurus, B. indicus*) coexist in large tracks of Africa. Both are large bovid species (but see Chapter 2) that are principally grazers with similar body sizes, and therefore rely on and compete for the same natural resources. Savannas are an important biome in Africa that have been maintained for the last millennia by the interaction of wild herbivores, livestock and their herders. Human–induced fire and livestock dung-related nutrient cycling play an important role in the enrichment and heterogeneity of these habitats (Marshall et al., 2018). Savannas offer important grazing that is more or less degraded or constrained by the footprint of human activities, including agricultural expansion and the scarcity of surface water, especially during the dry season (Valls-Fox et al., 2018). Today, most savanna African buffalo populations live in protected areas (Chapter 4), often with no physical separation to prevent interactions with livestock living on the periphery of, and more and more frequently within, these protected areas. Savanna buffalo populations outside protected areas live in areas where they can also encounter livestock (e.g. Garissa district, Kenya). Interactions between buffalo and cattle have increased significantly during the second half of the twentieth century due to the wider use of anti-trypanosomiasis drugs and the reduction of the range of trypanosomiasis vectors, *Glossina* sp. This provided an opportunity for herders to penetrate into grazing areas where cattle previously would have simply died, including in protected areas of West, Central and Eastern Africa. As livestock populations in these regions grew, so did demand for grazing resources, increasing competition with crop producers and placing livestock in closer proximity to buffalo populations relatively isolated from them until recently (e.g. Cuisance, 1996). This phenomenon is not limited to savannas, as it can also be observed in rainforests in which forest buffalo (*S. c. nanus*) are increasingly interacting with intruding cattle.

Buffalo/cattle interactions are a source of conflict not only because both species compete for resources, but also due to the risk of disease transmission in both directions (Miguel et al., 2017). These interactions can contribute to the disease burden of small-scale livestock production systems as buffalo can maintain or spread some diseases detrimental to the health of cattle (e.g. tick-borne diseases, bovine tuberculosis; Caron et al. 2013; Chapter 9). Commercial livestock production, especially that intended for international trade, is very sensitive to some diseases that cannot be eradicated in buffalo, and therefore important trade regulations are imposed on producers depending on their exposition to buffalo/cattle interactions (e.g. foot and mouth disease, FMD; Scoones et al., 2010; Thomson et al., 2013; Chapter 12). Some of the diseases mentioned above are zoonoses, most of them hardly studied in African contexts and therefore with an (often unknown) impact on public health (e.g. Rift valley fever, brucellosis; Gadaga et al., 2016). Finally, the interactions work both ways, and cattle can transmit diseases that can threaten the survival of wildlife such as rinderpest, a cattle disease imported during European colonization that decimated wildlife populations in Africa (van Onselen, 1972; Chapter 12). Buffalo/cattle interactions are therefore an important aspect of the management of African savannas and forests with socioeconomic, environmental and political implications. For example, the success of Transfrontier Conservation Areas in southern Africa connecting parks across borders and promoting wildlife mobility can be weakened by sanitary regulations aiming to protect cattle production from transboundary animal diseases (Ferguson et al., 2013).

In this chapter, we will review the knowledge on the characterization of the buffalo/cattle interaction, the related ecology of pathogen transmission, and how this transmission can be modelled to improve the management and control of diseases. The geographical distribution of studies on buffalo/cattle interactions and the associated disease ecology is uneven, with almost none undertaken in rainforest habitats and most focused on savanna habitats in eastern and mainly southern Africa.

Characterizing the Buffalo/Cattle Interface

Wildlife/livestock interactions occur in wildlife/livestock interfaces that exist worldwide and represent a matter of concern for various reasons, including predation by wildlife, competition for resources, biodiversity conservation, cross-breeding and crop-raiding (Osofsky and Cleaveland, 2005). However, the risk of disease transmission at these interfaces has probably been the most burning issue in modern times (Kock, 2005). Frameworks to define and characterize these interfaces have also been proposed recently, including the definition of the interface that is used in this chapter: 'the physical space in which wild and domestic species, as well as humans, overlap in range and potentially interact' (Caron et al., 2021). They principally focus on defining the geographic (e.g. spatial), physical (hard–soft edge) and dynamics (e.g. seasonality, small-scale and interannual dynamics) properties of the interface to understand if, where and when wild and domestic species interact.

For both buffalo and cattle, access to scarce water and grazing resources in the savanna ecosystem, including agricultural fields (which attract buffalo), is the main driver of buffalo and cattle movements across their respective land-use boundaries (i.e. protected areas and communal land). In addition, rainfall, natural and human-induced fires, as well as human activities and infrastructure are key factors influencing the distribution of buffalo and cattle in space and time (Higgins et al., 2007; Cornélis et al., 2011; Naidoo et al. 2012; Ogutu et al., 2012). These movements determine a spatial use that may or may not trigger contact between buffalo and cattle and create the buffalo/cattle interface.

In Africa, buffalo/cattle interfaces are found mainly in savanna ecosystems. Forest buffalo (*S. caffer nanus*) seldom interact with cattle, given their exclusive dwelling in forest habitats in which cattle husbandry seldom exists. However, recent changes in pastoral practices in Central Africa (e.g. south-west of the Central African Republic) have pushed cattle closer to forest buffalo habitat, especially during the dry season (Chardonnet, personal commmunication). In savannas, the buffalo/cattle interface can exist under the form of a 'hard edge', a type of interface found mainly in southern Africa and especially South Africa (e.g. the fence surrounding Kruger National Park on the South African side), but not exclusively (e.g. also in Botswana, Namibia; Figure 10.1). The remaining majority of the interfaces found in West, Central, Eastern and Southern Africa should be classified as 'symmetric soft interfaces' where both species can cross the edge and exploit resources a few kilometres maximum from the edge (Caron et al., 2021; see e.g. Figure 10.2). In

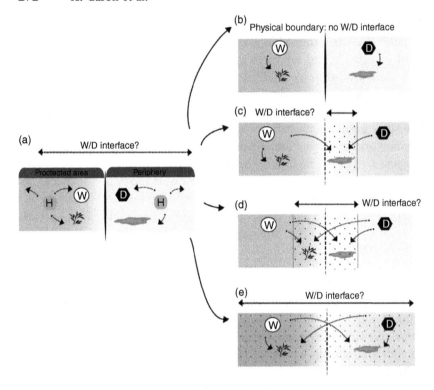

Figure 10.1 (a) Theoretical conceptual model of a wildlife/livestock (W/L) interface including wild buffalo (W) and domestic cattle (D) populations, human actors (H) as well as key landscape features including land-use boundaries (dark line separating a hypothetical protected area and its periphery) and key resources (pasture and surface water for example, represented by icons) that will help define hypotheses about the W/L interface (horizontal bidirectional arrow on top); the human component is only represented in panel (a) but it is assumed that the human driver is one of the most important to define W/L interfaces, defining cattle production practices, buffalo management and resource distribution. (b) Hard-edge interface: a fence or a natural impassable barrier (e.g. non-crossable river) limits the movements of buffalo and cattle: this is a hard edge; this type of interface is theoretical for many national park boundaries as animal movement-proof edges are rare. (c) Asymmetric semi-hard interface: only one of the two species (i.e. buffalo here) can cross the edge to use natural resources; the interface is limited to a small band in the cattle side; the reverse is of course also possible. (d) Symmetric soft interface: both species can cross the edge and exploit resources across the edge; this type of interface exists for many unfenced protected areas. (e) Diffuse interface: there is no edge and the home range of buffalo and cattle overlap extensively. In (c)–(e), the temporal dimension of the interface is crucial to understanding the dynamics of the interfaces. Adapted from Caron et al. (2021), with permission from Springer.

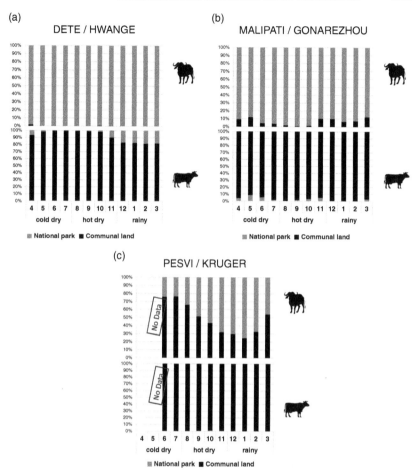

Figure 10.2 Three asymmetric and seasonal interfaces in southern Africa characterized by GPS localizations of cattle and buffalo in protected areas or communal land used for extensive subsistence livestock farming. (a) The Dete/Sikumi Forest interface in Zimbabwe without any fence: a mainly asymmetric interface during the rainy season when cattle enter the protected Sikumi Forest. (b) The Malipati/Gonarezhou national park interface in Zimbabwe separated by the Mwenezi River that dries part of the year: asymmetric interface with buffalo entering the communal land most of the year but with some cattle incursions into the protected area during the cold-dry (and hot-dry) seasons. (c) The Pesvi/Kruger national park in Zimbabwe/South Africa separated by the (large) Limpopo River that dries part of the year: an asymmetric interface with buffalo entering the communal land most of the year but with seasonal variations (Miguel, 2012).

practice, few 'diffuse interfaces', where both cattle and buffalo permanently coexist on the same production unit, currently exist in Africa. These may occur locally within extensive mixed ranches associating cattle and buffalo for diversified ecotourism, hunting and meat productions. However, veterinary regulations applicable in most African countries prevent such associations to protect livestock from buffalo-borne disease transmission that would put a high burden on meat production both from a production and regulatory perspective. Early attempts in southern Africa to produce 'disease-free' buffalo herds, which could be associated with cattle herds on the same ranges, proved technically and financially difficult to maintain in the long run. From a spatial perspective, other types of interfaces such as 'asymmetrical interfaces' can exist but are rare, despite their potential to promote buffalo/cattle coexistence systems. The asymmetry can, however, emerge from 'symmetric soft interfaces' and produce some opportunities for coexistence between buffalo and cattle. For example, where cattle are penned at night to protect them from natural predation or theft, buffalo can use this nocturnal temporal window to use space previously used by cattle (Miguel et al., 2017).

Characterizing wildlife/livestock interfaces has been the focus of recent research, supported by the development of technologies such as telemetry and remote sensing technologies (e.g. Richomme et al., 2006; Pruvot et al., 2014; Woodroffe et al., 2016; Campbell et al., 2019; Triguero-Ocana et al., 2021). To characterize interfaces, multidisciplinary approaches are often required. They can range from behavioural studies of wild and domestic species (e.g. telemetry or capture–marking–recapture techniques) to emerging non–invasive molecular techniques to assess the presence or absence of specific species (e.g. faecal or environmental sampling), as well as sociological studies to understand people's perceptions, knowledge and practices regarding the state and management of the interface. Focusing on the characterization of buffalo/cattle interfaces, satellite remote sensing (SRS) offers an array of methodologies to monitor, characterize and quantify how natural resources impact buffalo and cattle movements in their respective environments (Rumiano et al., 2020). Optical and radar SRS imagery can be used efficiently to discriminate surface water and land covers at a landscape scale due to a wide range of sensors, with various spatial and temporal resolutions available (Corbane et al., 2015; Bioresita et al., 2018; Huang et al., 2018). The effects of fire on vegetation can spatially and temporally be detected using vegetation spectral signature as their intrinsic characteristics change over time (Meng and Zhao, 2017). Whereas precipitation can be measured with advanced infrared (IR), passive microwave (MW) and radar sensors provide a complementary alternative to in situ records (Camberlin et al., 2019). These SRS techniques are available to characterize interfaces across the range of buffalo and cattle in Africa at the spatial and temporal scale deemed most relevant to the issue at hand. Combining these SRS methodological approaches with telemetry studies on both species and the pastoralist and agro-pastoralist practices can provide a good understanding of buffalo/cattle interfaces.

Most of this research on wildlife/livestock interfaces has been done in the field of ecology (e.g. Hibert et al., 2010) and especially in the emergent field of disease ecology. The study of the ecology of pathogen and disease transmission at the wildlife/livestock interface seeks to: (1) understand the patterns of contact between wild and domestic species, especially the intensity and frequency of these contacts as well as their driving factors; (2) assess the proportion of these contacts that could trigger an 'infectious contact' defined as the interspecies transmission of a pathogen; and (3) model the host and pathogen population dynamics in this context and assess the efficiency of potential management options to mitigate or control diseases (de Garine-Wichatitksy et al., 2021).

Measuring Infectious Contact at the Buffalo/Contact Interface

Measuring Contacts between Two Species

Determining the relative location of two individuals to each other (e.g. individual cattle and buffalo) is the first step to be able to estimate if there is a risk of interspecies pathogen transmission. This risk will be defined by the evaluation of potential infectious contacts between two individuals. As the observation of infectious contact *per se* is almost impossible (i.e. pathogens are invisible to the naked eye), interspecies contacts are used as a proxy. For a given pathogen, a direct mode of transmission requires close contact between an infected and a healthy individual, that is both hosts are at the same place and at the same time (Bengis et al., 2002; Altizer et al., 2003). Indirect transmission can occur when a pathogen is excreted by the infected individuals in the environment at a specific location (e.g. directly on the ground or water) and subsequently infects a susceptible host using the same location after the infected host. Until recently, direct observation was the only way to determine the position of wild individuals, a time-consuming technique difficult to implement on two species. The advent of satellite telemetry using a global position-ing system (GPS) has transformed the possibility to assess the temporal and spatial positions of animals in a given area with high precision and temporal accuracy (Cagnacci and Urbano, 2008). This breakthrough in technology can generate a lot of data: a GPS collar collecting one GPS point every hour for two years will produce 17,520 locations of the individual in addition to its speed, the position of its head and the tem-perature among numerous data that can now be collected with captors integrated into the GPS collar. This technology has thus enabled new insights into the ecology of animal movements (e.g. patterns of bio-diversity, ecological characteristics of individual species and ecosystem function; Kays et al., 2015; Eikelboom et al., 2021). Data describing the movements made by individual animals during their entire lifetime, and species-wide sampling from multiple populations, are now becoming available and offer new opportunities to measure and estimate contacts (Flack et al., 2016). Wielgus et al. (2020) used GPS telemetry to describe fission–fusion dynamics of buffalo in various groups at several sites. This example shows how GPS telemetry can define and improve species-inherent ecological behaviours that can potentially be used, by exten-sion, to characterize intra- and interspecies contacts. Proximity loggers are another recently developed tool. While they only provide a measure of direct contacts between individuals (i.e. they detect and log events when tagged individuals are located within a predefined distance thresh-old; Böhm et al., 2009; Drewe et al., 2013), they cost considerably less than GPS collars. This allows a larger number of individuals of a given wildlife or livestock population to be equipped, depending on the dif-ficulties and costs associated with the capture/fitting of the collars.

Both technologies allow researchers to determine when, and for how long, two animals have been in proximity and, therefore, describe the contact patterns relevant for a directly or indirectly (only for GPS) trans-mitted pathogen. However, few studies on large herbivores occupy-ing African savanna environments using these technologies have been conducted so far (Owen-Smith et al., 2020). These new technologies have several constraints that can potentially limit their use. The most apparent is the cost of recording units (until recently between €1500 and €2500 per buffalo unit) to be fitted to individual animals (until recently between €1500 and €2500 per buffalo unit) (Cooke et al., 2004) and the cost of the capture and then recapture to remove the collars (€1000–1500 per head). These devices are also not robust enough to study adult male buffalo and can be damaged by cattle during, for example, dipping for tick-borne disease control (Caron, personal communication). Moreover, GPS telemetry can affect animal behaviour, survival and well-being in some instances, and its system function is influenced by environmental variables (e.g. climatic factors, habitat types, terrain roughness) and animal behaviour (e.g. movement, orientation of the collar) (Tomkiewicz et al., 2010). As a result, spatial inaccuracy of the acquired locations, and missing data in the form of failed location attempts, can potentially impact derived GPS telemetry data and lead to mistaken inferences on animal spatial behaviour, especially those involving movement paths and habitat selection (Frair et al., 2010). Finally, movement is a continuous process that can only be tracked by sampling, usually at constant time intervals. This sampling is constrained by the limits of the technology used (battery life), which forces a trade-off between the sampling frequency of the displacement and the duration of the tracking. This trade-off is especially important when working on contacts between two individuals as we can assume that most of these contacts occur between sampling points. However, telemetry technology is developing rapidly and future systems may overcome some of these constraints.

Contact Estimation at the Buffalo/Livestock Interface

Few studies have investigated wildlife/livestock contacts for epidemiological or other purposes. Some of the main models studied so far are: the interface between the European badger (*Meles meles*) and cattle in the UK in relation to bovine tuberculosis (e.g. Woodroffe et al., 2016; Campbell et al., 2019); the interface between wild boar (*Sus scrofa*) and cattle in relation to the same disease in Spain (e.g. Barasona et al., 2014; Triguero-Ocana et al., 2019); the interface between white-tailed deer (*Odocoileus virginianus*) and cattle in the United States in relation to bovine tuberculosis (Ribeiro-Lima et al., 2017); the interface between elk (*Cervus canadensis nelson*) and cattle in relation to brucellosis in the US (Proffitt et al., 2011); and the buffalo/cattle interface in relation to FMD and bovine tuberculosis (e.g. Miguel et al. 2013, 2017; Valls-Fox et al., 2018).

By combining telemetric and epidemiological approaches to sympatric cattle and buffalo, recent studies have provided good evidence that the contact rate with buffalo significantly influences FMD dynamics in cattle populations living at the periphery of conservation areas in Zimbabwe (Miguel et al., 2013, 2017). In the latter study, 36 GPS collars were deployed on African buffalo and cattle to assess proximity patterns at the symmetric soft interface of three protected areas in Zimbabwe, namely Hwange and Gonarezhou in Zimbabwe and Kruger in South Africa. GPS acquired one location per hour and data collection ran between 14 and 17 months between 2010 and 2011. One head of cattle was equipped per herd (herd size averaged 12) on the assumption that the movement of one of the lead cows would significantly represent the daily movement of the herd. At night, cattle herds were penned in 'kraals' (a case of partial asymmetrical interface between cattle and buffalo at night; Figure 10.1) to protect them from predation and theft. Adult female buffalo were equipped and their movements were assumed to represent mixed herd movements (Chapter 6). To assess interspecies contacts relevant for FMD, direct and indirect contacts were calculated based on the buffalo–cattle dyad being: (1) at the same place together (i.e. direct contact); the 300 m radius accounts for GPS precision and herd size; or (2) one or the other being in a 300 m radius from a location of the other up to 15 days later; this spatial–temporal window was decided based on the potential survival of the FMD virus in the environment.

Contacts between buffalo and cattle varied between sites and seasons and individual cattle. Of importance, almost no direct contact was recorded during the entire study. The locations of indirect contacts were both inside the national parks and in the communal land and varied greatly between sites, with most of the spatial overlap occurring in the Kruger–Pesvi interface area (Pesvi is a small village across the Limpopo River in Zimbabwe, along the northern section of Kruger National Park; Figures 10.3 and 10.4). Contacts increased from the rainy season towards the late dry season.

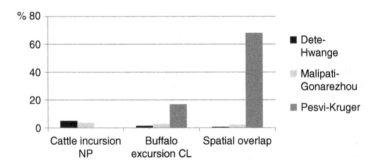

Figure 10.3 Percentage of cattle/buffalo contacts relative to sites and land-use (inside national park – NP – or inside the Communal Land – CL): during the study by Miguel et al. (2013).

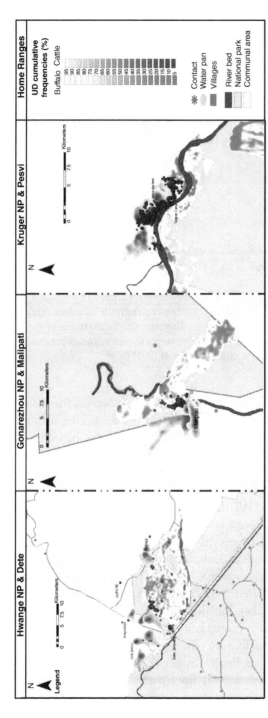

Figure 10.4 Maps of cattle and buffalo home ranges (red-brown and red-yellow, respectively) and contacts at three national parks (NP borders in southern Africa (KAZA–TFCA: Hwange–Dete and GL–TFCA: Gonarezhou–Malipati and Kruger–Pesvi). The locations of contact events between cattle and buffalo are represented by pink stars (i.e. cattle position recorded within 300 m of a buffalo position less than 15 days after the buffalo position has been recorded). Source: Miguel (2012).

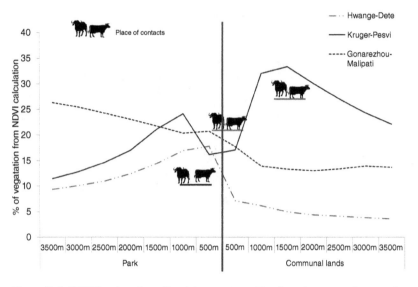

Figure 10.5 NDVI estimations (lines) in communal lands and protected areas of the three sites studied in relation to the distance from the interface (dark vertical line). The cattle and buffalo pictogram illustrates the localizations of the contacts between the two species and the line below these pictograms represents the 95 per cent range of these contacts. Source: Miguel (2012).

Because buffalo and livestock use similar resources, particularly water and grazing areas during the dry season, they use similar habitats, which explains the contact patterns observed. Quantitative observations of the density of vegetation on each side of the boundaries (National Park/ Communal Land) were obtained, for the three interfaces, using satellite images and the calculation of NDVI (Normalized Difference Vegetation Index). Although NDVI does not allow grassland to be distinguished from shrubland and forest areas, this index can be used to measure the plant phenology and by extention, the distribution of available vegetation in communal lands and adjacent protected areas. High variability in terms of habitat use was observed across sites with NDVI structuring the buffalo habitat use. When NDVI was higher outside the protected areas (Kruger–Pesvi interface), buffalo exited from the Kruger NP boundaries to range inside the communal land areas (Figure 10.5).

Surface water distribution among study sites varied significantly. Two river systems for Pesvi–Kruger (Limpopo River) and Malipati–Gonarezhou (Nuanetsi River) flow part of the year and only offer a few stagnant pools of water during the dry season. In Dete–Hwange, scattered water pans provide water across the year, with their number decreasing as the dry season proceeds. This contrast in water distribution patterns could explain the difference in contact rates between the three study areas. For example, in the Hwange–Dete study site, cattle and buffalo preferred open grassland habitats found close to water. During the rainy season, cattle entered the protected forest area daily, pushed by herders to avoid feeding on the crops growing just outside the protected forest border, and buffalo avoided cattle completely. During the dry season, when cattle ranged further into the protected area in search of forage, buffalo and cattle spatial overlap increased as water dependence took precedence over avoidance (Valls-Fox et al., 2018).

The role of lions in buffalo–cattle contacts was also explored in the same study site (Miguel et al., 2017). Buffalo and cattle avoided the use of the same pasture up to 2 months after one species had used a specific location. Lions made frequent incursions in the interaction zone a few days to weeks after buffalo had used that zone and buffalo avoided areas recently used by lions. Lions could therefore impact the spatiotemporal overlap between cattle and buffalo and therefore buffalo–cattle contacts.

Finally, buffalo/cattle contacts were structured by land-use and resource gradients (mainly water and grazing) as well as the presence of wild predators. The small sample size of these studies (i.e. a few individuals tracked for a dozen months) limits the extrapolation of results at population levels. However, this limit is somehow attenuated by the gregarious organization of both buffalo (in mixed herds) and cattle (in managed herds) for which the movements of a few individuals represent the behaviour of the herd.

From Interspecies Contact to Infectious Contact

Besides direct contacts, the capacity of the pathogen to survive in the environment and to be able to infect another host will determine the temporal window in which transmission can occur. The same applies to vector-borne transmission (e.g. arthropod-borne) with the difference that a spatial window will need to be taken into account in addition to the temporal window to account for the potential mobility of the vector in the environment (Dougherty et al., 2018).

Infectious contacts, that is contacts that result in the transmission of one or more pathogens, are invisible ecological processes that are currently impossible to characterize in real-time. An assessment of contacts as presented in the previous section provides some information about the spatial and temporal dynamics of infectious transmission but cannot be directly translated into an assessment of infectious contacts. For example, in the study by Miguel et al. (2013), the GPS protocol at the buffalo/cattle interface was completed by a longitudinal survey of 300 cattle, with five repeated sampling sessions undertaken on known individuals over 16 months. Immunological assays, which allow the production of antibodies following infection or vaccination to be tracked, were used to assess serological transitions (i.e. incidence and reversion) in the surveyed cattle. The incidence in the cattle populations of FMD antibodies produced following infection varied among sites and as a function of contact rates with African buffalo. The incidence was higher for sites with higher contact rates between the two species and varied according to the season.

The use of genomics on hosts and pathogens can help in inferring infectious contacts and their direction. Kamath et al. (2016) in the Greater Yellowstone ecosystem estimated the date and the frequency of brucellosis introduction events and found that the disease was introduced into elk (a.k.a. wapiti, *Cervus elaphus*) from cattle in this region at least five times. The diffusion rate varies among *Brucella* lineages and over time. They were also able to estimate the direction of transmission between hosts from different species with 12 host transitions from bison (*Bison bison*) to elk, and five from elk to bison. However, up to now, such a large-scale study using both telemetry and pathogen genetic studies has not been implemented for the characterization of buffalo/cattle interfaces (but see Musoke et al., 2015).

Space–Time Window as a Proxy of Modes of Transmission

Infectious diseases spread through transmission routes between hosts, and each pathogen can use one or more modes of transmission to 'jump' from one host to another. Therefore, as seen for FMD in the previous section, the pathogen of interest and its specific mode(s) of transmission will define the space–time window in which a pathogen can spread from an infected to a susceptible host. The behaviour of both hosts (e.g. cattle and buffalo), the characteristic of the pathogen, and, when relevant, the ecology of the vector will therefore be crucial to estimating the risk of interspecies pathogen spread. This also means that a given contact network between buffalo and cattle can produce very different risks of interspecies spread when considering pathogens with different modes of transmission and similar risks when the modes of transmission and the characteristic of two pathogens are converging. Finally, the data collection method also can impact the quality of the assessment.

To define contacts responsible for FMD transmission between buffalo and cattle, Miguel et al. (2013) used a spatial window of 300 m and a temporal window of 15 days. The spatial window took into account both the inaccuracy of the GPS measure and the ability of and cattle to move during a one-hour period. The temporal window accounted for the potential environmental transmission of the virus. Bovine tuberculosis is most often transmitted by respiratory routes, requiring close contact between buffalo and cattle, but the pathogen also can spread by indirect contacts, as the mycobacteria *Mycobacterium bovis* can survive in faeces for up to 1 month in natural conditions in southern Africa (Tanner and Michel, 1999). A space–time window to assess the probability of bovine tuberculosis transmission between buffalo and cattle (or vice versa) must take into account direct contacts between both hosts, as well as indirect contacts, with up to 30-day intervals to reflect the survival of the pathogen in faeces. Therefore, a single data set of contact patterns between buffalo and cattle will result in different estimations of the risks of pathogen transmission between species depending on the modes of transmission of the pathogen considered.

Modelling Pathogen Transmission at the Buffalo/Cattle Interface

The dynamics of pathogens in multi-species assemblages are complex. They are influenced by the interaction of each host–pathogen dyad (e.g. morbidity, mortality rate), host population dynamics (e.g. social dynamics, size of groups, intergroup contacts) and interspecies contacts. Various approaches exist to model each of these components, but they have yet to be integrated to produce a holistic model of the buffalo/cattle interface. Here we present examples of modelling approaches to buffalo and cattle population dynamics as well as of interspecies contacts that could support the integration of a pathogen or disease transmission model.

Contact Network and Graph Models

Contact networks, where individuals are represented as nodes and interactions between them as edges, expand the relevance of epidemiological models by capturing the patterns of interaction between individuals (Hamede et al., 2009, 2012; Yin et al., 2020). However, realism and precision can limit the applicability of contact data to general contexts (White et al., 2015), especially as contact networks are rarely fully described for wildlife species. To address these issues, we can infer the rules behind the generation of contacts within the network and use them to extrapolate the contact structure in the entire population. Exponential random graphs models (ERGMs) provide an appropriate framework to do so. The purpose of ERGMs is to describe parsimoniously the local forces that shape the global structure of a network (Silk et al., 2017, 2018). To this end, a network data set may be considered as the response variable in a regression model, where the predictors are based on individual traits (gender, age, group), such as 'the propensity for individuals of the same sex to form partnerships', or structural metrics of the network (degree, two-stars, triads), such as 'the propensity for individuals to form a cluster'. The information gleaned from the use of an ERGM may thus be used to understand how contact networks are generated and to simulate new random realizations of networks that retain the essential properties of the observed network, which can be used to simulate disease dynamics (Reynolds et al., 2015). Such an approach was attempted using the GPS data of 84 collared African buffalo from four populations (Wielgus et al., 2020). Unfortunately, no non-random structure of contact was found within the sampled networks because they were missing individuals representing, for example, adult males or juveniles. Nevertheless, ERGMs hold great potential for pathogen transmission modelling within buffalo populations if GPS data from a significant number of individuals within the same population can be sampled for several years.

Spatialized Mechanistic Modelling Approaches

Spatial models integrating the environmental drivers of buffalo and cattle mobility can be developed to assess the potential contacts between the two species and their variations in space and time. For example, the Ocelet domain-specific language and open modelling platform (www.ocelet.fr), based on the tool of interaction graphs (Degenne and Seen, 2016), allows the implementation of spatialized mechanistic modelling approaches (e.g. Grégoire et al., 2003) that connect 'entities' of different nature (e.g. buffalo, cattle, water bodies, grazing areas), define their interactions (e.g. interspecies relations, species-natural resources dependencies), and simulate their spatiotemporal dynamics. As a result, such models allow the assessment and visualization of the location and frequency of potential contacts between different species based on a wide range of variables that can evolve through time (e.g. animal behaviour, natural resources distribution, human-based social and economic processes, pathogen transmission). Such an approach was used to simulate the impact of the surface water spatial distributions and its seasonal variation on African buffalo movements in a given area (Rumiano et al., 2021; Figure 10.6). From there, cattle movements can be added to assess the potential contact areas between the two species (Rumiano et al., in prep.), provided that ecological empirical knowledge on focal species is available to feed the model and determine its design. Of note, GPS telemetry data collected from previous works (Miguel et al., 2013; Valls-Fox et al., 2018) provide necessary information for calibration (conceptual phase) and validation (assessment phase) of the models.

Combining Host Contact and Pathogen Transmission

Once interspecies host population dynamics have been modelled using one of the methodologies presented above, pathogen data can then be coupled with host population modelling to better understand the relationship between environmental drivers, host contacts and pathogen dynamics. This coupling will resolve an important limitation of most epidemiological models that assume homogeneous mixing between naïve and infected hosts, and thus omit the heterogeneity of host behaviour (Lloyd-Smith, 2005; Paull et al., 2012). Thus far, the use of such applications in disease ecology has been limited, especially at an interspecies level, despite the importance of interspecies contact patterns on pathogen transmission and the impact of infection on host behaviour (Dougherty et al., 2018). New insights into buffalo social dynamics will modify the dynamics of pathogens spread in buffalo groups (Chapter 6; Wielgus et al., 2020, 2021). Gregarious species with connected and unfragmented social units (classical definition of a mixed herd) should facilitate pathogen spread compared to gregarious species with a higher level of fusion–fission dynamics (Sah et al., 2017). Similarly, these fusion–fission patterns will have an impact on the risk of pathogen spread between cattle and buffalo (both ways) at interface areas.

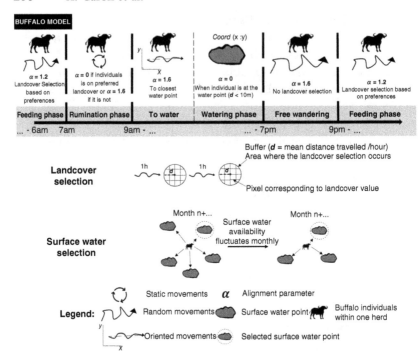

Figure 10.6 Designed mechanistic model of buffalo movements according to surface water seasonality, geographic location and type of land cover. This movement model is divided into five behavioural phases per 24-hour period (Feeding phase, Rumination phase, To water phase, Watering phase, Free wandering phase) that are based on buffalo behaviour (i.e. median speed per hour) derived from collected telemetry data of three study sites (Miguel et al., 2013; Valls-Fox et al., 2018). All individuals move from their starting location to the next at discrete time steps by a fixed distance, their direction defined for each time step as an angle. This angle is correlated to the alignment (α) of each individual with respect to their close neighbours, thus allowing simulation of a collective movement of interdependent individuals (Grégoire et al., 2003). The value given to α will determine the behaviour of the buffalo. During the 'Feeding phase', the buffalo will move until they reach a 'feeding' land cover type. During the 'Rumination phase', the buffalo stay in motion in the same land cover type. For these two behavioural phases, land cover selections occur within a determined buffer area corresponding to the mean distance travelled per hour (Rumiano et al., in prep.). In the 'To water phase', buffalo move towards the closest surface water (varies seasonally) from the buffalo's herd centroid position at the beginning of the phase. Once buffalo individuals are within 10 m of the targeted surface water point, the 'Watering phase' starts and all individuals stop their movements. During the 'Free wandering' phase, buffalo move freely in space. Land cover and surface water have been characterized at the landscape scale (10 m of spatial resolution) using supervised and unsupervised classifications on a selected time series of Sentinel-2 satellite images (Rumiano, 2021). The spatialized classifications have then been integrated into the model thanks to the spatial modelling language Ocelet (Degenne and Seen, 2016).

Perspectives and Conclusion

Buffalo and cattle interactions and the sustainability of the systems that maintain both species are relevant to the coexistence between humans and nature in Africa. The potential spillover and spillback of pathogens between sympatric buffalo and cattle populations threaten biodiversity conservation, local and national agricultural economies and public health. If buffalo and cattle are to coexist in an open landscape, the sanitary risk will need to be managed according to a new paradigm relative to the level and types of risks that are acceptable. Currently, production systems have not managed to conceive a management process in which both species coexist (Chapters 12 and 14).

Different spatial models of animal movement, contact and interaction taking into account biotic and abiotic ecological features as well as behavioural mechanisms have been developed in recent years (Rastetter et al., 2003; Moorcroft 2012; Westley et al. 2018). Nonetheless, there is a need to further develop mechanistic animal movement, contact and interaction models that integrate independent and validated environmental SRS data enabling landscape-scale analysis of interspecies contact and interaction. Such models could benefit from the integration of especially characterized environmental SRS data while extending their application capacities to different environmental and ecological contexts (Neumann et al., 2015; Rumiano et al., 2020). Several SRS methodologies have already been developed to characterize spatial and temporal variations of environmental drivers, such as surface water (Naidoo et al., 2020) and vegetation (Zengeya et al., 2015), in relation to buffalo and cattle movements. By allowing the characterization of these environmental drivers at the landscape scale, SRS can improve the understanding of buffalo/cattle contacts and associated disease transmission estimations where in-situ environmental data are lacking.

Mechanistic models, even if they involve significant development and implementation costs, are less dependent on a correlation between ecological processes and environment properties than empirical modelling approaches (Dormann et al., 2012). By mathematically simulating interactions and mutual constraints among animal species, mechanistic models improve the transferability to different environments (Kearney and Porter, 2009). Such models can therefore be adapted specifically for interspecies contacts and interactions by improving focal species ecological behaviour simulations regarding habitat selection and spatial and temporal distributions of natural resources. Advances in GPS telemetry, such as decreasing size, weight and cost of tags, computing power enhancement, and improving battery autonomy and durability, are allowing this technology to be used more efficiently on an expanded range of animal species, but also on animal population subcategories (e.g. female, juvenile, male) while increasing their temporal resolution (Kays et al., 2015). Improved GPS telemetry technology combined with the rapid growth of SRS use in functional ecology and the enhancement of specialized mechanistic models offer tremendous potential for evaluating inter-species interactions (Rumiano, 2021). This type of approach can prove to be very valuable in environments such as the buffalo/cattle interfaces in African savannas that are limited in terms of natural resources, highly sensitive to climate condition fluctuations and prone to constant changes in land-use/management practices.

Despite the limits and constraints of these studies, the understanding of buffalo/cattle interactions is crucial to managing the interface and mitigating its negative consequences. Modelling is important to investigate the consequences of some management options that cannot be tested in situ. For example, as resources drive these interactions, appropriate water management could reduce contacts between buffalo and cattle (e.g. Mwakiwa et al., 2013; Hilbers et al., 2015). One could suggest manipulating cattle management practices or buffalo behaviours, taking into consideration ethical aspects of animal welfare and transdisciplinary approaches when working with local stakeholders. Modelling also can be important to explore how these interactions will evolve: buffalo/cattle interactions are a moving target as both cattle herding (e.g. pastoralism and agro-pastoralism) and wildlife populations are currently adapting to changing environments (e.g. climate change, human demographic explosion, global markets; Kock et al., 2014). Modelling can also trigger essential discussions and debates between different actors (e.g. scientists, breeders, political institutions, etc.) and different research disciplines. This implies a participatory platform potentially allowing the integration of virtuous solutions for all (e.g. One Health).

In combination with other emerging initiatives such as commodity-based trade in southern Africa (Thomson et al., 2013), the management of buffalo/cattle interactions can be a pillar of a sustainable coexistence between humans and nature in African landscapes (du Toit et al., 2017). The current focus of the study of these interfaces in southern Africa (and to a lesser extent to East Africa) calls for more studies in different contexts including pastoralism of Central Africa, and different biomes including rainforests in which encroachment by cattle creates new types of interfaces.

References

Altizer, S., C.L. Nunn, P.H. Thrall, et al. (2003). Social organization and parasite risk in mammals: integrating theory and empirical studies. *Annual Review of Ecology, Evolution, and Systematics* **34**(1): 517–547.

Barasona, J.A., M.C. Latham, P. Acevedo, et al. (2014). Spatiotemporal interactions between wild boar and cattle: implications for cross-species disease transmission. *Veterinary Research* **45**: 122.

Bengis, R.G., R.A. Kock and J. Fisher (2002). Infectious animal diseases: the wildlife/livestock interface. *Revue Scientifique et Technique de l'OIE* **21**(1): 53–65.

Bioresita, F., A. Puissant, A. Stumpf and J.-P. Malet (2018). A method for automatic and rapid mapping of water surfaces from Sentinel-1 imagery. *Remote Sensing* **10**(2): 217.

Böhm, M., M.R. Hutchings and P.C.L. White (2009). Contact networks in a wildlife–livestock host community: identifying high-risk individuals in the transmission of bovine TB among badgers and cattle. *PLoS One* **4**(4): e5016.

Cagnacci, F. and F. Urbano (2008). Managing wildlife: a spatial information system for GPS collars data. *Environmental Modelling & Software* **23**(7): 957–959.

Camberlin, P., G. Barraud, S. Bigot, et al. (2019). Evaluation of remotely sensed rainfall products over Central Africa. *Quarterly Journal of the Royal Meteorological Society* **145**(722): 2115–2138.

Campbell, E.L., A.W. Byrne, F.D. Menzies, et al. (2019). Interspecific visitation of cattle and badgers to fomites: a transmission risk for bovine tuberculosis? *Ecology & Evolution* **9**(15): 8479–8489.

Caron, A., J.A. Barasona, E. Miguel, et al. (2021). Characterization of wildlife/livestock interfaces: the need for interdisciplinary approaches and a dedicated thematic field. In J. Vicente, K. Vercauteren and C. Gortazar (Eds.), *Disease at the Wildlife/Livestock Interface: Research and Perspectives in a Changing World*. Wildlife Research Monographs. New York: Springer.

Caron, A., E. Miguel, C. Gomo, et al. (2013). Relationship between burden of infection in ungulate populations and wildlife/livestock interfaces. *Epidemiology and Infection* **141**(7): 1522–35.

Cooke, S.J., S.G. Hinch, M. Wikelski, et al. (2004). Biotelemetry: a mechanistic approach to ecology. *Trends in Ecology & Evolution* **19**(6): 334–343.

Corbane, C., S. Lang, K. Pipkins, et al. (2015). Remote sensing for mapping natural habitats and their conservation status – new opportunities and challenges. *International Journal of Applied Earth Observation and Geoinformation* **37**: 7–16.

Cornélis, D., S. Benhamou, G. Janeau, et al. (2011). Spatiotemporal dynamics of forage and water resources shape space use of West African savanna buffalo. *Mammalogy* **92**(6): 1287–1297.

Cuisance, D. (1996). Réactualisation de la situation des tsé-tsé et des trypanosomoses animales au Tchad. Phase II/Zone du Lac, Guera, Salamat. Enquête réalisée du 22 mars au 20 avril 1996.

de Garine-Wichatitksy, M., E. Miguel, D. Cornélis, et al. (2021). The Ecology of Disease Transmission at the Wildlife-Livestock Interface: Beyond Disease Ecology, Towards Socio-Ecological System Health. In J. Vicente, K. Vercauteren and C. Gortazar (Eds.), *Disease at the Wildlife/Livestock Interface: Research and Perspectives in a Changing World*. Wildlife Research Monograph. New York: Springer.

Degenne, P. and D.L. Seen (2016). Ocelet: simulating processes of landscape changes using interaction graphs. *SoftwareX* **5**: 89–95.

Dormann, C.F., S.J. Schymanski, J. Cabral, et al. (2012). Correlation and process in species distribution models: bridging a dichotomy. *Journal of Biogeography* **39**(12): 2119–2131.

Dougherty, E.R., D.P. Seidel, C.J. Carlson, et al. (2018). Going through the motions: incorporating movement analyses into disease research. *Ecology Letters* **21**(4): 588–604.

Drewe, J., H. O'connor, N. Weber, et al. (2013). Patterns of direct and indirect contact between cattle and badgers naturally infected with tuberculosis. *Epidemiology & Infection* **141**(7): 1467–1475.

du Toit, J.T., P.C. Cross and M. Valeix (2017). Managing the livestock–wildlife interface on rangelands. In D.D. Briske (Ed.), *Rangeland Systems: Processes, Management and Challenges*. Cham: Springer Nature, pp. 395–425.

Eikelboom, J., W. Spruyt and H. Prins (2021). Timely poacher detection and localization using sentinel animal movement. *Scientific Reports* **11**(1): 4596–4596.

Ferguson, K.J., S. Cleaveland, D.T. Haydon, et al. (2013). Evaluating the potential for the environmentally sustainable control of foot and mouth disease in Sub-Saharan Africa. *EcoHealth* **10**(3): 314–22.

Flack, A., W. Fiedler, J. Blas, et al. (2016). Costs of migratory decisions: a comparison across eight white stork populations. *Science Advances* **2**(1): e1500931.

Frair, J.L., J. Fieberg, M. Hebblewhite, et al. (2010). Resolving issues of imprecise and habitat-biased locations in ecological analyses using GPS telemetry data. *Philosophical Transactions of the Royal Society B: Biological Sciences* **365**(1550): 2187–2200.

Gadaga, B.M., E.M. Etter, B. Mukamuri, et al. (2016). Living at the edge of an interface area in Zimbabwe: cattle owners, commodity chain and health workers' awareness, perceptions and practices on zoonoses. *BMC Public Health* **16**(1): 84.

Grégoire, G., H. Chaté and Y. Tu (2003). Moving and staying together without a leader. *Physica D: Nonlinear Phenomena* **181**(3–4): 157–170.

Hamede, R., J. Bashford, M. Jones and H. McCallum (2012). Simulating devil facial tumour disease outbreaks across empirically derived contact networks. *Journal of Applied Ecology* **49**(2): 447–456.

Hamede, R.K., J. Bashford, H. McCallum and M. Jones (2009). Contact networks in a wild Tasmanian devil (*Sarcophilus harrisii*) population: using social network analysis to reveal seasonal variability in social behaviour and its implications for transmission of devil facial tumour disease. *Ecology Letters* **12**(11): 1147–1157.

Hibert, F., C. Calenge, H. Fritz, et al. (2010). Spatial avoidance of invading pastoral cattle by wild ungulates: insights from using point process statistics. *Biodiversity and Conservation* **19**(7): 2003–2024.

Higgins, S.I., W.J. Bond, E.C. February, et al. (2007). Effects of four decades of fire manipulation on woody vegetation structure in savanna. *Ecology* **88**(5): 1119–1125.

Hilbers, J.P., F. Van Langevelde, H.H. Prins, et al. (2015). Modeling elephant-mediated cascading effects of water point closure. *Ecological Applications* **25**(2): 402–415.

Huang, C., Y. Chen, S. Zhang and J. Wu (2018). Detecting, extracting, and monitoring surface water from space using optical sensors: a review. *Reviews of Geophysics* **56**(2): 333–360.

Kamath, P.L., J.T. Foster, K.P. Drees, et al. (2016). Genomics reveals historic and contemporary transmission dynamics of a bacterial disease among wildlife and livestock. *Nature Communications* **7**(1): 1–10.

Kays, R., M.C. Crofoot, W. Jetz and M. Wikelski (2015). Terrestrial animal tracking as an eye on life and planet. *Science* **348**(6240).

Kearney, M. and W. Porter (2009). Mechanistic niche modelling: combining physiological and spatial data to predict species' ranges. *Ecology Letters* **12**(4): 334–350.

Kock, R. (2005). What is this infamous "wildlife/livestock interface?" A review of current knowledge. In S. Osofsky, S. Cleaveland, W. B. Karesh, et al. (Eds.), *Conservation and Development Interventions at the Wildlife/Livestock Interface: Implications for Wildlife, Livestock and Human Health*. Gland, Switzerland/Cambridge, UK: IUCN.

Kock, R., M. Kock, M. de Garine-Wichatitksy, et al. (2014). Livestock and buffalo (*Syncerus caffer*) interfaces in Africa: ecology of disease transmission and implications for conservation and development. In M. Melletti and J. Burton (Eds.), *Ecology, Evolution and*

Behaviour of Wild Cattle: Implications for Conservation. Cambridge: Cambridge University Press, pp. 431–445.

Lloyd-Smith, J.O. (2005). Disease transmission in heterogeneous populations. PhD dissertation, University of California.

Marshall, F., R.E.B. Reid, S. Goldstein, et al. (2018). Ancient herders enriched and restructured African grasslands. *Nature* **561**: 387–390.

Meng, R. and F. Zhao (2017). Remote sensing of fire effects. A review for recent advances in burned area and burn severity mapping. In G.P. Petropoulos and T. Islam (Eds.), *Remote Sensing of Hydrometeorological Hazards*. Boca Raton: CRC Press, pp. 261–276.

Miguel, E. (2012). Contact et diffusion de pathogènes des ongulés sauvages aux ongulés domestiques africains. PhD, Ecole Doctorale SIBAGHE, Université de Montpellier II.

Miguel, E., V. Grosbois, A. Caron, et al. (2013). Contacts and foot and mouth disease transmission from wild to domestic bovines in Africa. *Ecosphere* **4**(4): art51.

Miguel, E., V. Grosbois, H. Fritz, et al. (2017). Drivers of foot-and-mouth disease in cattle at wild/domestic interface: insights from farmers, buffalo and lions. *Divers Distrib* **23**(9): 1018–1030.

Moorcroft, P.R. (2012). Mechanistic approaches to understanding and predicting mammalian space use: recent advances, future directions. *Journal of Mammalogy* **93**(4): 903–916.

Musoke, J., T. Hlokwe, T. Marcotty, et al. (2015). Spillover of *Mycobacterium bovis* from wildlife to livestock, South Africa. *Emerging and Infectious Diseases* **21**(3): 448–30(8): 51.

Mwakiwa, E., W.F. de Boer, J.W. Hearne, et al. (2013). Optimization of wildlife management in a large game reserve through waterpoints manipulation: a bio-economic analysis. *Journal of Environmental Management* **114**: 352–361.

Naidoo, R., A. Brennan, A.C. Shapiro, et al. (2020). Mapping and assessing the impact of small-scale ephemeral water sources on wildlife in an African seasonal savannah. *Ecological Applications* 30(8): e02203.

Naidoo, R., P. Du Preez, G. Stuart-Hill, et al. (2012). Home on the range: factors explaining partial migration of African buffalo in a tropical environment. *PLoS One* **7**(5): e36527.

Neumann, W., S. Martinuzzi, A.B. Estes, et al. (2015). Opportunities for the application of advanced remotely-sensed data in ecological studies of terrestrial animal movement. *Movement Ecology* **3**(1): 1–13.

Ogutu, J.O., N. Owen-Smith, H.-P. Piepho, et al. (2012). Dynamics of ungulates in relation to climatic and land use changes in an insularized African savanna ecosystem. *Biodiversity and Conservation* **21**(4): 1033–1053.

Osofsky, S.A., & S. Cleaveland (Eds.) (2005). *Conservation and Development Interventions at the Wildlife/livestock Interface: Implications for Wildlife, Livestock and Human Health: Proceedings of the Southern and East African Experts Panel on Designing Successful Conservation and Development Interventions at the Wildlife/Livestock Interface – Implications for Wildlife, Livestock and Human Health, AHEAD (Animal Health for the Environment and Development) Forum*, IUCN Vth World Parks Congress, Durban, South Africa, 14–15 September 2003 (No. 30). Gland: IUCN.

Owen-Smith, N., G. Hopcraft, T. Morrison, et al. (2020). Movement ecology of large herbivores in African savannas: current knowledge and gaps. *Mammal Review* 50(3): 252–266.

Paull, S.H., S. Song, K.M. McClure, et al. (2012). From superspreaders to disease hotspots: linking transmission across hosts and space. *Frontiers in Ecology and the Environment* **10**(2): 75–82.

Proffitt, K.M., J.A. Gude, K.L. Hamlin, et al. (2011). Elk distribution and spatial overlap with livestock during the brucellosis transmission risk period. *Journal of Applied Ecology* **48**(2): 471–478.

Pruvot, M., D. Seidel, M.S. Boyce, et al. (2014). What attracts elk onto cattle pasture? Implications for inter-species disease transmission. *Preventive Veterinary Medicine*.

Rastetter, E.B., J.D. Aber, D.P. Peters, et al. (2003). Using mechanistic models to scale ecological processes across space and time. *Bioscience* **53**(1): 68–76.

Reynolds, J.J.H., B.T. Hirsch, S.D. Gehrt, et al. (2015). Raccoon contact networks predict seasonal susceptibility to rabies outbreaks and limitations of vaccination. *Journal of Animal Ecology* **84**(6): 1720–1731.

Ribeiro-Lima, J., M. Carstensen, L. Cornicelli, et al. (2017). Patterns of cattle farm visitation by white-tailed deer in relation to risk of disease transmission in a previously infected area with bovine tuberculosis in Minnesota, USA. *Transboundary and Emerging Diseases* 64(5): 1519–1529.

Richomme, C., D. Gauthier and E. Fromont (2006). Contact rates and exposure to inter-species disease transmission in mountain ungulates. *Epidemiology and Infection* **134**(1): 21–30.

Rumiano, F. (2021). The combined use of remote sensing and spatial modelling for animal movement – application to the study of wildlife/livestock contacts and the risk of pathogen transmission in Southern Africa. PhD dissertation, Ecology, University of Montpellier.

Rumiano, F., C. Gaucherel, P. Degenne, et al. (2021). Combined use of remote sensing and spatial modelling: when surface water impacts buffalo (*Syncerus caffer caffer*) movements in savanna environments. *International Archives of the Photogrammetry, Remote Sensing and Spatial Information Sciences* XLIII-B3-2021: 631–638.

Rumiano, F., E. Wielgus, E. Miguel, et al. (2020). Remote sensing of environmental drivers influencing the movement ecology of sympatric wild and domestic ungulates in semi-arid savannas, a review. *Remote Sensing* **12**(19): 3218.

Sah, P., S.T. Leu, P.C. Cross, et al. (2017). Unraveling the disease consequences and mechanisms of modular structure in animal social networks. *Proceedings of the National Academy of Sciences of the United States of America* **114**(16): 4165–4170.

Scoones, I., A. Bishi, N. Mapitse, et al. (2010). Foot-and-mouth disease and market access: challenges for the beef industry in southern Africa. *Pastoralism: Research, Policy and Practice* **1**(2): 135–164.

Silk, M.J., D.P. Croft, R.J. Delahay, et al. (2017). Using social network measures in wildlife disease ecology, epidemiology, and management. *Bioscience* **67**(3): 245–257.

Silk, M.J., K.R. Finn, M.A. Porter and N. Pinter-Wollman (2018). Can multilayer networks advance animal behavior research? *Trends in Ecology and Evolution* **33**(6): 376–378.

Tanner, M. and A.L. Michel (1999). Investigation of the viability of *M. bovis* under different environmental conditions in the Kruger National Park. *Onderstepoort Journal of Veterinary Research* **66**(3): 185–190.

Thomson, G.R., M.L. Penrith, M.W. Atkinson, et al. (2013). Balancing livestock production and wildlife conservation in and around southern Africa's transfrontier conservation areas. *Transboundary and Emerging Diseases* **60**(6): 492–506.

Tomkiewicz, S.M., M.R. Fuller, J.G. Kie and K.K. Bates (2010). Global positioning system and associated technologies in animal behaviour and ecological research. *Philosophical Transactions of the Royal Society B: Biological Sciences* **365**(1550): 2163–2176.

Triguero-Ocana, R., J.A. Barasona, F. Carro, et al. (2019). Spatio-temporal trends in the frequency of interspecific interactions between domestic and wild ungulates from Mediterranean Spain. *PLoS One* **14**(1): e0211216.

Triguero-Ocana, R., E. Laguna, S. Jimenez-Ruiz, et al. (2021). The wildlife–livestock interface on extensive free-ranging pig farms in central Spain during the "montanera" period. *Transboundand and Emerging Diseases* 68(4): 2066–2078.

Valls-Fox, H., S. Chamaillé-Jammes, M. de Garine-Wichatitsky, et al. (2018). Water and cattle shape habitat selection by wild herbivores at the edge of a protected area. *Animal Conservation* **21**(5): 365–375.

van Onselen, C. (1972). Reactions to Rinderpest in Southern Africa 1896–97. *The Journal of African History* **13**(3): 473–488.

Westley, P.A., A.M. Berdahl, C.J. Torney and D. Biro (2018). Collective movement in ecology: from emerging technologies to conservation and management. *Philosophical Transactions of The Royal Society B: Biological Sciences* 373(1746): 20170004.

White, L.A., J.D. Forester and M.E. Craft (2015). Using contact networks to explore mechanisms of parasite transmission in wildlife. *Biological Reviews of the Cambridge Philosophical Society*.

Wielgus, E., A. Caron, E. Bennitt, et al. (2021). Inter-group Social behavior, contact patterns and risk for pathogen transmission in Cape buffalo populations. *Journal of Wildlife Management* **85**(8): 1574–1590.

Wielgus, E., D. Cornélis, M. de Garine-Wichatitsky, et al. (2020). Are fission–fusion dynamics consistent among populations? A large-scale study with Cape buffalo. *Ecology & Evolution* **10**(17): 9240–9256.

Woodroffe, R., C.A. Donnelly, C. Ham, et al. (2016). Badgers prefer cattle pasture but avoid cattle: implications for bovine tuberculosis control. *Ecology Letters* 19(10): 1201–1208.

Yin, S., H.J. de Knegt, M.C. de Jong, et al. (2020). Effects of migration network configuration and migration synchrony on infection prevalence in geese. *Journal of Theoretical Biology* **502**: 110315.

Zengeya, F.M., A. Murwira, A. Caron, et al. (2015). Spatial overlap between sympatric wild and domestic herbivores links to resource gradients. *Remote Sensing Applications: Society and Environment* **2**: 56–65.

11 · Host–Parasite Interactions in African Buffalo: A Community-Level Perspective

B. BEECHLER, E. GORSICH, C. GLIDDEN, A. JOLLES AND V. O. EZENWA

Introduction

Parasites, spanning viruses, bacteria, helminths, protozoa and arthropods, live within or on a host, often affecting individual host health, survival and reproduction. Furthermore, these individual-level effects of parasites can have consequences that cascade to the population, community and ecosystem levels (Wilson et al., 2019). Historically, host–parasite interactions were studied from a one host–one parasite perspective. However, given that most hosts are infected with more than one type of parasite simultaneously (Cox, 2001), the study of concurrent infection (i.e. coinfection) has gained increasing attention from ecologists, epidemiologists, veterinarians and biomedical scientists (Hoarau et al., 2020; Mabbott, 2018; Salgame et al., 2013). Crucially, wildlife studies occupy a unique niche in this research area because they can help uncover the real-world contexts in which coinfection, and the interactions occurring between coinfecting parasites, are most important (Ezenwa, 2016).

Just like free-living species in ecological communities, parasite species live in communities within their hosts where they interact by competing against or facilitating one another, with consequences for parasite community structure, host health and host fitness (Beechler et al., 2019; Graham, 2008; Pedersen and Fenton, 2007; Telfer et al., 2010). Many of the initial efforts to study parasite interactions in wildlife focused on co-occurrence patterns, revealing that coinfection is common, and that parasites and pathogens interact within hosts both directly and indirectly (e.g. Bush and Holmes, 1986; Lello et al., 2004). For instance, parasites may compete for space or resources (Budischak et al., 2018a; Clerc et al., 2019), such that the presence of one parasite decreases the likelihood another succeeds at growth and replication. Alternatively, one parasite may increase the success of another by providing resources or space (Dutt et al., 2021; Zélé et al., 2018). Parasite community interactions are further governed by the host immune response, where cross-immunity may cause one parasite to negatively affect the establishment and growth of another (Raberg et al., 2006), or where one parasite may suppress the host immune response in a way that is beneficial to other parasites (Graham, 2008). Recently, advances in molecular, immunological and statistical methods have enabled an increasingly mechanistic and/or predictive understanding of these types of parasite interactions in wild species (e.g. Clerc et al., 2019; Fountain-Jones et al., 2019; McDonald et al., 2020).

Studies of African buffalo have played a key role in advancing research on wildlife coinfection. Multiple facets of African buffalo ecology and life history make them an excellent system for understanding parasite interactions in free-living animals (Ezenwa et al., 2019). Buffalo are relatively long-lived, large-bodied, gregarious animals that are common throughout sub-Saharan Africa. Furthermore, buffalo are host to a broad diversity of parasites, including bacteria, viruses, protozoa and helminths (Ezenwa et al., 2019). These attributes allow parasite studies to be conducted on relatively large numbers of individuals across multiple spatiotemporal scales (Garabed et al., 2020). Physiological similarity between domestic cattle and African buffalo further enables the use of readily available physiological (Couch et al., 2017), immunological (Beechler et al., 2012) and diagnostic tools (Glidden et al., 2018), as well as therapeutics to measure animal responses to infection, describe parasite community composition (Beechler et al., 2019), and manipulate host–parasite interactions (Ezenwa and Jolles, 2015). In this chapter, we describe insights on parasite interactions derived from the study of African buffalo. Focusing on results drawn from two large studies performed in Kruger National Park (KNP), South Africa (see Box 11.1), we discuss how pairwise and multi-parasite perspectives have been used to understand which parasite taxa interact most strongly, the mechanisms accounting for these interactions and the implications for both hosts and parasites. We also highlight general patterns that have emerged across parasite systems. We outline key technical tools, both computational and laboratory, that facilitate the ability to draw strong inferences and link phenomena across scales. We conclude by identifying future research directions that will help advance scientists' understanding of the causes and consequences of parasite interactions.

Box 11.1 *Studying Parasite Interactions in the Wild*

Experimental and longitudinal approaches are important ingredients for studying parasite interactions in natural systems. By directly manipulating parasites in situ, researchers can identify how co-occurring parasites, as well as hosts, respond to changes in the parasite community and simultaneously investigate factors both internal and external to the host that govern variation in observed responses. Likewise, longitudinal approaches allow for parasite and host characteristics to be tracked over time, providing insight about the order in which events occur and helping to distinguish cause from effect. Either approach is valuable on its own, but in combination, these two methods represent a powerful tool for unravelling the causes and consequences of parasite interactions in free-ranging wildlife. Studies on wild African buffalo in KNP used these approaches to address a range of questions about parasite interactions.

Study 1 followed ~200 free-ranging young female buffalo captured from two herds in southern KNP over a four-year period. The animals were fitted with VHF collars (see Figure 11.1a) with recaptures occurring every 6 months to monitor changes in parasite communities, host physiology, health and performance (see Table 11.1). These animals were captured in the south-eastern portion of the park and animals were allowed to move and disperse as normal (Spaan et al., 2019). A goal of the study was to understand how gastrointestinal worms and bovine tuberculosis (bTB) interact, so half of the study animals received a long-acting anthelmintic drug applied every 6 months to reduce their worm burdens, while the other half were used as controls. Study animals were bTB-free at the onset of the experiment so that effects of anthelmintic treatment on bTB infection incidence and severity could be quantified.

Study 2 followed one herd of ~80 mixed age and sex buffalo, housed in a 900 ha semi-natural, predator-free enclosure in central KNP (see Figure 11.1b) that had been in place since the early 2000s and managed by KNP veterinary wildlife services. In this 'mesocosm' setting, study animals were captured every 2–3 months to collect finer-scale information on parasite communities and host traits. This short capture interval allowed for a better understanding of transmission patterns of microparasites like viruses and bacteria that are quick to spread throughout a population.

(a)

(b)

Figure 11.1 (a) African buffalo fitted with a VHF collar. (b) Double fence surrounding the 900 ha semi-natural enclosure containing the buffalo herd of Study 2.

Table 11.1 *Measures of health and immunity used in African buffalo.*

Measure	Method	Citation
Physiology and health		
Body condition	Manual palpation of buffalo	Ezenwa et al. (2009)
Pregnancy status	Rectal palpation	Beechler et al. (2015)
Lactation status	Manual milking of teats	NA
Cortisol as a measure of stress	Radioimmunoassay of faecal samples	Spaan et al. (2017)
Haematocrit and red blood cell measurements	Haematological assessment of whole blood	Beechler et al. (2009)
Total protein, albumin, kidney and liver enzymes	Chemistry profile on plasma	Couch et al. (2017)
Immunity		
White blood cell counts	Blood smear on whole blood	Beechler et al. (2009)
Bacteriacidal ability	Bacterial killing assay on plasma and whole blood	Beechler et al. (2012)
Lymphocyte proliferation ability (LPA)	Whole blood LPA	Beechler (2013)
Cytokines (IFNy, IL4, TNFa, IL12)	Enzyme-linked immunosorbent assay (ELISA) of plasma	Beechler et al. (2015); Ezenwa and Jolles (2015); Glidden et al. (2018)
Acute phase proteins (SAA, Hapto)	ELISA of plasma	Glidden et al. (2018)
Total globulins	Chemistry profile on plasma	Couch et al. (2017)

For both studies, samples (e.g. blood, faeces) collected at capture were used to quantify and describe the parasite community. These samples were also used to perform a suite of assays to assess host physiology, immunity and overall health (see Table 11.1). In combination with information about external environmental conditions (e.g. seasonality), the data on host traits and parasites were used to test a range of hypotheses about the nature and implications of parasite interactions. For both studies, animal handling and scientific permits were acquired from appropriate institutions (see Ezenwa and Jolles, 2015 for Study 1 and Jolles et al., 2021 for Study 2 permit information).

Parasite Interactions: Combining Pairwise and Multi-Species Perspectives

Studies of parasite interactions in African buffalo have ranged in scale from studies focused on pairwise parasite interactions to studies examining interactions among multiple co-occurring parasites using taxonomic and trait-based approaches (Table 11.2). In most cases, a key goal of the work has been to uncover how the presence of more than one parasite modifies host and parasite responses to infection. Below, we review these studies to identify notable commonalities across them as well as methods used to develop a multi-parasite perspective. Findings highlight the value of pairwise and multi-parasite perspectives: integrating both perspectives identified immunological and ecological mechanisms underlying pairwise interactions and assessed the relative importance of those mechanisms in more complex parasite communities.

The studies of pairwise parasite interactions cover a broad taxonomic scope, including bacteria, viruses, protozoa and helminths (Table 11.2, Theme 1). They investigate parasite interactions and the consequences for hosts and parasites in real-world settings. For example, in laboratory studies, immunological mechanisms of interaction between parasites are well described, but if and how these interactions manifest in wild populations has been unclear. Early work in African buffalo provided seminal evidence that cross-regulated immune responses can shape parasite population dynamics (Jolles et al., 2008), and that as in laboratory rodents, infection with parasites like gastrointestinal helminths can induce immune cross-regulation (Ezenwa et al., 2010). Studies in the KNP buffalo population (Box 11.1) expanded on this foundation using manipulative experiments and longitudinal tracking of individuals to confirm that in a wild setting, clearance of one type of parasite (gastrointestinal helminths) has ramifications for host immunity and the severity of infection with a second parasite, in this case *Mycobacterium bovis*, the causative agent of bovine tuberculosis (bTB) (Ezenwa and Jolles, 2015). Another key result from the pairwise studies was the broad importance of bTB on host immunity, health and survival. *M. bovis* infection was associated with lower innate immunity and higher inflammatory cytokine secretion, measured as *Escherichia coli* killing capacity and interleukin-12 concentration, respectively (Beechler et al. 2012, 2015). Accordingly, prior infection with bTB was associated with an increased likelihood of acquiring both *Brucella abortus* (the causative agent of brucellosis) and Rift Valley fever virus (RVF) (Beechler

Table 11.2 *Summary of research on parasite interactions in African buffalo. The studies span a range of designs, including experimental (E), longitudinal (L) and case control (CC) studies. The design column indicates the study design type and whether the data were derived from Study 1 or 2 as described in Box 11.1. The scale column indicates whether the study focused on two parasites (pairwise), a group of parasites (e.g. helminths or Theileria), or all of the parasites that were screened (WC, for whole community). It also describes whether the interaction was between microparasites (micro–micro), macroparasites (macro–macro) or both (macro–micro). The interaction type and effects columns define whether the parasites positively (facilitation) or negatively (competition) influenced each other during a subsequent observation or across multiple observations (succession).*

Parasites (diseases)	Design	Scale	Interaction type	Effects on other parasite/parasite communities/host	Citation
Theme 1: Pairwise studies					
Mycobacterium bovis (bTB) *vs. Brucella abortus* (brucellosis)	L – 1	Pairwise. Micro–micro	Facilitation and competition	Effects on other parasite: Brucellosis infection was twice as likely in buffalo with bTB compared to uninfected buffalo, but brucellosis infection was not correlated with risk of bTB. Mathematical modelling suggests the net effect of bTB on transmission and mortality results in competition at the population-level: R_0 and endemic prevalence predictions for bTB were lower in populations in which both pathogens co-occur. Effects on host: Mortality rates were higher after individuals became infected with either bTB or brucellosis, with the highest risk occurring in co-infected buffalo. Neither infection reduced fecundity, measured by calf observations.	Gorsich et al. (2018),
bTB *vs.* helminths	E – 1	Pairwise. Micro–macro	Competition	Effects on other parasite: Experimental anthelmintic treatment did not influence risk of bTB. The predicted R_0 of bTB is 8-fold higher in treated populations due to decreases in mortality when worm burdens decline. Effects on host: Mortality rates were lower in buffalo that received the treatment compared to controls.	Ezenwa and Jolles (2015),

Parasites	Code	Interaction type		Effects	Reference
bTB vs. helminth resistance	L/E – 1	Pairwise, Micro–macro	Competition	Effects on other parasite: There was no effect of natural host resistance to worms on bTB infection risk. Effects on host: Worm-resistant individuals were more likely to die of bTB than were non-resistant individuals despite having lower worm burdens, and bTB progressed more quickly in the lungs of non-resistant individuals. Anthelmintic treatment moderated but did not eliminate this pattern, implicating 'resistance' to worms and not simply current worm infection as a driver of the interaction.	Ezenwa et al. (2021)
bTB vs. Rift Valley fever virus	L – 1	Pairwise. Micro–micro	Facilitation	Effects on other parasite: RVF infection was twice as likely in buffalo with bTB compared to uninfected buffalo. Mathematical modelling suggests this results in larger and faster spreading RVF outbreaks. Effects on host: Foetal abortion rates were 6.6 times higher in coinfected buffalo compared to infection with RVF alone.	Beechler et al. (2015)
Helminths, namely *Haemonchus* spp. vs. *Cooperia fuelleborni*	E – 1	Pairwise. Macro–macro	Facilitation	Effects on host: Host body condition was lower in buffalo that underwent experimental anthelmintic treatment compared to controls. In controls, increases in *Haemonchus* egg counts were negatively associated with changes in condition, while increases in *Cooperia* egg counts were associated with increases in condition. Neither parasite directly influenced survival or fecundity (likelihood of being pregnant or lactating). However, treated buffalo had higher survival and both treated and untreated buffalo in good condition had both higher survival and fecundity.	Budischak et al. (2018b)
Schistosoma matthei vs. *Cooperia fuelleborni*	–L – 1	Pairwise. Macro–macro	Facilitation	Effects on other parasite: Schistosome burdens varied seasonally. Wet season gains in burden were not correlated with helminth coinfection, but coinfection did influence the magnitude of dry season reductions in burden. Buffalo infected with *Cooperia* maintained higher schistosome burdens throughout the dry season.	Beechler et al. (2017)

(cont.)

Table 11.2 (*cont.*)

Parasites (diseases)	Design	Scale	Interaction type	Effects on other parasite/parasite communities/host	Citation
Theme 2: Multi-parasite studies applying taxonomic approaches					
6 gastrointestinal helminths[a]	–E – 1	Helminths	Succession	Effects on parasite community: After anthelmintic treatment, helminth communities in treated buffalo had a lower total abundance and higher diversity compared to communities in undisturbed control buffalo. With increasing time since treatment, treated helminth communities resembled those found in undisturbed control buffalo.	Budischak et al. (2016)
6 respiratory pathogens associated with bovine respiratory disease[b]	L – 1	WC	Facilitation	Effects on parasite community: Five of the respiratory pathogens were continuously circulating. Viral coinfection was the best predictor of viral infection; host physiology and season had little effect on odds of viral infection. Coinfection with bTB was positively associated with risk of BRSV but none of the other pathogens. Anti-helminthic treatment was not associated with any of the respiratory pathogens.	Glidden et al. (2021)
10 *Theileria* phylotypes[c]	–L – 1	*Theileria*	Facilitation, competition, succession	Effects on parasite community: Interaction networks change over time; young animals are infected with *Theileria* interaction networks composed of many negative and positive interactions, while adult interaction networks are composed of three positive interactions. 7/10 phylotypes exist with 80–90% prevalence in adult animals, this coexistence is likely the result of phylotype-specific immunity and facilitation. Two phylotypes infect young animals early (within 1 month), but are later displaced in adult animals and facilitation.	Glidden et al. (2021),

Theme 3: Multi-parasite studies applying trait-based perspectives

Parasites	Code		Interaction	Effects	Reference
bTB, brucellosis, 3 haemoparasites,d 6 respiratory pathogens[b] coccidia, strongyle nematodes, Schistosoma matthei	C–C –1	WC	—	Effects on parasite community: Animals that acquired bTB experienced a greater increase in parasite assemblage richness and functional richness compared to age-matched buffalo that did not acquire bTB. The traits of parasite communities after bTB were less variable (measured as multivariate dispersion) and dominated by contact-transmitted parasites with simple life cycles and fast replication times.	Beechler et al. (2019),
11 haemoparasites[d] vs. BTB, brucellosis, helminths, coccidia, ticks (Amblyomma hebraeum, Rhipicephalus spp.)	L – 1	WC	Facilitation and competition	Effects on parasite community: Parasites infecting the same tissue type were associated with the probability of haemoparasite infection (e.g. other haemoparasites). For pairs of haemoparasites, the direction of the association can be predicted based on shared resources, cross immunity, and having a shared vector. In contrast, associations between haemoparasites and parasites infecting other tissue types were weak or non-existent.	Henrichs et al. (2016)
Tick-borne parasites Gastrointestinal parasites Respiratory pathogens	–L – 2	WC	—	Effects on parasite community: Parasite communities follow patterns of succession similar to free-living communities. The median age of first infection differs between parasite taxa, with tick-borne and helminths parasites first occurring in animals less than 1 year old and directly transmitted infections first occurring after 2 years.	Combrink et al. (2020)

a Cooperia fulleborni, Haemonchus sp., Parabronema sp., Trichostrongylus sp., Africanastrongylus giganticus, Africanastrongylus buceros.

b Bovine adenovirus-3 (AD-3), bovine herpes virus (BHV), bovine parainfluenza-3 (Pi-3), bovine respiratory syncytial virus (BRSV), Mycoplasma bovis (MB), Mannheimia haemolytica (MH).

c T. parva, T. sp (buffalo), T. sp (bougasvlei), T. velifera B, T. mutans-like 1, T. mutans-like 2, T. mutans, T. mutans MSD. T. mutans-like 3, T. mutans, T. sp (buffalo),

d Anaplasma centrale, A. marginale, A. sp. Omatjenne, A. phagocytophilum, Babesia sp., Ehrlichia ruminantium, Theileria parva, T. mutans, T. sp (buffalo), T. sp (sable), T. velifera.

et al., 2015; Gorsich et al., 2018). These studies provide a starting platform for investigating the consequences of bTB for a wider range of co-occurring parasites. Given the broad effects of bTB on African buffalo survival, health and susceptibility to other parasites, mechanistic models are useful to predict the consequences of bTB for the population-level dynamics of a second parasite. For example, Gorsich et al. (2018) parameterized a mechanistic model of bTB–brucellosis dynamics that represented a host's increased likelihood of acquiring brucellosis and increased mortality rates if the host was also infected with bTB. The model predicted the net consequences of these effects for prevalence and R_0, thereby linking the within-host mechanisms explored in previous papers (Beechler et al., 2012, 2015) to population-level patterns of disease spread.

Further studies investigated multi-parasite interactions by applying a multi-parasite approach (Table 11.2, Themes 2 and 3). These studies can be conceptually divided into those that quantify higher-order association patterns that emerge from complex multi-parasite interactions (Theme 2) and those that simplify complex multi-parasite interactions into generalizable patterns (Theme 3). The former relies on taxonomic approaches where parasites are classified according to their taxonomy, while the latter applies a trait-based perspective where parasites are classified by their biological features, such as how they differ in physiological, morphological or life-history traits. The two approaches reveal how different dimensions of the parasite community respond to change. However, because traits or trait distributions can be directly linked to host or environmental conditions, trait-based approaches allow for more mechanistic predictions about how a community may change in response to coinfection (see McGill et al., 2006 for a review of traits-based approaches in ecology).

Importantly, the multi-parasite approaches (Table 11.2, Themes 2 and 3) and the pairwise approaches (Table 11.2, Theme 1) have proven highly complementary. For example, Beechler et al. (2019) applied a trait-based approach to evaluate how parasite community composition – including 14 parasites ranging from viruses, bacteria, protozoa and helminths – differed before versus after buffalo were infected with bTB. Interestingly, parasite communities tended to have higher taxonomic and functional richness (e.g. unique parasite traits) after hosts acquired bTB infection (Figure 11.4a). Furthermore, while the number of unique parasites tended to increase after bTB, the traits of these parasites were functionally similar to each other, as quantified by multivariate dispersion. Multivariate dispersion measures the amount of trait space occupied by a given community; thus, after bTB infection, parasite communities became more homogenous in terms of their traits even though the communities contained more species. This pattern was associated with communities becoming dominated by certain traits (e.g. contact transmission, fast replication rate), with less representation of other traits (slow transmission rate, environmental transmission).

Taxonomic studies occurring in the same system corroborate this result. The dominance of contact-transmitted, fast-replicating parasite taxa is supported by a longitudinal, multi-parasite study investigating associations among five contact-transmitted, fast-replicating respiratory pathogens (Theme 2). This analysis showed that after accounting for bTB infection, pathogen co-occurrence explained the largest proportion of variation in three focal viruses (bovine adenovirus-3, bovine herpes virus-1, bovine parainfluenza-3), with all three positively influenced by coinfection (Glidden et al., 2021). Additionally, the lack of slowly transmitted or environmentally transmitted pathogens is supported by pairwise-longitudinal and experimental studies investigating associations between bTB, brucellosis and gastrointestinal nematodes (Theme 1). Coinfection with both gastrointestinal nematodes and brucellosis was associated with higher mortality in bTB-positive individuals (Ezenwa and Jolles, 2015; Gorsich et al., 2018). These examples illustrate the value of combining approaches to investigate parasite communities.

Notable Commonalties Across Studies

Studying diverse parasite interactions can reveal commonalities across combinations of parasites that provide new insight into how the consequences of coinfection manifest in nature. At least one such common thread has emerged from studies of parasite interactions in wild African buffalo – the presence of conflicting outcomes across scales. Two studies of pairwise parasite interactions, one focused on interactions between gastrointestinal helminths and bTB (Ezenwa and Jolles, 2015), the other focused on interactions between brucellosis and bTB (Gorsich et al., 2018), both found evidence that from a host perspective, whether the outcome of coinfection is negative or positive differs at the individual host versus population scale.

Understanding the mechanisms that cause interactions between parasites is a cornerstone of coinfection research, in large part because uncovering these mechanisms should facilitate the development of effective disease intervention and control strategies. Immunological mechanisms are widely implicated as a driver of interactions between helminth parasites and many microbial pathogens (e.g. viruses, bacteria). For example, in mammals, helminth infections typically trigger a T-helper cell 2 (Th2)-type immune response, but the upregulation of this response can suppress T-helper cell 1 (Th1)-type immune responses directed against microbial pathogens (Mosmann and Sad, 1996). The individual-level repercussions of this immune cross-regulation can include any or all the following: increased susceptibility to microbial infection, faster disease progression and more severe disease (Ezenwa and Jolles, 2011). Moreover, these individual-level effects may scale up to influence the spread of microbes at the population-level if their combinatorial effects are sufficient to alter microbial population growth rates (Fenton, 2008). Consequently, in populations where hosts are faced with concurrent helminth and microbe infection, treating individuals for their worms (e.g. via anthelmintic drug therapy) may be an effective strategy for mitigating the negative health impacts of certain microbial infections and reducing the population-level spread of these microbes (Hotez et al., 2006). However, how eliminating helminths will affect the population dynamics of a coinfecting microbe depends on the net effect of helminths on the different parameters relevant to microbial transmission.

The anthelmintic treatment study of wild buffalo in KNP (Box 11.1, Study 1) tracked the effect of experimental deworming on two key parameters that influence bTB dynamics in buffalo: (i) the probability that an individual becomes infected with the disease, and (ii) the disease-associated mortality rate. Results showed that although treatment boosted buffalo anti-bTB immunity, treated animals were equally likely as untreated controls to acquire bTB (Ezenwa and Jolles, 2015). In contrast, treatment drastically reduced bTB-associated mortality, with treated animals almost nine times less likely to die of their bTB infections compared to controls (Ezenwa and Jolles, 2015). The population-level consequences of these effects were estimated by considering the impact of treatment on the basic reproductive number (R_0) of bTB, a metric that generally reflects how fast a pathogen can spread in a host population. Theoretically, anthelmintic treatment can either decrease or increase the R_0 of bTB, but in this case, treatment was associated with a nearly eight-fold increase in bTB's R_0 (Ezenwa and Jolles, 2015). As R_0 is defined as the number of secondary cases produced by a single infected individual in a fully susceptible population, this means that, on average, an anthelmintic-treated buffalo infects eight conspecifics with bTB for every one infected

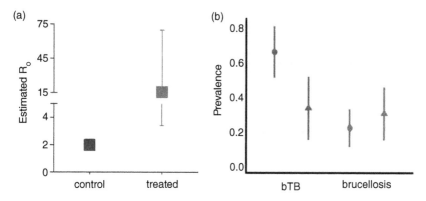

Figure 11.2 (a) The estimated reproductive number (R_0) of bTB in buffalo subpopulations that did (treated) versus did not (control) receive anthelmintic drug treatment. R_0 was approximately eight times higher for treated individuals (2 vs. 15.5), with upper and lower estimates of 3.4 and 69.8, respectively. (b) The estimated prevalence of bTB in buffalo populations with single bTB (left panel, line with circle) or concurrent bTB and brucellosis (left panel, line with triangle) infections. bTB prevalence declined in the presence of brucellosis, but there was no reciprocal effect of bTB on *Brucella* prevalence (right panel, line with circle vs. line with triangle).

by an untreated buffalo. Thus, although anthelmintic treatment has a positive outcome for individual health (i.e. bTB infected buffalo that receive treatment survive better), there appears to be a population-level cost of this strategy in terms of faster bTB spread (Figure 11.2a). This conflicting outcome likely arises because of the asymmetrical effects of worm treatment on bTB infection probability and mortality – as anthelmintic-treated, bTB-infected buffalo live longer (positive individual-level effect), they have more time to spread the disease to others (negative population-level effect). In the real world, therefore, broad-scale anthelmintic treatment and elimination or eradication of helminth parasitism may have unintended effects on the dynamics of certain microbial infections like bTB, despite vastly improving individual health outcomes.

In many cases, the within-host mechanisms underlying interactions between parasites are unknown, and *a priori* hypotheses about potential modes of intervention or control are lacking. Nevertheless, longitudinal studies can be used to understand the impacts of coinfection on both individuals and populations and extract insight about potential consequences of control strategies. Interactions between bTB and brucellosis in buffalo were studied in this way, with results pointing to another intriguing case of conflicting outcomes for individuals and populations. Taking

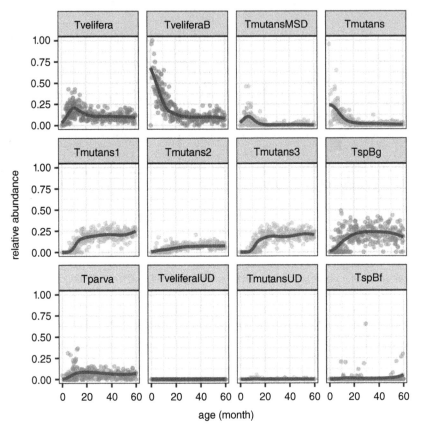

Figure 11.3 The succession of *Theileria* subtypes in African buffalo demonstrates the unique applicability of combining longitudinal study designs with high-throughput sequencing to identify how pathogen communities change over time. By combining infection time series with information on host traits (Table 11.1) we can determine the assembly processes that shape African buffalo parasite communities. Here, the bTB axis represents within-host parasite relative abundance, the x-axis represents animal age. The regression line is the output of a general additive mixed model with a Dirichlet-multinomial distribution, allowing for modelling composition and clustered data.

advantage of the coupled longitudinal design of Study 1 (Box 11.1), the interactions between these two chronic bacterial infections on the risk of infection of buffalo to each pathogen and mortality were examined. While bTB infection increased brucellosis risk, there was no consistent effect of brucellosis on bTB infection risk, revealing an asymmetry in the effects of these pathogens on one another (Gorsich et al., 2018). In terms of mortality risk, buffalo infected with both bTB and brucellosis

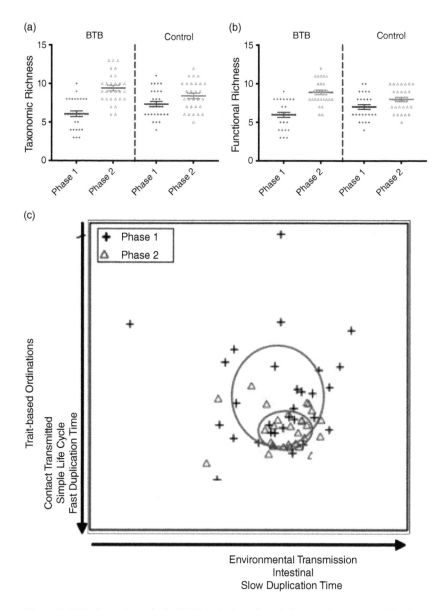

Figure 11.4 Bovine tuberculosis (bTB) infection altered the parasite communities in buffalo. By assessing changes in parasite communities both taxonomically (by species and genus) as well as functionally (e.g. using parasite traits such as speed and site of replication), Beechler et al. (2019) showed that animals that acquired bTB had higher parasite richness after bTB (phase 2) than before (phase 1) both taxonomically (panel a) and functionally (panel b). Furthermore, the magnitude of this increase was greater than that experienced in non-bTB infected control animals. Additional analysis suggested that becoming infected with bTB shifted the parasite community to be dominated by parasites with three key traits (panel c): direct contact transmission, fast replication time and simple life cycle (rather than complex with intermediate hosts). These results suggest that bTB altered the parasite community in buffalo in particular ways, lending the ability to predict how the invasion of bTB in other host populations may affect parasite communities.

experienced a more than eightfold increase in mortality compared to uninfected buffalo (Gorsich et al., 2018). A mathematical model exploring how these changes in infection risk and mortality affected the R_0 and prevalence of both pathogens showed that the presence of brucellosis reduced both the R_0 of bTB and population-level prevalence, whereas the presence of bTB had no consistent effect on brucellosis (Gorsich et al., 2018). Thus, even though bTB infection renders individual buffalo more susceptible to brucellosis, the presence of brucellosis moderates the prevalence of bTB at the population level (Figure 11.2b), highlighting yet another conflicting pattern across scales. In this case, the conflict arises because buffalo infected with bTB are more likely to acquire brucellosis and die (a negative individual-level outcome); however, this decreases the timeframe over which they can spread bTB to others, thereby reducing bTB prevalence at the population level (a positive population-level outcome). This result means that coinfection can help moderate the population-level spread of pathogens in certain circumstances, even if the individual-level outcomes of coinfection are undesirable.

These two case studies reveal an intriguing contrast between individual- and population-level consequences of infectious diseases in multi-parasite systems. Both examples suggest that the presence of one parasite or pathogen (helminths, brucellosis) can moderate the spread of another (bTB). In both contexts, cross-scale contrasts arise because the relative effects of helminths and brucellosis on individual host susceptibility to bTB are negligible compared to effects on mortality during coinfection (Gorsich et al., 2018). If this imbalance between mortality and susceptibility/transmission effects is general, the implications for designing disease control and intervention strategies may be applicable to multiple host–pathogen systems. In wildlife, single-pathogen focused disease control and management programmes may inadvertently increase the prevalence of non-target infections or facilitate the invasion of novel pathogens. More generally, the presence of conflicting cross-scale outcomes raises intriguing new questions about parasite interactions. Among these questions, identifying the circumstances in which such conflicting outcomes are most likely, including the host and parasite attributes that contribute to this pattern, represent new frontiers in research on coinfection.

Tools for Studying Parasite Interactions

The growing understanding of the community ecology of buffalo parasites is in part attributable to the variety of empirical approaches (e.g. experiments, longitudinal tracking, case control designs) that have been used to draw inference as well as the parallel development of new computational and laboratory tools. Here, we highlight these tools as they apply to the studies described in Table 11.2.

Pairwise Interactions: Causes and Consequences

Expanding our knowledge of host- versus parasite-level outcomes of coinfection is one of the largest contributions the buffalo study system has made to parasite community ecology. The ability to track large numbers of individual buffalo make them well suited for revealing these processes. Specifically, following animals through time allowed for parameterization of dynamical compartmental models as the number of susceptible, infected, coinfected and recovered (in some cases) individuals could be accurately assessed in real-time, and fecundity and/ or survival rates could be parameterized using time-to-event analyses (Beechler et al., 2015; Ezenwa and Jolles, 2015; Gorsich et al., 2018). As dynamic compartmental models integrate multi-scale information to describe mechanistic processes, this methodological framework paints a clear and robust picture of multi-scale outcomes of parasite coinfection. Notably, in Ezenwa and Jolles (2015), the application of an anthelmintic drug typically used for cattle supported causal inference as well as guaranteed a relatively even sampling design of helminth infection status across animals.

A longitudinal study design and application of an anthelmintic drug also aided Budischak et al. (2016) in revealing patterns of parasite succession and in characterizing the outcome of a *gain* in infection on host health. Likewise, Beechler et al. (2017) benefited by uncovering seasonally dependent effects of helminth infection on schistosome *loss*. In both of these studies, mixed effects models were able to parse out the effect of explicit covariates and animal-level random variation. As such, not only do these methods account for repeated measures and non-independence among samples, but they also identify the presence of latent animal traits not included in the model.

Community-Wide Analyses: Characterizing Complexity and Emergent Patterns

Advancing statistics and diagnostic approaches have been crucial in understanding communities beyond pairwise interactions. The ubiquity of concomitant infections in African buffalo has made it an ideal system for application of these techniques. For example, Glidden et al. (2021) used diagnostic tools initially developed for cattle to identify five respiratory pathogens infecting buffalo. Conditional Markov-random field models were then used to estimate the relative effect of the associations among all pathogens versus animal traits related to animal exposure and susceptibility on odds of infection. Notably, these methods can also be used to estimate how association strength among pathogens varies with host traits. In the study described here, the authors found that association strength differed with herd membership and animal lactation status (Glidden et al., 2021). If examining interaction networks at multiple scales (individual, population, meta-population) joint-species distribution models can yield similar results (Fountain-Jones et al., 2019; Tikhonov et al., 2017).

Advanced time series analyses can also be used to detect causal associations (i.e. true interactions) between parasites in longitudinal observational data, without an experimental component, thereby making it possible to quantify multidimensional parasite communities. In Glidden (2020), empirical dynamical modelling, a technique that uses time series to detect information transfer among variables (Clark et al., 2015), was paired with high throughput sequencing of an 18S genus-specific marker specific to describe non-linear and time-varying interactions among 12 subtypes of *Theileria*. This empirical dynamical modelling revealed that parasite interaction complexity decreases as animals age, with adult animals' interaction networks containing only four facilitative interactions and no competitive interactions, whereas the *Theileria* community was connected via a dense web of both facilitative and competitive interactions in juvenile animals. General additive mixed models were then used to estimate the non-linear relationships among interaction strengths and host immune response, detecting a correlation between antibody concentration and mean interaction strength, suggesting that change in interaction networks may be related to shifts in immune dynamics. In this context, panel regression models are also a powerful tool as they use time series of multiple units (e.g. individuals) to detect causal relationships (Dudney et al., 2021). If considering linear interactions, autoregressive models (Solvang and Subbey, 2019) can similarly leverage time series data to identify causal interactions and characterize true interaction networks (Clark et al., 2015). Overall, increasingly accessible computational tools have expedited insight on the complex and interacting factors shaping high-dimensional pathogen community assemblages, with particularly novel tools allowing for causal inference from observational studies.

Trait-Based Analyses: Bridging Complexity to Prediction and General Rules

In recent years, the community ecology of free-living organisms has moved to expand characterization of biodiversity to include functional and trait-based descriptions. The sharing of pathogens of veterinary importance between livestock and buffalo has resulted in a fairly detailed knowledge of pathogen traits in African buffalo (e.g. infected tissue, transmission route), enabling classification of functional diversity. Unsupervised machine learning methods were used by Beechler et al. (2019) to cluster pathogen communities by functional traits pre- and post-bTB infection. Classification by traits has also eased interpretation of grouped analyses such as in Combrink et al. (2020), where time-to-event analyses were used to measure age of first infection across a range of parasite and pathogen taxa, and clear patterns emerged based upon pathogen transmission route and taxonomic group where animals were typically first infected by tick-borne protozoa and last infected with directly transmitted respiratory viruses and bacteria. Combrink et al.'s (2020) investigation was made possible by the ability to track African buffalo from birth, allowing observation of natural parasite succession. The same study system (Study 2, Box 11.1) was used to identify patterns of succession of *Theileria* subtypes, while the application of non-linear regression and high-throughput sequencing allowed for a fine-scale identification of groups of *Theileria* subtypes with unique life-histories (colonization, relative abundance in adults; Figure 11.3).

Advances Making Work More Feasible

Advances in genomic techniques have accelerated the ability to describe pathogen communities in African buffalo across a multitude of taxa from the genera to strain level (Glidden et al., 2020) and explore relationships between pathogens and microbiomes (Couch et al., 2021; Sabey et al., 2021). Pairing genomic tools with non-invasive sampling, such as 18S sequencing of faecal samples to exhaustively characterize gastrointestinal parasite communities (e.g. Gogarten et al., 2020), will continue to further our understanding of pathogen community assembly, the effect of coinfection on host fitness, and variation in pathogen communities across scales. Improvement in contact and GPS collars will support a better integration of pathogen exposure and host movement data into our understanding of pathogen community dynamics (Owen-Smith et al.,

2020). The development and reduction in cost of transcriptomics will further help to characterize complex immune responses to infection and coinfection (Sallé et al., 2020).

At the forefront of parasite community ecology, these genomic tools are starting to be used to uncover evolutionary drivers of observed coinfection patterns, helping to explain how trade-offs among evolved pathogen defences may drive responses to coinfection (Ezenwa et al., 2021). These tools have the capacity to answer long-standing ecological questions, in a range of wildlife host–parasite systems.

Conclusions and Future Directions

Our past studies on parasite communities in African buffalo have contributed novel insights into the mechanisms by which parasites interact within their hosts, and how these interactions scale up to affect individual hosts, population-level disease dynamics, and parasite community structure. We have employed experimental and longitudinal approaches to infer causal links between infection patterns by different parasites, and have viewed coinfections both through the lens of pairwise species interactions, and at a broad community-wide scale. Along the way, we have developed and refined methods for diagnosing a range of infections in African buffalo and quantifying buffalo immune responses, other aspects of host physiology, and fitness. We have also taken advantage of new methods for analysing multivariate longitudinal data sets including interacting networks of dozens of parasite taxa. This work has set the stage for African buffalo to serve as a tractable model system for the study of disease processes in natural populations. However, our studies have raised more questions than they have answered. With new technologies and tools becoming available for data collection and analysis, there is broad scope for future disease ecological investigations in African buffalo. In particular, this model system is poised to: (i) help advance our understanding of ecological and evolutionary disease dynamics in the context of environmental change, and (ii) provide an empirical basis for evaluating whole-system impacts of disease interventions.

Current environmental changes are presenting wild animals with novel physiological challenges and assemblages of infectious organisms. In this context, mechanistic disease models are essential to providing robust predictions of disease dynamics and impacts of disease control interventions. Statistical extrapolation relies on previously observed variation to predict future conditions; however, when environments shift outside the boundaries of previously observed state space, non-linearities in host and pathogen functional responses may lead to novel infection patterns and outcomes (Kock et al., 2018). Improvements in animal tracking technologies and metabolic loggers can provide continuous, fine-scale data on animal movement, interactions, activity levels and metabolic rate. Coupled with high-resolution environmental data streams, and non-invasive sampling for infectious diseases, these technological advances set the stage for studies connecting environmental variation with host physiological and behavioural responses (Williams et al., 2021), contact patterns (Hamilton et al., 2020) and, ultimately, disease dynamics (Devan-Song, 2021). Building on this, assessing the metabolic and fitness costs of infections in natural populations becomes tractable, yielding insights on selection gradients imposed on hosts by parasites and pathogens. Complementary to this, quantitative molecular diagnostics provide detailed information on life-history variation among parasite strains and across different hosts. Faster, cheaper, deeper genetic sequencing techniques can elucidate host immunogenetic variation and parasite population genetics (Galen et al., 2020; Jax et al., 2021). Taken together, these data streams promise to provide an unprecedented empirical foundation for coevolutionary studies in model natural host–pathogen systems, such as African buffalo and their parasite community.

Our previous work has uncovered the ubiquity of interactions among coinfecting parasites, and their importance in shaping disease dynamics and host fitness. However, host–microbe interactions include the full spectrum of mutualistic to parasitic interactions. Elucidating the involvement of the microbiome in host health and disease in natural populations confronted with the full gamut of environmental variability and infectious challenges is an exciting frontier in disease ecology (Leung et al., 2018; Williams et al., 2018). Importantly, disease control interventions are likely to affect not only the specific target organisms, but also – directly or indirectly – the host's extended infracommunity of parasites and microbiota. Previous work on successional processes in parasite communities of African buffalo has used novel analytical techniques for disentangling host and microbial factors that shape microbial infracommunity dynamics (Budischak et al., 2016; Combrink et al., 2020; Glidden, 2020). However, the glimpse into parasite life-history variation and succession that we have provided is far from comprehensive. The intersection of quantitative molecular diagnostics (e.g. Glidden et al., 2020; Sisson et al., 2017) and analytical techniques for resolving community dynamics in complex, interacting species networks (e.g.

Sugihara et al., 2012) as applied in Glidden (2020) allows causal inferences to be drawn from observational parasite community data sets. This places a much broader understanding of parasite community responses to perturbations – such as disease control interventions, pathogen invasions or environmental change – within reach.

Overall, the foundational work on parasite interactions and community dynamics in African buffalo we describe in this chapter helps sets the stage for future studies in this model system addressing what is one of the central challenges in disease ecology: how to predict and mitigate infectious disease threats during a time of unprecedented, rapid environmental change.

References

Beechler, B. (2013). *Rift Valley fever in African buffalo (Syncerus caffer): basic epidemiology and the role of bovine tuberculosis coinfection.* PhD thesis, Oregon State University.

Beechler, B.R., K.S. Boersma, P.E. Buss, et al. (2019). Bovine tuberculosis disturbs parasite functional trait composition in African buffalo. *Proceedings of the National Academy of Sciences of the United States of America* **116**(29): 14645–14650.

Beechler, B.R., H. Broughton, A. Bell, et al. (2012). Innate immunity in free-ranging African buffalo (*Syncerus caffer*): associations with parasite infection and white blood cell counts. *Physiological and Biochemical Zoology* **85**(3): 255–264.

Beechler, B.R., A.E. Jolles, S.A. Budischak, et al. (2017). Host immunity, nutrition and coinfection alter longitudinal infection patterns of schistosomes in a free ranging African buffalo population. *PLoS Neglected Tropical Diseases* **11**(12): e0006122.

Beechler, B.R., A.E. Jolles and V.O. Ezenwa (2009). Evaluation of hematologic values in free-ranging African buffalo (*Syncerus caffer*). *Journal of Wildlife Diseases* **45**(1): 57–66.

Beechler, B.R., C.A. Manore, B. Reininghaus, et al. (2015). Enemies and turncoats: bovine tuberculosis exposes pathogenic potential of Rift Valley fever virus in a common host, African buffalo (*Syncerus caffer*). *Proceedings of the Royal Society of London B: Biological Sciences* **282**(1805): 20142942.

Budischak, S.A., E.P. Hoberg, A. Abrams, et al. (2016). Experimental insight into the process of parasite community assembly. *The Journal of Animal Ecology* **85**(5): 1222–1233.

Budischak, S.A., D. O'Neal, A.E. Jolles and V.O. Ezenwa (2018a). Differential host responses to parasitism shape divergent fitness costs of infection. *Functional Ecology* **32**(2): 324–333.

Budischak, S.A., A.E. Wiria, F. Hamid, et al. (2018b). Competing for blood: the ecology of parasite resource competition in human malaria–helminth co-infections. *Ecology Letters* **21**(4): 536–545.

Bush, A.O. and J.C. Holmes (1986). Intestinal helminths of lesser scaup ducks: an interactive community. *Canadian Journal of Zoology* **64**(1): 142–152.

Clark, T., H. Ye, F. Isbell, et al. (2015). Spatial convergent cross mapping to detect causal relationships from short time series. *Ecology* **96**(5): 1174–1181.

Clerc, M., A. Fenton, S.A. Babayan and A.B. Pedersen (2019). Parasitic nematodes simultaneously suppress and benefit from coccidian coinfection in their natural mouse host. *Parasitology* **146**(8): 1096–1106.

Combrink, L., C.K. Glidden, B.R. Beechler, et al. (2020). Age of first infection across a range of parasite taxa in a wild mammalian population. *Biology Letters* **16**(2): 20190811.

Couch, C.E., K. Stagaman, R.S. Spaan, et al. (2021). Diet and gut microbiome enterotype are associated at the population level in African buffalo. *Nature Communications* **12**(1): 2267.

Couch, C., M. Movius, A.E. Jolles, et al. (2017). Serum biochemistry panels in African buffalo (*Syncerus caffer*): defining references intervals and assessing variability across season, age and sex. *PLoS One* **12**(5): e0176830.

Cox, F.E. (2001). Concomitant infections, parasites and immune responses. *Parasitology* **122**(Suppl): S23–S38.

Devan-Song, A. (2021). *Contact Patterns in African Buffalo*. PhD, Oregon State University.

Dudney, J., C.E. Willing, A.J. Das, et al. (2021). Nonlinear shifts in infectious rust disease due to climate change. *Nature Communications* **12**: 5102.

Dutt, A., R. Anthony, D. Andrivon, et al. (2021). Competition and facilitation among fungal plant parasites affect their life-history traits. *Oikos* **130**(4): 652–667.

Ezenwa, V.O. (2016). Helminth–microparasite co-infection in wildlife: lessons from ruminants, rodents and rabbits. *Parasite Immunology* **38**(9): 527–534.

Ezenwa, V.O., S.A. Budischak, P. Buss et al. (2021). Natural resistance to worms exacerbates bovine tuberculosis severity independently of worm coinfection. *Proceedings of the National Academy of Sciences of the United States of America* 118(3): e2015080118.

Ezenwa, V.O., R.S. Etienne, G. Luikart, A. Beja-Pereira and A.E. Jolles (2010). Hidden consequences of living in a wormy world: nematode-induced immune suppression facilitates tuberculosis invasion in African buffalo. *The American Naturalist* **176**(5): 613–624.

Ezenwa, V.O. and A.E. Jolles (2011). From host immunity to pathogen invasion: the effects of helminth coinfection on the dynamics of microparasites. *Integrative and Comparative Biology* **51**(4): 540–551.

Ezenwa, V.O. and A.E. Jolles (2015). Epidemiology. Opposite effects of anthelmintic treatment on microbial infection at individual versus population scales. *Science* **347**(6218): 175–177.

Ezenwa, V.O., A.E. Jolles, B.R. Beechler, S.A. Budischak and E.E. Gorsich (2019). The causes and consequences of parasite interactions: African buffalo as a case study. In: K. Wilson, A. Fenton and D. Tompkins (Eds.), *Wildlife Disease Ecology: Linking Theory to Data and Application*. Cambridge: Cambridge University Press, pp. 129–160.

Ezenwa, V.O., A.E. Jolles and M.P. O'Brien (2009). A reliable body condition scoring technique for estimating condition in African buffalo. *African Journal of Ecology* 47(4): 476–481.

Fenton, A. (2008). Worms and germs: the population dynamic consequences of microparasite–macroparasite co-infection. *Parasitology* **135**(13): 1545–1560.

Fountain-Jones, N.M., C. Packer, M. Jacquot, et al. (2019). Endemic infection can shape exposure to novel pathogens: pathogen co-occurrence networks in the Serengeti lions. *Ecology Letters* **22**(6): 904–913.

Galen, S.C., J. Borner, J.L. Williamson, et al. (2020). Metatranscriptomics yields new genomic resources and sensitive detection of infections for diverse blood parasites. *Molecular Ecology Resources* **20**(1): 14–28.

Garabed, R.B., A. Jolles, H. Garira, et al. (2020). Multi-scale dynamics of infectious diseases. *Interface Focus* **10**(1): 20190118.

Glidden, C.K. (2020). *Individual Host to Population Scale Dynamics of Parasite Assemblages in African Buffalo of Kruger National Park, South Africa*. PhD thesis, Oregon State University.

Glidden, C.K., B. Beechler, P.E. Buss, et al. (2018). Detection of pathogen exposure in African buffalo using non-specific markers of inflammation. *Frontiers in Immunology* **8**: 1944.

Glidden, C.K., C.A.C. Coon, B.R. Beechler, et al. (2021). Co-infection best predicts respiratory viral infection in a wild host. *The Journal of Animal Ecology* **90**(3): 602–614.

Glidden, C.K., A.V. Koehler, R.S. Hall, et al. (2020). Elucidating cryptic dynamics of *Theileria* communities in African buffalo using a high-throughput sequencing informatics approach. *Ecology and Evolution* **10**(1): 70–80.

Gogarten, J.F., S. Calvignac-Spencer, C.L. Nunn, et al. (2020). Metabarcoding of eukaryotic parasite communities describes diverse parasite assemblages spanning the primate phylogeny. *Molecular Ecology Resources* **20**(1): 204–215.

Gorsich, E.E., R.S. Etienne, J. Medlock, et al. (2018). Opposite outcomes of coinfection at individual and population scales. *Proceedings of the National Academy of Sciences of the United States of America* **115**(29): 7545–7550.

Graham, A.L. (2008). Ecological rules governing helminth–microparasite coinfection. *Proceedings of the National Academy of Sciences* **105**(2): 566–570.

Hamilton, D.G., M.E. Jones, E.Z. Cameron, et al. (2020). Infectious disease and sickness behaviour: tumour progression affects interaction patterns and social network structure in wild Tasmanian devils. *Proceedings of The Royal Society Biological Sciences* **287**(1940): 20202454.

Henrichs, B., M.C. Oosthuizen, M. Troskie, et al. (2016). Within guild co-infections influence parasite community membership: a longitudinal study in African Buffalo. *The Journal of Animal Ecology* **85**(4): 1025–1034.

Hoarau, A.O.G., P. Mavingui and C. Lebarbenchon (2020). Coinfections in wildlife: focus on a neglected aspect of infectious disease epidemiology. *PLoS Pathogens* **16**(9): e1008790.

Hotez, P.J., D.H. Molyneux, A. Fenwick, et al. (2006). Incorporating a rapid-impact package for neglected tropical diseases with programs for HIV/AIDS, tuberculosis, and malaria. *PLoS Medicine* **3**(5): e102.

Jax, E., I. Müller, S. Börno, et al. (2021). Health monitoring in birds using bio-loggers and whole blood transcriptomics. *Scientific Reports* **11**(1): 10815.

Jolles, A.E., V.O. Ezenwa, R.S. Etienne, et al. (2008). Interactions between macroparasites and microparasites drive infection patterns in free-ranging African buffalo. *Ecology* **89**(8): 2239–2250.

Jolles, A., E. Gorsich, S. Gubbins, et al. (2021). Endemic persistence of a highly contagious pathogen: foot-and-mouth disease in its wildlife host. *Science* **374**(6563): 104–109.

Kock, R.A., M. Orynbayev, S. Robinson, et al. (2018). Saigas on the brink: multidisciplinary analysis of the factors influencing mass mortality events. *Science Advances* **4**(1): eaao2314.

Lello, J., B. Boag, A. Fenton, et al. (2004). Competition and mutualism among the gut helminths of a mammalian host. *Nature* **428**(6985): 840–844.

Leung, J.M., A.L. Graham and S.C.L. Knowles (2018). Parasite–microbiota interactions with the vertebrate gut: synthesis through an ecological lens. *Frontiers in Microbiology* **9**: 843.

Mabbott, N.A. (2018). The influence of parasite infections on host immunity to co-infection with other pathogens. *Frontiers in Immunology* **9**: 2579.

McDonald, C.A., A.V. Longo, K.R. Lips and K.R. Zamudio (2020). Incapacitating effects of fungal coinfection in a novel pathogen system. *Molecular Ecology* **29**(17): 3173–3186.

McGill, B.J., B.J. Enquist, E. Weiher and M. Westoby (2006). Rebuilding community ecology from functional traits. *Trends in Ecology and Evolution* **21**(4): 178–185.

Mosmann, T.R. and S. Sad (1996). The expanding universe of T-cell subsets: Th1, Th2 and more. *Immunology Today* **17**(3): 138–146.

Owen-Smith, N., G. Hopcraft, T. Morrison, et al. (2020). Movement ecology of large herbivores in African savannas: current knowledge and gaps. *Mammal Review* **50**(3): 252–266.

Pedersen, A.B. and A. Fenton (2007). Emphasizing the ecology in parasite community ecology. *Trends in Ecology and Evolution* **22**(3): 133–139.

Raberg, L., J.C. de Roode, A.S. Bell, et al. (2006). The role of immune-mediated apparent competition in genetically diverse malaria infections. *The American Naturalist* **168**(1): 41–53.

Sabey, K.A., S.J. Song, A. Jolles, et al. (2021). Coinfection and infection duration shape how pathogens affect the African buffalo gut microbiota. *The ISME Journal* **15**(5): 1359–1371.

Salgame, P., G.S. Yap and H.C. Gause (2013). Effect of helminth-induced immunity on infections with microbial pathogens. *Nature Immunology* **14**(11): 1118–1126.

Sallé, G., V. Deiss, C. Marquis, et al. (2020). Strongyle-resistant sheep express their potential across environments and leave limited scope for parasite plasticity. *bioRxiv* 161729. https://doi.org/10.1101/2020.06.19.161729

Sisson, D., J. Hufschmid, A. Jolles, et al. (2017). Molecular characterisation of Anaplasma species from African buffalo (*Syncerus caffer*) in Kruger National Park, South Africa. *Ticks and Tick-Borne Diseases* 8(3): 400–406.

Solvang, H.K. and S. Subbey (2019). Correction: An improved methodology for quantifying causality in complex ecological systems. *PLoS One* 14(6): e0217195.

Spaan, J.M., N. Pitts, P. Buss, et al. (2017). Experimental validation of fecal glucocorticoid metabolites as a non-invasive measure of stress response in African buffalo (*Syncerus caffer*) reveals resilience to immobilization and captivity. *Journal of Mammalogy* 98(5): 1288–1300.

Spaan, R.S., C.H. Epps, V.O. Ezenwa and A.E. Jolles (2019). Why did the buffalo cross the park? Resource shortages, but not infections, drive dispersal in female African buffalo (*Syncerus caffer*). *Ecology and Evolution* 9(10): 5651–5663.

Sugihara, G., R. May, H. Ye, et al. (2012). Detecting causality in complex ecosystems. *Science* 338(6106): 496–500.

Telfer, S., X. Lambin, R. Birtles, et al. (2010). Species interactions in a parasite community drive infection risk in a wildlife population. *Science* 330(6001): 243–246.

Tikhonov, G., N. Abrego, D. Dunson and O. Ovaskainen (2017). Using joint species distribution models for evaluating how species-to-species associations depend on the environmental context. *Methods in Ecology and Evolution* 8(4): 443–452.

Williams, C.L., A.M. Caraballo-Rodríguez, C. Allaband, et al. (2018). Wildlife–microbiome interactions and disease: exploring opportunities for disease mitigation across ecological scales. *Drug Discovery Today. Disease Models* 28: 105–115.

Williams, H.J., J.R. Shipley, C. Rutz, et al. (2021). Future trends in measuring physiology in free-living animals. *Philosophical Transactions of the Royal Society of London. Series B, Biological Sciences* 376(1831): 20200230.

Wilson, K., A. Fenton and D. Tompkins (2019). *Wildlife Disease Ecology: Linking Theory to Data and Application.* Cambridge: Cambridge University Press.

Zélé, F., S. Magalhães, S. Kéfi and A.B. Duncan (2018). Ecology and evolution of facilitation among symbionts. *Nature Communications* 9(1): 4869.

12 · *African Buffalo and Colonial Cattle: Is 'Systems Change' the Best Future for Farming and Nature in Africa?*

R. A. KOCK*, R. G. BENGIS*,
D. FEKADU SHIFERAW, F. GAKUYA,
D. MDETELE, H. H. T. PRINS, A. CARON
AND M. D. KOCK

Introduction

The African buffalo (*Syncerus caffer*) has historically been maligned in African colonial and post-colonial veterinary and livestock communities because of its reputation for being maintenance hosts for several infectious diseases that can impact the viability of the commercial livestock industry (Michel and Bengis, 2012). We provide here some historical context that justified this position, but will argue that this is an unfortunate and perhaps misguided and out-of-date narrative. The dogma perpetrated throughout colonial times that African livestock systems would naturally follow northern hemisphere production systems and disease control models has been, through retrospective social and economic analysis, challenged: '(...) the assumptions that the high-value/high cost option [in terms of livestock industry] is necessarily the best [in Africa] – and the one that should be striven for – and the low value/low cost [of extensive livestock] is automatically bad news are not upheld' (Scoones et al., 2010). The mandates of veterinary services are almost exclusively set up to protect intensive animal-based agriculture investments and trade. This paradigm is promoted by high-income industrialized countries, and most international trade ignores the impacts on wildlife economic opportunities and the realities of domestic livestock limitations in African countries that face restricted international trade

---

* Joint first authors.

opportunities. There is also a vested interest in maintaining this situation of perceived risk from disease, especially for the expansion of European breeds and modern intensive systems of livestock agriculture, which are often described as 'improved, productive and efficient' in contrast to African extensive and pastoral systems, reflecting a kind of neo-colonialism.

We argue that as the 'new deal' required by recognition of the Anthropocene becomes accepted, the dogma will change. Future economic, agricultural and overall development models will need to fit into the finite environmental envelop that will constrain human activities by choice or by force. There is a greater appreciation of the negative environmental, climate, health and socioeconomic externalities of intensive livestock systems, and of the need for more inclusive landscapes where biodiversity conservation and local citizens' well-being meet and more value is put on indigenous knowledge and value systems (cf. Gordon et al., 2016). African continental ownership of future policy has been controversial for decades and may well be the final arbiter on this controversy (Artz et al., 1991; Prins, 1989).

The Development of Coexistence of African Pastoralism with Wildlife

Contemporary views on buffalo reach back to the introduction of Eurasian cattle along with the colonization of the African continent. In the following sections, we focus on eastern and southern regions of Africa where most of the 'conflict' is expressed, and mostly exclude western and northern regions of the continent, where cattle herds have deep histories, including truly African breeds (Prins, 2000). Issues between cattle and buffalo in relation to disease are less pronounced in these regions, if only because buffalo are absent in the north and there are only small, scattered buffalo populations in the west where pastoral systems dominate (Kock et al., 2014; Chapter 4).

Before colonization, in the seventeenth century, large areas of the southern and western regions of southern Africa were sparsely populated by the nomadic hunter-gatherer San people and nomadic farmers (Khoikhoi/Khoisan) who were probably the first livestock owners in these southern lands. The more eastern and northern areas of southern Africa were inhabited by primarily Bantu groups who were also pastoralists, owning Sanga (Nguni) cattle, sheep and goats, and also growing edible crops (Maggs, 1986).

The situation in East Africa in the pre-colonial context was composed of extensive grasslands and traditional cattle owning coexisting with abundant wildlife. Wildlife behaviour and traditional livestock practices such as pastoralism and transhumance coevolved in East Africa, sharing space and participating in the engineering of open grassland savannas (Chapter 2). *Bos taurus africanus* or Sanga cattle is generally considered the indigenous African cattle from eastern African origins. African cattle were likely derived from complex introductions over centuries, and even from aurochs in Egyptian times from the Near East (Prins, 2000). Some species from North Africa are recognized to have existed beyond Egypt but are now extinct, for example *Bos primigenius mauretanicus* (Tikhonov, 2008). Along with hybridization between *B. taurus* and *B. indicus* or zebu cattle, a variety of breeds now constitute cattle populations in sub-Saharan Africa. These breeds coexisted with wildlife for over a thousand years and developed some resilience to infection, parasites and drought. Both pastoralism and wildlife may have benefited from each other, co-creating integrated landscapes. Wild ungulates used human-occupied areas to avoid predation by wild carnivores or, in the case of smaller antelopes, to benefit from areas grazed by cattle, feeding off early shoots after heavy cattle grazing (Augustine et al., 2011; Georgiadis et al., 2007; Odadi et al., 2011). In the case of the hirola antelope (*Beatragus hunteri*), the most endangered artiodactyl in Africa today, its survival in a narrow range in Kenya was closely linked to local pastoralists. Hirola, having become extinct elsewhere apart from a small part of Kenya, often concentrate, feeding around nutrient-rich old boma sites and short grasses established by livestock grazing pressure where predators are persecuted. Hence, they benefited inadvertently from traditional pastoralism while indigenous people considered the presence of hirola as a good sign for their cattle (Andanje, 2002). The relationship with wildlife was used to predict resource availability (tracking movements) and as a source of culture and food when necessary (Lankester and Davis, 2016). Presently, with the wide availability of guns, rifles and other weaponry in the hands of pastoralists, this has changed, and the hirola is now next-to-extinct and features on the IUCN Red List.

Archaeological data indicate that diseases at the wildlife/livestock interface may also have been an important component of this interaction. Even with indigenous breeds of cattle, the establishment of pastoralism in some African ecosystems was constrained by wildlife and vector-mediated diseases, such as tick-borne diseases (e.g. East Coast fever, ECF), trypanosomiasis and malignant catarrhal fever (MCF).

Practices such as fire, bush-clearing and contact avoidance, respectively, have taken time to evolve to counter sanitary threats and allow pastoralism to colonize new landscapes (Gifford-Gonzalez, 2000). Most of Africa's livestock farmers practiced (and still do) unfenced extensive systems with indigenous breeds of cattle (historical hybrid *B. indicus* and *B. taurus africanus*). These breeds and systems have proven to be more sustainable and resilient to infectious diseases, parasites, heat and droughts when compared to most *B. taurus* breeds and livestock systems imported from Europe (Mattioli et al., 2000; Morris, 2007). Under conditions of widespread vectors and pathogens in Africa, acquired resistance enables greater sustainability of traditional livestock keeping and resilience in the face of epidemic and endemic diseases. Little control is practiced, and fencing is very limited in its use in African rangeland, mostly to separate a few historical ranches from open range. Most of the separation between buffalo and African cattle herds derives from behavioural determinants, mostly human aggression and use of dogs for reasons other than disease, with an avoidance response from buffalo herds leading to their predominance in protected areas where humans and domestic animals are mostly excluded.

Re-Drawing of the African Landscape – Colonization and De-Colonization – Emergence of Production-Oriented Livestock Systems in Africa

Southern Africa was one of the earliest subregions to be colonized by European settlers, which took place in the seventeenth and eighteenth centuries. The settlers landing in the southern Cape were European with a drive towards settled agriculture and land tenure, which was not part of indigenous tribal cultures. These moves led to major conflicts not only between different European cultures but with several tribes over land and resources. This territorial expansionism by the settlers accelerated in the nineteenth century and culminated in the forming of several nation-states. These included the Boer republics in South Africa and periods of British sovereignty over large areas of southern Africa up to the miombo belts and forests of East and Central Africa, as well as the German colonization of South West Africa (Namibia) and East Africa (Tanganyika, Ruanda-Urundi). In addition, around the end of the nineteenth century, serious colonization of East Africa by the Germans and British happened with Tanganyika ultimately falling under British rule on behalf of the League of Nations.

During these territorial expansion periods, settlers, European hunters, war and disease all eventually had major impacts on wildlife populations. The settlers were heavily reliant on hunting to supply their daily protein needs, and there are many historical accounts of wild herds stretching from 'horizon to horizon' (e.g. Beard, 1977; Prins and De Jong, 2022). There was also a large amount of commercial hunting for dried meat and hides as well as sport hunting for trophies, the slaughter continuing unabated as though the resource was limitless and infinite. These practices were also used to clear land to make space for grazing domestic stock, with wildlife numbers suffering through depredation and competition. In South Africa, the kwagga (*Equus quagga*), Cape lion (*Panthera leo melanochaita*) and bluebuck (*Hippotragus leucophaeus*) were driven to extinction, and the bontebok (*Damaliscus dorcas dorcas*), white rhinoceros (*Ceratotherium simum*) and Cape mountain zebra (*Equus zebra*) were pushed to the brink. Countless animals were killed to feed trading safaris, and colonial armies also were fed meat from game. Lands were cleared of wildlife species to create space for white settlers and local farmers alike, as in Kenya (Adamson, 1968, pp. 97 ff, 120) and many other places. The total number of African elephants (*Loxodonta africana*) killed by elephant control officers in East and southern Africa may perhaps be equal to the number that was poached for their ivory. The onslaught on Kenyan wildlife during World War II is jaw-dropping, where herds of game were used as targets to represent enemy troops and elephant herds were even bombed (Prins and De Jong, 2022).

In southern Africa, the power lay with cattle keeping and agriculture communities during colonization, while National Parks (NPs) were seen as the only way to address perceptions of irrational pastoralism (Lankester and Davis, 2016). Ironically, the strong militarization of protected areas, including the post-independence exclusion of people from traditional lands and even the banning of hunting (both sport and traditional), generated animosity which may even have laid the foundations for the poaching of elephant, rhinoceros and other species after the colonies collapsed. In each of these arenas, there was inevitably conflict. For example, in southern Rhodesia, wildlife were culled extensively to create buffer zones between wildlife-rich areas and colonial farmer production areas for various reasons (Mutwira, 1989), and to target the preferred hosts of tsetse flies in order to reduce tsetse-infested areas and the occurrence of trypanosomiasis (e.g. Zululand; Andersson and Cumming, 2014).

With colonization, pastoralism was also catastrophically reduced through the introduction of contagious bovine pleuropneumonia, followed by the great rinderpest pandemic (the Masai–Maa cultural group was reduced by two-thirds: Prins and De Jong, 2022; Box 12.1). Some wildlife species also suffered huge losses in East and southern Africa, deregulating African savannas' trajectories in the following decades with alteration of the habitat (e.g. bush encroachment; Holdo et al., 2009) and wildlife diversity and abundance (reduction then increase following the space liberated by human populations). The phylogenetic relationship between African buffalo and cattle, although quite distant (Chapter 2), leads to shared pathogens and led to the frequent

---

Box 12.1 *Impact of the Great African Plague Rinderpest on Livestock Development*

A major event that influenced agricultural thinking was the emergence of novel pathogens exotic to Africa, for example, rinderpest and contagious bovine pleuropneumonia or CBPP (Chapter 9). The great pandemic of the late nineteenth century caused by Rinderpest (a morbillivirus) killed almost all cattle it infected and wiped out a large proportion of the indigenous wildlife herds from North to South Africa, resulting in huge epidemics in buffalo with massive mortality. In many cases, only small relict populations of some species survived in remote pockets or were entirely extirpated from their former ranges. Impacts were seen on some keystone species including migrating East African wildebeest (*Connochaetes taurinus*). This had major impacts on the scale of migration and habitat with a transformation in vegetation types and distribution (Holdo et al., 2009).

Veterinary services were launched at about the same time as colonial administration became established, with the task of disease control to support the further development of livestock systems. Ironically, the loss of indigenous breeds made way for the colonists to import European breeds and hybrids favoured for their high potential for milk and meat production. These colonial cattle herds, with their innate vulnerabilities, soon came into conflict with buffalo in southern Africa.

These changes were reversed, with the elimination of the virus (officially in 2011) proving a strong disease and ecology relationship, uncommonly proven.

accusations of the buffalo being a reservoir of key livestock diseases during colonial and post-colonial eras. The buffalo became synonymous with the early concept of the so-called wildlife–livestock interface in Africa (Kock, 2006), showing the buffalo's prominent role in several diseases (Chapter 9). During colonial times, the epidemiology was poorly understood and quantified, and most of the evidence was derived from a few human-altered ecosystems, mainly in southern Africa. At least in this region, the negative perception of wildlife and diseases led to clear segregation of land uses dedicated to livestock production and the separation of domestic and wild ecosystems. New diseases and pressure from white colonialists forced traditional pastoralists and their livestock into newly emerging tsetse fly (*Glossina* spp.) belts (Prins and De Jong, 2022). In East Africa, this was less of an issue because local livestock and forestry, for instance, could be combined (Brasnett et al., 1948). This divergence between concepts of 'modern' livestock agriculture and traditional pastoralism, between the south and the north, took on sociocultural and political dimensions. During colonial or European rule, a narrative against traditional local livestock keeping in Africa developed, and this has persisted to some extent, frequently justified by the disease paradigm and from where the power in control policies lies, which is mostly within industrialized western nations. This was understandable given that epidemic and vector-borne livestock diseases were a major constraint to the expansion of European livestock systems in southern Africa (e.g. Gunn, 1932), while in the east and west of the continent, the pastoral systems thrived. Attempts at ranching cattle gradually declined over the twentieth century in East Africa, with large landholdings reverting successfully to wildlife–cattle integrated management with meat and tourism activities and, sometimes, communal ownership (NRT, 2020).

Positively, the colonial era inspired protection of game and areas of land in law. However, as royalty had given hunting rights exclusively to the wealthy in Europe, colonialists discriminated against local people and limited people of pastoral communities' access, making wildlife a preserve of the rich behind a conservation banner. People and animals were negotiated or shifted away and excluded from extensive productive rangelands, and this has persisted to this day.

The pattern of wildlife decline was repeated in eastern and Central Africa during the period of decolonization from the mid-twentieth century. Indigenous communities and rebel armies slaughtered game in the transition periods, partly during conflict for food, and to push back against colonial masters, conducting revenge killings after years of exclusion and to avoid future restrictions by eliminating game. However, some positive post-colonial developments based on the colonial systems should be noted. For example, in Kenya, these included much-debated bans on hunting (Anon., 1977) in attempts to slow the decline in wildlife; improved protection agencies; and eradication of rinderpest, a big killer of buffalo (Kock, 2006). These measures appear to have stabilized buffalo numbers, at least in Kenya, over the last three decades (Grunblatt et al., 1996; KWS, 2021). Ironically, after the end of the colonial era, the same colonial model of disease management was adopted by emerging states with identical results. For the natural ecologies in these areas to recover, old paradigms had to be overturned or remain to be challenged. Interestingly, in the fields of human health and global health, this theme has also been gathering momentum as shackles remain on poor countries and a few high-income countries dictate the human health and health industry agenda (Büyüm et al., 2020).

Current Situation at The Interface, The Burden of History and the Weight of Changes

Today, many new pressures, including climate change, human population growth, associated buffalo–cattle–human conflicts (Matseketsa et al., 2019) and agriculture (Prins and De Jong, 2022) are reducing the viability of buffalo populations, now highly dependent on protection. In much of sub-Saharan Africa, with under-investment from abroad, land-use pressure is mounting with heavy investment in extractive industries, including forestry, and mining, while the human population is growing at a particularly high rate. This human population impact on land is, to some extent, compensated by urbanization, but demand for food continues to grow. As a result, the lands that were designated for wildlife and pastoralism are being encroached on and put under increasing pressure. Increasing populations of livestock, more or less replacing wild ungulates, have been documented in some countries and regions such as Ethiopia (Gebretsadik, 2016), and countries with strong wildlife economies like Kenya have also been affected, but at a slower rate (Ogutu et al., 2016). Political power lies in the hands of urban communities and agriculturalists, while pastoralists are weakly represented in government. These communities have historically been persecuted and discriminated against through land-use policy that removes key resource areas from their control. Some of these conflicts, especially in West and Central Africa, remain serious and violent, with recent examples within the Fulani (a.k.a. Peul) pastoralists community around the Lake Chad basin. Today, there is an East and Central African model, where open rangeland remains available and true pastoralism and transhumance are still practiced, and a southern African model, where land tenure has dominated the scene for the past 200 years, and little 'open' rangeland still exists.

The 'trade sensitivity' around the main diseases impacting livestock production that were prominent in Europe at the time of colonization was simply transplanted into African colonial systems (see, for instance, Empire Marketing Board, 1930). In some regions of sub-Saharan Africa, disease in wildlife is still seen by animal health agencies as a significant barrier to agricultural development. However, we posit, that is mostly a result of residual dogma and supporting narrow policies that benefit the main agribusinesses trading in a globalized world. Veterinary fencing, with a primary role to separate buffalo from cattle populations, has been used extensively across southern Africa (Chigwenhese et al., 2016; Ferguson and Hanks, 2010), but is cropping up in Europe too (like the wild boar fence separating Denmark from Germany) and has been in place in Australia since the end of the 1800s. Even until the present day, the government veterinary services of South Africa, Zimbabwe, Botswana and Namibia all practice so-called 'hard edge' disease control measures, which include barrier fences such as the Kruger NP (KNP) western and southern boundary fence (restricting contact with livestock in South Africa – while the eastern Mozambique fence is only partially closed), the Ngamiland buffalo fence (partly separating the Okavango Delta from livestock areas in Botswana) and the Namibian veterinary cordon fence to prevent contact between commercial livestock and wildlife, particularly buffalo. In Zimbabwe, 55 per cent of the buffalo population is fenced today, and this policy is sometimes supported by conservation non-governmental organizations (NGOs) sharing an interest in preventing cattle and people from entering the protected areas and wildlife from getting out. A similar cordon line exists between Western Zambia and Angola. These veterinary measures clearly separate commercial livestock production that is protected for their markets versus wildlife systems and small-scale livestock production imprisoned in the fenced areas and unable to be marketed. Indeed, Botswana's fences protect blocks that are designated for commercial trade with a foreign region (European Union) and certainly constrain local production and compromise local food security, with devastating consequences on wildlife communities and ecosystems. To show the tenacity of such beliefs and practices, the Veterinary Cordon Fence in Namibia was enacted by the German Reichstag in 1905, and still discriminates between livestock producers from beyond the fence and those 'on the right side' of it (e.g. Miescher, 2012; Tjaronda, 2008). In addition, certain designated geographical control zones have been declared for diseases such as foot and mouth disease (FMD), African swine fever and corridor disease (buffalo-associated theileriosis) in South Africa. As in Botswana, these are primarily intended to protect designated production zones exporting to high-end meat markets. Its mirror side, however, is that by framing cattle meat as coming from potentially 'dangerous' areas where veterinary control may be wanting, farmers in these importing countries are enabled to prevent competing meat from coming to 'their' market (Robinson, 2017; Whittington et al., 2019). This fencing policy, mostly imposed by the state on local stakeholders is costly, opposed by pastoralists and accepted by commercial livestock and crop farmers for obvious reasons. In all but a few cases (UNEP, 2011), fences are detrimental to wildlife movements and conservation, and they require significant maintenance (De Jong et al., 2020; Gadd, 2012). In the absence of good maintenance, fencing deteriorates and becomes porous (Chigwenhese et al., 2016).

However, to some extent fencing for disease control and for reducing wildlife conflict with people and agriculture has taken hold in much of the continent. In East Africa, arguments against this approach seem to have helped to slow any progression down this path for reasons of disease control (Kock, 2010). In many situations, with open interfaces between protected areas and communal land, buffalo's natural and adaptive avoidance of cattle reduces the risk of disease spillover, and these systems show high tolerance to infection without many diseases expressed (Caron et al., 2016; Meunier et al., 2017; Valls-Fox et al., 2018). In times of drought, contact rates can change dramatically and disease epidemics are more likely to occur (Bengis et al., 2002; Kock, 2005). A severe drought in Kenya from 1993 to 1994 probably precipitated the large rinderpest outbreak in the 1990s in East Africa (Kock et al., 1999, 2006), killing 60 per cent of buffalo in the Tsavo National Park ecosystem. However, this drought killed some 70 per cent of the buffalo in the Masai Mara even before the disease arrived (Dublin and Ogutu, 2015). In East Africa, livestock remained in open pastoral systems and coexisted with wildlife, which thrived (Homewood et al., 2012), but mostly with buffalo only surviving in protected areas and buffer zones. Agropastoral, farm or ranching communities and pastoralists are known to use self-managed movement control to avoid epidemics. However, increasing densities of people and their livestock ultimately can continue to lead, in the absence of new policy, to the demise of wildlife (Prins, 1992; Prins and de Jong, 2022). This is not inevitable; for example, more integrated developments in pastoral land use, such as in Kenya, have led to remarkable overall stability in wildlife populations over decades, despite rapid development, human population expansion and declines of wildlife on state lands (KWS, 2021).

When there is insistence on disease elimination rather than control in livestock, the interface becomes more threatening. De Vos et al. (2016) clearly described, for example, the challenge in South Africa of perceptions around certain species and diseases stating,

The majority of endemic pathogens found in protected areas do not kill large numbers of wild animals or infect many people, and may even play valuable ecological roles; but occasional disease outbreaks and mortalities can have a large impact on public perceptions and disease management, potentially making protected areas unviable in one or more of their stated aims. Neighbouring landowners also have a significant impact on park management decisions. The indirect effects triggered by disease in the human social and economic components of protected areas and surrounding landscapes may ultimately have a greater influence on protected area resilience than the direct ecological perturbations caused by disease.

In more extensive pastoral systems, wildlife and livestock remain integrated to some degree, with designated protected areas allowing the survival of core buffalo populations. The protected area models adopted in West and Central Africa, with core protected areas surrounded by buffer zones with limited human activities (e.g. game hunting, some pastoral activities) offered management of the buffalo/cattle interface that has allowed the survival of core buffalo populations, even if isolated (Bauer et al., 2020), as long as there was no security crisis. That system has subsequently collapsed in many places in West and Central Africa (Scholte et al., 2021), and perhaps only timber concessions and privately managed reserves appear to maintain buffalo (Chapter 4). Even though open systems have allowed wildlife to thrive, buffalo are not tolerated by pastoral livestock owners due to the aggression sometimes shown by buffalo to pastoralists and direct competition for water and grazing. This has led to the virtual extirpation of buffalo from some communal lands (Metzger et al., 2010). There are a few exceptions with forest buffalo (*Syncerus caffer nanus*) and some savanna buffalo in forested areas such as Boni Dodori in Kenya, where large populations >10,000 share habitat with hunter-gatherer/small-scale cropping communities (Chapter 4). A similar peaceful coexistence can be seen in along the Kazinga Channel between Lakes Edward and George in Uganda (Kock, personal observation).

Where a wildlife economy dominates as a source of foreign exchange revenue over agriculture, such as in Kenya and Tanzania, the political establishment lends a more sympathetic ear. In addition, and perhaps as a result, all attempts at draconian veterinary measures detrimental to the wildlife and pastoral economy have never been applied successfully, even if policies exist on paper. A sustainable balance is often achieved, allowing for livestock keeping and healthy wildlife populations to be conserved and contributing to tourism and the economy. Increasingly this tourism industry is locally owned and beneficial to indigenous communities (Mureithi et al., 2019; Tyrrell et al., 2017; Western et al., 2020). While in the south of the continent, where livestock owners were well connected politically and largely dominated the land-use arguments in favour of agriculture for over a century (Munangándu et al., 2006), this has been reversed to some extent more recently, with an expansion of wildlife ranching and conservancies (Chapter 13). In many of these ranches and conservancies in South Africa, integrated farming with livestock and wildlife now takes place, but with the exclusion of buffalo and large predators. Legislation dictates that buffalo and cattle may not be kept on the same property.

In addition to these influences, a failure to invest in local communities around wildlife protected areas brings more pressure. Estimates of locally shared revenue from conservation areas like the Serengeti are only 5 per cent of total annual income and only go to a few households, with the majority of beneficiaries being a distant private sector and government exchequers (Homewood et al., 2012; Lankester and Davis, 2016). In Zimbabwe, where *Operation CAMPFIRE* first resulted in much higher revenue sharing with local communities, this community benefit fell to only a few euros per year after the CAMPFIRE strategy was 'invaded' by local politicians and bureaucrats (Poshiwa et al., 2013a, 2013b). We are not judging what was or is right or wrong in this debate on 'human versus biodiversity rights', but are trying to present the different perspectives and historical precedence around disease which may explain past and current actions.

Recovery of African Pastoralism and Wildlife in Africa – Is This Possible?

With ongoing climate change and continuing human population growth, as resources decline and drylands increase, the use of available water from rivers and wetlands will probably increase the likelihood of buffalo and cattle meeting. Increased grazing pressure may result in ecological disturbance and degradation of natural resources. If this progresses, the natural disease regulation benefits of the ecosystems may begin to decline and vector–host–pathogen dynamics may be disturbed, which will impact livestock more. Eventually, wildlife may also suffer as malnutrition and stress erode even their resilience to disease, and whole ecosystems may begin to decline with population crashes. As buffalo are removed from pastoral or agriculturally designated lands, they are still frequently blamed as a source of diseases for livestock kept by communities surrounding the conserved areas where buffalo are mostly found. In addition, the ecological consequences of agriculture, ranching and overall degradation of fenced land, especially with high stocking rates, create poor conditions for ungulates and increased vulnerabilities to disease irrespective of the presence of carrier animals peripherally or in the parks (Glover et al., 2020; Kinne et al., 2010). However, the conflict remains high in livestock keepers' minds. As populations of cattle grow, the domestic animals themselves become more epidemiologically significant, through a mere numerical relationship, and become the main carriers of diseases and a preferred food source for disease vectors (Channumsin et al., 2019; Clausen et al., 1998). This can change the epidemiological dynamics of pathogens locally, shifting the role of wild and domestic species, and can drive the further spread of disease within the domestic population, the community of wild and domestic ungulates, which may include spillback to wildlife.

With today's improved epidemiological knowledge, better diagnostic tests and better livestock vaccines, it is hoped that African endemic disease control can become less conflictual and more environmentally friendly. The movement of diseases between wildlife and livestock is in fact bi-directional. With dwindling wildlife numbers in many countries (especially in West and Central Africa: Chapter 4), wild animals can also be threatened by persistent livestock disease spillover (e.g. bovine tuberculosis, peste des petits ruminants and brucellosis) to naive and sometimes critically endangered wildlife (Pruvot et al., 2020; Shury et al., 2015; Viggers et al., 1993; White et al., 2011; Chapter 9).

More recently, changing views on livestock management and values of wildlife have resulted in the fading away of earlier red lines on diseases such as FMD (Ferguson et al., 2013; Weaver et al., 2013). Strengthening wildlife-based economies in Africa, and innovative thinking around integrative management of wildlife and livestock and the rangelands in which they coexist, are increasing environmentally friendly land uses (Ferguson et al., 2013). Development of softer disease policies such as the use of commodity-based trade (CBT) to circumvent FMD trade restrictions renders FMD elimination an obsolete goal (Thomson et al., 2013) even if currently its acceptance remains slow. Nevertheless, there are now increasing opportunities for trade without disease control burdens. The emphasis on intensive husbandry of livestock with production and profit as the main goal is shifting towards more sustainability in food systems. Other benefits of mixed rangeland management include climate change mitigation and reduction in disease control costs. Perhaps the ultimate arbiter of future livestock systems will be the concerns over their role in biodiversity loss, as competitors for food crops which might otherwise be used for humans and climate change ramifications. A shift from animal- to plant-based diets is gaining momentum in many countries in Africa where meat consumption remains low per capita compared to other continents while biodiversity remains high (Figure 12.1).

In South Africa, a buffalo production model emerged in the 1990s and has evolved to this today with controversial outcomes (Box 12.2). The more visionary wildlife ranching and community-based natural resource management (CBNRM) practiced in Namibia and Zimbabwe since the 1970s, utilizing mainly the extensive and relatively free-range systems and conservancies, has been important in bringing communities on board. Kenya and Tanzania have taken strides in recent decades, with integrated pastoral livestock and wildlife ecosystems such as the Northern Rangeland Trust and Ngorongoro Conservation Area, respectively. However, upheavals and violence in the latter area in 2022 may throw another light on the success of this narrative (Kihwele et al., 2021; ROAPE, 2022). In regard to such initiatives, South Africa is lagging behind, with Uganda and Ethiopia and countries in West Africa (with large and small buffalo populations) even more so.

Under several proposed future alternative development scenarios, if land is released from animal production for rewilding, disease epidemics are likely to decrease without abundant domestic animal host populations. Historic concerns about wildlife as disease reservoirs will dissipate, resource competition will decline and wildlife-based economic opportunities will arise.

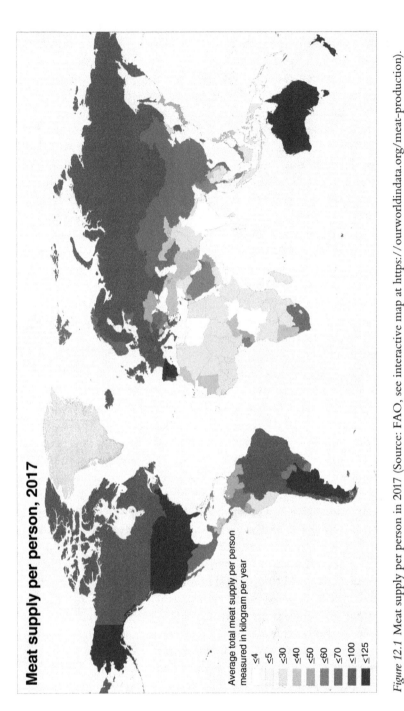

Meat supply per person, 2017

Average total meat supply per person
measured in kilogram per year

≤4
≤5
≤30
≤40
≤50
≤60
≤70
≤100
≤125

Figure 12.1 Meat supply per person in 2017 (Source: FAO, see interactive map at https://ourworldindata.org/meat-production). This illustrates how the narratives around Africa and meat consumption are largely distorted. Africa has much more sustainable low-impact animal-based agriculture and wild meat consumption in terms of environment, biodiversity and climate change. A wildlife economy continuing and developing alongside an agricultural economy in Africa could address and prevent many of the challenges currently facing advanced economies.

Box 12.2 *Buffalo as a Production Animal in South Africa: A Case Study*

The uses of buffalo as a production animal or for trophy hunting are covered in Chapters 13 and 16. However, it is pertinent to showcase the intensification of buffalo production (semi-intensive and intensive production systems: Chapter 13), separated from cattle production but along the modern northern hemisphere economic model (privatization, compartmentalization, commodification of nature for capitalist markets) within a sector sometimes disconnected from nature.

In South Africa, KNP authorities developed a project between 1996 and 2006 in response to concerns about invasive bovine tuberculosis (bTB) and the unique genetics of their infected buffalo population, as well as commercial interests (Bengis and Grobler, 2000). The objective was to breed specific pathogen-free (SPF) buffalo calves from infected parent stock. Approximately 460 SPF buffalo calves free of FMD, theileriosis, bTB and bovine brucellosis were produced during the lifetime of the Kruger project. Many more so-called SPF calves were also produced from infected parent stock in private facilities within the FMD control zone. The offspring of these original buffalo were translocated to other NPs that did not have buffalo, which was in itself a major conservation goal, and today, Pilanesberg, Vaalbos, Marikele, Mountain Zebra and Mokala NPs all have viable, relatively free-ranging populations of Kruger buffalo in multi-species and extensive systems. Some SPF offspring were also supplied to private wildlife ranches throughout South Africa. Today, these privately owned SPF buffalo are being kept under intensive, semi-intensive and extensive conditions. Under more 'controlled' and intensive ranching conditions, population health appears to deteriorate and any resilience benefit of wildlife over cattle is diminished. Diseases in intensively managed captive buffalo further show this tendency for a shift in pathogenicity when animals are removed from their natural ecosystems with, for example, FMD expressed through weight loss and lymphadenopathy (Vosloo et al., 2007), bTB and Rift Valley fever-associated morbidity and mortality also expressed under certain conditions (Beechler et al., 2015). With these more intensive systems, endo- and ectoparasite control also became important. In addition, some SPF buffalo raised under conditions of minimal exposure to disease vectors have actually died from theileriosis, MCF and even heartwater after significant tick exposure or contact with wildebeest or sheep. These are diseases to which buffalo are normally totally resistant.

The fact that these SPF buffalo are now present on wildlife ranches in all nine provinces of South Africa has been problematic for the State Veterinary Services. Legislation requires that all farms that have buffalo must be registered, and any buffalo movement from one property to another requires animals to be retested for all four diseases. There is also concern over veterinary management options should an outbreak of any of these dreaded diseases occur in this diffuse privately owned population. This concern has continued to lead to discrimination against buffalo in the last decades; for example, SPF buffalo breeding project expansion in South Africa has been curtailed by the Veterinary Department. As the evidence shows, replacing a commercial domestic cattle model with a wildlife ranch model may not work as any intensification and interruption of natural ecological processes is fraught with problems and disease is clearly one.

Some of these trends relate to the veterinary controls and historical separation of animals and subsequent commercialization of wildlife species. In this regard, the difference between extensive versus more intensive forms of buffalo production needs to be appreciated. While extensive systems can certainly achieve important conservation goals, in contrast, the more intensive forms of production, despite claiming to be contributing to species conservation, are not recognized by conservation bodies such as IUCN. The recent legal change in South Africa where some of these species may be listed as farming animals for intensive commercialization further demonstrates this shift and effectively disconnects these populations from nature. Animals raised in these intensive production systems should not be used for conservation purposes, such as reintroductions or reinforcements of natural populations, due to the risk of introduction of production diseases or of animals which are 'disease-free' becoming exposed to natural disease cycles. In addition, a potential genetic shift and/or altered production genes may be deleterious to natural ecologies (cf. wild boar *Sus scrofa*; Martínez-Avilés et al., 2020). Land uses in which SPF buffalo are produced intensively and artificially selected should not be connected to natural ecosystems or protected areas for conservation purposes.

Are Buffalo and the Diseases They Carry Still a Concern in the Modern African Landscape?

As observed, the diseases which have been much thought of in the context of buffalo and cattle are African strains of FMD, corridor disease (theileriosis), bTB, brucellosis, trypanosomiasis, heartwater and Rift Valley fever (Michel and Bengis, 2012; Chapter 9). African buffalo are believed to serve as maintenance or incidental hosts and amplifiers of these cattle diseases with potential spillback (Musoke et al., 2015). However, there is relatively little supportive evidence for spillback happening, and new evidence is challenging long-held assumptions. In truth, cross-species infections are rarely documented or confirmed, but epidemics can occur, especially where there is a policy on disease elimination in livestock, and a hard boundary between disease-free and infected populations created by fencing. The following paragraphs provide examples to illustrate the trends.

There is no doubt that FMD SAT strains are maintained by buffalo, and they may represent the original coevolved host (Anderson et al., 1979; Thomson and Bastos, 2004). However, as with many 'emerging' infectious diseases, confirming origins retrospectively is nearly impossible. Cattle that are FMD-free can be at risk of a breakdown in status at any interface with buffalo and other carriers of the virus (Guerrini et al., 2019; Hargreaves et al., 2004; Miguel et al., 2013). However, even this strong narrative of buffalo being the original sole 'source' of SAT strains of FMD in Africa is now in question. Buffalo may perhaps have been so historically, but more recent evidence in certain regions of the continent shows that cattle can also maintain cattle-adapted SAT strains for extended periods (Omondi et al., 2020; Wekesa et al., 2015). Not all cattle outbreaks with SAT viruses might have been from buffalo, but in several southern African countries, cattle outbreaks have been shown to be caused mainly by buffalo isolates. Many of these buffalo isolates that are regularly mutating have subsequently been incorporated into cattle vaccines.

Some vector-borne diseases – for example, the tick-borne disease theileriosis and heartwater – can cause very high mortality (up to 100 per cent) in naive African cattle (Lawrence, 1992; Neitz et al., 1955), while certain exposed cattle populations living at extensive buffalo/cattle interfaces suffer fewer losses (Young, 1981). As with FMD, cattle-adapted *Theileria* strains have evolved and emerged, causing the diseases known as East Coast fever (ECF) and Zimbabwe theileriosis (January disease), and these diseases can circulate independently in cattle without any buffalo presence. In addition, with regards to heartwater, the development of premunity and endemic stability has resulted in fewer losses. Other vector-borne diseases can have multiple reservoir hosts. With trypanosomiasis, wildlife certainly provides reservoir hosts, some preferred by tsetse flies, such as buffalo, wild porcines, spiral-horned antelopes and elephants, but from a risk perspective, these populations can also dampen environmental infection loads away from livestock and humans, reducing disease risk and impacts (Channumsin et al., 2019; Clausen et al., 1998). As with the Rift Valley fever virus, buffalo are susceptible but are only one among a myriad of susceptible wild and domesticated ruminants (Swanepoel, 1976).

On the bacterial side, even if livestock-origin brucellosis and bTB have crossed the 'species barrier' many times, their impact on free-ranging populations of buffalo appears to be ecologically insignificant. For brucellosis, this is true even in populations where brucella spp. antibody prevalence is quite high, as in KNP, South Africa (De Vos and van Niekerk, 1969; Herr and Marshall, 1981; Ndengu et al., 2017) with occasional reports of disease in buffalo and spillover to other species (Condy and Vickers, 1972; Gradwell et al., 1977). Certainly, the observation of hygromas in older buffalo is not uncommon throughout the buffalo range. Much more has been published on bTB in buffalo, but almost exclusively focused on South Africa (but see Sintayehu et al., 2017a), where it is thought to have been introduced with cattle imports in the eighteenth and nineteenth centuries (Paine and Martinaglia, 1928). The most attention is given to the 'compressed' fenced or semi-fenced protected areas such as KNP and Hluluwe/Umfolozi NP (Bengis et al., 1996; de Garine-Wichatitsky et al., 2010), with high buffalo densities. Here, there are concerning trends with buffalo apparently suffering some disease and mortality. There is evidence that this species is also driving infection in other wildlife species such as lions, *Panthera leo* (Keet et al., 1996), greater kudu, *Tragelaphus strepsiceros* (Keet et al., 2001) and chacma baboons, *Papio ursinus* (Keet et al., 2000). This has raised conservation concerns regarding less-populous species and predator/scavenger impacts. In more open unfenced systems in Uganda, bTB was confirmed around the 1960s and seroprevalence for bTB has been consistently high in buffalo over the intervening years, yet the disease is rarely reported (Guilbride et al., 1963; Meunier et al., 2017; Woodford, 1982a, 1982b). In Ethiopian pastoral systems, and likely in other pastoral systems too, the patterns of bTB are closely linked to human social networks (Sintayehu et al., 2017a). There are also efforts in Ethiopia to establish risk factors for cattle TB associated with wildlife (Sintayehu et al., 2017b). These are multi-species and slowly developing diseases with a long time course before clinical expression, and they are both zoonoses, so need to be monitored.

Anthrax is another multi-species disease that occurs on most continents, and in Africa epidemics occur in wildlife and these are sometimes associated with epidemics in livestock (Mukarati et al., 2020). Epidemiologically, this spillover may well be mostly driven by insect mechanical vectors such as blowflies and biting flies and through contamination of browse, pasture or water (Bengis, 2012; De Vos and Turnbull, 2004; Ebedes, 1976; Hugh-Jones and De Vos, 2002; Prins and Weyerhauser, 1987). Evidence from Ethiopia suggests some significant recorded events in wildlife occurred after a series of livestock outbreaks (Shiferaw et al., 2002), and in the Serengeti, wildlife anthrax epidemics tend to occur during droughts, clustered around contaminated sites such as water holes/salt licks and similar locations where aggregation and mixing of species can occur (Hampson et al., 2011).

It certainly can be argued that introduced cattle diseases on the African continent have had impacts on both the cattle industry and wildlife. Indirectly, the impact on wildlife has been seen through the implementation of control measures. Fortunately, in open mixed rangelands systems, these introduced diseases and the buffalo-endemic diseases are of little consequence to wildlife populations, other than rinderpest. There is a need to re-evaluate historic and modern disease dialogues, rather than perpetuating the old narratives and the prejudice against wildlife as disease reservoirs.

Buffalo have attracted significant research, often becoming the centre of investigations, with this focus perhaps reinforcing preconceptions of their relative disease role and significance. Of 79 publications recorded in a scoping review on viruses in ungulates (Swanepoel et al., 2021), 41 were on FMD in buffalo. This high number is most probably due to the funding available and international interest among researchers for this disease. Buffalo are overstudied without considering other species found in the same environment or the role of cattle themselves in the persistence and spread of infection. As a consequence, the roles of these other wild ungulates (e.g. greater kudu, Thompson's gazelle [*Gazella thomsonii*], impala [*Aepyceros melampus*] or blue wildebeest [*Connochaetes taurinus*]) are relatively unknown despite evidence of their role in a few specific breakdowns and cattle epidemics historically (Weaver et al., 2013). In KNP, which has an endemically infected buffalo population, clinical spill-over FMD has also been confirmed in impala, greater kudu, bushbuck (*Tragelaphus scriptus*), common warthog (*Phacochoerus africanus*) and giraffe (*Giraffa cameleopardalis*), but with relatively mild symptoms observed rarely (e.g. impala; Vosloo et al., 2009).

Towards a New Vision

In the context of disease transfer between buffalo and cattle, who is to blame? The most significant problems for wildlife and cattle stem from the introduction of exotic breeds and their diseases into Africa and the production and trade model that came with them. Models of coex-istence between buffalo and African cattle breeds existed during the pre-colonial era only to be disturbed by the introduction of susceptible European breeds and their northern hemisphere pathogens during the colonial period. In addition, the endemic disease risks to introduced cattle, especially for the so-called improved breeds, are very high. The full benefits of buffalo (as a comparable bovid) in the context of the animal and land use are clear but are not being realized, except in some specific land use examples. Most buffalo populations have been reduced to small relict herds, especially in West and Central Africa. If buffalo go extinct, cattle will provide poor compensation for this highly adapted species.

On the other hand, from a disease risk perspective, the manage-ment of wildlife species such as buffalo along similar lines to livestock production makes little sense. Extensive free-ranging unfenced sys-tems are already of proven value for harvesting, sport hunting and tourism, and as bulk grazers in maintaining ecosystem's integrity and function. The history of the development of both cattle and wildlife managed systems in Africa and trends in associated disease problems provide abundant evidence for this conclusion. The resilience and health of species are highly connected to the ecological resilience of the systems in which they have coevolved. Therefore, it is likely that community-based (pastoral) systems that can be mixed, rather than agribusiness-driven fenced monoculture (wild or domestic), are a route to sustainable tourism and animal-based food production sys-tems and economies in Africa. Much of African livestock and wildlife will remain more or less in open conditions for the foreseeable future, and thus these systems should be reinforced by appropriate policy and investment rather than discriminated against. This approach has the added value of ecological recovery of highly degraded landscapes from over-intensive livestock agriculture, reinforcing biodiversity conservation, supporting the delivery of natural ecosystem goods and services as well as related income streams. It could innovatively contribute to the target of 30 per cent of land protected by 2030 recently set by the High Ambition Coalition adopted by 69 countries (HAC, 2021). The ambition is high indeed, but realities on the ground suggest it will simply be too late in many countries to progress before major land-use changes and settlements have degraded habitats, especially in Central African savannas (Scholte et al., 2021). Climate change mitigation benefits will also accrue, while still contributing high-quality protein and food security, in a continent that has the lowest meat consumption per capita on Earth. However, to achieve this means shedding colonial legacies around land use and tenure, livestock development and animal health production systems imposed on Africa. It may require reversion to more traditional views on extensive animal use, harvesting and integrated low-cost–low-risk systems of management that are not new and were widely discussed in the twentieth century (Asibey,1974; Dasmann, 1964; Ledger, 1964).

As a new community of scientists and veterinarians emerges across Africa with a novel vision, knowledge from the past and ideas about future agro-ecologies and mixed land use will likely come into play. What may help is that there is now a major shift in perception of animal-based food systems in the very countries that promoted intensive livestock production in Africa. The question that really matters is what do Africans think of alternate futures? Will they remain embedded in old development dogma, or will they surf on the economic and cultural opportunities offered by wildlife? Could mixed land use become a dominant policy? Already, new land management, with mixed livestock and conservation initiatives, has shown considerable success in Namibia and Kenya, building on earlier innovation in Zimbabwe under the CAMPFIRE project, which under difficult political and economic circumstances remains nascent.

New ideas and opportunities beyond conventional systems of agriculture and wildlife protected areas will undoubtedly emerge, becoming hopefully more conducive to both local economic growth, ecosystem stability, resilience and biodiversity conservation. Planetary health demands it. In this chapter, we have shown the need for a reappraisal of history and the risk in the context of buffalo and diseases of concern to the livestock industry. Much of the narrative for 'land clearing' of wildlife is historic and 'blames' buffalo for diseases such as FMD, tick-borne infections, brucellosis and bTB, which early on justified fencing and the compartmentalization of land. In many cases their roles in the epidemiology of these pathogens are tangential and no longer highly significant in evolving contexts in which cattle populations are exploding and buffalo populations are maintained or decreasing in many ecosystems.

The genetic modification of farmed animals for objectives of higher production creates breeds more susceptible to pathogens when buffalo are disease-resistant in African contexts. Putting them together does not make the buffalo the culprit. The current industrial approach may work in highly transformed temperate systems but not in Africa's landscapes, where there is high microbial and vector diversity and a multitude of hosts. This failure of livestock intensification to develop in Africa without subsidization has led to the narrative that it is only through promoting greater separation and higher biosecurity that animal-based food economies can develop and reduce the risk of catastrophic disease epidemics in heavily invested livestock industries. This is basically underpinning policy on disease control and has been supported by unrealistic standards in disease management generated by the World Animal Health Organization (WOAH). These industries are effectively highly subsidized through international funding, and agencies are dedicated to forcing through these agricultural development agendas. Ironically, most of the benefits from these policies accrue to high-income countries that are not African, for instance through blocking access to their lucrative markets. Globally, these policies have come at a major cost to biodiversity and ecosystems in return for little more than cheap protein and high profits for agribusinesses. Africa now stands to gain substantially from shifts in diet, with reduced meat consumption and an increasing acknowledgement of the value of natural land and biodiversity. None of the externalities from, for example, climate change impacts to the loss of habitats or biodiversity are currently born by the livestock industry, although the internalization of these externalities has been called for by the Ecosystem Approach (Principle 4) under the Convention of Biological Diversity (CBD Decision COP V/6) and again under the Principles for Sustainable Use by the same (binding) Convention (CBD Decision COP VII/12). This situation will change as there is increasing pressure for accountability and determination of externalities of various industries for future sustainable development. Buffalo may well still have a bright future.

Acknowledgements

The co-authors would like to dedicate this chapter to Dr Gavin Thomson, who died in April 2021 just before finalizing this text. His passing is a great loss to the veterinary and wildlife health communities. He was an African who had a long research history working on FMD, including as one-time Chair of the FMD Commission of the OIE. He was a convert to supporting contemporary views on buffalo and the reappraisal of FMD control policies for Africa, inspiring commodity-based trade in his later years. Gavin was in the end a true conservationist.

References

Adamson, G. (1968). *Bwana Game: The Life Story of George Adamson*. Collins: London.

Andanje, S.A. (2002). *Factors Limiting the Abundance and Distribution of Hirola (Beatragus hunteri) in Kenya*. PhD thesis, University of Newcastle-upon-Tyne.

Anderson, E.C., W.J. Doughty, J. Anderson and R. Paling (1979). The pathogenesis of FMD in African buffalo and the role of this species in the epidemiology of the disease in Kenya. *Journal of Comparative Pathology* **89**: 541–550.

Andersson, J.A. and D.H.M. Cumming (2014). Defining the edge: boundary formation and TFCAs in southern Africa. In J. A. Andersson, M. de Garine-Wichatitsky, D. H. M. Cumming, V. Dzingirai and K.E. Giller (Eds.), *Transfrontier Conservation Areas: People Living on the Edge*. London: Earthscan, pp. 25–61.

Anon. (1977). Legal Notice 120. *Kenya Gazette* **79**(22): 330.

Artz, N., B. Motsamai, P. Zacharias and P. Tueller (1991). The Grassland Society of Southern Africa's first international conference. *Rangelands Archives* **13**: 237–239.

Asibey, E.O. (1974). Wildlife as a source of protein in Africa south of the Sahara. *Biological Conservation* **6**: 32–39.

Augustine, D.J., K.E. Veblen, J.R. Goheen, et al. (2011). Pathways for positive cattle–wildlife interactions in semi-arid rangelands. *Smithsonian Contributions to Zoology* **632**: 55–71.

Bauer, H., B. Chardonnet, P. Scholte,et al. (2020). Consider divergent regional perspectives to enhance wildlife conservation across Africa. *Nature Ecology and Evolution* **5**: 149–152.

Beard, P.H. (1977). *The End of the Game: The Last Word from Paradise – A Pictorial Documentation of the Origins, History and Prospects of the Big Game Africa*. New York: Chronicle.

Beechler, B.R., R. Bengis, R. Swanepoel, et al. (2015). Rift Valley Fever in Kruger National Park: do buffalo play a role in the inter-epidemic circulation of virus? *Transboundary and Emerging Diseases* **62**: 24–32.

Bengis, R.G. (2012). Anthrax in free-ranging wildlife. In R.E. Miller and M. Fowler (Eds.), *Fowler's Zoo and Wild Animal Medicine: Current Therapy*, Vol 7. St Louis: Elsevier Saunders Press, pp. 98–107.

Bengis, R.G. and D.G. Grobler (2000). Breeding of "disease free" buffalo. Proceedings of the North American Veterinary Conference, Orlando, FL, 5–19 January 2000, pp. 1032–1033.

Bengis R.G., R.A. Kock and J. Fischer (2002). Infectious animal diseases: the wildlife livestock interface. *Revue Scientifique et Technique de l'OIE* **21**: 53–62.

Bengis, R.G., N.P. Kriek, D.F. Keet, et al. (1996). An outbreak of bovine tuberculosis in a free-living African buffalo (*Syncerus caffer*) population in the Kruger National Park: a preliminary report. *Onderstepoort Journal Veterinary Research* **63**: 15–18.

Brasnett, N.V., R.D. Richmond, G.W. Dimbleby, et al. (1948). Fifth Empire Forestry Conference, 1947: reviews of papers submitted. *Empire Forestry Review* **27**: 83–128.

Büyüm, A.M., C. Kenney, A. Koris, et al. (2020). Decolonising global health: if not now, when? *BMJ Global Health* **5**(8): e003394.

Caron, A., D. Cornélis, C. Foggin, et al. (2016). African buffalo movement and zoonotic disease risk across Transfrontier Conservation Areas, Southern Africa. *Emerging Infectious Diseases* **2**: 277–280.

CBD [Convention on Biological Diversity]. Ecosystem Approach, as endorsed by COP5 of the convention Decision V/6, Principle 4. www.cbd.int/decision/cop/?id=7148

CBD [Convention on Biological Diversity]. Sustainable Use Principles, as accepted by COP7 of the convention Decision VII/12, Principle 13. www.cbd.int/decision/cop/?id=7749

Channumsin, M., M. Ciosi, D. Masiga, et al. (2019). Blood meal analysis of tsetse flies (*Glossina pallidipes*: Glossinidae) reveals a reduction in host fidelity when feeding on domestic compared to wild hosts. *BioRxiv* 69205.

Chigwenhese, L., A. Murwira, F.M. Zengeya, et al. (2016). Monitoring African buffalo (*Syncerus caffer*) and cattle (*Bos taurus*) movement across a damaged veterinary control fence at a Southern African wildlife/livestock interface. *African Journal of Ecology* **54**: 415–423.

Clausen, P.-H., I. Adeyemi, B. Bauer, et al. (1998). Host preferences of tsetse (Diptera: Glossinidae) based on bloodmeal identifications. *Medical and Veterinary Entomology* **12**: 169–180.

Condy J.B. and D.B. Vickers (1972). Brucellosis in Rhodesian wildlife. *Journal South African Veterinary Medical Association* **3**: 175–179.

Dasmann, R.F. (1964). *African Game Ranching*. London: Pergamum Press.

de Garine-Wichatitsky, M., A. Caron, C. Gomo, et al. (2010). Bovine tuberculosis in buffaloes, Southern Africa. *Emerging Infectious Diseases* **16**: 884–885.

De Jong, J.F., P. van Hooft, H.J. Megens, et al. (2020). Fragmentation and translocation distort the genetic landscape of ungulates: Red Deer in the Netherlands. *Frontiers in Ecology and Evolution* **8**: 365.

De Vos, A., G.S. Cumming, D. Cumming, et al. (2016). Pathogens, disease, and the social–ecological resilience of protected areas. *Ecology and Society* **21**(1): 20.

De Vos, V. and P.C. Turnbull (2004). Anthrax. In J.A.W Coetzer and R.C. Tustin (Eds.), *Infectious Diseases of Livestock*, 2nd ed. Oxford: Oxford University Press, pp. 1788–1818.

De Vos, V. and C.A.W.J. van Niekerk (1969). Brucellosis in the Kruger National Park. *Journal South African Veterinary Medical Association* **40**: 331–334.

Dublin, H.T. and J.O. Ogutu (2015). Population regulation of African buffalo in the Mara–Serengeti ecosystem. *Wildlife Research* **42**: 382–393.

Ebedes, H. (1976). Anthrax epizootics in Etosha National Park. *Madoqua* **10**: 99–118.

Empire Marketing Board (1930). *The Dissemination of Research Results Among Agricultural Producers: Answers to a Questionnaire Issued by the Empire Marketing Board*. London: His Majesty's Stationary Office.

Ferguson, K.J., S. Cleaveland, D.T. Haydon, et al. (2013). Evaluating the potential for the environmentally sustainable control of foot and mouth disease in Sub-Saharan Africa. *Ecohealth* **10**: 314–322.

Ferguson, K. and J. Hanks (2010). *Fencing Impacts: A Review of the Environmental, Social and Economic Impacts of Game and Veterinary Fencing in Africa with Particular Reference to the Great Limpopo and Kavango–Zambezi Transfrontier Conservation Areas*. Pretoria: Mammal Research Institute.

Gadd, M.E. (2012). Barriers, the beef industry and unnatural selection: a review of the impact of veterinary fencing on mammals in Southern Africa. In M.J. Somers and M.W. Hayward (Eds.), *Fencing for Conservation: Restriction of Evolutionary Potential or a Riposte to Threatening Processes?* Berlin: Springer, pp 153–186.

Gebretsadik T. (2016). Causes for biodiversity loss in Ethiopia: a review from conservation perspective. *Journal of Natural Sciences Research* **6**: 32–40.

Georgiadis, N.J., F. Ihwagi, J.N. Olwero and S.S. Romanach (2007). Savanna herbivore dynamics in a livestock dominated landscape. II: ecological, conservation, and management implications of predator restoration. *Biological Conservation* **137**: 473–483.

Gifford-Gonzalez, D. (2000). Animal disease challenges to the emergence of pastoralism in Sub-Saharan Africa. *African Archaeological Review* **17**: 95–139.

Glover, B., M. Macfarlane, R. Bengis, et al. (2020). Investigation of *Brucella melitensis* in sable antelope (*Hippotragus niger*) in South Africa. *Microorganisms* **8**: 1494.

Gordon, I.J., H.H.T. Prins and G. Squire (Eds.) (2016). *Food Production and Nature Conservation: Conflicts and Solutions*. London: Routledge.

Gradwell, D.V., A.P. Schutte, C.A.W.J. Van Niekerk and D.J. Roux (1977). The isolation of *Brucella abortus*, biotype1 from African buffalo in the Kruger National Park. *Journal South African Veterinary Medical Association* **48**: 41–43.

Grunblatt, J., M. Said and P. Wargute (1996). *DRSRS National Rangelands Report: Summary of Population Estimates for Wildlife and Livestock, Kenyan Rangelands 1977–1994*. Nairobi: Department of Resource Surveys and Remote Sensing (DRSRS), Ministry of Planning and National Development.

Guerrini, L., D.M. Pfukenyi, E. Etter, et al. (2019). Spatial and seasonal patterns of FMD primary outbreaks in cattle in Zimbabwe between 1931 and 2016. *Veterinary Research* **50**(1): 73.

Guilbride, P.D.L., D.H.L. Rollison and E.G. McAnulty (1963). Tuberculosis in free-living African (Cape) buffalo (*Syncerus caffer*). *Journal Comparative Pathology and Therapeutics* **73**: 337–348.

Gunn, G.H. (1932). Milk supplies, with special reference to legislation. *South African Medical Journal* **6**: 251–256.

HAC (2021). www.hacfornatureandpeople.org/home

Hampson, K., T. Lembo, P. Bessell, et al. (2011). Predictability of anthrax infection in the Serengeti, Tanzania. *Journal of Applied Ecology* **48**: 1333–1344.

Hargreaves, S.K., C.M. Foggin, E.C. Anderson, et al. (2004). An investigation into the source and spread of foot and mouth disease virus from a wildlife conservancy in Zimbabwe. *Revue Scientifique et Technique de l'OIE* **23**: 783–790.

Herr, S. and C. Marshall (1981). Brucellosis in free-living African buffalo (*Syncerus caffer*): a serological survey. *Onderstepoort Journal Veterinary Research* **48**: 133–134.

Holdo, R.M., A.R.E. Sinclair, A.P. Dobson, et al. (2009). A disease-mediated trophic cascade in the Serengeti and its implications for Ecosystem C. *PLoS Biology* **7**(9): e1000210.

Homewood, K., P.C. Trench and D. Brockington (2012). Pastoralist livelihoods and wildlife revenues in East Africa: a case for pastoralism. *Research, Policy and Practice* **2**: 19.

Hugh-Jones, M.E. and V. De Vos (2002). Anthrax and wildlife. *Revue Scientifique et Technique de l'OIE* **21**: 359–383.

Keet, D.F., N.P.J. Kriek, R.G. Bengis, D.G. Grobler and A. Michel (2000). The rise and fall of tuberculosis in a free-ranging chacma baboon troop in the Kruger National Park. *Onderstepoort Journal of Veterinary Researc* **67**: 115–122.

Keet, D.F., N.P.J. Kriek, R.G. Bengis and A.L. Michel (2001). Tuberculosis in kudus (*Tragelaphus strepsiceros*) in the Kruger National Park. *Onderstepoort Journal of Veterinary Research* **68**: 225–230.

Keet, D.F., N.P.J. Kriek, M.-L. Penrith, A. Michel, and H.F. Huchzermeyer (1996). Tuberculosis in buffaloes (*Syncerus caffer*) in the Kruger National Park: spread of the disease to other species. *Onderstepoort Journal Veterinary Research* **63**: 239–244.

Kihwele, E.S., M.P. Veldhuis, A. Loishooki, et al. (2021). Upstream land-use negatively affects river flow dynamics in the Serengeti National Park. *Ecohydrology and Hydrobiology* **21**: 1–12.

Kinne, J., R. Kreutzer, M. Kreutzer, U. Wernery and P. Wohlsein (2010). Peste des petits ruminants in Arabian wildlife. *Epidemiology and Infection* **138**: 1211–1214.

Kock, R.A. (2005). What is this infamous 'Wildlife/Livestock Disease Interface?': a review of current knowledge for the African continent. In S.A. Osofsky, S. Cleaveland, W.B. Karesh et al. (Eds.), *Proceedings of the Southern and East African Experts Panel on Designing Successful Conservation and Development Interventions at the Wildlife/Livestock Interface: Implications for Wildlife, Livestock and Human Health, AHEAD (Animal Health for the Environment And Development) Forum*, IUCN Vth World Parks Congress, Durban, South Africa, 14 and 15 September, 2003. Gland: IUCN, pp. 1–13.

Kock, R.A. (2006). Rinderpest and wildlife. In T. Barrett, P.P. Pastoret and W. Taylor (Eds.), *Rinderpest and Peste des Petits Ruminants Virus: Plagues of Large and Small Ruminants*. London: Elsevier, pp. 144–162.

Kock, R.A. (2010). The newly proposed Laikipia disease control fence in Kenya. In K. Ferguson and J. Hanks (Eds.), *Fencing Impacts: A Review of the Environmental, Social and Economic Impacts of Game and Veterinary Fencing in Africa with Particular Reference to the Great Limpopo and Kavango–Zambezi Transfrontier Conservation Areas*. Pretoria: Mammal Research Institute, pp. 71–74.

Kock, R., M. Kock, M. de Garine-Wichatitksy, P. Chardonnet and A. Caron (2014). Livestock and buffalo (*Syncerus caffer*) interfaces in Africa: ecology of disease transmission and implications for conservation and development. In M. Melletti and J. Burton (Eds.), *Ecology, Evolution and Behaviour of Wild Cattle: Implications for Conservation*. Cambridge: Cambridge University Press, pp. 431–445.

Kock, R.A., J.M. Wambua, J. Mwanzia, H. Wamwayi, et al. (1999). Rinderpest epidemic in wild ruminants in Kenya 1993–7. *Veterinary Record* **145**: 275–283.

Kock, R.A., H.M. Wamwayi, P.B. Rossiter, et al. (2006). Re-infection of wildlife populations with rinderpest virus on the periphery of the Somali ecosystem in East Africa. Rinderpest in East Africa: continuing re-infection of wildlife populations on the periphery of the Somali ecosystem. *Preventive Veterinary Medicine* **75**: 63–80.

KWS [Kenya Wildlife Service] (2021). *National Wildlife Census Report 2021*. Nairobi: Ministry of the Environment, Government of Kenya Publisher.

Lankester, F. and A. Davis (2016). Pastoralism and wildlife: historical and current perspectives in the East African rangelands of Kenya and Tanzania. *Revue Scientifique Technique L'OIE* **35**: 473–484.

Lawrence, J.A. (1992). History of bovine theileriosis in southern Africa. In R. A. I. Norval, B. D. Perry and A. S. Young (Eds.), *The Epidemiology of Theileriosis in Africa*. London: Academic Press, pp. 1–39.

Ledger, H.P. (1964). The role of wildlife in African agriculture. *East African Agricultural and Forestry Journal* **30**: 137–141.

Maggs, T. (1986). The early history of the black people in southern Africa. In T. Cameron and S.B. Spies (Eds.), *Illustrated History of South Africa*. Johannesburg and London: J. Ball.

Martínez-Avilés, M., I. Iglesias and A. De La Torre (2020). Evolution of the ASF infection stage in Wild boar within the EU (2014–2018). *Frontiers in Veterinary Science* **7**: 155.

Matseketsa, G., N. Muboko, E. Gandiwa, D.M. Kombora and G. Chibememe (2019). An assessment of human–wildlife conflicts in local communities bordering the western part of Save Valley Conservancy, Zimbabwe. *Global Ecology and Conservation* **20**: e00737.

Mattioli, R.C., V.S. Pandey, M. Murray and J.L. Fitzpatrick (2000). Immunogenetic influences on tick resistance in African cattle with particular reference to trypanotolerant N'Dama (*Bos taurus*) and trypanosusceptible Gobra zebu (*Bos indicus*) cattle. *Acta Tropica* **75**: 263–277.

Metzger, K.L., A.R.E. Sinclair, R. Hilborn, J.G.C. Hopcraft and S.A.R. Mduma (2010). Evaluating the protection of wildlife in parks: the case of African buffalo in Serengeti. *Biodiversity and Conservation* **19**: 3431–3444.

Meunier, N.V., P. Sebulime, R.G. White and R. Kock (2017). Wildlife–livestock interactions and risk areas for cross-species spread of bovine tuberculosis. *Ondersterpoort Journal of Veterinary Research* **84**: 1–10.

Michel, A.L. and R.G. Bengis (2012). The African buffalo: a villain for interspecies spread of infectious diseases in southern Africa. *Ondersterpoort Journal of Veterinary Research* **79**: 26–30.

Miescher, G. (2012). *Namibia's Red Line: The History of a Veterinary and Settlement Border.* New York: Palgrave MacMillan.

Miguel, E., V. Grosbois, A. Caron, et al. (2013). Contacts and foot and mouth disease transmission from wild to domestic bovines in Africa. *Ecosphere* **4**: 1–32.

Morris, C.A. (2007). A review of genetic resistance to disease in *Bos taurus* cattle. *The Veterinary Journal* **174**: 481–491.

Mukarati, N.L., G. Matope, M. de Garine-Wichatitsky, et al. (2020). The pattern of anthrax at the wildlife–livestock–human interface in Zimbabwe. *PLoS Neglected Tropical Diseases* **14**(10): e0008800.

Munangándu, H.M., V.M. Siamudaala, A. Mambota, et al. (2006). Disease constraints for utilisation of the African buffalo (*Syncerus caffer*) on game ranches in Zambia. *Japanese Journal of Veterinary Research* **54**: 3–13.

Mureithi, M.M., A. Verdoodt, J.T. Njoka, J.S. Olesarioyo and E. Van Ranstithi (2019). Community-based conservation: an emerging land use at the livestock–wildlife interface in northern Kenya In J.R. Kideghesho and A.A. Rija (Eds.), *Wildlife Management – Failures, Successes and Prospects.* London: IntechOpen, pp. 62–77.

Musoke, J., T. Hlokwe, T. Marcotty, B.J. du Plessis and A.L. Michel (2015). Spillover of *Mycobacterium bovis* from wildlife to livestock, South Africa. *Emerging Infectious Diseases* **21**: 448–451.

Mutwira, R. (1989). Southern Rhodesia wildlife policy (1890–1953): a question of condoning wildlife slaughter. *Journal of Southern African Studies* **15**: 250–262.

Ndengu, M., G. Matope, M. de Garine-Wichatitsky, et al. (2017). Seroprevalence of brucellosis in cattle and selected wildlife species at selected livestock/wildlife interface areas of the Gonarezhou National Park, Zimbabwe. *Preventive Veterinary Medicine* **146**: 158–165.

Neitz, W.O., A.S. Canham and E.B. Kluge (1955). Corridor disease: a fatal form of bovine theileriosis encountered in Zululand. *Journal South African Veterinary Medical Association* **26**: 79–87.

NRT [Northern Rangelands Trust] (2020). State of Conservancies Report Northern Rangelands Trust. www.nrt-kenya.org

Odadi, W.O., M.K. Karachi, S.A. Abdulrazak and T.P. Young (2011). African wild ungulates compete with or facilitate cattle depending on season. *Science* **333**: 1753–1755.

Ogutu, J.O., H.-P. Piepho, M.Y. Said, et al. (2016). Extreme wildlife declines and concurrent increase in livestock numbers in Kenya: what are the causes? *PLoS One* **11**(9): e0163249.

Omondi G., F. Gakuya, J. Arzt, et al. (2020). The role of African buffalo in the epidemiology of foot-and-mouth disease in sympatric cattle and buffalo populations in Kenya. *Transboundary and Emerging Diseases* **67**: 2206–2221.

Paine, R. and G. Martinaglia (1928). Tuberculosis in wild buck living under natural conditions. *Journal South African Veterinary Medical Association* **1**: 87–92.

Poshiwa X., R.A. Groeneveld, I.M.A. Heitkönig, et al. (2013a). Reducing rural households' annual income fluctuations due to rainfall variation through diversification of wildlife use: portfolio theory in a case study of south eastern Zimbabwe. *Tropical Conservation Science* **6**: 201–220.

Poshiwa, X., R.A. Groeneveld, I.M.A. Heitkonig, et al. (2013b). Wildlife as insurance against rainfall fluctuations in a semi-arid savanna setting of southeastern Zimbabwe. *Tropical Conservation Science* **6**: 108–125.

Prins, H.H.T. (1989). East African grazing lands: overgrazed or stably degraded? In W.D. Verwey (Ed.), *Nature Management and Sustainable Development.* Amsterdam/Tokyo: IOS, pp. 281–306.

Prins, H.H.T. (1992). The pastoral road to extinction: competition between wildlife and traditional pastoralism in East Africa. *Environmental Conservation* **19**: 117–123.

Prins, H.H.T. (2000). Competition between wildlife and livestock. In H.H.T. Prins, J.G. Grootenhuis and T.T. Dolan (Eds.), *Conservation of Wildlife by Sustainable Use*. Boston: Kluwer Academic, pp. 51–80.

Prins, H.H.T. and J.F. de Jong (2022). The ecohistory of Tanzania's northern Rift Valley – can one establish an objective baseline as endpoint for ecosystem restoration? In M. Bond, C. Kiffner and D. Lee (Eds.), *Tarangire: Human–Wildlife Coexistence in a Fragmented Landscape*. Cham: Springer Nature, pp. 129–161.

Prins, H.H.T. and F.J. Weyerhaeuser (1987). Epidemics in populations of wild ruminants: anthrax and impala, rinderpest and buffalo in Lake Manyara National Park, Tanzania. *Oikos* **49**: 28–38.

Pruvot, M., A.E. Fine, C. Hollinger et al. (2020). Outbreak of peste des petits ruminants in critically endangered Mongolian saiga and other wild ungulates. *Emerging Infectious Diseases* **26**: 51–62.

ROAPE (Review of African Political Economy) (2022). The struggles of the Ngorongoro Maasai. https://roape.net/2022/02/11/the-struggles-of-the-ngorongoro-maasai/

Robinson, P.A. (2017). Framing bovine tuberculosis: a 'political ecology of health' approach to circulation of knowledge(s) about animal disease control. *The Geographical Journal* **183**: 285–294.

Scholte, P., O. Pays, S. Adam, et al. (2021). Conservation overstretch and long-term decline of wildlife and tourism in the Central African savannas. *Conservation Biology* **36**(2): e13860.

Scoones, I., A. Bishi, N. Mapitse, et al. (2010). Foot-and-mouth disease and market access: challenges for the beef industry in southern Africa. *Pastoralism* **1**: 135–164.

Shiferaw, F., S. Abditcho, A. Gopilo, M.K. Laurenson (2002). Anthrax outbreak in Mago National Park, southern Ethiopia. *Veterinary Record* **150**: 318–320.

Shury, T.K., J.S. Nishi, B.T. Elkin and G.A. Wobeser (2015). Tuberculosis and brucellosis in wood bison (*Bison bison athabascae*) in northern Canada: a renewed need to develop options for future management. *Journal of Wildlife Diseases* **51**: 543–554.

Sintayehu, D.W., I.M.A. Heitkönig, H.H.T. Prins, et al. (2017b). Effect of host diversity and species assemblage composition on bovine tuberculosis (bTB) risk in Ethiopian cattle. *Parasitology* **144**: 783–792.

Sintayehu, D.W., H.H.T. Prins, I.M.A. Heitkönig and W.F. de Boer (2017a). Disease transmission in animal transfer networks. *Preventive Veterinary Medicine* **137**: 36–42.

Swanepoel, H., J. Crafford and M. Quan (2021). A scoping review of virald diseases in African ungulates. *Veterinary Science* **8**: 17.

Swanepoel, R. (1976). Studies on the epidemiology of Rift Valley fever. *Journal South African Veterinary Medical Association* **47**: 93–94.

Thomson, G.R. and D.S. Bastos (2004). Foot and mouth disease. In J.A.W. Coetzer and R.C. Tustin (Eds.), *Infectious Diseases of Livestock*, 2nd ed. Cape Town: Oxford University Press, pp. 1324–1365.

Thomson, G.R., M.L. Penrith, M.W. Atkinson, et al. (2013). Balancing livestock production and wildlife conservation in and around southern Africa's transfrontier conservation areas. *Transboundary and Emerging Diseases* **60**: 492–506.

Tikhonov, A. (2008). *Bos primigenius*. IUCN Red List of Threatened Species. 2008: e.T136721A4332142.

Tjaronda, W. (2008). Namibia: VCF hampers market access. New Era (Windhoek), 14 April 2008. https://allafrica.com/stories/200804140810.html.

Tyrrell, P.R, S. Russell and D. Western (2017). Seasonal movements of wildlife and livestock in a heterogenous pastoral landscape: implications for coexistence and community-based conservation. *Global Ecology and Conservation* **12**: 59–72.

UNEP (2011). *Environmental, Social and Economic Assessment of the Fencing of the Aberdare Conservation Area*. A report for: The Kenya Wildlife Service, Kenya Forest Service, Kenya Forests Working Group, United Nations Environment Programme and Rhino Ark Biotope Consultancy Services: Nairobi.

Valls-Fox, H., S. Chamaillé-Jammes, M. de Garine-Wichatitsky, et al. (2018). Water and cattle shape habitat selection by wild herbivores at the edge of a protected area. *Animal Conservation* **21**(5): 365–375.

Viggers, K.L., D.B. Lindenmayer and D.M. Spratt (1993). The importance of disease in reintroduction programmes. *Wildlife Research* **20**: 687–698.

Vosloo, W., L.-M. de Klerk, C.I. Boshoff, et al. (2007). Characterisation of a SAT-1 outbreak of foot-and mouth disease in captive African buffalo (*Syncerus caffer*): clinical symptoms, genetic characterisation and phylogenetic comparison of outbreak isolates. *Veterinary Microbiology* **120**: 226–240.

Vosloo, W., P.N. Thompson, B. Botha, et al. (2009). Longitudinal study to investigate the role of impala (*Aepyceros melampus*) in foot-and-mouth disease maintenance in the Kruger National Park, South Africa. *Transboundary and Emerging Diseases* **56**: 18–30.

Weaver, G.V., J. Domenech, A.R. Thiermann and W.B. Karesh (2013). Foot and mouth disease: a look from the wild side. *Journal of Wildlife Diseases* **49**: 759–785.

Wekesa, S.N., A.K. Sangula, G.J. Belsham, et al. (2015). Characterisation of recent foot-and-mouth disease viruses from African buffalo (*Syncerus caffer*) and cattle in Kenya is consistent with independent virus populations. *BMC Veterinary Research* **11**: 17.

Western, D., P. Tyrrell, P. Brehony, et al. (2020). Conservation from the inside-out: winning space and a place for wildlife in working landscapes. *People and Nature* **2**: 279–291.

White, P.J., R.L. Wallen, C. Geremia, et al. (2011). Management of Yellowstone bison and brucellosis transmission risk – implications for conservation and restoration. *Biological Conservation* **144**: 1322–1334.

Whittington, R., K. Donat, M.F. Weber, et al. (2019). Control of paratuberculosis: who, why and how. A review of 48 countries. *BMC Veterinary Research* **15**: 1–29.

Woodford, M.H. (1982a) Tuberculosis in wildlife in the Ruwenzori National Park, Uganda (Part 1). *Tropical Animal Health and Production* **14**: 81–88.

Woodford, M.H. (1982b). Tuberculosis in wildlife in Ruwenzori National Park, Uganda (Part 2). *Tropical Animal Health and Production* **14**: 155–159.

Young, A.S. (1981). The epidemiology of theileriosis in East Africa. In A.D. Irvin, M.P. Cunningham and A.S. Young (Eds.), *Advances in the Control of Theileriosis*. Dordrecht: Springer, pp. 38–55.

Part IV
Management

P. CHARDONNET

From a Commodity to a High-Value Species

The African buffalo has always been taken for granted. Due to its massive body size and vast herds, the species has constantly been perceived as an infinite source of wealth. Local hunters were fairly certain to bring home lots of valuable meat for their neighbours, friends and family. Scientists paid little attention to this abundant and rather unattractive cattle-looking beast compared to charismatic creatures threatened with extinction. Foreign hunters knew that a hunt for buffalo would not be in vain, that they would most certainly be challenged by a formidable adversary, with at least a thrilling fair chase as a result. Even conservationists were disinterested after the spectacular recovery of the species from the rinderpest onslaught. It is no surprise that such a commodity animal remained largely unnoticed and overlooked for so long.

Until things changed. With the human demographic upsurge, the escalating demand for game meat overtook the ability of wildlife – including buffalo – to match the needs. Buffalo habitats shrunk under unrestrained assaults of agro-pastoral encroachment. With the spread of modern weapons all over the continent, the fear of stalking buffalo faded. Buffalo started to struggle to cope with death tolls that were exceeding birth rates. They disappeared from large parts of their range, and were cornered in a few strongholds, mainly National Parks. Hunting Areas, another category of Protected Areas, became their last frontier outside National Parks, acting as critical buffer zones of National Parks and corridors in between.

Then the time came when visionary scientists such as Anthony Sinclair and Herbert Prins focused their minds on the species. Increasing numbers of tourists were excited to tick buffalo off their wish list as one of the Big Five. A new generation of veterinarians became conscious of the unique capacity of the indigenous African buffalo to resist or tolerate diseases that devastated exotic livestock. They also gained expertise in capturing and moving buffalo individuals and herds. Innovative cattle-ranchers initiated buffalo ranching as a new animal production system for multiple uses, both consumptive and non-consumptive, with a wider scope than dairy and beef, and as a means to rewild former cattle ranches.

Nearly restricted to very few countries in southern Africa, the private ownership of wildlife has changed the picture quite dramatically. By adapting livestock farming science and technology, the productivity of buffalo herds in captivity has improved. With optimized nutrition, especially during the dry season, buffalo ranchers get rid of the seasonality for breeding year-round and obtain earlier attainment of sexual maturity. However, the quest to produce ever larger trophy horns, driving prices up to at times unsustainable levels, is resulting in contentious breeding practices that include genetic manipulations such as outbreeding with East African buffalo and extreme inbreeding. Therefore, the large stock of captive buffalo is not considered part of the wild free-ranging populations for the long-term conservation of the taxon.

More recently, several non-African countries started to peremptorily impose bans on the importation from Africa of hunting trophies from charismatic wildlife species such as elephant and lion. This effectively posed an embargo on hunters from their jurisdictions to hunt for most trophies in range states of the African buffalo. Although buffalo (a non-controversial species) is not targeted by the bans, it is impacted by them. By downsizing the hunting market, the bans leave many Hunting Areas vacant and exposed to poaching and habitat conversion, rendering the buffalo a collateral victim of bans directed at other species. In the meantime, the bans are elevating the value of the buffalo, making it a foremost game in an attempt to compensate for the loss of other huntable game. Although less profitable than more prominent game, the buffalo finds itself in a position to financially contribute more to sustain hunting concessions so that they can continue to function as Protected Areas for preserving vast tracts of wilderness and their biodiversity. Hunting the African buffalo, if done judiciously and with restraint, could showcase the concept of sustainable use, which is one of the two pillars on which the Convention on Biological Diversity rests, the other being conservation.

When well-managed, the buffalo is a typical example of a high-value species producing high income from a low percentage of the population harvested. After being a commodity species throughout history, the African buffalo is now appearing as a promising prospect for Africa. It is time for buffalo to be considered a prominent asset for people rather than a banal species.

However, there are limitations that constrain the necessary change in paradigm. One is related to southern Africa, where the modified ("augmented") buffalo stock in captivity makes an ex-situ population incompatible with conservation. Another is external to Africa, because foreign standards dictated by non-African countries are working hard to prevent Africa from using its own renewable natural resources such as wildlife, including buffalo (meat and trophies). This is leading the intrinsic values (existence values) advocated by many in the North to prevail over the use-values (utilitarian values) needed by the South. It is as if African wildlife only exist to make nice movies and serve as tourist attractions for temporary visitors. One more constraint is the need to make more progress in some fields, notably in veterinary science, for example how to manage diseases where cattle and buffalo cohabitate, and how to develop physical restraint technologies that rely less on chemical immobilization, especially opioids.

The information provided in this section is not only based on different forms of academic research, but also on extensive field experience, gained by hard work, successes and also failures. As such, the expertise acquired from field experience forms part of what is known as 'experiential knowledge', important in fields such as conservation science, biomedical research, farming and veterinary science. While often difficult to collate, this information is commonly useful in practice. Therefore, in this section, we formalize some of the experiential knowledge that we have acquired over the years.

13 · *African Buffalo Production Systems*

D. FURSTENBURG, E. GANDIWA, Pa. OBEREM AND Pe. OBEREM

Historical Perspective and Current Situation

Before the eighteenth century, the African buffalo *Syncerus caffer* was widespread and abundant in Africa (Furstenburg, 2015). Across the African continent, humans had used buffalo for millennia, well before domestic cattle were introduced, as a source of meat and co-products such as hides. The meat from buffalo and other game was the product of hunting, including trapping and even kleptoparasitism. Unfortunately, the use of buffalo has not always been sustainable, in particular since European explorers and settlers arrived with their guns (Chapter 12). In more modern times, human population growth, associated agricultural encroachment and modern weaponry has greatly impacted the conservation status of the African buffalo across its continental range, reducing its natural habitat and population size. In southern Africa especially, culling by white settlers from the 1650s to 1800s had a major impact. The great rinderpest epidemic of the 1890s spread south across the continent, further reducing the remaining buffalo population while also eradicating large numbers of other wildlife. This compounded the earlier impacts on the geographic distribution, population size, structure of herds, migration patterns, and hence production of buffalo.

Buffalo are asymptomatic carriers of SAT serotypes of foot-and-mouth disease (FMD), various species of *Theileria* causing East Coast fever, corridor disease and January disease, as well as tsetse-transmitted nagana (Chapter 9). To control and prevent the spread of these diseases to domestic stock, veterinary fences to control the movement of buffalo, other disease carriers and susceptible animals consequently have been used in southern Africa. This has had a further dramatic impact on the buffalo's range and numbers (Oberem and Oberem,

Figure 13.1 Various categories of African buffalo production systems. Adapted from Chardonnet, 2011; background picture: © Christophe Morio.

2016). It is only recently, with the introduction of community-based natural resource management, private ownership and game ranching, that the concept of sustainable utilization has again, this time consciously, become widely practiced in southern Africa. Regional wildlife populations have grown in southern Africa with the increase of private ownership.

Globally, from the year 1900 to 2000, domestic animal numbers increased by a multiple of 4.5 while wildlife numbers were halved (Smil, 2011). Across African savanna areas, after evolving at varying times and speeds in different regions, the conservation status of habitat and species is today similar, with up to 80 per cent of wild animals lost and replaced in large areas by domestic stock, especially cattle. These developments across the continent have reached a point today where domestic livestock, although an exotic taxon, has virtually replaced buffalo, an indigenous taxon, and restricted the remaining buffalo populations to residual scattered wilderness.

Today, buffalo populations across Africa are broadly conserved in three major land-use systems, that is public protected areas owned by the State, communal land and private properties, the latter in only about five countries, all in southern Africa, out of the 37 African buffalo range countries. Variations in management objectives across these land-use regimes strongly influence the resultant production systems and the extent of the species' utilization by land managers. Consequently, buffalo production systems have evolved and diversified between extensive models with free-ranging buffalo at low densities on large land areas and, at the other extreme, intensive models with enclosed buffalo at high stocking rates on small, fenced properties (Figure 13.1). The various categories of buffalo production systems are not compartmented; there is a continuum between categories.

Buffalo farms are always fenced, most buffalo ranches are fenced, while most hunting areas with buffalo as a game animal are unfenced. In South Africa, however, all reserves, parks, ranches and farms where buffalo production occurs are enclosed by fences that restrict animal movement.

Buffalo Production Systems

Wildlife production systems can be classified on a scale of intensity of management. Here they are structured into three categories of property size and management intensity: (1) extensive production systems, (2) semi-extensive systems (game ranches) and (3) intensive systems (game farms).

In Zambia, the 200 game ranches existing there in 2012 (with a growth rate of six (6 per cent) per year over the past 32 years) were classified in three similar categories: (i) large-size game ranches of over 500 ha (75 ranches, that is 38 per cent of the national total), (ii) intermediate-size game farms of between 50 and 499 ha (27 game farms, 13.5 per cent of the national total) and (iii) small-size ornamental properties of less than 50 ha (98 ornamental properties, 49 per cent of the national total) (Chomba et al., 2014).

This structure and these definitions are made in a quest to clarify and better understand the concepts. However, there are no strict limits between the three categories, it is rather a gradient of intensity.

Extensive Production Systems

In extensive production systems, buffalo are free-ranging and occur at natural densities, with or without the ability to migrate between natural resources and without managerial or veterinary intervention, as seen through most of the range states in Africa. Wildlife in extensive production systems is managed to be utilized for ecotourism and/or regulated hunting (Bothma and Du Toit, 2016).

Multispecies Bushmeat Hunting in Natural Ecosystems

Africa's diverse ecosystems are endowed with wild large carnivores and herbivores that hold both ecological and socio-economic importance, and bushmeat hunting is probably as old as humans and still occurs today throughout Africa, both legally (hunting) and illegally (poaching).

In large areas, managers generally employ a more hands-off (extensive) management style utilizing multi-species in natural ecosystems. The smaller the area, the higher the likelihood that fewer species are more intensively managed.

The Cape buffalo *Syncerus caffer caffer* (hereafter, buffalo), given its large size and gregarious gathering in herds, was once one of the southern and eastern African mega-herbivores with the largest distribution (Hildebrandt, 2014). In Africa, humans have, with some exceptions, mostly been transformed from traditional hunter-gatherers into sedentary village hunters and farmers (Wilkie et al., 2016). Historically, subsistence hunting for consumption (bushmeat) in traditional systems was not considered to have a detrimental effect on wildlife populations, because hunting was regulated (Fa and Brown, 2009). Traditional hunting or human predation in multi-species natural wildlife production systems for animal protein (bushmeat) and other wild animal products characterize many tropical indigenous communities (Marks, 1977a; Manyanga and Pangeti, 2017). For example, the African buffalo is among the important target species for the Valley Bisa community in the Luangwa Valley, Zambia. Their hunting techniques and selection of prey is related to the ecology and behaviour of the prey and influence the hunting patterns and timing of hunts (Marks, 1977a, 1977b). This traditionally organized form of wild animal hunting has facilitated the persistence of wild animals due to its selectivity and associated cultural conservation practices (Marks, 1973). However, with the general decline in large wildlife populations (Craigie et al., 2010; Mabeta et al., 2018), species such as buffalo tend to be progressively substituted by medium to small-sized wild herbivores in response to the increasing demand of bushmeat consumption and trade in urban markets (Davies and Brown, 2007).

Around the start of the twentieth century, the declines in wildlife populations prompted many African countries, most then under colonial rule, to criminalize the traditional livelihood strategy of bushmeat hunting (Child et al., 2012). This led to negative relationships and conflict among local people, wildlife and the state as most local communities' access to bushmeat was controlled. Any local hunting of wildlife now is labelled as poaching, and wildlife are mostly confined to protected game areas and national parks (Child et al., 2012; Hildebrandt, 2014; Mutanga et al., 2015).

Today, bushmeat hunting is generally non-selective and indiscriminate with regard to the animal's sex and age and, when it is commercial, to the number of individuals taken. As rural populations grew, hunting methodologies became more modern, effective and less selective (firearms as opposed to the more traditional methods). As the land available for wild animal populations became limited by the expansion of farming and agriculture, bushmeat hunting concentrated in the remaining natural habitats was reported to threaten wildlife populations (Child et al., 2012; Wilkie et al., 2016). Literature points to hunting by humans, since the advent of modern firearms, having led to the extinction of wildlife species inclusive of large carnivores and herbivores (Martin, 1966; Ripple et al., 2019). Today, wildlife provides many ecosystem services in the form of ecotourism, trophy hunting, meat, medicinal products, aesthetic enjoyment and inspiration (Tchakatumba et al., 2019).

Community-Based Natural Resources Management
and Multi-Species Hunting
The introduction of community-based natural resources management (CBNRM) in the early 1980s was perceived as a necessary intervention to benefit wildlife and communities (Child et al., 2012). Where CBNRM is implemented properly, wildlife can be used sustainably as an economic engine in communal lands while simultaneously encouraging conservation (Child et al., 2012). For example, the Communal Areas Management Programme for Indigenous Resources (CAMPFIRE) is an example of a CBNRM programme that was designed and implemented by the Government of Zimbabwe in 1989 to stimulate the long-term development, management and sustainable use of natural resources in the country's communal farming areas adjacent to state-protected areas. Thus, under CAMPFIRE, extensive natural wildlife areas were actively managed by local communities in order to reduce unsustainable exploitation of wildlife and human–wildlife conflicts, while also providing local communities with conservation benefits and incentives (Muboko and Murindagomo, 2014). A major shift in the business model was the sharing of benefits inclusive of bushmeat derived from organized trophy hunting of multiple species of wild animals based on a participatory and sustainable quota setting system.

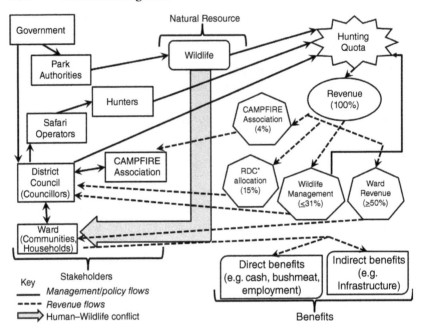

Figure 13.2 Flow of direct and indirect benefits from CAMPFIRE programmes (Tchakatumba et al., 2019). ★RDC refers to Rural District Council. Source: with permission of Taylor & Francis.

In 2022, a total of 58 of 60 districts in Zimbabwe were under CAMPFIRE programmes with a total area of 50,000 km² (12 per cent of Zimbabwe's surface area), which supports approximately 200,000 households (Machena et al., 2017; Campfire Association Zimbabwe, 2022). On average, CAMPFIRE generates about €1.85 million per year with trophy hunting, constituting the major source of revenue while other sources of revenue include ecotourism and lease fees (Machena et al., 2017). Thus, under CAMPFIRE, local communities realize both direct and indirect benefits from the sustainable management of local natural resources (Figure 13.2). The buffalo is identified as one of the 'Big Five' species, is valuable for both meat and trophy hunting and is a high-value species for photographic tourism. Local communities are tasked with conducting anti-poaching patrols and general resource monitoring in CAMPFIRE areas. Studies on CAMPFIRE show that wildlife habitats are being maintained well and have created conditions for increased wildlife populations outside protected areas (Gandiwa et al., 2013; Musiwa and Mhlanga, 2020). Nonetheless, there has been some criticism of the CAMPFIRE experience (e.g. Dzingirai, 2003). Elsewhere, similar CBNRM programmes (e.g. Botswana and Namibia) have led to enhanced conservation, benefits for local communities and recovery of wildlife populations (Mogomotsi et al., 2020; Stoldt et al., 2020).

Semi-Extensive Production Systems: Game Ranches

A semi-extensive production system is a natural area that is large enough for self-sustaining wildlife populations to be managed, that is a game ranch or a national, provincial or private park or reserve (Cloete et al., 2015). It can be fenced or unfenced, but humans need to intervene to provide either water, supplementary and/or complementary feeding, control of parasites, control of predation or the provision of health care (Cloete et al., 2015). Camp sizes (subportion of a game ranch/reserve) vary from several hundred to several thousand hectares depending on the habitat, climate, environment, other herbivore species, topography of the land and the nature and scope of the business. Every production system is unique, with specific ecological and animal management parameters addressed scientifically and professionally by experts. Game ranches may be considered as an innovative, sustainable form of agriculture or animal husbandry where an important outcome is the rewilding of an area.

Buffalo ranching often occurs in semi-extensive multi-species production systems as one element of the herbivory with or without natural predation. Stocking rates may exceed the natural carrying capacity of the rangeland; hence, in such cases, the need to supply supplemental feed during the dry season. Without careful rangeland management, there is subsequently a risk of ecological deterioration of natural habitat conditions. Buffalo ranching is often practiced on marginal agricultural land that was formerly severely degraded due to monocropping or domestic stock farming, and there is a need over time for sophisticated habitat rehabilitation programmes to be implemented (Chapter 14).

Such systems also require the management of sex and age structure by (i) limiting the number of mature breeding bulls (selective per individual animal profiling), normally 1 bull per 20–40 mature cows; (ii) removing surplus young bulls, mostly allowing only one bachelor group of <10, or complete removal of all young bulls, to limit social confrontation and fighting with the usually very valuable breeding bull; and (iii) removing and/or replacing post-age and non-productive females from the population.

Its reputation has given the buffalo the status of being recognized worldwide as one of the 'Big Five'. The buffalo is the most dangerous of

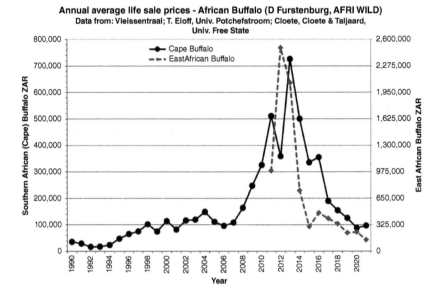

Figure 13.3 Auction prices of live breeding buffalo bulls over time and illustrating the value initially placed by purchasers on buffalo of East African origin for reasons discussed in the section dealing with production of buffalo with large horn size, below. East African buffalo, formerly recognized as a subspecies, is phenotypically 12 per cent larger in body size, 10–20 cm higher shoulder height, with greater horn spread, lesser curve-drop and smaller bosses, than the southern African buffalo. East African buffalo was introduced into the South African production systems adding specific value market traits. © Deon Furstenburg.

all African game species, especially if wounded or solitary. Its economic value has been further enhanced (Figure 13.3) by veterinary restrictions that prevent its translocation due to the danger of spreading disease. Consequently, the captive breeding of disease-free buffalo in semi-extensive confinement has become a lucrative business, but one which must be approached properly to ensure success. There was a boom in prices after the worldwide economic crises of 2008, reaching a record high in 2017 (Figure 13.3), followed by a fall to more normal pricing trends during 2018–2019.

Intensive Production Systems: Game Farms

Intensive wildlife production systems occur in small fenced areas where wild animals are intensively managed for the production of meat, hides

Figure 13.4 Horizon, the most expensive African buffalo bull ever bred so far, was sold at an auction for €10.8 million. Horizon was bred by Jacques and Caroline Malan of Lumarie. According to the SCI method (following the external curve of the horns, in inches), he measures an impressive 55 6/8". © Nyumbu Game.

and live animals. Buffalo farming is also sometimes practiced intensively in small camps on game farms, mainly to produce highly priced animals for live sales, that is specific disease-free and specifically selected for phenotypes (e.g. body size, horn size and shape) of trophy buffalo (Figures 13.5 and 13.6; Bothma and Du Toit, 2016). A camp is fenced off to more closely manage rare and valuable animals that cannot move freely. These small camps vary in size from 5 ha pens to 80 ha camps. As a result of the small surface areas of the camps, daily supplement feeding, or even a complete feed, is provided all year round, the ratio depending on the camp size and quantity (biomass) and quality (nutritional contents) of the grass production. The animal load in the camps exceeds natural vegetative carrying capacity generally by two- to threefold or more. One mature bull (selected by its animal and genetic profile) and 10–40 mature cows depending on the specific situation are usually kept as a herd in a camp. As a result of socio-spatial restrictions, only one bull is kept and all male progeny are removed to a different camp before reaching sexual maturity and the risk of intersocial confrontation, that is fighting. However, because of the recent dramatic decline in prices attained for

Figure 13.5 Aerial view of a 460-ha intensified multi-camp buffalo production system in savanna habitat with centred pens for handling, supplement feeding and rotation of stocking between camps. Optimal habitat management entitles (i) a 2-camp system per buffalo herd and rotated every 8 months, or (ii) a 3-camp system per herd and rotated every 4 months (Furstenburg, 2017a).

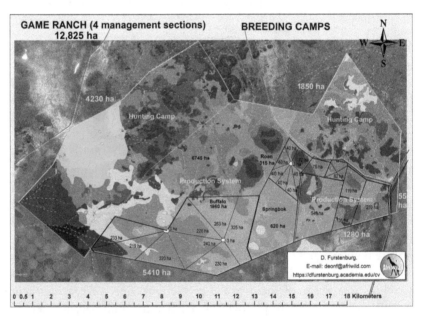

Figure 13.6 Example outlay of a semi-extensive buffalo production camp system (2-camps, on average 230 ha each, per breeding herd, including two free-roaming areas >4,000 ha each for surplus animals) constructed per vegetation survey map in arid Kalahari savanna habitat (Furstenburg, 2017b).

buffalo and due to the cost of management, feed, veterinary services and medication in these intensive systems, the truly intensive breeding facilities have begun to turn more to semi-intensive methods of ranching.

Buffalo Products

All of the above production systems rely on one or more of the four sustainable use pillars of 'game ranching', namely (i) breeding for sale to new properties being converted to game ranches and rewilding; (ii) non-consumptive tourism, that is ecotourism; (iii) consumptive tourism, that is hunting; and (iv) production of meat and other animal products such as skins/leather, curios from horns, skins, hooves, bones, etc.

Live Sales of Breeding Animals

Many game ranchers took the opportunity to breed game animals for live sales. Most of these specialized in specific so-called rare species, for example bontebok, black wildebeest, sable antelope, roan antelope. Others specialized in specific, sought-after characteristics such as buffalo and sable with trophy-quality horns and body conformation. Yet others focused on multiplying colour variants that occur naturally but rarely in nature, such as black impala, golden wildebeest, etc. The breeding, sale and translocation of these animals resulted in the rewilding of marginal conventional agricultural land that was converted into game ranches. Today, this market segment is less lucrative than at its summit in 2017 but is still thriving.

Non-Consumptive 'Ecotourism'/Wildlife-Viewing Tourism

Non-consumptive tourism in the form of wildlife-viewing tourism can also be regarded as a production system where the product or service is a photographic, educational or recreational safari sold to clients who buy a period of time spent in nature to watch fauna and flora including buffalo. Buffalo, as one of the 'Big Five' and with a reputation of being dangerous, are highly prized by wildlife-viewing tourists. With appropriate management, both consumptive and non-consumptive tourism can be conducted in the same area to increase and diversify the value of the ecosystem service.

Consumptive Tourism/Hunting Tourism = Sustainable Utilization

By definition, hunting tourism harvests a very low percentage of individuals within populations, old males or excess animals only, with the

ecological and economic objectives of (i) conserving a buffalo population and its habitats through sustainable hunting and (ii) sustaining the
hunting enterprise as well as the ranch. The trophy-hunting model aims
to produce large trophies, while the sport-hunting model aims to offer
fair chase hunts to tourist hunters who are more interested in the quest
than in the trophy.

These buffalo-hunting production systems operate over large to very
large areas where the buffalo densities appear at their natural levels, which
are low compared to intensive systems. In all of the countries where buffalo
tourism hunting occurs, hunting areas are unfenced open range extending
in size from between 50,000 and 300,000 ha. South Africa, where buffalo
are hunted in fenced hunting areas of smaller but still physically substantial
sizes such as a few thousand hectares, is an exception. Given the demand
and value realized by these forms of buffalo hunting, hunting buffalo for
meat in these semi-extensive systems is rare, in contrast with the hunting
of more common, less expensive game species (Chapter 16).

Animal Products

Game meat is considered a delicacy in many parts of the world where
it is in demand for its rarity and its health benefits, such as high protein
and low fat content. There are specialist harvesters who harvest excess
animals for the purpose of supplying specialist game meat processors.
The jurisprudence with respect to the South African Meat Safety Act
40, 2000 still needs (after >12 years of negotiations) to be amended to
ensure that game meat can reach its true potential as a source of good,
healthy, natural protein.

Many different curios are manufactured, formally and informally,
from many parts of carcasses used for trophies and meat, including from
skins (leather goods such as skin floor mats, shoes, handbags and belts,
even furniture coverings), horns (door handles, lamps, wall decorations),
bones (carved salt and pepper cellars, knife handles, lamp stands), etc.

Case Study: The Wildlife Ranching Industry in South Africa

The Buffalo in South Africa

In South Africa, the game ranching industry was born with the prom-
ulgation of the Stock Theft Act in South Africa in 1991, which confers

Table 13.1 *Percentage of various species, some endangered, on private land owned by private game ranches versus those on state reserves in South Africa (Nel, 2021; Furstenburg et al., 2022).*

Species	% on private land	% on state land
Black wildebeest	87	13
Blesbok	90	10
Bontebok	88	12
Buffalo	63	37
Oribi	97	3
Roan antelope	95	5
Sable antelope	97	3
White rhinoceros	65★	15★

★ Of the world population.

ownership of game to the owner of the land so long as the land is adequately fenced. It got a further growth boost in 1996 when the new South African Constitution was adopted; Section 24 of this constitution recognizes the principle of the sustainable use of natural resources in South Africa.

The 2008 economic crisis played a further role with investors seeking different ways to invest their money. At its summit in 2015/2017, 8,000–10,000 game ranches covered almost 20 million ha (i.e. 14 per cent of the national estate, an area 2.2 times larger than the formally protected areas of the country). Many game ranches were established on marginal land, that is farmland with low agricultural production potential. Others were established on degraded agricultural farmland that was previously occupied by monocultures of domestic stock and/or crops such as maize (Cloete et al., 2015), thus rewilding and converting former farms into wildlife-based enterprises.

Sustainable use as a form of conservation was at the beginnings of a massive private and privately funded 'rewilding' of the country. This brought about a major turnaround in the numbers of many endangered species, as well as in the 'ownership profile' of animals in the country. As can be seen from Table 13.1, the numbers of species, including endangered species, are much higher on privately owned game ranches compared to state land.

The same successful contribution has been made by private owners on private land to the survival of buffalo in South Africa. Table 13.2

Table 13.2 *Numbers and disease status of buffalo in South Africa; bTB = tuberculosis; CA = brucellosis; FMD = foot and mouth disease (personal research of P.T. Oberem).*

Facility: State Protected Areas *versus* private ranches	Size (Ha)	Buffalo numbers	Sanitary status
Kruger NP	2,000,000	>35,000	bTB, CA, FMD positive, theileriosis positive
Addo Elephant NP	170,000	440	bTB, CA, FMD, *Theileria* free
Mountain Zebra NP	28,400	80	bTB, CA, FMD, *Theileria* free
Hluhluwe–Imfolozi	96,000	>7000	bTB, theileriosis positive CA free, FMD free?
Camdeboo	19,400	75	bTB, CA, FMD, *Theileria* free
Marakele	61,000	20 plus	bTB positive?, CA, FMD, *Theileria* free
Mokala	26,485	50	bTB, CA, FMD, *Theileria* free
Madikwe	72,000	800	CA, *Theileria*, FMD free, bTb positive
Total in State Protected Areas	**2,401,285**	**>43,465**	**Only 645 disease-free**
Total on private ranches	**>7,000,000 (available)**	**>75,000**	**ALL DISEASE-FREE** bTB, CA, FMD, *Theileria* free

indicates the number of buffalo in national and provincial parks versus game ranches as well as their disease status. There are only 645 disease-free buffalo in state parks compared with 75,000 disease-free buffalo on private ranches.

Legal Status of Buffalo in South Africa

The South African Government Gazette No. 42464 dated 17 May 2019 amended table 7 of the Animal Improvement Act (Act no. 62 of 1998) and now lists 32 new wild animal species, including 24 indigenous mammals (e.g. the African buffalo), to provide for the breeding, identification and utilization of genetically superior animals to improve the production and performance of animals in the interest of the Republic. By declaring these wild animals as landrace breeds (in table 7 of the regulations), the Act typically provides for landrace breeds to be bred and 'genetically improved' to obtain superior domesticated animals with enhanced production and performance. Similarly, provision is made for the Breeders Association to lay claim to the breed and to establish specific breed standards for animals to be included in stud books. Animals declared as landrace breeds can also be used for genetic manipulation, embryo harvesting, in-vitro fertilization and embryo transfers.

Numerous concerns about the new legislation have been raised, including from scientists, over negative genetic consequences, ecological and economic risks, as well as direct conflict with other biodiversity laws in South Africa (e.g. IUCN SSC Antelope Specialist Group, 2015; IUCN, WCC 2016; Somers et al., 2020). However, many if not all of these concerns could be mitigated by the Code of Conduct of the game breeder association (Wildlife Ranching South Africa), which intends to become the administrative and implementing agent under this legislation.

Macroeconomics

On the 20 million hectares occupied by game ranches, an income stream of €1.2 billion (ZAR 20 billion; €1 = ZAR 16.31) is generated annually, resulting in numerous decent jobs and outperforming the national economy (Oberem and Oberem, 2016).

Surveys of game ranch usage in South Africa (Taylor et al., 2020) revealed important facts about the benefits of private game ranching. Eighty per cent of private ranches utilized some form of consumptive sustainable use, with 5 per cent of the total land area covered by these private properties utilized for intensive breeding of rare species or colour variants. While profitability varied greatly between the properties, they produced an average return on investment (ROI) of 0.068 and employed more people at higher wages than equivalent domestic livestock operations. From the survey, it was concluded that the South African model could be a suitable option for other African countries seeking sustainable land-use alternatives.

A further survey (Taylor et al., 2021) assessed how the wildlife ranching sector (including intensive and semi-extensive) contributes to the conservation of herbivores. It concluded that individual ranches had a mean of 15.0 ($\pm$4.8) species, 1.9 ($\pm$1.5) threatened species and 3.6 ($\pm$3.1) extralimital species per property. In comparison to 54 state Protected Areas, wildlife ranches had significantly higher species richness, more threatened species but also more extralimital species, with total herbivore numbers estimated to be as many as 7.5 million. The report concluded that private game ranching in South Africa represents one of the few examples on earth where indigenous mammal populations are thriving and demonstrating how sustainable use can lead to rewilding.

Table 13.3 *Income from various economic activity pillars on game ranches in South Africa (Nel, 2021) (€1 = ZAR16.31).*

Activity	Annual income (€1 = ZAR16.31)
Subsistence hunting (meat)	€735.9 million (ZAR 12 billion)
International hunting (sport/trophy)	€122.7 million (ZAR 2 billion)
Processed products (meat/leather/curios)	€306.6 million (ZAR 5 billion)
Live animal sales @ formal auctions	€61. million (ZAR 1 billion)
Total	**€1.2 billion (ZAR 20 billion)**

Nel (2021) reported that 50 per cent of game ranches obtain an income from hunting, with hunting being the main income stream for 30 per cent of these ranches. Of these game ranches, 5 per cent conduct photographic tourism and 52 per cent are engaged in all four of the economic activity pillars. Table 13.3 indicates the income obtained from the economic activity pillars on game ranches.

In South Africa, buffalo was the number one income-generating species in 2016 (North-West University, 2017; Table 13.4), although it does not appear on the list of the top ten most hunted species. This is an outstanding demonstration of a high-value species that produces high income with a small number of harvested individuals.

Basics of the Game Ranching Technology

In general, smaller properties require far more management inputs than larger ones where the size, diversity and lower density levels of animals allow for less close oversight and interventions.

Infrastructure

Fences around game farms in South Africa are regulated by law. To own wild animals the property is required to have a Certificate of Adequate Enclosure (CoAE), which is issued by the Department of Environmental Affairs. The specifications (height, number of stands, etc.) are dictated by the law. In order to introduce and release African buffalo onto the property, a permit (WR number for the property) is required from Veterinary Services. Properties with buffalo also have specific minimum fencing requirements. Fences are not generally electrified, they are so usually only when very valuable animals are kept in small camps (<80 ha), and

Table 13.4 *Top 10 income generators (€1 = ZAR16.31) (North-West University, 2017).*

Species	2014	2015	2016	% CHANGE
Buffalo	€7.8 million (ZAR127 million)	€8.9 million (ZAR145 million)	€13.5 million (ZAR220 million)	+73
Sable	€3.5 million (ZAR57 million)	€4.5 million (ZAR73 million)	€7.2 million (ZAR117 million)	+106
Lion	€12 million (ZAR195 million	€11.1 million (ZAR181 million)	€6.8 million (ZAR111 million)	−43
Kudu	€4.8 million (ZAR78 million	€6.4 million (ZAR104 million)	€6.7 million (ZAR110 million)	+40
White rhino	€4.4 million (ZAR72 million)	€4.7 million (ZAR76 million)	€5.1 million (ZAR83 million)	+14
Nyala	€2.8 million (ZAR45 million)	€2.8 million (ZAR46 million)	€4.7 million (ZAR76 million)	+71
Waterbuck	€2.2 million (ZAR36 million)	€2.5 million (ZAR40 million)	€3.1 million (ZAR51 million)	+39
Blue wilde-beest	€2.2 million (ZAR36 million)	€2.4 million (ZAR39 million)	€3.1 million (ZAR50 million)	+39
Burchell's zebra	€2.4 million (ZAR39 million)	€2.8 million (ZAR45 million)	€3.1 million (ZAR51 million)	+29
Oryx/gems-buck	€2.4 million (ZAR39 million)	€3.1 million (ZAR51 million)	€3 million (ZAR49 million)	+27

this to keep aggressive bulls in adjacent camps from fighting and to prevent predation of the calves.

In order for any buffalo to be moved from one property to another, both properties need to be approved and registered (WR numbers) by Veterinary Services, the animals have to be tested for the four controlled diseases, namely FMD, corridor disease (i.e. theileriosis), bovine brucellosis/contagious abortion (CA) and bovine tuberculosis (bTB). Permits must then be issued by the Department of Environmental Affairs in the provinces involved (two if moving the animals from one province to the other).

Bomas, or small, sturdily built camps of 1 ha or less, are not often used. When they are, it is mainly only for temporary housing, for example when holding animals while waiting for disease test results and permits (no animals may be moved without permits, see above), while in quarantine and/or for adaptation purposes to new farms in new and different geographic areas (Figures 13.7 and 13.8).

Figure 13.7 Buffalo in boma. © Q. Strauss – MLP Media.

Figure 13.8 Buffalo in boma. © J. Malan.

The sectoral focus that is the main economic driver and the size of the game ranch determine the need and type of water provision and/ or water facilities provided. The biggest ranches would most likely rely mainly on natural water resources and sources such as rivers, dams and wetlands with perhaps (as is seen even in the 2 million ha Kruger National Park) some additional artificial drinking reservoirs and troughs to supplement the resource and ensure better utilization of the available habitat (pasture). At the other extreme, smaller farms and camps may rely entirely on such artificial sources.

Habitat and Feeding Management
Habitat management includes restoring the natural habitat and vegetation that generally has/had been damaged to varying degrees by earlier agricultural practices, including ploughing, overgrazing with a monoculture of species (e.g. cattle) and internal fencing/camping. It also includes providing artificial water sources, boreholes, reservoirs and dams to improve the utilization of the natural habitat across the property. Many of these former cattle farms also may be damaged as a result of bush encroachment (e.g. *Dicrostachys* sp., *Stoebe vulgaris*, various thorn trees of *Senegalia* and *Vachellia* sp.), which requires expensive interventions to restore the vegetative value and carrying capacity. It may also entail the removal of toxic invasive plants (often aliens) such as *Lantana camara* and *Asclepias* spp.

Especially on smaller properties, supplementary feeding needs to be practiced, in particular during the dry season (in South Africa this is mainly during the austral winter months) to ensure optimum health and reproductive rates. This would include vitamin and mineral supplements, protein supplements during the winter, and compounds to counteract the plant's own defences, for example inclusion of polyethylene glycol (PEG) and propylene glycol (PG) to bind terpines and tannins allowing better utilization of especially browse but also lignified sour grasses during the winter (van Hoven and Oberem, 2018).

Breeding and Health Management
The first most important breeding management interventions are reducing the number of male animals that are kept for breeding to allow a higher percentage of female animals, that is altering the sex ratio from 1:1 to 1 male for 25–40 females. Males that are not selected for breeding are used either for trophy/sport hunting or for harvesting game meat. The

second most important breeding management intervention is the selection of specific males for breeding to (i) maintain the natural characteristics of the species, (ii) improve adaptedness to that specific environment and (iii) improve general health by selecting against characteristics predisposing to parasites and diseases. For example, it is not recommended to breed with animals, in particular bulls, that habitually carry large numbers of ticks ('tick taxis'). In the case of buffalo, selection is often specifically to restore the 'lost' horn length and character, which was selected against by heavy trophy hunting over many decades. A further important reason for selecting specific males and keeping records thereof is to prevent inbreeding.

Reproductive performance can be greatly improved by supplementary feeding in particular, and by reducing the numbers of male animals – and hence competition. Production management reduces the average inter-calving rate of cows from extensive areas (as seen in the larger protected areas) from 22 to 14.5 months. This increases the maximum number of progeny per lifespan (20 years, first mating at age 5) from a natural $n = 8$ calves to $n = 12$ per lifespan (i.e. a 50 per cent increase per breeding cow). The age at first calving can also be reduced through the provision of constant quality feeding.

Wild animals have various adaptations to reduce the impact of parasites such as ticks and helminths on them. In some cases, this consists of migrating away from heavily parasitized areas, which often is not possible on fenced properties. This requires management interventions to reduce parasite numbers. Various 'self-medication' forms of acaracide applications have been developed. However, they all have negative aspects (e.g. not being able to control which animals are treated, frequency of dose and/or rate/size dose are difficult to control). Recently, acaricidal balls have been developed, shot by paintball sporting guns, meaning that the correct pour-on acaricide dose can be applied to the correct animal at the required time. Helminth treatment is usually only necessary on small properties with a higher numbers of animals per hectare and is most commonly applied to the supplementary feed.

Genetic Perspective of Buffalo Ranching

In South Africa, all buffalo are in fenced areas, either on private game ranches or National or Provincial Protected Areas. Similarly, veterinary fences and national boundaries in many cases prevent the migration and free movement of buffalo. This has created separate genetic pockets in regions, countries, reserves and private ranches. Given the earlier genetic bottlenecks the African buffalo has suffered, namely the great rinderpest epidemic, and hunting and veterinary controls, this further genetic isolation is of great concern. Private game ranchers, however, have by the nature of their businesses traded and moved animals, in particular bulls, from farm to farm, a practice of metapopulation species management. The purpose was and is twofold, namely to (i) mitigate against inbreeding and loss of genetic diversity and (ii) enhance the quality of the animals on a property by being healthy specimens of the typical buffalo in line with the descriptions recorded by Skinner and Chimimba (2005).

A study of 4,000 buffalo from 26 private ranches (Greyling et al., 2013) revealed that 11 ranches had a genetic diversity 3 per cent lower, and nine ranches had a genetic diversity greater than that of Kruger National Park. The latter indicates the enhancement obtained from metapopulation outbreeding because of frequent trading between private populations. In comparison, relative heterozygosity of private production populations ranges from 1.05 to 0.7 (disease-free) compared to protected conservancy-based populations of (i) Kruger National Park = 1 (diseased, meaning with the four main diseases cited above, that is bTB, CA, FMD and theleiriosis), (ii) Hluhluwe–iMfolozi = 0.85 (diseased), (iii) Addo = 0.65 (disease-free) and St Lucia Estuary = 0.62 (diseased) (Greyling, 2017).

Metapopulation macro-genetic management by private production systems could not only enhance, but also restore historically depleted genetic diversity of game species, with a positive contribution to the survival of the species. The combination of climate change and human industrial development poses increased risk to species adaptation and survival (Furstenburg and Scholtz, 2009; Scholtz et al., 2010). Consequently, increased species and population heterozygosity (genetic integrity) has become directly essential for species survival, and sustained species marketing traits as incentive for production breeding being indirectly essential (Chapter 3).

Production of Specific Disease-Free Buffalo

After detecting bTB in Kruger National Park in 1990, a project was developed to preserve the Kruger buffalo genotype. In 1998, 11 disease-free calves were successfully bred and moved to private land outside of Kruger National Park. As a result of the subsequent successful breeding of more than 27,000 privately owned disease-free buffalo in South Africa, the project was terminated in 2011 (Bengis et al., 2016).

In contrast to state and provincial parks, all buffalo in the private buffalo sector are thus currently disease-free (Table 13.2; Chapter 12).

Production of Large Horn Size Buffalo

Early travellers' journal entries and many scientific studies indicate that buffalo, like many other species (e.g. sable, *Hippotragus niger*; greater kudu, *Tragelaphus strepsiceros*; eland, *Tragelaphus oryx*; elephant, *Loxodonta africanus*; and more), were exploited during the eighteenth and nineteenth centuries by continuous selective hunting. Trophy hunters in particular often first shot the largest individual in a herd, consequently possibly gradually depleting the natural genetic integrity and quality of the species. Studies of kudu populations by Furstenburg (2005) in both free-roaming conservancy production and semi-extensive production systems in the Eastern Cape and in Namibia revealed genetic quality depletion in under 20 years by continuous selective harvesting/hunting.

During the wildlife price boom of the 2010s, East African buffalo had greater trade value for having a 12 per cent larger body size and a greater horn spread than the Kruger and Addo phenotypes. Kruger buffalo are known for thick bosses and a deep drop at the side of the head before curving upwards, and Addo buffalo have smaller body sizes and smaller bosses. East African buffalo were introduced and bred with the Southern African private populations during the late 1990s. Gradually, trophy quality increased, and the first 50-inch trophy bull was auctioned in September 2013 for €1.6 million (ZAR 26 million), and re-auctioned in February 2016 at an all-time record for buffalo of €10.8 million (ZAR 176 million; the animal shown in Figure 13.4). Indications from auctions are that today there are more than 50 bulls with greater than 50-inch trophies among the breeding stock in private production systems in South Africa.

The extent to which this is manipulated genetic engineering versus the restoration of historic natural genetic integrity continues to be debated at the national and international levels. At the national level, disagreements between various organizations are flaring, including between hunting organizations (Selier et al., 2018). Somers et al. (2020) point out numerous concerns in the new legislation, including the process of consultation, and argue that the law will not improve the genetics of the species mentioned but will have considerable negative genetic consequences and pose ecological and economic risks. At the international level, there is much concern about intentional genetic manipulations of wildlife, for

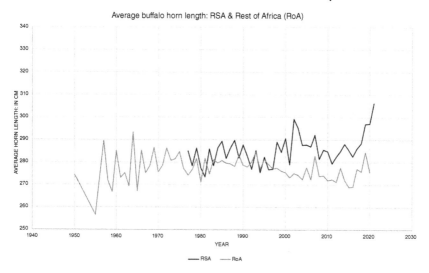

Figure 13.9 Average horn length in Cape buffalo (*Syncerus caffer caffer*) in South Africa (*n* = 777, 22 per cent) and in the 'Rest of Africa' (RoA), a variable composed of data from 11 countries from eastern and southern Africa: Angola, *n* = 19; Botswana, *n* = 35; Kenya, *n* = 89; Mozambique, *n* = 100; Namibia, *n* = 16; Rwanda, *n* = 3; Tanzania, *n* = 857; Uganda, *n* = 4; Zambia, *n* = 482; Zimbabwe, *n* = 811. All buffalo were hunted for trophy hunting in South Africa when buffalo in other countries may have been hunted for other reasons. Graph drawn from data published by Safari Club International (2022).

example (i) the World Conservation Congress at its session in Hawaii, United States of America, 1–10 September 2016, adopted the recommendation WCC-2016-Rec-100-EN on management and regulation of selective intensive breeding of large wild mammals for commercial purposes (IUCN WWC, 2016); and (ii) the Antelope Specialist Group of IUCN released in 2015 a position statement warning about intentional genetic manipulation of antelopes (IUCN SSC Antelope Specialist Group, 2015).

The twin impacts of indiscriminate hunting of the better trophy buffalo bulls in the rest of Africa and the managed breeding and sustainable use of these animals in South Africa are clearly visible in Figure 13.9 (Safari Club International, 2022). The growth of hunted buffalo's average horn length in South Africa can be seen in the graph of records from the 1990s. In comparison, the horn lengths of hunted buffalo from the rest of eastern and southern Africa have shown a steady decline, probably as a result of indiscriminate hunting of the better horned bulls.

Domestication

Domestication of a species is a process whereby, over time, and via genetic selection and modification of a species, it may be adapted for human association and use. Some species, through their genetic plasticity, are better suited for this process (e.g. the dog). It is important to distinguish domestication from 'taming' and 'habituation', both processes being short-term, individual- or small group-based and not involving genetic modification. Habituation can occur even in areas as large as Kruger National Park, where animals of all types become accustomed to and accepting of, for example, tourists in their vehicles on the roads and behave as if the latter were not there. Similarly, the concept of buffalo herding as practiced recently in Zimbabwe and historically in Mozambique is another example of habituation rather than domestication.

Domestication of the African/savanna buffalo, although unsuccessfully attempted on a few occasions, is not something to consider. First, the buffalo's aggressive temperament, massive size and huge horns renders this a risky exercise. Second, its value as a tourism (both consumptive and non-consumptive) icon would be eroded. As domestication would require genetic selection for docility and other 'agriculturally favourable' traits it might, if not very carefully managed, lead to a weakening of the desirable survival traits/genes of the species.

Perspectives and Prospects

The hunger for land to feed the growing human population is rapidly driving the spread of agriculture into the remaining wilderness areas of Africa. With the disappearing wilderness and the loss of species, the need for formal conservation through the declaration of National Parks and the like increases. This in turn often leads to growing wildlife–human conflicts. Governments in many of the poorer developing countries just do not have the financial resources to fund, create and manage Protected Areas or compensate adequately those evicted from the declared areas, fuelling illegal bushmeat harvesting or, in other words, poaching.

Community-based resource management and private rewilding, funded through sustainable use, of the huge areas of marginal land already in use for other forms of agriculture should be considered to ensure the restoration and conservation of biodiversity, such as has been the case in South Africa. When the natural human inclination to want to determine one's own destiny on one's own piece of land is overcome through cooperation and the formation of a cooperative landscape on much larger areas, then it becomes so much easier to sustainably create wealth and create decent jobs for communities previously excluded from tourism (consumptive and non-consumptive), meat harvesting and processing, and the production of many other products. This is a system somewhere in-between the CAMPFIRE programme and the smaller private game ranching as currently found in some southern African states, particularly South Africa. The benefits are habitat conservation, improved biodiversity, improved production, sustainable job creation, integrated community economic development and improved food security and welfare through sustainable use. The iconic buffalo, as one of the Big Five, and valuable as a hunting trophy, for photographic tourism and for meat production, plays a pivotal role in such developments.

References

Bengis, R., D. Govender, E. Lane, et al. (2016). Eco-epidemiological and pathological features of wildlife mortality events related to cyanobacterial bio-intoxication in the Kruger National Park, South Africa. *Journal of the South African Veterinary Association* **87**(1): 1–9.

Bothma, J. du P. and J.G. Du Toit (2016). *Game Ranch Management*, 6th ed. Pretoria: Van Schaik Publishers.

Campfire Association Zimbabwe (2022). *Community Benefits Summary*. Campfire Association. www.campfirezimbabwe.org/article/community-benefits-summary.

Chardonnet, P. (2011). Wildlife ranching: ensuring present and future conservation benefits. 7th International Wildlife Ranching Symposium, 10–14 October 2011, Kimberley, South Africa.

Child, B.A., J. Musengezi, G.D. Parent and G.F. Child (2012). The economics and institutional economics of wildlife on private land in Africa. *Pastoralism* **2**(1): 1–32.

Chomba, C., C. Obias and V. Nyirenda (2014). Game ranching: a sustainable land use option and economic incentive for biodiversity conservation in Zambia. *Open Journal of Ecology* **4**: 571–581.

Cloete, F.C., P. van der Merwe and M. Saayman (2015). *Game Ranch Profitability in South Africa*. Cape Town: ABSA, pp. 1–192.

Craigie, I.D., J.E. Baillie, A. Balmford, et al. (2010). Large mammal population declines in Africa's protected areas. *Biological Conservation* **143**(9): 2221–2228.

Davies, G. and D. Brown (2007). *Bushmeat and Livelihoods: Wildlife Management and Poverty Reduction*. London: Blackwell Publishing.

Dzingirai, V. (2003). 'CAMPFIRE is not for Ndebele migrants': the impact of excluding outsiders from CAMPFIRE in the Zambezi Valley, Zimbabwe. *Journal of Southern African Studies* **29**(2): 445–459.

Fa, J.E. and D. Brown (2009). Impacts of hunting on mammals in African tropical moist forests: a review and synthesis. *Mammal Review* **39**(4): 231–264.

Furstenburg, D. (2005). The greater kudu. In J. du P. Bothma and N. van Rooyen (Eds.), *Intensive Wildlife Production in Southern Africa*. Pretoria: Van Schaik Publishers, pp. 14–168.

Furstenburg, D. (2015). *Game Species Window*. Amazon E-Books, pp. 832–1263.

Furstenburg, D. (2017a). Bestuur en Produksie, Basis van Wildplaasontwikkeling. *Wildlife Ranching* 2017(**4**): 66–73.

Furstenburg, D. (2017b). Wildlife Scoping Technical Report, 257 pp. Afri Wild Services (formerly Geo Wild Consult), South Africa (unpublished report).

Furstenburg, D., Otto, M., Van Niekerk, P., Lewitton, D. (2022). Contribution of private game ranching and captive bred operationjs in South Africa to White rhino Ceratotherium simum species survival conservation. J. Vet. Health Sci. 3(4):331-360. DOI: 10.33140/JVHS.03.04.05

Furstenburg, D. and M. Scholtz (2009). Global climate change and animal production in southern Africa: a short review. Paper submitted to the *Livestock Science* Supplement on the 10th World Congress on Animal Production.

Gandiwa, E., I.M. Heitkönig A.M. Lokhorst, et al. (2013). CAMPFIRE and human–wildlife conflicts in local communities bordering northern Gonarezhou National Park, Zimbabwe. *Ecology and Society* **18**(4): 7.

Greyling, B. (2017). Buffalo genetics, highlights from two decades of research. *The Buffalo Journal*, pp. 14–16.

Greyling, B., D. Furstenburg and P. van Hooft (2013). Ranched populations: the implications for conservation management of the African buffalo from a genetics point of view. National Parks Board Symposium, Skukuza.

Hildebrandt, W.R. (2014). *Management and reproduction of the African savanna buffalo Syncerus caffer caffer*. Doctoral dissertation, Stellenbosch University.

IUCN SSC Antelope Specialist Group (2015). IUCN SSC ASG Position Statement on the Intentional Genetic Manipulation of Antelopes Ver. 1.0 (30 April 2015).

IUCN WCC (2016). World Conservation Congress Recommendation WCC-2016-Rec-100-EN. WCC-2016-Rec-100-EN Management and regulation of selective intensive breeding of large wild mammals for commercial purposes.

Mabeta, J., B. Mweemba and J. Mwitwa (2018). *Key drivers of biodiversity loss in Zambia*. Policy Brief # 3. Zambia: Biodiversity Finance Initiative (BIOFIN).

Machena, C., E. Mwakiwa and E. Gandiwa (2017). *Review of the communal areas management programme for indigenous resources (CAMPFIRE) and community based natural resources management (CBNRM) models*. Harare: Government of Zimbabwe and European Union.

Manyanga, M. and G. Pangeti (2017). Pre-colonial hunting in Southern Africa: a changing paradigm. In M. Manyanga and S. Chirikure (Eds.), *Archives, Objects, Places and Landscapes: Multidisciplinary Approaches to Decolonised Zimbabwean Pasts*. Bamenda, Cameroon: Langaa RPCIG, pp. 277–294.

Marks, S.A. (1973). Prey selection and annual harvest of game in a rural Zambian community. *African Journal of Ecology* **11**(2): 113–128.

Marks, S.A. (1977a). Buffalo movements and accessibility to a community of hunters in Zambia. *African Journal of Ecology* **15**(4): 251–261.

Marks, S.A. (1977b). Hunting behavior and strategies of the Valley Bisa in Zambia. *Human Ecology* **5**(1): 1–36.

Martin, P.S. (1966). Africa and Pleistocene overkill. *Nature* **212**(5060): 339–342.

Mogomotsi, P.K., L.S. Stone, G.E.J. Mogomotsi and N. Dube (2020). Factors influencing community participation in wildlife conservation. *Human Dimensions of Wildlife* **25**(4): 372–386.

Muboko, N. and F. Murindagomo (2014). Wildlife control, access and utilisation: Lessons from legislation, policy evolution and implementation in Zimbabwe. *Journal for Nature Conservation* **22**(3): 206–211.

Musiwa, A.R. and W. Mhlanga (2020). Human–wildlife conflict in Mhokwe Ward, Mbire District, North-East Zimbabwe. *African Journal of Ecology* **58**(4): 786–795.

Mutanga, C.N., S. Vengesayi, N. Muboko and E. Gandiwa (2015). Towards harmonious conservation relationships: a framework for understanding protected area staff-local community relationships in developing countries. *Journal for Nature Conservation* **25**: 8–16.

Nel, L. (2021). Sustainability in wildlife-based enterprises. The conservation of biodiversity and landscapes: is sustainable use an option? WESSA Lowveld Conference, 4 September 2021.

North-West University (NWU) (2017). A marketing and spending analysis of trophy hunters, 2015/16 season. Tourism Research in Economic Environs and Society.

Oberem, P. and P.T. Oberem (2016). *The New Game Rancher*. Pretoria: Briza Publications.

Ripple, W.J., C. Wolf, T.M. Newsome, et al. (2019). Are eating the world's megafauna to extinction? *Conservation Letters* **12**(3): e12627.

Safari Club International (2022). Online Record Book: Species Detail – Cape or Southern Buffalo. www.scirecordbook.org/species, accessed 21 April 2022.

Scholtz, M., D. Furstenburg, N. Maiwashe, et al. (2010). Environmental–genotype responses in livestock to global warming: a Southern African perspective. *South African Journal of Animal Science* **40**: 408–413.

Selier J., L. Nel, I. Rushworth, et al. (2018). *An assessment of the potential risks of the practice of intensive and selective breeding of game to biodiversity and the biodiversity economy in South Africa*. Report: Xvi, 172 pp.

Skinner, J.D. and C.T. Chimimba (2005). *The Mammals of the South African Sub-Region*. Cambridge: Cambridge University Press.

Smil, V. (2011). Harvesting the biosphere: the human impact. *Population and development review* **37**(4): 613–636.

Somers M.J., M. Walters, J. Measey, et al. (2020). The implications of the reclassification of South African wildlife species as farm animals. *South African Journal of Science* 116(1/2): Art. #7724.

Stoldt, M., T. Göttert, C. Mann and U. Zeller (2020). Transfrontier conservation areas and human–wildlife conflict: the case of the Namibian component of the Kavango-Zambezi (KAZA) TFCA. *Scientific Reports* **10**(1): 1–16.

Taylor, W.A., M.F. Child, P.A. Lindsey, et al. (2021). South Africa's private wildlife ranches protect globally significant populations of wild ungulates. *Biodiversity and Conservation* **30**, 4111–4135.

Taylor, W.A., P.A. Lindsey, S.K. Nicholson, et al. (2020). Jobs, game meat and profits: the benefits of wildlife ranching on marginal lands in South Africa. *Biological Conservation* **245**: 108561.

Tchakatumba, P.K., E. Gandiwa, E. Mwakiwa, et al. (2019). Does the CAMPFIRE programme ensure economic benefits from wildlife to households in Zimbabwe? *Ecosystems and People* **15**(1): 119–135.

van Hoven, W. and P.T. Oberem (2018). Afrivet Business Management (Pty) Ltd. Video: https://youtube/xRCWnEflITg.

Wilkie, D.S., M. Wieland, H. Boulet, et al. (2016). Eating and conserving bushmeat in Africa. *African Journal of Ecology* **54**(4): 402–414.

14 · *Management Aspects of the Captive-Bred African Buffalo (Syncerus caffer) in South Africa*

L. C. HOFFMAN, C. A. SHEPSTONE,
K. ROBERTSON AND T. NEEDHAM

Introduction

The objective of most buffalo production systems is to produce offspring that meet specific requirements. In the case of captive-bred African buffalo in South Africa, the main aim is to produce trophy-quality animals for breeding and hunting. Managing nutrition and feeding is of the utmost importance when working with high-value species such as the African buffalo, as their nutritional status has a direct effect on their (re-)production and the profitability of the enterprise. In natural systems (game reserves, national parks), droughts cause buffalo numbers to decline due to animals not being able to source the necessary nutrients for reproduction in the available dry grazing (Chapter 7), thus reducing the animals' reproductive performance and production. Within intensive systems focusing on individual and herd performance, particularly reproductive performance, there is a need to create management programmes and practices to assuage potential poor performance due to a lack of necessary nutrients at different times of the year. Although numerous factors, such as sexually transmitted diseases, libido, age of first mating, season and nutrition, influence reproduction rate, this section will discuss how nutrition may be used to support reproduction and production in intensively and semi-extensively housed/ranched African buffalo herds. In this chapter, we discuss the feeding preferences under semi-extensive systems together with the estimation of stocking rates for buffalo of differing physiological stages, as well as the nutritional requirements of buffalo, the effects of season on these, and how supplementary feeding may be used to ensure adequate nutrition – most of the knowledge/experience presented in this chapter comes from southern Africa, given their development of the private wildlife sector (see Chapter 13).

Furthermore, fundamental information regarding buffalo reproduction and their utilization for meat production is summarized using real-time ranch experience originating from the disease-free buffalo breeding ranches that flowed out into commercial buffalo ranching in South Africa. It is essential to give credit where it is due; the origin of buffalo ranching started with the cattle industry's husbandry techniques, and as time progressed, more and more scientific data were collected. This scientific knowledge allowed the game industry to not only gain the knowledge of breeding disease-free buffalo, but also to introduce these animals back into the wild.

Nutrition

Buffalo are broadly classified as bulk grazers, spending 40–80 per cent of their time feeding and ruminating depending on the season. Rumination is the process through which selected forage, already in the rumen, is repeatedly regurgitated into the mouth and back to the rumen to decrease particle size and buffer rumen pH via saliva; these fine food particles are degraded in the rumen by microbial action and fermentation. These small particles pass through into the omasum, then the abomasum, and then the small and large intestine for further degradation, digestion and nutrient absorption. The African buffalo consumes a wide variety of grass species, with grass constituting a relatively high proportion of their diet (75–100 per cent), but utilize more browse during the dry season or in different vegetation zones (woodlands or forest) when they are forced to graze less selectively and browse on woody shrubs, increasing the browse proportion of their diet.

African buffalo are relatively unselective grazers, but prefer highly palatable nutrient-rich grass. In extensive systems of southern Africa within granite and basalt landscapes (Macandza et al., 2004), they depend primarily on *Panicum* spp. (mostly *P. maximum*) throughout the year, and as the dry season progresses, *Digitaria eriantha* and *Urochloa mosambicensis* (previously also known as *U. usambarensis*) and *Cynodon dactylon* are the predominant species consumed. Some *Bothriochloa* spp. become important contributors to the buffalo's diet during the transition from wet to dry seasons, but mostly not *B. insculpta*, while *Eragrostis* spp. contribute towards the end of the dry season. On the other hand, important cattle forage species, like *Themeda triandra*, which generally hold more fibrous content during the dry season, are less favoured by African buffalo under low-input management conditions Furthermore, *Cymbopogon plurinodis*, *Bothriochloa* spp., *Pogonarthria squarrosa*, *Aristida* spp. and *Setaria* spp. tend to be rejected by buffalo, regardless of the season.

The quantity (amount) and quality (nutrients) of grazing is influenced by soil type, topography, rainfall, ambient temperature and animal stocking rate/density. In semi-extensive ranching systems, these factors need to be taken cognisance of, as the manager only has control over the number of animals placed in the ranch/camp/paddock (stocking rate/density), keeping in mind factors such as carrying capacity (see below).

Extensive Grazing and Stocking Rates

Safe stocking rate (referred to as 'carrying capacity' by many game and livestock ranchers) can be defined as the number of animals that a specific piece of land can accommodate annually without degrading the quality of the forage, and can be measured in different animal units, generally known as large stock or large animal units (LSU or LAU), grazing and browsing units (GU/BU) in southern Africa. With irregularities existing in stocking rate methodology and the interpretation of the animal units in these methods, researchers developed a model where the different methods could be interpreted on a metabolizable energy basis measured in megajoules (MJ ME), establishing a calculated large stock unit (LSU^C), grazing and browsing unit (GU^C/BU^C) to be used in the model. One LSU is equivalent to a steer (cattle) with a body mass of 450 kg that is growing 500 g per day by feeding on grazing that has a mean digestible energy concentration of 55 per cent, thus supplying 75 MJ ME per day (Meissner, 1982). A grazing unit (GU) is a 180 kg blue wildebeest and a browsing unit (BU) is a 180 kg kudu (Van Rooyen and Bothma, 2016) requiring 29.71 MJ ME per day (Shepstone et al., 2022). These methods are conservative ways to calculate a piece of land's safe stocking rate if its grazing and browsing capacity has been assessed. This prevents overutilization of the available forage and ensures that the quantity and quality of grazing do not deteriorate over time.

When estimating the carrying capacity and stocking rate on semi-extensive systems, the average LSU^C or GU^C/BU^C value for the specific species should be used. Using averages for all production phases mentioned in Table 14.1 will undersupply energy to lactating females,

Table 14.1 *Calculated large stock unit equivalents and metabolizable energy values for different physiological stages of African buffalo.*

Physiological stage	Mass (kg)	ME (MJ/day)*	LSU$^{C\#}$	BU^C/GU$^{C\#}$
Calf, 8 months	145	29.6	0.39	1.00
Heifer, dry, 4 years	460	78.1	1.04	2.63
Cow, dry, 10 years	530	72.6	0.97	2.44
Cow, with calf, 4 years	460	99.1	1.32	3.34
Cow, with calf, 10 years	530	93.2	1.24	3.14
Young bull, 4 years	500	80.2	1.07	2.70
Adult bull, 10 years	640	81.9	1.09	2.76

* Calculated metabolizable energy.
\# Calculated large stock, grazing and browsing units.
Adapted from Shepstone et al. (2022).

as well as growing and adult males. Intensive systems should either use the fixed values in Table 14.1, where the number of animals is multiplied by the LSU^C or GU^C/BU^C value for each respective physiological state in a spreadsheet, or use the lactating cow (cow with calf) LSU value of 1.32 as the baseline parameter. For example, using the LSU^C value of 1.32, a herd of 20 breeding buffalo will need 264 ha if the carrying capacity of the property is 10 ha/LSU. On commercial ranches in southern Africa, stocking rates vary and range between 2.6 and 13.3 ha/ LSU (Hildebrandt, 2014). The methodology behind calculating the ME requirements, calculated large stock, grazing and browsing unit values and dry matter intake (DMI), is described by Shepstone et al. (2022).

When the stocking rate exceeds the assessed safe stocking rate, the property is overstocked, making it necessary to purchase or supply stored roughage of a suitable quality to reach the desired reproductive goals. In circumstances where the stocking rate equals, or is lower than, the assessed safe stocking rate, and the quality of the available grazing is not suitable for optimal reproductive performance, the specific nutrients that nature cannot supply must be provided so the ranch can reach the desired production goal. The production constraining nutrients normally found in dry grasses are digestible protein, minerals and vitamins. It is important to note that no specific nutrient guidelines currently exist for buffalo, so cattle data are used to extrapolate the nutrient requirements for buffalo and other similar species. When supplying animals with supplemental feed formulated to mitigate a deficiency, it is important to understand that content and quantity of a particular nutrient will differ from one production system to another, and from one ranch to another. The nutrient concentration and the amount to be fed are directly influenced by the nutrient requirements of the animals/herds at that specific time, the quantity and quality of the natural grazing (high correlation with rainfall) or supplied roughage, seasonal changes, availability of raw materials, manufacturing equipment and storage of the mixed feed and raw materials. In order to ensure optimal rangeland utilization on a piece of land, and to limit rangeland degradation by overutilization (i.e. too many animals), routine vegetation studies are necessary to calculate its respective annual safe stocking rate and to take measures to ensure a conservative stocking rate using either or both the calculated LSU^C, GU^C and BU^C methods. Similar animal unit methods are used internationally, such as the animal unit (AU) used in North America and the tropical livestock unit (TLU) used in tropical countries. Be aware of the differences before translating values 1 to 1.

Nutrient Requirements

When considering nutrient requirements for wild animals, a similar well-studied species is used as a proxy when formulating feeds; when considering the bulk-grazing African buffalo, other bulk grazing species such as beef cattle and water buffalo (*Bubalis bubalus*) data can be used. In this document, we use nutrient requirements of beef cattle in the United States (National Academies of Sciences Engineering and Medicine, 2016) as the baseline comparative nutrition proxy because rangeland beef cattle in southern Africa select a similar diet, live in similar habitats and have a similar daily water requirement to the African buffalo. On the other hand, water buffalo are animals housed and raised similarly to how the dairy industry houses and raises their dairy cattle, making this species less comparable to the African buffalo from a comparative nutrition point of view. Using cattle nutrient requirement data to estimate the daily nutrient requirements of buffalo is of little value if the buffalo's average weight, physiological state and daily DMI are unknown; thus, these are important factors to account for when formulating a supplement/feed for buffalo. Knowing the physiological state and average weight aids in calculating the animal's nutrient requirements, and nutrient analysis of the grass or roughage supplied to the animals will aid in calculating what shortfalls exist.

In addition to providing sufficient quantities of feed, the quality (nutrients) of feed, which includes the energy, protein, fibre and trace elements (vitamins and minerals) content, is important for ensuring optimal production and reproduction based on the animals' nutrient requirements. The calculated LSU^C, GU^C and BU^C methods discussed above is currently the most accurate method to calculate the energy requirements for game animals (Shepstone et al., 2022), where the energy used by the animal is expressed as ME, measured in megajoules (MJ). When conditions are favourable, ruminants eat to meet their energy requirements rather than to fill their rumens (intake capacity). However, during the dry season, when the available ME in the selected grazing is too low to meet maintenance/lactation requirements, the animals cannot consume more grass or browse to satisfy their requirements, the main reason being that the total amount of feed intake per unit of time is restricted by their thoracic cavity (restricted rumen capacity). Furthermore, a cow in her last trimester of pregnancy has even less space (as the calf is taking up a lot of the abdominal cavity) for food in her rumen. The average voluntary feed intake (VFI) for buffalo is calculated to be approximately 1.8–2.3 per cent of their live body mass (530 kg) for a dry cow and a lactating cow, respectively (Shepstone et al., 2022), which compares well to the published value of 2.5 per cent of live body mass on a dry mass (DM) basis (Prins, 1996).

The supply and intake of protein are the main factors controlling production performance in ruminants like cattle (Köster et al., 1996) and buffalo on dry rangeland. The minimum crude protein requirement of buffalo is 7–8 per cent (Prins, 1996), which may be provided by browse when available. When considering dietary protein supply in ruminants, it can generally be broken down into rumen-degradable protein (RDP) and rumen-undegradable protein (UDP). Ruminants require protein (nitrogen and amino acids) for two important functions. First, specific amino acids are needed for their metabolic processes (UDP). Second, and more importantly, protein from grass and supplemental feed is needed to supply the necessary nitrogen (RDP) to the rumen microbes to multiply, playing a pivotal role in increasing the VFI of dry forage. A ruminant's RDP requirement in general can be calculated using the following equation: $RDP = \text{live body weight}^{0.75} \times 4$. The VFI of dry grass is directly related to the concentration of RDP in the forage and/or feed.

While buffalo can increase their dietary protein intake by increasing their VFI, they are constrained by the need to ruminate, which competes with grazing time. In addition to selecting more browse during periods when high quantities of mixed quality food are available or under food scarcity/poor quality conditions, buffalo apply bulk grazing, whereby they graze during periods of adequate or high grazing volume availability and spend equal amounts of time grazing and ruminating (Prins, 1996). When the quantity and quality of grazing is poor, buffalo spend more time in search of food, therefore they have less time for rumination and digestion on a daily basis, and are limited by rumen fill (capacity) regardless of passage rate. Feed supplementation should be considered to meet the nutrient requirements of buffalo, especially with regards to RDP during the dry season or during periods of increased productive/reproductive performance.

The most important goal of supplementation, particularly RDP (nitrogen), is to maximize the VFI of dry roughage during the dry season to ensure optimal ruminal microbe proliferation and supply of microbial protein. With a limited supply of RDP (nitrogen), fewer microbes are available to ferment the finer particles of grass that have been masticated into small particles by rumination, thereby reducing the fermentation rate of the ingested food, causing food to stay in the rumen for longer periods. As it takes the animal a longer amount of time to degrade and digest the food, the animal starts losing condition, forcing it to mobilize stored energy (fat) and protein (muscle) to survive. When this problem can be diminished or even prevented by increasing the VFI of dry grass, the animal will have more nutrients to maintain its good body condition. This can be done by ensuring adequate amounts of RDP are available all year round. Green grazing normally has sufficient RDP to maintain the animal's condition, but as the dry season progresses the plants dry out, causing the quality and supply of protein to become limited for the rumen bacteria first, thereby making it necessary to supply additional RDP. Supplements formulated to supply the appropriate amount and ratio of RDP and other nutrients will enable beneficial microbes to proliferate. With a larger microbe population, the animals can degrade and ferment more food, thereby increasing their VFI of dry grass, resulting in improved production, body condition, health, milk, and colostrum quality and strong calves. As buffalo are ruminants, they can utilise nitrogen from non-protein nitrogen (NPN) sources such as urea and convert this into microbial protein (McDonald et al., 2002), making it possible to design supplements that include NPN sources such as urea.

In addition to energy and protein, minerals (macro-minerals > 100 mg/kg feed and micro-/trace minerals < 100 mg/kg feed) and vitamins are nutrients important for herbivorous animals including buffalo. Macro-minerals, micro-minerals and vitamins are important components of supplementary feed if optimal reproductive performance is desired. As grass is the main component of a buffalo's diet, the animal relies on the minerals and vitamins that grass supplies. The mineral content and the availability of grass to the animal are influenced by different factors, including grass species and stage of maturity of the grazing, the type of soil, climate and seasonal conditions, and the condition of the soil, such as pH and mineral content as well as fertilization and liming (McDonald et al., 2002). The (trace) elements that are typically deficient are phosphorous, sodium, chloride, sulphur, iron, iodine, copper, cobalt, manganese, and selenium (Schmidt and Snyman, 2016), although there may be specific minerals that are deficient in specific areas.

Vitamins are needed in small quantities by herbivorous animals, and ruminants require even less as they have microorganisms that synthesize some vitamins in the rumen that can be used in the buffalo's body. Under natural extensive conditions, vitamin levels in green grazing are generally high enough to meet the animals' requirements. The exception is vitamin A, which normally is found in low concentrations in dry mature grass and grains used in formulated feeds. As with most supplementation of shortages, the most effective starting point to control or manage a mineral or vitamin shortage is to accurately predict its extent. A possible way of predicting the mineral shortages of buffalo is to analyse the grass species selected by the animal on the ranch at different stages of growth, and then formulate a mineral supplement that makes up for the shortfalls of the grazing (Schmidt and Snyman, 2016). However, this method might prove impractical and/or costly. Alternatively, basic knowledge of the animal's well-being and behaviour, regular observation and accurate record-keeping combined with basic knowledge of the environment (type of veld, general shortages in the area, weather patterns, parasites, etc.) should suffice to identify most shortages. The buffalo themselves are the best indicators of mineral shortages, and if the animals maintain good health with 13-month intercalving periods, and the calves display optimal growth and health, then any changes made are likely unwarranted. Any unnecessary changes to the 'environment' may have an adverse effect on production and cause monetary losses.

The planting of additional grazing (pastures) is an effective management method in areas that provide low-quality natural grazing (such as sourveld in the dry months; 'sourveld' is the term used in Southern Africa for nutrient-poor, dystrophic savannas and grassland types), especially for overwintering. By irrigating these planted pastures, the feed production of the pasture can be raised substantially, and the expense of feed costs can be lowered. Nonetheless, these planted pastures can be a potential reservoir for parasites, especially in cases where the grazing forms a thick matt at the base, such as kikuyu (*Pennisetum clandestinum*, also known as *Cenchrus clandestinus*) and should be managed accordingly. Additional advantages include the fact that many of these grasses are perennial grasses, and once established, all that is needed for growth is sufficient water and, depending on the soil type, at times fertilizer. The grass not used for grazing can be baled and either stored for drought years or sold as an additional source of income.

Influence of Season on Nutrition and Feeding

Three factors need to be taken into consideration to estimate what nutrient shortfalls exist, if any, namely: (i) a nutrient analysis of the grass or roughage supplied to the animals; (ii) an assessment of the physiological state of the particular class of animals, including body condition, to gauge their nutrient requirements; and (iii) for the same reason, an estimate of the typical weights of the particular class of animals for which one wants to estimate the possible nutrient shortfall. The available grass on reserves and game ranches is normally a combination of annual and perennial grass species. These grasses have a green growing phase and a dry phase (Figure 14.1). During the dry phase, perennial grasses go into dormancy and store most of their nutrients in their roots and seeds, while the annual grass species release their seeds and die. Under free-ranging conditions, many buffalo populations would migrate shorter or longer distances, grazing higher-quality food elsewhere, but within ranches they are stuck in an area (due to fencing) where the grass nearly always deteriorates to a point where the buffalo lose condition. Buffalo in a poor body condition have lower conception rates, fewer calves, less milk and fewer calves that reach adulthood (see Chapter 7); in addition, the general health of the adult and subadult deteriorates over time.

The changes in nutrient quality from a high-/higher-quality green plant to a dry, brownish, poor-quality plant have a direct effect on the buffalo's ability to break down and digest the available grass. Protein, energy, macro-minerals, trace minerals and vitamin concentrations decrease as the plant dries out, while the fibre portion increases. The drastic decrease in nutrient concentration, particularly RDP, results in fewer microbes proliferating, slowing down the degradation and digestion of the ingested fibrous feed, and thus the production of volatile fatty acids (VFA). VFAs produced by these microbes are the main energy source for ruminants and thus buffalo. The small population of microbes present when buffalo feed on poor-quality feed takes longer to degrade

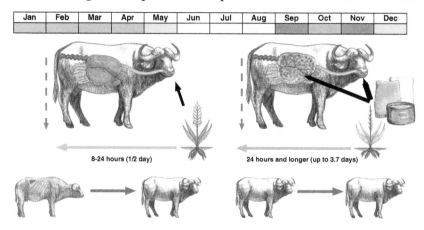

Jan	Feb	Mar	Apr	May	Jun	Jul	Aug	Sep	Oct	Nov	Dec

8-24 hours (1/2 day)

24 hours and longer (up to 3.7 days)

Figure 14.1 How the season affects the quality of the grazing and animals' body condition in southern Africa. Considering the months of January through to December (a full year), each month has a shade of green (rainy season), or yellow to orange (dry season). The green blocks correspond with the rumen and plant (in green) and the green arrow below it, portraying the time of the year when the selected feed gets degraded and digested in less than 24 h. The yellow to orange blocks correspond with the rumen and plant (in yellow/orange) and the orange arrow below it, portraying the time of the year when the selected takes longer than 24 h to be degraded and digested. Source: Craig Shepstone.

the fibrous feed, resulting in the feed remaining in the rumen for a longer period, forcing the animals to mobilize stored nutrients to survive (Figure 14.1) and resulting in the animal losing body condition.

As shown in Figure 14.1, the nutrient-rich green grass available from January to April supplies enough nutrients for increased VFI. Bulk grazing ruminants like buffalo then only need between 8 and 24 h to digest the green grass, resulting in an improved body condition (poor to improved body condition). However, in the dry season (June to November), buffalo can take as long as 3.7 days to digest the nutrient-poor grazing available, resulting in poorer body condition. The lower the RDP concentration in the dry grazing, the longer it takes to be digested in the rumen. Supplying the correct amounts of the necessary nutrients in the dry season will aid in reaching the desired production/reproduction goals, reducing feed digestion time from 3.7 days (worst case scenario) to 24 h.

For optimal production, managers should pre-empt the negative effects of the upcoming dry season and supply supplemental feed in small amounts before the grass deteriorates and the animals start losing condition. As the dry season progresses, it may be necessary to supply more nutrients for optimal body condition; the reason for this is that grass nutritional quality deteriorates further as the dry season progresses, particularly the protein and energy contents. Supplementing ranched/ managed animals with the feed nutrients they need during the times when nature cannot supply these nutrients will not only speed up the time taken to digest the ingested food, but will also improve body condition, conception, milk production and general health. Not unimportant, it will assist in raising healthy calves. Furthermore, when considering optimal production in times of drought where the quality and the quantity of the available feed gets poorer, it is imperative that animal numbers are reduced, or additional high-quality roughage be supplied. Droughts have deleterious effects on production, reproduction and growth, with young and weaned animals being the most vulnerable (Chapter 7).

Supplementary Feeding of Ranched Buffalo

High-quality feeds can be used to supplement buffalo during critical periods (without having to decrease the number of animals) and can be found in different forms. These include everything from pellets to home-mixed rations, which are normally supplied in an amount smaller or equal to one-third of total daily intake. Supplementary feed for buffalo on dry grazing focuses on supplying RDP, energy, minerals and vitamins. In situations where grazing is limited or not available (in a 'boma', also known as 'kraal' or 'corral'), feed must be supplied daily with all of the above nutrients together with ample high-quality roughage. In the rainy season, when the quantity and quality of grazing are high, supplying adequate amounts of protein and energy, some minerals may nonetheless remain deficient. For example, phosphorus, copper and zinc are deficient in most parts of southern Africa, making it advisable to supply some minerals to the animals throughout the year. Mineral licks composed of salt, macro-, and trace minerals will supply the nutrients for the animals to reach their owners' production goals.

For any rancher/manager interested in obtaining well-balanced feeds, licks in both meal and block form for supplying buffalo the nutrients nature cannot, feed companies throughout southern Africa (South Africa, Namibia, Zimbabwe, Zambia) can be contacted, who will formulate and supply custom diets for the game ranches' specific need. Purchased or self-mixed feeds usually come in the form of a supplement (concentrated feed) providing $\leq \frac{1}{3}$ of total DMI a semi-ad-libitum feed supplying approximately ⅔ of total DMI and full feeds, otherwise known as total mixed rations (TMR). Semi-ad-libitum feeds are usually 50:50 concentrated nutrients: high-quality roughage. Some pellets on the market, known as high-fibre pellets, are designed to be fed as semi-ad-libitum feeds. A TMR for buffalo usually contains roughly one-third (33–40 per cent) of the total daily amount of feed as concentrated nutrients that supply all of the desired trace minerals and vitamins, and most of the protein and energy, with the rest of the roughage making up the difference. To ensure optimal rumination in the bulk-grazing African buffalo, fibre length should be at least 2.5–3.5 cm.

Intakes of concentrated supplemental feed, known in Africa as lick, in a meal (powder) or block form can be controlled by increasing or decreasing the concentration of salt, ammonium sulphate and mono-calcium phosphate and by hardening the licks in block form by adding binders like calcium hydroxide, magnesium oxide and molasses syrup.

When pellets or fine meals are used as ⅔ of the total DMI, the concentrations of the nutrients, particularly protein, energy and copper, should be kept in mind. Do not supply a pellet or fine meal that is designed as a supplement as a semi-ad-libitum feed at approximately two-thirds of DMI or as a full feed at three-thirds. This will result in the overconsumption of some nutrients or minerals, which could cause deleterious effects. Additives like Poly Ethylene Glycol (PEG) can be added to a supplemental diet to aid the buffalo in degrading and digesting tannin-rich browse when they need to consume browse as a food source. Mycotoxin binders should be added to all self-mix recipes. If self-mix recipes are stored for periods longer than 2 or 3 days, the addition of a mould inhibitor is advised. The addition of an active yeast product will aid in the control of rumen pH (reducing the risk of acidosis) and enhance fibre digestion (Chaucheyras-Durand et al., 2016). All dry or semi-dry feed should be stored in a well-ventilated (dehumidified if necessary) storeroom or container (rodent-, insect- and bird-free), preferably on pallets, and never in direct sunlight.

Buffalo should receive good-quality grass hay as the largest portion of their diet. When hays (alfalfa, grass, oat or other cereal hays) are supplied to the animals in the camp (ad-libitum if limited or no grazing is available), place them in or near the feeding area, in a separate bowl or hay rack that keeps the hay off the ground (reducing losses and cost). All hay that falls on the ground should be removed, preventing young animals from eating wet/soiled/mouldy hay. Mouldy or dusty hay can cause pneumonia, colic and/or heaves. All roughage with any visible signs of mould should not be used, as it usually contains high levels of mycotoxins. If poor-quality grass is the only source of grass hay available to the animals, it would be advisable to mix 10–20 per cent legume hay (alfalfa) into the roughage diet to augment the amount of protein. Legume hay roughage, such as soya bean or peanut, can be used as a roughage source if the products are free of mycotoxins, as the pods often house the fungus. When in doubt, use a suitable mycotoxin binder when using any such roughage as feed. Macronutrient analysis of all hay should be done routinely. This will not only help illustrate what the buffalo are eating, but it will also assist in deciding how much legume hay is needed to be mixed into a ration if the grass hay is of poor nutrient quality. Exclusive use of small grain hay and alfalfa hay for the Cape buffalo is discouraged as it may lead to mineral imbalances, laminitis, colic and diarrhoea, and other dietary abnormalities.

When the season changes and the nutrient quality of the grass drops to levels where it is necessary to supplement the animals with a supplemental (concentrated) feed to keep them in good condition, it is critical to remember that the animals need to be slowly adapted to the feed (over 5 weeks) to avoid conditions like acidosis, rumenitis and *Clostridium*-related illnesses, which can be fatal. This is also important when changing concentrated feeds, where the new feed is mixed with the old in increasing increments of $\frac{1}{5}$ over the 5 weeks. Animals should be vaccinated against red gut (frequently caused by sudden feed changes to ruminant diets, thought to be caused by excess growth of *Clostridium perfringens* type A, which causes an enterotoxaemia or torsion of the gut). During the growing season, it is necessary to supply a well-balanced mineral lick, and a well-balanced supplement/semi-ad-libitum feed in the dry season.

When a particular spot in a camp is used continuously as a feeding site, problems could arise in the long term, namely parasite build up (wire and other roundworms and coccidia) and a breeding place for disease due to the high number of flies and mould growing in old food, leading to possible mycotoxicosis. Unfortunately, feeding sites that are used continuously are often associated with accumulated faeces and urine. To prevent the build up of the abovementioned problems, and to encourage the animals to eat grass in a different part of the reserve or game ranch, feeding sites should be moved regularly. Small enclosures are an exception, making dedicated feeding sites necessary. These feeding areas need to be designed so they can be cleaned and disinfected routinely. Feed should not be placed near water troughs, and placing feed bowls a short distance away will limit the amount of collected feed falling out of

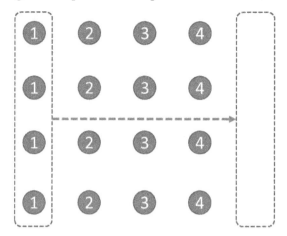

Figure 14.2 Feed bowl placement in a camp and movement suggestions. The circles represent bowls, and the figures refer to a column of bowls that need to be moved together periodically, from left to right as shown in the diagram. Spaces between bowls should be 2.5 the animal's length. Source: Craig Shepstone.

the animal's mouth into the water. Water troughs and feed bowls must be cleaned routinely, and new feed should not be added on top of old remaining feed.

A rule of thumb suggested to ranchers who keep animals where both male and female animals have horns is to place a bowl per animal and an extra bowl for every four animals, but observation of the competition at feeding is necessary, and it may be necessary to increase the number of bowls. Place the bowls 2.5 animal lengths apart in a rectangular chessboard-like fashion and only feed the animals when they are near the feed bowls. Move one line of bowls every second or third day (Figure 14.2). This not only saves time but also gives the keeper the chance to clean all the bowls at least once a month.

Water Provision

The importance of water in ruminant nutrition is often overlooked; water being the basis of rumen fluid creates a suitable environment in which the beneficial anaerobic bacteria can degrade (ferment) and digest the selected food, making it imperative that animals like buffalo need a regular supply of clean water.

The water requirements of buffalo differ according to the different circumstances and environments. Factors affecting water requirements include the gestation, age and physiological condition of the buffalo, the composition of the vegetation fed on and environmental conditions. Watering points are needed at regular intervals to supply adequate water without the buffalo having to travel long distances. Buffalo can utilize most types of water sources but seem to prefer artificial water holes and dams over troughs. In the case of intensive ranching, it is advisable to use water sources that can be controlled. Controlled water points can be tested and analysed for quality and contaminants (which is advised when ranching intensively with high-value species) and filtered if harmful agents are found in the water, as opposed to open and stagnant ground-/rainwater which could contain toxin-producing bacteria or other harmful agents. Open groundwater also doubles as a potential mud hole for wallowing, which is a part of daily activity in warm months, especially by bulls. As buffalo tend to urinate or defecate in these mud holes, it is advised to limit these to only wallowing (and not drinking as well) to prevent any potential diseases emanating from these activities.

Reproduction

The reproduction efficiency of buffalo is influenced by body condition (like cattle), and thus nutrition plays a crucial role in a herd's reproductive performance. It is influenced by the fact that buffalo show some degree of seasonality in their breeding activities under extensive conditions, with most births occurring during seasons when food quality and availability are at their highest (Bertschinger, 1996). However, the degree of breeding seasonality may differ under semi-extensive/intensive conditions where nutrition is optimal and health challenges are minimized. The attainment of sexual maturity is primarily influenced by body condition and thus nutrition; sexual maturity in buffalo is estimated to occur when they attain two-thirds of their genetically determined adult body mass which, depending on their condition, is generally 4–5 years of age for wild free-ranging southern African buffalo heifers. Typically, mature males can weigh 650–850 kg while females can weigh 520–635 kg at maturity. In captive-bred/supplemented herds, buffalo heifers, due to better nutrition and consequently faster growth rates, regularly become sexually mature in the latter stages of their third year. The average lifespan of the buffalo is 11 years under wild conditions (disease and predation being mostly responsible for mortalities) and 16 years in captivity. Females become senescent at 15 years (Prins, 1996). Maximum lifespans are 24 and 20 years on average, for males and females, respectively.

African buffalo are promiscuous, and under extensive, so-called natural conditions, adult buffalo bulls constitute 10–15 per cent of the herd and adult females 55 per cent (Sinclair, 1977), and thus a 1:5 adult sex ratio typically exists. As reported in the survey of Hildebrandt (2014), southern African ranches tend to have a male:female ratio of 1:2 under intensive ranching conditions, with a ratio of active breeding bulls:cows being 1:27, within herds that ranged from 56 to 290 buffalo (mean = 156 animals/enterprise). Hildebrandt concluded that the optimal ratio of breeding bulls:cows would be 1:30, provided that their nutritional requirements are met and body condition is maintained.

The buffalo cow is polyoestrous, and her oestrous cycle is 23 days long, with oestrus lasting 24 h, and the ovulation of two ova is rare (the second is often resolved). The buffalo is a long-day breeder, being sensitive to photoperiod effects. The gestational period of buffalo is ~340 days, with an intercalving period varying from 13 to 29 months, depending on nutritional conditions (Prins, 1996). Hildebrandt (2014) conducted surveys of a number of ranches in southern Africa and reported an average intercalving period of 443 days (14,6 months), with the optimum period being under 400 days. Typically, lactation lasts 10–15 months (Carmichael et al., 1977). Calves are on average 40 kg at birth. When the calf is removed shortly after birth (3 days), oestrus occurs within 5 weeks, but post-partum anoestrus depends on the conditions of the cow and population dynamics. Cows with good body condition at parturition, receiving a high-energy diet, resume oestrus within 90 days post-partum. On the contrary, poor nutrition of the cow may result in low fecundity for up to 2 years thereafter (Ryan et al., 2007). The body condition of the cow during gestation also affects the calf's growth and survival.

Thus, prior to parturition and during lactation, the cow would benefit from improved nutrition and her body condition should be monitored. It is important to remember that as soon as implantation of the embryo takes place during gestation, the feed intake of the cow becomes the feed intake of the calf too. This continues after parturition, as the calf is now dependent on the milk from the cow, although less direct than when in the uterus, but the quality of the milk has a direct effect on the development of the calf and its performance as an adult (McDonald et al., 2002). The energy requirement of lactation is extremely high and can reach between 93 and 99 MJ/day at peak milk production (~5 weeks after parturition; Shepstone et al., 2022). The weaning age of buffalo in southern African ranches ranges from 6, 12 to 18 months (Hildebrandt, 2014). In the wild, it appears to tend more to 18 months than to shorter periods (Prins, 1996).

The feeding of weaned male buffalo bulls is often neglected, as most of them are placed in a bull camp to grow out with as little expense as possible to the rancher. As some of the weaned bulls might prove to be the best sellers, especially when from a good genetic background, it may be worthwhile to also attend to their feed requirements to optimize growth and obtain the maximum expression of their genetic potential.

From a trophy-hunting perspective, the 'solid boss' of a bull is its most desirable characteristic. Wild, free-ranging southern African buffalo, which occur south of the Zambezi River in areas with 450–750 mm of annual rainfall, become sexually mature in their fifth year, but their bosses only become sufficiently hard enough to become a desirable 'trophy' by their ninth year (Pienaar, 1969). This is the same in East Africa (Prins, 1996). Better nutrition enables captive-bred bull buffalo to grow faster and attain their sexual maturity weight at a younger age, which makes their bosses develop sooner; a 6-year-old bull buffalo may have the appearance of a solid-bossed 9-year-old simply by providing better nutrition, which in turn enables them to be hunted as 'trophies' at a much younger age.

Meat Production

Presently, with the exception of Kruger National Park (KNP, South Africa), no other entity in southern Africa has sufficient numbers of buffalo to ensure a constant supply of buffalo carcasses. However, as commercial ranchers reach their safe stocking rates and the supply of trophy bulls surpasses the demand, more inferior animals will become available (and cheaper) for so-called 'biltong' (traditional dried lightly salted/spiced meat product) or meat hunters to hunt, or to start harvesting on a more commercial scale. Nonetheless, there are still some buffalo hunted for trophy purposes whose meat is available to enter the consumption market. In addition, the culling of animals for various management reasons is an essential component of wildlife management, and there is interest in economic opportunities for game ranchers and ecotourism. However, concerns have been raised over the practicality and financial benefits of using culled buffalo as a source of meat in South Africa, where buffalo are not normally utilized for their meat. Cape buffalo have carcass yields similar to those of domestic beef cattle and produce meat with favourable organoleptic properties (Van Zyl and Skead, 1964). Cape buffalo carcasses are typically from subadults (280–430 kg live weight), adult cows (450–680 kg) or adult bulls

(600–850 kg), who yield carcass weights of 140–220 kg, 260–330 kg and 300–440 kg, respectively (Grobler, 1996). Thus, buffalo typically have a dressing percentage of 48–58 per cent depending on their gut fill at point of slaughter – similar to that of *Bos taurus* cattle (Hoffman et al., 2020). Under extensive conditions, the mass gains (kg/year) from up until 42 months can be expected to be for different regions of Africa (Bothma and van Rooyen, 2005):

- Kruger National Park, South Africa: 113 kg/year for bulls and 108 kg/year for cows
- Serengeti, Tanzania: 103 kg/year for bulls and 99 kg/year for cows
- Ruwenzori, Uganda: 103 kg/year for bulls and 92 kg/year for cows
- Northern Uganda: 105 kg/year for bulls and 100 kg/year for cows.

Currently, there is a lack of scientific information regarding expected growth rates for intensively farmed buffalo.

As outlined in Figure 14.3, the culling and processing of African savanna buffalo meat typically involve five stages, namely (1) field operation, (2) slaughter, (3) deboning, (4) production of products, and finally (5) marketing. Moreover, these logistical points (phases) will utilize a set of activities required to process a raw material into a value-added product.

Field Operation and Slaughter

Two of the challenges involved in the large-scale harvesting of buffalo in the field is to shoot a sufficient number of animals rapidly and efficiently ensuring that the procedures comply with animal welfare standards and human safety requirements, and to ensure that the carcasses all fall in an area as small as possible to facilitate the further slaughtering and loading of the carcasses for transport to the abattoir. Due to these challenges, a typical system that has been shown to work efficiently is to shoot a group of buffalo out of a helicopter with darts containing scoline (suxamethonium chloride, also known as suxamethonium or succinylcholine). This is a medication used to cause short-term paralysis; in most countries the use of scoline has to be managed by a veterinarian. The helicopter pilot can herd the darted group of buffalo (four to eight, depending on terrain, herd size and abattoir capacity) into a small compact group until all of the darted animals have dropped (± 5 min from the first dart). Before the cull, careful selection of the 'killing zone' needs to be made to ensure that the animals are close to this area and that it is accessible to

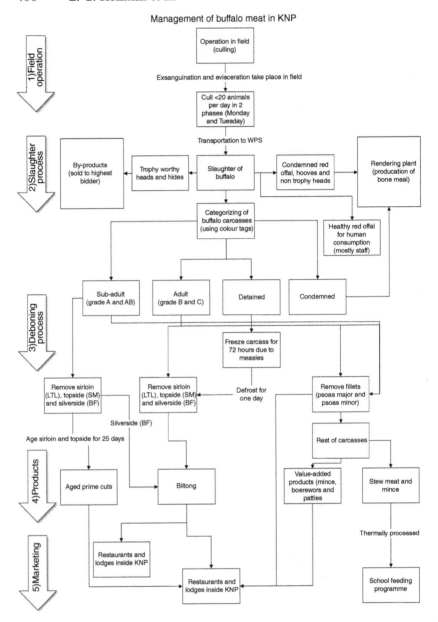

Figure 14.3 Standard operating system for the major logistical operational points to be considered in a typical buffalo culling scheme, as demonstrated in Kruger National Park (KNP, South Africa). LTL = *longissimus thoracis et lumborum*; BF = *biceps femoris*; SM = *semimembranosus* muscles; WPS = Wildlife Processing Structure. Source: Louwrens Hoffman.

the ground team and all vehicles. After dropping, the animals are killed with a free bullet shot in the head with a heavy-calibre rifle.

Although cost-effective, safe for the operators and widely used since the 1980s, the use of scoline is prone to ethical issues. Herding, darting buffalo with scoline and resulting asphyxia was shown to generate high levels of cortisol concentrations compared to animals shot at a stand-still (Hattingh et al., 1984). Such response could partly be ascribed to conscious perception of asphyxia in conscious animals with resulting fear (Button and Mülders, 1983). Previous studies suggested that residues of scoline in meat and biltong are apparently considered acceptable by public health authorities (Button et al., 1981). This statement should be re-examined in the light of recent technologies and standards, also taking into consideration that using scoline alters physical meat quality attributes (pale, soft and exudative meat; Hoffman, 2001). In a context of evolving animal welfare standards, the cost–benefits associated with the use of scoline should also be reconsidered.

After shooting, the animals are bled/exsanguinated, preferably on a slope or suspended. Using a terrain vehicle that is equipped with a con-veyer belt whereupon the buffalo carcasses are placed helps to speed up the time between exsanguination and the hanging process. Removal of the internal organs from the carcass takes place in the field to ensure that there is no bloating of the carcass (which increases the risk of contamina-tion). Ideally, transportation to the abattoir should not take longer than 2 h. It is important to ensure that knives are sterilized throughout and that hand-cleaning facilities are available. The primary meat inspection is conducted by a state veterinarian in the field and includes inspecting the head, pluck (red offal), feet, abdominal and reproductive organs of a par-tially dressed game carcass with the pluck and carcass then being sent to a registered game abattoir. Most of the white offal is left in the field for predators or vultures. However, some of the white offal will be cleaned and taken for consumption by the staff, such as the plies (third stomach) and set of tripe (weasand, first, second and fourth stomach and rectum).

Following the field operation, buffalo arrive at the abattoir offload-ing section (Figure 14.3). The carcasses are hoisted up, suspended from both Achilles tendons, and weighed. The head is removed, and trophy-worthy heads are cleaned and dried in the sun to be sold as trophies to hotels and restaurants as decoration or to individuals, while the smaller heads and the condemned (i.e. rejected) carcasses go to the rendering plant to produce an end product known as bone meal that can be sold as fertilizer. The skin is then removed, and to prevent contamination, removal of the hides should be done carefully, preferably when the carcass is warm, and all of the cuts are made from the inside to the outside to prevent contamination of the meat, using the two knife principles. The hides are normally processed (salted and dried) to be sold at auctions.

Red offal is preferably removed at the abattoir and is hung on a separate line, in the same order as the carcasses, for inspection by the veterinarians so that they may be correlated with the carcass, which is also individually inspected. The carcasses should be split with a saw blade along the spinal column to promote chilling. Lastly, the carcasses are washed with potable water, to remove all blood and bone sawdust, quartered between the ninth and tenth ribs, and weighed before being placed in the cold room (<7°C).

If only the red offal is affected, and the rest of the carcass is normal, only the red offal is condemned (lungs, heart and liver). However, if the intestines are linked to general diseases such as enlargement of the lymph glands, fever, or hepatitis, etc. the whole carcass is condemned. The condemned carcasses and condemned organs are sent to the rendering plant to create bone meal. Carcasses can be partially or totally condemned. Affected areas are condemned for various reasons, such as infections caused by systematic or generalized lesions.

Older buffalo, depending on where they have been reared and with which other species (generally wild dogs and carnivores) they have interacted, can contain intermediate stages of tapeworm parasites (cysticerci and hydatid cysts) and need to be frozen for a minimum of 72 h with an air temperature of at least −18°C before being deemed fit for human consumption. However, the freezing compromises the quality of the meat and it is no longer suitable for selling as tender prime meat and should thus be processed further.

Deboning and Products

While no official carcass grading system is currently used for buffalo, or any other game species really, Table 14.2 provides a suggested grading system that could be utilized to class buffalo carcasses according to age. The application of a grading system helps to categorize buffalo carcasses, guiding the deboning team to know which carcasses will go for prime steaks, ageing, value-added products and processed meat. Incorporating the grading of buffalo at the abattoir will help speed up the process and prevent adult/old buffalo meat from being sold as prime tender (and expensive) steaks.

Table 14.2 *Suggested grading of African savanna buffalo (Syncerus caffer caffer) carcasses.*

Grade	Permanent incisors	Buffalo age	Category
A	0	<2 years	Juvenile
AB	1–2	2.5; 3–3.5 years	Subadult
B	3–6	4; 4.5; 5; 5.5 years	Adult
C	7–8	6; 6–10; >12 years	Old

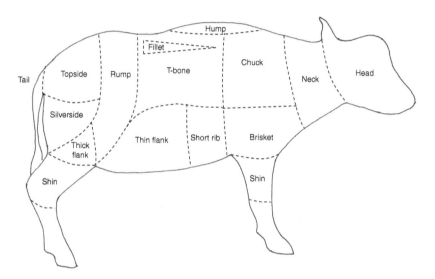

Figure 14.4 Primal cuts of African buffalo carcasses for further processing and marketing. Source: Tersia Needham.

Grades A and AB (subadult) buffalo carcasses should be used for aged primal cuts as well as processing for value-added products. Grades B, C (adult) and detained (frozen) buffalo carcasses can be used for processed meats (mainly biltong, a traditional dried lightly salted/spiced meat product) and value-added products. However, the fillets of all the carcasses can be sold as primal steaks at the highest price.

Deboning is the process whereby the fore and hind quarters of the carcass are taken and processed into various primal cuts (similar to those from beef carcasses, and illustrated in Figure 14.4) at 24–36 h post-mortem. The primal cuts from the hind quarter are silverside (*biceps femoris*), fillet (*psoas major* and *psoas minor*), sirloin (*longissimus thoracis et lumborum*), prime rump (*gluteus medius*), T-bone, topside (*semimembranosus*), knuckle (*vastus medialis* and other related muscles) and hind shin (*Peronaeus terius, extensor digitorum longus* and *extensor digiti terii proprius*).

Block tests are a measure established for wholesalers and retailers to price a variety of cuts given a certain producer price. By using the block test, the quantity of meat that will be produced can be predicted, and the price per carcass can be calculated. Therefore, block tests (Table 14.3 on a buffalo with a carcass weight of 277 kg) should ideally be conducted regularly to help determine the number of different cuts that will be produced from a buffalo carcass.

Primal cuts should be vacuum-packed and matured for a minimum of 25 days under refrigerated conditions (and labels should clearly indicate the day in and suggested sale date) before being sold, with the sirloin and topside muscles in particular identified as valuable cuts. The fillets of all animals can be sold as soon as they are removed; due to their

Table 14.3 *Block test conducted on an African savanna buffalo (carcass weight of 277 kg).*

Retail cuts	Weight (kg)	% whole carcass
Topside	11.4	4.11
Silverside	15.2	5.49
Rump steak	10.9	3.93
Thin flank	8.5	3.07
Thick flank	8.9	3.21
Short fillet	1.9	0.68
Soft shin	11	3.97
Shin	3.3	1.19
Tail	0.5	0.18
T-bone steak	15.8	5.7
Blade steak	13.7	4.94
Brisket	17.3	6.24
Short rib	6.3	2.27
Chuck/prime	22.7	8.19
Neck	11	3.97
Trimming	21	7.58
Stew	43.6	15.74
Goulash	3.1	1.12
Hump	4.5	1.62
Bones	34	12.27
Sinew and fat	10.7	3.86
Band saw loss	1.7	0.67
Total	**277**	**100**

inherent nature/composition, they need not be aged. In contrast, the silverside is ideal for biltong production, as toughness will not decrease over a more extended ageing period, and it will thus remain a tough muscle. The offcuts and trimmings could be used for value-added meat products, including biltong, droëwors (traditional dried sausage product made from meat off-cuts, sheep/beef fat and traditional spices), patties, boerewors (traditional fresh sausage) and minced meat. Biltong can be produced from frozen-thawed (detained) carcasses using different drying methods, which creates a larger profit margin because frozen carcasses can only be used for processing biltong, stewing meat and mince.

References

Bertschinger, H.J. (1996). Reproduction in the African buffalo: a review. In B.L. Penzhorn (Eds.), *The African Buffalo as a Game Ranch Animal*. Pretoria: University of Pretoria.

Bothma, J.D.P. and N. van Rooyen (2005). *Intensive Wildlife Production in Southern Africa*. Pretoria: Van Schaik.

Button, C., H. Bertschinger and M.S. Molders (1981). Haemodynamic and neurological responses of ventilated and apnoeic calves to succinyldicholine. *Journal of the South African Veterinary Association* **52**(4): 283–288.

Button, C. and M. Mülders (1983). Responses of unanaesthetised and pentobarbitone-anaesthetised sheep to a lethal dose of succinyldicholine. *Journal of the South African Veterinary Association* **54**(1): 63–64.

Carmichael, I.H., L. Paterson, N. Drager and D.A. Breto (1977). Studies in reproduction in the African Buffalo (*Syncerus caffer*) in Botswana. *South African Journal of Wildlife Research* **7**: 45–52.

Chaucheyras-Durand, F., A. Ameilbonne, A. Bichat, et al. (2016). Live yeasts enhance fibre degradation in the cow rumen through an increase in plant substrate colonization by fibrolytic bacteria and fungi. *Journal of Applied Microbiology* **120**(3): 560–570.

Grobler, D.G. (1996). The potential utilization of the African buffalo with regard to hunting and meat production. In B.L. Penzhorn (Ed.), *The African Buffalo as a Game Ranch Animal*. Pretoria: University of Pretoria, pp. 37–42.

Hattingh, J., P. Wright, V. De Vos, et al. (1984). Blood composition in culled elephants and buffaloes. *Journal of the South African Veterinary Association* **55**(4): 157–164.

Hildebrandt, W.R. (2014). *Management and reproduction of the African savanna buffalo (Syncerus caffer caffer)*. PhD, Stellenbosch University.

Hoffman, L.C. (2001). A comparison between the use of scoline (succinyldicholine chloride) and killing by means of a head shot on the physical meat quality attributes of buffalo (*Syncerus caffer*). International Congress of Meat Science and Technology.

Hoffman, L.C., J.S. Van As, P.A. Gouws and D. Govender (2020). Carcass yields of African savanna buffalo (*Syncerus caffer caffer*). *African Journal of Wildlife Research* **50**(1): 69–74.

Köster, H., R. Cochran, E. Titgemeyer, et al. (1996). Effect of increasing degradable intake protein on intake and digestion of low-quality, tallgrass-prairie forage by beef cows. *Journal of Animal Science* **74**(10): 2473–2481.

Macandza, V., N. Owen-Smith and P. Cross. (2004). Forage selection by African buffalo (*Syncerus caffer*) through the dry season in two landscapes of the Kruger National Park. *South African Journal of Wildlife Research* **34**(2): 113–121.

McDonald, P., R.A. Edwards, J.F.D. Greenhalgh and C.A. Morgan (2002). *Animal Nutrition*, 6th ed. Pearson Education.

Meissner, H. (1982). Theory and application of a method to calculate forage intake of wild southern African ungulates for purposes of estimating carrying capacity. *South African Journal of Wildlife Research* **12**(2): 42–47.

National Academies of Sciences Engineering and Medicine (2016). *Nutrient Requirements of Beef Cattle: Eighth Revised Edition.* Washington, DC: The National Academies Press.

Pienaar, U.V. (1969). Observations on developmental biology, growth and some aspects of the population ecology of African buffalo (*Syncerus caffer caffer* Sparrman) in the Kruger National Park. *Koedoe* **12**: 29–52.

Prins, H.H.T. (1996). *Ecology and Behaviour of the African Buffalo.* London: Chapman & Hall.

Ryan, S., C. Knechtel and W. Getz (2007). Ecological cues, gestation length, and birth timing in African buffalo (*Syncerus caffer*). *Behavioral Ecology* **18**(4): 635–644.

Schmidt, A.G. and D. Snyman (2016). Nutritional and mineral deficiencies, and supplementary feeding. In J. Du P Bothma and J. G. Du Toit (Eds.), *Game Ranch Management.* Pretoria: Van Schaik Publishers, pp. 372–384.

Shepstone, C., H. Meissner, J. Van Zyl, et al. (2022). Metabolizable energy requirements, dry matter intake and feed selection of sable antelope (*Hippotragus niger*). *South African Journal of Animal Science* **52**(3): 326–338.

Sinclair, A. (1977). *The African Buffalo. A Study of Resource Limitation of Populations.* Chicago: University of Chicago Press.

Van Rooyen, N. and J.D.P. Bothma (2016). Veld management. In J. du P. Bothma and J.G. Du Toit (Eds.), *Game Ranch Management.* Pretoria: Van Schaik Publishers, pp. 808–872.

Van Zyl, J. and D. Skead (1964). The meat production of South African game animals 2: the African buffalo. *Fauna and Flora* **15**: 34–40.

15 · *Handling and Moving the African Buffalo*

M. LA GRANGE, N.J. LA GRANGE,
J. MOSTERT, J. MOSTERT-LA GRANGE,
R. HOARE, M. D. KOCK, I. L. LEKOLOOL
AND P. CHARDONNET

Introduction

Archaeology and literature provide evidence that African wild animals have been live captured for a very long time, at least since the ancient Egyptians (e.g. Trinquier, 2002; Mark, 2016) and Romans (e.g. Bertrandy, 1987; Mackinnon, 2006; Christesen and Kyle, 2014). However, modern wildlife capture methods are only a few decades old, and considerable progress has been achieved recently in innovative chemical and physical restraint techniques for all wildlife species. While these methods are now used all over the continent, southern Africa appears today as the leading region in wildlife capture. In South Africa, the Wildlife Translocation Association's members annually capture and translocate approximately 130,000 game animals, and the game capture industry now has an annual turnover in excess of €7.4 million (Snyman et al., 2021).

As a member of the famous 'Big Five', the African buffalo (*Syncerus caffer*) adds significantly to the value of the wildlife economy everywhere, both for consumptive and non-consumptive use. However, with its historical range severely impacted by human activity, attaining this value today is often dependent upon being able to physically 'manage' them. The conservation of buffalo is consequently massively enhanced and facilitated today by being able to capture, handle and move the species. All of these actions are very specialist undertakings because buffalo are large-bodied, live in sizeable herds and can become aggressive and dangerous to humans.

Reasons for Capturing and Moving Buffalo

Buffalo may need to be captured and released on-site for diverse reasons. Depending on the type of management (extensive or intensive;

Chapter 13), a manager can request a licensed veterinarian to examine or treat injured or sick individuals. Similarly, buffalo populations at risk of disease outbreaks, posing a sanitary risk to other species (such as livestock or humans) or subject to sanitary regulations may be required to be captured for mass vaccinations to control the targeted diseases. Under extensive management (i.e. natural conditions), contexts necessitating the capture of buffalo may be more restricted (i.e. for a suffering individual).

Disease investigations or pre-movement health checks, notably for foot and mouth disease (FMD – including setting up FMD-free herds), bovine tuberculosis (bTB), tick-borne diseases (especially theileriosis) and other zoonotic or livestock diseases, are additional reasons to sample buffalo populations after immobilization. In addition to sanitary knowledge for production purposes, ecological or ecosystem research, for example collaring individuals with satellite tracking devices, may require captures for a few minutes in order to fit or release the devices.

Finally, buffalo may be captured for translocation for diverse reasons (Box 15.1). These include establishing founder populations, either for reintroduction or introduction purposes; numerically or genetically reinforcing depleted, isolated or small populations; moving vulnerable individuals or populations; and finally moving individuals to mitigate human–wildlife conflicts. Table 15.1 provides a sample of recent translocation events in eastern and southern Africa showcasing these diverse reasons for moving buffalo.

Box 15.1 *Definitions of Translocations (IUCN/SSC, 2013)*

Conservation translocation is the intentional movement and release of a living organism where the primary objective is conservation. This will usually comprise improving the conservation status of the focal species locally or globally, and/or restoring natural ecosystem functions or processes. Conservation translocations are classified according to the intended benefit of the process, entailing releases either within (population restoration) or outside (conservation introduction) the species' indigenous range.

- **Population restoration** involves:
  - **Reinforcement,** which is the intentional movement and release of an organism into an existing population of conspecifics, aiming to enhance population viability.

- **Reintroduction,** which is the intentional movement and release of an organism inside its indigenous range from which it has disappeared, aiming to re-establish a viable population of the focal species.
- **Conservation introduction** involves:
  - **Assisted colonization,** which is the intentional movement and release of an organism outside its indigenous range to avoid extinction of populations of the focal species.
  - **Ecological replacement,** which is the intentional movement and release of an organism outside its indigenous range to perform a specific ecological function. This is used to re-establish an ecological function lost through extinction and will often involve the most suitable existing subspecies, or a close relative of the extinct species within the same genus.

For whatever reason a capture operation is decided, it should be carefully thought through, and planned with strict adherence to veterinary regulations with respect to disease control, dangerous drugs, etc. The planning exercise should pay particular attention to behavioural characteristics and stress management.

Most of the knowledge and information presented in this chapter is based on massive experience and skills developed after many years of practice by the authors and other colleagues (La Grange, 2005, 2010).

Behavioural Characteristics to Consider for Capturing Buffalo

Like most bovids, buffalo are herd-orientated animals occupying distinct home ranges (Chapter 6). Therefore, they try to stay with one another while being driven towards the boma (a large funnel-shaped enclosure to physically capture buffalo – see below). Once in the boma, they will continue to follow the lead individual, who is likely to exploit any weakness in the integrity of the boma and try to initiate an escape response. Consequently, identifying and managing the lead individual effectively manages the herd.

Surprisingly, under capture pressure, the individual taking the lead to escape or attack is more often a cow that both defends and leads the way to safety. In the wild, bulls will join and separate depending upon age; subadult males will often leave to form bachelor groups while post-breeding old bulls

Table 15.1 *A few examples of capture and translocation operations of African buffalo*

Date	Place	Number of buffalo involved	Reason	Operations	Results
1984	Zambezi valley, Zimbabwe	Groups of around 100 each	Investigation of foot and mouth disease (FMD)	Capture, process, and release	Establishing strains and level of disease
1985, 1986	From Zambezi valley to central Zimbabwe	3 herds of around 100 each	Removal of female calves to establish FMD-free herds	Capture entire herds and remove calves	Release natal herds on site and remove calves to safe haven to be quarantined
1990 to 2020	Harare, Zimbabwe	Several groups of 1–10 individuals	FMD-free herds and redistribution of blood lines	Individual darting, loading and transportation	99% survival rate despite 5-day turn around
1995	Malilangwe, Zimbabwe	Several herds	Individual vaccination for anthrax	Capture, vaccination in crush and release	The buffalo population was saved
1997, 1998	Kariba dam, Zimbabwe	400, then 400	Rescue from lake Kariba	Capture in Bumi Hills, transport by ferry and release in Gache Gache	Successful relocation: 98% survival rate
2004	From Lake Nakuru National Park (NP) to Il Ngwesi Conservancy, Kenya	54	Population management at source and improving genetic diversity at recipient site	Capture, transport and release	100% survival rate
2004	From Lake Nakuru National Park to Il Lewa Wildlife Conservancy, Kenya	19	Population management at source and improving genetic diversity at recipient site	Capture, transport and release	100% survival rate

Year	Route	Number	Purpose	Action	Outcome
2008	From Solio Ranch to Aberdare National Park, Kenya	60	Mitigation of habitat destruction	Capture, transport and release	100% survival rate
2009	From Kibiku Forest, Ngong to Nairobi NP, Kenya	17	Mitigate human–wildlife conflict (HWC)	Capture, transport and release	100% survival rate
2009	Hwange NP, Zimbabwe	500	Reintroduction in Mwenezi Ranch	Capture and translocation from Robins camp to Mwenezi Ranch	Successful reintroduction
2010	Marromeu National Reserve (NR), Mozambique	99	Investigation of bovine tuberculosis (BTb)	Capture, sampling and release	Status of bTB in Marromeu buffalo
2012	From Marromeu NR and Gorongoza NP to Gilé NR, Mozambique	20	Reintroduction of buffalo in Gilé NR (species formerly extinct)	Capture, transport, and release	Species reintroduced in Gilé NR
2013	From Niassa NR to Gilé NR, Mozambique	47	Reinforcement in Gilé NR (consolidation of the reintroduction)	Capture in Niassa NR, transport over 900 km and release in Gilé NR	The reintroduction of the species is consolidated (150 buffalo in 2021)
2015 to 2017	From Marromeu NR to Coutada 9, Mozambique	50 in 2015 and 200 in 2017	Reinforcement of the relict buffalo population in Coutada 9	Capture in Marromeu NR, transport and release in Coutada 9	Successful reinforcement in Coutada 9 (380 buffalo in 2020)
2017	From Marromeu NR to Zinave NP, Mozambique	250	Reintroduction	Capture, transport and release	Successful reintroduction, 99% survival rate
2017, 2018	From Chinhoyi, Zimbabwe, to DRC	50, then 50	Introduction	Airlift to Luanda and drive to Lubumbashi	99% survival rate
2019	From Kitengela to Nairobi NP, Kenya	8	Mitigation of HWC	Capture, transport and release	100% survival rate

Source: *Author*.

will separate. These older bulls, often referred to as 'dagga' bulls in southern Africa, frequently have impaired eyesight and hearing. They sometimes seek the safety (i.e. from natural predators) of areas surrounding human habitations and can become exceedingly dangerous if stumbled upon.

Mothers are strongly bonded to their calves, recognizing them immediately from the bawling vocalizations of their respective offspring. They will respond aggressively to investigate and retrieve them even under stampede situations. Yearlings are reliant on parent herd knowledge, become lost in unrecognizable environments and need to be close to their mothers and other herd members. The cow–calf bond lasts for longer periods than for many other species (a comparatively long time between birth and puberty).

Home range dispersal is generally forced through large predator interactions or human-induced disturbances. Individual adult animals driven out into surrounding communities because of forced dispersal tend to be harassed and therefore can become exceedingly dangerous and often attack with little provocation. These individuals are unlikely to be returned successfully to the area they originated from.

Behaving in many respects like sable, once cornered and unable to escape in a boma, the buffalo herd will form a tight circular gathering often referred to as 'laager' in southern Africa, providing an effective defence strategy, especially against predators such as lions. This strategy prevents losses which likely would occur if the herd panicked and ran in several directions.

However, in a herding situation during capture, depending upon the pressure exerted on them, buffalo will readily attack when deemed threatened. The correct reading of the situation is necessary and relies on experience in order to apply just enough pressure to solicit the required response. It may be necessary to back off before this pressure becomes too much and invokes an attack or unnecessary panic. In this way, the lead cow becomes both ally and foe, and given the opportunity, would prefer to find a way out of the capture boma. She and the herd may be cleverly manipulated through good boma design and management to achieve smooth capture of the herd. Experienced operators and helicopter pilots do make a difference!

Stress Management

Fifty years of capture experience by professional operators have proven that for all species, stress cannot be removed completely, but its intensity can be minimized during every stage of the capture operation. Observations indicate that the main activity compounding stress is uncontrolled panic and running with attempts to attack or to escape. Struggling and overexertion prior to restraint must be quickly brought under control. Uncontrolled running up and down a boma, for example, is sufficient to overexert animals, resulting in potential health complications. Similarly, continued stress observed during physical restraint requires quick, deft action to control and calm animals throughout the operation. Basic application, for example, of a blindfold prior to or during immobilization and tranquillization, will provide a calming effect. Fortunately, buffalo are less prone to panic than many other species, but these principles still apply.

Any capture operation must minimize mortality and stress. Currently, advances in translocation knowledge have resulted in minimal mortalities, even when moving entire herds over long distances. An acceptable mortality rate is considered to be <2 per cent. However, modern capture techniques have been so refined that almost zero or very low mortality is now achievable. A thorough understanding of the subtleties of buffalo herd behaviour is important to overall success. Such knowledge allows potential problems to be anticipated before they occur, providing for timely management decisions that can be corrected and adapted throughout the entire capture process, effectively minimizing stress at all stages with the goal of zero mortality.

Physical Capture/Mass Capture

Physical capture is the capture of wild animals without using drugs. Mass capture of herd animals using a temporarily erected boma is a revolutionary technique of physical capture that originated in the 1960s in Namibia (Oelofse, 1970). In the animals' natural habitat, opaque or 'blind' plastic polyweave sheeting is erected on poles and supported top and bottom by tension cables in the formation of a large funnel-shaped enclosure, usually named mass boma capture, often referred to simply as boma capture (Figure 15.1). The principle employed is that animals are herded into the large open end of the funnel, and while being forced to traverse it to the narrow end, will not challenge the tall, flimsy barrier because they cannot see an escape route to the outside. The funnel ends in a crush in which animals can be individually selected or handled and thereafter either released or loaded onto a custom-made transporter vehicle already situated on an exit road.

(a)

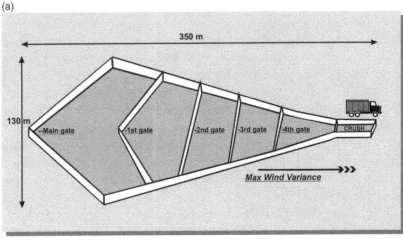

(b)

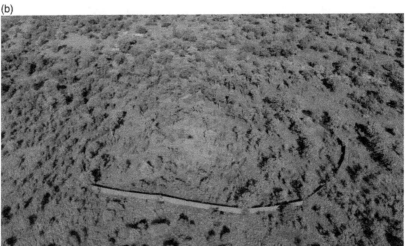

Figure 15.1 (a) Diagram of a temporary mass capture boma constructed out of woven plastic sheeting. (b) In practice, the boma is camouflaged in the vegetation and the narrow 'crush' section curves towards a ramp into transport vehicles on an exit road (transport vehicle on the top). Source: Author.

Using a small, manoeuvrable helicopter is the preferred method of driving animals to a boma (using horses, vehicles or people would be cheaper but is impractical for many reasons). It is absolutely essential that the pilot is not simply a commercially rated licence holder but someone who has experience in both low-level game capture flying *and* wild animal observation and behaviour. While flying the pilot has to be able to separate a workable number of animals from a herd, move them as calmly as possible in a downwind direction towards the boma, and avoid having them panic, separating far from each other and escaping from the group. At the same time, the pilot must communicate via radio and thus coordinate the activity of members of a ground team strategically positioned in and around the capture boma. The helicopter pilot flies alone to reduce helicopter mass enabling more power for manoeuvring.

The overhead noise and presence of a helicopter provide sufficient stimulus to move most wild animals including buffalo. The disturbance readily groups them while moving them in the required direction. The pilot must vary altitude and position judiciously, strategically moving around the herd, and applying varying levels of pressure to direct and keep the selected herd/group together. Directional pressure is gradually increased (lower altitude, closer distance) as the herd approaches the well-concealed wide boma entrance. Near the mouth of the boma, the helicopter is flying low, and finally activates a loud siren to provide the final stimulus while directing ground staff to close the main gate, with the process repeated to close secondary gates as the herd funnels down through the boma.

Ground teams stationed on the boma partition gates rapidly draw these plastic curtains across in sequence behind the buffalo as the herd progresses forward towards the narrow end of the boma. Employing this strategy, the herd is confined in a manageable sized space (a boma compartment), with individual movement restricted and less chance of escape. It is essential to limit outside stimuli while the boma is occupied to allow buffalo to regain their rest composure following the stressful chase. In large capture operations, the manageable number of animals driven in per helicopter drive is around 30–40 buffalo. This number is considered practical to handle and load, adding further subdrives to fill additional boma compartments if required or carrying out additional drives after the loading of the previous subdrive.

Placing buffalo under stress during mass capture is akin to them being hunted as prey in the wild where they display equivalent behavioural responses. Initially, they bunch into a circular defensive formation to prevent losses that would likely occur from individuals panicking and running in several directions. They often attack under extreme or persistent pressure, with a number of individuals charging in one direction behind a leader.

Pushing captured wild buffalo one by one into a narrow 'cattle-like crush' is obviously not easy and cannot be done by people on foot inside the boma. A modified four-wheel drive vehicle with strong front and side

Figure 15.2 Final stage of a buffalo mass capture: (a) buffalo are chased into the boma by the helicopter; (b) then pushed into desired sections of the boma or lorry using an adapted vehicle. © Philippe Chardonnet.

protection can be used to achieve this by slow 'persuasion' (Figure 15.2). Buffalo will attack the vehicle, especially the front and wheels, rather than target the people inside. Adding a curve to the handling facility, or hanging vegetation at the far end of the boma to camouflage the dead end, leads the herd into thinking that there is an attractive way of escape, and its leaders will eventually move on towards that (Figure 15.1).

All procedures in the capture of wildlife are in effect stress management exercises. Put simply, physical capture without drugs is achieved through a sequence of induced animal behaviours: naturally moving away from the disturbance source, encouraged to take the escape opportunity given, enabled by loss of geo-location and reluctance to challenge the unknown (see some tips in Box 15.2).

Chemical Capture/Individual Capture

Chemical immobilization of buffalo is achieved by darting or injecting drugs. Darting and handling of immobilized wild animals require very comprehensive training in specialized courses that are available in a few selected countries. Even veterinarians are advised to attend these courses because this very detailed and specialist field is usually not fully covered in general veterinary training. Dangerous drugs, especially opioids, fall under very strict veterinary regulations. In cases of accidental exposure

Box 15.2 *Tips for Managing Buffalo within the Mass Boma*

- The helicopter drive for separating the required number of buffalo is important to avoid driving too many in at once. Too many animals will be difficult to manage in the boma. Instead, position the main herd nearby ±200 m and separate 30–40 animals for each subdrive into the boma, filling the respective boma compartments providing further options. Rather than filling each compartment, more often additional drives are conducted after the loading of the previous subdrive.
- Identify and work with the lead cow as discussed. This requires lots of patience – offer a way to escape and capitalize on any advantage emerging.
- Provide a suitable boma herding vehicle within the boma as operating on foot would be extremely dangerous. As indicated, prevent direct confrontation, applying targeted pressure, following or backing off, observing the response. Any old 4×4 vehicle will do as buffalo tend to attack the vehicle, especially the front and wheels, rather than the people inside.
- The secret is: 'Give n'take!' Avoid applying too much pressure and AVOID direct contact!
- The boma is flexible in design to provide for a wide range of capture applications, including:
  - Combining physical and chemical capture to enable the selection of specific animals for testing or capture. Basically, instead of a crush, providing a sufficiently large circular working area at the boma end to drive the herd in and dart individual animals selected from a vehicle. Individual animals can be marked and released back to the herd or following bulk knockdown, for example, veterinary testing, before releasing the herd back to the wild.
  - Calf removal for FMD-free buffalo breeding programmes is basically a variant of this technique, capturing the entire herd, then employing a vehicle to drive among the herd as they mill around, 'fishing' out the calves individually with a rope and pole noose. Male calves are separated from the females into different bulk crates. Finally, the males are released back to the herd before the final herd is released back to the wild.

- o Conducting large immunizing programmes against diseases such as anthrax. This is done by providing an extended crush at the boma end to hold 30–50 buffalo. These are pole syringed and, importantly, marked for identification before release.
- o The first gate (Figure 15.1) serves to first contain the driven buffalo herd, aiming to keep the area between it and the main gate pristine for subsequent drives.

Figure 15.3 Individual darting on foot of a West African savanna buffalo. © Daniel Cornélis.

to these, such as the potent opioids used for buffalo, humans are unfortunately extremely susceptible to the same effects, which can rapidly be fatal. Safety procedures are paramount and must be thoroughly applied.

Darting on the ground requires approaching a buffalo within close range (maximum about 40 m), which requires knowledge of the behaviour of the species and judgement of each circumstance. It is safest and easier to approach by vehicle if the terrain allows. However, in West and Central Africa where many landscapes do not allow driving off track, and where helicopters are difficult to hire, buffalo darting is often carried out on foot (Figure 15.3). Compared to many other large mammals,

Figure 15.4 Chemical capture of a free-ranging herd of Cape buffalo by individual darting from a helicopter. © Samy Julliand.

buffalo are quite easy to approach on foot provided the stalking is done very strictly against the wind. However, approaching buffalo by foot close enough for darting becomes a difficult exercise in poorly managed areas where harassed buffalo become very shy. Operational success hence may drop from darting a few buffalo each day to just one buffalo every few days, especially if specific individuals are targeted (e.g. an adult female or collared individual for device removal). Lone males are the easiest to get close to, followed by male coalitions. Herds are more difficult, however, often with males following behind.

Darting from a helicopter requires a pilot with experience in both low-level flying techniques and interpreting animal behaviour (Figure 15.4). The darter and the pilot must have excellent intercom communication in the air. Aircraft reliability and aviation and veterinary safety procedures must be established and adhered to as there is very little margin for error (see tips in Box 15.3).

The darting of individual buffalo or small groups uses combinations of opioid drugs and tranquillizers (Table 15.2). Such combinations are designed to provide synergistic effects; the opioid is the 'knockdown' component, inducing a physiological state called 'narcosis' which is much different from the deeper unconscious state of 'anaesthesia', familiar to most humans. The

Box 15.3 *Tips to Consider with Aerial Darting of Buffalo*

- Capitalize on the 'window-of-opportunity' offered by confusion, separating out smaller, manageable subgroups of buffalo, driving them to more accessible open ground away from the principal herd, forcing them to circle on themselves to promote confusion, and quickly darting all the individuals comprising the group. It is important to keep them together in suitable recovery terrain until they all go down. This process requires skill and experience from the helicopter pilot and darter working together with ground teams, who should be directed in to render timely assistance to potentially compromised animals. It is important to minimize the total downtime of the group.
- Positive knockdown of the targeted animals is paramount, requiring correct dart placement and the appropriate drug combination. Generally, with free-range darting of wild buffalo, apply the **high-dose opioid protocol** (Table 15.2), avoiding underdosing that is more problematic with the potential for complications. Buffalo herded by a helicopter are more likely to be stressed and hyperthermia can be a problem, especially with a dark-skinned animal. Consider combining thiafentanyl with etorphine in a 50:50 combination dose, which significantly reduces the excitement phase, reducing time running and therefore distance travelled. Thiafentanyl alone in combination with azaperone provides quick knockdown, but thousands of buffalo in southern Africa have been successfully immobilized with etorphine and azaperone.
- It is especially recommended to immediately redart if poor dart placement is suspected rather than waiting for drug sign. Be prepared to manage possible overdose using butorphanol.

addition of a tranquillizer reduces stress by smoothing the 'induction period' (the time for a drug's full effect over several minutes), counters muscle rigidity during the immobilization phase, and improves the recovery process.

Historically, the traditional choice of drug combinations has been etorphine hydrochloride (M99, Captivon® Wildlife Pharmaceuticals): 5–8 mg etorphine combined with 40–50 mg azaperone for a free-ranging adult, reducing this marginally (by 20 per cent) for penned and tamer animals (Figure 15.2). With free-range darting of wild buffalo, apply the high-dose opioid protocol. In holding boma situations, pens or where buffalo are calm or habituated, the low-dose opioid protocol can be

Table 15.2 *Drug recommendations for the African buffalo (taken with the kind permission of Kock and Burroughs, 2021).*

Buffalo	Opioid	Tranquillizer	Opioid antagonist	α-2 agonist
		High-dose opioid protocol		
Free-ranging bulls	Etorphine 7–8 mg or	Azaperone 40–60 mg	Naltrexone 140–160 mg	
	Thiafentanil 7–8 mg	Azaperone 40–60 mg	Naltrexone 70–80 mg	
	Mix etorphine 4 mg and thiafentanil 4 mg	Azaperone 40–60 mg	Naltrexone 120 mg	None
Free-ranging cows	Etorphine 4–6 mg	Azaperone 40–60 mg	Naltrexone 80–120 mg Diprenorphine at 12–18 mg is useful in loading	
	Thiafentanil 4–6 mg	Azaperone 40–60 mg	Naltrexone 40–60 mg	
	Mix etorphine 3 mg and thiafentanil 3 mg	Azaperone 40–60 mg	Naltrexone 90 mg	
Adults in boma	Etorphine 3–5 mg	Azaperone 40–60 mg	Diprenorphine 9–15 mg or naltrexone 60–100 mg	
		Low-dose opioid protocol		
Adult bull	Thiafentanil 1.5–2 mg	Medetomidine 4 mg plus Azaperone 40mg	Naltrexone 15–20 mg	Atipamezole 4 mg plus yohimbine at 0.5 ml per mg of medetomidine
Adult cow	Thiafentanil 1–1,5 mg	Medetomidine 3–4 mg plus Azaperone 40 mg	Naltrexone 10–15 mg	Atipamezole 4 mg plus yohimbine at 0.5 ml per mg of medetomidine
0–6 months	Thiafentanil 1 mg		Naltrexone 10 mg	

(cont.)

Table 15.2 (*cont.*)

Buffalo	Opioid	Tranquillizer	Opioid antagonist	α-2 agonist
6–12 months	Thiafentanil 1 mg	Medetomidine 0.5 mg plus azaperone 15 mg	Naltrexone 10 mg	Atipamezole 0.5 mg plus yohimbine at 0.5 ml per mg of medetomidine
12–24 months	Thiafentanil 1 mg	Medetomidine 1 mg plus azaperone 20 mg	Naltrexone 10 mg	Atipamezole 1 mg plus yohimbine at 0.5 ml per mg of medetomidine
24–36 months	Thiafentanil 1 mg	Medetomidine 2 mg plus azaperone 30	Naltrexone 10 mg	Atipamezole 2 mg plus yohimbine at 0.5 ml per mg of medetomidine

Notes:

• Azaperone is recommended in all buffalo immobilizing combinations.

• Ketamine given intravenously (IV) is effective as a 'top-up' drug in animals that are not sufficiently immobilized by the opioid and sedative/tranquillizer mixture. Administer 100–200 mg IV and further doses can be given if required. Doses of 50–100 mg will often be sufficient.

• Naltrexone for free release is preferred and for transport a mixture of diprenorphine and naltrexone is useful.

• Diprenorphine at 12–18 mg is useful in loading.

• In forest buffalo, the same drug combinations can be used but reduce doses accordingly due to smaller size. Carfentanil (4 mg) has been used successfully to immobilize this subspecies – reverse with 200–300 mg naltrexone. The use of carfentanil may result in knuckling problems post-recovery in savanna buffalo and is not recommended for them.

• The addition of hyaluronidase to the mixture in the dart is advisable in buffalo, particularly with the high-dose opioid protocol.

• Azaperone is the better drug to use. Buffalo are generally sensitive to the effects of the α-2 agonists so take due precautions in free-living animals. When complete reversal of the α-2 agonist is required, use atipamezole.

substituted. Either on the ground or from the air, if poor dart placement occurs or dart failure is suspected, it is generally recommended to redart immediately rather than waiting for signs of drug effect.

Following chemical capture, the recumbent buffalo is given an opioid antagonist, a rapidly acting antidote drug which allows the animal to regain full consciousness to normal mobility with all its vital functions intact. Recovery drugs (variously called 'antidotes', 'reversals' or 'antagonists') and their dosages vary according to what management procedure is required following capture. If a buffalo needs to be moved from an area inaccessible to transport, 'partial antagonists' drugs may be used. The remarkable efficacy of these drugs is to allow the buffalo to get to its feet and be slowly physically guided by well-trained handlers. Obviously, this is while it is still blindfolded and well restrained with ropes, but in a heavily tranquilized state and not sufficiently awake to injure the handlers or escape uncontrollably.

It is far easier to manage the effects of 'overdosage' of immobilizing drugs on a wild animal than 'underdosage'. To most people, this would seem counterintuitive. The reason, however, is that if a recumbent animal is physiologically compromised, there are various ways of quickly improving its vital functions to keep it alive while it remains recumbent and manageable. In the worst-case scenario, should the procedure not be able to continue, an intravenous opioid antidote drug can quickly wake the animal up and bring it back to normality. By contrast, if the animal receives an insufficient dose, it will remain 'half-immobilized' on its feet and continually try to escape, whereupon its uncontrolled mobility and associated high stress levels can cause it to become rapidly compromised physiologically, which is often fatal (see tips in Box 15.4).

The choice of a commercially available darting system is a matter of personal preference. There are two main types of 'remote injection devices', distinguished by the method of dart propulsion from the gun and drug injection from the dart. Powder-charged guns use small blank cartridges while gas-powered guns are fitted with small cylinders containing compressed carbon dioxide (CO_2). Drugs are expelled from darts by either small powder charges or the release of compressed air. Two of the most used systems are called 'Pneudart®' and 'DanInject®'. These darting systems are versatile enough that they can be used with darts from different manufacturers (11 mm and 13 mm barrel bore size), such as Palmer Cap-Chur® (0.50 calibre or 13 mm). It is important to select the correct needle size and length (2 × 50 mm) when darting buffalo (Kock and Burroughs, 2021).

Box 15.4 *Tips for Monitoring the Immobilized Buffalo*

- The immobilized animal should be approached slightly from behind. A blindfold should be gently lowered over its eyes, this will significantly reduce stress, effectively assisting in relaxing the animal and protecting the eyes. Earplugs are optional.
- Immediately upon approach, the buffalo must be placed and maintained in a sternal recumbency position with the head lowered. Over the years the potential for regurgitation and aspiration of ruminal contents into the lungs has proven an issue, especially with drug combinations using α-2 agonists.
- Throughout the whole procedure until the end, respiration must be monitored with a normal rate of 6–8 breaths/minute. Less than this, butorphanol can be injected in increments of 5 mg but beware of complete reversal at doses higher than 30 mg. Doxapram given at 5–15 ml IV also provides respiratory stimulation, but is short-acting and can produce some arousal, so constant monitoring is required. A rate of 10–12 means the animal is light and, depending on the time from darting, may require a top-up of 100–200 mg of ketamine. Avoid adding more opioid into the animal, ketamine is highly effective and safe.
- A large buffalo's limbs folded under a heavy body are very susceptible to lack of blood supply during longer procedures; thus, the body position must be regularly adjusted to maintain adequate circulation to the limbs and to avoid any nerve damage due to pressure.
- The drugs to either terminate or prolong immobilization must be on hand and the required procedures known in detail by the operators. For reversal, a combination of naltrexone (25 to 100mg depending on opioid dose) and diprenorphine (12-18mg) can be used IV or IM, especially when more than one animal are woken up at the same time in a recovery crate – the lower dose of naltrexone helps with the recovery of buffalo. A significant cost reduction can be achieved using this in combination with the full diprenorphine dose.

Transport of Buffalo

Transporting wild animals as large as buffalo by road is a very detailed and specialized undertaking, requiring large amounts of equipment, logistical support and organizational capability. Unless only a few individual buffalo are to be transported a very short distance (which could be done by tranquillizing and transporting them recumbent in a pickup truck), moving buffalo requires experienced 'capture operators'.

In some African countries, there may be detailed veterinary and other legal requirements for moving buffalo, resulting in extensive prior paperwork. Buffalo can share several diseases and parasites with livestock, so official health requirements can be very stringent, expensive and time-consuming.

Customized crates replicating 'shipping containers' are the most used equipment for road transport. Obvious requirements for these containers are non-slip flooring, good ventilation, sliding doors and operator access via the roof for observation or animal behaviour intervention. Buffalo travel well in groups when well-designed crates and good management practices are used, and can travel for up to 36 hours after capture without food and water en route. Watering and feeding can be done at both ends of the journey. Tranquillization using injectable drugs should be limited to bulls and/or truculent animals only. Never tranquillize juveniles or yearlings because there is the risk that they may lie down in transit and be trampled by adults (see tips in Box 15.5).

Box 15.5 *Tips for Loading Buffalo and Managing Their Transportation*

- Buffalo travel well as mixed groups.
- Need to employ fully enabled management crates to properly distribute the captured animals – considered essential.
- Compartments fitted with fully functional sliding doors – capable of separating buffalo, allowing the movement of animals back and forth between compartments as required.
- Cross-loading capabilities – extra truck units may be needed to cross-load as required.
- Crates providing full access from the top to inspect, move, sort, tranquillize and operate partition gates.
- Watch packing density. Buffalo are prone to hyperthermia, which can be exacerbated by too many animals packed into a compartment.
- Not too many animals at one time should be in a crush. It is a good idea to split the load into 20–25 subgroups at the crush (a suitable number for a truck and trailer load). Where large numbers are to be moved, consider cross-loading into additional truck units linked up.
- Generally, calves at foot do not load and transport well; therefore, avoid the breeding season.

- Bulls tend to be easier to load, but they will occupy a larger space and should be appropriately tranquillized.
- *Tranquillization of truculent individuals only.*
- *Never* tranquillize calves and yearlings that are then prone to be trampled upon!
- Buffalo can travel for up to 36 hours after capture without food and water.
- Should watering and feeding prove necessary, this may be achieved by moving animals into an adjacent compartment, for example, when undertaking time-consuming cross-border operations.

Box 15.6 *Checklist Tips Prior to Transportation*

- Ensure animals are settled before transporting! Unload and reload should animals remain unsettled requiring group resorting.
- Tranquillize as required.
- Ensure correct paperwork is in hand: wildlife permits, vehicle clearance, border crossing. Experience dictates that it is best to use the services of an experienced clearing agent to facilitate border crossing.
- Consider best travel route: terrain, condition and directions.
- Weather conditions en route are more often overlooked. Consider potential for chill factor problems en route when travelling through the coldest part of the night. Wherever possible, avoid these situations, remembering the chill factor may often reduce ambient temperatures by a factor of 4–8°C.
- Consider GPS track monitoring of the vehicle.
- Cell/smartphone–satphone enabled.
- Stop and rest frequently, every 200 km. Select quiet stopping places, not near gatherings of people, for example, a village.
- Watering and feeding are not normally an issue if delivering within 24 hours. Empty one compartment and place flat troughs and fresh grass should this become necessary.
- It is very important to ensure rehydration on final release.
- Consider refuelling requirements for the trucks: identify places and the currency required. Think logically through all these requirements, addressing any that have the potential to interrupt smooth passage.
- Drivers should be experienced and well briefed.

Long-distance considerations

- Use alternate drivers.
- Stop and rest frequently, every 200 km.
- Emergency tranquillization may be needed (azaperone and diaz-epam) for particularly truculent individuals.
- An accompanying 'chase' vehicle is important with a qualified person to assist the animals for cross-border deliveries.
- May need to water down animals, drinking considerations become more important with long distances (avoid excessive water in crate, beware of danger of slipping).
- Monitor weather en route, especially whether hot or cold spells.

To transport live animals, drivers of heavy vehicles must be extensively trained and experienced. The best travel route must be researched and planned, and very reliable communications guaranteed between drivers and support staff. The weather en route is often overlooked: in hot daytime conditions buffalo can overheat if too tightly packed; on the other hand, when travelling during the coldest part of the night, a wind chill factor can reduce the ambient temperature by up to 8°C. On long journeys, vehicle stops in quiet locations at a maximum of every 200 km are essential. Extra requirements for unforeseen problems arising are a senior staff member in an accompanying 4WD 'chase vehicle' and an empty crate for cross-loading should some animals need to be removed during transit (see checklist in Box 15.6).

Release at Destination

Herbivores with social behaviour like buffalo are easier to translocate than many other taxa, but a successful capture does not end upon reaching the destination, where much remains to be done. Possibly one of the greatest pitfalls to concluding a successful capture and translocation is the problem of subsequent maladaptation when wild animals are introduced to new surroundings.

If the transport arrives late at night, leave the buffalo inside the crates and unload them early the following day. Allowing buffalo immediate and full rehydration at the destination is essential. Immediate free release (also named 'hard release') might be practiced in a fenced environment. However, the construction of an adaptation boma is recommended where the buffalo can settle into new surroundings via an initial captive

Box 15.7 *Tips for Pen Management*

- In carrying out the daily chore management of the pens, it is important to establish a routine. Animals are naturally routine-orientated as they go about their daily business of feeding and resting. This should be maintained as much as possible during the penning process.
- It is extremely important to respect the midday siesta routine. Naturally, animals rest in shade during the hot part of the day, so pen cleaning, sorting and animal feeding should be limited to early morning before 11h00 and late afternoon from 16h00 onwards.
- Move animals to a new pen once a week. This allows for pen cleaning and rotation, which greatly helps when they finally need to be loaded and transported.
- Ensure that any disturbances remain on the outside of the pens, never on the inside. The pen attendant and family should be accommodated nearby the pen complex, effectively providing disturbance to the outside but not invading the privacy within. This greatly assists with the taming process; animals realize that the pens represent safety.
- For further reading, refer to Raath (1996).

period. If the new habitat is substantially different from the source area, for example, subtle complications involving rumen microflora adaption can be very important. Dietary maladaptation can seriously impact the animals' health and future survival.

When boma management is carried out correctly, buffalo do settle down relatively quickly compared to some other wild herbivores (see tips in Box 15.7). A few main points relating to this phase of handling are to allow an area of about 1 ha (100 × 100 m) for up to 25 buffalo and increase accordingly. As in a capture boma, the walls must be opaque or blanked off (e.g. woven plastic sheeting on fences), adequate shade for the entire group should be available, and good-quality grass and/or hay *ad libitum* should be provided, concentrate supplements can be added but only in small quantities daily. Human activity inside the pen (cleaning/animal sorting) should be kept to a minimum and during the cooler hours of the day and any disturbance, especially from spectators, must be strictly limited and only outside the boma. Domestic dogs should never be allowed anywhere near wildlife-holding bomas or pens. For final release back to the wild, pick a quiet day early in the morning and simply leave the enclosure gate open to allow the buffalo to find their own way out in their own time.

The Case of Virtual Boundary

The more that wildlife are managed, the more there are indications that a virtual component is playing out. This is particularly noticeable upon releasing animals into a new environment that they do not know; essentially, they are rendered lost. In the wild, animals are fully geo-located to their home ranges and always know accurately where they are. The establishment of 'remembered' boundary positions, risky areas and food and water locations is information imprinted virtually in their mindset, logged against time and season. If they are suddenly uplifted and moved in a dramatic fashion to where a new reality is foisted upon them, it renders them rather lost and unable to recognize much of their new surroundings. Experience over the years has demonstrated that release stress is best cushioned by placing animals in a blanked off and confined space (boma or pen) that they cannot see out of. In this, they quickly establish the basic information relating to the whereabouts of food, shelter and most importantly, a refuge. This position becomes 'virtually logged', so that release into a new wild area is undertaken from this remembered position as they gradually move away from it, exploring their new surroundings. The virtual boundary concept is interesting for future management in that this virtual knowledge is proving invaluable in developing innovative approaches to mitigate capture complications and human–wildlife conflict (La Grange et al., 2022).

Conclusion

The cardinal rule of buffalo or any wildlife capture, translocation and release is to regard all human interventions as potentially stressful to the animals, and therefore to strive to conduct them as far as possible as 'short-term and low-stress management exercises'. Achieving this objective involves well-coordinated teamwork with individual team members practicing an eclectic mixture of activities that add up to 'an art as much as a science'. However, that said, there is still room for progress. The chemical capture of large mammals remains overly dependent upon opioids, which are problematic for two main reasons: (i) they are extremely dangerous for humans and animals, and (ii) strict procurement protocols have severely hampered access for most countries outside the few with substantial experience in wildlife capture. Hence, there is a real need to actively research non-opioid drugs, especially the alpha-2s (e.g. medetomidine) and combinations thereof. Physical capture methods also could be improved, and maybe even new strategies developed, including for example virtual applications such as a drone capture technique (under review), and applying scent technology through a guided, one-way camouflaged crush arrangement into a compacted mobile crate management arrangement, obviating the necessity for large plastic mass boma equipment, helicopters and expensive labour commitment.

References

Bertrandy, F. (1987). Remarques sur le commerce des bêtes sauvages entre l'Afrique du Nord et l'Italie (IIe siècle avant J.-C.–IVe siècle après J.-C.). *Mélanges de l'école française de Rome* **99**(1): 211–241.

Christesen, P. and D.G. Kyle (Eds.) (2014). *A Companion to Sport and Spectacle in Greek and Roman Antiquity*. Weinheim: Wiley-Blackwell.

IUCN/SSC (2013). *Guidelines for Reintroductions and Other Conservation Translocations*. Version 1.0. Gland: IUCN Species Survival Commission.

Kock, M.D. and R. Burroughs (Eds.) (2021). *Chemical and Physical Restraint of African Wild Animals*, 3rd ed. International Wildlife Veterinary Services (Africa) Greyton, South Africa. 2021. 476 pp. ISBN: 978-199121725-7.

La Grange, M. (2005). *The Capture, Care and Management of Wildlife in Southern Africa*. Pretoria: Van Schaike Publishers.

La Grange, M. (2010). Chapters 33 and 34, Capture and transport of wild animals. In J. du P. Bothma and J.G. Du Toit (Eds.), *Game Ranch Management*, 5th ed. Pretoria: Van Schaik Publishers.

La Grange, M, C. Matema, B. Nyamukure and R. Hoare (2022). The virtual fence dynamic: a breakthrough for low-cost and sustainable mitigation of human-elephant conflict in subsistence agriculture? *Frontiers in Conservation Science* **3**: 863180.

Mackinnon, M. (2006). Supplying exotic animals for the Roman amphitheatre games: new reconstructions combining archaeological, ancient textual, historical and ethnographic data. *Mouseion: Journal of the Classical Association of Canada* **6**(2): 137–161.

Mark, J.J. (2016). Pets in Ancient Egypt. *World History Encyclopedia*, 18 March 2016.

Oelofse, J. (1970). Plastic for game catching. *Oryx* **10**(5): 306–308.

Raath, J.P. (1996). Boma management. In B.L. Penzhorn (Ed.), *Proceedings of a Symposium on the Management of the African Buffalo as a Game Ranch Animal*. Onderstepoort: South African Veterinary Association Wildlife Group.

Snyman, S., D. Sumba, F. Vorhies, et al. (2021). *State of the Wildlife Economy in Africa. South Africa Case Study*. Kigali: African Leadership University, School of Wildlife Conservation.

Trinquier, J. (2002). Localisation et fonctions des animaux sauvages dans l'Alexandrie lagide: la question du «zoo d'Alexandrie». *Mélanges de l'école française de Rome* **114**(2): 861–919.

Wildlife Translocation Association (2020). www.wtass.org/Default.aspx

16 · *Buffalo Hunting: From a Commodity to a High-Value Game Species*

P. CHARDONNET, R. TAYLOR,
W. CROSMARY, S.P. TADJO, F.A. LIGATE,
R. BALDUS, L. SIEGE AND D. CORNELIS

A Story Longer Than Thought

Early Days

January 1895. Makanga country, now in Mozambique. Edouard Foa, a French explorer, is struggling to gain an audience with the powerful and feared Chief Tchanetta Mendoza. Foa had come there on his way to cross the continent by foot from the Indian Ocean to the Atlantic Ocean. Eventually, after having threatened Foa, the Chief consented to grant him a clearance to walk across and hunt on this land. At that time, the country was rich in game and Tchanetta forbade unnecessary shooting. Because Arabs used to come there from the North once a year for times immemorial, the Chief had them hunt elephants exclusively, measuring the powder for each hunter himself. Buffalo (*Syncerus caffer*), antelope, and other game were reserved to indigenous hunters for feeding his people. The tribute to be paid to the Chief for hunting elephant was one tusk per elephant killed. When the beast had fallen, the tusk that was on the ground side was the property of the Chief of the territory. Locally, in Portuguese, this tax was named '*o dente da terra*', the Earth's tooth (Foa, 1900).

The price to pay for the right to hunt existed long before Foa. As early as the sixteenth century, Portuguese records state that no elephant could be killed and consumed without the consent of the Chief in the lands south of the Zambezi, where the '*dente da terra*' tax already existed by unwritten law (Manyanga and Pangeti, 2017). Such hunting levies were not only restricted to this area. In western Tanzania, Foa had to pay the '*hongo*', a tribute to walk and hunt on a Chief's land (Foa, 1900).

In western Zimbabwe, Lobengula (1836–1894), Chief of the Ndebele, was issuing hunting concessions for foreign hunters as a way to protect Ndebele hunting rights (Moyo et al., 1993).

These ancient situations reveal extremely important historical traits: systems of governance and management of wildlife were already in place in precolonial times, mainly enacted by traditional leaders and their ruling families (Sansom, 1974; Campbell, 1995; Carruthers, 1995), even endorsed by spirit mediums, at least in the Zambezi valley (Hasler, 1996). These systems did not disappear abruptly under colonial rule and often coexisted with new foreign regulations.

Today, the current trophy fee paid by the hunting tourist is nothing other than a modern form of the historical '*dente da terra*'. The present listing of particular species as fully protected is nothing other than ancient rules such as the prohibition by Lobengula of hunting hippopotamus, and the fee paid by the hunting operator to lease a hunting concession from the State is nothing other than the historical tribute to be paid to the landlord for being allowed to walk and hunt on his land. Today, by delegating the appropriate authority from central to local levels, the now widespread mechanism of community-based natural resources management is in a way reviving precolonial systems, but with more democratic efforts than under the past feudal regimes.

Colonial Times

With the establishment of colonies, foreign powers assumed that the traditional sanctions and precolonial institutions that regulated hunting were an inadequate means of conserving wildlife in the face of growing human populations and competition for wildlife resources (Child, 2004). By transposing their foreign laws, many colonial regimes prescribed wildlife as *res nullius*: with wildlife now belonging to no one and managed by the State, traditional rulers were disempowered from controlling hunting. It is even assumed that some of them let poaching happen to steal State goods in revenge for having lost control.

The settlers who began arriving at the Cape of Good Hope in 1652 hunted wildlife for food and commercial gain (Booth and Chardonnet, 2015), and to open land to develop agriculture and livestock husbandry. In less than two centuries, wildlife had been deeply impacted by the introduction of millions of muzzleloaders, metal gin-traps, etc. (Richards, 1980), the development of agriculture, and the expansion of livestock accompanied by several exotic diseases. The rinderpest outbreak in the 1880s wiped out up to 95 per cent of the buffalo populations (Robertson, 1996; Spinage, 2003; Chapters 9 and 12). Regarded as common game, buffalo did not benefit from special protection and were even destroyed in southern Africa in the attempt to eradicate tsetse flies. Most colonial regimes maintained special, relatively cheap meat hunting licences to feed populations and plantation workers (Anderson, 2017).

At the end of the nineteenth century, a number of hunters throughout Africa recognized the harm of uncontrolled hunting and played a key role in establishing protected areas (Kruger National Park in 1894 in South Africa, Selous Game Reserve in 1896 in Tanzania). In the meantime, they also introduced modern protective game laws. All over Africa, many if not most of the Hunting Reserves that were gazetted at that time are the ancestors of today's National Parks. The turn of the century was the period when hunting for trading ivory and skins or for collecting specimens for museums (Roosevelt, 1910) gave birth to hunting for sport, adventure and exotic travels named safari (*safari* means travel in Swahili). Hunting tourism arose in East Africa with pioneer farmers and explorers guiding foreign hunters (Lindsey et al., 2007). After the First World War, the hunting safari industry expanded, policed by law and administration. After the Second World War, sport hunting became more organized and regulated as a business (Booth and Chardonnet, 2015).

Independence

After independence, game and hunting laws were progressively modernized and the network of Protected Areas developed. Safari hunting continued except for a few countries like Kenya, where it was banned in 1977, which precipitated the steep decline of game numbers in the country (Western et al., 2009; Ogutu et al., 2016). In contrast, neighbouring Tanzania, after a temporary hunting ban between 1973 and 1977, has maintained until today safari hunting on vast areas while also succeeding in maintaining the highest numbers on Earth of large mammals such as lion and buffalo. Unexpectedly, the bans on hunting in Kenya and temporarily in Tanzania made both safari hunting clients and professional hunters look for new hunting fields in other regions of Africa, which boomed following the bans in East Africa (Hurt and Ravn, 2000).

While buffalo remained common in some areas, more and more situations were arising, especially in West and Central Africa, where local buffalo populations were diminishing as human population growth drove demand for more land at the expense of wilderness, with agriculture and livestock encroachment, and with increasing poaching pressure for bushmeat. Gradually, hunting became controlled by sustainability norms and integrated into conservation strategies. The rationale was to create sustainable revenue streams for rural communities and State wildlife agencies, thus providing incentives to preserve Hunting Areas as duly gazetted Protected Areas, in a challenging attempt to prevent their conversion into agriculture or other environment-unfriendly land uses (Prins and de Jong, 2022). In several African countries, there was a gradual alignment of trophy-hunting industries with conservation and development policies, supported by a number of international donor agencies (Lindsey et al., 2007).

Starting in the 1980s with the Communal Areas Management Programme for Indigenous Resources (CAMPFIRE) programme in Zimbabwe, new approaches aiming at increasing benefits from hunting and other wildlife uses for local populations led to a paradigm shift towards connecting sustainable use and hunting with rural development and livelihoods (Murphree, 2000; Chapters 1 and 13). This approach progressively expanded throughout Africa with the Administrative Management Design programme (ADMADE) in Zambia, the *Programme de Développement des Zones de Chasse Villageoises* (PDZCV) in CAR, the *Zones d'Intérêt Cynégétique à Gestion Communautaire* (ZICGC) programme in Cameroon, the *Gestion Participative des Ressources Naturelles et de la Faune* (GEPRENAF) programme in Burkina Faso, and the *Ecosystèmes Protégés d'Afrique Soudano-Sahélienne* (ECOPAS) programme (Lindsey et al., 2007). The foundation of this Community-Based Natural Resources Management (CBNRM) approach is to allocate user rights to local people, thereby allowing for benefits from wildlife use and creating conservation incentives (Baldus, 2009). However, the implementation of this approach is not always that simple. In south-eastern Zimbabwe, for example, Poshiwa et al. (2013) show the limitations of revenues from wildlife diversification, even though wildlife income is less volatile than income from the agro-pastoral system, and wildlife can be used as a hedge asset to offset risk from agricultural production without compromising on return.

In these utilization schemes, hunting tourism has in most cases the highest income potential (Booth, 2010). As one of the most numerous large game animals, the buffalo is a core species for high-income hunting tourism (Lindsey et al., 2012). Buffalo hunts contribute a high share to community hunting income under CBNRM, for example in CAR (Bouché, 2010) and Tanzania (TAWA, 2019).

Hunting Buffalo Today

Hunting Buffalo for Meat and Other Reasons

Informal Bushmeat Hunting Throughout Africa

Hunting for food began millennia ago with the first humans. Today, many rural communities across the continent still heavily rely on bushmeat, both for food security and income (e.g. Loibooki et al., 2002; van Vliet and Mbazza, 2011; Friant et al., 2020). Consumption of buffalo meat occurs broadly across the wide range of wild animal species consumed (Table 16.1). The pay-off for hunting a buffalo is high: a single buffalo represents one of the greatest amounts of meat that can be obtained per capita, and buffalo meat is one of the most nutritive among the wild species usually hunted (Cawthorn and Hoffman, 2015). Buffalo is highly prized in urban markets and restaurants. While not the case everywhere, in some places like in Bangui, Central African Republic (Fargeot et al., 2017), or Manica Province, Mozambique (Lindsey and Bento, 2012), its meat is among the most expensive. This makes buffalo one of the species most targeted by poaching in several areas (Skikuku et al., 2018; Gaodirelwe et al., 2020). Buffalo meat may also be obtained as a by-product of conflicts between the species and the local communities; several communities hunt buffalo in retaliation after the species has raided their crops or attacked people (Long et al., 2020).

Local communities also hunt buffalo for purposes other than meat (Table 16.1). In Ethiopia, for instance, poachers hunt buffalo as trophies to increase their social acceptance and respect in society (Erena, 2014). For the Bisa people in Zambia, there are multiple dimensions to hunting buffalo, including social positioning and cohesion of their society (Marks, 1976). In many areas, buffalo body parts are used for cultural ceremonies and in traditional medicine (Whiting et al., 2011).

There are some communities that are reluctant to hunt buffalo. First, because hunting buffalo may be perceived as too dangerous by local hunters (Dell et al., 2020). In many traditional systems, hunters also have to share the meat from their hunts with a large number of community members. They therefore tend to avoid large species such as buffalo to limit the expense of delivering parts of the hunted animals to relatives living in distant places (Eniang et al., 2017). Finally, for some communities, the buffalo is regarded as a totem or taboo animal, and its hunt is not allowed (FAO/CIG, 2002; Duda et al., 2018; Chapter 1).

That said, hunting for bushmeat largely contributes to local declines of buffalo populations, even sometimes to the vanishing of the species (Prins,

Table 16.1 Uses (either legal or illegal) of African buffalo by local communities: examples across the species range by region, in West, Central, East and Southern Africa (based on data/sources in the table).

Region	Country	Area	Buffalo product	Use	Details	Reference
West Africa	*Burkina Faso*	Bobo-Dioulasso	Meat	Food	Buffalo hunted in groups for commercial purpose, sold to restaurants	Montcho et al. (2020)
			Testis	Traditional medicine	Aphrodisiac potions	
			Trophy	Social prestige		
	Ghana		Meat	Food	Species previously regarded as totems, such as buffalo, started to appear openly on major bushmeat markets because of increasing poverty and the growing scarcity of preferred wildlife species	FAO/CIG (2020)
	Ivory Coast	Comoé National Park	Meat	Food	All the local residents surveyed feed on buffalo flesh and/or skin	Atta et al. (2021)
			Organs and other body parts	Traditional medicine	E.g. tail, heart, leg bones, horns, poop, urine fat, brain, bile to cure diarrhoea, eye aches, folie, heartache, bone weakness, sexual impotence, etc.	
				Witchcraft	Turning away bad luck, banish fear, repulse bad spells, etc.	
			Meat	Food	Near extinction of buffalo because of hunting for food	P. Henschel, unpublished data in Lindsey et al. (2015)

Country	Location	Body part	Use	Remarks	Reference
Nigeria	Abia, Bauchi, Edo, Kogi, Ondo and Zamfara State	Meat	Food		Alarape et al. (2021)
		Penis	Traditional medicine	Used as an aphrodisiac	Adeola (1992)
	Ibadab, Oyo State	Bone	Traditional medicine	Used as anti-vomiting	Oduntan et al. (2012)
	Cross River State	Meat	Food	Hunters prefer not to hunt buffalo because the traditional system demands them to share the meat with community members, sometimes in distant places. However, Fulani herdsmen reported that they responded to the conflict between buffalo and cattle by setting wire snares along trails and shooting buffalo	Eniang et al. (2017)
	South-western towns	Skin, eyeballs, liver, tail, penis, etc.	Traditional medicine	Elephantiasis, loss of hearing/speech/ eyesight vertebral column fracture, prolonged pregnancy; extrusion of placenta after parturition, human skull fracture, fertility	Sodeinde and Soewu (1999)
		Nose, head	Witchcraft	Invoking witches appeasing traditional gods	

(cont.)

Table 16.1 (*cont.*)

Region	Country	Area	Buffalo product	Use	Details	Reference
Central Africa	*Cameroon*	Kimbi-Fungom National Park	Meat	Food	Buffalo hunting is a source of income	Nda et al. (2018)
					Buffalo is generally avoided in the Pygmy groups because it is considered as having a potential harmful effect on humans	Duda et al. (2018)
	Central African Republic	Bangui	Meat	Food	Buffalo, with snakes, are the most expensive species sold in the markets	Fargeot et al. (2017)
		Yangambi Landscape, Yangambi Biosphere Reserve and the Ngazi Forest Reserve	Meat	Food	The local extirpation of buffalo is explained as the result of overhunting by armed groups (Armed Forces of the DRC, Congolese, Rwandans, and Ugandans from eastern DRC) during the periods of rebellion	Van Vliet et al. (2018)
		Around Lomani National Park	Meat	Food	Buffalo nearly disappeared because of overhunting	Batumike et al. (2021)
	Democratic Republic of Congo	Garamba National Park	Meat	Food	During peacetime, protected species such as elephant and buffalo rarely appeared in the rural markets, but they comprised more than half of all bushmeat sales in the urban markets. During wartime, the sales of protected species in the urban markets increased fivefold	De Merode and Cowlishaw (2006)
		South of the Salonga–Lukenie–Sankuru Landscape	Meat	Food	Buffalo meat sold in large quantities, accounting for the highest percentage of total weight of carcasses found in the local market	Steel et al. (2008)

Region	Country	Location	Product	Use	Description	Reference
	Democratic Republic of Congo and Republic of the Congo	Kinshasa and Brazzaville	Meat	Food	Buffalo meat illegally sold in the restaurants. Buffalo is the most expensive meat among the ungulate species	Gluszek et al. (2021)
	Gabon	Gambia Complex of Protected Areas	Meat	Food	In most locations with buffalo, signs of poaching were found as well. Buffalo meat sold at a price of 2200 CFA-Franc	Litjens (2017)
	Republic of the Congo	Pointe Noire	Meat	Food	Buffalo is among the species most frequently bought and sold in markets and restaurants	Boratto and Gore (2018)
East Africa	*Ethiopia*	Western Ethiopia			Bushmeat and illegal trophy hunting are the key causes of buffalo collapse. Bushmeat hunting is carried out by local poachers or local militias, whereas most illegal trophy hunters come from the remote parts of Limu, Gidda Ayana and Ebantu districts of the East Wollega Administrative Zone	Erena et al. (2019)
		Oromia Regional State	Trophy	Social prestige	Hunting buffalo for trophies was frequently practised in the area	Erena (2014)
	Kenya	Mount Elgon Biosphere Reserve	Meat	Food	Buffalo is the mostly targeted species, after antelopes. Also hunted by poachers from Uganda	Skikuku et al. (2018)
			Tail	Cultural ornamentation, sign of prestige		
		Nationwide		Retaliatory killing	Buffalo is the second most commonly killed species in retaliation for damage caused	Long et al. (2020)

(cont.)

Table 16.1 (cont.)

Region	Country	Area	Buffalo product	Use	Details	Reference
	Rwanda	Volcanoes National Park	Meat	Food	Hunting buffalo for meat was the most common forest activity in the past. Less common now because of increased law enforcement	Munanura et al. (2018)
	Sudan	Dinder Biosphere Reserve	Meat	Food	During periods of famine, conflict and critical fallback of food sources (crop and domestic livestock), many Sudanese consume all types of wild fauna, including buffalo	Adam (2019)
	Tanzania	Uzungwa Scarp Forest and Mwanihana Forest	Meat	Food	Locally extinct in the Reserve by the early 1970s as a result of intensive hunting for bushmeat trade	Rovero et al. (2012); Hegerl et al. (2017)
		South West Rungwa Game Reserve	Meat	Food	Communities get meat through resident hunting. Buffalo meat is mostly used for trade to generate income	Nachihangu et al. (2018)
		Western Serengeti	Meat	Food	The ethnic groups in Western Serengeti prefer medium–large wildlife such as buffalo for protein and income	Holmern et al. (2006); Ndibalema and Songorwa (2007); Mfunda and Røskaft (2010)

		Tarime District	Meat	Food	The harvesting rates of buffalo are alarming. Buffalo was reported to be reduced by 50–90% out of their range	Holmern et al. (2002, 2006); Kideghesgo et al. (2006)
	Uganda	Northern Uganda	Meat	Food	Buffalo meat found in local markets	Dell et al. (2021)
		Near Murchison National Park	Meat	Food	Buffalo is perceived by poachers as the most dangerous wild animal to hunt and the most dangerous to trap	Dell et al. (2020)
Southern Africa	*Botswana*	Okavango Delta	Meat	Food	Approximately 1800 illegal hunters each harvest an average of 320 kg of bushmeat annually, although some reported harvesting ≥1000 kg. While impala was the most commonly hunted species, buffalo accounted for 30% of all bushmeat production	Rogan et al. (2017)
		In and outside Wildlife Management Areas around the Moremi Game Reserve	Meat	Food	CBNRM communities mostly target impala, followed by Cape buffalo	Gaodirelwe et al. (2020)
	Mozambique		Meat	Food	Illegal hunters commonly use gin traps, which are manufactured from steel car springs and used to kill animals as large as buffalo	Lindsey and Bento (2012)
		Manica Province	Meat	Food	Bushmeat from large species such as buffalo is less frequently sold today than during the civil war. However, buffalo is one of the most commonly cited bushmeat species by interviewees	Lindsey and Bento (2012)

(cont.)

Table 16.1 (*cont.*)

Region	Country	Area	Buffalo product	Use	Details	Reference
	South Africa	Pafuri in the Makuleke concession	Meat	Food	Cable from the dilapidated western boundary fence frequently stolen by illegal hunters to make snares to capture hippo and buffalo	C. Roche, unpublished data in Lindsey et al. (2015)
		Xhosa and Sotho communities in the Western Cape Province	Bones	Traditional medicine	Buffalo bone is one of the most expensive animal items sold	Nieman et al. (2019)
		Faraday market, Johannesburg	Skull, horns, skin	Traditional medicine	Buffalo is one of the ungulate species most represented in the market	Whiting et al. (2011)
	Zambia	Luangwa Valley, Upper and Lower Lupande, Lumimba and Sandwe game management areas	Meat	Food	Declining population of buffalo in areas close to human settlements, close to boundary of the National Park	R. McRobb, M. Becker and D. Lewis, unpublished data in Lindsey et al. (2015)

1996; Batumike et al., 2021). Basically, bushmeat hunting is unselective and unlimited; where snares and gin-traps are set for buffalo and other game, any calf, female or male can be taken, and with no limitation in numbers given that traps can be reset. Bushmeat hunting is often considered one of the greatest threats to biodiversity in African savannas and forests, often ahead of other major threats such as deforestation and habitat fragmentation (Wilkie et al., 2011; van Velden et al., 2018).

Regulated Bushmeat Hunting

Some countries, such as Tanzania, allow hunting quotas for meat purposes (including buffalo), while others allow subsistence community hunting, like CAR (Snyman et al., 2021). In most countries, trophy-hunting concessionaries are mandated by their lease agreements to provide local communities – free of charge – the meat obtained by tourist hunters. This is quite stringent in West and Central Africa, where wild meat is extremely sought after. In Zambia, 130 tons of fresh game meat – of which 24 per cent is from buffalo – are provided annually by the hunting tourism industry to rural communities at an approximate yearly value for the meat alone of over €500,000 exclusive of distribution costs (White and Belant, 2015).

In some southern African countries, the production of wild meat constitutes a real industry, one that is organized and regulated. In Namibia, with an annual mean of between 60 and 75 kg of venison produced per square kilometre in 2013 on farmland, hunting for venison is an important sector which contributes more to national food security than livestock, as beef is mainly exported (Lindsey et al., 2013). However, most of the venison is from antelopes, not from buffalo, which is restricted by veterinary regulations. In South Africa, 'biltong hunting' is a recreational hunting by local hunters who harvest wild meat and process it into biltong (dried meat) or sausage (Taylor et al., 2015). It is a major value chain in this country, much larger than trophy hunting; however, it mainly targets common game rather than buffalo.

Buffalo Hunting Tourism

What Are We Talking About?

This section addresses lawful and regulated hunting only, in contrast with outlawed and unregulated hunting, commonly called poaching (see Prins, 2020). The terminology of hunting categories has been debated at length (Booth and Chardonnet, 2015). One reason is that the terms used in each language are often difficult to translate literally into other languages. Another reason is that the various categories of hunting often overlap (IUCN, 2016). For IUCN, 'trophy hunting is hunting of animals with specific characteristics and involves the payment of a fee by a foreign or local hunter for a hunting experience, usually guided; it may be a distinct activity or overlap with recreational or meat hunting'. While trophy hunting reflects the quest for an outstanding trophy, sport hunting rather reflects the quest for a challenging fair chase of the game by tracking on foot, whatever the trophy. The trophy is a key part of a safari, but the hunting experience and adventure in the bush are also what attracts clients, and there also has to be the feeling of a fair chase to the proper hunter with no guarantee of success (Hurt and Ravn, 2000). While some authors prefer the term 'regulated hunting' (Dickson et al., 2009; Booth and Chardonnet, 2015), many other terms are commonly used, for example safari hunting, recreational hunting, tourism hunting, hunting tourism. For Spenceley (2021), 'hunting tourism is a consumptive mode of nature-based tourism that uses renewable natural resources in a wild or undeveloped form for the purpose of enjoying natural areas or wildlife and contribute to conserve and value wilderness areas'. It is a typical tourism value chain with (i) emitting countries, that is countries of origin of the clients (hunting tourist or tourist hunter), and (ii) receiving countries, that is countries selling operating rights to tourism operators (hunting company or hunting operator or outfitter), themselves selling tourism services (hunting safari or hunting trip or hunting party or hunt) to their clients.

Throughout Africa

To most hunters, the buffalo is a fascinating game for being (i) one of the so-called 'dangerous game' and (ii) one of the 'Big Five', the term commonly used to describe the five major big game species. Hunting accidents with buffalo are not uncommon, even with experienced professional hunters. The buffalo is widely regarded as dangerous to hunt, which certainly adds to the attractiveness of its hunt: '*He looks as if you owe him money*' (Ruark, 1987, italics added for emphasis). In 2022, buffalo can be legally hunted by hunting tourists in 16 sub-Saharan African countries, that is in 43 per cent of the 37 buffalo range countries (Figure 16.1). The COVID-19 pandemic in 2020 and 2021 prevented hunting tourists from travelling, which severely impacted hunting tourism like all forms of tourism. The situation slightly returned to normal in 2022.

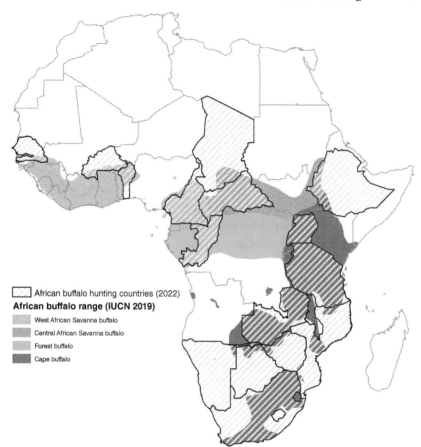

Figure 16.1 Buffalo range countries where hunting tourism is lawful in 2022 for the four subspecies of buffalo recognized by the IUCN Red List so far. Note: Buffalo in northern and central Angola were categorized as 'Cape buffalo' by IUCN (2019), but phenotypically and perhaps even genetically they are 'forest buffalo'. Source: Author.

Among the four subspecies thus far recognized by the IUCN Red List (Chapters 3 and 4), the Cape buffalo is by far the most hunted, being legally hunted in nine countries. This obviously reflects its much higher abundance than the other subspecies, but also other factors like a greater development of the tourism industry, a safer security situation, a larger expansion of CBNRM programmes, etc. The forest buffalo is the least hunted subspecies with only three countries where it can be hunted legally, a situation resulting from a more restricted range, landlocked hunting grounds, the difficulty of the hunt in thick habitats, and also probably a degraded conservation status. The West and Central African savanna buffalo, both subspecies being rather similar and intermixed, can be hunted in eight countries. However, the overall number of buffalo trophy-hunted annually in these two regions has always been quite low, about 300 a year. We need to mention that the hunting community recognizes a fifth subspecies, the Nile buffalo, which ranges in Ethiopia, northern and western Uganda, and appears as an intermediate form between the Central African savanna buffalo and the Cape buffalo. The reality of the transitional shape of its trophy explains that hunters specifically hunt this particular buffalo and register their trophies distinctly in the records books.

Hunting quotas (the maximum number of adult male buffalo allowed to be hunted per year per Hunting Area) and offtakes (number of buffalo effectively harvested per year per Hunting Area) vary greatly between regions, with the highest figures in Tanzania and Southern Africa and the lowest in West and Central Africa (Table 16.2). The national offtake rate (ratio of offtake to quota) is not only the result of the number of buffalo taken per Hunting Area, but also of the percentage of Hunting Areas being leased and operational, which is a sign of the functionality of the industry in the country. In nearly all of the hunting countries, the hunt concerns free-ranging buffalo in unfenced Hunting Areas. South Africa, where buffalo hunting happens behind fences, is a major exception. Another peculiar feature of South Africa is that hunting quotas are set by the landowner, while they are generally set by government authorities quasi-everywhere else.

West Africa

Three countries of West Africa allow legal hunting of buffalo. In Senegal, with a relict population of West African savanna buffalo in the far southeastern corner of the country, buffalo trophy hunting is anecdotal. In contrast, Benin and Burkina Faso have developed a well-organized and regulated big game hunting tourism industry with the West African savanna buffalo as the main attraction together with the roan antelope (*Hippotragus equinus*). Buffalo hunting there is renowned for being a challenging, fair chase by stalking on foot with excellent local trackers.

In Burkina Faso, in 2017, 303 hunting tourists (9 per cent of all tourists) harvested 424 mammals for a production of 86 tons of meat and a direct revenue of about €827,000 (Ouedraogo, 2018). Over seven years between 2012 and 2018, the average national annual quota was 166

Table 16.2 *Buffalo hunting quotas and offtakes in selected countries throughout Africa.*

		2011/ 2012	2012/ 2013	2013/ 2014	2014/ 2015	2015/ 2016	2016/ 2017	2017/ 2018	2018/ 2019	2019/ 2020	Average
West Africa	*Benin* (PNP, 2018, 2019; PNW, 2018, 2019)	Buffalo quota (N buffalo)	n/a	n/a	n/a	n/a	n/a	n/a	75	75	n/a	75
		Buffalo offtake (N buffalo)	n/a	n/a	n/a	n/a	n/a	n/a	57	59	n/a	58
		Buffalo offtake rate (%)	n/a	n/a	n/a	n/a	n/a	n/a	76	79	n/a	**77**
	Burkina Faso (DFRC, 2018)	Buffalo quota (N buffalo)	147	163	153	153	183	183	181	n/a	n/a	166
		Buffalo offtake (N buffalo)	115	136	129	82	115	81	81	n/a	n/a	106
		Buffalo offtake rate (%)	78	83	84	54	63	44	45	n/a	n/a	**64**
Central Africa	*Cameroon* (MINFOF, 2020)	Buffalo quota (N buffalo)	n/a	n/a	n/a	n/a	n/a	352	341	356	381	358
		Buffalo offtake (N buffalo)	n/a	n/a	n/a	n/a	n/a	156	184	125	99	141
		Buffalo offtake rate (%)	n/a	n/a	n/a	n/a	n/a	44	54	35	26	**39**
East Africa	*Tanzania* (Wildlife Division, personal communication, 2021)	Buffalo quota (N buffalo)	2130	2130	2130	1948	1456	1456	1456	1456	1456	1735
		Buffalo offtake (N buffalo)	1129	901	889	940	828	672	655	625	737	820
		Buffalo offtake rate (%)	53	42	42	48	57	46	45	43	51	**47**

(cont.)

Table 16.2 (*cont.*)

		2011/ 2012	2012/ 2013	2013/ 2014	2014/ 2015	2015/ 2016	2016/ 2017	2017/ 2018	2018/ 2019	2019/ 2020	Average
Southern Africa	*Zimbabwe* (ZPWMA, personal communication, 2022)	Buffalo quota (*N* buffalo)	n/a	n/a	1794	1751	1205	1308	1343	1252	1289	1420
		Buffalo offtake (*N* buffalo)	n/a	n/	717	699	593	642	592	585	200	575
		Buffalo offtake rate (%)	n/	n/	40	40	49	49	44	47	16	**41**
	Namibia (only for Communal Conservancies) (MEFT and NACSO, personal communication, 2022)	Buffalo quota (*N* buffalo)	n/a	n/a	106	106	108	122	122	122	132	117
		Buffalo offtake (*N* buffalo)	n/a	n/a	88	93	93	110	99	114	61	94
		Buffalo offtake rate (%)	n/a	n/a	83	85	86	90	81	93	46	**80**

buffalo/year (147–183), and the average national annual offtake was 106 buffalo hunted/year (81–136) for a national annual offtake rate of 64 per cent (44–84) (DFRC, 2018; Table 16.2).

In Benin, over the two hunting seasons 2017–2018 and 2018–2019, the five existing Hunting Areas (only four of which were operational) harvested an annual average of 58 buffalo out of an average annual quota of 75 for an average annual offtake rate of 77.3 per cent (PNP, 2018, 2019; PNW, 2018, 2019; Table 16.2). In 2018, the W National Park ecosystem earned 76 per cent of its revenue from 19 hunting tourists visiting the Mekrou Hunting Area and 2 per cent from 476 photographic tourists visiting the W National Park (PNP, 2018, 2019; PNW, 2018, 2019; Table 16.2).

Since 2019, the severe degradation of the security situation in the region (with terrorism taking over vast wilderness areas) has prevented many National Parks and Hunting Areas from operating in West Africa.

Central Africa

Central Africa is the region where buffalo are the most diverse, with three subspecies occurring out of four. Buffalo there is not the first game of appeal for tourist hunters, who mainly look for the Eastern giant eland (*Tragelaphus derbianus gigas*) and the Western or lowland bongo (*Tragelaphus eurycerus eurycerus*). However, buffalo is part of the hunting package and is sought after for providing serious stalking by foot with outstandingly skilful trackers from local communities.

Cameroon is the country with the highest number of legal big game hunters in all of West and Central Africa in recent years. In 2018, 285 tourists came to Cameroon for hunting (MINFOF, 2019). In this country, Hunting Areas are a major component of the national network of Protected Areas: 71 gazetted Hunting Areas (*Zones d'Intérêt Cynégétique*) cover 57,000 km² (11.9 per cent of the country), that is 1.5 times the size of National Parks and Reserves (39,000 km², 8.2 per cent of the country; MINFOF, 2019). Over four hunting seasons between 2016 and 2020, the average annual quota was 358 buffalo (341–381) with 69 per cent savanna buffalo and 31 per cent forest buffalo. During this period, an annual average of 141 buffalo (99–184) were hunted for an average annual offtake rate of 39 per cent (MINFOF, 2020; Table 16.2). Such a low offtake rate reflects an important proportion of unleased Hunting Areas, as a number of them are no longer operational due to degradation by all sorts of activities which are illegal in protected

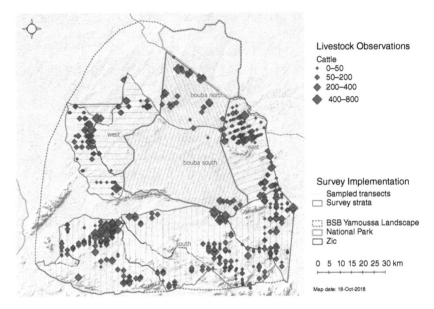

Figure 16.2 Livestock sightings in the BSB landscape covering the transboundary national parks of Bouba Ndjidda (Cameroon) and Sena Oura (Chad) as well as the seven neighbouring Hunting Areas (Cameroon), during the aerial wildlife survey in 2018 (total surface of about 10,500 km²). The estimated livestock population (117,134 heads) was six times higher than the estimated population of the 11 largest wild mammals (20,136 individuals), and located mostly within the Hunting Areas surrounding the National Parks (data and illustration reproduced from WCS and MINFOF, 2018, with permission).

areas: poaching, livestock invasion (Figure 16.2), cotton encroachment, gold mining, logging, and the charcoal trade.

The Central African Republic (CAR) could be named the 'buffalo country', as it is the only one on the continent where three subspecies of buffalo occur and can be legally hunted, although the forest buffalo is rarely hunted there. In this country, 89 gazetted Hunting Areas cover 220,000 km² (35 per cent of the country), that is 3.6 times the size of the National Parks and Reserves (61,000 km², 10 per cent of the country). Before the political unrest initiated in 2012, CAR was a prime destination for big game hunting. It is still practiced in 2022, but so far remains marginal. Before the collapse of tourism, the buffalo was the second most abundant large game species after the giant eland in the *Zones cynégétiques villageoises* (ZCV, Village Hunting Zones) of northern CAR, with a density of 1.1 buffalo per km² (Bouché, 2010). In these ZCV only, the buffalo was the most hunted game species: in the 2008–2009 hunting season, 44 buffalo were harvested by hunting tourists, ahead of 26 giant eland (Bouché, 2010).

Chad is renowned for hosting the typical form of *Syncerus caffer aequinoctialis* with its wide, flattened horn shape. The country used to be famous for big game hunting until the contemporary civil turmoil. Despite these constraints, hunting tourism continued to be practiced in 2022, but at a lower scale.

In the Republic of Congo, hunting tourism has recently resumed with only a few forest buffalo harvested per year.

The security situation in Central Africa has been deteriorating for a longer time than in West Africa, and this has undermined the hunting industry as well as conservation. The region is experiencing what Scholte et al. (2021) call a conservation overstretch: with increasing insecurity and declining revenues, governments find themselves confronted with too few resources to protect vast areas.

East Africa

In East Africa, three countries have developed a well-structured hunting tourism industry. In Ethiopia, few buffalo are hunted for the simple reason that the Hunting Areas are not exactly located within the buffalo range in this country. The buffalo is not the game of appeal for tourist hunters coming to this country. In Uganda, the hunting industry has developed over the last 20 years to a point where it is now a real alternative to the other East and Central African hunting destinations. A special attraction is the so-called Nile buffalo, and Uganda is the place to find it (Siege and Siege, 2020).

Tanzania, which hosts the largest number of African buffalo on Earth, unsurprisingly comes first among all African countries for regulated hunting of free-ranging buffalo. Tanzanian buffalo are famous for their large herds and their magnificent wide horns.

The hunting domain is an essential pillar of the national network of Protected Areas in this country. In 2004, proclaimed Protected Areas gazetted as Hunting Areas covered over 250,000 km² (26.4 per cent of the country), nearly twice the size of the National Parks (134,881 km², 14.1 per cent; Baldus and Cauldwell, 2004). The number of Hunting Areas was progressively reduced from 164 to 113 in 2020 with the gazetting of several Game Reserves as National Parks. However, Hunting Areas still cover nearly a quarter of Tanzania's surface. Many if not most

Hunting Areas are not viable for other conservation options such as eco-tourism due notably to remoteness, lack of scenery and poor visibility of wildlife compared to the top National Parks.

Hunting tourism is an important and organized sector in Tanzania. For the 2013–2018 period, out of 164 Hunting Areas, 149 were awarded to 60 hunting companies. However, there was considerable financial pressure during this period due to adverse publicity regarding sport hunting, and the impact of hunting bans on elephant and lion trophy imports to the USA, Europe and Australia (TAWA, 2019). With fewer hunting clients visiting Tanzania than in previous years, hunting tourism revenues dropped from €44 million in 2008 with 1673 hunters (Booth, 2010) to €28.3 million in 2014 with 708 hunters (Booth, 2017). When the cost of maintaining Hunting Areas became higher than the income, many hunting companies returned their Hunting Areas to the wildlife authorities. By the end of 2018, 81 Hunting Areas were handed back, representing slightly less than 130,000 km^2 (approximately 52 per cent) of the area set aside for hunting (TAWA, 2019).

This downtrend also impacted buffalo conservation in two contrasting ways. First, when the Hunting Areas formerly leased for hunting were abandoned, these 13 million ha of wilderness became vacant, and hence were exposed to poaching and encroachment by other land uses detrimental to the environment. Highly susceptible to these threats, buffalo became a collateral victim of the bans on the importation of hunting trophies directed at elephants and lions, two species listed on CITES Appendices. Second, as the buffalo is not a CITES-listed species, the bans turned the buffalo, once considered a secondary game species, into a first-choice species for hunters travelling to Tanzania. The character of the Tanzania hunting industry has changed over the last 10 years from being a 'big four' game hunting destination to one that is now heavily dependent on leopard and buffalo (TAWA, 2019).

However, although the trophy fee for buffalo is cheaper than that of the flagship game species, buffalo remains the first tax-earning species in this country due to the larger number harvested: in 2019/2020, the trophy fees (€2080 per buffalo) of 737 buffalo hunted in 77 Hunting Areas earned €1.53 million, to which all other revenue sources should be added, that is hunting block fees, licences, daily fees (Wildlife Division, personal communication).

Over eight years between 2012 and 2020, the average national annual quota was 1681 buffalo/year (1456–2130), and the average national annual offtake was 781 buffalo hunted/year (625–940) for a national annual offtake rate of 46.3 per cent (41.7–56.8; Wildlife Division, personal communication). A yearly offtake of 781 individuals represents an annual taking of about 0.3 per cent of the roughly evaluated 250,000 buffalo population in Tanzania (see Chapter 4 for actual best estimates).

Southern Africa

In Southern Africa, there are six countries with legal hunting tourism, and the Cape buffalo is a major game. In Botswana, buffalo hunting was resumed in 2020. Hunting is organized in registered Hunting Areas covering 75,000 km² (13 per cent of the country) for an annual revenue of €40 million in 2012 (Di Minin et al., 2016). In Zambia, buffalo is a major game species for 36 hunting concessions within Game Management Areas covering 170,000 km² (23.6 per cent of Zambia; Snyman et al., 2021). In Zimbabwe, hunting is undertaken in 78,000 km² (20 per cent of the country) and generated €24.4 million revenue in 2015 (Chitauro, 2016 in Snyman et al., 2021). Buffalo is an important game outside the central plateau in both State land and in the 10 CAMPFIRE communal areas. In Mozambique, buffalo is also a major game species for the various categories of Hunting Areas (*Coutadas, Fazendas do bravio*, etc.) covering 135,000 km² (17 per cent of the country) (Di Minin et al., 2016). In Namibia, buffalo hunting is restricted to the Caprivi strip because existing veterinary policies prevent the reintroduction of buffalo, although it is a key species for tourism and safari hunting (Lindsey et al., 2013). Hunting is a major driver of the wildlife-based tourism in Namibia, with €26.6 million direct revenue in 2016 (Snyman et al., 2021) over 287,000 km² (Lindsey et al., 2013). Hunting is undertaken in two land categories: (i) communal conservancies (86 of them in 2021 cover 166,000 km², i.e. 20.2 per cent of Namibia), which collect 100 per cent of the hunting fees (€2.3 million in 2018) in their 48 hunting concessions (Snyman et al., 2021); and (ii) private game ranches (so-called 'freehold lands'), which contain 21–33 times more wildlife than Protected Areas (Snyman et al., 2021).

South Africa has the largest African hunting industry in terms of numbers of operators, visiting hunters, animal collected, and revenues generated (Lindsey et al., 2007). South Africa also hosts the highest number of buffalo in southern Africa, yet with a peculiar situation that contrasts sharply with the rest of the continent: there are no free-ranging buffalo in this country, all of them being enclosed, so that buffalo are always hunted behind fences (Chapter 13). Hunting Areas there are hence considerably smaller in size than anywhere else in Africa, largely due to the requirement for fencing (Taylor et al., 2020). The average size of a game ranch is slightly less than 3000 ha (Cloete et al., 2015), that is in the order of between 10 and 100 times smaller than Hunting Areas in the rest of Africa (e.g. the average size of the 17 Hunting Areas of Niassa Special Reserve in Mozambique is 2486 km²). Overall, Hunting Areas cover 150,000 km² in South Africa, that is 12 per cent of the country (Snyman et al., 2021). Since the Game Theft Act of 1991, properly fenced wildlife in South Africa is the property of the landowner, a situation almost non-existent in most other African countries. This ownership of wildlife allowed the private sector to develop a dynamic wildlife industry providing substantial benefits to local and national economies (Snyman et al., 2021). For half of the nearly 10,000 game ranches, hunting is a source of income, and for 30 per cent of them hunting is the main source of income (Nel, 2021).

Buffalo in South Africa is a typical example of a high-value species producing high income from a very low percentage of the population harvested. It does not appear on the list of the 10 most hunted game species in South Africa (NWU, 2017 in Snyman et al., 2021), yet it is the top income-earning species with €13.2 million generated in 2016 and €9.2 million in 2019 (South African Professional Hunters statistics, 2019), well ahead of the second high-value game species, sable (*Hippotragus niger*).

Since the amendment in 2019 of the Animal Improvement Act of 1998, buffalo are legally subject to selection programmes for enlarging and reshaping their horns in order to raise their commercial value for live sales and hunting trophies (e.g. the first 50-inch-wide trophy live bull in South Africa was auctioned at an all-time record for buffalo of €10.5 million). The selection methods combine (i) extreme inbreeding among the most desired individuals and (ii) outbreeding with East African buffalo, which have greater horn spread than South African buffalo. Whether this development is a matter of manipulated genetic engineering or the restoration of historic natural genetic integrity is an issue of tense debate, including in the international arena (IUCN SSC Antelope Specialist Group, 2015; IUCN WCC, 2016). There is considerable concern about the negative genetic consequences of intensive selective breeding of wildlife, as well as about the image and tourism economy of South Africa (e.g. Selier et al., 2018; Russo et al., 2019; Somers et al., 2020). Game ranching in South Africa is certainly a success story in many ways (socioeconomic, rewilding, recovery of endangered species, etc.; Chapter 13), for example there are roughly three times more wildlife in private game ranches than in the National Parks

(Kitshoff-Botha, 2020). The sustainable-use approach of wildlife ranching has furthermore proved to be a legitimate way to conserve biodiversity, and one that may even be advisable for other African countries to be considered (Taylor et al., 2020). However, a great many stakeholders and observers disapprove of the creation of so-called 'superior' bigger trophy animals, as well as of introducing exotic taxa and canned or put-and-take hunting (Snyman et al., 2021).

Administration and Management of Buffalo Hunting

Legal Framework at a Glance

International Scene

The Convention on International Trade in Endangered Species of Wild Fauna and Flora (CITES) does not list the African buffalo in any of its Appendices of protected animals (CITES, 2022). No CITES Party has passed stricter domestic measures for the African buffalo to date. For example, the European Union does not list this species in the Annexes of the EU Wildlife Trade Regulations (European Commission, 2010), and the USA do not include this species in the list of foreign species of its Endangered Species Act (ESA) (US Fish and Wildlife Service, 2022). Therefore, international trade of buffalo and their parts including trophies is not subject to specific controls beyond general custom, wildlife and veterinary regulations. In 2022, the African buffalo is listed in the 'Near Threatened' Category of the IUCN Red List, the second lowest category on the risk scale (IUCN SSC Antelope Specialist Group, 2019). Thus far, the Red List does not distinguish between buffalo subspecies, a matter for discussion as the conservation status of each subspecies is evolving differently (Chapter 4).

National Settings

Each buffalo range country has established its own environmental legislation with an array of laws and regulations to protect and manage biodiversity. All of the countries that allow the legal hunting of buffalo have set their respective permit systems with precise rules, so that hunting buffalo without the proper licences is taken as poaching and subject to penalties. In most countries, the rules, taxes and fees are different between citizens, resident expatriates and foreigners. The cost to hunt a buffalo is much higher for foreign hunting tourists than for citizens.

Costs consist of government levies, payments for the services of safari operators and royalties or retention schemes for local communities and landowners (Hurt and Ravn, 2000). The revenues generated by buffalo hunting provide incentives for (i) the State to preserve the national network of Protected Areas, and (ii) communities and landowners to keep game on their lands and avoid landscape conversion into alternative land uses that are environmentally unfriendly.

Monitoring Buffalo Hunting

Monitoring is an essential process for the assessment of population trends in evaluating the conservation status of species at multiple scales over time. For management purposes, monitoring helps determine whether an intervention like hunting is on track to meet its objective and, if not, when, where and how changes may need to be made (Bell, 1983, 1984; CSIR, 1983; Martin, 1984).

Monitoring Buffalo Populations

Knowing how many animals there are in a given area at different times helps to measure the population trend. However, this is not simple, and a selection of appropriate methods and techniques (Collinson, 1985) is crucial, underpinned by clear objectives and a decision-making process (Caughley, 1977). While the aerial survey is often the method of choice in open savanna landscapes (Norton-Griffiths, 1978), it is not appropriate for forest or savanna–forest mosaics. However, as a herding species, buffalo are usually non-randomly distributed in clusters, which makes the count less reliable than for more evenly distributed species (Norton-Griffiths, 1978; Taylor and Mackie, 1997). Nevertheless, the aerial survey (with photography) remains the most cost-effective approach in large savanna landscapes (1000–10,000 km² and above). Ground counts using distance sampling methods (Buckland et al., 2001), also referred to as road strip or line transect counts, are also used either on foot or in vehicles, including for community-based game counts (NACSO, 2021).

Counting buffalo in forest landscapes is much more tedious and time- and money-consuming, using either transect surveys (line, recce or strip transects) or point sampling in, for example, forest clearings. More recently, camera traps have been utilized to assess densities by using distance sampling methods (Hofmeester et al., 2017; Howe et al., 2017). Another method, the Pooled Local Expert Opinion (PLEO) method, is based on traditional knowledge. A number of local hunters are asked to estimate wildlife abundance in a specified area, after which densities are calculated per species, and the estimates are pooled and extrapolated for the whole area (Van der Hoeven et al., 2004). Using citizen science and local communities as resource managers contribute to improving conservation monitoring (Rigava et al., 2006; Keeping et al., 2018).

Quota Setting for Hunting

The primary objective of monitoring a hunted population is to assess the demographic trend in that population in order to set hunting quotas that allow sustainable hunting. However, detecting trends on a regular basis is often fraught with the difficulty of making decisions based on inadequate and/or imprecise data (Taylor, 2001). Consequently, it is important to consider multiple sources or lines of evidence that can provide more robust data or information on the species being hunted. In addition to survey data, other indices of abundance should be used as well as the local knowledge of multiple stakeholders ultimately involved in the management and use of the species. Fortunately, the buffalo lends itself comparatively easily to this approach.

In a number of African countries, annual trophy hunting quotas are still set by the wildlife management authorities as a percentage of the total population size of the given species, for example 1–2 per cent of the buffalo population size. However, such a method appears impractical in most African conditions where population sizes are usually either unknown or imprecisely known or not updated on a yearly basis (Bell, 1984). Quota-setting methods relying on wildlife censuses face serious limitations because estimating the density or population size of large herbivores with high precision and accuracy is difficult, especially over large areas, and requires considerable investment of time, people and money (Morellet et al., 2007). In these situations, it is meaningless to attempt to set quotas on a percentage basis, and it is preferable to set quotas either (i) by specifying biological rules such as minimum trophy size or age of individuals to be taken (Morellet et al., 2007) and/or (ii) by adjusting quotas according to participative assessments of population trends (WWF, 1997, 2000) as has been done with success for decades in several southern African countries as well as in North America and Europe.

The quota-setting method based upon trends requires the involvement of an 'extended peer community' consisting of those with a stake in the issue of concern (Funtowicz and Ravetz, 1993). This is counter to conventional wisdom, which seeks to maintain centralized control (Bell, 1987). Failure to integrate knowledge held among all stakeholders undermines effective resource management (Hulme and Taylor, 2000). Participatory quota setting for the harvesting of wildlife species reflects a relatively recent departure from the conventional norm, whereby local resource managers become active participants in an adaptively managed process with greater devolution of responsibility and accountability (Taylor, 2001; Rigava et al., 2006).

The Participatory Quota-Setting Process

The process should ideally bring together all of the parties involved in establishing a quota and its subsequent use. Typically, this would include wildlife authority managers and ecologists, land occupiers (farmers or resource managers), safari operators and hunters, local communities and even hunting trackers as applicable, regardless of background, education or training. Each stakeholder brings different sets of information, recognizing the importance and value of the information and its source. The use of a facilitator provides greater understanding and demystifies the process of establishing and using a quota. This information provides a set of matrices that can be triangulated. Triangulation comprises an iterative process of examining, assessing and sense-making of information, which results in a reliably informed decision being made (Greyson, 2018). Trend data are assembled by participants and graphically represented for each species and entered into the matrix. The current quota is assessed against the available data and information, and the proposed quota adaptively determined using the full set of indices (Table 16.3). The proposed quota can be submitted to the regulatory wildlife authority for review and approval with or without adjustment, and subsequently used by the safari operator in the coming hunting season.

Monitoring Buffalo Hunts

Hunting during the season is monitored by representatives of the stakeholders and in compliance with applicable laws and regulations as required by specific countries. Regardless of such requirements, completion of a 'Hunt Return Form' (HRF) is essential. This is a crucially important monitoring tool that captures key biological and economic variables associated with every individual hunt. At the end of the hunting season, the set of HRFs collected per hunting area is analysed and

Table 16.3 *An example of the participatory triangulation matrix summarizing the trends in key indicators for individual species in view of proposing new hunting quota.*

Species (males only)	Current quota (Year N)	Aerial survey grounds	Ground count trends	Trends from other monitoring methods	Trophy quality trends	Catch-effort	Illegal activity	HWC and PAC	Other type of info	New quota (Year N + 1)
Greater kudu	8	⇔	⇔	UNK	⇔	⇓	⇑	⇑	X	6
Buffalo	10	⇑	⇔	UNK	⇓	⇔	⇔	⇒	X	8
Impala	20	⇑	⇑	UNK	⇔	⇑	⇔	X	X	20
Other species	...	...	...	...	...	...	...	...	...	...

X, information not available or irrelevant; UNK, information unknown; HWC, human–wildlife conflict; PAC, problem animal control. ⇑, indicator shows a population increasing trend; ⇓, indicator shows a population decreasing trend; ⇔, indicator shows a stable population.

used at both national and hunting area levels for the establishment of further sustainable hunting quotas. Subsequent data analysis provides insights into trends in quotas, offtakes, trophy quality and assessments of 'catch-effort' (Grobbelaar and Muselani, 2003).

Using Quotas for Buffalo

Hunting quotas for buffalo are only set for adult males, ideally old ones. Neither females nor subadult males are hunted by trophy hunters. However, hunting buffalo for trophies is challenged by the fact that the size of the trophy does not well reflect the age of the individual because the horns of old buffalo tend to wear down (Grobbelaar and Muselani, 2003). The largest trophies are thus obtained from animals at or just above middle age, which coincides with the age at which males are breeding bulls. Males aged 5–10 years constitute the breeding cohort, a period when they wear their largest horns. Moreover, trophy males have to be replaced by maturing younger males in order to have trophies available in the next seasons. Trophy hunting will be unsustainable if inappropriate hunting practices take place that remove these younger males in their prime instead of harvesting the oldest bulls. For this reason, trends in trophy quality and age should be carefully monitored (Crosmary et al., 2013).

Trophy Quality

For most species, trophies only represent a small fraction of the older adult males in the population, mainly after their breeding time, and therefore a very small proportion of the total population. Removing this segment of the population does not impact the survival of the population because no females are hunted and only a tiny proportion of the old males are harvested as trophies. However, selection pressure on bulls actively breeding can impact on characters in a population such as horn length. Removing breeding animals with superior horns can possibly result in a decrease in such specimens in the population, and increase specimens with inferior horns (Crosmary et al., 2013). Therefore, trophy quality should be monitored per hunting area per hunting season. The trophy quality is indexed by the trophy size of hunted individuals.

The Rowland Ward (RW) system of measurement, founded in 1870, has been the traditional method for measuring hunting trophies, for example 30th Edition for Africa in 2020 of Rowland Ward's Records

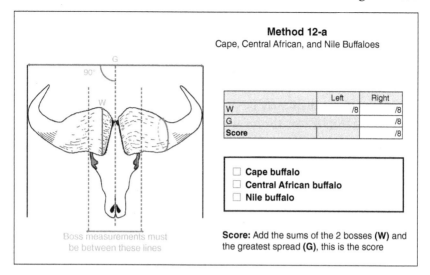

Method 12-a
Cape, Central African, and Nile Buffaloes

	Left	Right
W	/8	/8
G		/8
Score		/8

☐ **Cape buffalo**
☐ **Central African buffalo**
☐ **Nile buffalo**

Boss measurements must
be between these lines

Score: Add the sums of the 2 bosses **(W)** and
the greatest spread **(G)**, this is the score

Figure 16.3 Method for measuring the trophies of Cape, Central African and Nile buffalo according to Rowland Ward's Records of Big Game, Rowland-Ward-Method-12-a-Cape.pdf (rowlandward.org). Illustration reproduced from © RowlandWard.org with permission.

of Big Game (Rowland Ward, 2020). In 1977, North American trophy hunters introduced the Safari Club International (SCI) Record Book of Trophy Animals (SCI, 2022) with a measurement system built upon the original RW system, but nonetheless quite different. For buffalo, the RW system measures the greatest outside spread of the horns, which is not affected by the wear of the horns (RW method 12-a for Cape, Central African and Nile buffalo, rowlandward.org; Figure 16.3). Note that RW uses a different method (12-b) for West African and Dwarf buffalo. The SCI system measures the so-called 'tip to tip length of the horns' following the curves all along both horns, which is obviously much affected by the horns' wear (SCI method 4 for African buffalo, safariclub.org). Thus, by penalizing worn horns, the SCI system encourages hunters to hunt younger breeding bulls with longer tip-to-tip lengths (Grobbelaar and Muselani, 2003; Taylor, 2005). Using Taylor's (1988) predictive tooth wear and age relationship, and relating this to trophy score with both RW and SCI systems (Taylor, 2005), it is clear that the SCI scoring system favours the attributes of younger individuals and leads to rates of offtake that are too high for sustaining trophy quality. The Namibian Professional Hunters Association is considering adopting an Age-Related Measuring System that scores according to age in addition to other criteria, and where immature animals are disqualified (NAPHA, 2021).

While determining the age of individual hunted animals provides an additional refinement to monitoring, it can also be considered as a further imposition on safari operators, professional hunters and their hunters. However, where there may be concern over sustainability and possible diminishing trophy size, the measurement of the first molar tooth for age determination of hunted buffalo (Taylor, 1988) should be implemented as part of good adaptive management. This will necessitate the proper collection, labelling and storing of lower jaws (mandible).

Overall and simply, when hunting a male trophy buffalo, ideally:

(i) do not hunt buffalo males in herds; rather, hunt males in bachelor groups or individually,
(ii) think RW not SCI when selecting the individual to hunt,
(iii) select the oldest of the old males; however, if none of the bulls is old enough refrain from hunting,
(iv) post-hunt measure trophy using RW should be mandatory and SCI optional,
(v) hunter/hunting guide/hunting operator must determine age of hunted buffalo by extracting the first permanent molar and measuring tooth cusp height.

Strengths and Weaknesses of Buffalo Trophy Hunting

Buffalo Hunting, Conservation and Livelihood

According to IUCN (2016), legal, well-regulated trophy hunting can, and does, play an important role in delivering benefits for both wildlife conservation and for the livelihoods and wellbeing of indigenous and local communities living with wildlife.

Hunting Areas More Than Double the Land Area
Dedicated to Wildlife Conservation
Buffalo hunting tourism is conducted in officially gazetted Hunting Areas proclaimed as such by the law of each country. Hunting Areas are recognized by IUCN as Protected Areas under both IUCN Categories IV and VI. They contribute to the national networks of Protected Areas covering the percentage of a country's surface internationally declared

as set aside by the country as Protected Areas. In sub-Saharan Africa, Hunting Areas cover a minimum area of 1,394,000 km^2, exceeding the area encompassed by National Parks (Lindsey et al., 2007). This means that financial incentives from trophy hunting effectively more than double the land area that is used for wildlife conservation, relative to the area that would be conserved by national parks alone (Lindsey et al., 2007). Hence, trophy hunting sustains these immense wilderness areas acting as biodiversity reservoirs, carbon sinks and ecosystem service providers.

The large proportion of Hunting Areas that neighbour National Parks act as buffer zones amortizing the human pressure from outside. Many Hunting Areas are also the last ecological corridors linking National Parks that otherwise would become conservation islands in a human landscape devoid of wildlife. In the final analysis, Hunting Areas are the 'last frontier' of buffalo and large wildlife outside National Parks. Typical examples are two buffalo strongholds: the three National Parks (W, Arly, Pendjari) of the transboundary WAP complex (Benin, Burkina Faso, Niger) in West Africa, and the three National Parks (Faro, Bénoué, Bouba Ndjidda) of northern Cameroon in Central Africa. These National Parks are all embedded in Hunting Areas that also link the parks together with no discontinuity.

In South Africa and Zimbabwe, trophy hunting has been the entry point for the conversion of thousands of livestock ranches to wildlife ranches with the reintroduction of locally extinct species like buffalo and the subsequent multiplication of wildlife populations (Bond et al., 2004; Leader-Williams et al., 2005). Similarly, trophy hunting was the initial driver for local communities to establish the CAMPFIRE programme in Zimbabwe, Community Conservancies in Namibia, Wildlife Management Areas in Tanzania, and Village Hunting Zones in CAR, etc. where wildlife often are more abundant than in neighbouring National Parks. In Mozambique, trophy hunting played an important role in facilitating the recovery of wildlife populations in Hunting Areas after the war (Lindsey et al., 2006) by permitting income generation from wildlife without jeopardizing wildlife population growth (Bond et al., 2004). Buffalo in particular is making a remarkable comeback in this country, with Hunting Areas within Niassa Special Reserve and Marromeu complex as sources of founders for reintroducing locally extinct or depleted buffalo populations in National Parks like Gilé and Zinave (Chardonnet et al., 2017; Fusari et al., 2017; Macandza et al., 2017). Trophy hunting may be a viable alternative for Protected Area-based wildlife conservation in countries or areas where National Parks fail to protect their wildlife (e.g. Western et al., 2009), in regions of political instability, in remote wilderness areas, or where wildlife densities are low (Lindsey et al., 2006).

Conservation Funding from Buffalo Hunting

Not only are Hunting Areas the only Protected Areas that cost nothing to the State, they also provide funds to the State through leasing taxes, hunting taxes, income taxes, etc. that sustain wildlife administrations and, in several countries, even represent the main source of income for the wildlife administration. In Tanzania, while the funding of TANAPA (Tanzania National Parks, in charge of wildlife within National Parks) mainly comes from park entry fees, 80 per cent of the funding of TAWA (Tanzania Wildlife Management Authority, responsible for wildlife all over the country outside the jurisdiction of TANAPA) comes from hunting tourism (TAWA, 2019). Buffalo is the top tax-earning game in this country (TAWA, 2019), making it crucial for TAWA to maintain all of the Protected Areas other than National Parks in a country where 68 per cent of the Protected Areas rely on income from trophy hunting (Lindsey et al., 2020). In South Africa, becaue buffalo is the top income-earning game species for the hunting tourism sector (DEA, 2016; South African Professional Hunters statistics, 2019), it is a pillar sustaining the privately owned wildlife conservation areas. In this country, trophy hunting contributed more than €341 million and supported more than 17,000 employment opportunities in 2015/2016 (Saayman et al., 2018). In Zimbabwe, 80 per cent of the budget of the Zimbabwe Parks and Wildlife Management Authority comes from tourism, including trophy hunting (Lindsey et al., 2020). In Benin, in 2018, the W National Park ecosystem earned 33 times more money from hunting tourism in the neighbouring Hunting Areas (which provide income to the State) than from photographic tourism within the National Park (which costs the State) with 25 times fewer hunting tourists (19) than photographic tourists (476) (PNW, 2019). In South Africa, in 2013, each foreign leisure hunter spent about €8250, that is about 14 times more than that spent by the average foreign tourist arriving by plane (Oberem and Oberem, 2016). According to Hurt and Ravn (2000), safari hunting produces an income per hectare some seven times higher than that from cattle or game ranching and from far fewer animals harvested. They also reckon that wildlife-viewing tourism can generate even higher returns, but only in areas that are scenic and have very high concentrations of wildlife, and from massive numbers of tourists (Earnshaw and Emerton, 2000). Lindsey et al. (2012) hold a different view, observing that net returns from livestock in semi-arid African rangelands (\$10–30/km²/year in areas with 400–800 ml of annual rainfall according to Norton-Griffiths 2008) are similar to those from trophy hunting in some areas (\$24–164/km²). However, they conclude that maximizing returns from hunting is key to ensuring the competitiveness of wildlife-based land uses.

Some critiques of the socioeconomic effects of trophy hunting suggest that its contributions to country-level gross domestic product (GDP) are small relative to non-hunting wildlife tourism (Ghasemi, 2021). 't Sas-Rolfes et al. (2022) disagree, arguing that the claim is misleading because national GDP contributions are a poor indicator in terms of both broader socioeconomic relevance and appropriate scale of analysis: (i) GDP metrics fail to consider essential ecosystems services and natural capital (Costanza et al., 1997) and (ii) nation states are an arbitrary level at which to make such assessments. More relevant are the global benefits of effective species conservation and ecosystem services provided by intact habitats, functionally populated with large game, and the more localized benefits that flow to specific rural landowners and communities, who are thereby incentivized to actively support conservation ('t Sas-Rolfes et al., 2022).

Overall, hunting tourism drives a virtuous chain with financial flows of hard currency originating from developed countries (tourist-emitting countries) and directed to developing countries (tourist-receiving countries), from wealthy individuals to poorer people, and supporting vast conservation areas and local communities, as well as providing States of the South with revenues from their renewable natural resources.

Buffalo Hunting Sustaining Livelihood

When sustainable, consumptive utilization of wildlife can promote conservation beyond the borders of National Parks while at the same time generating revenue for local communities (Crosmary et al., 2015a). Where properly managed, trophy hunting can provide income for impoverished and often landlocked rural communities (IUCN, 2016), that is royalties, employment, venison, community infrastructures, social services, etc. Namibia is one of the best examples in this regard, well ahead of many other countries. Trophy hunting finances the budgets of 82 communal conservancies, which cover ~20 per cent of the country (162,000 km²) and encompass ~189,000 community members, or 9 per cent of Namibia's population (Naidoo et al., 2016). However, a number of other countries or areas are not as successful for various reasons, for example when the benefits from hunting are captured by local elites (Leader-Williams et al., 2009) or when the benefits are substantial at the community level but too small at the household level. In northern Cameroon, Mayaka et al. (2005) proposed a series of recommendations to improve the benefits of wildlife harvesting, notably by increasing the return to local communities for resource custodianship. In the same area, Akito Yasuda (2011) pointed out that while sport hunting certainly generates tax revenues and provides profit sharing and employment opportunities to local communities, the latter two are too limited and inequitably distributed in the community. Similarly, in south-eastern Zimbabwe, Poshiwa et al. (2013) described the benefits of wildlife tourism but emphasized their limited magnitude. Because high levels of poverty (Matseketsa et al., 2022) and poor governance, such as the leakage of hunting revenues for communities (Burn et al., 2011), are powerful drivers to poaching by local communities, the allocation of sufficient benefits of Hunting Areas to communities is an absolute critical factor for a successful deal between the local community (living on the land), the State (owning the land) and the hunting operator (protecting and valorizing the land).

Access to natural resources is also important for the livelihoods of local communities. In northern Cameroon, populations complain that locals' rights over natural resource use are regulated (Akito Yasuda, 2011). However, while National Parks are strict exclusion areas for local communities, most Hunting Areas are less stringent and allow for some activities by local communities, such as harvesting firewood and non-timber forest products.

Finally, concerns about the negative cultural and environmental impacts of tourism are growing with mass wildlife tourism in Africa (Spenceley, 2005; Lindsey et al., 2007), for example in the Okavango Delta, Botswana (Mbaiwa, 2003). However, due to their very small number, the impacts of hunting clients, such as habitat conversion for infrastructure development and all sorts of pollution, are considerably lower compared to mass tourism.

Threats to Buffalo Hunting

Ill-Managed Hunting Undermines Well-Managed Hunting

There have been and there are cases of hunting poorly conducted by some hunting operators and of hunting sectors poorly regulated by some wildlife administrations (IUCN, 2016). A variety of problems may hamper the proper functioning of the hunting tourism industry and undermine the conservation role of sustainable wildlife utilization, for example depending on countries, poor governance of the hunting sector (Burn et al., 2011), lack of professionalism in the administration and control of the hunting activity (Booth and Chardonnet, 2015) and risk of corruption (Leader-Williams et al., 2009). We concur with Lindsey et al. (2007) that the inequitable distribution of hunting revenues represents the most serious threat to the long-term sustainability of the industry. In some countries, there is insufficient sharing of hunting taxes by government administrations reluctant to decentralize and empower communities. Too often, benefits are centralized into the hands of elites or captured by local rulers so that promises from trophy hunting fail to materialize at the grassroots level (Nelson et al., 2007). In a number of situations, the management of Hunting Areas certainly needs to be improved. One failure, for example, is the reduction of anti-poaching activity outside the hunting season. Another is the lack of proper monitoring by hunting operators, which weakens their credibility and constraints the sustainability of the activity (Selier and Di Minin, 2015). Nevertheless, all of these problems are far from being specific to the hunting industry, they are also fully shared by other industries, including photographic ecotourism (Christie and Crompton, 2001; Walpole and Thouless, 2005). Finally, poorly managed trophy hunting can cause local wild population declines (Packer et al., 2011). However, in the case of buffalo, no example is known of a buffalo population driven to extinction by hunting tourism, while poaching is well recognized as being responsible for many local extinctions across the buffalo's range.

Hunters Their Worst Enemies?

While the hunting community is certainly skilled, with a great deal of field experience and knowledge of the bush, members rarely produce or publish peer-reviewed scientific articles which nevertheless largely make the basis of conservation politics. Moreover, a number of hunting professionals tend to be reluctant to seek the collaboration of scientists. As a result, reliable standardized data on the hunting sector are certainly missing (Lindsey et al., 2007; Snyman et al., 2021). This situation appears detrimental to the hunting industry at a time it badly needs more science in all sorts of domains, for example biological, socioeconomic, management. In Western Zimbabwe, Crosmary et al. (2015b) showed that harvested populations of large herbivores in trophy Hunting Areas may perform as well, and sometimes even better, than in National Parks where trophy hunting is not authorized. However, Buckley and Mossaz (2015) pointed out that this study represented only one example, concluding that more studies are needed to understand the benefits of hunting tourism to wildlife conservation. Crosmary et al. agree and concur with Selier and Di Minin (2015) that scientists are needed to establish long-term wildlife monitoring systems that also integrate the social and financial benefits of trophy hunting for local communities.

There is probably some kind of misunderstanding on the part of hunting stakeholders, who find it difficult to accept critics in a polemic context. However, and counterintuitively, the hunting activity holds a broad set of very strong assets in favour of conservation, not only of the hunted game, but also of non-game species and their habitats, of the entire biodiversity in fact (fauna and flora), of all ecosystem services, without even talking about the livelihoods of local communities. In other words, hunters are poor advocates of their achievements. This said, some poorly performing individuals, companies and administrations certainly jeopardize the profession, like in any profession, whether because they lack training, professionalism, ethics or something else. While these kinds of internalities probably affect all sectors, they cannot be hidden in the hunting industry.

Beyond these internalities, there are also powerful externalities that fall beyond the responsibility of the hunting community and severely affect Hunting Areas and the hunting activity. The current hunting industry inherited ancient situations that are no longer suitable today, for example Hunting Areas that are very (too?) large to take care of in view of the fast-growing human population, and which require much more funding than before for their proper management (Scholte et al., 2021). The profession is also facing newly arising tricky situations such as increasing numbers of all sorts of new arrivals claiming to be local communities despite not being indigenous people, more pastoralists with ever larger herds of livestock replacing wildlife in Hunting Areas (e.g. Figure 16.2 in Cameroon; Bouché et al., 2012 and Aebischer et al., 2020 in CAR; Musika et al., 2021 and Musika et al., 2022 in Tanzania), illegal goldminers, wild loggers, without mentioning bandits and even terrorists. Other contemporary constraints are the intense pressure of lobbies promoting commercial crops at all costs, especially the cotton value chain, which are heavily supported by national and international agencies with hardly any exception. Overall, many externalities have appeared on the scene and reshuffle the game, making hunting work more difficult, less viable and threatening ever more the conservation of natural resources. There is definitely a need to reform the governance and administration of hunting tourism (Booth and Chardonnet, 2015), but given the above-mentioned externalities, the reform should not be considered in isolation (Leader-Williams et al., 2009).

Poaching Versus Hunting
The African buffalo does not give the impression of being a fragile animal. However, it is indeed extremely sensitive to poaching, notably because it is quite easy to stalk on foot provided you strictly approach against the wind. The buffalo shows little resilience under poaching pressure. Poaching means limitless and indiscriminate offtake of any kind of buffalo, whatever sex and age, whereas tourism hunting harvests a tiny percentage of only old bulls (Table 16.4). Legal and illegal hunting are mutually exclusive: where poaching flourishes, hunting tourism deteriorates and even fails. Just like National Parks, Hunting Areas require anti-poaching engagement to be protected and avoid wildlife depletion.

Hunting Bans and the Future of Buffalo
One of the biggest challenges facing the hunting industry is the prescriptive unilateral decision by Western countries to ban imports of hunting trophies from Africa (Ares, 2019), which could have a long-lasting negative impact on many economies, and in turn on conservation, in Africa (Snyman et al., 2021). For local communities in northern Botswana, the safari hunting ban of 2014 led to a reduction of tourism benefits to local communities, for example income, employment opportunities, social services and scholarships. This led to the development of negative attitudes by community-based organizations of rural residents towards wildlife conservation and to an increase in incidents of poaching (Mbaiwa, 2018; Blackie, 2019; Strong and Silva, 2020). For game ranchers and other owners of private conservation areas in South Africa, most believe that the economic viability of their enterprises, biodiversity conservation and the livelihoods of owners and employees would be lost following a hunting ban (Parker et al., 2020). Without hunting activity, most Hunting Areas would no longer protect buffalo, which means that the persistence of buffalo outside of National Parks would be short-lived, as experienced in CAR after the 2012 political events when buffalo was

Table 16.4 *Comparison between poaching and tourism hunting.*

	Illegal unregulated hunting (poaching)	Legal regulated tourism hunting
Wildlife offtake Species	All wildlife species with value as food or trophy, e.g. ivory, claws, etc.	Only a few selected game species
Number of individuals	Unlimited	Small % (approx. 1%) of the population
Sex of individuals	Males and females	Only males (exceptions in South Africa)
Age of individuals	Any age including calves	Mostly old individuals, often beyond reproductive age
Impacts of the wildlife offtake For local communities	Meat and other wildlife products	Meat
	Livelihood but with limited income from trade of meat and trophies	Livelihood and formal employment by hunting companies
	Negative impact due to overexploitation leading to depletion of the wildlife resource	According to countries: share of the taxes (% of leasing tax, trophy fees, etc.), royalties
	Conflict with law enforcement leading to fines and prison sentences	Community infrastructures and services (schools, dispensaries, wells, etc.)
For illegal wildlife traders	High financial gains	No business
For the Government finances	Negative impact due to absence of revenue from the activity	Taxes (income tax, etc.)
For the wildlife administration	Negative impact due to the cost of anti-poaching	Taxes (leasing fees for hunting areas, trophy fees, hunting permits, operating licenses, etc.)

For the private sector	Negative impact due to the cost of anti-poaching and the depletion of the wildlife resource	Return from daily fees, paid hunting services
For the national network of Protected Areas	Negative impact due to the degradation of the Protected Areas	Hunting Areas as Protected Areas of the IUCN Cat. VI are maintained by the income of hunting tourism (ecotourism rarely viable in these areas)
For animal welfare	Long death and suffering for animals caught by snares, gin traps, pits or other trapping devices	Instant death in most cases
For the conservation of biodiversity	Negative impact due to the degradation of the wildlife conservation status leading to loss of biodiversity	Improved conservation status of (i) the few income-generating game species, and (ii) all the non-game species of fauna and flora

one of the first large mammals to disappear from the Hunting Areas (Matthieu Laboureur, personal communication). With the authoritarian restrictions by Western countries on imports of elephant and lion hunting trophies from Africa, many Hunting Areas were returned to the governments in Tanzania and Zambia. Without funding or surveillance, these areas are left to poaching, greatly impacting the fate of buffalo.

Hunting trophies import bans dictated by some northern countries without an alternative global conservation framework providing conservation incentives will likely reverse the gains in wildlife conservation and rural development in some southern countries where sustainable utilization is an integral part of the wildlife conservation practice (e.g. Di Minin et al., 2016; Dickman et al., 2019; Nyamayedenga et al., 2021). Where trophy hunting is planned to end, alternatives should be implemented to avoid land conversion and biodiversity loss in Hunting Areas (Di Minin et al., 2013). However, most of these areas appear unsuitable for alternative wildlife-based land uses such as photographic ecotourism because of, for example, difficult and expensive access, absence of infrastructure, lack of attractive scenery and of high densities of viewable wildlife (Wilkie and Carpenter, 1999; Lindsey et al., 2006; Winterbach et al., 2015). IUCN (2016) states that unless better land-use alternatives exist, hunting reforms should be prioritized over bans, while such reforms have proved effective (Booth and Chardonnet, 2015; Begg et al., 2018).

Surprisingly, bans and restrictions on importing hunting trophies of game species listed on CITES Appendices diverted the attention of the hunting industry to buffalo, a non–CITES-listed species. While becoming a new focus, the buffalo has either reinforced or taken the lead as a flagship game in an attempt to compensate the loss of CITES-listed game, even though it does not attract as much income. Buffalo hunting does not draw much public awareness, in contrast with the hunting of the four other representatives of the Big Five, a bit like the wild boar in Europe compared to red deer or chamois. Therefore, the less–charismatic member of the Big Five is now gaining more importance for sustaining Hunting Areas and for wildlife conservation outside National Parks. In other words, from a commodity game, buffalo is turning out to be a high-value game species.

In 2021, Van Houdt et al. surveyed international networks to investigate the divergent views on trophy hunting in Africa. Unlike European respondents, African respondents showed significantly more support for trophy hunting and, unlike North Americans, African respondents supported external subsidies of wildlife areas presently funded by hunting.

Oddly, while Europeans and North Americans carry out trophy hunting in their own countries, they tend to oppose it in African countries. The inquiry concluded that policies on African hunting should better integrate African perspectives, in particular those of rural communities (Van Houdt et al., 2021). While opponents to hunting tourism in Africa often qualify this activity as a colonial relic, it cannot be denied that most Protected Areas have deep roots in the colonial period, either National Parks for wildlife viewing tourism or Hunting Areas for hunting tourism, 'but that makes it even more important that today, the decisions-making and rights of African countries and communities are respected; Westerners must not continue to externally impose their own ideals upon Africans, such as pushing trophy hunting bans and restrictions' (Dickman et al., 2021). A group of African countries called for a 'New Deal' for rural communities (Southern Africa Trust, 2019) that allows them to achieve the self-determination to sustainably manage wildlife and reduce poverty. Dickman et al. (2019) stated that it is incumbent on the international community not to undermine that. More recently, in response to the call of a UK parliamentary committee in 2022 for ending trophy hunting in Africa (but not in the UK), the Community Leaders Network of Southern Africa responded: 'It's a form of colonialism to tell us Africans what to do with our wildlife' (Louis, 2022).

References

Adam, S.A.M. (2019). *Impact of some wildlife offenses on wild animals and their habitats in selected states in Sudan and Dinder Biosphere Reserve during 2013–2017.* MSc thesis, Sudan University of Science and Technology, College of Animal Production Science and Technology, Khartoum.

Adeola, M.O. (1992). Importance of wild animals and their parts in the culture, religious festivals, and traditional medicine of Nigeria. *Environmental Conservation* **19**: 125–134.

Aebischer, T, T. Ibrahim, R. Hickisch, et al. (2020). Apex predators decline after an influx of pastoralists in former Central African Republic hunting zones. *Biological Conservation* **240**: 108326.

Alarape, A.A., R.B. Shuaibu and Z.B. Yaduma (2021). The impacts of bushmeat exploitations on the conservation of wildlife in Nigeria. *Asian Journal of Social Science and Management Technology* **3**: 84–94.

Anderson, J. (2017). The natural history and management of the Cape buffalo. In P. Flack (Ed.), *Hunting the African Buffalo. Nature's Debt Collector – The Six Subspecies.* South Africa: Peter Flack Productions.

Ares, E. (2019). Trophy hunting. House of Commons Library Briefing Paper Number 7908: https://researchbriefings.parliament.uk/ResearchBriefing/Summary/CBP-7908

Atta A.C.-J., O. Soulemane, B. Kadjo and Y.R. Kouadio (2021). Some uses of the African buffalo *Syncerus caffer* (Sparrman, 1779) by the populations living around the Comoé National Park (North-East Ivory Coast). *Journal of Animal and Plant Sciences* **47**: 8484–8496.

Baldus, R. (2009). *A Practical Summary of Experiences after Three Decades of Community-Based Wildlife Conservation in Africa: "What are the Lessons Learnt?"* Budapest: joint publication of FAO and CIC.

Baldus, R. and A. Cauldwell (2004). Tourist hunting and its role in development of wildlife management areas in Tanzania. In: *Proceedings of the 6th International Game Ranching Symposium,* Paris, 6–9 July 2004. Paris: Office National de la Chasse et de la Faune Sauvage.

Batumike, R., G. Imani, C. Urom and A. Cuni-Sanchez (2021). Bushmeat hunting around Lomami National Park, Democratic Republic of the Congo. *Oryx* **55**: 421–431.

Begg, C.M., J.R. Miller and K.S. Begg (2018). Effective implementation of age restrictions increases selectivity of sport hunting of the African lion. *Journal of Applied Ecology* **55**(1): 139–146.

Bell, R.H.V. (1983). Decision making in wildlife management with reference to problems of overpopulation. In R.N. Owen-Smith (Ed.), *Management of Large Mammals in African Conservation Areas.* Pretoria: Haum.

Bell, R.H.V. (1984). Chapter 11, Carrying capacity and off-take quotas. In R.H.V. Bell and E. McShane-Caluzi (Eds.), *Conservation and Wildlife Management in Africa.* The proceedings of a workshop organized by the US Peace Corps, Kasungu National Park, Malawi, October 1984. Washington, DC: Office of Training and Support Program, Forestry and natural Resources Sector, US Peace Corps.

Bell, R.H.V. (1987). Conservation with a human face: conflict and reconciliation in african land use planning. In D. Anderson and R. Grove (Eds.), *Conservation in Africa: People, Policies and Practice.* Cambridge: Cambridge University Press.

Blackie, I. (2019). The impact of wildlife hunting prohibition on the rural livelihoods of local communities in Ngamiland and Chobe District Areas, Botswana. *Cogent Social Sciences* **5**: 1.

Bond, I., B. Child, D. de la Harpe, et al. (2004). Private land contribution to conservation in South Africa. In B. Child (Ed.), *Parks in Transition.* London: Earthscan, pp. 29–61.

Booth, V.R. (2010). The contribution of hunting tourism: how significant is this to national economies? In *Contribution of Wildlife to National Economies.* Budapest: joint publication of FAO and CIC.

Booth, V.R. (2017). *Economic Assessment of the Value of Wildlife to the Tanzania Hunting Industry.* Dar es Salaam, Tanzania: USAID, USFWS and MNRT.

Booth, V.R. and P. Chardonnet (Eds.) (2015). *Guidelines for Improving the Administration of Sustainable Hunting in sub-Saharan Africa.* Rome: The Food and Agriculture Organization of the United Nations. www.fao.org/3/bo583e/bo583e.pdf

Boratto, R. and M.L. Gore (2018). The bushmeat supply chain in Pointe Noire, Republic of the Congo: a conservation criminology analysis. Report prepared for the Wildlife Conservation Society. Michigan State University, Michigan.

Bouché, P. (2010). *Les Zones Cynégétiques Villageoises du Nord de la République Centrafricaine: 15 ans déjà ! June 2010.* Liege: University of Liege Gembloux Agro-Bio Tech.

Bouché, P, R.N.M. Mange, F. Tankalet, et al. (2012). Game over! Wildlife collapse in northern Central African Republic. *Environmental Monitoring and Assessment* **184**(11): 7001–7011.

Buckland, S.T., D.R. Anderson, K.P. Burnham, et al. (2001). *Introduction to Distance Sampling: Estimating Abundance of Biological Populations.* New York: Oxford University Press.

Buckley, R. and A. Mossaz (2015). Hunting tourism and animal conservation. *Animal Conservation* **18**: 133–135.

Burn, R.W., F.M. Underwood and J. Blanc (2011). Global trends and factors associated with the illegal killing of elephants: a hierarchical Bayesian analysis of carcass encounter data. *PLoS One* **6**: e24165.

Campbell, A. (1995). Historical utilisation of wildlife. In *Proceedings of a Symposium on the Present Status of Wildlife and its Future in Botswana, 7–8 November 1995*. Gaborone: Kalahari Conservation Society and Chobe Wildlife Trust, pp 45–68.

Carruthers, J. (1995). *The Kruger National Park: A Social and Political History*. Pietermaritzburg: University of Natal Press, p. 289.

Caughley, G (1977). *Analysis of Vertebrate Populations*. New York: Wiley-Interscience.

Cawthorn, D.M. and L.C. Hoffman (2015). The bushmeat and food security nexus: a global account of the contributions, conundrums and ethical collisions. *Food Research International* **76:** 906–925.

Chardonnet, P., A. Fusari, J. Dias, et al. (2017). *Lessons Learned from the Reintroduction of Large Mammals in Gilé National Reserve, Mozambique*. Saint-Louis, Senegal: SSIG 17.

Child, G. (2004). Growth of modern nature conservation in southern Africa. In B. Child (Ed.), *Parks in Transition: Biodiversity, Rural Development and the Bottom Line*. London: Earthscan.

Chitauro (2016). Status of the hunting sector in Zimbabwe. Internal report prepared by the Director of Exchange Control on behalf of the Reserve Bank of Zimbabwe. Unpublished.

Christie, I.T. and D.E. Crompton (2001). Tourism in Africa. World Bank Africa Region Working Paper Series Number 12. www.worldbank.org/afr/wps/wp12.pdf

CITES (2022). The CITES species: https://cites.org/eng/disc/species.php

Cloete, F.C., P. Van der Merwe and M. Saayman (2015). *Game Ranch Profitability in South Africa*. Johannesburg: ABSA, pp. 1–192.

Collinson, R (1985). *Selecting Wildlife Census Techniques*. Monograph 6. Durban: Institute of Natural Resources, University of Natal.

Costanza, R., R. d'Arge, R. de Groo, et al. (1997). The value of the world's ecosystem services and natural capital. *Nature* **387**(6630): 253–260.

Crosmary, W.G., A.J. Loveridge, H. Ndaimani, et al. (2013). Trophy hunting in Africa: long-term trends in antelope horn size. *Animal Conservation* **16:** 648–660.

Crosmary, W.G., S.D. Côté and H. Fritz (2015a). The assessment of the role of trophy hunting in wildlife conservation. *Animal Conservation* **18:** 136–137.

Crosmary, W.G., S.D. Côté and H. Fritz (2015b). Does trophy hunting matter to long-term population trends in African herbivores of different dietary guilds? *Animal Conservation* **18:** 117–130.

CSIR (1983). *Guidelines for the Management of Large Mammals in African Conservation Areas*, ed. A.A. Ferrar. Report No. 69, South African National Scientific Programmes. Pretoria: CSIR.

DEA (2016). *Biodiversity and Tourism Lab briefing report*, May 2016. Pretoria: Department of Environmental Affairs.

Dell, B., C. Masembe, R. Gerhold, et al. (2021). Species misidentification in local markets: Discrepancies between reporting and molecular identification of bushmeat species in northern Uganda. *One Health* **13**: 100251.

Dell, B.A.M., M.J. Souza and A.S. Willcox (2020). Attitudes, practices, and zoonoses awareness of community members involved in the bushmeat trade near Murchison Falls National Park, northern Uganda. *PLoS One* **15**(9): e0239599.

De Merode, E. and G. Cowlishaw (2006). Species protection, the changing informal economy, and the politics of access to the bushmeat trade in the Democratic Republic of Congo. *Conservation Biology* **20**: 1262–1271.

DFRC (2018). *Rapports Bilans des campagnes d'exploitation fauniques de la Direction de la Faune et des Ressources Cynégétiques (DFRC) de 2012 à 2018*. Ouagadougou, Burkina Faso: DFRC.

Dickman, A., R. Cooney, P.J. Johnson, et al. (2019). Trophy hunting bans imperil biodiversity. *Science* **365**(6456): 874.

Dickman, A., B. Child, A. Hart and C. Semcer (2021). Misinformation about trophy hunting is wrong. Dead wrong. *Changing America*, Feb. 16, 2021.

Dickson, B., J. Hutton and W.A. Adams (Eds.) (2009). *Recreational Hunting, Conservation and Rural Livelihoods: Science and Practice*. Oxford: Wiley-Blackwell.

Di Minin E., D. MacMillan, P. Goodman, et al. (2013). Conservation businesses and conservation planning in a biological diversity hotspot. *Conservation Biology* 27(4): 808–820.

Di Minin, E., N. Leader-Williams and C.J.A. Bradshaw (2016). Banning trophy hunting will exacerbate biodiversity loss. *Trends in Ecology and Evolution* 31(2): 99–102.

Duda, R., S. Gallois and V. Reyes-García (2018). Ethnozoology of bushmeat: importance of wildlife in diet, food avoidances and perception of health among the Baka (Cameroon). *Revue d'ethnoécologie* 14: 41.

Earnshaw, A. and L. Emerton (2000). The economics of wildlife tourism: theory and reality for landholders in Africa. In: Prins, H.H.T., J.G. Grootenhuis and T.T. Dolan (Eds.). *Wildlife Conservation by Sustainable Use*. Conservation Biology Series, vol 12. Dordrecht: Springer.

Eniang, E., C. Ebin, A. Nchor, et al. (2017). Distribution and status of the African forest buffalo *Syncerus caffer nanus* in south-eastern Nigeria. *Oryx* 51: 538–541.

Erena, M.G. (2014). The indirect socioeconomic impact of illegal hunting of African buffalo (*Syncerus caffer*) for trophy in East Wollega, Ethiopia. *American Scientific Research Journal for Engineering, Technology, and Sciences* 9: 64–75.

Erena, M.G., H. Jebessa and A. Bekele (2019). Consequences of land-use/land-cover dynamics on range shift of Cape Buffalo in Western Ethiopia. *International Journal of Ecology and Environmental Sciences* 45: 123–136.

European Commission (2010). Wildlife Trade Regulations in the European Union. An Introduction to CITES and its Implementation in the European Union. https://ec.europa.eu/environment/cites/pdf/trade_regulations/short_ref_guide.pdf.

FAO/CIG (2002). *Assessment of Bushmeat Trade During The Annual Closed Season on Hunting in Ghana (1st August–1st December 2001)*. Ghana: Food and Agricultural Organization and Conservation International.

Fargeot, C., N. Drouet-Hoguet and S. Le Bel (2017). The role of bushmeat in urban household consumption: insights from Bangui, the capital city of the Central African Republic. *Bois et Forêts des Tropiques* 332: 31–42.

Foa, E. (1900). De l'océan Indien à l'océan Atlantique. *La traversée de l'Afrique du Zambèze au Congo français*. Paris: Librairie Plon.

Friant, S., W.A. Ayambem, A.O. Alobi, et al. (2020). Eating bushmeat improves food security in a biodiversity and infectious disease "hotspot". *EcoHealth* 17: 125–138.

Funtowicz, S.O. and J.R. Ravetz (1993). Science for the post-normal age. *ScienceDirect* 25: 739–755.

Fusari, A., C. Lopes Pereira, J. Dias, et al. (2017). Reintroduction of large game species to Gilé National Reserve, Mozambique. In IUGB 33rd Congress, Montpellier, 22–25 August 2017.

Gaodirelwe, I., G.S. Masunga and M.R. Motsholapheko (2020). Community-based natural resource management: a promising strategy for reducing subsistence poaching around protected areas, northern Botswana. *Environment, Development and Sustainability* 22: 2269–2287.

Ghasemi, B. (2021). Trophy hunting and conservation: do the major ethical theories converge in opposition to trophy hunting? *People and Nature* 3(1): 77–87.

Gluszek, S., J. Viollaz and M.L. Gore (2021). Using conservation criminology to understand the role of restaurants in the urban wild meat trade. *Conservation Science and Practice* 3(5): e368.

Greyson, D. (2018). Information triangulation: a complex and agentic everyday information practice. *Journal of the Association for Information Science and Technology* 69(7): 869–878.

Grobbelaar, C and R. Masulani (2003). Review of offtake quotas, trophy quality and "catch effort" across four wildlife species: elephant, buffalo, lion and leopard. Unpublished report prepared for WWF SARPO and USAID NRMP II.

Hasler, R. (1996) *Agriculture, Foraging and Wildlife Resources Use in Africa: Cultural and Political Dynamics in the Zambezi Valley*. London: Kegan Paul.

Hegerl, C., N.D. Burgess, M.R. Nielsen, et al. (2017). Using camera trap data to assess the impact of bushmeat hunting on forest mammals in Tanzania. *Oryx* **51**: 87–97.

Hofmeester, T.R., J.M. Rowcliffe and P.A. Jansen (2017). A simple method for estimating the effective detection distance of camera traps. *Remote Sensing in Ecology and Conservation* **3**(2): 81–89.

Holmern, T., E. Røskaft, J. Mbaruka, et al. (2002). Uneconomical game cropping in a community-based conservation project outside the Serengeti National Park, Tanzania. *Oryx* **36**: 364–372.

Holmern, T., S.Y. Mkama, J. Muya, et al. (2006). Intraspecific prey choice of bushmeat hunters outside the Serengeti National Park, Tanzania: a preliminary analysis. *African Zoology* **41**: 81–87.

Howe, E.J., S.T. Buckland, M.L. Després-Einspenner and H.S. Kühl (2017). Distance sampling with camera traps. *Methods in Ecology and Evolution* **8**(11): 1558–1565.

Hulme, D and R. Taylor (2000). Integrating environmental, economic and social appraisal in the real world: from impact assessment to adaptive management. In N. Lee and C. Kirkpatrick (Eds.), *Sustainable Development and Integrated Appraisal in a Developing World*. Cheltenham: Edward Elgar.

Hurt, R. and P. Ravn (2000). Hunting and its benefits: an overview of hunting in Africa with special reference to Tanzania. In H.H.T. Prins, J.G. Grootenhuis and T.T. Dolan (Eds.), *Wildlife Conservation by Sustainable Use*. Conservation Biology Series, vol 12. Dordrecht: Springer.

IUCN (2016). Informing decisions on trophy hunting: A Briefing Paper regarding issues to be taken into account when considering restriction of imports of hunting trophies. Briefing paper April 2016. www.wwf.de/fileadmin/user_upload/IUCN-Informing-decision-on-trophy-hunting.pdf.

IUCN SSC Antelope Specialist Group (2015). IUCN SSC ASG Position Statement on the Intentional Genetic Manipulation of Antelopes Ver. 1.0 (30 April 2015) www.iucn.org/sites/dev/files/import/downloads/asg_igm_posnsment_2015_final_19may_2015.pdf.

IUCN SSC Antelope Specialist Group (2019). *Syncerus caffer*. The IUCN Red List of Threatened Species 2019: e.T21251A50195031. https://dx.doi.org/10.2305/IUCN.UK.2019-1.RLTS.T21251A50195031.en.

IUCN WCC (2016). WCC-2016-Rec-100-EN Management and regulation of selective intensive breeding of large wild mammals1 for commercial purposes. https://portals.iucn.org/congress/assembly/motions/print?langua.

Keeping, D, J.H. Burger, O. Keitsile, et al. (2018). Can trackers count free-ranging wildlife as effectively and efficiently as conventional aerial survey and distance sampling? Implications for citizen science in the Kalahari, Botswana. *Biological Conservation* **223**: 156–169.

Kideghesho, J.R., J.W. Nyahongo, S.N. Hassan, et al. (2006). Factors and ecological impacts of wildlife habitat destruction in the Serengeti ecosystem in northern Tanzania. *African Journal of Environmental Assessment and Management* **11**: 17–32.

Kitshoff-Botha, A. (2020). Introduction to the South Africa Wildlife Industry and Wildlife Ranching South Africa. Presented to ALU SOWC MBA students, July 2020.

Leader-Williams, N. and J.M. Hutton (2005). Does extractive use provide opportunities to reduce conflicts between people and wildlife? In R. Woodroffe, S.J. Thirgood and A.

Rabinowitz (Eds.), *People and Wildlife: Conflict or Coexistence*. Cambridge: Cambridge University Press, pp. 140–161.

Leader-Williams, N., R.D. Baldus and R.J. Smith (2009). The influence of corruption on the conduct of recreational hunting. In B. Dickson, J. Hutton and W.M. Adams (Eds.), *Recreational Hunting, Conservation and Rural Livelihoods: Science and Practice*. Oxford: Wiley-Blackwell, pp. 296–316.

Lindsey, P.A. and C. Bento (2012). *Illegal hunting and the bushmeat trade in Central Mozambique: a case-study from Coutada 9, Manica Province*. Harare, Zimbabwe: TRAFFIC East/ Southern Africa.

Lindsey, P.A., R. Alexander, L.G. Franket, et al. (2006). Potential of trophy hunting to create incentives for wildlife conservation in Africa where alternative wildlife-based land uses may not be viable. *Animal Conservation* 9: 283–298.

Lindsey, P.A., P.A. Roulet and S.S. Romañach (2007). Economic and conservation significance of the trophy hunting industry in sub-Saharan Africa. *Biological Conservation* 134(4): 455–469.

Lindsey, P.A., G.A. Balme, V.R. Booth and N. Midlane (2012). The significance of African lions for the financial viability of trophy hunting and the maintenance of wild land. *PLoS One* 7(1): e29332.

Lindsey, P.A., C.A. Havemann, R.M. Lines, et al. (2013). Benefits of wildlife-based land uses on private lands in Namibia and limitations affecting their development. *Oryx* 47(1): 41–53.

Lindsey, P.A., G. Balme, M. Becker, et al. (2015). *Illegal Hunting and the Bush-Meat Trade in Savanna Africa: Drivers, Impacts and Solutions to Address the Problem*. New York: Panthera/ Zoological Society of London/Wildlife Conservation Society report.

Lindsey, P., J. Allan, P. Brehony, et al. (2020). Conserving Africa's wildlife and wildlands through the COVID-19 crisis and beyond. *Nature Ecology and Evolution* 4(10): 1300–1310.

Litjens, J. (2017). *African forest buffalo in the Gamba Complex of Protected Areas Gabon*. MSc thesis, Wageningen University, Netherlands.

Loibooki, M., H. Hofer, K. Campbell and M. East (2002). Bushmeat hunting by communities adjacent to the Serengeti National Park, Tanzania: the importance of livestock ownership and alternative sources of protein and income. *Environmental Conservation* 29: 391–398.

Long, H., D. Mojo, C. Fu, et al. (2020). Patterns of human–wildlife conflict and management implications in Kenya: a national perspective. *Human Dimensions of Wildlife* 25: 121–135.

Louis, M.P. (2022). It's a form of colonialism to tell us Africans what to do with our wildlife. Community Leaders Network of Southern Africa. *Daily Mail*, June 29, 2022.

Macandza, V.A., C.M. Bento, R.M. Roberto, et al. (2017). *Relatório da contagem aérea de fauna bravia na reserva nacional do Gilé*. CEAGRE, FAEF, UEM and ANAC.

Manyanga, M. and G. Pangeti (2017). Precolonial hunting in southern Africa: a changing paradigm. In M. Manyanga and S. Chirikure (Eds.), *Archives, Objects, Places and Landscapes: Multidisciplinary Approaches to Decolonised Zimbabwean pasts*. Mankon, Bamenda: Langaa RPCIG, chapter 12.

Marks, S.A. (1976). *Large Mammals and a Brave People: Subsistence Hunters in Zambia*. Seattle: University of Washington Press.

Martin, R.B. (1984). Goals of conservation and wildlife management. In R.H.V. Bell and E. McShane-Caluzi (Eds.), *Conservation and Wildlife Management in Africa*. Proceedings of a Workshop at Kasungu National Park, Malawi, October 1984. Washington, DC: US Peace Corps.

Matseketsa, G., K. Krüger and E. Gandiwa (2022). Rule-breaking in terrestrial protected areas of sub-Saharan Africa: a review of drivers, deterrent measures and implications for conservation. *Global Ecology and Conservation* 37: e02172.

Mayaka, T.B., T. Hendricks, J. Wesseler and H.H.T. Prins (2005). Improving the benefits of wildlife harvesting in Northern Cameroon: a co-management perspective. *Ecological Economics* **54**(1): 67–80.

Mbaiwa, J.E. (2003). The socio-economic and environmental impacts of tourism development on the Okavango Delta, north-western Botswana. *Journal of Arid Environments* **54**(2): 447–467.

Mbaiwa, J.E. (2018). Effects of the safari hunting tourism ban on rural livelihoods and wildlife conservation in Northern Botswana. *South African Geographical Journal* **100**(1): 41–46.

MINFOF (2019). *Annuaire statistique 2019 du MINFOF.* Yaoundé, Cameroon: Ministère des Forêts et de la Faune.

MINFOF (2020). *Annuaire statistique 2020 du MINFOF.* Yaoundé, Cameroon: Ministère des Forêts et de la Faune.

Mfunda, I.M. and E. Røskaft (2010). Bushmeat hunting in Serengeti, Tanzania: an important economic activity to local people. *International Journal of Biodiversity and Conservation* **2**: 263–272.

Montcho, M., J.-B. Ilboudo, E.D. Dayou, et al. (2020). Human use-pressure and sustainable wildlife management in Burkina Faso: a case study of bushmeat hunting in Bobo-Dioulasso. *Journal of Sustainable Development* **13**: 60–70.

Morellet, N., J.M. Gaillard, A. Hewison, et al. (2007). Indicators of ecological change: new tools for managing populations of large herbivores. *Journal of Applied Ecology* **44**: 634–643.

Moyo, S., P. O'Keefe and M. Sill (1993). *The Southern African Environment.* London: Earthscan.

Munanura, I.E. K.F. Backman, E. Sabuhoro, et al. (2018). The perceived forms and drivers of forest dependence at Volcanoes National Park, Rwanda. *Environmental Sociology* **4**: 343–357.

Murphree, M. (2000). Community-based conservation, old ways, new myths and enduring challenges. Paper delivered at a Conference on African Wildlife Management, Mweka, Tanzania.

Musika, N.V., J.V. Wakibara, P.A. Ndakidemi and A.C. Treydte (2021). Spatio-temporal patterns of increasing illegal livestock grazing over three decades at Moyowosi Kigosi Game Reserve, Tanzania. *Land* **10**(12): 1325.

Musika, N.V., J.V. Wakibara, P.A. Ndakidemi and A.C. Treydte (2022). Using trophy hunting to save wildlife foraging resources: a case study from Moyowosi-Kigosi Game Reserves, Tanzania. *Sustainability* **14**(3): 1288.

Nachihangu, J., K. Kiondo and J. Lwelamira (2018). Community participation in resident hunting in southwest Rungwa Game Reserve. *Journal of Scientific Research and Reports* **18**: 1–15.

NACSO (2021). www.nacso.org.na/resources/game-count-data

Naidoo, R., L.C. Weaver, R.W. Diggle, et al. (2016). Complementary benefits of tourism and hunting to communal conservancies in Namibia. *Conservation Biology* **30**: 628–638.

NAPHA (2021). Age Related Trophy (ART) Measurement System Manual. Working Group for the Erongo Verzeichnis for African game animals. Namibian Hunting Trophy Measurement System (napha-namibia.com).

Nda, N.F., E.A. Tsi, C. Fominyam, et al. (2018). Status of bushbuck (*Tragelaphus scriptus*) and buffalo (*Syncerus caffer*) in the north and southeastern parts of the Kimbi-Fungom National Park, northwest region of Cameroon. *International Journal of Forest, Animal and Fisheries Research* **2**: 1–25.

Nel, L. (2021). Sustainability in wildlife-based enterprises. The conservation of biodiversity and landscapes: is sustainable use an option? WESSA Lowveld Conference, 4 September 2021.

Nelson, F., R. Nshala and W.A. Rodgers (2007). The evolution and reform of Tanzanian wildlife management. *Conservation and Society* **5**(2): 232–261.

Ndibalema, V.G. and A.N. Songorwa (2007). Illegal meat hunting in Serengeti: dynamics in consumption and preferences. *African Journal of Ecology* **46**: 311–319.

Nieman, W.A., A.J. Leslie and A. Wilkinson (2019). Traditional medicinal animal use by Xhosa and Sotho communities in the Western Cape Province, South Africa. *Journal of Ethnobiology and Ethnomedicine* **15**(1): 34.

NORAD (2008). *Results Management in Norwegian Cooperation: A Practical Guide*. Oslo: Norwegian Ministry of Foreign Affairs.

Norton-Griffiths, M. (1978). *Counting Animals. Handbooks on Techniques Currently Used in African Wildlife Ecology*, 2nd ed. (ed. J.J.R. Grimsdell). Nairobi: African Wildlife Leadership Foundation.

Norton-Griffiths, M. (2008). How many wildebeest do you need? *World Economics* **8**: 41–64.

Nyamayedenga, S., C. Mashapa, R.J. Chateya and E. Gandiwa (2021). An assessment of the impact of the 2014 US elephant trophy importation ban on the hunting patterns in Matetsi Hunting Complex, north-west Zimbabwe. *Global Ecology and Conservation* **30**: e01758.

Oberem, P. and P. Oberem (2016). *The New Game Rancher*. South Africa: Briza Publications.

Oduntan, O.O., A. Akinyemi, O. Ojo, et al. (2012). Survey of wild animals used in zoo-therapy at Ibadan, Oyo State, Nigeria. *International Journal of Molecular Zoology* **2**: 70–73.

Ogutu, J.O., H.P. Piepho, M.Y. Said, et al. (2016). Extreme wildlife declines and concurrent increase in livestock numbers in Kenya: what are the causes? *PLoS One* **11**(9): e0163249.

Ouedraogo, A. (2018). Campagne d'exploitation faunique 2017–2018: accroître la contribution du secteur faunique à l'économie nationale. *Faso Actu* 10.01.2018, Ouagadougou, Burkina Faso.

Packer, C., H. Brink, B.M. Kissui, et al. (2011). Effects of trophy hunting on lion and leopard populations in Tanzania. *Conservation Biology* **25**(1):142–53.

Parker, K., A. De Vos, H. Clements, et al. (2020). Impacts of a trophy hunting ban on private land conservation in South African biodiversity hotspots. *Conservation Science and Practice* **2**: e214.

PNP (2018). Saison cynégétique 2017–2018. Août 2018, Parc National de la Pendjari, Bénin.

PNP (2019). Saison cynégétique 2018–2019. Septembre 2019, Parc National de la Pendjari, Bénin.

PNW (2018). Rapport de fin de saison touristique et cynégétique 2017–2018. Août 2018, Parc National du W, Bénin.

PNW (2019). Rapport de fin de saison touristique et cynégétique 2018–2019. Juin 2019, Parc National du W, Bénin.

Poshiwa, X., R.A. Groeneveld, I.M.A. Heitkönig, H.H.T. Prins and E.C. van Ierland (2013). Reducing rural households' annual income fluctuations due to rainfall variation through diversification of wildlife use: portfolio theory in a case study of southeastern Zimbabwe. *Tropical Conservation Science* **6**(2): 201–220.

Prins, H.H.T. (1996). *Ecology and behavior of the African buffalo – Social Inequality and Decision Making*. Dordrecht: Springer.

Prins, H.H.T. (2020). Preserving nature: artificial intelligence against green violence. Farewell address upon retiring as Professor of Resource Ecology at Wageningen University. Wageningen University Press, Wageningen.

Prins, H.H.T. and J.G. de Jong (2022). The ecohistory of Tanzania's Northern Rift Valley – can one establish an objective baseline as an endpoint for ecosystem restoration? In C. Kiffner, M.L. Bond and D.E. Lee (Eds.), *Tarangire: Human–Wildlife Coexistence in a Fragmented Ecosystem*. Ecological Studies, vol. 243. Cham: Springer.

Richards, W. (1980). The import of firearms into West Africa in the eighteenth century. *The Journal of African History* **21**(1): 43–59.

Rigava, N, R. Taylor and L. Goredema (2006). Participatory wildlife quota setting. *Participatory Learning and Action* **55**: 30–36.

Robertson, K. (1996). *Nyati, The Southern Buffalo*. Harare: Mag-Set Publications (Pvt) Ltd p. 4.

Rogan, M.S., P.A. Lindsey, C.J. Tambling et al. (2017). Illegal bushmeat hunters compete with predators and threaten wild herbivore populations in a global tourism hotspot. *Biological Conservation* 210: 233–242.

Roosevelt, T. (1910). *African Game Trails: An Account of the African Wanderings of an American Hunter-Naturalist*. London: Murray's Imperial Library.

Rovero, F., A.S. Mtui, A.S. Kitegile and M.R. Nielsen (2012) Hunting or habitat degradation? Decline of primate populations in Udzungwa Mountains, Tanzania: an analysis of threats. *Biological Conservation* 146: 89–96.

Rowland Ward (2020). *Rowland Ward's Records of Big Game*. 30th ed. Huntington Beach, CA: Rowland Ward.

Ruark, R.C. (1987). *Horn of the Hunter*. Long Beach, CA: Safari Press, p. 285.

Russo, I.-R., S. Hoban, P. Bloomer, et al. (2019). 'Intentional Genetic Manipulation' as a conservation threat. *Conservation Genetics Resources* 11(2): 237–247.

SCI (2022). Big Game Hunting Records – Safari Club International online record book. (www.scirecordbook.org).

Sansom, B. (1974). Traditional economic systems. In W.D. Hammond Tooke (Ed.), *The Bantu Speaking People of Southern Africa*. London: Routledge and Kegan Paul.

Saayman, M., P. van der Merwe and A. Saayman (2018). The economic impact of trophy hunting in the south African wildlife industry. *Global Ecology and Conservation* 16(2018): e00510.

Scholte, P., O. Pays, S. Adam, B. Chardonnet, et al. (2021). Conservation overstretch and long-term decline of wildlife and tourism in the Central African savannas. *Conservation Biology* 36(2), e13860.

Selier, S.A.J. and E. Di Minin (2015). Monitoring required for effective sustainable use of wildlife. *Animal Conservation* 18: 131–132.

Selier, J., L. Nel, I. Rushworth, et al. (2018). An assessment of the potential risks of the practice of intensive and selective breeding of game to biodiversity and the biodiversity economy in South Africa Scientific Authority Report 2018. www.iucn.org.

Siege, H. and L. Siege (2020). *Die Sache mit der Auslandsjagd*. Melsungen: Neumann-Neudamm, p. 289.

Skikuku, K.R., P. Makenzi and P. Muruthi (2018). Poaching in the Mount Elgon Transboundary Ecosystem. *UNESCO Biosphere Reserves* 2: 1–14.

Snyman, S., D. Sumba, F. Vorhies et al. (2021). *State of the Wildlife Economy in Africa*. Kigali: African Leadership University, School of Wildlife Conservation.

Sodeinde, O.A. and D.A. Soewu (1999). Pilot study of the traditional medicine trade in Nigeria. With reference to wild fauna. *TRAFFIC Bulletin* 8: 35–40.

Somers, M.J., M. Walters, J. Measey, et al. (2020). The implications of the reclassification of South African wildlife species as farm animals. *South African Journal of Science* 116(1–2): 1–2.

South African Professional Hunters statistics (2019). *Game and Hunt Daily*. South African Professional Hunting Statistics – Game & Hunt Daily (gameandhuntdaily.co.za).

Southern Africa Trust (2019). Declaration – Voices of the communities: A new deal for rural communities and wildlife and natural resources. www.southernafricatrust.org/2019/06/25/declaration-voices-of-the-communities-a-new-deal-forrural-communities-and-wildlife-and-natural-resources/

Spenceley, A. (2005). Nature-based tourism and environmental sustainability in South Africa. *Journal of Sustainable Tourism* 13(2): 136–170.

Spenceley, A. (2021). *The Future of Nature-Based Tourism, Impacts of COVID-19 and paths to sustainability*. Gland: Luc Hoffmann Institute.

Spinage, C.A. (2003) The great African rinderpest panzootic. In *Cattle Plague*. Boston: Springer. https://doi.org/10.1007/978-1-4419-8901-7_22

Steel, L., A. Colom, F. Maisels and A. Shapiro (2008). *The Scale and Dynamics of wildlife Trade Originating in the South of the Salonga–Lukenié–Sankuru Landscape.* WWF Democratic Republic of Congo.

Strong, M. and J.A. Silva (2020). Impacts of hunting prohibitions on multidimensional well-being. *Biological Conservation* **243**: 108451.

TAWA (2019). *Review of Trophy Hunting in Tanzania. The Case of Selous Game Reserve, Buffer Zones and Selous–Niassa Corridor.* Morogoro, Tanzania: TAWA.

Taylor, R.D. (1988). Age determination of the African buffalo, *Syncerus caffer* (Sparrman) in Zimbabwe. *African Journal of Ecology* **26**: 207–220.

Taylor, R.D. (2001). Participatory natural resource monitoring and management: implications for conservation. In D. Hulme and M. Murphree (Eds.), *African Wildlife and Livelihoods: The Promise and Performance of Community Conservation.* Oxford: James Currey.

Taylor, R.D. and C.S. Mackie (1997). Aerial census results for elephant and buffalo in selected Campfire areas. *CAMPFIRE Association Publication Series* **4**: 4–11.

Taylor, W.G. (2005). *The influence of trophy measurement on the age of sport hunted buffalo, Syncerus caffer (Sparrman), in the Zambezi valley, Zimbabwe, and its implications for sustainable trophy hunting.* Unpublished undergraduate dissertation in Environmental Biology, Oxford Brookes University.

Taylor, W.A., P.A. Lindsey and H. Davies-Mostert (2015). *An Assessment of the Economic, Social and Conservation Value of the Wildlife Ranching Industry and its Potential to Support the Green Economy in South Africa.* Johannesburg: The Endangered Wildlife Trust.

Taylor, W.A., P.A. Lindsey, S.K. Nicholson, et al. (2020). Jobs, game meat and profits: the benefits of wildlife ranching on marginal lands in South Africa. *Biological Conservation* **245**: 108561.

't Sas-Rolfes, M., R. Emslie, K. Adcock and M. Knight (2022). Legal hunting for conservation of highly threatened species: the case of African rhinos. *Conservation Letters* **15**: e12877.

US Fish and Wildlife Service (2022). Endangered Species Act. www.fws.gov/law/endangered-species-act.

Van der Hoeven C.A., W.F. de Boer and H.H.T. Prins (2004). Pooling local expert opinions for estimating mammal densities in tropical rainforests. *Journal for Nature Conservation* **12**: 193–204.

Van Houdt, S., R.P. Brown, T.C. Wanger, et al. (2021). Divergent views on trophy hunting in Africa, and what this may mean for research and policy. *Conservation Letters* **14**(6): e12840.

Van Velden, J., K. Wilson, K. and D. Biggs (2018). The evidence for the bushmeat crisis in African savannas: a systematic quantitative literature review. *Biological Conservation* **221**: 345–356.

Van Vliet, N. and P. Mbazza (2011). Recognizing the multiple reasons for bushmeat consumption in urban areas: a necessary step toward the sustainable use of wildlife for food in Central Africa. *Human Dimensions of Wildlife* **16**: 45–54.

Van Vliet, N., J. Muhindo, J. Kambale Nyumu, et al. (2018). Mammal depletion processes as evidenced from spatially explicit and temporal local ecological knowledge. *Tropical Conservation Science* **11**: 1–16.

Walpole, M.J. and C.R. Thouless (2005). Increasing the value of wildlife through non-consumptive use? Deconstructing the myths of ecotourism and community-based tourism in the tropics. In R. Woodroffe, S.J. Thirgood and A. Rabinowitz (Eds.), *People and Wildlife: Conflict or Coexistence.* Cambridge: Cambridge University Press, pp. 122–139.

Western, D., S. Russell and I. Cuthill (2009). The status of wildlife in Protected Areas compared to non-protected areas of Kenya. *PLoS One* **4**(7): e6140.

Whiting, M.J., V.L. Williams, T.J. Hibbitts, et al. (2011). Animals traded for traditional medicine at the Faraday market in South Africa: species diversity and conservation implications. *Journal of Zoology* **284**: 84–96.

White, P.A. and J.L. Belant (2015). Provisioning of game meat to rural communities as a benefit of sport hunting in Zambia. *PLoS ONE* **10**(2): e0117237.

WCS and MINFOF (2018). *Aerial Survey of Wildlife and Human Activity in the BSB Yamoussa Landscape, Cameroon, Dry Season 2018.* New York: Wildlife Conservation Society, Ministry of Forestry and Wildlife. Funded by the KfW.

Wilkie, D.S. and J.F. Carpenter (1999). The potential role of safari hunting as a source of revenue for protected areas in the Congo Basin. *Oryx* **33**: 339–345.

Wilkie, D.S., E.L. Bennett, C.A. Peres and A.A. Cunningham (2011). The empty forest revisited. *Annals of the New York Academy of Sciences* **1223**(1): 120–128.

Winterbach, C.W., C. Whitesell and M.J. Somers (2015). Wildlife abundance and diversity as indicators of tourism potential in northern Botswana. *PLoS One* **10**(8): e0135595.

WWF (1997). *Quota Setting Manual.* Wildlife Management Series of Guideline Manuals. Harare: WWF Zimbabwe Programme Office.

WWF (2000). *District Quota Setting Toolbox.* Wildlife Management Series of Guideline Manuals Harare: WWF Zimbabwe Programme Office.

Yasuda, A. (2011). The impacts of sport hunting on the livelihoods of local people: a case study of Bénoué National Park, Cameroon. *Society and Natural Resources* **24**(8): 860–869.

Part V
Concluding Chapters

17 · Knowns and Unknowns in African Buffalo Ecology and Management

H. H. T. PRINS, D. CORNELIS, A. CARON
AND P. CHARDONNET

On Knowledge

The definition of 'knowledge' is 'a justified true belief'. Philosophers of science took a few centuries to arrive at this definition. The reasoning on which it is based is that knowledge is a 'belief' because a belief is defined as 'conviction of the truth of some statement' and is related to the verb 'to believe', which means 'to hold something as true' or 'to give credence that something is true'. Because science does not deal with revelations or their interpretation, the justification of holding a particular belief can only be found in evidence, which thus makes it a 'true belief'. Finally, as many things are seen by people and taken as evidence (even if not true – think of Cold Fusion), the belief and the evidence for it must be 'justified'. Justification is found in an entire corpus of other, related, evidence.

Ecologists have been studying the African buffalo in the wild for about 70 years. Before that time, most knowledge came from hunters, and with hindsight it is reasonable to assume that the information so gathered was often more closely related to storytelling than to what we consider science. Prins and Sinclair (2013) and Cornélis et al. (2014) provide good recent summaries of what we think we know about the African buffalo. New knowledge added since the publication of these works is reported in the different chapters of the present book. We dare to assert that with this book and all of the publications referred to in it, the African buffalo is now the best-known animal of all Bovidae, so even better known than the American bison (*Bison bison*), the European wisent (*B. bonasus*) or any antelope, wild sheep, or goat. Are there other terrestrial wild mammals that are better known than the African buffalo? We believe that two or three species can compete for that honour, namely the red deer (wapiti, American elk; *Cervus elaphus*), the white-tailed deer (*Odocoileus virginianus*) and, perhaps, the mule deer (*O. hemionus*). The white-tailed deer is said to be the most studied large mammal in the world (Hewitt, 2011). Many books have been published on this species, but, like for the mule deer, most are on its management for hunting. However, the knowledge gathered on reindeer (*Rangifer tarandus*) (Leader-Williams, 1988; Forbes et al., 2006; Tryland and Kutz, 2019) and especially red deer has contributed much more to science, as exemplified by Clutton-Brock et al. (1982). The other mammal species that has been of great significance for science is the elephant seal (*Mirounga angustirostris*; Le Boeuf and Laws, 1994; Le Boeuf and Le Boeuf, 2021). Yet of all these species, the African buffalo may present the biggest challenge because of its intricate relationships with domestic cattle in its network of diseases and parasites.

However, after exulting and crowing about how good we, students of the African buffalo are and have been, we would like to identify the knowledge deficits that remain. Our aim is to bring our science of '*nyatology*' (from '*Nyati*' = buffalo in kiSwahili and other Bantu languages) to such a level that it morphs into deep-seated contributions to the theory of evolutionary ecology, behavioural ecology, functional ecology, disease ecology and, perhaps, biology. Too much of our '*nyatology*' remains basically descriptive and is, at best, testing hypotheses derived from more general science. Yet we believe that this amazing species, comprising phenomenally robust and well-adapted individuals with a social organization so intricate that it approaches eusociality, has more in store for us to learn, and its students will be able to generate hypotheses that can be tested on other organisms. Indeed, the house mouse (*Mus domesticus*) or the fruit fly (*Drosophila* spp.) may be wonders of adaptation too, but they became model organisms probably more as historical accidents than because of their wonderful resistance against diseases, their enormous distribution associated with complicated clinal variations in (eco-) morphs and richness of genetic patterning, or their social organization. So, where are the knowledge deficits that we must fill? To identify the holes in our knowledge, we surveyed this book's authors, who collectively may be the most knowledgeable group of scientists and practitioners concerning the African buffalo alive (Figure 17.1).

Former Secretary of Defence of the United States of America Donald Rumsfeld once made a famous distinction between the different sorts of knowledge that one has. He said on 12 February 2002, 'There are

Figure 17.1 Four African lions about to kill a juvenile male of Cape African buffalo, Mana Pools National Park, Zimbabwe. © Alexandre Caron.

known knowns; there are things we know we know. We also know there are known unknowns; that is to say we know there are some things we do not know. But there are also unknown unknowns – the ones we don't know we don't know ...it is the latter category that tends to be the difficult ones'. We scientists are very good at reporting on 'known knowns'. This book and earlier publications such as those of Sinclair (1977), Prins (1996) and the many, many good papers on the African buffalo (check all references in this book) offer a wealth of information about what we know on African buffalo. However, what about the 'known unknowns' and 'unknown unknowns'? And we would like to add a category, namely, 'unknown knowns' – which we posit refers to sound scientific knowledge that appears to have been forgotten. Too many scientists do not read scientific papers that are older than 10 years or so, or they only read abstracts, and knowledge that used to be in the scientific domain thus tends to fall out of it. This is called 'knowledge decay'. The term does not describe the process through which knowledge becomes outdated, but rather one through which knowledge is forgotten.

On purpose, we have not formulated 'hypotheses' in this chapter for several reasons. We believe that what we need most is 'descriptive ecology' and 'natural history' (see Prins and Gordon, 2014; Gordon and Prins, 2019), while the use of storylines (linked to the assessment of their plausibility) probably offers better heuristic tools to approach best understanding (see De Jong and Prins, 2023; Prins and Gordon, 2023). The following knowledge deficits were identified in a process of questioning the collective of authors who contributed to this book.

Known Unknowns – These Are the Next Research Questions Sitting in the Backs of Our Minds

These research issues represent, relatively speaking, low-hanging fruit – others already have given them much thought, allowing one to delve deeper. The following thoughts and ideas were shared among us, which we have collected under a suite of subsections.

Natural History, Climate Change and Conservation

1. As compared to the Cape buffalo from the area ranging between Kenya and South Africa, precariously little is known about the buffalo ranging between Senegal and Sudan. Perhaps the only exception is the work of Cornélis et al. (2011), and only little is known on forest buffalo despite the work of especially Korte (see Cornélis et al., 2014) but also of others (e.g. Bekhuis et al., 2008).

2. In a number of countries where African buffalo still occur or did occur in the recent past, the respective 'departments of wildlife' (whatever their name) are not allocated sufficient funds to survey animal populations on a regular basis. In some of these countries, trend analyses and/or population estimates are thus frequently not very reliable. Offtake quotas are ideally set on reliable and precise population estimates (from which reliable and trustworthy trends can be deduced), and thus may not be set correctly (see e.g. Hagen et al., 2014; Milner-Gulland and Shea, 2017; see also Pellikka et al., 2005; Morellet et al., 2007). Additionally, offtake quotas may be set on the wrong premise of population stability (Chapter 5). Does this uncertainty in the data and the application of the wrong models negatively impact some local populations of buffalo?

3. The IPCC (2022) predicts that temperatures will rise in coming decades over much of the African buffalo's range. Heatwaves are on the increase (ACSS, 2021), implying that heat stress for African buffalo (and other large mammals) may become severe. The search terms 'heat stress' associated with 'cattle' or 'water buffalo' yield thousands of publications. Much more research on the thermal ecology of the species is needed (see Hetem et al., 2009, 2010, 2013; Shrestha et al., 2012, 2014; Fuller et al., 2014, 2021; Strauss et al., 2016).

4. Increasing CO_2 levels could lead to a strengthening of the woody layer, resulting in an inexorable march to a thicker tree layer competing strongly with the grass layer (e.g. Bond and Midgley, 2000; Kgope et al., 2010), although the simplicity of the mechanism has been contested (Gosling et al., 2022; Raubenheimer and Ripley, 2022). Regardless, many former grasslands in African savannas have densified. In extreme circumstances where grazing pressure is high and the grass layer is stressed, a drought pushes grazers such as buffalo into a marginal space for survival. Most past research findings may hence no longer be applicable.

5. Even though there is much arm-waving about climate change and its impact, there is a significant lack of fundamental knowledge on the habitats of the African buffalo (in the Sahel, the savannas of East and Southern Africa, but also in the rainforests).

6. What are the exact workings of the transcription of DNA, the translation of RNA and the functionality of proteins in relation to the development and physiology of the African buffalo? In cattle, much progress has been made (see e.g. Drackley et al., 2006; Beerda et al., 2008; Kirkpatrick, 2015; Cesar et al., 2016; Barshad et al., 2018). There are some intriguing findings by Van Hooft et al. (2007) that have yet to be clearly explained (Van Hooft et al., 2018). Indeed, many techniques are already in place (see e.g. Smitz et al., 2016) for tackling this.

7. For the forest buffalo, there may be more unknowns than for the Cape buffalo. As shown elsewhere in this book, it appears as if the forest buffalo evolved later than the savanna buffalo. Yet there are many gaps in our knowledge concerning gene flow between the different forms. Too much credit is given to subjective assessments of horn forms or the proportions of calves with reddish coats versus blackish ones. The exchange of individuals between groups of forest buffalo is an identified knowledge gap.

Ecology

1. Research is needed to understand the causal factors underlying behavioural avoidance between buffalo groups. Many studies have shown very little spatial overlap between neighbouring groups of buffalo, but the mechanism by which segregation is maintained remains poorly understood (scent marking, perhaps). Research is also needed that goes beyond mere speculation about the functionality of this spatial segregation of groups. One can think, of course, about competition for resources or the prevention of transmission of pathogens. However, exhaustive systematic reviews of the literature to discover whether competition has been proven show a lack of evidence for interspecific competition (Prins, 2016; Schieltz and Rubenstein, 2016) but good evidence for intraspecific competition (see e.g. Prins, 1989b).

2. Information is needed on male contact patterns – males could be important vectors of pathogens at the population level due to group affiliation behaviour between groups of females and bachelor groups. More work should focus on understanding the movements of adult males (e.g., how often they encounter mixed groups, how long and where). Such work also is needed to better understand the socioecological organization of the species (see also Prins, 1989a). For forest buffalo, this lack of knowledge is even more prevalent.

3. Research is needed on how extractive industries (notably, for instance, mining gold using mercury) might impact buffalo and their habitat across their range. It is known that extractive industries influence the habitat (e.g. Foster et al., 2019). In water buffalo, health effects have been measured (e.g. Singh et al., 2018), in cattle as well (e.g. Ranjan et al., 2008; Pati et al., 2020), and mining has been shown to have unexpected consequences for African elephant distribution (Sach et al., 2020). The effects of gold mining using mercury have been studied in South America (e.g. Markham and Sangermano, 2018), North America (e.g. Eagles-Smith et al., 2016) and the Arctic (e.g. Dietz et al., 2013). It appears that most problems can be expected in aquatic environments (Basu et al., 2018), but because buffalo are closely tied to water, the problem may be large.

4. The expansion of cotton growing (most of it *Gossypium hirsutum*, a native to Central America), especially in West and Central Africa (but also elsewhere in Africa), is a threat especially to the northern savanna buffalo because cotton appears to thrive where this buffalo form has its native range. Cotton growers rely heavily on

phytosanitary procedures, and the widespread use in Africa of highly dangerous chemicals prohibited by, for example, the Stockholm Convention since 2001 (see, for instance, Hagen and Walls, 2005) is putting at risk entire ecosystems but is very much understudied. The presence of these chemicals has been found in African animals living in 'cotton regions' (e.g. Aïkpo et al., 2017; Houndji et al., 2020). Simple toxicology analysis would easily help to describe and measure the phenomenon, its magnitude, risk analysis, etc. (cf. Baudron et al., 2009).

5. Do buffalo use auditive clues in their communication? There is much we do not understand concerning hearing (see e.g. Benoit et al., 2020) in ungulates and there is much to learn about vocalization (e.g. Blank, 2021). Who would have thought that Sumatran rhinoceros (*Dicerorhinus sumatrensis*) have song-like vocalizations (Von Muggenthaler et al., 2003) or that giraffe (*Giraffa camelopardalis*) and okapi (*Okapi johnstonii*) use infrasound (Badlangana et al., 2011; Von Muggenthaler and Bashaw, 2013)? Given the fact that buffalo are generally so silent in the audible range for humans, one would not be surprised if they use infrasound too in their communication, especially in dense vegetation.

6. The mechanisms underlying collective movements, particularly at the time of group fission, are still unknown in buffalo. In other words, how do individuals decide to join one of the subgroups that form at the time of fission? The probability of following one of the subgroups could depend on the number of individuals already involved in the movement, regardless of their identity, social or affiliative relationships with individuals already moving or still at rest or their needs at the time. It would be interesting to examine decision-making during group fission in buffalo to measure the weight of social influence, compared to ecological influence (often examined), on group stability. This lack of knowledge appears to be even stronger in the forest buffalo.

7. Group decision-making has been studied in buffalo (e.g. Prins, 1996, p. 218 ff), but also in other mammals. Theory has been developed by for example Conradt and Roper (2003) and reviewed by Conradt and Roper (2005). See also Couzin et al. (2005). Much can be gained by further studying this under different ecological circumstances.

8. What is the effect of genetic relatedness on fission and fusion patterns (see Prins, 1996, p. 77 ff; p. 54 ff)?

9. What are the impacts of human disturbance on buffalo grouping patterns and social decisions? Do buffalo groups tend to be more

transient when encounters and disturbances from human activities are higher (human–wildlife interfaces versus within a park)? A testable idea could be that the higher the intensity and frequency of buffalo–human (including livestock) interactions, the higher frequency of the fission–fusion events, which would perhaps lead to smaller groups of buffalo closer to the borders of protected areas without fences (as compared to areas that are fenced). This ought to be controlled for possible competitive effects and poaching (see for instance Clegg, 1994; Leweri et al., 2022; cf. Dave and Jhala, 2011). One can also imagine that undisturbed animals maintain diseases within their own groups (e.g. Delahay et al., 2000), but disturbed animals do so less (cf. Smith and Wilkinson, 2003). Network analysis (e.g. Jacoby et al., 2012; Yin et al., 2020) will need to be applied to buffalo in disturbed and undisturbed situations.

10. What are the effects of poaching on social cohesion and fission–fusion patterns in buffalo? In the African elephant (*Loxodonta africana*), poaching has been shown to affect social patterns (e.g. Prins et al., 1994; Archie et al., 2008), but it is not known how poaching affects buffalo.

11. While more is understood about the functioning of key resource areas in animal migrations (e.g. Scholte and Brouwer, 2008; Moritz et al., 2010; Cornélis et al., 2011, 2014; Fynn et al., 2015; Moritz et al., 2015), much less is understood regarding how buffalo maintain themselves in areas without such green floodplains during the late dry season, for example in Kruger National Park (South Africa). Where do buffalo get sufficient (crude) protein and energy to support foetus development or peak lactation, which is even more demanding? Indeed, perhaps it can be found in the maintenance of grazing lawns (e.g. Vesey-FitzGerald, 1969; 1974; Cromsigt et al., 2013; Muthoni et al., 2014; Hempson et al., 2015). Gut morphology (e.g. Hofmann, 1973) is key to gaining a better understanding, as is the digestibility of the forage.

12. There is no understanding of the forage traits that buffalo select under different constraints and demands. In other words, the proximate factors in food selection are not understood, and a simple description, 'roughage selector', does not do justice to either the animals or the plants. What forage traits help buffalo to maximize intake of energy, protein and minerals for growth and reproduction, and what is the optimal height of the sward? What forage traits provide optimal reserves of forage for the early dry season, the late

dry season and during droughts? For example, we know that buffalo rather select for leafy, medium-height grasses such as *Themeda triandra*, *Digitaria eriantha* and the lawn-forming grass *Cynodon dactylon*, but what is it about these grasses that they like? Are the leaves more digestible, is it the leaf-to-stem ratio, is it the height and the bite size they offer for a tongue-sweeping forager, or some combination of the above? What are the traits of drought refuges – that is what level of leaf and stem toughness can they tolerate to avoid severe loss of body stores and starvation during droughts? See also below under 'unknown knowns', point ii.

13. Much modern buffalo research nowadays depends on darting animals, immobilizing them and fitting them with a measuring device (like a GPS collar). The assumption is that the animal, once given its antidote, 'immediately' reverts to its normal behaviour, finds its herd and assumes its normal social position. In human patients, the standards are set high, but much has still to be learned before one really knows what one does to memory (Borrat et al., 2018; Galarza Vallejo et al., 2019; Veselis and Arslan-Carlon, 2021). In companion animals, rather in-depth analysis is carried out to investigate what is done to the animals (e.g. Biermann et al., 2012; Reader et al., 2019; Abouelfetouh et al., 2021) and likewise in horses (e.g. Hubbell and Muir, 2006; Schauvliege et al., 2019; Cock et al., 2022). Even in ruminants, precious little is known about the effects of key processes in the intact animal (e.g. Nicol and Morton, 2020; Waite et al., 2021). Research is urgently needed not only on the effects on the animals' well-being, but also on their social behaviour and ranging behaviour.

14. Time series of total population alone may lead to erroneous predictions about the population without detailed knowledge of its age structure (Chapter 5). Without this detailed knowledge, incorrect deductions may be made about possible density-related effects or sustainable harvesting regimes. Nyatiologists need to find a way to more precisely identify the age of individuals in the field.

Disease

1. Some key resource areas, like floodplains, play a critical role in supporting buffalo over the late dry season. Yet, these areas also may harbour internal parasites, such as giant fluke (*Fasciola gigantea*) and the small fluke (*Dicrocoelium hospes*), and many other Platyhelminthes and Trematodes that can make cattle very sick if they are not properly

treated (e.g. Swai and Wilson, 2017). How do buffalo contend with liver flukes? Indeed, they are widely infected (Hammond, 1972), but in the Central African Republic, 12 of 33 inspected buffalo that were infested with both flukes had no apparent clinical signs (Graber et al., 1972). It is worrying to note that African buffalo that are not infected with such parasites are resistant to bTB (Ezenwa et al., 2010; c.f. Budischak et al., 2012), but it is gratifying to know that a grazing alternation between ruminants and hindgut fermenters may reduce parasite burdens (Odadi et al., 2011).

2. Do buffalo use natural plant chemicals to treat themselves for flukes and other parasites? Species that spring to mind are *Lippia javanica* and *Tarchonanthus camphoratus* (e.g. Koné et al., 2012; Kosgei, 2014; Hassen et al., 2022), and an evolutionary arms race may already have been on for a long time (see Beesley et al., 2017). By and large, however, evidence is scant and the literature abounds with 'potential effects' versus real ones, and ethnoveterinary storytelling instead of proven remedies.

3. What is the influence of group formation dynamics on pathogen dynamics in buffalo? Cross et al. (2004) and Wielgus et al (2021) studied the influence of contact patterns within groups on pathogen dynamics. However, the aggregation of contact indices across time (e.g. per month) may lead to a misleading prediction of pathogen dynamics, as it ignores short-term interactions that change due to ecology and social behaviour (i.e. fission–fusion behaviour), which could have a significant effect on pathogen transmission patterns. See also Prins (1989a), Cross et al. (2012), Sintayehu et al. (2017a, 2017b) and Davis et al. (2018).

4. What are the veterinary standards for health, or good reproduction, in buffalo (or for other wild mammals)? Little is known about the normal parameter values of blood, liver or other tissue, and too often one must rely on cattle standards. However, African buffalo are not at all closely related to cattle or Asian buffalo (see Chapter 2), and it is thus not very plausible that cattle standards are informative for African buffalo.

5. More research is needed on foot and mouth disease (FMD), (bovine) tuberculosis ([b]TB) and brucellosis in free-ranging buffalo populations in unfenced ecosystems of central, eastern and western Africa; for the latter, these diseases pose public health problems as they are. Work on FMD in cattle in East Africa has shown how the model developed for this disease in southern Africa does not capture the whole story, nor do controls need to be so draconian with the options

of commodity-based trade. This potential for a different perspective in terms of management of landscape and animal agriculture/wildlife economy and tolerance/control of the disease needs to be investigated further. This will need an integrated programme of socioeconomic, cultural, environmental (including climate change), biodiversity, agricultural, political and ecological benefits of living with FMD. The work of Sintayehu (2017a, 2017b) provides good pointers.

6. Buffalo are resistant to a number of diseases, but the mechanisms for such resistances are not well known (for trypanosomiasis it remains quite unclear). Strikingly, even livestock-focused scientists have expressed little interest in understanding how to take advantage of such mechanisms in buffalo to apply to livestock production. Cases in point are: how are African buffalo capable of maintaining FMD on a permanent basis without expressing any symptoms (asymptomatic, or are they healthy carriers)? Applied to domestic artiodactyls, meat commercial trade rules would be reshuffled with new FMD policies. How do African buffalo resist African trypanosomes (genus *Trypanosoma*) and how can they live and thrive in areas that are heavily infested with the vector tsetse flies? What causes buffalo to be insensitive to CBPP (contagious bovine pleuropneumonia), Peste des petits ruminants (PPR), East Coast fever (ECF), heart water, babesiosis, streptothricosis/dermatophylosis and many other potential diseases which are so deadly for cattle? If we knew, we would not need to spend billions in yearly national cattle vaccination campaigns. Once again, African buffalo are probably not bovids (Chapter 2).

7. The role of closed (i.e. fenced) versus open (i.e. non-fenced) systems with bTB expression and prevalence needs further research, but again in areas other than the southern African region where much of the work has been done already. The nature of the force of infection in a mixed livestock–buffalo system needs to be explored in the context of different cattle breeds. The potential risks of buffalo zoonotic bTB transmission through hunting or sustainable use of infected buffalo herds (managed culling and processing) needs to be explored.

Management

1. What is the economic value of different land uses, namely, buffalo hunting (but also other species), agriculture (without buffalo but with livestock), conservation without hunting (but with buffalo) or any form of co-management including cattle and buffalo? Some work

has been done on this (e.g. Hearne et al., 1996; chapters in Hearne et al., 2000; Prins et al., 2000; Mayaka et al., 2005; Mwakiwa et al., 2016; Poshiwa et al., 2013a, 2013b; Mwakiwa, 2019). Yet these economic analyses seem to encounter difficulties in entering more freely formulated, data-free discourses espoused by many conservationists. The implications of this are severe (see e.g. Scholte et al., 2022). These economic value assessments could be placed in the context of climate change scenarios in the contexts of Africa too. This lack of knowledge is even more pertinent for the forest and northern savanna buffalo.

2. The often-positive role of controlled trophy hunting is insufficiently acknowledged by too many conservationists even though the Sustainable Use Principles of the Convention on Biological Diversity, in which its role is acknowledged, have been endorsed by all signatory States (COP Decision VII/12: see www.cbd.int/decision/cop/?id=7749). There is much disagreement between NGOs, but also for instance Kenya does not acknowledge the acceptability and effectiveness of hunting as a conservation tool (although it is under ministerial review). This contrast between different parties is intensified by a lack of reliable data on the impact of trophy hunting on wildlife. Much information on African trophy hunting is still available only as unpublished grey literature, and thus is difficult to access (for instance, Snyman et al., 2021; but see Baker, 1997; Hurt and Ravn, 2000; Lindsey et al., 2007; Schalkwyk et al., 2010) and more efforts should be done to collate information.

3. Even though theories of non-equilibrium dynamics were formulated some 40 years ago (e.g. Ellis and Swift, 1988) and have been tested for savanna systems (e.g. Gillson, 2004; Accatino and De Michele, 2016; Engler and von Wehrden, 2018), too much work on buffalo and their ranging still is not placed in that context. African rangelands necessitate management strategies that acknowledge the unpredictability of weather, markets and politics. Many pastoralists realize this (e.g. Mace and Houston, 1989; Mace, 1990), but many managers do not (e.g. Shawiah, 2016) and are thus overwhelmed by so-called black swan events. In modelling for game ranching, some progress has been made (e.g. Joubert et al., 2007; Dlamini, 2011), but this is still unsatisfactory. The collapse of live buffalo prices, for example, made many an enterprise in South Africa suddenly unprofitable, and the effects of drought reverberate for many years through a population's age structure (Chapter 5).

4. The effect of trophy hunting is contested, as evidenced by parliamentary debates in, for example, Great Britain in 2022. Intriguingly, parliamentary members from western countries allow themselves to take decisions that would affect an industry (and positive outcomes for local people) in Zimbabwe or Namibia without encouraging parliaments in those countries to discuss red deer (*Cervus elaphus*) hunting (a.k.a. 'deer stalking') in Great Britain. Much more research along the lines of Gandiwa et al. (2014) is called for to reveal the hypocrisy in this debate (c.f. Curtin, 1940, p. 162 ff). Yet typical examples of successful management, at least partly based on utilization, occurred in South Africa where trophy hunting has facilitated the recovery of bontebok (*Damaliscus dorcas*), black wildebeest (*Connochaetes gnu*), cape mountain zebra (*Equus zebra*) and, until recently, southern white rhino (*Cerathoterium simum*). Furthermore, in recent years, trophy hunting has also facilitated the recovery of the buffalo and its habitat in several hunting areas of Mozambique and South Africa. It can be thought, however, that trophy hunting has a negative impact on buffalo and other wildlife (cf., #2), and the necessary data should lead to clear evidence to move the debate away from only emotions.

5. The fact that large buffalo herds are mobile also means that they seldom 'camp' on a patch for a long period of time but are continually moving through different landscapes. This means that unlike selective water-dependent grazers, buffalo will utilize an area and then move on, thus reducing the chance of overgrazing (a function of time and not necessarily number – the vegetation needs rest according to a number of range ecologists). On fragmented (fenced) areas, excessive artificially supplied surface water results in high densities of sedentary water-dependent species (e.g. impala *Aepyceros melampus*) and less space for buffalo to move. So, where and when should animal control (including culling) be exercised? Even in unfenced areas, animal control may need to be implemented where water point provision has resulted in increased animal numbers due to their increased distribution, resulting in insufficient forage for animals during dry periods (obviously more critical in fenced or fragmented situations). The alternative is that the population is allowed to fluctuate with the prevailing resource conditions, that is a die-off in drought (of buffalo in a poor condition or recent weanlings). This may be appropriate in unfenced, 'open' situations, but is it acceptable in fenced areas where animals are unable to move widely? The tricky issue if the 'laissez-faire' option is pursued is the long-term effect on the

resources resulting from overgrazing (see Peel and Smit, 2020) apart from the ethical issues surrounding enclosing animals in fenced-off areas where droughts occur.

6. Horn size and horn shape drive much of the economics of buffalo breeding in South Africa and buffalo hunting. However, little is known about the genetics around the inheritance of horn size and shape. Equally little is known about the effects of levels of nutrition (macro- and micro-nutrients) or of hormones on horn growth. In other species, the situation is slightly better (e.g. big horn sheep *Ovis canadensis*: Reich, 2021; domestic sheep: Pan et al., 2018), but even in cattle this field is understudied.

7. What are the effects of nutrition on calving rate, calf birth and weaning weight, intercalving interval, milk production, and calf growth? Similarly, what are the effects of nutrition on milk composition? Milk quality comparisons should be carried out on the milk of wild buffalo and those living in different forms of captivity (game ranches, farms and zoos). Apart from the scientific importance of these questions, they could lead to the formulation of standards for the nutrient requirements for African buffalo based on real research on buffalo rather than on comparative nutrition from cattle or water buffalo (as done at present). This is a common problem in wildlife ecology, and nutritional knowledge is detailed enough only in deer to have proper feeding standards (e.g. Hynd, 2019, p. 263 ff; Anonymous, 2020; Kim et al., 2020; Bao et al., 2021).

8. The former Resource Ecology Group under H.H.T. Prins has most consistently reported on forage quality parameters as espoused by Peter Van Soest (so, apart from crude protein, potassium, phosphorus, digestibility parameters such as neutral digestive fibre (NDF) and acid digestive fibre (ADF), but also in-vivo digestibility using rumen fluid; Van Soest, 1994). An important caveat is that the rumen fluids came from domestic cattle, and that NDF and ADF calibration was never done with African buffalo (or other African large mammals with the exception of blue wildebeest). To really understand buffalo fitness or merely performance, it is of paramount importance to establish a captive group of buffalo on which depth nutritional measurements can be done. There is not much known about the need for micro-nutrients either, and there are no feeding standards.

9. The reliance on opioids for buffalo immobilization (and other large mammals) is still enormous. Veterinary authorities and regulators are making very little progress to get rid of these substances that are very

dangerous to animals and humans. Similarly, we know little of the health effects of the use of helicopters for the mass capture of buffalo herds, and we are not aware of reliable and stress-free alternatives under development.

Unknown Knowns – Evidence-Based Scientific Knowledge on Buffalo That We Appear To Have Forgotten

The collective of buffalo scientists did not signal many insights that were forgotten. Of course, this may simply mean that this older knowledge truly has been forgotten or, alternatively, that the corpus of knowledge that has been garnered over the last decades is well integrated into our present-day knowledge. Finally, it may indicate that we have collectively reached the verdict that much of the older knowledge does not meet our standards and is thus rejected. However, there are three knowledge domains that were flagged as probably forgotten.

i.   There was possibly good knowledge of pastoral systems in which buffalo also could find a place, or, alternatively, good knowledge of systems that could not accommodate buffalo. If this knowledge exists or existed, it is probably indigenous knowledge of integrated pastoral systems tolerant/intolerant of buffalo. If such indigenous knowledge (still) exists, it is extremely likely that it was never written down and thus would need a socio-anthropological approach. If this knowledge could be 'tapped', or somehow 'resurrected', it could provide valuable insights into future land use possibilities.

ii. In contrast, the second field of knowledge that appears to have been forgotten can be found in the scientific literature. This relates to the bioenergetics of herbivores, including African buffalo. This field is, however, getting renewed attention (see e.g. Malishev and Kramer-Schadt, 2021). The great measuring systems of herbivores in metabolic chambers that were extremely important for understanding the physiology of ruminants (e.g. Blaxter, 1966; Moen, 1973) were hardly used for large African mammals. The great exception was the work of Martyn Murray. Careful feeding experiments of wild herbivores in captivity have been extremely rare (but see e.g. Murray and Brown, 1993) even though very important insights were obtained from shot individuals (e.g. Gordon and Illius, 1996). Much is known about domestic ruminants and small lagomorphs and geese, but we know little about large tropical wild ruminants (see e.g. Illius and Jessop, 1996). Proper measurements of energy expenditure of wild ruminants are rare, and non-existent for African buffalo.

Work that was nearly forgotten concerned the horns of bovids as possible cooling organs (Taylor, 1966; see also Picard et al., 1999; Cain et al., 2006), which was not used in some important reviews on thermal adaptation (e.g. McKinley et al., 2018) or just mentioned in passing (e.g. Henning et al., 2018), and experimental evidence has hardly been collected since (see Knierim et al., 2015). Many other important works on thermoregulation and water usage from the early 1970s by scientists like Taylor (Taylor, 1969, 1970a, 1970b; Taylor and Lyman, 1972; Taylor et al., 1969) deserve to be integrated better into tropical ungulate ecology, and especially that of the African buffalo. The current generation is, however, exploring this (e.g. Hetem et al., 2009, 2010, 2013; Shrestha et al., 2012, 2014; Strauss et al., 2016).

Lastly in this category is the non-use of non-Anglophone published literature. A good case in point are the books of Riviere (1978), De Vries and Djitèye (1982) and Boudet (1984) on forage and foraging, and those on parasites (e.g. Troncy, 1982).

iii. A third issue that has been flagged is the knowledge that is or was locked in the grey literature. Le Houérou's (1980) review of the knowledge on browse in Africa perhaps still has not been surpassed, but in July 2022 it had been cited only 149 times. Knowledge that remains hidden in the grey literature is especially relevant for wildlife inventories, game censuses and pest control reports in the archives of ministries or of consulting companies. All of this contributes to intergenerational amnesia and to the so-called 'shifting baseline syndrome' (e.g. Papworth et al., 2009; Soga and Gaston, 2009; Prins and De Jong, 2022).

Unknown Unknowns – Knowledge That, Once Obtained, Will Upset Our Present Thinking, Perhaps About African Buffalo, Perhaps About Ecology Evolution, or Aspects of Veterinary Sciences

We share these 'unknowns' without too much comment, but we hope that some of these thoughts may influence your own thinking and creativity.

Overarching in our thinking is Darwinism, which represents life as a continuous struggle, and which leaves scientists to think in terms of functionality and (negative) selection. To what extent does this paradigm cause us to overlook or misinterpret natural patterns and processes? The central tenet is that many features of an organism are not necessarily adaptive but may arise as a by-product of evolution, whatever their subsequent exaptive utility (Gould 1979; Gould and Lewontin, 1979). For example, it is assumed too easily that ungulates have coevolved with their food, yet the average duration of existence of a large mammalian chronospecies is about 1.5 million years (Prins and Gordon, 2023) while that of plant chronospecies is about 10 times longer (cf. Stanley, 1978). Plant families arise much slower than may be thought (see Harris and Davies, 2016). A trait-based approach may give false certainty (cf. Gordon and Prins, 2019), as many traits are interrelated and should not be viewed in isolation as promoted by the 'adaptationists'.

Much selection took place during the bull market for 'trophy animals', where especially in South Africa much effort was spent on breeding bulls with massive horns. We know very little of the possible pleiotropic effects of genes (or of proteins; pleiotropy is the property of a single gene or protein to act in a multiplicity of ways). If these occur in African buffalo, they immediately throw a stark light on the basis of the selection for adaptability of traits (see previous paragraph). In cattle, these pleiotropic effects have now been discovered (see e.g. Bolormaa et al., 2014; Saatchi et al., 2014; Xiang et al., 2021). It is intriguing to learn that many QTL (quantitative trait locus, a section of DNA that correlates quantitatively with phenotype) effects are linked to weight at birth, age of weaning, weaning weight and carcass weight in cattle, and that pleiotropy is involved (Saatchi et al., 2014; Gershoni et al., 2021; Li et al., 2021; Tiplady et al., 2021; Widmer et al., 2021). One may also assume that these vital life-history parameters are governed in a similar way in African buffalo. With the effects of inbreeding on the genetic make-up of the species and calving and weaning percentages, the lack of connectivity between buffalo populations across the continent may thus affect the essential life history of the remnant populations. We would think that an effective and rapid first approach would be to assume that genes and QTLs that have been discovered in cattle could be looked for as candidate genes in African buffalo. A next question to address would be: after what level of 'breeding' is a buffalo no longer 'natural' and thus lost to conservation? (See Child et al., 2019). We thus advise much caution when breeding for 'maximum trophy value', especially when the spill-back of animals into nature is not rigorously prevented.

Because African buffalo are very distantly related to other Bovini, and perhaps should not even be viewed as bovine but as boselaphine (Chapter 2), it is unlikely that 'genetic pollution' will occur at the level of interspecies hybridization. At the level of crossings between animals from widely different locations, as was done for the breeding of 'better' trophy buffalo (e.g. buffalo from Tanzania and Zimbabwe bred in South Africa), we know next to nothing. The genetic distance is not small (see Chapter 3). It is thus not clear really why IUCN voices concerns because the so-called intra-taxon biodiversity in reality may be minimal. Moreover, the suggested argument concerning the associated growing risk of diminishing the capacity of the taxon to resist 'all sorts of shocks, either expected or not expected' if buffalo from different regions within the same taxon ('*Syncerus caffer caffer*') are crossed, is countervailed by concepts of hybrid vigour. In red deer (*Cervus elaphus*) this type of crossbreeding has been measured and evaluated (De Jong et al., 2020), but not in buffalo. We thus call for an in-depth evaluation of this issue, taking into account societal effects, conservation considerations and genetics.

This crossbreeding and ranching of African buffalo may, under as yet unknown circumstances, perhaps lead to a change of perspective of wild-life versus domestic animals. For 150 years, the Midwest of the United States was nicknamed the '*Red Meat Republic*' (Specht, 2019; Dolan, 2021), yet it became possible to 'bring back the bison'. What would happen if in some African cultures the societal perceptions of 'bringing back the African buffalo' took hold? Would that be possible through greater use of communal land rather than limiting protected areas? That would herald a societal earth slide away from seeing wildlife merely as '*nyama*' (in kiSwahili, 'game' [alive] and 'meat' [the dead product]), towards a highly valued, iconic, cultural symbol for a form of African Renaissance. What if, as has rarely happened, an African leader actually embraced the conservation, sustainable use and pride of African wildlife?

This issue is important, because currently cattle populations are supplanting those of buffalo across much of Africa. In West and Central Africa this process nearly came to its fulfilment (Chapter 4; Scholte et al., 2022). The consequences of this replacement – from grazing by a once-dominant wild herbivore to its domestic surrogate – on soil, animal ecologies, resilience and animal and human health are totally unknown, although it has been speculated about through what was termed 'holistic management' (see Savory, 1983). Conversely, we also know next to nothing about the effects of compartmentalization of natural habitats and reinforcement (through protection) of buffalo enclaves on 'mini-ecosystems' (i.e. small protected or small game farms) from a variety of perspectives, including health and disease. There is much ecological thinking about the effects of isolation (and shrinking) of protected areas (based on Island Theory; e.g. Prins and Olff, 1998; Olff et al., 2002), but we are not aware of so-called 'before–after' evidence-based comparisons of ecosystem functioning during the process of this isolation and shrinking of protected areas with African buffalo.

The most extreme 'unknown unknown' could be this: what would happen if the proverbial black swan event occurred that conceivably could knock the whole wildlife system off its axis? From the experience of COVID-19, one may deduce that some horizon scanning to create anticipatory awareness (and perhaps the development of early warning systems) to build system recoverability after a major disturbance of nature and its wildlife is needed. Ecosystem managers should, we think, engage much more in scenario-thinking like big industry does (Chapter 18). We could possibly anticipate the effects of four major processes that take place in savanna Africa, namely rising CO_2 levels, changing weather systems, woody thickening which seem to supress the grass layer and probably African buffalo numbers, and the human population explosion with associated land hunger and need for fuel wood. Buffalo may feature in the development of scenarios not only as a casualty but perhaps also as some ecosystem architect (Prins and Van Oeveren, 2014).

Perhaps one day we will finally come to grips with the fact that we do not know much about buffalo communication (Figure 17.2). We hardly understand their cognitive processes, cognitive maps, or communal decision making (cf. Prins, 1996). Like most mammals, it is very likely that their sense of smell is linked to their perception of other buffalo, the world, and their detection of predators and strangers. This world of pheromones and smells is for us a closed book, but the emergence of 'electronic noses' may open this world. Indeed, dogs have learned to understand our language (e.g. Grassmann, 2014; Reeve and Jacques, 2022), while we – with our 'superior' brains and AI tools – do not understand theirs (e.g. Harris, 2017). When will we then understand African buffalo?

The number of doctoral candidates needed to answer the research questions presented in this chapter must be in the order of 100 or more (as compared to the 30-odd so far); after they are done, we definitely will be closer to understanding this splendid species. But truly

Figure 17.2 Herd of West African savanna buffalo, Konkombri Hunting Area, Benin. © Christophe Morio.

understanding your partner and family takes a lifetime of study, and be honest – did you succeed?

Acknowledgements

We are happy to recognize the input that we received from (alphabetically on given name) Craig Shepstone, Elodie Wielgus, John Hearne, Joost de Jong, Louw Hoffman, Mario Melletti, Mike Peel, Richard Fynn, Richard Kock and Thomas Breuer. We appreciate their collective knowledge and insights. Grace Delobel improved the clarity of the text, for which we thank her.

References

Abouelfetouh, M.M., L. Liu, E. Salah, et al. (2021). The effect of xylazine premedication on the dose and quality of anesthesia induction with alfaxalone in goats. *Animals* **11**(3): 723.

Accatino, F. and C. De Michele (2016). Interpreting woody cover data in tropical and sub-tropical areas: comparison between the equilibrium and the non-equilibrium assumption. *Ecological Complexity* **25**: 60–67.

ACSS (Africa Centre for Strategic Studies) (2021). How global warming threatens human security in Africa. https://reliefweb.int/report/world/how-global-warming-threatens-human-security-africa#:~:text=In%20East%20Africa%2C%20Uganda%2C%20Ethiopia,kill%20100%20people%20or%20more.

Aikpo, F.H., M.D.S. Ahouanse, L. Agbandji, et al. (2017). Assessment of contamination of soil by pesticides in Djidja's cotton area in Benin. *International Journal of Advanced Engineering Research and Science* **4**(7): 237202.

Anonymous (2020). *Animal Care Standards: Red Deer*. Middleburg, VA: Humane Farm Animal Care.

Archie, E.A., J.E. Maldonado, J.A. Hollister-Smith, et al. (2008). Fine-scale population genetic structure in a fission–fusion society. *Molecular Ecology* **17**: 2666–2679.

Badlangana, N.L., J.W. Adams and P.R. Manger (2011). A comparative assessment of the size of the frontal air sinus in the giraffe (*Giraffa camelopardalis*). *Anatomical Record (Hoboken)* **294**: 931–940.

Baker, J.E. (1997). Trophy hunting as a sustainable use of wildlife resources in southern and eastern Africa. *Journal of Sustainable Tourism* **5**: 306–321.

Bao, K., X. Wang, K. Wang, et al. (2021). Energy and protein requirements for the maintenance of growing male sika deer (*Cervus nippon*). *Frontiers in Veterinary Science* **14**: 1047.

Barshad, G., S. Marom, T. Cohen and D. Mishmar (2018). Mitochondrial DNA transcription and its regulation: an evolutionary perspective. *Trends in Genetics* **34**: 682–692.

Basu, N., M. Horvat, D.C. Evers, et al. (2018). A state-of-the-science review of mercury biomarkers in human populations worldwide between 2000 and 2018. *Environmental Health Perspectives* **126**: 106001.

Baudron, F., M. Corbeels, F. Monicat and K.E. Giller (2009). Cotton expansion and biodiversity loss in African savannahs, opportunities and challenges for conservation agriculture: a review paper based on two case studies. *Biodiversity and Conservation* **18**: 2625–2644.

Beerda, B., J. Wyszynska-Koko, M.F.W. Te Pas, et al. (2008). Expression profiles of genes regulating dairy cow fertility: recent findings, ongoing activities and future possibilities. *Animal* **2**: 1158–1167.

Beesley, N.J., D.J. Williams, S. Paterson and J. Hodgkinson (2017). *Fasciola hepatica* demonstrates high levels of genetic diversity, a lack of population structure and high gene flow: possible implications for drug resistance. *International Journal for Parasitology* **47**: 11–20.

Bekhuis, P.D.B.M., C. de Jong and H.H.T. Prins (2008). Diet selection and density estimates of forest buffalo in Campo-Ma'an National Park, Cameroon. *African Journal of Ecology* **46**: 668–675.

Benoit, J., L.J. Legendre, A.A. Farke, et al. (2020). A test of the lateral semicircular canal correlation to head posture, diet and other biological traits in "ungulate" mammals. *Scientific Reports* **10**: 1–22.

Biermann, K., S. Hungerbühler, R. Mischke and S.B. Kästner (2012). Sedative, cardiovascular, haematologic and biochemical effects of four different drug combinations administered intramuscularly in cats. *Veterinary Anaesthesia and Analgesia* **39**: 137–150.

Blank, D.A. (2021). Artiodactyl vocalization. In C.S. Rosenfeld and F. Hoffmann (Eds.), *Neuroendocrine Regulation of Animal Vocalization*. New York: Academic Press, pp. 159–188.

Blaxter, K.L. (1966). *The Energy Metabolism of Ruminants*. London: Hutchinson.

Bolormaa, S., J.E. Pryce, A. Reverter, et al. (2014). A multi-trait, meta-analysis for detecting pleiotropic polymorphisms for stature, fatness and reproduction in beef cattle. *PLoS Genetics* **10**(3): e1004198.

Bond, W.J. and G.F. Midgley (2000). A proposed CO_2-controlled mechanism of woody plant invasion in grasslands and savannas. *Global Change Biology* **6**: 865–869.

Borrat, X., M. Ubre, R. Risco, et al. (2019). Computerized tests to evaluate recovery of cognitive function after deep sedation with propofol and remifentanil for colonoscopy. *Journal of Clinical Monitoring and Computing* **33**: 107–113.

Boudet G. (1984). *Manuel sur les Pâturages Tropicaux et les Cultures Fourragères (4ème édition révisée)*. Paris: Institut d'Elevage et de Médecine Vétérinaire des Pays Tropicaux.

Budischak, S.A., A.E. Jolles and V. Ezenwa (2012). Direct and indirect costs of co-infection in the wild: linking gastrointestinal parasite communities, host hematology, and immune function. *International Journal for Parasitology: Parasites and Wildlife* **1**: 2–12.

Cain, J.W., P.R. Krausman, S.S. Rosenstock and J.C. Turner (2006). Mechanisms of thermoregulation and water balance in desert ungulates. *Wildlife Society Bulletin* **34**: 570–581.

Cesar, A.S., L.C. Regitano, M.D. Poleti, et al. (2016). Differences in the skeletal muscle transcriptome profile associated with extreme values of fatty acids content. *BMC Genomics* **17**: 1–16.

Child, M.F., S.J. Selier, F.G. Radloff, et al. (2019). A framework to measure the wildness of managed large vertebrate populations. *Conservation Biology* **33**: 1106–1119.

Clegg, K. (1994). *Density and Feeding Habits of Elk and Deer in Relation to Livestock Disturbance*. PhD thesis, Utah State University.

Clutton-Brock, T.H., F.E. Guinness and S.D. Albon (1982). *Red Deer: Behavior and Ecology of Two Sexes*. Chicago: Chicago University Press.

Cock, G., Z. Blakeney, J.A. Hernandez and S. DeNotta (2022). Opioid-free sedation for atlantoaxial cerebrospinal fluid collection in adult horses. *Journal of Veterinary Internal Medicine* **36**: 1812–1819.

Conradt, L. and Roper, T.J. (2003). Group decision-making in animals. *Nature* **421**: 155–158.

Conradt, L. and Roper, T.J. (2005). Consensus decision making in animals. *Trends in Ecology and Evolution* **20**: 449–456.

COP Decision VII/12: see www.cbd.int/decision/cop/?id=7749. This refers to the Convention on Biological Diversity.

Cornélis, D., S. Benhamou, G. Janeau, et al. (2011). Spatiotemporal dynamics of forage and water resources shape space use of West African savanna buffaloes. *Journal of Mammalogy* **92**: 1287–1297.

Cornélis, D., K. Melletti, L. Korte, et al. (2014). African buffalo *Syncerus caffer* (Sparrman, 1779). In M. Melletti and J. Burton (Eds.), *Ecology, Evolution and Behaviour of Wild Cattle: Implications for Conservation*. Cambridge: Cambridge University Press, pp. 326–372.

Couzin, I.D., J. Krause, N.R. Franks and S.A. Levin (2005). Effective leadership and decision-making in animal groups on the move. *Nature* **433**: 513–516.

Cromsigt, J.P., H.H.T. Prins and H. Olff (2009). Habitat heterogeneity as a driver of ungulate diversity and distribution patterns: interaction of body mass and digestive strategy. *Diversity and Distributions* **15**: 513–522.

Cross, P.C., J.O. Lloyd-Smith, J.A. Bowers, et al. (2004). Integrating association data and disease dynamics in a social ungulate: bovine tuberculosis in African buffalo in the Kruger National Park. *Annales Zoologici Fennici* **41**: 879–892.

Cross, P.C., T.G. Creech, M.R. Ebinger, et al. (2012). Wildlife contact analysis: emerging methods, questions, and challenges. *Behavioral Ecology and Sociobiology* **66**: 1437–1447.

Curtin, J. (1940). *Memoirs of Jeremiah Curtin, edited with notes and introduction by Joseph Schafer*. Madison: State Historical Society of Wisconsin.

Dave, C. and Y. Jhala (2011). Is competition with livestock detrimental for native wild ungulates? A case study of chital (*Axis axis*) in Gir Forest, India. *Journal of Tropical Ecology* **27**: 239–247.

Davis, G.H., M.C. Crofoot and D.R. Farine (2018). Estimating the robustness and uncertainty of animal social networks using different observational methods. *Animal Behaviour* **141**: 29–44.

De Jong, J.F., P. van Hooft, H.J. Megens, et al. (2020). Fragmentation and translocation distort the genetic landscape of ungulates: red deer in the Netherlands. *Frontiers in Ecology and Evolution* **8**: 365.

De Jong, J.F. and H.H.T. Prins (2023). Why there are no modern equids living in tropical lowland rainforests. In: H.H.T. Prins and I.J. Gordon (Eds.), *The Equids: A Suite of Splendid Species*. Cham: Springer Nature.

Delahay, R.J., S. Langton, G.C. Smith, et al. (2000). The spatio-temporal distribution of *Mycobacterium bovis* (bovine tuberculosis) infection in a high-density badger population. *Journal of Animal Ecology* **69**: 428–441.

De Vries, F.P. and M.A. Djiteye (1982). *La Productivité des Pâturages Sahéliens: une étude des sols, des végétations et de l'exploitation de cette ressource naturelle*. Wageningen: PUDOC.

Dietz, R., C. Sonne, N. Basu, et al. (2013). What are the toxicological effects of mercury in Arctic biota? *Science of the Total Environment* **443**: 775–790.

Dlamini, T.S. (2011). *The Economics of Converting a Sheep Farm into a Springbuck (Antidorcas marsupialis) Ranch in Graaf-Reinet: A Simulation Analysis*. PhD thesis, Rhodes University.

Dolan, K.C. (2021). *Cattle Country: Livestock in the Cultural Imagination*. Lincoln: University of Nebraska Press.

Drackley, J.K., S.S. Donkin and C.K. Reynolds (2006). Major advances in fundamental dairy cattle nutrition. *Journal of Dairy Science* **89**: 1324–1336.

Eagles-Smith, C.A., J.G. Wiener, C.S. Eckley, et al. (2016). Mercury in western North America: a synthesis of environmental contamination, fluxes, bioaccumulation, and risk to fish and wildlife. *Science of the Total Environment* **568**: 1213–1226.

Ellis, J.E. and D.M. Swift (1988). Stability of African pastoral ecosystems: alternate paradigms and implications for development. *Rangeland Ecology and Management/Journal of Range Management Archives* **41**: 450–459.

Engler, J.O., and H. von Wehrden (2018). Global assessment of the non-equilibrium theory of rangelands: revisited and refined. *Land Use Policy* **70**: 479–484.

Ezenwa, V.O., R.S. Etienne, G. Luikart, et al. (2010). Hidden consequences of living in a wormy world: nematode-induced immune suppression facilitates tuberculosis invasion in African buffalo. *The American Naturalist* **176**: 613–624.

Forbes, B.C., M. Bölter, L. Müller-Wille, et al. (2006). *Reindeer Management in Northernmost Europe: Linking Practical and Scientific Knowledge in Social–Ecological Systems*. Berlin: Springer.

Foster, K.R., C. Davidson, R.N. Tanna and D. Spink (2019). Introduction to the virtual special issue monitoring ecological responses to air quality and atmospheric deposition in the Athabasca Oil Sands region the Wood Buffalo Environmental Association's Forest health monitoring program. *Science of the Total Environment* **686**: 345–359.

Fuller, A., R.S. Hetem, S.K. Maloney and D. Mitchell (2014). Adaptation to heat and water shortage in large, arid-zone mammals. *Physiology* **29**: 159–167.

Fuller, A., D. Mitchell, S.K. Maloney, et al. (2021). How dryland mammals will respond to climate change: the effects of body size, heat load and a lack of food and water. *Journal of Experimental Biology* **224**(Suppl. 1): jeb238113.

Fynn, R.W.S., M. Murray-Hudson, M. Dhliwayo and P. Scholte (2015). African wetlands and their seasonal use by wild and domestic herbivores. *Wetlands Ecology and Management* **23**: 559–581.

Galarza Vallejo, A., M.C. Kroes, E. Rey, et al. (2019). Propofol-induced deep sedation reduces emotional episodic memory reconsolidation in humans. *Science Advances* **5**(3): eaav3801.

Gandiwa, E., S. Sprangers, S. van Bommel, et al. (2014). Spill-over effect in media framing: representations of wildlife conservation in Zimbabwean and international media, 1989–2010. *Journal for Nature Conservation* **22**: 413–423.

Gershoni, M., J.I. Weller and E. Ezra (2021). Genetic and genome-wide association analysis of yearling weight gain in Israel Holstein dairy calves. *Genes* **12**(5): 708.

Gillson, L. (2004). Testing non-equilibrium theories in savannas: 1400 years of vegetation change in Tsavo National Park, Kenya. *Ecological Complexity* **1**: 281–298.

Gordon, I.J. and A.W. Illius (1996). The nutritional ecology of African ruminants: a reinterpretation. *Journal of Animal Ecolog* **65**: 18–28.

Gordon, I.J. and H.H.T. Prins (2019). Browsers and grazers drive the dynamics of ecosystems. In I.J. Gordon and H.H.T. Prins (Eds.), *The Ecology of Grazing and Browsing II*, Ecological Studies Vol. 239. Berlin: Springer, pp. 405–444.

Gosling, W.D., C.S. Miller, T.M. Shanahan, et al. (2022). A stronger role for long-term moisture change than for CO_2 in determining tropical woody vegetation change. *Science* **376**: 653–656.

Gould, S.J. (1997). The exaptive excellence of spandrels as a term and prototype. *Proceedings of the National Academy of Sciences* **94**: 10750–10755.

Gould, S.J. and R.C. Lewontin (1979). The spandrels of San Marco and the Panglossian paradigm. *Proceedings of the Royal Society of London, Series B: Biological Sciences* **205**: 581–598.

Graber, M., J. Euzéby, P.M. Troncy and J. Thal (1972). Parasites recueillis en Afrique Centrale dans l'appareil circulatoire du buffle (*Bubalus (syncerus) caffer*, Sparrman 1779) et de diverses antilopes. *Revue d'Élevage et de Médecine Vétérinaire des Pays Tropicaux* **25**: 219–243.

Grassmann, S. (2014). Language learning in dogs. In P.J. Brooks and V. Kempe (Eds.), *Encyclopaedia of Language Development*. Los Angeles: SAGE, pp. 332–334.

Hagen, P.E. and M.P. Walls (2005). The Stockholm Convention on persistent organic pollutants. *Natural Resources and Environment* **19**: 49–52.

Hagen, R., S. Kramer-Schadt, L. Fahse and M. Heurich (2014). Population control based on abundance estimates: frequency does not compensate for uncertainty. *Ecological Complexity* **20**: 43–50.

Hammond, J.A. (1972). Infections with *Fasciola* spp. in wildlife in Africa. *Tropical Animal Health and Production* **4**: 1–13.

Harris, L.T. (2017). Do we understand what it means for dogs to experience emotion? *Animal Sentience* **2**(14): 8.

Harris, L.W. and T.J. Davies (2016). A complete fossil-calibrated phylogeny of seed plant families as a tool for comparative analyses: testing the 'time for speciation' hypothesis. *PLoS One* **11**(10): e0162907.

Hassen, A., M. Muche, A.M. Muasya and B.A. Tsegay (2022). Exploration of traditional plant-based medicines used for livestock ailments in north-eastern Ethiopia. *South African Journal of Botany* **146**: 230–242.

Hearne, J.W., R. Lamberson and P. Goodman (1996). Optimising the offtake of large herbivores from a multi-species community. *Ecological Modelling* **92**: 225–233.

Hearne, J.W., J.L. Korrûbel and K.J. Koch (2000). Modelling to optimise consumptive use of game. *Annals of Operations Research* **95**: 269–284.

Hempson, G.P., S. Archibald, W.J. Bond, et al. (2015). Ecology of grazing lawns in Africa. *Biological Reviews* **90**: 979–994.

Henning, B., B. de Sá Carvalho, J.L. Boldrini, et al. (2018). Statistical estimation of surface heat control and exchange in endotherms. *Open Journal of Statistics* **8**: 220.

Hetem, R.S., B.A. de Witt, L.G. Fick, et al. (2009). Body temperature, thermoregulatory behaviour and pelt characteristics of three colour morphs of springbok (*Antidorcas marsupialis*). *Comparative Biochemistry and Physiology Part A: Molecular and Integrative Physiology* **152**: 379–388.

Hetem, R.S., W.M. Strauss, L.G. Fick, et al. (2010). Variation in the daily rhythm of body temperature of free-living Arabian oryx (*Oryx leucoryx*): does water limitation drive heterothermy? *Journal of Comparative Physiology B* **180**: 1111–1119.

Hetem, R.S., D. Mitchell, B.A. de Witt, et al. (2013). Cheetah do not abandon hunts because they overheat. *Biology Letters* **9**: 20130472.

Hewitt, D.G. (2011). *Biology and Management of White-Tailed Deer*. Boca Raton: CRC Press.

Hofmann, R.R. (1973). *The Ruminant Stomach: Stomach Structure and Feeding Habits of East African Game Ruminants*. Nairobi: East African Literature Bureau.

Houndji, M.A., I. Imorou Toko, L. Guedegba, et al. (2020). Joint toxicity of two phytosanitary molecules, lambda-cyhalothrin and acetamiprid, on African catfish (*Clarias gariepinus*) juveniles. *Journal of Environmental Science and Health, Part B* **55**: 669–676.

Hubbell, J.A.E. and W.W. Muir (2006). Antagonism of detomidine sedation in the horse using intravenous tolazoline or atipamezole. *Equine Veterinary Journal* **38**: 238–241.

Hurt, R. and P. Ravn (2000). Hunting and its benefits: an overview of hunting in Africa with special reference to Tanzania. In H.H.T. Prins, G.J. Grootenhuis and T.T. Dolan (Eds.), *Wildlife Conservation by Sustainable Use*. Dordrecht: Kluwer, pp. 295–313.

Hynd, P. (2019). *Animal Nutrition: From Theory to Practice*. Canberra: CSIRO Publishing.

Illius, A.W. and N.S. Jessop (1996). Metabolic constraints on voluntary intake in ruminants. *Journal of Animal Science* **74**: 3052–3062.

IPCC (2022). *Climate Change 2022: Impacts, Adaptation, and Vulnerability. Contribution of Working Group II to the Sixth Assessment Report of the Intergovernmental Panel on Climate Change* (edited by H.-O. Pörtner, D.C. Roberts, M. Tignor, et al.). Cambridge: Cambridge University Press.

Jacoby, D.M., E.J. Brooks, D.P. Croft and D.W. Sims (2012). Developing a deeper understanding of animal movements and spatial dynamics through novel application of network analyses. *Methods in Ecology and Evolution* **3**: 574–583.

Joubert, J.W., M.K. Luhandjula, O. Ncube, et al. (2007). An optimization model for the management of a South African game ranch. *Agricultural Systems* **92**: 223–239.

Kgope, B.S., W.J. Bond and G.F. Midgley (2010). Growth responses of African savanna trees implicate atmospheric [CO_2] as a driver of past and current changes in savanna tree cover. *Austral Ecology* **35**: 451–463.

Kim, K.W., J. Lee, D.G. Kim, et al. (2020). Determination of protein requirements for maintenance of elk doe. *Journal of The Korean Society of Grassland and Forage Science* **40**: 177–181.

Kirkpatrick, B.W. (2015). Single genes in animal breeding. *Molecular and Quantitative Animal Genetics* **2**: 177.

Knierim, U., N. Irrgang and B.A. Roth (2015). To be or not to be horned: consequences in cattle. *Livestock Science* **179**: 29–37.

Koné, W.M., M. Vargas and J. Keiser (2012). Anthelmintic activity of medicinal plants used in Côte d'Ivoire for treating parasitic diseases. *Parasitology Research* **110**: 2351–2362.

Kosgei, C. (2014). *Larvicidal activity of extracts from* Lippia kituiensis, Lippia javanica, Phytolacca dodecandra, Pittosphorum viridiflorum *and* Synadenium compactum *against* Rhipicephalus appendiculatus. PhD thesis, Egerton University.

Leader-Williams, N. (1988). *Reindeer on South Georgia: The Ecology of an Introduced Population*. Cambridge: Cambridge University Press.

Le Boeuf, B.J. and R.M. Laws (1994). *Elephant Seals: Population Ecology, Behavior, and Physiology*. Berkeley: University of California Press.

Le Boeuf, B.J. and B.J. Le Boeuf (2021). *Elephant Seals*. Cambridge: Cambridge University Press.

Le Houérou, H.N. (1980). *Browse in Africa: The Current State of Knowledge*. Addis Ababa: International Livestock Centre for Africa.

Leweri, C.M., G.S. Bartzke, M.J. Msuha and A.C. Treydte (2022). Spatial and seasonal group size variation of wild mammalian herbivores in multiple use landscapes of the Ngorongoro Conservation Area, Tanzania. *PLoS One* **17**: e0267082.

Li, B., P.M. VanRaden, D.J. Null, et al. (2021). Major quantitative trait loci influencing milk production and conformation traits in Guernsey dairy cattle detected on *Bos taurus* autosome 19. *Journal of Dairy Science* **104**: 550–560.

Lindsey, P.A., P.A. Roulet and S.S. Romanach (2007). Economic and conservation significance of the trophy hunting industry in sub-Saharan Africa. *Biological Conservation* **134**: 455–469.

Mace, R. (1990). Pastoralist herd compositions in unpredictable environments: a comparison of model predictions and data from camel-keeping groups. *Agricultural Systems* **33**: 1–11.

Mace, R. and A. Houston (1989). Pastoralist strategies for survival in unpredictable environments: a model of herd composition that maximises household viability. *Agricultural Systems* **31**: 185–204.

Malishev, M. and S. Kramer-Schadt (2021). Movement, models, and metabolism: individual-based energy budget models as next-generation extensions for predicting animal movement outcomes across scales. *Ecological Modelling* **441**: 109413.

Markham, K.E. and F. Sangermano (2018). Evaluating wildlife vulnerability to mercury pollution from artisanal and small-scale gold mining in Madre de Dios, Peru. *Tropical Conservation Science* **11**: 1940082918794320.

Mayaka, T.B., T. Hendricks, T. Wesseler and H.H.T. Prins (2005). Improving the benefits from wildlife harvesting in Northern Cameroon: a co-management perspective. *Ecological Economics* **54**: 67–80.

McKinley, M.J., D. Martelli, G.L. Pennington, et al. (2018). Integrating competing demands of osmoregulatory and thermoregulatory homeostasis. *Physiology* **33**: 170–181.

Milner-Gulland, E.J. and K. Shea (2017). Embracing uncertainty in applied ecology. *The Journal of Applied Ecology* **54**: 2063–2068.

Moen, A.N. (1973). *Wildlife Ecology: An Analytical Approach*. San Francisco: Freeman.

Morellet, N., J.M. Gaillard, A.M. Hewison, et al. (2007). Indicators of ecological change: new tools for managing populations of large herbivores. *Journal of Applied Ecology* **44**: 634–643.

Moritz, M., E. Soma, P. Scholte, et al. (2010). An integrated approach to modeling grazing pressure in pastoral systems: the case of the Logone floodplain (Cameroon). *Human Ecology* **38**: 775–789.

Moritz, M., I.M. Hamilton, A.J. Yoak, et al. (2015). Simple movement rules result in ideal free distribution of mobile pastoralists. *Ecological Modelling* **305**: 54–63.

Murray, M.G. and D. Brown (1993). Niche separation of grazing ungulates in the Serengeti: an experimental test. *Journal of Animal Ecology* **62**: 380–389.

Muthoni, F.K., T.A. Groen, A.K. Skidmore and P. van Oel (2014). Ungulate herbivory overrides rainfall impacts on herbaceous regrowth and residual biomass in a key resource area. *Journal of Arid Environments* **100**: 9–17.

Mwakiwa, E. (2019). Optimisation of benefits from agriculture and wildlife land uses by wards in CAMPFIRE areas in Zimbabwe. *African Journal of Agricultural and Resource Economics* **14**: 120–136.

Mwakiwa, E., J.W. Hearne, J.D. Stigter, et al. (2016). Optimization of net returns from wildlife consumptive and non-consumptive uses by game reserve management. *Environmental Conservation* **43**: 128–139.

Nicol, A.U. and A.J. Morton (2020). Characteristic patterns of EEG oscillations in sheep (*Ovis aries*) induced by ketamine may explain the psychotropic effects seen in humans. *Scientific Reports* **10**: 1–10.

Odadi, W.O., M. Jain, S.E. Van Wieren, et al. (2011). Facilitation between bovids and equids in an African savanna. *Evolutionary Ecology Research* **13**: 37–252.

Olff, H., M.H. Ritchie and H.H.T. Prins (2002). Global environmental determinants of diversity in large herbivores. *Nature* **415**: 901–904.

Pan, Z., S. Li, Q. Liu, et al. (2018). Whole-genome sequences of 89 Chinese sheep suggest role of *RXFP2* in the development of unique horn phenotype as response to semi-feralization. *GigaScience* **7**(4): giy019.

Papworth, S.K., J. Rist, L. Coad and E.J. Milner-Gulland (2009). Evidence for shifting baseline syndrome in conservation. *Conservation Letters* **2**: 93–100.

Pati, M., G.S. Parida, K.D. Mandal and A. Raj (2020). Clinico-epidemiological study of industrial fluorosis in calves reared near aluminium smelter plant, at Angul, Odisha. *The Pharma Innovation Journal* **9**: 616–620.

Peel, M.J. and I.P. Smit (2020). Drought amnesia: lessons from protected areas in the eastern Lowveld of South Africa. *African Journal of Range and Forage Science* **37**: 81–92.

Pellikka, J., S. Kuikka, H. Lindén and O. Varis (2005). The role of game management in wildlife populations: uncertainty analysis of expert knowledge. *European Journal of Wildlife Research* **51**: 48–59.

Picard, K., D.W. Thomas, M. Festa-Bianchet, et al. (1999). Differences in the thermal conductance of tropical and temperate bovid horns. *Ecoscience* **6**: 148–158.

Poshiwa X., R.A. Groeneveld, I.M.A. Heitkönig, et al. (2013a). Reducing rural households' annual income fluctuations due to rainfall variation through diversification of wildlife use: portfolio theory in a case study of south eastern Zimbabwe. *Tropical Conservation Science* **6**: 201–220.

Poshiwa X., R.A. Groeneveld, I.M.A. Heitkönig, et al. (2013b). Wildlife as insurance against rainfall fluctuations in a semi-arid savanna setting of south-eastern Zimbabwe. *Tropical Conservation Science* **6**: 108–125.

Prins, H.H.T. (1989a). Condition changes and choice of social environment in African buffalo bulls. *Behaviour* **108**: 297–324.

Prins, H.H.T. (1989b). Buffalo herd structure and its repercussions for condition of individual African buffalo cows. *Ethology* **81**: 47–71.

Prins, H.H.T. (1996). *Behaviour and Ecology of the African Buffalo: Social Inequality and Decision Making*. London: Chapman & Hall.

Prins, H.H.T. (2016). Interspecific resource competition in antelopes: search for evidence. In J. Bro-Jorgensen and D.P. Mallon (Eds.), *Antelope Conservation: From Diagnosis to Action*. Conservation Science and Practice Series. Oxford: Wiley Blackwell, pp. 51–77.

Prins, H. H.T. and J.F. de Jong (2022). The ecohistory of Tanzania's northern Rift Valley – can one establish an objective baseline as endpoint for ecosystem restoration? In M. Bond, C. Kiffner and D. Lee (Eds.), *Tarangire: Human–Wildlife Coexistence in a Fragmented Landscape*. Cham: Springer Nature, pp. 129–161.

Prins, H.H.T. and I.J. Gordon (2014). A critique of ecological theory and a salute to natural history. In H.H.T. Prins and I.J. Gordon (Eds.), *Invasion Biology and Ecological Theory: Insights from a Continent in Transformation*. Cambridge: Cambridge University Press, pp. 497–516.

Prins, H.H.T. and I.J. Gordon (2023). Are equids evolutionary dead ends? In H.H.T. Prins and I.J. Gordon (Eds.), *The Equids: A Successful Suite of Species*. Cham: Springer Nature.

Prins, H.H.T. and H. Olff (1998). Species richness of African grazer assemblages: towards a functional explanation. In D.M. Newbery, H.H.T. Prins and N.D. Brown (Eds.), *Dynamics of Tropical Communities*. British Ecological Society Symposium Vol. 37. Oxford: Blackwell Science, pp. 449–490.

Prins, H.H.T. and H. van Oeveren (2014). Bovini as keystone species and landscape architects. In M. Melletti and J. Burton (Eds.), *Ecology, Evolution and Behaviour of Wild Cattle*. Cambridge: Cambridge University Press, pp. 21–29.

Prins, H.H.T. and A.R.E. Sinclair (2013). *Syncerus caffer* African buffalo. In J.S. Kingdon and M. Hoffmann (Eds.), *Mammals of Africa. Vol. 6. Pigs, Hippopotamuses, Cevrotain, Giraffes, Deer and Bovids*. London: Bloomsbury, pp. 125–136.

Prins, H.H.T., H.P. van der Jeugd and J.H. Beekman (1994). Elephant decline in Lake Manyara National Park, Tanzania. *African Journal of Ecology* **32**: 185–191.

Prins, H.H.T., J.G. Grootenhuis and T.T. Dolan (2000). *Conservation of Wildlife by Sustainable Use.* Boston: Kluwer Academic.

Ranjan, R., D. Swarup, B. Bhardwaj and R.C. Patra (2008). Level of certain micro and macro minerals in blood of cattle from fluoride polluted localities of Udaipur, India. *Bulletin of Environmental Contamination and Toxicology* **81**: 503–507.

Raubenheimer, S.L. and B.S. Ripley (2022). CO_2-stimulation of savanna tree seedling growth depends on interactions with local drivers. *Journal of Ecology* **110**: 1090–1101.

Reader, R.C., B.A. Barton and A.L. Abelson (2019). Comparison of two intramuscular sedation protocols on sedation, recovery and ease of venipuncture for cats undergoing blood donation. *Journal of Feline Medicine and Surgery* **21**: 95–102.

Reeve, C., and S. Jacques (2022). Responses to spoken words by domestic dogs: a new instrument for use with dog owners. *Applied Animal Behaviour Science* **246**: 105513.

Reich, M.H. (2021). *The Influence of Genetics on Horn Size in Bighorn Sheep.* MSc thesis, University of Alberta.

Riviere, R. (1978). *Manuel d'Alimentation des Ruminants Domestiques en Milieu Tropical (2ème édition).* Paris: Institut d'Elevage et de Médecine Vétérinaire des Pays Tropicaux.

Saatchi, M., R.D. Schnabel, J.F. Taylor and D.J. Garrick (2014). Large-effect pleiotropic or closely linked QTL segregate within and across ten US cattle breeds. *BMC Genomics* **15**: 1–17.

Sach, F., L. Yon, M.D. Henley, et al. (2020). Spatial geochemistry influences the home range of elephants. *Science of the Total Environment* **729**: 139066

Savory, A. (1983). The Savory grazing method or holistic resource management. *Rangelands Archives* **5**: 155–159.

Schalkwyk, D.L.V., K.W. McMillin, R.C. Witthuhn and L.C. Hoffman (2010). The contribution of wildlife to sustainable natural resource utilization in Namibia: a review. *Sustainability* **2**: 3479–3499.

Schauvliege, S., C. Cuypers, A. Michielsen, et al. (2019). How to score sedation and adjust the administration rate of sedatives in horses: a literature review and introduction of the Ghent Sedation Algorithm. *Veterinary Anaesthesia and Analgesia* **46**: 4–13.

Schieltz, J.M. and D.I. Rubenstein (2016). Evidence based review: positive versus negative effects of livestock grazing on wildlife. What do we really know? *Environmental Research Letters* **11**(11): 113003.

Scholte, P., and J. Brouwer (2008). Relevance of key resource areas for large-scale movements of livestock. In H.H.T. Prins and F. van Langevelde (Eds.), *Resource Ecology.* Dordrecht: Springer, pp. 211–232.

Scholte, P., O. Pays, S. Adam, et al. (2021). Conservation overstretch and long-term decline of wildlife and tourism in the Central African savannas. *Conservation Biology* **36**(2): e13860.

Shawiah, F.F.B. (2016). *Risk Management Strategies for Dealing with Unpredictable Risk in Saudi Arabian Organisations.* PhD thesis, University of Salford.

Shrestha, A.K., S.E. Wieren, F. van Langevelde, et al. (2012). Body temperature variation of South African antelopes in two climatically contrasting environments. *Journal of Thermal Biology* **37**: 171–178.

Shrestha, A.K., S.E. van Wieren, F. van Langevelde, et al. (2014). Larger antelopes are sensitive to heat stress throughout all seasons but smaller antelopes only during summer in an African semi-arid environment. *International Journal of Biometeorology* **58**: 41–49.

Sinclair, A.R.E. (1977). *The African buffalo. A Study of Resource Limitation of Populations.* Chicago: University of Chicago Press.

Singh, S.T., K. Dua, R. Singh, et al. (2018). Effects of drinking water defluoridation on mineral and haemato-biochemical status in fluorotic buffaloes. *Indian Journal of Animal Research* **52**: 1711–1714.

Sintayehu, D.W., H.H.T. Prins, I.M.A. Heitkönig and W.F. de Boer (2017a). Disease transmission in animal transfer networks. *Preventive Veterinary Medicine* **137**(part A): 36–42.

Sintayehu, D.W., I.M.A. Heitkönig, H.H.T. Prins, et al. (2017b). Effect of host diversity and species assemblage composition on bovine tuberculosis (bTB) risk in Ethiopian cattle. *Parasitology* **144**: 783–792.

Smith, G.C. and D. Wilkinson (2003). Modeling control of rabies outbreaks in red fox populations to evaluate culling, vaccination, and vaccination combined with fertility control. *Journal of Wildlife Diseases* **39**: 278–286.

Smitz, N., P. van Hooft, R. Heller, et al. (2016). Genome-wide single nucleotide polymorphism (SNP) identification and characterization in a non-model organism, the African buffalo (*Syncerus caffer*), using next generation sequencing. *Mammalian Biology* **81**: 595–603.

Snyman S., D. Sumba F. Vorhies, et al. (2021). State of the wildlife economy in Africa. African Leadership University, School of Wildlife Conservation, Kigali, Rwanda (unpublished).

Soga, M. and K.J. Gaston (2018). Shifting baseline syndrome: causes, consequences, and implications. *Frontiers in Ecology and the Environment* **16**: 222–230.

Specht, J. (2019). *Red Meat Republic: A Hoof-to- Table History of How Beef Changed America*. Princeton: Princeton University Press.

Stanley, S.M. (1978). Chronospecies' longevities, the origin of genera, and the punctuational model of evolution. *Paleobiology* **4**: 26–40.

Strauss, W.M., R.S. Hetem, D. Mitchell, et al. (2016). Three African antelope species with varying water dependencies exhibit similar selective brain cooling. *Journal of Comparative Physiology B* **186**: 527–540.

Swai, E.S. and R.T. Wilson (2017). Helminths and protozoa of the gastrointestinal tract of ruminants in Tanzania. *Animal Review* **4**: 21–34.

Taylor, C.R. (1966). The vascularity and possible thermoregulatory function of the horns in goats. *Physiological Zoology* **39**: 127–139.

Taylor, C.R. (1969). Metabolism, respiratory changes and water balance of an antelope, the eland. *American Journal of Physiology* **217**: 317–320.

Taylor, C.R. (1970a). Dehydration and heat: effects on temperature regulation of East African ungulates. *American Journal of Physiology* **219**: 1136–1139.

Taylor, C.R. (1970b). Strategies of temperature regulation: effects on evaporation in East African ungulates. *American Journal of Physiology* **219**: 1131–1135.

Taylor, C.R. and C.P. Lyman (1972). Heat storage in running antelopes: independence of brain and body temperatures. *American Journal of Physiology* **222**: 114–117.

Taylor, C.R., C.A. Spinage and C.P. Lyman (1969). Water relations of the waterbuck, an east African antelope. *American Journal of Physiology* **217**: 630–634.

Tiplady, K.M., T.J. Lopdell, E. Reynolds, et al. (2021). Sequence-based genome-wide association study of individual milk mid-infrared wavenumbers in mixed-breed dairy cattle. *Genetics Selection Evolution* **53**: 1–24.

Troncy, P.M. (1981). Les helminthoses du bétail et des oiseaux de basse-cour en Afrique Tropicale. In *Précis de parasitologie vétérinaire tropicale*. Paris: Institut d'Élevage et de Médicine vétérinaire des Pays tropicaux, Ministère de la Coopération en du Développment, pp. 27–300.

Tryland, M. and S.J. Kutz (2019). *Reindeer and Caribou: Health and Disease*. Boca Raton: CRC Press.

Van Hooft, P., E.R. Dougherty, W.M. Getz, et al. (2018). Genetic responsiveness of African buffalo to environmental stressors: a role for epigenetics in balancing autosomal and sex chromosome interactions? *PLoS One* **13**(2): e0191481.

Van Hooft, P., B.J. Greyling, H.H.T. Prins, et al. (2007). Selection at the Y chromosome of the African buffalo driven by rainfall. *PLoS One* **2**(10): e1086.

Van Soest, P.J. (1994). *Nutritional Ecology of the Ruminant*. Ithaca: Cornell University Press.

Veselis, R.A. and V. Arslan-Carlon (2021). Sedation: is it sleep, is it amnesia, what's the difference? In *Pediatric Sedation Outside of the Operating Room*. Cham: Springer, pp. 223–245.

Vesey-FitzGerald, D.F. (1969). Utilization of the habitat by buffalo in Lake Manyara National Park. *African Journal of Ecology* **7**: 131–145.

Vesey-FitzGerald, D.F. (1974). Utilization of the grazing resources by buffaloes in the Arusha National Park, Tanzania. *African Journal of Ecology* **12**: 107–134.

Von Muggenthaler, E. and B. Bashaw (2013). Giraffe Helmholtz resonance. *The Journal of the Acoustical Society of America* **133**: 3259.

Von Muggenthaler, E., P. Reinhart, B. Lympany and R.B. Craft (2003). Songlike vocalizations from the Sumatran rhinoceros (*Dicerorhinus sumatrensis*). *Acoustics Research Letters Online* **4**: 83–88.

Waite, S.J., J.E. Cater, G.C. Waghorn and V. Suresh (2021). Effect of sedatives on rumen motility in sheep. *Small Ruminant Research* **196**: 106284.

Widmer, S., F.R. Seefried, P. von Rohr, et al. (2021). A major QTL at the LHCGR/FSHR locus for multiple birth in Holstein cattle. *Genetics Selection Evolution* **53**: 1–15.

Wielgus, E., A. Caron, E. Bennitt, et al. (2021). Inter-group social behavior, contact patterns and risk for pathogen transmission in cape buffalo populations. *Journal of Wildlife Management* **85**: 1574–1590.

Xiang, R., I.M. MacLeod, H.D. Daetwyler, et al. (2021). Genome-wide fine-mapping identifies pleiotropic and functional variants that predict many traits across global cattle populations. *Nature Communications* **12**: 1–13.

Yin, S., H.J. de Knegt, M.C.M. de Jong, et al. (2020). Effects of migration network configuration and migration synchrony on infection prevalence in geese. *Journal of Theoretical Biology* **502**: 110315.

18 · *Futures of the African Buffalo*

A. CARON, R. BOURGEOIS,
P. CHARDONNET, D. CORNELIS
AND H.H.T. PRINS

Introduction

While the health of the African buffalo (*Syncerus caffer*) population in Africa is generally good, it is threatened in some regions of the continent, as described in Chapter 4. A few African buffalo are kept outside Africa, for example, in parts of the United States (e.g. Texas) where they can be hunted, and in zoo collections across the world (e.g. in European collections there are estimated over 100 *Syncerus caffer caffer* and 150 *S. c. nanus*). Yet it is utterly unlikely that modern governments will allow the population of an exotic mammal, one that can become an exotic invasive species, to be built up. It is consequently unlikely that relatively safe havens for the African buffalo will develop outside Africa; if the species is going to survive, it must be in Africa. On the other hand, the build-up of large populations of nilgai (a.k.a. blue bull, *Boselaphus tragocamelus*) in the USA provide food for thought (Presnall, 1958; Butts, 1979; Foley et al., 2017), as does that of the Canada goose (*Branta canadensis*) and raccoon (*Procyon lotor*) in Europe and banteng (*Bos javanicus*) in northern Australia. Nonetheless, it seems reasonable to anticipate that the futures of the African buffalo will take place in the context of the African continent only. As a result, these futures will depend on how the many and multidimensional factors that impact them develop or unfold.

It is not easy to forecast the fates of biodiversity and biodiversity conservation in Africa. On the one hand, African biodiversity is unique. In some parts of Africa, biodiversity is well conserved compared to other continents, and some African economies (e.g. Namibia) have managed to rely on its sustainable use, mainly through international tourism. Other countries are losing their biological heritage hand over fist, mainly in West and Central Africa (e.g. Scholte et al., 2022). On the other hand, Africa is currently undergoing significant transformations generated by, among other factors, a booming human population, growing urbanization, shifting geopolitical relationships, increasing pressures on natural resources and political variability and sometimes volatility. These transformations are likely to induce conflicts over land between agricultural production and biodiversity conservation if the land-sparing versus land-sharing debate does not deliver a sustainable framework to conciliate both dynamics (e.g Fischer et al., 2014; Kremen, 2015; Baudron et al., 2021). The fate of the African buffalo residing in and outside protected areas will be impacted by both the politics of conservation (currently mainly centred on protected areas and less so on sustainable use) and the relationship between the people of Africa and Nature in the decades to come. Both the COVID-19 crisis and several bans on hunting also have profoundly incapacitated the international tourism industry, cutting a significant material incentive for protecting wildlife in Africa. The consequences of these crises could say a lot about the resilience of natural resource management on the continent.

Is there any chance that the African forest buffalo (*Syncerus caffer nanus*) will survive in the ransacked forests of West Africa? Or that the northern savanna buffalo will survive in the swath of land stretching between Senegal and Ethiopia? And if so, what has to be realistically and concretely done to safeguard a future for this magnificent animal?

Methodology

The more than 60 contributors to this book, many members of the African Buffalo Interest Group (AfBIG) belonging to the IUCN Antelope Specialist Group, hold a large body of knowledge and experience on the focal species. Drawing from their collective and diverse expertise on the species, and from the updated information contained in the chapters of this book, we created a list of *factors of change* based on the question: what are the factors of change that could impact (positively or negatively) African buffalo populations in the future? We chose a time horizon of 30 years because it is approximately equivalent of one human generation. From this perspective, looking backwards is then what is termed 'within living memory' (e.g. Fanta et al., 2019), while looking forward is what most people feel capable of imagining within their lifetime (see e.g. Ebel, 2009; Vecchi and Gatti, 2020). We drafted a preliminary list of factors and submitted it to all co-authors of this book for comments and additions. For each 'factor of change' added to the list, a definition was agreed upon and its relevance was discussed and assessed.

Table 18.1 *Influence/dependence matrix used to categorize the factors of change that are thought to shape the African buffalo's futures over the next three decades.*

Factor of change	Weakly dependent	Strongly dependent
Strongly influent	Driver	Leverage
Weakly influent	Outlier/singular	Outputs

Adapted from Godet (1986).

From the list of factors of change, we also implemented a *structural analysis* (Godet, 1986). Structural analysis is performed on a set of factors that are considered as interconnected, thus forming a 'system'. Its final purpose is to uncover *driving forces* that are transforming the system (Godet, 2000). Through structural analysis based on expert knowledge (in this case the authors of this chapter), a systematic pairwise discussion of the direct influences of each factor on all other factors makes it possible to discover how we perceive the structure of the system, that is, the set of dominant factors and their interactions that may shape futures for African buffalo populations. This analytical process leads to the creation of an influence/dependence matrix associated with graphs displaying the position of each factor of change in different categories according to their level of influence on the other factors, and dependence to other factors, as per Table 18.1.

Subsequently, we discussed the list of the important factors of change based on the authors' selections, and the most influential factors of change (based on the structural analysis). Hence, we identified the driving forces that we think drive the futures of African buffalo populations (i.e. the most influential factors of change), and then reflected about the potential *future states* of these driving forces. Given that the most influential factors of change were 'external', that is beyond the control or influence of the core actors involved in the management of the buffalo population, we applied the *critical uncertainty matrix* approach (Curry and Schultz, 2009) to explore alternative futures for buffalo. This approach, also called the 2×2 matrix or the 2×2 scenario method, has been developed and widely used in strategic foresight for exploring contextual futures (Ramirez and Wilkinson, 2014) to the point of being called a 'golden tool' (Bradfield et al., 2005). It consists of (i) selecting one pair of driving forces with a strong impact on the system and a very uncertain development, (ii) imagining for each of the driving forces two contrasting future states by the time horizon selected and (iii) combining these future states to

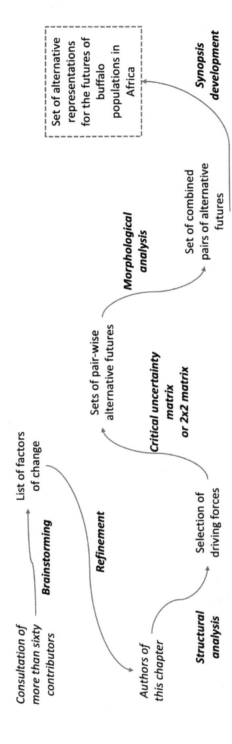

Figure 18.1 The methodological steps used for the development of alternative futures of the buffalo population in Africa. Source: Authors.

portray four alternative futures. Thus, each future represents a possible systems context for the question, here the potential futures of buffalo populations. This approach has well-known advantages and drawbacks (Ramirez and Wilkinson, 2014) and the most important ones for our study will be discussed later. Due to these shortcomings, we modified the approach, applying it to several pairs using all of the driving forces selected. For this, the pairwise combination respected the rule of non-related forces and privileged a combination of different dimensions such as societal, technical, economic, environmental, political and values ('STEEPV' dimensions). We then used an adapted *morphological analysis* (Álvarez and Ritchey, 2015; Duczynski, 2017) to combine these different sets of four alternative futures, thus producing a final set of mutually exclusive and contrasting *synopses* incorporating the different states of these driving forces.

Each synopsis was then further developed with plausible states of the factors of change that the authors considered as being directly related to the description of the state of the buffalo population and its management in Africa. Figure 18.1 displays the entire sequence of the methodology.

Results

Factors of Change and Structural Analysis

The first outputs of this methodological approach included a list of 29 factors of change with their definition and some examples (Table 18.2).

Each of the five authors then conducted a structural analysis of these 29 factors and the results were combined into a merged influence/dependence matrix where each cell was filled with the value that was attributed to it by at least three of five authors. Figure 18.2 displays the position of the factors of change in accordance with their respective relative direct influence on the other factors, and their respective relative dependency on the other factors.

To select the key variables for the 2×2 matrix approach, we decided to temporarily discard climate change because the selection of inputs for the matrix was based on a criterion of high uncertainty. For the selected time horizon of 2050, there is a relatively low level of uncertainty about the future state of this factor for much of sub-Saharan Africa. We also decided to put aside 'Colonial legacy', as this factor of change was closely linked to, and therefore represented in, the 'External influence' and 'Western worldviews' factors of change. Although thought to be highly

Table 18.2 *List of factors of change (in alphabetical order) potentially impacting positively or negatively African buffalo populations at the continent level. The most influential factors of change are displayed in grey. The fourth column indicates the domain(s) in which a factor of change falls using the STEEPV dimensions: S, societal; T, technical; Ec, economic; En, environmental; P, political; V, values.*

Factor of change	Acronym	Definition	STEEPV	Notes
African buffalo production systems	Prod_Sys	The use of African buffalo for production purposes as a domestic species	Ec	e.g. trophy/meat production, selective breeding
African worldviews	Afr_WorldV	African cultural values regarding wildlife and nature	V	e.g. relation with wild meat consumption, wildlife as cultural heritage
Buffalo uses in natural systems	Buff_Use	The types of use of African buffalo under extensive and natural systems	Ec	e.g. trophy hunting, sustainable harvesting, subsistence hunting
Climate change	Clim_Chg	The change of local climate in terms of frequency and intensity of events	En	
Climate mitigation measures	Clim_Mit	The measures adopted to mitigate the effects of climate change	T	e.g. forest conservation, carbon sequestration in savannas
Colonial legacy	Col_Leg	The influence of colonial era on current international political processes	P	e.g. current conservation models were designed in the context of colonial era
Conservation funding	Conserv_Fund	The status and modalities of conservation funding	Ec	
Conservation models	Conserv_Mod	The diversity and specificities of conservation models	En, Ec	e.g. co-management, role of state, non-governmental organizations, local communities

Conservation priorities	Cons_Prio	The orientation of conservation towards particular species or habitats	V	e.g. focus on large carnivores and pachyderms
Food production	Food_Prod	The quantity and quality of food production, including the balance of animal-based to crop-based agriculture	Ec	Land sparing versus land sharing
Genetic adaptability of African buffalo	Buf_Gen	On an evolutionary timescale, the capacity of the African buffalo to adapt to its changing environment	En	e.g. gene flow and inbreeding depression, deleterious alleles
Habitat fragmentation	Hab_Frag	The emergence of discontinuities (fragmentation) in a given environment	En	
Human/livestock diseases	H/L_Dis	Political and economic importance of animal and zoonotic diseases involving the African buffalo	Ec	e.g. foot and mouth disease, brucellosis
Human population growth	Hum_Pop	The growth of the human population	S	e.g. ratio urban/rural population
Influence of environmental movements	Env_Mouv	Nature and influence of environmental movements of societal values, perceptions and actions	P	e.g. shift towards plant-based diet (versus meat-based diet)
Influence of non-African states	Ext_Infl	The level of political and economic influence of external state in African politics and economy	P, Ec	e.g. land grabbing, infrastructure development
Intersectoral collaboration	Inter_Coll	State of intersectoral collaboration between ministries/governmental services	P	
Land tenure	Land_Cons	The quantity of land converted for agriculture	P, Ec	e.g. green revolution/State versus private ownership
Livestock production	Liv_Prod	The quantity of land use for extensive livestock production	Ec	

(cont.)

Table 18.2 (*cont.*)

Factor of change	Acronym	Definition	STEEPV	Notes
Political governance	Pol_Gov	The quality of state and local political governance	P	e.g. threat of state capture
Political stability	Pol_Stab	The political stability of states and regions	P	e.g. war, terrorism
state of african tourism	Afr_Tour	The state of African nature tourism	Ec	e.g. dependency to international tourism
State of global tourism	Glo_Tour	State of global tourism	Ec	e.g. restriction of global tourism due to COVID-19 pandemic
State of poverty	Stat_Pov	The extent of poverty in African populations	S	
Surface water availability	Surf_Wat	The state of natural and human-induced availability of water	En	e.g. changes in rainfall, water abstraction, leading to loss of wetland habitats
Technological innovation	Tech_Inov	Capacity for researchers and practitioners to access and use new technologies and knowledge to study the African buffalo	T	e.g. democratization and improvement of drones and/or telemetry tools
Transfrontier activities	Trans_Front	Activities implemented from one state into another, formally or informally	Ec	e.g. poaching, transfrontier tourism
Western worldviews	West_WorldV	The state of Western public opinion on African wildlife, nature and it uses	V	e.g. ban on hunting by European and African states

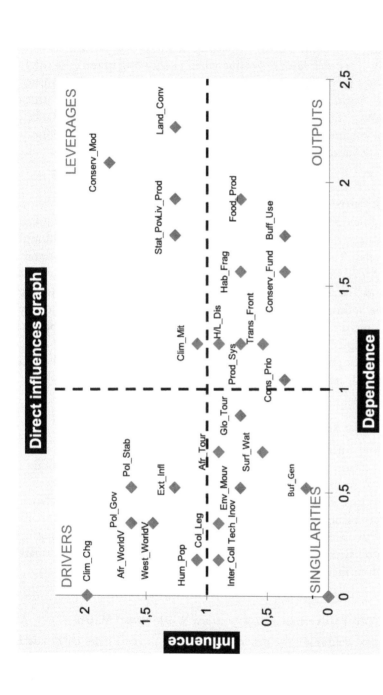

Figure 18.2 Structural analysis direct influence matrix (some squares overlap). The dotted lines represent the 'average' influence and dependence of the factors in this system centred on the value 1. They define for quadrants or categories of factors as indicated in Table 18.1. Each factor of change is visualized on this graph with its influence and dependence coordinates. As a result, eight factors of change appeared to be located in the 'drivers' (top-left) quadrant plus one very influential leverage (i.e. conservation models) as summarized in Table 18.2.

significant, we set aside 'Conservation model' due to its extremely high dependency, which implies that it is not really a driving force. 'Human population' as a global variable is also quite predictable for the next 30 years, but it is much less predictable when its meaning in terms of rural/ urban ratios is considered. We therefore kept it with this specific meaning after checking that this would not change the results of the structural analysis. The key variables selected are thus 'Political governance', 'Political stability', 'External influences', 'Western worldviews', 'African worldviews' and 'Human population'.

Creating Pairwise Alternative Futures with the 2×2 Matrix

We combined these six variables into three pairs, avoiding closely linked dimensions in these pairs and ensuring that diverse STEEPV dimensions were mixed. The resulting set of three pairs comprised 'Political stability and African worldviews', 'Political governance and Western worldviews' and 'External influence and Human population'. For each driving force, the authors together selected two contrasting alternative states by 2050. These are included in the three sets of matrices presented below. The resulting 12 alternative futures were each given a metaphoric name or descriptive phrase as a way to refer to them, but also to help others to imagine such an alternative future.

The 'Political Stability and African Worldviews' Matrix

Positioning on an axis for 'Political stability' the two opposite states, 'political chaos' versus 'generalized political stability', and on another axis for 'African worldviews' the two opposite states, 'Preservation of nature' versus 'Exploitation of nature', and placing them in a Cartesian coordinate plane results in what has been named a 'scenario cross' consisting of two axes with extremes and four scenario stories. The resulting four futures with their metaphoric names are displayed in the quadripartite graph in Figure 18.3.

The 'Political Governance and Western Worldviews' Matrix

This matrix yields four alternative futures when the two states of 'Political governance', that is 'fulfilling the aspiration of all the people' versus 'serving the interest of a few' and the two states of 'Western worldviews', that is 'preservation with sustainable consumptive use' versus 'preservation without

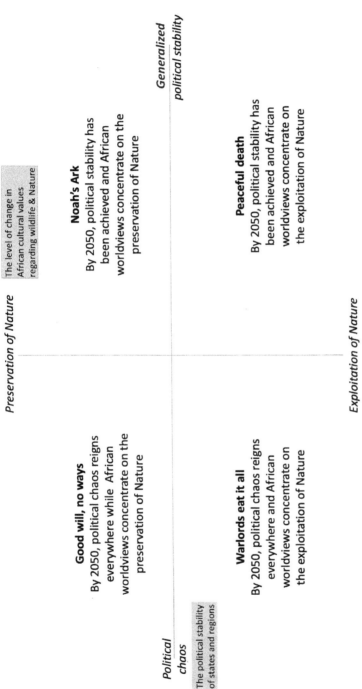

Figure 18.3 Alternative futures from the 'Political stability and African worldviews' matrix.

consumptive use' are placed in an orthogonal Cartesian plane. The resulting four futures are displayed in a quadripartite graph in Figure 18.4.

The 'External Influence and Human Population' Matrix

This matrix yields four alternative futures when the two states of 'External influence', that is 'Africa independent from the world economy and politics' versus 'external influence dictates politics and economy' and the two states of 'Human population', that is 'people live in rural areas' versus 'people live in urban areas' are placed in an orthogonal Cartesian plane. The resulting four futures are displayed in a quadripartite graph in Figure 18.5.

Using Morphological Analysis to Create Integrated Synopses of the Six Driving Forces

We proceeded by developing a morphological table combining the future states of the first two matrices where we discarded incompatible futures, that is futures whose combination would make an inconsistent synopsis (results displayed in the first two columns in Table 18.3). For example, we discarded futures where 'political chaos' was associated with 'political governance fulfilling the aspirations of all the people' under the postulate that political stability figures among the aspirations of at least some people. In a second morphological analysis step, the eight resulting combinations were put in relation with the four alternative futures produced with the third matrix (Table 18.3). The purpose was to identify where each of these four futures best fitted with the preceding eight ones. We ensured that all four futures were used in the results. We noted that the presence of the future state, 'independent from the rest of the world' of the 'External influence' driving force made automatically inessential some of the first eight futures whose differences came from discrepancies between African worldviews and Western worldviews on Nature. Hence, not all eight futures were selected.

We gave a metaphoric name to each of the seven resulting differentiated futures and scripted them in the form of synopses combining the related states of the six driving forces. Each synopsis thus represented a contextual future environment for the buffalo population that was detailed enough to logically conjecture what would be the credible state of the buffalo population and its related internal factors, that is the factors that the actors directly involved in the management of the buffalo population could influence/control. Among these, the factor 'Conservation model' plays a crucial role

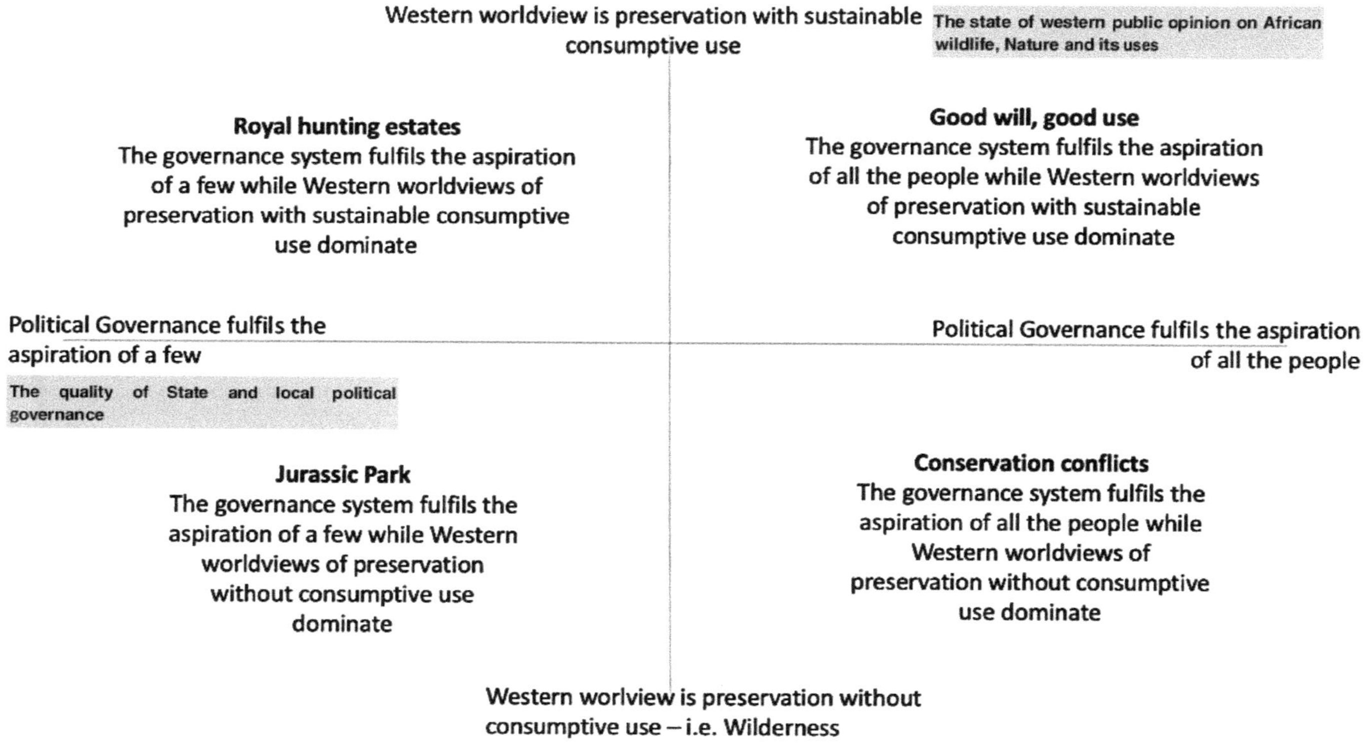

Western worldview is preservation with sustainable consumptive use

The state of western public opinion on African wildlife, Nature and its uses

Good will, good use

The governance system fulfils the aspiration of all the people while Western worldviews of preservation with sustainable consumptive use dominate

Political Governance fulfils the aspiration of all the people

Conservation conflicts

The governance system fulfils the aspiration of all the people while Western worldviews of preservation without consumptive use dominate

Royal hunting estates

The governance system fulfils the aspiration of a few while Western worldviews of preservation with sustainable consumptive use dominate

Political Governance fulfils the aspiration of a few

The quality of State and local political governance

Jurassic Park

The governance system fulfils the aspiration of a few while Western worldviews of preservation without consumptive use dominate

Western worlview is preservation without consumptive use – i.e. Wilderness

Figure 18.4 Alternative futures from the 'Political governance and Western worldviews' matrix.

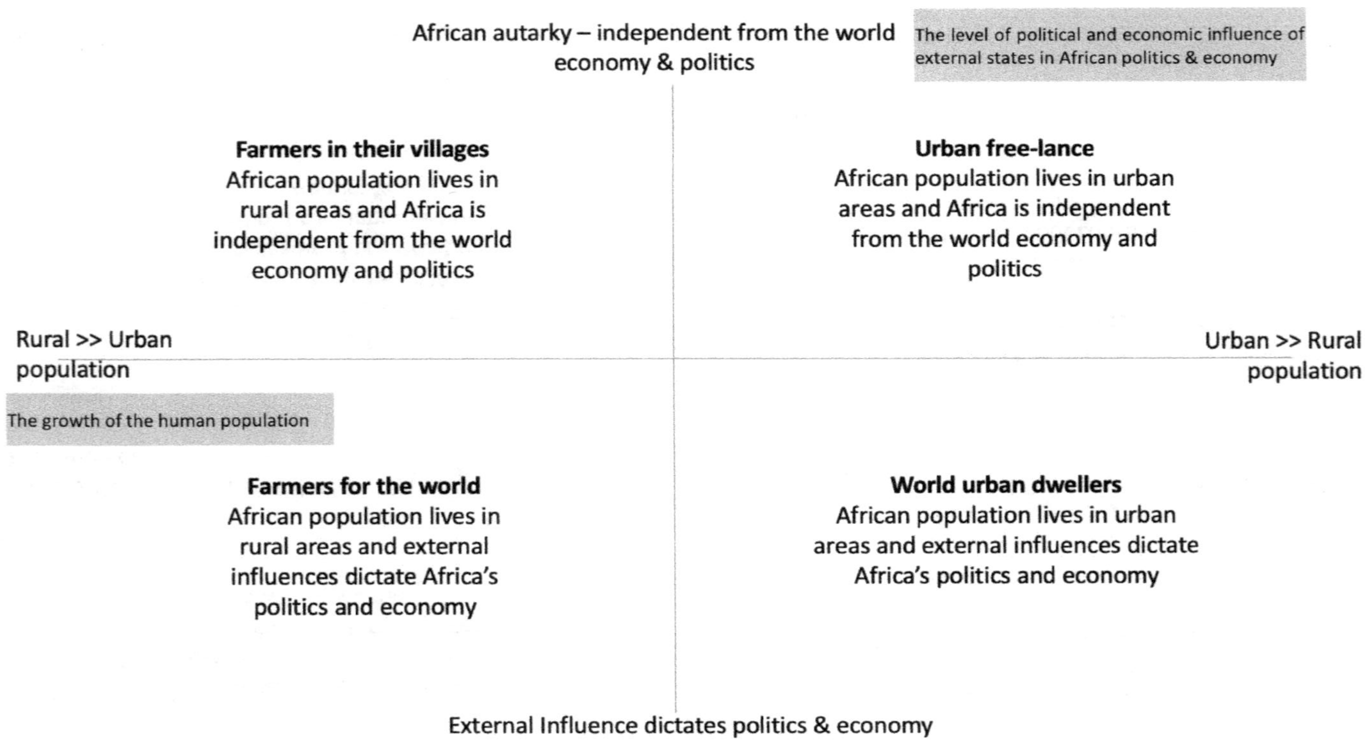

The level of political and economic influence of external states in African politics & economy

African autarky – independent from the world economy & politics

Urban free-lance
African population lives in urban areas and Africa is independent from the world economy and politics

Urban >> Rural population

World urban dwellers
African population lives in urban areas and external influences dictate Africa's politics and economy

Farmers in their villages
African population lives in rural areas and Africa is independent from the world economy and politics

Rural >> Urban population

The growth of the human population

Farmers for the world
African population lives in rural areas and external influences dictate Africa's politics and economy

External Influence dictates politics & economy

Figure 18.5 Alternative futures from the 'External influence and human population' matrix.

Table 18.3 *Second morphological analysis step: after putting in relation the first 2×2 matrices and developing metaphoric names and short synopses (first two columns), the eight resulting combinations were put in relation with the four alternative futures produced with the third matrix. White backgrounds indicate the 7 combinations of 6 driving forces' states selected, including the metaphoric names of these synopses, ensuring that all driving forces' states were used in the results. Dark backgrounds indicate combinations that were discarded because of an incompatibility between the driving forces' states. Light grey backgrounds indicate possible combinations that were not selected because of inessential selected combinations.*

Metaphoric names of 2×2 matrix	Combination of the first two matrices: African worldviews × Political stability and Western worldviews × Political governance	Synopsis of 2×2 matrix: External Influence × Human population			
		1. Urban freelance	2. World urban dwellers	3. Farmers in their villages	4. Farmers for the world
		African population lives in urban areas and Africa is independent from the world economy and politics	African population lives in urban areas and external influence dictates Africa's politics and economy	African population lives in rural areas and Africa is independent from the world economy and politics	African population lives in rural areas and external influence dictates Africa's politics and economy
1. Noah's universal Ark	By 2050, political stability has become generalized and the governance system fulfils the aspiration of all people. African worldviews concentrate on the preservation of nature while Western worldviews concentrate on preservation with sustainable consumptive use.				**African renaissance**

(cont.)

Table 18.3 (*cont.*)

Synopsis of 2×2 matrix: External Influence × Human population

		Happy nature	
2. Noah's controversial Ark	By 2050, political stability has become generalized and the governance system fulfils the aspiration of all people. African worldviews concentrate on the preservation of nature while Western worldviews concentrate on preservation without consumptive use.		Even more difficult if Western dictates wilderness and all people live in rural areas
3. Into the wild	By 2050, political chaos reigns everywhere and governance system fulfils the aspiration of few people. African worldviews concentrate on the preservation of nature as do Western worldviews but without consumptive use.		Even more difficult if Western dictates wilderness and all people live in rural areas
		Pauper's hell	
4. Private games	By 2050, political chaos reigns everywhere and the governance system fulfils the aspiration of few people. Western worldviews concentrate on preservation with sustainable consumptive use while African worldviews concentrate on the preservation of nature.		**Conservation islands**

		Self-service	Battleground 2050	Agro-Africa	
5. We profit all	By 2050, political stability has become generalized and the governance system fulfils the aspiration of all people. While Western worldviews concentrate on preservation with sustainable consumptive use, African worldviews concentrate on the exploitation of nature.				Not very consistent: opposition of worldviews while Western dictates
6. All against the West	By 2050, political stability has become generalized and the governance systems fulfil the aspiration of all people. African worldviews concentrate on the exploitation of nature while Western worldviews concentrate on preservation without consumptive use.				Not very consistent: opposition of worldviews while Western dictates
7. The lords of nature	By 2050, political chaos reigns everywhere and the governance systems fulfil the aspiration of few people. African worldviews concentrate on the exploitation of nature while Western worldviews concentrate on preservation without consumptive use.		Not very consistent: opposition of worldviews while Western dictates		Not very consistent: opposition of worldviews while Western dictates
8. The hunting lords	By 2050, political chaos reigns everywhere and the governance systems fulfil the aspiration of few people. African worldviews concentrate on the exploitation of nature while Western worldviews concentrate on preservation with sustainable consumptive use.				Not very consistent: opposition of worldviews while Western dictates

Table 18.4 *Resulting synopsis setting contextual futures for the future of buffalo population in Africa.*

African renaissance	By 2050, external influences dictate Africa's politics and economy; political stability has been reached in Africa now for one generation and the governance system fulfils the aspiration of all people. In the context of the doubling of the human population, the urban population remained stable while the rural population tripled. Western worldviews have changed and adopted relevant preservation of nature modes that promote sustainable consumptive use in recognition of local culture and knowledge, echoing re-emerging African worldviews rooted in ancestral beliefs about the interconnectivity between all human beings and nature and the need to respect them. These ancestral beliefs are now ruling once again the relationship of man to nature. New locally relevant conservation models have emerged, promoting land sharing between conservation and local development for the benefit of both. As external influences led to improved agriculture, agricultural intensification took place as the rural population embraced conservation, preventing expansion into the bush. Climate change has pushed most farmers to focus on livestock production systems integrated within rangeland management programmes, sustainable resource use and local livestock markets to maintain a low livestock density. The state of poverty thus drastically reduced in Africa. *The African buffalo is a key economic asset of these new conservation models (for tourism, hunting, meat) and free-roaming populations thrive in protected areas and community-based managed areas.*
Happy nature	By 2050, external influences dictate Africa's politics and economy; political stability has been reached in Africa now for one generation and the governance system fulfils the aspiration of all people. The African human population has almost doubled, the urban population more than tripled while the rural population drastically decreased, leading to extreme agricultural intensification. Africans live in urban areas, allowing for biodiversity to flourish in almost deserted rural areas since Western worldviews pushed for and imposed preservation without consumptive use over African worldviews. African cities are fed by international trade and some local concentrated intensive livestock production units. A luxury local agricultural market exists for citizens on the little land left in African landscape protected at 50%. The state of poverty in rural Africa is now much lower because fewer people live there with a few job opportunities such as those generated by the private sector, which has developed a highly profitable wildlife economy, for example in southern Africa. The dominant conservation model is still largely based on National Parks with no human activities apart from safari tourism. In southern Africa, the private sector has developed a highly profitable wildlife economy that generate many jobs. *The African buffalo is free-roaming in protected areas and a large private population, genetically selected, exists in intensively managed farms.*

Pauper's hell

By 2050, Africa is independent from the world economy and politics. Political chaos reigns everywhere and the governance system fulfils the aspiration of few people. African populations find shelters in cities to make a living. The ones who stayed in rural areas can only produce for subsistence and rely on nature for the rest of their needs. The state of poverty has remained as in the 2020s. Due to shrinking state services, the tsetse fly and sleeping sickness have returned in large parts of the continent and therefore prevent livestock production in large tracks of land. The dominant African worldviews is the preservation of nature, not because the pauperized people would not like to harvest it, but because the elite want to hunt or enjoy these animals for themselves and they enforce strict rules about the (inequitable) access to wildlife. The Western worldviews focusing on sustainable use cannot reach Africa, which is completely disconnected from the rest of the world. *The African buffalo is free-roaming in protected areas that are classified as 'National Parks' but are, in reality, more like royal domains.*

Self-service

By 2050, political stability has become common and widepread and the governance system fulfils the aspiration of all people. Africa is independent from the world economy and politics. Thus, while Western worldviews try to promote preservation with sustainable consumptive use, the worldviews of the African populations, who live in urban areas, concentrate on the exploitation of nature. As a result, a small rural population exploits unsustainably most of the landscape, which is becoming drier and subject to extreme events. Livestock is produced in vast quantities feeding the local markets but the density on the land is high. Poverty has increased as the land produces less and less. Conservation models advanced by the West do not convince African populations to change their mind on the preservation of nature apart from a few places. *The African buffalo populations are isolated in protected areas, under the pressure of livestock farming and numbers are decreasing. The highest number of living individual buffalo are private property in intensive farms, profiting a few.*

Conservation islands

By 2050, political chaos reigns everywhere and the governance systems fulfil the aspiration of few people. Africa is independent from the world economy and politics. The worldview of African populations, who live in rural areas, concentrates on the exploitation of nature while Western worldviews still try to promote preservation without consumptive use where it can. Thirty per cent of the land is under strict conservation since 2030, following international agreements, but the need for land for the ever-increasing rural population puts pressure on protected areas. Livestock farming is dominating in the arid landscape and the level of poverty has increased since the 2020s. There are no conservation models beside the willingness of the powerful to keep a few animals for their own pleasure in their private holdings. *The African buffalo is not a key species for conservation in Africa and its populations have declined and are on the brink of extinction.*

(*cont.*)

Table 18.4 (*cont.*)

AgroAfrica By 2050, political stability has become common and widespread and the governance systems fulfil the aspiration of all the people. Africa has taken independence from the world economy and politics and now concentrates on its food security with African populations living mostly in rural areas. African worldviews concentrate on the exploitation of nature against the Western worldviews incapable of imposing the preservation of nature without consumptive use anymore. The land use is dominated by agriculture as a booming sector sustained by intensification principles that have been adapted to African contexts. Livestock production is integrated in crop–livestock systems. Poverty is on the verge of being eradicated in Africa. The conservation of nature is an old story of Western dreamers: as Europe, Africa has made its green revolution to the expense of nature. African states have conserved National Parks to follow international treatiesn but their state is poor. *The African buffalo population remains in protected areas, isolated, including fading populations in small parks under human pressure.*

Battleground 2050 By 2050, external influence dictates Africa's politics and economy; political chaos reigns everywhere and the governance systems fulfil the aspiration of few people. Western worldviews are preservation with sustainable consumptive use. As most people now live in cities, land tenure has shifted towards dominant conservation landscapes at low human density with integrated management of livestock and rangeland management. The level of poverty is relatively low. However, urban African populations have developed worldviews that concentrate on the unsustainable exploitation of nature, creating a demand for natural resources. This includes bush meat, which makes environmental criminal organizations thrive. Conservation models that have emerged are now locally relevant, promoting land sharing between conservation and agriculture. The unsustainable exploitation of wildlife threatens this fragile equilibrium. *The African buffalo is an important asset of the new conservation models, but the constant poaching activities prevent a true success story of the sustainable use for the benefit of all.*

Figure 18.6 Herd of Cape African buffalo, central Botswana. © Rudi van Aarde.

as a leverage as its future is determined by the contextual environment set by influential factors and at the same time an influential one for the buffalo system in particular. Three other factors also play roles, to a lesser extent, as leverages as indicated in Table 18.2, namely 'Land Tenure', 'Livestock Production' and 'State of Poverty'. We thus incorporated them in the refinement of the synopses along with the other internal factors directly associated with the buffalo population as indicated in Table 18.4.

Discussion

The list of factors of change identified by the co-authors of this book who responded to our calls for input includes two groups of separate factors. The first consists of external factors (e.g. 'Climate change', 'External influence of States'), which put together sets a general context for Africa. The second group consists of more internal factors (e.g. African buffalo production systems, conservation funding). The results of the structural analysis shows that the first group strongly influences the second group, and thus contributes largely to shaping the future of African buffalo populations in Africa (Figure 18.6).

Regarding the full process, we considered Africa as a whole for the sake of the exploratory nature of this reflection. The resulting synopses (Table 18.4) should not be understood as continent-wide alternative futures. A synopsis represents a possible contextual situation, which could occur only in parts of the continent or of countries, coexisting with others in other parts as discussed later. These alternative futures are not predictions either. They are exploratory imaginaries of possible futures, and as such constitute only one way of anticipating amidst several alternative ways (Amer et al., 2013; Crawfords, 2019). They serve as a basis to enlarge our reflection on the future of the buffalo population beyond and in complement to the conventional use of trends and projections. As such they are intended to shed additional lights on how we '...make sense of change (difference) in the emergent present' (Miller, 2015), that is the current situation of the buffalo population, and what that could mean for the future.

While we discarded 'Climate change' from our selection of drivers due to its high level of predictability at the time horizon selected, this factor of change cannot be removed from the discussion. Climate evolves 'slowly', will exert continuous pressure across the century and cannot be represented by different and contrasting states in the 30-year horizon that we set for this futures exercise. The climate is already changing and symptoms of these changes already can be felt in the buffalo range, especially in semi-arid areas (e.g. southern Africa; Kupika et al., 2018). Future buffalo in Africa will most probably live under a changed climate including more extreme events but also with a larger human population. Droughts or lack of surface water, their frequency and intensity in particular, will be a direct threat for buffalo that are quite susceptible to them, with substantial declines in some populations as witnessed in the Sahel at the end of the 1960s and during the 1990s in Tsavo, Serengeti/Mara, Gonarezhou and Kruger (East, 1999; Cornélis et al. 2014) and in 2022 in Amboseli, Lewa Downs and Tsavo in Kenya (Prins, personal observation). Without access to drought refuge resources such as extensive wetlands, some populations could suffer high mortality.

Against this general backdrop, the other factors of change that we perceived as setting the context of Africa in 2050 are mainly political and value-based. First, the quality and stability of African States' political systems, including their governance, seem to be decisive with regard to their capacity to design and implement environmental policies, and to control or enable illegal activities. Consequently, the occurrence of wars and other conflicts can have serious impacts on wildlife populations, especially buffalo herds that can feed troops with good quantities of quality meat, as observed in the past. For bygone centuries, African politics have been largely impacted by the influence of colonial powers, and since independence by the influence of former colonial powers and emerging players on the African continent such as China, Russia, Israel and Turkey. The status of these future international relationships will impact the global context in terms of development, politics and ultimately the management of natural resources (e.g. extractive industries). Alternative futures with stronger or ruptured ties can be framed with secondary impacts on other factors of change (e.g. differences between 'Pauper's hell' and 'Self-service' synopses). The influence of external States is impacting African conservation. Historically, the pre-eminence of Western countries in African affairs was associated with their capacity to globally impose the now dominant Western worldviews regarding conservation. Today, these Western worldviews have shown some limits (e.g. a land-sparing system too often neglecting local communities triggering negative local perceptions towards conservation and conflicts) and some voices have expressed the need for a decolonization of conservation policies (Domínguez and Luoma, 2020). This process, only started recently, could create a space for the re-emergence of the multiple African worldviews that pre-existed the colonial era and fell silent or went extinct since then, such as in 'African renaissance'. If and how these African worldviews will reinvent themselves in the new contexts and redefine the relationship between African populations and nature is a major uncertainty for the future of conservation in Africa, and therefore for buffalo.

This group of contextual factors of change sets the scene in which future conservation models will succeed or fail to preserve African buffalo and perhaps associated biodiversity. The different synopses in Table 18.4 depict alternative futures considering different states of each of these factors of change articulated together to build a possible future. The aim is once again not to predict the future but to explore the maximum range of the possible futures in which the African buffalo could exist. As for most large wild mammals, the fate of the buffalo in Africa will be mirrored by the fate of conservation. The current status of buffalo in the West and Central savannas, where they only remain as a few isolated (but relatively robust) populations in national parks and well-guarded hunting areas and reserves, can serve as a picture of the future of African buffalo populations in a context of fortress conservation imposed by strong pressure from human activities (e.g. mobile pastoralism, both nomadic and transhumant and sedentary livestock husbandry, the former impacting more buffalo populations) such as in the 'AgroAfrica', 'Self-service' and 'Conservation islands' synopses. However, even if this future is possible, it does not mean that future buffalo populations will be restricted to protected areas only. In many parts of Africa today, the expansion of cotton growing (with unsustainable farming practices), pastoralism and the development of mining are only a few examples of elements that are already putting growing pressure on land, pushing buffalo into protected areas and sometimes encroaching into protected areas, including rainforests in the central parts of the continent. The demand for land for the growing human population superimposed on climate change could drive the conversion of more land for agriculture and other extractive activities and leave less land for natural habitat and buffalo. This will create a difficult context for achieving the objective of 30 per cent of land under protected areas by 2030 (even if some African countries have already reached this proportion, albeit some areas have been called 'paper parks'; Blom et al., 2004; Di Minin and Toivonen, 2015; IUCN, 2022; e.g. 'Conservation islands'). Another key for the future of buffalo in Africa will be its capacity to exist outside protected areas.

Disruptive developments could unfold in the management of land, its uses and the relationship between conservation and local development. These developments could be attractive for all stakeholders, but would require quite systemic changes in conservation. The previous paragraph demonstrates that land conversion for conservation could take place in two cases: either if conservation delivers decent livelihoods for the local human population (e.g. 'African renaissance'), or if the majority of African populations live in cities as the current trend points at (e.g. 'Happy nature'). In relation to the former, community-based natural resource management programmes (CBNRM) have been tested in Africa since the mid-1980s with failures and successes (Dressler et al., 2010). Their central tenet is the devolution to local communities of the right to access natural resources such as wildlife, and to encourage the sustainable management of the resources through consumptive (e.g. hunting, meat production) and/or non-consumptive (e.g. ecotourism or photographic safari) uses. Given many cases where this CNBRM failed (for instance, because of resource capture by local elites, weak safeguarding against short-term profiteering versus long-term sustainability, rent-seeking behaviour, weak embedding in existing legislation if at all, non-understanding of cultural differences, etc.), we do not plea for a blanket application of CBNRM at all. We thus call for a critical analysis of success factors as was done for fisheries (e.g. Cunningham and Bostock, 2005; Squires et al., 2017) instead of blind faith in self-regulation of natural resource use not by local peoples. Possible futures could go beyond the initial CBNRM concept to embrace further the framework of environmental justice that not only calls for more equal distribution (i.e. benefits) between stakeholders, but also for more equal involvement in decision-making processes, an aspect partially covered by CBNRM, and more recognition of local identities and cultural difference, meaning more recognition of local (African) world-views (Martin et al., 2016; e.g. 'African renaissance'). This would mean a progressive shift from (conservation) projects that are designed outside of local contexts, without the involvement of the final beneficiaries and are imposed on the latter by national or international external experts. The decision for a community to use its land for some form of conservation would be their own decision (they would have the right not to do so as well), under their terms and their governance and management system, and with enough benefits to be sustainable in the long term (after the end of external funding if this is not long term). The result would be mixed conservation–agricultural or conservation land, preferentially adjacent to protected areas to promote connectivity between natural habitats and/or between protected areas (e.g. 'African renaissance' and 'Battleground 2050'). Pockets of this future already exist today, although they remain in a minority, with a progressive paradigm shift in some stakeholders (donors, practitioners, researchers) towards exploring these new forms of land use (Caron et al., in prep.). Any form of Half Earth concept (50 per cent of land protected globally) could only emerge in Africa through these types of new conservation models that would not concentrate solely on the management of protected areas as disconnected land use, but on larger landscapes in which protected areas are integrated with pro-conservation or coexistence land uses, benefiting a larger set of (local) stakeholders and benefiting from them. The concept of 'Other effective area-based conservation measure' (or OEACM) means 'a geographically defined area other than a Protected Area, which is governed and managed in ways that achieve positive and sustained long-term outcomes for the *in situ* conservation of biodiversity, with associated ecosystem functions and services and, where applicable, cultural, spiritual, socioeconomic, and other locally relevant values' and was adopted in 2018 by the 14th Conference of the Parties of the Convention on Biological Diversity and could provide a framework for such land-sharing options (OECMs, 2019; Figure 18.7).

The African buffalo could be a key species, if not the most important species, for these new conservation models that would be based on the consumptive use of wildlife. The reason for this is that only a small fraction of African landscapes and wildlife communities can offer proper products for clients of wildlife viewing. Alternative uses are trophy hunting and meat production through sustainable management. Today, trophy hunting is a very sensitive topic that divides Western opinion, sometimes violently (Chapter 16). An influential and powerful part of Western opinion opposes consumptive use in Africa and has succeeded in imposing bans

Figure 18.7 Forest buffalo calf, Odzala National Park, Republic of Congo. ©
Thomas Breuer.

on trophy imports in countries from which important populations of
hunters come from, reflecting a combination of three drivers, 'Western
worldviews', 'External influence of States' and 'Colonial legacy'. There
is no such fracture in mainstream African worldviews, where consumptive uses of natural resources are often allowed with access rules (e.g.
seasonal, geographical, social, mystical, specific hunting rules). Chapters
13 and 16 present the central role that buffalo already play in the wildlife
and trophy-hunting industry (i.e. it would be difficult to run a trophy-
hunting business without buffalo except in cases where very iconic species can be hunted), and Chapter 14 focuses on meat production, which
is also a valuable use of buffalo if markets for this meat exist. The new
land-use options in which the buffalo may play an important role could,
in possible futures (e.g. 'Battleground 2050'), compete with traditional
agricultural land uses such as rainfed crops, irrigated crops and livestock
production (Cumming et al., 2014). They would require a new paradigm
in which African populations take ownership of the buffalo as an indigenous species replacing the exotic breeds of cattle imported during the
colonial era (as in 'African renaissance'). This paradigm could percolate
into the tourism industry by developing tourism products that offer the
exploration of these rich and diverse landscapes in which biological and

cultural diversity are nurtured. These products could attract emergent African middle and rich urban classes that may desire to reconnect with their culture and localities. In this future, African buffalo would thrive in and outside protected areas and be a symbol of the decolonization of Africa and the ownership of its landscapes and natural resources.

African worldviews also could fail to embrace the conservation of nature and do the minimum for conservation to respect signed treaties (as in 'Battleground 2050') or completely ignore their wildlife in order to make sure they reach food security through conventional agriculture (e.g. 'AgroAfrica' and 'Self-service'). These contexts would restrict buffalo populations in protected areas while raising issues related to genetic bottlenecks if metapopulation management does not exist. The relationship with non-African states would be important as the funding for conservation would be, as it is today, dependent on external sources. Modalities for subsidizing nature for its conservation by local stakeholders would be a way to maintain protected areas in good shape. The conditions linked to this funding would be important if a sustainable management of natural resources and habitats is targeted; notions of appropriation, empowerment and recognition would still be important in these contexts.

Among possible futures, the commodification of buffalo through private ownership and under semi-extensive or intensive management (Chapter 13) could spread beyond South Africa as a business model in which buffalo already play an important role. However, this alternative raises two important questions: can this model produce enough benefits (through employment) to local communities to be accepted, and not only for a rich elite (as in 'Self-service' or 'Conservation 'islands')? To what extent can artificially genetically selected (e.g. for horn size) or disease-free buffalo (including endemic diseases to African wildlife) still be considered as suitable to join free-roaming populations and benefit conservation? In recent decades, a few countries in southern Africa have also experienced strict sanitary measures regarding important cattle diseases (the main one being foot-and-mouth disease – see Chapters 9 and 12) that imposed strict separations between buffalo and cattle land uses, with devastating consequences for wildlife populations and small-scale subsistence farmers living close to protected areas with buffalo (Ferguson and Hanks, 2010; Cumming et al., 2015). In a context of higher economic dependence on external states, fencing to control diseases with consequences for wildlife and costs to the poorest farmers could spread to other region of Africa, mainly to the benefit of states. Due to these consequences, and to the fact that Africa needs to produce for itself, the disease issue did not appear as very important in the synopses. However, this vision could become a possible future for southern Africa.

The synopses of Table 18.4 draw possible futures that may or may not seem relevant for the different regions of Africa regarding the context and the future of African buffalo. Projecting current trends into the future, buffalo populations in West and Central savannas appear to follow some elements of the synopses 'AgroAfrica', 'Self-service' and 'Conservation islands' with a restriction in protected areas under pressure from human activities. The existing harsh competition between agro-pastoralists and pastoralists in these areas would require massive investments to keep conservation land as it is, and neo-military approaches currently appear to be the only short-term solution to protect what exists in war zones. Too little information exists on the state of the forest buffalo in West and Central Africa (albeit to a lesser extent in the latter; Chapter 4); the connectedness between populations, the impact of hunting, subsistence slash-and-burn agriculture and the relation with extractive industries are unknowns (Chapter 17), which prevent wild guesses. Sustainable management of forests by the timber industry is emerging and it could be interesting to further consider the place that the African buffalo could play in these managed forests, and likewise in well-managed, well-guarded oil concessions. Finally, Eastern and southern Africa are the regions in which pockets of the future are currently visible, such as some innovative conservation models (e.g. Kenya, Zambia, Mozambique) and experiences of the commodification of buffalo through private ownership.

The selected methodology has some inherent limits. It is widely acknowledged that the 2×2 matrix carries a very reductionist and quite Manichean view of the world, based on the opposition of extremes. This methodology helps to define a 'framework of the extremes' within which potential futures will likely be located on a region or country basis. In addition, one could very well criticize the results as ultimately the products of Westerners' perceptions about Africa and the dynamics of the African buffalo. While this seems quite opposed to the philosophy of some recent publications about decolonizing the future (Bourgeois et al., 2022), what needs to be taken into account here is that in this process our ways of imagining the future do not intend to frame anyone's future. To the contrary, we wish to contribute to opening imaginaries and not closing or restricting them. If this work and its methodology give ideas to different people with different origins and backgrounds to undertake such a study, producing additional non-Western imaginaries, we would consider our endeavour successful.

Table 18.5 *The seven synopses ranked according to what is perceived as good for African buffalo.*

#1	African renaissance	Excellent for buffalo and probably stable	Because this is so good for buffalo, conservationists should support these factors in the coming years.
#2	Happy nature	Very good for buffalo but undermining perhaps in the long term	Even though this is good for buffalo there may be inherent danger of changing the genetic disposition of the species, thus making it less resilient. Conservationists should support these socioeconomic factors now, but probably not the selective breeding.
#3	Pauper's hell	Excellent for buffalo but probably not stable	Even though this is very good for buffalo, its inherent risk of lack of (social) stability leads to the conclusion that the factors leading to this scenario should not be supported by conservationists at present.
#4	AgroAfrica	Reasonably acceptable for buffalo	This appears to be reasonably good for buffalo, but this scenario necessitates on the long term the exchange of buffalo between large protected areas as already is the case for African wild dogs (*Lycaon pictus*) in southern Africa.
#5	Battleground 2050	Not good for buffalo	This scenario is quite bad for buffalo, necessitating present-day conservationists not to support this political reality and avoid unsustainable use in a land-sharing context.
#6	Self-service	Bad for buffalo as this will not sustain them in the longer term	Even though this appears to be reasonably good for buffalo in the short term, this synopsis is not sustainable, leading to the conclusion that the factors leading to this scenario should not be supported by conservationists at present.
#7	Conservation islands	Very bad for buffalo	Even though this appears to be reasonably good for buffalo in the short term, this scenario is not sustainable, leading to the conclusion that the factors leading to this scenario should not be supported by conservationists at present even though it appears to be the mainstream conservation model at present.

Figure 18.8 West African savanna buffalo female, Konkombri Hunting Area, Benin. © Christophe Morio.

Implications for the Futures of the African Buffalo

The seven synopsis that emerge from Table 18.4 generate different possible futures for African buffalo based on extreme states of the most influential factors on buffalo populations. Among these, some are more or less 'good' for African buffalo populations, at least if we consider the number of buffalo as a good indicator of the robustness of the species (as one cannot yet measure the well-being of a buffalo and they cannot tell us when and where they are happy). We have therefore ranked these seven synopses in a gradient of what we perceived as good for buffalo in Table 18.5 and their consequences for conservationists (and others of good will).

The best scenario appears to be characterized by (i) good governance for all, (ii) sparing land for conservation, (iii) economic intensification on agricultural lands and (iv) land sharing with conservation in combination with sustainable use. The worst scenarios appear to be characterised by (i) African autarky, (ii) high numbers of people farming and/or high numbers of livestock in the countryside and (iii) any unsustainable use of natural resources, including buffalo. A futures analysis can thus objectively guide present-day priority setting and conservationists' programme choices in a way that is independent of political leanings or contemporary foibles (Figure 18.8).

References

Álvarez, A. and T. Ritchey (2015). Applications of general morphological analysis. *Acta Morphologica Generalis* **4**: 1–40.

Amer, M., T.U. Daim and A. Jetter (2013). A review of scenario planning. *Futures* **46**: 23–40.

Baudron, F., B. Govaerts, N. Verhulst, et al. (2021). Sparing or sharing land? Views from agricultural scientists. *Biological Conservation* **259**: 109167.

Blom, A., J. Yamindou and H.H. Prins (2004). Status of the protected areas of the Central African Republic. *Biological Conservation* **118**(4): 479–487.

Bourgeois, R., G. Karuri-Sebina and K.E. Feukeu (2022). The future as a public good: decolonising the future through anticipatory participatory action research. *Foresight* ahead-of-print.

Bradfield, R., G. Wright, G. Burt, et al. (2005). The origins and evolution of scenario techniques in long range business planning. *Futures* **37**(8): 795–812.

Butts, G.L. (1979). The status of exotic big game in Texas. *Rangelands*, **1**(4): 152–153.

Caron, A., P. Mugabe, R. Bourgeois, et al. (in prep.). Reframing Transfrontier Conservation Areas in southern Africa: promoting sustainable livelihoods towards social and environmental justice.

Cornélis, D., M. Melletti, L. Korte, et al. (2014). African buffalo *Syncerus caffer* (Sparrman, 1779). In M. Melletti and J. Burton (Eds.), *Ecology, Evolution and Behaviour of Wild Cattle: Implications for Conservation*. Cambridge: Cambridge University Press, pp. 326–372.

Crawfords, M.M. (2019). A comprehensive scenario intervention typology. *Technological Forecasting and Social Change* **149**: 119748.

Cumming, D.H.M., V. Dzingirai and M. de Garine-Wichatitksy (2014). Land- and natural resource-based livelihood opportunities in TFCAs. In J.A. Andersson, M. de Garine-Wichatitsky, D.H.M. Cumming, V. Dzingirai and K.E. Giller (Eds.), *Transfrontier Conservation Areas: People Living on the Edge*. London: Earthscan, pp. 163–191.

Cumming, D.H.M., S.A. Osofsky, S.J. Atkinson and M.W. Atkinson (2015). Beyond fences: wildlife; livestock and land use in southern Africa. In J. Zingsstag et al. (Eds.), *One Health: The Theory and Practice of Integrated Health Apporaches*. Wallingford: CAB, pp. 243–257.

Cunningham, S. and T. Bostock (2005). *Successful Fisheries Management: Issues, Case Studies and Perspectives*. Utrecht: Eburon Uitgeverij BV.

Curry, A. and W. Schultz (2009). Roads less travelled: different methods, different futures. *Journal of Futures Studies* **13**: 35–60.

Di Minin, E. and T. Toivonen (2015). Global protected area expansion: creating more than paper parks. *Bioscience* **65**(7): 637–638.

Domínguez, L. and C. Luoma (2020). Decolonising conservation policy: how colonial land and conservation ideologies persist and perpetuate indigenous injustices at the expense of the environment. *Land* **9**(3): 65.

Dressler, W., B. Buscher, M. Schoon, et al. (2010). From hope to crisis and back again? A critical history of the global CBNRM narrative. *Environmental Conservation* **37**(1): 5–15.

Duczynski, G. (2017). Morphological analysis as an aid to organisational design and transformation. *Futures* **86**: 36–43.

East, R. (1999). *African Antelope Database*. Edited by IUCN/SSSC, Vol. 21. Antelope Specialist Group. Gland/Cambridge: IUCN.

Ebel, R.E. (2009). *The Geopolitics of Russian Energy: Looking Back, Looking Forward*. Washington, DC: CSIS.

Fanta, V., M. Šálek and P. Sklenicka (2019). How long do floods throughout the millennium remain in the collective memory? *Nature Communications* **10**(1): 1–9.

Ferguson, K. and J. Hanks (2010). *Fencing Impacts: A Review of the Environmental, Social and Economic Impacts of Game and Veterinary Fencing in Africa with Particular Reference to the Great Limpopo and Kavango-Zambezi Transfrontier Conservation Areas*. Pretoria: South Africa.

Fischer, J., D.J. Abson, V. Butsic, et al. (2014). Land sparing versus land sharing: moving forward. *Conservation Letters* **7**(3): 149–157.

Foley, A.M., J.A. Goolsby, A. Ortega-S Jr, et al. (2017). Movement patterns of nilgai antelope in South Texas: implications for cattle fever tick management. *Preventive Veterinary Medicine* **146**: 166–172.

Godet, M. (1986). Introduction to la prospective. *Futures* **18**: 134–157.

Godet, M. (2000). The art of scenarios and strategic planning: tools and pitfalls. *Technological Forecasting and Social Change* **65**(3): 22.

IUCN (2022). IUCN's position. Third meeting of the Open-Ended Working Group on the Post-2020 Global Biodiversity Framework (OEWG3), Twenty-fourth meeting of the Subsidiary Body on Scientific, Technical and Technological Advice (SBSTTA24), Third meeting of the Subsidiary Body on Implementation (SBI3), Geneva, 14–29 March 2022.

Kremen, C. (2015). Reframing the land-sparing/land-sharing debate for biodiversity conservation. *Annals of the New York Academy of Sciences* **1355**(1): 52–76.

Kupika, O.L., E. Gandiwa, S. Kativu and G. Nhamo (2018). Impacts of climate change and climate variability on wildlife resources in Southern Africa: experience from selected protected areas in Zimbabwe. In B. Sen and O. Grillo (Eds.), *Selected Studies in Biodiversity*. London: IntechOpen.

Martin, A., B. Coolsaet, E. Corbera, et al. (2016). Justice and conservation: the need to incorporate recognition. *Biological Conservation* **197**: 254–261.

Miller, R. (2015). Learning, the future, and complexity. An essay on the emergence of futures literacy. *European Journal of Education* **50**(4): 513–523.

OECMs, I.-W.T.F.o. (2019). *Recognising and Reporting Other Effective Area-Based Conservation Measures*. Gland: IUCN.

Presnall, C.C. (1958). The present status of exotic mammals in the United States. *The Journal of Wildlife Management* **22**(1): 45–50.

Ramirez, R. and A. Wilkinson (2014). Rethinking the 2×2 scenario method: grid or frames? *Technological Forecasting and Social Change* **86**: 254–264.

Scholte, P., O. Pays, S. Adam, et al. (2022). Conservation overstretch and long-term decline of wildlife and tourism in the Central African savannas. *Conservation Biology* **36**(2): e13860.

Squires, D., M. Maunder, R. Allen, et al. (2017). Effort rights-based management. *Fish and Fisheries* **18**(3): 440–465.

Vecchi, T. and D. Gatti (2020). *Memory as Prediction: From Looking Back to Looking Forward*. Cambridge, MA: MIT Press.

Index

Printed in the USA
CPSIA information can be obtained
at www.ICGtesting.com
LVHW020251151123
763991LV00003B/31